ANNUAL REVIEW OF IRISH LAW 1993

Annual Review
of Irish Law 1993

Raymond Byrne
B.C.L., LL.M., Barrister-at-Law
Lecturer in Law, Dublin City University

William Binchy
B.A., B.C.L., LL.M., Barrister-at-Law
Regius Professor of Laws, Trinity College Dublin
Formerly, Research Counsellor, The Law Reform Commission

ROUND HALL SWEET & MAXWELL
DUBLIN

The typesetting for this book was produced by
Gough Typesetting Services, Dublin for
ROUND HALL SWEET & MAXWELL
4 Upper Ormond Quay, Dublin 7.

A catalogue record for this book
is available from the British Library.

ISBN 1-85800-052-1

ISSN 0791-1084

Printed by
Redwood Books, Wiltshire

Content

Preface

In this seventh volume in the Annual Review series, our purpose continues to be to provide a review of legal developments, judicial and statutory, that occurred in 1993. In terms of case law, this includes those judgments which were delivered in 1993, regardless of whether they have been (or will be) reported and which were circulated up to the date of the preface. Once again, it is a pleasure to thank those who made the task of completing this volume less onerous. Mr Justice Brian Walsh (who, as we have mentioned in previous volumes, was the originator of the concept of an Annual Review of Irish Law) continues to be most supportive and we remain very grateful for this. Once again, we are in the debt of a number of people for providing access to library facilities. In particular, Ms Peggy McQuinn, of the Office of the Supreme Court, Ms Margaret Byrne and Ms Mary Gaynor, of the Library of the Incorporated Law Society of Ireland, and Mr Johnathon Armstrong and Ms Therese Broy, of the King's Inns Library, were as helpful as ever with a number of difficult queries from the authors. And once again, Ms Jennifer Aston, Librarian in the Law Library, Four Courts, was also especially helpful in facilitating access to statutory material which is otherwise very difficult to source. We would also like to express our heartfelt thanks to the staffs of the Dublin City University and Trinity College libraries for their assistance in the research for this volume. This seventh volume in the Annual Review series also marks a departure from previous years. The authors are delighted to have had the benefit of specialist contributions on Company Law, Contract Law, Land Law and Social Welfare included in the volume. The authors continue to take final responsibility for the overall text as in the past, but are especially grateful for the contributions of David Tomkin and Adam McAuley in Company Law, Eoin O'Dell in Contract Law, Paul Coughlan in Land Law and Gerry Whyte in Social Welfare.

Finally, we are very grateful to Round Hall Sweet & Maxwell and Gilbert Gough, whose professionalism ensures the continued production of this series.

Raymond Byrne and William Binchy,
Dublin

August 1996

Table of Cases

Other Tables

TABLE OF CONSTITUTIONAL ARTICLES

TABLE OF IRISH STATUTES

TABLE OF STATUTORY INSTRUMENTS

TABLE OF UK LEGISLATION

INTERNATIONAL TREATIES AND CONVENTIONS

ANNUAL REVIEW OF IRISH LAW 1993

Administrative Law

GOVERNMENT FUNCTIONS

Appropriation   The Appropriation Act 1993 provided as follows. For the year ended 31 December 1993, the amount for supply grants was £8,789,118,000 and for appropriations-in-aid was £1,006,586,000. A short-fall for the year 1991, amounting to £10 in respect of the grant to the State Laboratory, was also included. The 1993 Act came into effect on its signature by the President on 29 December 1993.

Civil service   In *O'Reilly v Minister for Industry and Commerce*, High Court, 4 March 1993, the question of retirement of a civil servant on reaching the age of 60 arose, albeit indirectly. The plaintiff was, in 1990, the Assistant Secretary in the Department of Industry and Commerce and had reached the age of 60. He had applied for the post of Secretary but was unsuccessful. The successful candidate, on being informed of his appointment by the then Minister, had a conversation with the Minister about the reorganisation of the Department and specifically about the plaintiff. There was some discussion about the applicant's retirement and the new Secretary was to ask the plaintiff if he would retire voluntarily. No decision was made as to whether the plaintiff would be requested to retire under the terms of s. 8(2A) of the Civil Service Regulations Act 1956 by which the Minister 'may . . . require any civil servant who has attained the age of sixty years to retire and such civil servant shall retire accordingly.'

   At a subsequent meeting between the Secretary and the plaintiff, the purpose of which was not indicated to the plaintiff in advance, the plaintiff indicated that he did not wish to retire. He stated his wish to continue but was told that the end of June would be the best time to go. At some time in the meeting, he was informed by the Secretary of the terms of s. 8(2A) of the 1956 Act. The plaintiff considered that, in effect, he had no option but to retire and the following Wednesday he wrote a one line memorandum stating: 'Secretary, I wish to retire from the Civil Service with effect from 15 April 1991.'

   The plaintiff brought proceedings in which he claimed damages for the loss he had sustained through retiring before the normal retirement age of 65. Carroll J held in his favour. The defendant Minister pointed out that the issue of compulsory retirement had never been decided on and that, in fact, the plaintiff did have a choice to decline to retire voluntarily. Carroll J considered that, whatever the intent of the Secretary, the effect of the meeting between the two was that the plaintiff considered he was required to retire. She held that the failure of the Secretary to correct this misapprehension, which she held 'must have been obvious' was effectively a misstatement and therefore the defendant could not rely on the plaintiff's letter of resignation to defeat his claim. She also held, citing the decision of the Supreme Court in *Garvey v Ireland* [1981] IR 75, that in exercising his powers under s. 8(2A) of the 1956 Act the Minister was bound to act fairly and that, equally, the Secretary was bound to act fairly where the plaintiff had reasonable grounds for believing that he had no option but to go. Accordingly, she awarded the plaintiff the loss he incurred arising from his early retirement.

Development and management of State buildings   The State Authorities (Development and Management) Act 1993 is a short Act enacted in the wake of *Howard v Commissioners of Public Works in Ireland* [1993] ILRM 665 (SC); [1994] 1 IR 101 (HC & SC), in which it had been held, *inter alia*, that the Commissioners of Public Works, commonly known as the Office of Public Works, lacked a general legislative power to develop and manage State buildings.

   Given the extent to which many public buildings, whether government buildings or national monuments, have traditionally been constructed and maintained by the Office of Public Works, the decision in *Howard* necessitated an immediate legislative response. This was forthcoming, the 1993 Act being enacted within six days of the High Court decision in the case. The *Howard* case is discussed in the Local Government chapter, 430-2, below, in the context of the Local Government (Planning and Development) Act 1993, another legislative result of the case.

   To revert to the State Authorities (Development and Management) Act 1993, s. 2(1) of the Act, the main substantive provision, states that:

   A State authority shall have, and be deemed always to have had, power
   —

   (a) to carry out, or procure the carrying out of, development,
   (b) to maintain, manage, repair, improve, alter, enlarge, reduce in size, remove or otherwise deal with buildings or structures or other works or property of, or provided under paragraph (a) of this subsection by, a State authority. . . .

   S. 1 of the Act provides that 'State authority' means any authority being either a Minister of the Government or the Commissioners of Public Works in Ireland, while s. 2(6) provides that 'development' means the carrying out of any works on, in or under the land or the making of any material change in the use of any structures or other land.

Clearly, the 1993 Act is very extensive in potential scope, and by its terms s. 2(1) appears to have full retrospective effect. However, s. 2(3) provides that s. 2(1) shall be subject to such limitations as are necessary in the event that the exercise of the powers in the 1993 Act are in breach of any constitutional rights. This provision mirrors a similar proviso in the Courts (No. 2) Act 1988 (as to which see the 1988 Review, 337-8 and the 1990 Review, 155-57). The terms of s. 2 were subsequently litigated in a follow-up to the original *Howard* case: see *Howard v Commissioners of Public Works in Ireland (No. 2)* [1994] 2 ILRM 301, in which Lynch J upheld the validity of s. 2. We will return to *Howard (No. 2)* in the 1994 Review.

Diplomatic relations
Immunity: INTELSAT The INTELSAT (Designation of Organisation and Immunities of Organisation and its Officers and Employees) (Amendment) Order 1993 (SI No. 191) amended the 1972 Order of the same title in order to enable the 1978 Protocol on Privileges and Immunities of the International Telecommunications Satellite Organisation (INTELSAT) to be implemented pursuant to the Diplomatic Relations and Immunities Act 1967.

Immunity: EUMETSAT The EUMETSAT (Privileges and Immunities) Order 1993 (SI No. 192) enabled the 1986 Protocol on Privileges and Immunities of the European Organisation for the Exploitation of Meteorological Satellites (EUMETSAT) to be implemented pursuant to the Diplomatic Relations and Immunities Act 1967.

Immunity: EUTELSAT The European Telecommunications Satellite Organisation (EUTELSAT) (Designation and Immunities) Order 1993 (SI No. 193) enabled the 1987 Protocol on Privileges and Immunities of the European Telecommunications Satellite Organisation (EUTELSAT) to be implemented pursuant to the Diplomatic Relations and Immunities Act 1967. One can only speculate as to why the organisation's full title was used in the title of this Order whereas, in the two previous Orders referred to above, acronyms were used.

Diplomatic services
Diplomatic and consular officers The Diplomatic and Consular Officers (Provision of Services) Act 1993 is a relatively short Act which provides for an updating of the terms used to describe diplomatic and consular officers so that they confrom to those contained in the 1961 Vienna Convention on Diplomatic Relations and the 1963 Vienna Convention on Consular Rela-

tions. Both Conventions, of course, had already been incorporated into Irish law by the Diplomatic Relations and Immunities Act 1967. S. 2 of the 1993 Act describes four types of persons to whom the Act applies: a civil servant employed as a head of mission, a member of the diplomatic staff of a mission, a career consular officer and an honorary consular officer appointed by the Minister. S. 3 of the 1993 Act provides for the making of Regulations by the Minister for Foreign Affairs fixing the fees to be charged for services provided under the Regulations by the diplomatic and consular officers referred to in s. 2. Such persons are empowered by s. 5 of the 1993 Act to administer any oath and take any affidavit as well as do any act which a notary public could do in the State. S.6 of the 1993 Act makes the false swearing of any oath or affidavit made under s. 5 a matter of perjury. S. 8 of the 1993 Act provides for the repeal of the Commissioners for Oaths (Diplomatic and Consular) Act 1931 and the Diplomatic and Consular Fees Act 1939, subject to the saver of any Regulations made under those Acts. For examples of such Regulations, see below. In accordance with s. 9(2) of the 1993 Act, the Act came into force on 21 January 1994, one month after its passing, that is, one month after its signature by the President.

Fees The Diplomatic and Consular Fees (Amendment) Regulations 1993 (SI No. 107), the Diplomatic and Consular Fees (Amendment) (No.2) Regulations 1993 (SI No. 251) and the Diplomatic and Consular Fees (Amendment) (No. 3) Regulations 1993 (SI No. 417) amended the 1982 Regulations of the same title, updating the fees payable for certain services under the Diplomatic and Consular Fees Act 1939. These Regulations were continued in force by s. 8 of the Diplomatic and Consular Officers (Provision of Services) Act 1993, notwithstanding the repeal of the 1939 Act by the 1993 Act: see above.

Government Departments In January 1993, a number of Orders were made under s. 6(1) of the Ministers and Secretaries (Amendment) Act 1939 to give effect to changes in the titles of certain government Departments, the creation of new government Departments and the allocation of different functions between the Departments.

Agriculture, Food and Forestry The Agriculture and Food (Alteration of Name of Department and Title of Minister) Order 1993 (SI No. 11) altered the name of the Department of (and Minister for) Agriculture and Food to that of Agriculture, Food and Forestry. Connected to this, the functions formerly vested in the Minister for Energy under the Forestry Acts 1946 to 1988 were transferred to the Minister for Agriculture, Food and Forestry by the Energy (Transfer of Departmental Administration and Ministerial Functions) Order 1993 (SI No. 10).

Arts, Culture and the Gaeltacht The Gaeltacht (Alteration of Name of Department and Title of Minister) Order 1993 (SI No. 22) altered the name of the Department of (and Minister for) the Gaeltacht to that of Arts, Culture and the Gaeltacht. Connected to this, functions concerning broadcasting, arts and culture were transferred to the Minister for the Arts, Culture and the Gaeltacht by the Broadcasting (Transfer of Departmental Administration and Ministerial Functions) Order 1993 (SI No. 13), the Arts and Culture (Transfer of Departmental Administration and Ministerial Functions) Order 1993 (SI No. 21) and the the Arts and Culture (Transfer of Departmental Administration and Ministerial Functions) (No.2) Order 1993 (SI No. 35).

Enterprise and Employment The Industry and Commerce (Alteration of Name of Department and Title of Minister) Order 1993 (SI No. 19) altered the name of the Department of (and Minister for) Industry and Commerce to that of Enterprise and Employment. Pursuant to the Labour (Transfer of Departmental Administration and Ministerial Functions) Order 1993 (SI No. 18), the Minister for Enterprise and Employment took charge, in effect, of the majority of the functions formerly exercised by the Ministers for Labour and of Industry and Commerce, apart from those vested in the Ministers for Equality and Law Reform and Tourism and Trade: see below.

Equality and Law Reform The Labour (Alteration of Name of Department and Title of Minister) Order 1993 (SI No. 20) altered the name of the Department of (and Minister for) Labour to that of Equality and Law Reform. This newly-created Department took charge of equality law functions, such as those concerned with the Employment Equality Agency, of the Department of Labour not transferred to the Department of Enterprise and Employment by the Labour (Transfer of Departmental Administration and Ministerial Functions) Order 1993 (SI No. 18): see above. Pursuant to the Justice (Transfer of Departmental Administration and Ministerial Functions) Order 1993 (SI No. 34), the Minister for Equality and Law Reform also took over from the Department of Justice the law reform functions connected with family and property matters, including functions concerning the non-statutory Legal Aid Board as well as responsibility for family legislation.

Tourism and Trade The Energy (Alteration of Name of Department and Title of Minister) Order 1993 (SI No. 11) altered the name of the Department of (and Minister for) Energy to that of Tourism and Trade. Connected to this, functions concerning foreign trade and tourism, formerly vested in the Minister for Industry and Commerce (now the Minister for Enterprise and Employment: see above) and the Minister for Tourism, Transport and Communications (now the Minister for Transport, Energy and Communications: see below) were transferred to the Minister for Tourism and Trade by the Foreign Trade (Transfer of Departmental Administration and Ministerial Functions) Order 1993 (SI No. 14) and the Tourism (Transfer of Departmental Administration and Ministerial Functions) Order 1993 (SI No. 15).

Transport, Energy and Communications The Tourism, Transport and Communications (Alteration of Name of Department and Title of Minister) Order 1993 (SI No. 17) altered the name of the Department of (and Minister for) Tourism, Transport and Communications to that of Transport, Energy and Communications. Connected to this, the functions formerly vested in the Minister for Energy (apart from those concerning forestry refered to in SI No. 10, above) were transferred to the Minister for Transport, Energy and Communications by the Energy (Transfer of Departmental Administration and Ministerial Functions) (No.2) Order 1993 (SI No. 12).

Industrial development The Industrial Development Act 1993 represented one legislative element of the Government's response to the 1992 Report of the Industrial Policy Review Group, *A Time for Change*, commonly called the Culliton Report, and the 1993 Report of the Moriarty Task Force, which had been established in the wake of Culliton. The government's overall response to Culliton and Moriarty, *Employment Through Enterprise* (Pl.9763), effectively a White Paper on Industrial Development, anticipated the changes effected in the 1993 Act.

The 1993 Act involved a substantial change in the functions and structures of the existing industrial development bodies. The changes were not, however, as radical as those suggested in the Culliton Report, which had recommended the creation of a single 'super agency' with responsibility for all elements of industrial development, domestic and foreign. Instead s. 5 of the 1993 Act provided for the creation of Forfás, the principal co-ordinating and advisory agency on industrial development, together with two subsidiary agencies of Forfás, namely Forbairt and the Industrial Development Authority (Ireland), hereinafter IDA Ireland.

S. 6 of the 1993 Act provides that the functions of Forfás are to advise the Minister for Enterprise and Employment on matters relating to the development of industry in the State as well as to co-ordinate the policies of Forbairt, IDA Ireland and other development agencies such as An Bord Trachtála, the export trade agency. S.7 of the Act provides that Forbairt, as an agency of Forfás, has responsibility for the development of industry in the State, that is indigenous industry, while s. 8 provides that IDA Ireland, as an agency of Forfás, is responsible for promoting the establishment and development in the State of industrial undertakings from outside the State. S.9 of the 1993 Act provides that the functions formerly exercised by the Industrial Development Authority and Eolas, the Science and Technology Agency, were vested in Forfás on the coming into force of the 1993 Act, and s. 18 provided that these two bodies would then stand dissolved. The 1993 Act came into effect on 1 January 1994: Industrial Development Act 1993 (Establishment Day) (Forfás, Forbairt and Industrial Development Agency (Ireland)) Order 1993 (SI No. 376).

The terms of the 1993 Act are very general in nature and, while in formal terms Forfás appears in the Act as the predominating entity with Forbairt and IDA Ireland being 'mere' agencies of Forfás, it was clear when the 1993 Act came into force that the driving forces behind industrial development would be the 'mere' agencies and that Forfás would, in effect, become a 'holding company' for industrial development.

International Development Association The International Development Association (Amendment) Act 1993 provided for a further contribution from this State of £13 million to the International Development Association. On the work of the Association, see the discussion of the International Development Association (Amendment) Act 1990, in the 1990 Review, 4. The contribution mandated by the 1993 Act represented 0.11% of the total contribution of almost £13 billion. The 1993 Act came into effect on its signature by the President on 27 October 1993.

State Bodies
Aer Lingus The Air Companies (Amendment) Act 1993, which concerned the restructuring plan for the State airline Aer Lingus, is discussed in the Transport chapter, 583, below.

B & I Line The B & I Line Act 1991 (Section 8) (Commencement) Order 1993 (SI No. 302) brought s. 8 of the 1991 Act, insofar as it applies to Part II of the Schedule to the Act, into force on 15 October 1993. The effect of this was to repeal s. 4 of the B & I Steampacket Co. Ltd (Acquisition) Act 1965 and ss. 2 and 4 of the B & I Steampacket Co. Ltd (Acquisition) (Amendment) Act 1971 from that date. On the 1991 Act, which provided for the privatisation of the B & I Line, see generally the 1991 Review, 4, and for a more detailed discussion, see the Annotation in *Irish Current Law Statutes Annotated*.

Bord Gáis The Gas (Amendment) Act 1993 increases the borrowing powers of the State body Bord Gáis Éireann (BGE) and makes other necessary adjustments to the Gas Acts 1976 to 1987 in order to provide a statutory footing for the completion of a gas interconnector pipeline between Ireland and Scotland. The interconnector is intended to ensure continuity of gas supply for Irish consumers who currently receive supplies from the Kinsale and Ballycotton Gas Fields. In the event of further gas finds being made off the Irish coast, the interconnector can also be operated from Ireland to Britain. For previous legislation in this area, see the 1987 Review, 4, 297.

Bord na gCon The Greyhound Industry (Amendment) Act 1993 is discussed the Agriculture chapter, 37, below.

Central Statistics Office The Statistics Act 1993 provides for the first time a clear legislative basis for the operation of the Central Statistics Office (CSO) and an advisory body, the National Statistics Board which, prior to the 1993 Act, like the CSO itself, had operated in a non-legislative framework. The terms of the 1993 Act implement the government's 1985 White Paper, *A New Institutional Structure for the Central Statistics Office* (Pl.3483). The 1993 Act also provides for the repeal and replacement of the Statistics Acts 1926 and 1946. Provisions relating to the confidentiality of, and disclosure of, information collected by the CSO is also provided for in the 1993 Act. The 1993 Act came into effect on 1 November 1994: Statistics Act 1993 (Commencement) Order 1994 (SI No. 323 of 1994).

Conditions of service in State bodies In *Ó Cearbhaill and Ors v Bord Telecom Éireann* [1993] ELR 253 (HC); [1994] ELR 54 (SC), the correct interpretation of s. 45(2) of the Postal and Telecommunications Services Act 1983, which is a standard provision concerning the transfer of civil servants to a newly-created State body, was considered: see the discussion in the Labour Law chapter, 374-6, below.

Development and management of State buildings The State Authorities (Development and Management) Act 1993 is discussed separately above, 4.

ICC Bank The ICC Bank Act 1992 (Section 3) Regulations 1993 (SI No. 24) were referred to in the 1992 Review, 5.

Industrial development The effect of the Industrial Development Act 1993 is discussed above, 8.

Irish Aviation Authority The Irish Aviation Authority Act 1993 provides for the establishment of a company called the Irish Aviation Authority. Although not established as a State body as such, the Authority has many of the characteristics of a State body, including close control by a government Department: see the discussion of the 1993 Act in the Transport chapter, 584-5, below.

Irish Film Board The Irish Film Board (Amendment) Act 1993 is discussed in the Communications chapter, 73, below.

National Roads Authority The Roads Act 1993 provides for the establishment of a State body called the National Roads Authority: see the discussion of the 1993 Act in the Transport chapter, 588-93, below.

National Stud S. 2 of the National Stud (Amendment) Act 1993 provides for an increase in the share capital of the State body, the National Stud Company Ltd, from £5 million to £10 million. S. 3 of the 1993 Act increases the National Stud's borrowing powers from £500,000 to £5 million. These changes were regarded as essential if the National Stud was to continue to be a viable operation in the face of increased competition from private horse studs. The extent of the increases involved also reflect the inability of the National Stud to purchase stallions in recent years.

NET The Nitrigín Éireann Teoranta Act 1993 provides, *inter alia*, for an increase in the borrowing powers of the State body Nitrigín Éireann Teo (NET). While originally involved in the manufacture of agricultural fertilizers, NET is nowadays primarily responsible for the management of the enormous debt incurred by itself in the 1970s connected in part with the construction of the Marino Point manufacturing plant in Cork. Since 1987, a joint venture between Irish Fertilizers Industries plc (a subsidiary of NET) and Imperial Chemical Industries plc has been responsible for the manufacturing side, while NET continues to manage the pre-1987 debt: see the Nitrigín Éireann Teoranta Act 1987 (1987 Review, 6). The 1993 Act reflects the fact that the NET debts are increasing rather than diminishing since its 1987 figure of £164 million, with NET's borrowing power being increased from £180 million to £200 million by s. 2(b) of the 1993 Act.

RTE The Broadcasting Authority (Amendment) Act 1993 is discussed in the Communications chapter, 70, below.

Údarás na Gaeltachta The Údarás na Gaeltachta (Amendment) Act 1993 provides for certain changes to the Údarás na Gaeltachta Act 1979 in order to place An tÚdarás, the State's job creation agency for the Irish language Gaeltacht areas, on a more secure financial footing. S. 2 of the 1993 Act amends s. 22 of the 1979 Act and provides that grants to an tÚdarás from the Minister for the Arts, Culture and the Gaeltacht shall henceforth be on an annual basis. For the previous regime, see the 1989 Review, 5. Finally, s. 3 of the 1993 Act provides that previous advances to an tÚdarás under the 1979 Act were non-repayabale.

Tribunals of Inquiry In May 1991, the Minister for Agriculture and Food decided to establish a Tribunal of Inquiry into the Beef Industry, arising from certain allegations made in an ITV 'World in Action' programme and other allegations made in Dáil Éireann. The subsequent resolutions of both Houses of the Oireachtas concerning the Tribunal had the effect of conferring on it the powers contained in the Tribunals of Inquiry (Evidence) Acts 1921 and 1979. The Tribunal's sole member and Chairman was Mr Justice Hamilton, then President of the High Court, since Chief Justice.

In the 1992 Review, 6, we outlined the substantial case law which had emerged from the Tribunal's deliberations. In this Review, we complete our discussion of this case law. *Attorney General v Mr Justice Hamilton (No. 2)* [1993] ILRM 821; [1993] 3 IR 227, *Goodman International v Mr Justice Hamilton (No. 2)* [1993] 3 IR 307 and *Goodman International v Mr Justice Hamilton (No. 3)* [1993] 3 IR 320, in which the privilege for members of the Oireachtas under Article 15.13 of the Constitution was considered, are discussed in the Constitutional Law chapter, 165-9, below. *Kiberd v Mr Justice Hamilton* [1992] 2 IR 257; [1992] ILRM 574, in which a claim to privilege by a journalist was rejected, is discussed in the Criminal Law chapter, 219, below. We should also add to the list of case law arising from the Tribunal the decision of Costello J in *Council of the Bar of Ireland v Sunday Business Post Ltd*, High Court, 30 March 1993, discussed in the Criminal Law chapter, 217, below.

The Report of the Tribunal was published in 1994, and we will return to its contents in the 1994 Review.

JUDICIAL REVIEW

Availability and scope   Three decisions under discussion in this Review dealt with different aspects of the scope of judicial review. In *Duff and Ors v Minister for Agriculture and Food (No. 2)*, High Court, 10 July 1992 (the judgment in which was not circulated in time for inclusion in the 1992 Review), Murphy J declined to judicially review a decision which, he concluded, had been based on grounds of national policy. By way of contrast, in *Browne v Dundalk UDC* [1993] ILRM 328; [1993] 2 IR 512, Barr J granted judicial review in respect of a 'politically motivated' decision. In the third case, *Rajah v Royal College of Surgeons in Ireland* [1994] 1 ILRM 233; [1994] 1 IR 384, Keane J held that judicial review did not lie against the respondent college.

In the first of these cases, *Duff and Ors v Minister for Agriculture and Food (No. 2)*, High Court, 10 July 1992, the plaintiffs were a group of farmers who had been advised during the 1970s and 1980s by ACOT agricultural advisers (who were servants or agents of the Minister) to prepare expansion, or modernisation, plans for their dairy farms. The modernisation plans were part of the national implementation of a 1972 EEC Directive aimed at encouraging milk production. The plaintiffs put in train the plans agreed with the ACOT advisers and substantially increased their output in the early 1980s. By this time, milk production had grown to such an extent in the European Community that Community policy began to turn in the direction of imposing limits on production. In 1984, EC Regulation 857/84 imposed national reference amounts, commonly called milk quotas, which effectively imposed a cap on milk production. Punitive sanctions, introduced by means of another EC Regulation, and dubbed the super-levy, were introduced for excess production. This amounted to a monetary penalty on States and, ultimately, on individual dairy farmers who exceeded their allotted quotas.

The then Irish Minister for Agriculture had strongly opposed the impostion of milk quotas and, in response to this, Regulation No. 857/84 granted a relatively generous quota to Ireland, based on 1983 production levels as opposed to the 1981 levels which formed the basis for most other member States' quotas. Regulation 857/84 also envisaged that, in order to assist farmers engaged in expansion at the cut-off date for the quotas, member States could use part of their national alloctaion to create a national reserve quota which could be distributed among such farmers and others with special difficulties.

After consultation with the dairy industry in early 1984 as to the best method of allocating the milk quota, the Minister determined that existing producers would be allocated the entire quota by reference to their production levels in 1983 and that no national reserve would be created. This resulted in farmers who were in production for 1983 receiving a quota over their actual production levels, the figures presented to Court in the instant case indicating that the national quota alloted to the State exceeded 1983 milk production by 3.6%. The result for the plaintiffs, as developing farmers, was that while they received a share of this extra 3.6%, they did not obtain a milk quota commensurate with their actual level of production. Accordingly, they faced the prospect of paying the super-levy on production over their quota. In the case of the first-named plaintiff, a super-levy bill of £13,717 was due to his creamery which, it appeared, he was obliged to pay if the creamery was to accept any more milk from him in 1992.

The plaintiffs, in essence, challenged the Minister's failure to create a national reserve quota or to make provision in some other way for development farmers who had not qualified for a quota. They argued that they had a legitimate expectation, arising from the advice given to them by the ACOT advisers, that their expansion plans would not be thwarted by subsequent Community action.

Murphy J agreed that the plaintiffs had a legitimate expectation 'of

bringing their farming plans to fruition.' However, he held that this did not
end the matter, since the plaintiffs had accepted in their argument to Court
that the Irish High Court could not question the validity of Regulation 857/84,
and the effect of that Regulations had been, in practice, to frustrate the
plaintiffs' plans. The case therefore turned, in Murphy J's view, on the correct
interpretation of Article 3 of that Community Regulation, which concerned
the reserve quota. In this respect, Murphy J accepted decisions of the Court
of Justice, in particular *Cornee v Cooperative Agricole Laitiere de Loudeac*
[1989] ECR 2309, that the Minister had a discretion to choose not to create
a national reserve. The plaintiffs' case then turned on whether the courts
would review the discretion thus conferred on the Minister.

Accepting that judicial review had developed and expanded in scope
considerably in recent years, Murphy J ultimately held that the Minister's
decision was not reviewable. He said:

> Even leaving aside any question of the application of the doctrine of the
> separation of powers it seems to me impossible for the courts to review
> decisions based on questions of national policy. To do so would involve
> the State disclosing publicly details of highly confidential national and
> international planning and strategy, and even if that were done some
> yardstick would have to be found by which the courts could be invited
> to say that such policies were irrational [within the meaning of *The State
> (Keegan) v Stardust Victims Compensation Tribunal* [1987] ILRM 202;
> [1986] IR 642]. I do not think that the first of these propositions is
> desireable or that the second is possible. . . . Political decisions of a
> policy nature are inherently far removed from the relatively compact
> arguments concerning the legal or constitutional rights of parties to
> litigation before the courts.

While one might cavil at the suggestion that constitutional claims do not
involve the courts in determining very difficult issues of policy with a
political dimension — *Murphy v Attorney General* [1982] IR 241 seems a
case in point — the general thrust of this passage reflects the well-established
view that the courts should resist becoming involved in 'political controversies' (as to which see generally *McKenna v An Taoiseach*, High Court, 8 June
1992 and *Slattery v An Taoiseach* [1993] 1 IR 286, discussed in the 1992
Review, 217-9). However, by way of contrast, we also draw attention to the
decision of Barr J in *Browne v Dundalk UDC* [1993] ILRM 328, discussed
below, 15-17.

In any event, in the *Duff* case, it appeared to have been conceded that it
was impossible to restore the *status quo ante* for the plaintiffs. In this context,
Murphy J cited with approval a passage from the judgment of Henchy J in

the *Murphy* case, above, to the effect that the passage of time would, in some instances, render into an accepted part of the *corpus juris* certain unconstitutional acts. It is, perhaps, ironic, that what might be regarded as this 'policy' approach of the courts aimed at avoiding retrospection of their constitutional decisions was quoted by Murphy J in the immediate aftermath of the passage which supported the avoidance of 'political' questions. Indeed, that such an argument was accepted in the context of ruling on an issue of European law seems to deny the fact that the Court of Justice has accepted that, in certain instances, its decisions should have retrospective effect: see for example the discussion of *Carbery v Minister for Social Welfare*, High Court, 28 April 1989 (1989 Review, 395-6).

Finally, Murphy J rejected a claim by the plaintiffs for damages, which had been based on the suggestion that the ACOT agricultural advisers, servants and agents of the Minister, had acted in breach of a duty of care to the plaintiffs in failing to warn them about the effect of the EC Regulation on the milk super-levy which was under consideration at the same time as the plaintiffs were being advised to proceed with their development plans. Murphy J accepted the general proposition that such a claim could be made, referring to his judgment in *Cotter v Minister for Agriculture and Ors*, High Court, 15 November 1991, subsequently upheld by the Supreme Court, 1 April 1993. However, in the instant case, Murphy J concluded that, since the plaintiffs were equally aware of the impending EC Regulation, and as no material piece of information was withheld from them, the plaintiffs' belief that they 'would be looked after' was in the political arena and not one for which there was a remedy available at law.

It may be that, in reaching this conclusion, Murphy J did not have directly in mind the decision of the Supreme Court in *Webb v Ireland* [1988] ILRM 565; [1988] IR 353 (see the 1987 Review, 162-4). However, it is worth pointing out that, whereas in the *Webb* case, a positive statement was made to the effect that the plaintiffs in that case would be 'treated honourably', which gave rise to a legally enforceable legitimate expectation, the plaintiffs in the *Duff* case received no such assurance. See also the discussion of legitimate expectation, below, 23-9.

The second case concerning the scope of judicial review which we discuss here involved more localised issues of politics. In *Browne v Dundalk UDC* [1993] ILRM 328; [1993] 2 IR 512, the applicant was an elected representative of Dundalk UDC and a member of the Sinn Féin party. He and two other colleagues entered into a contract on 2 October 1992 with the respondent Council for the hiring of its town hall for use in connection with the annual conference of Sinn Féin to be held in February 1993. A sum of £100 was paid to the Council as a booking fee and to cover insurance for the town hall. The contract was duly approved and sanctioned by the town clerk and county manager for County Louth. However, on 27 October 1992, a resolution was passed by the UDC to the effect that the booking of the town hall by Sinn Féin 'be cancelled on the basis that this organisation publicly supports the use of violence. . . .' On foot of this resolution, the town clerk informed the applicant by letter that the booking of the town hall 'has been cancelled' and the sum of £100 was also returned with the letter.

The applicant sought judicial review of the purported cancellation of the booking on the ground, primarily, that the UDC resolution was void and of no effect. Barr J accepted this argument. It was conceded by counsel for the respondent that the resolution could not be brought within the terms of s. 4 of the City and County Management (Amendment) Act 1955, as amended by the Local Government Act 1991 (see the 1991 Review, 310-13), since the procedural requirements attaching to such resolutions had not been complied with (as to which see the 1988 Review, 296-301 and the 1992 Review, 458-9). In addition, Barr J concluded that, even if the resolution could have been brought within s. 4 of the 1955 Act, it would be unlawful since it purported to direct reccission of a valid contract. In view of this fact, Barr J stated that the town clerk, in accordance with s. 4 of the 1955 Act, would have been obliged to have consulted the law agent for advice as to whether he should give effect to the resolution.

The respondent put forward one further argument to suggest why the applicant should be refused relief. This was that, since the applicant was seeking, in effect, to enforce a private contract, judicial review did not lie, citing in support the decision of the Supreme Court in *Beirne v Garda Commissioner* [1993] ILRM 1 (see the 1992 Review, 382). Barr J quoted with approval the views of Finlay CJ in the *Beirne* case to the effect that judicial review does not reach to decisions which are 'solely and exclusively derived from an individual contract made in private law.' In the instant case, Barr J considered that the town clerk's purported rescission of the contract was not 'solely and exclusively' derived from the contract with the applicant, because it had been based on the council resolution which 'was patently motivated solely by political factors.' Barr J continued:

> As the council's resolution was in terms politically motivated, it was clearly within the public domain. . . . I am satisfied that in the premises the conduct of the town clerk acting on behalf of the local authority in purporting to terminate unlawfully its contract with the applicant is properly the subject-matter of an application for judicial review.

On this basis, Barr J quashed the town clerk's decision and granted the applicant an injunction restraining the council from breaching the contract for the hire of the town hall.

When the *Browne* case is placed beside the *Duff* case, discussed above, they clearly involve very different aspects of the scope of judicial review.

Nonetheless, they highlight the difficulty which the judiciary have faced in recent years where, on the one hand, there has been a tendency to widen the scope of judicial review while, at the same time, there has been some concern expressed that limits should be placed on its reach. Recent decisions, such as those in the *Beirne* case, have indicated that there is no clear consensus on the matter: see the discussion in the 1990 Review, 12-4. Because of this lack of consensus, it is not easy to give full support to the view expressed by Murphy J in the *Duff* case that the courts must shy away from issues which involve 'national policy'. On the other hand, the robust approach of Barr J in the *Browne* case that a 'politically motivated' decision, being in the public domain, *ipso facto* was one amenable to judicial review must be treated with some caution also.

While the courts are in agreement on the general scope of judicial review, the range of application of those principles remains difficult to quantify. And although Murphy J expressed the hope in the Duff case that 'academic writers will provide further assistance in providing a comprehensive and cohesive analysis' of developments in the area of judicial review over the past 30 years, the nature of the grounding principles may be such that hard and fast rules of application will continue to prove elusive. However, it appears to the present authors that the discussion in Hogan and Morgan, *Administrative Law in Ireland*, 2nd ed. (Sweet & Maxwell, 1991) provides the best point of departure for those seeking to begin a principled analysis.

The third case under discussion in this Review concerning the availability and scope of judicial review is *Rajah v Royal College of Surgeons in Ireland* [1994] 1 ILRM 233; [1994] 1 IR 384, in which Keane J held that judicial review did not lie against the respondent college.

The applicant, a medical student at the Royal College of Surgeons in Ireland, had failed her pre-medical course in the Summer 1992 sittings, and again at the Autumn repeat examinations. Under the rules of the college, a student who had failed at the repeat examination was considered discontinued. Such a student could appeal to the student progress committee who, in the case of mitigating circumstances, could grant permission to repeat the year. Provision was made for a further appeal to an academic appeals board. The applicant, who claimed that her studies had been affected by her suffering from an illness and personal problems, appealed unsuccessfully to the student progress committee. She then appealed, again unsuccessfully, to the academic appeals board. The applicant sought judicial review to quash the decision of the academic appeals board on a number of grounds. As indicated, Keane J held that judicial review did not lie.

Referring to the decisions in *Murphy v Turf Club* [1989] IR 172 (1989

Review, 14) and *Beirne v Garda Commissioner* [1993] ILRM 1 (1992
Review, 382), Keane J held that since the appeals committee of the college
derived its jurisdiction solely from the private contract of membership
between the applicant and the college, it was not subject to judicial review.
He added that the fact that the college, like other third level institutions,
derives its existence from a charter or act of parliament, was not a sufficient
ground for bringing matters relating to the conduct and academic standing
of its students within the ambit of judicial review.

However, Keane J also dealt with the actual grounds raised by the
applicant in view of the importance of the issues for her. He held that the
appeals committee had heard the appeal in a fair and reasonable manner, and
without breaching fair procedures. Nor did he consider that the appeals board
had misconstrued its appellate jurisdiction. Finally, he held that the decision
made by the respondents was not of such a nature as to necessitate the giving
of reasons. For a comprehensive discussion of the issues raised in the *Rajah*
case, together with a comparative analysis of similar decisions in England,
see Alex Carroll's article (1994) 12 ILT 259.

Basis of decision: whether clear   In *Lang v Government of Ireland*, High
Court, 7 July 1993, the applicant was a prison officer whose employment
had been terminated by direction of the government under s. 5 of the Civil
Service Regulations Act 1956 for persistent absenteeism. The applicant
claimed that the reason given was ambiguous and he also claimed that the
requirements of fair procedures had not been complied with. The applicant
accepted that his attendance record had not been satisfactory but claimed that
this was due to an on-going illness. O'Hanlon J reviewed the substantial
correspondence which had passed between the personnel section of the
prison service and the applicant in the years leading up to the termination, in
which the applicant's absences had been variously described as 'appalling',
'unacceptable', 'not due to a health problem' and 'a flagrant abuse of the
privilege' of uncertified sick leave. O'Hanlon J noted that at no stage did the
applicant attempt to refute these allegations prior to the termination of his
employment. In these circumstances, O'Hanlon J concluded that the requirements of fair procedures had been complied with, citing in support decisions
such as *Hynes v Garvey* [1978] IR 174, *The State (Duffy) v Minister for
Defence* [1979] ILRM 65 and *The State (Burke) v Garvey* [1979] ILRM 232.

To the same effect, see the decisions in *Doran v Garda Commissioner*
[1994] 1 ILRM 303, below, 31 and *Gormley v Ireland and Ors (No. 2)*, High
Court, 1 December 1993, below, 33.

For a case where fair procedures were not adopted in this respect, see
O'Shea v Garda Commissioner, High Court, 25 March 1993, discussed in
the Garda Síochána chapter, 340, below.

Bias In *Huntsgrove Developments Ltd v Meath County Council* [1994] 2 ILRM 36, Lardner J rejected the applicant's claim that the respondent Council had arrived at a decision influenced by bias: see the discussion in the Local Government chapter, 427-8, below.

Decision within reasonable time In *Twomey v Minister for Tourism and Transport*, Supreme Court, 12 February 1993, the question of whether a decision should be made within a reasonable period from the time of application was considered. The background to the case was as follows.

The applicant had been in the road haulage business since 1973. After the promulgation of the European Communities (Merchandise Road Transport) Regulations 1977, he applied to the Department of Tourism and Transport for a road freight certificate, but the application was refused in 1978 and 1979 on the basis that the applicant did not bring himself within the terms of the Regulations. The applicant did not disclose at the time that his business did, in fact, come within the terms of the 1977 Regulations.

No further application for a licence was made by the applicant until 1986, by which time another piece of legislation became particularly important. S. 3(1) of the Road Transport Act 1986 provided that, on the commencement of the section, the holder of a current road freight certificate issued under the 1977 Regulations was entitled to be granted a road freight carrier's licence. S. 3(1) of the 1986 Act came into operation on 30 September 1986 by means of a Commencement Order made by the respondent Minister. The applicant applied on 2 September 1986 for a certificate under the 1977 Regulations and on this occasion, his application included the relevant information that he had operated a road haulage business up to the date of the application and thus came within the terms of the 1977 Regulations. This application was not replied to by the Department until a letter dated 22 September 1986 and the applicant replied to the matters raised in this letter by further letter of 26 September 1986. However, by 30 September 1986, the date when s. 3(1) of the 1986 Act came into effect, no certificate had been issued to the applicant though one was issued in May 1987. The applicant applied for judicial review, seeking, *inter alia*, a declaration to the effect that he was entitled to a licence pursuant to s. 3(1) of the 1986 Act.

In the High Court, Barron J refused the relief sought: see the 1988 Review, 292. He stated:

> There may well be circumstances in which it would be unfair for the attainment of statutory rights to be dependent upon the speed with which an application for the same is processed.

However, he went on to hold that this was not such a case. He took the view that it had been the applicant's own delays and abandonment of his application for a certificate prior to 1986 which prevented him from obtaining the certificate in time. Taking an avowedly literal interpretation of s. 3(1) of the 1986 Act, Barron J concluded that the applicant did not fulfil the conditions set out therein.

On appeal, the Supreme Court (Finlay CJ, Egan and Blayney JJ) unanimously reversed Barron J. Delivering the Court's decision, Egan J recapitulated the proposition contained in Barron J's judgment, quoted above. Egan J commented:

> I agree that this is a correct statement of the law but disagree that the present case is not such a case. There was a statutory duty on the Minister [under the 1977 Regulations] to consider the application dated 2 September 1986. The applicant was entitled to this as a matter of right and the Minister did not have a discretion. His obligation was to deal with it within a reasonable time and where, as in this case, there was a critical 'cut-off' time within which the applicant would be entitled to the grant of a merchandise licence under the 1986 Act and this 'cut-off' time had been fixed by the Minister himself [in the Commencement Order], the road freight certificate should have been granted on or before this critical date. . . . Otherwise the applicant would have had no practical remedy and delay beyond that date would be wholly unjust.

On this basis, therefore, the Court granted the applicant the declaration sought. However, a further claim by the applicant to have the May 1987 certificate 'back-dated' to 30 September 1986 could not be pursued as it would have been of no avail to the applicant. This was because, under s. 3(7) of the 1986 Act, such a certificate would have lapsed three years after the date on which it was granted, and since six years had elapsed by the time of the Supreme Court decision, any backdating would leave the applicant without a certificate under the 1977 Regulations. Egan J noted that this was particularly unfortunate as the applicant would have been within the three year period at the time of the High Court judgment.

In what he described as the 'very special circumstances of this case', Egan J stated that the applicant should be permitted to amend his claim pursuant to O.84, r.23(2) of the Rules of the Superior Courts 1986 to include a claim for damages resulting from the failure to grant him a certificate on or before 30 September 1986. He acknowledged, in line with previous decisions of the Court (see the 1992 Review, 473-4), that it was 'most undesirable that relief should be sought in this Court in cases where it was not sought in the High Court' but considered that the unusual circumstances and the requirements of justice necessitated a breach of the general rule.

On this area, see also *Point Exhibition Co. Ltd v Revenue Commissioners* [1993] ILRM 621; [1993] 2 IR 551, discussed in the Licensing chapter, 408, below.

Hearing both sides
Advance notice In *TV 3 Television Co. Ltd and Ors v Independent Radio and Television Commission*, High Court, 4 May 1992; Supreme Court, 26 October 1993; [1994] 2 IR 439, Blayney J and, on appeal, the Supreme Court, considered the requirements of advance notice in the context of the award of a television franchise: see the Communications chapter, 71, below. The decision in *Ó Scanaill v Minister for Agriculture and Food* [1993] ELR 176, discussed in the Agriculture chapter, 34, below, also considered the question of notice.

Legal advice not communicated *Georgopoulos v Beaumont Hospital Board* [1994] 1 ILRM 58; [1993] ELR 246 was not a case of judicial review but it surveyed some elements of fair procedures which may be dealt with here. The plaintiff had been appointed as registrar in neurosurgery at Beaumont Hospital. The appointment was renewed and extended for a period of 12 months with effect from 1 July 1990. The plaintiff made written complaints to the hospital's medical administrator alleging the existence of certain practices in the hospital which compromised the treatment of patients. An aspect of this was discussed in *Georgopoulos v Fitness to Practice Committee of the Medical Council*, High Court, 3 March 1992 (1992 Review, 392-3). Subsequently, complaints were made about the plaintiff's conduct and he was dismissed from his post without being heard by the defendants in relation to the complaints. The plaintiff challenged the validity of his dismissal, but these proceedings were compromised on the basis that the defendants would consider afresh the complaints regarding the plaintiff's conduct.
    Both the hospital and the plaintiff were legally represented at these hearings, and the board retained the services of a legal assessor. Following the inquiry the chairman of the board informed the plaintiff by letter that his failure to perform his contractual duties had been established and that this warranted his dismissal. The plaintiff challenged this decision and claimed a declaration that the board had acted *ultra vires* and breached the requirements of natural and constitutional justice. Murphy J dismissed the claim.
    As to the retention by the hospital of a legal assessor, Murphy J was of the view that where, as here, a tribunal is engaged in determining only a question of fact, it is not in itself a breach of natural or constitutional justice which would invalidate its decision for it to receive advice on a matter of law without informing the parties as to the fact or nature of that advice. He acknowledged that, in *The State (Polymark (Ireland) Ltd) v Labour Court*

[1987] ILRM 357, Blayney J had suggested that where the Labour Court obtained legal advice from its Registrar it should inform the parties of this and hold a resumed hearing to consider such advice. Murphy J agreed with this view and that 'it is, at the very least, a desirable practice.' However, he noted that the defendants' function was to determine, as a matter of fact, whether the allegations made against the plaintiff were well founded. Unlike the Labour Court, therefore, they were not engaged in determining any question of law, and since the legal guidance was sought solely for the purpose of ensuring that they were acquainted with the requirements of natural and constitutional justice, they were not required to disclose it to the parties. However, Murphy J also added the following comment:

> If, however, the result of such advice is that the tribunal falls into error — and in that regard it does not matter whether their error was due to ignoring submissions on law made to them or relying on advice which had not been the subject matter of any such submission — if at the end of the day the procedures adopted by the tribunal are flawed, it would be no answer to a claim for judicial review to say that a particular procedure was adopted in pursuance of expert legal advice.

In the instant case, therefore, the key issue was whether, in making its decision, the defendants had fallen into error. In this context, Murphy J accepted the argument that, as the defendants were not in the position of a disciplinary tribunal but instead were acting as an employer reviewing the conduct of an employee, it was not incumbent upon them to enquire as to whether any further submissions were to be made in mitigation of the penalty of dismissal imposed on the plaintiff. In any event, he concluded, the plaintiff had been given ample opportunity to deal fully with the allegations made against him and the consequences which an adverse finding might have for him.

One might disagree with Murphy J when he appeared to accept that the defendants as employer owe a somewhat lower duty to the plaintiff in dismissing him than a disciplinary body imposing a penalty: the question must surely simply be whether legal rights are affected by the decision. However, the actual outcome can be supported if one is to assume that the defendants provided the plaintiff with a full hearing and that all possible penalties were considered. Nonetheless, one is left with the impression that Murphy J's conclusions may have been influenced by his expression of opinion earlier in his judgment that 'it is alarming to find that such an elaborate inquiry conducted with such obvious care and no doubt consider-able expense and inconvenience is not impervious to challenge.' There are many examples of hearings conducted in the courts themselves which have been challenged successfully whether on judicial review or through other procedures, but even where those hearings have been conducted with great care — and at great expense — the failure to comply with what may sometimes be regarded as technicalities has led to many such decisions being quashed.

Finally, one could only agree with Murphy J's comment that the criminal standard of proof was not applicable to the instant case as the matter arose out of a civil claim between an employer and an employee. Citing the Supreme Court's decision in *Banco Ambrosiano SPA v Ansbacher & Co. Ltd* [1987] ILRM 669 (1987 Review, 165), Murphy J concluded that the case fell to be determined on the balance of probabilities.

Legitimate Expectation   The somewhat inconsistent development of the doctrine of legitimate expectation was illustrated by two cases decided in 1993. Both cases involved the exercise of statutory powers. In *Carbury Milk Products Ltd v Minister for Agriculture and Ors*, High Court, 23 April 1993, the plaintiff successfully invoked the doctrine, but in *Tara Prospecting Ltd v Minister for Energy* [1993] ILRM 771, it proved of no avail.

In the first case concerning legitimate expectation, *Carbury Milk Products Ltd v Minister for Agriculture and Ors*, High Court, 23 April 1993, Hamilton P considered a claim which arose in the context of the granting of export refunds under the EC Common Agricultural Policy (CAP). Pursuant to the European Communities (Common Agricultural Policy) (Market Intervention) Regulations 1973, the Minister for Agriculture was designated the agent in Ireland responsible for the payment, *inter alia*, of export refunds under Regulation 804/68, as amended.

The plaintiff sought to have one of its products, known as lactalbumen powder, a by-product of cheese production, classified for the purposes of Regulation 804/68 to determine if it would qualify for export refunds. As requested by the Department of Agriculture, in 1977 the company submitted samples of the product for analysis by the State Chemist in order for the Revenue Commissioners to make a determination on the classification of the product. Resulting from this analysis, the Revenue Commissioners classified the product as 'milk protein powder', thus coming within a category which qualified for export refunds under Regulation 804/68.

As a result, the plaintiff exported the product in 1977 and 1978, and claimed and received export refunds from the Department of Agriculture in the sum of £963,270. Further exports occurred in 1979, giving rise to a claim by the plaintiff for export refunds in the sum of £902,531, but the plaintiff had not been paid this sum when an event occurred that precipitated these proceedings. A sample from a consignment of the product was tested by the Dutch authorities and was classified as 'whey powder', which did not qualify for export refunds under Regulation 804/68, as amended.

Further samples were then analysed by the State Chemist, which reached a conclusion similar to that of the Dutch authorities. It was accepted that the product had not changed in any way from that which had been originally tested, and Hamilton P concluded in his judgment that the original classification had been 'incorrect' and that the 'Revenue Commissioners and the State Chemist were negligent' in classifying the product as milk protein powder when in fact it was whey powder.

When the error was discovered, the Minister then purported to 'back-date' the new classification of the product to all exports of the product and declined to grant export refunds in respect of the 1979 exports for which the company had claimed refunds but which had not yet been paid by the Department. The company claimed that a legitimate expectation arose in its favour by virtue of the original classification by the State laboratory of its product and that, having entered into export contracts on foot of that classification, it was entitled to be paid the export refunds claimed. The Minister denied the plaintiff was entitled to export refunds for the 1979 exports and also counterclaimed for the export refunds which, it was claimed, had been wrongly paid to the company in respect of the 1977 and 1978 exports of the product.

Hamilton P (as he then was) found in favour of the plaintiff, holding that the doctrine of legitimate expectation was applicable in the circumstances which had arisen. In terms of Irish case law, he quoted the well-known passage from the judgment of Finlay CJ in *Webb v Ireland* [1988] ILRM 565; [1988] IR 353 (see the 1987 Review, 162-4) in support of his view that legitimate expectation is well recognised in Irish law. It is unfortunate that, by contrast with the judgment of Costello J one week later in *Tara Prospecting Ltd v Minister for Energy* [1993] ILRM 771, which we discuss below, Hamilton P did not further address the subsequent domestic case law on this area, including the significant jurisprudence to which he himself has contributed, such as *Conroy v Garda Commissioner* [1989] IR 140 (see the 1988 Review, 259) and *Duggan v An Taoiseach* [1989] ILRM 710 (see the 1988 Review, 21-4). This may be explained by the European dimension to the case, because in his judgment Hamilton P also invoked the case law of the Court of Justice in outlining the breadth of the legitimate expectation doctrine, quoting passages from the judgments in *Tomadini v Amministrazione della Finanze dello Stato* [1979] ECR 1801 and *Durbeck* [1981] ECR 1095.

It is particularly unfortunate that Hamilton P was not referred to the Supreme Court's decision in *Wiley v Revenue Commissioners* [1989] IR 350 (HC); [1993] ILRM 482 (SC), discussed in the 1992 Review, 8-10, a decision which might usefully have been cited in the *Carbury* case. Hamilton P noted that, in the instant case, all the exports in respect of which the plaintiff claimed export refunds involved contracts entered into prior to the discovery of the incorrect classification of the plaintiff's product. This may be contrasted with the situation in *Wiley* where, as the applicant was aware that a mistake had been made, the Supreme Court held that legitimate expectation could not arise. In the *Carbury* case, Hamilton P pointed out that the company had relied on the original classification of its product in deciding to export the product in the belief that it would attract export refunds under Regulation 804/68, as amended. On this basis, he stated:

> The Minister for Agriculture is estopped from denying the company's entitlement to its claim for export refunds. . . . Having regard to the circumstances . . . in which the product was classified by the Revenue Commissioner's at the request of the Department of Agriculture, the reliance placed on such classification by the company, . . . the fixing of its prices by the company . . . in the legitimate expectation based on such classification that it would be entitled to export refund[s] . . . and that the company was in no way at fault or contributed in any way to the situation, it would be unjust and inequitable if the company were held not to be entitled to export refunds.

Accordingly, Hamilton P granted the plaintiff a declaration that it was entitled to the claimed refunds in respect of the 1979 exports and dismissed the Minister's counterclaim in respect of the 1977 and 1978 exports. In this respect, it can be said that *Carbury* is the mirror image of the *Wiley* case.

In the second decision in 1993 on legitimate expectation, *Tara Prospecting Ltd v Minister for Energy* [1993] ILRM 771, the Minister for Energy had granted prospecting licences in 1981 and 1984 to the first applicant in respect of areas which included part of Croagh Patrick, Co. Mayo, a well known place of religious pilgrimage. Tara and another company, Burmin Exploration Ventures Ltd, the second applicant, subsequently entered into a joint venture agreement, with the Minister's approval, confined exclusively to gold exploration.

When gold was found in the Croagh Patrick area, there was public opposition to mining proposals. Unsuccessful efforts were made to use planning legislation to block any mining in the area: see *Glencar Explorations plc v Mayo County Council* [1993] 2 IR 237 (1992 Review, 457). There was also opposition on the ground that Croagh Patrick was a traditional place of pilgrimage. Costello J summarised the position thus:

> Croagh Patrick is not only a place of outstanding natural beauty; it is also a place of pilgrimage associated with Ireland's national saint since

the early middle ages. Many thousands of pilgrims climb the mountain every year, pray at its stations and hear Mass in a chapel at its summit. There is an annual national pilgrimage on the last Sunday in July attended by believers from all over Ireland and abroad. The association of Saint Patrick with the mountain is recorded in the Book of Armagh, and historical records establish its unique place in the religious life of the nation for over a millennium. It was reasonable to assume, therefore, that the establishment of mining operations on a commercial scale might well be deeply disturbing to those who regarded Croagh Patrick as hallowed ground.

Although the applicants had anticipated such objections, the local Roman Catholic Archbishop voiced objection to the proposed mining at the 1989 pilgrimage to Croagh Patrick. The problems were discussed in detail between the prospecting companies and the Department of Energy. At a press conference in May 1990, the Minister announced that he had decided to use his powers under s. 12 of the Mineral Development Act 1940 to exclude Croagh Patrick from the prospecting licence 'because of the unique importance of this pilgrim site which is part of our national, cultural and religious heritage.'

The applicants challenged the Minister's decision as being *ultra vires*, in breach of the principles of natural and constitutional justice and contrary to the legitimate expectations which the Minister had caused them to entertain in relation to the licences. They also sought an order of *mandamus* directing the Minister to renew the licences. Costello J dismissed the claim for judicial review.

As to whether the Minister's decision was *ultra vires* s. 12 of the 1940 Act, Costello J noted that since the Minister, in the exercise of his statutory authority, is required to have regard to the public interest, he was entitled to bear in mind that the 'Preamble [to the Constitution] contains a clear affirmation that the Irish are a religious people'. Thus, it was not *ultra vires* for the Minister to prohibit activities which he concluded were offensive on religious grounds to many members of the Irish public. He also held that the Minister was entitled to reject the applicants' views and that he had not breached the rules of natural justice.

Turning to the question of legitimate expectation, Costello J engaged in an extended analysis of the English and Irish case law which had developed in recent years, tracing the doctrine's origin to the judgment of Lord Denning in *Schmidt v Secretary of State for Home Affairs* [1969] 2 Ch 149. He noted that the principle of procedural fairness which underlay the *Schmidt* case had later been extended to a legitimate expectation that a benefit would be received rather than simply that a hearing would be afforded: *R. v Liverpool Corporation, ex p. Liverpool Taxi Fleet Operators' Association* [1972] 2 QB

299. However, he characterised the applicants' claim as amounting to something quite different:

> It is not that the legitimate expectations which the applicants held entitled them to a *fair hearing* (such a right arising from constitutional and well established common law principles I have already considered), but that they created a right to the *benefit itself* which should be enforced by an order of *mandamus*. [emphasis in original]

He pointed out that in *R. v Secretary of State for Health, ex p. US Tobacco International* [1991] 3 WLR 529, which involved a challenge to a statutory ban on oral tobacco products, a Divisional High Court had rejected such a claim and he found the reasoning in the case persuasive, notwithstanding some criticisms voiced by Craig, (1992) 108 LQR 79. Note also the decision of Blayney J in *United States Tobacco (Ireland) Ltd v Ireland* [1993] 1 IR 267, which also involved an unsuccessful challenge to a statutory ban on oral tobacco products (1991 Review, 376-7). Costello J also referred with approval to the decision of the High Court of Australia in *Attorney General for New South Wales v Quin* (1990) 170 CLR 1 in which the Court had also rejected the type of extension sought in the instant case.

Costello J then went on to a discussion of the Irish authorities in this area, beginning with the Supreme Court decision in *Webb v Ireland* [1988] IR 353; [1988] ILRM 565 (1987 Review, 162-4). He also noted that, in the Court's decision in *Wiley v Revenue Commissioners* [1989] IR 350 (HC); [1993] ILRM 482 (SC) (1992 Review, 8-10), the limits to legitimate expectation voiced in the Australian *Quin* case had been approved. He also referred to the judgment of Lardner J in *Devitt v Minister for Education* [1989] ILRM 639 (1989 Review, 12) and his own in *Hempenstall v Minister for the Environment* [1993] ILRM 318 (1992 Review, 210-11). He summarised the legal principles arising from the existing case law in an important passage:

> (1) There is a duty on a Minister who is exercising a discretionary power which may affect rights or interests to adopt fair procedures in the exercise of the power. Where a member of the public has a legitimate expectation arising from the Minister's words and/or conduct that (a) he will be given a hearing before a decision adverse to his interests will be taken or (b) that he will obtain a benefit from the exercise of the power then the Minister also has a duty to act fairly towards him and this may involve a duty to give him a fair hearing before a decision adverse to his interests is taken. There would then arise a correlative right to a fair hearing which, if denied, will justify the court in quashing the decision.

(2) The existence of a legitimate expectation that a benefit will be conferred does not in itself give rise to any legal or equitable right to the benefit itself which can be enforced by an order of *mandamus* or otherwise. However, in cases involving public authorities, other than cases involving the exercise of statutory discretionary powers, an equitable right to the benefit may arise from the application of the principles of promissory estoppel to which effect will be given by appropriate court order.

(3) In cases involving the exercise of a discretionary statutory power the only legitimate expectation relating to the conferring of a benefit that can be inferred from words or conduct is a conditional one, namely, that a benefit will be conferred provided that at the time the Minister considers that it is a proper exercise of the statutory power in the light of current policy to grant it. Such a conditional expectation cannot give rise to an enforceable right to the benefit should it later be refused by the Minister in the public interest.

(4) In cases involving the exercise of a discretionary statutory power in which an explicit assurance has been given which gives rise to an expectation that a benefit will be conferred no enforceable equitable or legal right to the benefit can arise. No promissory estoppel can arise because the Minister cannot estop either himself or his successors from exercising a discretionary power in the manner prescribed by parliament at the time it is being exercised.

In the instant case, Costello J concluded that any assurance given by the Minister was entirely conditional, namely that renewal of the prospecting licences would remain in the public interest. He rejected the claim that any unqualified assurance of renewal had emanated from the Minister's officials who had dealt with the applicants. Since the Minister had given the applicants' case a fair hearing, he had complied with all relevant legal principles. Thus, Costello J rejected the applicants' case.

The judgments in the *Carbury* and *Tara Prospecting* cases may be contrasted in that *Carbury* represented a traditional 'estoppel' case of legitimate expectation while the *Tara Prospecting* case involved a rejection of any further development of the doctrine outside the boundaries now fixed by English and Irish case law. The summary of relevant principles by Costello J in the *Tara Prospecting* case are also a very useful list for future cases in this area.

See also the decision of Murphy J in *Duff and Ors v Minister for Agriculture and Food (No. 2)*, High Court, 10 July 1992, discussed above, 12-5. and the judgment of Lardner J in *Huntsgrove Developments Ltd v Meath County Council* [1994] 2 ILRM 36, discussed in the Local Government chapter, 427-8, below. In the latter case, Lardner J expressly followed the principles laid down in the *Tara Prospecting* case.

Notice In *Ó Scanaill v Minister for Agriculture and Food* [1993] ELR 176 (discussed in the Agricuture chapter, 34, below), Lynch J considered the need to give notice of the purpose of a meeting at which a decision adverse to a person may be made. See also *TV 3 Television Co. Ltd and Ors v Independent Radio and Television Commission*, High Court, 4 May 1992; Supreme Court, 26 October 1993, discussed in the Communications chapter, 71, below.

Practice and Procedure

Amendment of claim In very unusual circumstances, the Supreme Court in *Twomey v Minister for Tourism and Transport*, Supreme Court, 12 February 1993 allowed an amendment to a claim for judicial review under O.84, r.23(2) of the Rules of the Superior Courts 1986 to include a claim which had not been made in the High Court: see 19-20, above.

Leave to seek judicial review In *G. v Director of Public Prosecutions* [1994] 1 IR 374, the Supreme Court considered the burden of proof at the leave to apply stage under O.84, r.20 of the Rules of the Superior Courts 1986: see the discussion in the Criminal Law chapter, 234, below.

Locus standi The question of standing was raised in *Bargaintown Ltd v Dublin Corporation* [1993] ILRM 890.

Public law/private law The reach of O.84 of the Rules of the Superior Courts 1986, in terms of the distinction between public and private law, was discussed in *Rajah v Royal College of Surgeons in Ireland* [1994] 1 ILRM 233; [1994] 1 IR 384 (see above, 17) and in *Geoghegan v Institute of Chartered Accountants in Ireland*, High Court, 9 July 1993 (see below in the Constitutional Law chapter, 141-7).

Remittal The circumstances in which the courts will remit a case pursuant to O.84, r.26 of the Rules of the Superior Courts 1986 are considered in the context of criminal cases in the Criminal Law chapter, 234, below.

Reasonableness In *Doran v Garda Commissioner* [1994] 1 ILRM 303 (discussed below, 31), *Brandon Book Publishers Ltd v Radio Telefís Éireann* [1993] ILRM 806, *Brandon Book Publishers Ltd v Independent Radio and Television Commission*, High Court, 29 October 1993 (both considered in the Communications chapter, 69-70, below), *Carton v Dublin Corporation*

[1993] ILRM 467 (discussed in the Local Government chapter, 421, below) and *Truloc Ltd v McMenamin* [1994] 1 ILRM 151 (see the Safety and Health chapter, 472-4 below) the test of reasonableness laid down in the decisions of the Supreme Court in *The State (Keegan) v Stardust Victims Compensation Tribunal* [1987] ILRM 202; [1986] IR 642 and *O'Keeffe v An Bord Pleanála* [1992] ILRM 237; [1993] 1 IR 39 (see the 1991 Review, 16-8) was applied in a number of High Court decisions.

The Supreme Court itself also applied the *Keegan* test in *Garda Representative Association and Ors v Ireland and Ors* [1989] ILRM 1 (HC); [1994] 1 ILRM 81 (SC) (see the Garda Síochána chapter, 339, below) and in *Dumbrell and Ors v Governor of Limerick Prison*, Supreme Court, 20 December 1993 (see the Prisons chapter, 468, below).

Reasons for decision   Four cases decided in 1993 concluded that reasons need not be given by the decision-makers whose decisions were under review. These were *Manning v Shackleton* [1994] 1 ILRM 346; [1994] 1 IR 397, *Rajah v Royal College of Surgeons in Ireland* [1994] 1 ILRM 233; [1994] 1 IR 384 (discussed above, 17), *Doran v Garda Commissioner* [1994] 1 ILRM 303 and *Gormley v Ireland and Ors (No. 2)*, High Court, 1 December 1993. We will discuss here the *Manning, Doran* and *Gormley* cases.

In the first of these cases, *Manning v Shackleton* [1994] 1 ILRM 346; [1994] 1 IR 397, Barron J considered in some depth the case law concerning the circumstances in which a decision-making body is required to give reasons for its decisions. The case arose against the background of an arbitration following the compulsory acquisition of some of the applicant's land.

In the course of this arbitration, an unconditional offer was made by the County Council which had compulsorily acquired the land of £175,000, exclusive of costs, in full and final settlement of the applicant's claim. On 12 December 1991 the respondent arbitrator made an award of £156,280. As the award did not exceed the offer which had already been made, the applicant was ordered to pay the costs from the date of the offer.

The applicant's solicitors subsequently wrote to the respondent requesting that he furnish a written judgment setting out his findings of fact and of law as well as a breakdown of the content of the award, but the respondent declined. On judicial review, Barron J upheld this approach. He surveyed the case law in this area, including two judgments delivered by Barron J himself, *The State (Daly) v Minister for Agriculture* [1988] ILRM 173; [1987] IR 165 (1987 Review, 10-12) and *Anheuser Busch Inc. v Controller of Patents, Designs and Trademarks* [1988] ILRM 247; [1987] IR 329 (1987 Review, 10-11). He also quoted with approval passages from the judgment of Finlay

CJ in *The State (Creedon) v Criminal Injuries Compensation Tribunal* [1989] ILRM 104; [1988] IR 51 (1988 Review, 17-8). He commented:

> These cases indicate that the giving of reasons by a person or body required to act judicially may be compelled by this Court when such reasons are necessary to determine whether such a power has been validly exercised. It is not an essential obligation and arises only when required to prevent an injustice or to ensure that not only has justice been done but is seen to have been done.

However, he concluded that, in the instant case, the applicant had not indicated how he was likely to suffer prejudice or injustice as a result of the failure to state reasons. He commented that, if the applicant had wished to ensure that, contrary to the normal practice, the respondent should give reasons for his award, he should have made a submission to that effect at the outset of the hearing. By allowing the hearing to continue and by failing to seek reasons from the respondent, he had accepted the normal practice.

Turning to whether any legal issues were at issue before the respondent, Barron J stated that the applicant could have brought these before the High Court by asking the respondent to make his report in the form of a special case under s. 6(1) of the Acquisition of Land (Assessment of Compensation) Act 1919, but he had not done so. The applicant had likewise waived his right under s. 3(3) of the 1919 Act to require the respondent to specify the amount awarded in respect of any particular matter.

However, as to the question of costs, Barron J accepted that the applicant had some grounds to complain. It appeared that the amount of compensation which was awarded might have been affected by the nature of certain undertakings given by the Council at the time that the unconditional offer had been made. Barron J noted that it would not be possible to say whether the award was more or less than the unconditional offer until there was a determination as to the amount, if any, which the respondent deducted from the compensation by reason of the undertakings which were given in the unconditional offer and were added at the hearing. Accordingly, he remitted the matter to the respondent arbitrator for a determination of these issues. He noted that, in any event, this was a ground for remitting a matter to an arbitrator under s. 36 of the Arbitration Act 1954.

The second case in 1993 we consider here on the issue of giving of reasons by decision-making bodies is the judgment of O'Hanlon J in *Doran v Garda Commissioner* [1994] 1 ILRM 303. Here, the applicant was a detective garda officer who had been stationed in a particular town for approximately 14 years. His wife was employed in a clerical position in the same garda station. The marriage broke down and the applicant formed a relationship with a local married woman who was the only pharmacist in the town. The applicant's superior officers were concerned by the operational difficulties caused by his estranged wife continuing to work in the same station and his association with someone who was subject to supervision by the gardaí under statutory provisions pertaining to drugs and poisons.

He was interviewed by his superintendent and later the chief superintendent in relation to both matters. It was suggested that the applicant should end his relationship with the pharmacist but he refused to do so. Soon after these discussions the Garda Commissioner required that the applicant should be transferred to a station in another county. The Garda Review Board rejected the applicant's appeal against this decision. Following receipt of the board's decision the applicant's solicitor sent a letter indicating that no reason for the proposed transfer had been given and demanding that a statement of the reasons should be supplied within a stated number of days. No reply was received within this time and an application for leave to apply for judicial review was made seeking an order of *certiorari* quashing the decision. O'Hanlon J refused the relief sought.

In an approach which mirrored that taken by O'Hanlon J himself earlier in 1993 in *Lang v Government of Ireland*, High Court, 7 July 1993 (see above, 18) and that taken just two months later by Costello J in *Gormley v Ireland and Ors (No. 2)*, High Court, 1 December 1993 (below, 33), O'Hanlon J stated that given the discussions which took place prior to the making of the decision, the applicant had been aware in general terms of the matters which were causing concern to his superior officers. Likewise, when the transfer decision was appealed to the Garda Review Board, only the breakdown of the applicant's marriage was discussed and in his submissions he had addressed this issue and his alleged association with a local person. Thus the applicant had known about the case which he had to meet and had an opportunity to make submissions to the effect that it was not a sufficient basis for a decision to transfer him.

Although the view that a pharmacist was subject to special garda supervision was not specifically identified as the basis for the concern regarding the applicant's relationship prior to the filing and service of the affidavit, O'Hanlon J concluded that this was known to the applicant and it had been open to him to argue in court that no reasonable tribunal could have reached a decision to transfer him based on the grounds referred to in the affidavit.

Finally, on the reasoanbleness of the transfer order, O'Hanlon J concluded that the decision to transfer the applicant was not so unreasonable that no reasonable authority could have come to it nor was it fundamentally at variance with reason and common sense. In this respect he applied the Supreme Court decisions in *The State (Keegan) v Stardust Victims' Compensation Tribunal* [1987] IR 202; [1986] IR 642 and *O'Keeffe v An Bord*

Pleanála [1992] ILRM 237; [1993] 1 IR 39 (see the 1991 Review, 16-8).

The third case in 1993 we consider here on the issue of giving of reasons by decision-making bodies was the judgment of Costello J in *Gormley v Ireland and Ors (No. 2)*, High Court, 1 December 1993. The case arose from circumstances going back to the late 1950s.

Between July 1957 and November 1958, the plaintiff, then aged 21, was interned pursuant to the Offences against the State (Amendment) Act 1940. At the time of his internment, he was a civil servant, being a clerical officer in a post office, then under the control of the Department of Posts and Telegraphs. During his internment, he was requested to sign a declaration to respect the Constitution of Ireland and not to support or assist any unlawful organisation. The plaintiff refused and, in August 1957, the Department wrote to the plaintiff stating that he was being suspended from duty. Shortly after his release from internment, the plaintiff was again requested to sign a declaration in the form submitted to him earlier. The plaintiff replied in writing that, in view of his Republican principles, he was not prepared to sign the declaration.

Between 1958 and 1983 the plaintiff declined to sign this declaration and he remained suspended as a clerical officer. In 1983, after obtaining the services of a solicitor, the plaintiff signed the declaration and he was restored to his position. He instituted proceedings claiming that he was entitled to a salary without regard to the interruption arising in his suspension from duties. He argued, *inter alia*, that the defendants had engaged in actionable wrongs in failing to give reasons for the decision to suspend him in 1958. An earlier discovery motion in the case, *Gormley v Ireland* [1993] 2 IR 75, was considered in the 1991 Review, 339-40.

Costello J dismissed the claim at the end of the plaintiff's evidence in the case. Quoting with approval the decision of the Supreme Court in *McHugh v Garda Commissioner* [1987] ILRM 181, Costello J concluded that the Department was not required to give reasons for the decision to suspend the plaintiff in the circumstances which arose. In particular, he noted that the plaintiff had been requested to sign the relevant declaration while he was interned and that the Department had informed him of his suspension after he had declined to sign the declaration. Costello J stated:

In the *McHugh* case, as in this case, the reason for the suspension was obvious, and it is not necessary for the suspending authority to spell out the reasons in order to do justice in the case.

Similar considerations applied to the continuing refusal of the plaintiff to sign the undertaking requested between 1958 and 1983 and, accordingly, the plaintiff's claim was dismissed.

Agriculture

ANIMAL DISEASE ERADICATION

Levies The Bovine Diseases (Levies) Regulations 1993 (SI No. 115) revoked the 1990 Regulations of the same title (1990 Review, 21) and update the levies payable under the Bovine Diseases (Levies) Act 1979.

Revocation of veterinary authorisation to test In *Ó Scanaill v Minister for Agriculture and Food* [1993] ELR 176, the applicant was a veterinary surgeon who had been authorised to test animals under s. 25 of the Diseases of Animals Act 1966 for the purposes of the bovine TB and Brucellosis eradication schemes. The applicant had been requested to attend a meeting in the Department of Agriculture 'to discuss your testing' of named herds. The applicant had previously been notified that his testing of these herds had not been satisfactory. At the conclusion of the meeting in the Department, the applicant was informed that the nature of his testing would be drawn to the attention of the Minister, and subsequently he was informed that his authorisation to test animals was being revoked. The applicant successfully applied for judicial review of this decision.

Lynch J quashed the revocation decision by the respondent Minister on the ground that, in view of the effect which the decision would have on the applicant's ability to earn his livelihood, he should have been informed 'in advance in plain language that the Minister would be considering whether or not to revoke his authorisation under s. 25 of the 1966 Act. . . .' As in many other cases on procedural fairness, Lynch J made the point in his judgment that he was not considering whether the decision of the Minister was justified or not, but merely whether the decision had been made in accordance with principles of fair procedures.

ANIMAL REMEDIES

The Animal Remedies Act 1993 is a comprehensive consolidation, with substantial amendments, of the statutory regime for the control of animal remedies, including growth promoters. The 1993 Act repealed the Animal Remedies Act 1956 and brought under its remit the numerous Regulations made under the European Communities Act 1972 which had implemented

EC Directives on the control of animal remedies.

The 1993 Act was brought before the Oireachtas as a matter of urgency arising from the challenge to the Regulations made under s. 3 of the 1972 Act in *Meagher v Minister for Agriculture and Food* [1994] 1 ILRM 1; [1994] 1 IR 329 (HC & SC), which is discussed in detail in the European Community chapter, 299-304, below. It will be recalled that, in *Meagher*, Johnson J held in April 1993 that the Regulations in this area were invalid on the ground that s. 3 of the 1972 Act was itself unconstitutional. In view of the importance to the agri-sector of an effective legal basis for combatting illegal use of growth promoters, the 1993 Act was enacted by the Oireachtas by the end of July 1993. While the High Court decision in *Meagher* was successfully appealed to the Supreme Court, which delivered judgment in November 1993, the 1993 Act had already largely been brought into force on 1 October 1993: Animal Remedies Act 1993 (Commencement) Order 1993 (SI No. 283). In hindsight, therefore, it might be argued that the 1993 Act was thus not required, but its terms introduce a significant modernising of an important aspect of Irish trade so that it can easily be justified in those terms.

S. 1 of the 1993 Act, *inter alia*, defines an 'animal remedy' to mean any substance or combination of substances intended for administration to animals for the purpose, amongst others, of treating or preventing disease in animals or for improving the health of animals. S. 2 of the 1993 Act provides that its terms apply to all mammals (other than humans, birds, fish, reptiles, molluscs, crustaceans and honey bees) and any other animal kept for human consumption. It also provides that the Minister for Agriculture, Food and Forestry may, by Order, apply all or any of the Act's provisions to any other domestic or wild animal.

S. 3 of the Act provides for the continuation in being of the Animal Remedies Consultative Committee, established by the Animal Remedies Act 1956. As already noted, the 1956 Act was repealed by the 1993 Act.

S. 4 of the 1993 Act requires that all animal remedies be clearly marked and labelled and include the name of the ingredients of the remedy in question. In addition, any animal remedy must comply with any Regulations made by the Minister for the time being in force, including those carried over by the 1993 Act under s. 31. S. 4 also provides that any requirements under connected legislation, for example the Therapeutic Substances Act 1932, shall not be affected by the terms of the 1993 Act (though it should be noted that the 1932 Act will, ultimately be repealed and replaced by the 1993 Act and other legislation connected with medical products: see below, 36). S. 4 of the 1993 Act also provides the first clear link between the 1993 Act and the extensive EC-based code concerning veterinary products: s. 4(5) provides that the 1993 Act does not override the requirements of the European

Communities (Veterinary Medicinal Products) Regulations 1986, which implemented Directive 81/851/EEC. S. 5 of the 1993 Act expressly prohibits any adverstising of an animal remedy which contravenes the provisions of the 1993 Act.

S. 6 of the Act provides that it is an offence for any person to have in their possession an animal remedy except where this is authorised by the Act. S. 7 of the Act provides that, in any contract for the sale of an animal to which the Act applies, 'there shall be an implied condition on the part of the seller that all reasonable precautions have been taken and all due diligence has been exercised to ensure' that the animal was not treated with any animal remedy save in accordance with the terms of the Act.

S. 8 of the 1993 Act is extremely signifciant since it confers on the Minister for Agriculture, Food and Forestry substantial Regulation-making powers in connection with the manufacture, sale and use of animal remedies. S. 8 expressly provides that such Regulations may include such as give effect to the requirements of past or future acts of the institutions of the European Communities in this area. This is clearly a very wide-ranging power, and its terms may be linked to the genesis of the Act arising from the *Meagher* case, referred to above. Worthy of note also was that the European Communities (Control of Oestrogenic, Androgenic, Gestagenic and Thyrostatic Substances) Regulations 1988, the Regulations challenged in the Meagher case, were expressly brought under the 'umbrella' of the 1993 Act in an attempt to save them from the apparent invalidity attached to them by the High Court decision in *Meagher*. Whether such an attempt to cloak the Regulations in retrospective validity could be regarded as *intra vires* must now be considered a moot point in view of the ultimate decision of the Supreme Court in *Meagher* to uphold the 1988 Regulations: see the European Community chapter, 299-304, below.

The remainder of the 1993 Act provides for the administrative arrangements required to implement the terms of the Act, including the appointment of authorisied officers of the Department of Agriculture, Food and Forestry to act as inspectors for the purposes of the Act (ss. 10, 11, 16 and 17); the issuing of search warrants by a judge of the District Court (s. 12); the searching of persons suspected of being in possession of an animal remedy in contravention of the Act (s. 13); powers of arrest for the Gardaí (s. 14); provisions for offences and penalties under the Act (ss. 18 to 23); possible disqualification from keeping animals on foot of a conviction under the Act (s. 24) and the forfeiture and disposal of animals (ss. 25 to 27).

As already indicated, the 1993 Act largely came into force on 1 October 1993: Animal Remedies Act 1993 (Commencement) Order 1993 (SI No. 283). In fact, the entire Act came into effect on that date, save for the repeal of the Therapeutic Substances Act 1932. In accordance with the terms of s.

32(1)(b) of the 1993 Act, the repeal of the 1932 Act will occur pursuant to an Order made by the Minister for Agriculture, Food and Forestry after consultation with the Minister for Health. The latter Minister has responsibility for the operation of the 1932 Act insofar as it has an effect on human health. See for example the European Communities (Therapeutic Substances Act 1932) (Cesser of Application) Regulations 1992 (1992 Review, 393).

GREYHOUND INDUSTRY

Bord na gCon and coursing The Greyhound Industry (Amendment) Act 1993 amended the Greyhound Industry Act 1958 in a number of respects. S. 2 of the Act amended s. 9 of the 1958 Act by altering the basis on which members are appointed to Bord na gCon, the Greyhound Board which controls the industry. S. 3 of the 1993 Act amended s. 36 of the 1958 Act by empowering the Minister for Agriculture, Food and Forestry to provide, by Regulations, for the muzzling of greyhounds at coursing meetings. The 1993 Act should be seen against the background of a comprehensive review of the greyhound industry in Ireland which is likely to produce future substantial re-structuring of the industry and its legislative base. The 1993 Act came into effect on 22 December 1993 on its signature by the President.

HORSE INDUSTRY

Equine studs and equine competitions The European Communities (Equine Stud-Book and Competition) Regulations 1993 (SI No. 305) gave effect to Directives 90/427/EEC and 90/428/EEC as well as the associated Decisions 92/216/EEC, 92/353/EEC and 92/354/EEC. In implementing Directive 90/427/EEC, the Regulations set out the criteria which a body must meet if it is to maintain an officially recognised stud-book. In relation to Directive 90/428/EEC, the Regulations provide that any equine competitions organised in the State must not involve discriminatory conditions for horses which originate in other EC member States.

INTRA-COMMUNITY CO-OPERATION

The European Communities (Mutual Assistance as Regards Correct Application of Legislation on Veterinary and Zootechnical Matters) Regulations 1993 (SI No. 150) implement Directive 89/608/EEC. The Regulations empower the Minister and authorised officers to provide information to relevant authorities in other Member States or to the European Commission concerning the application of domestic legislation on veterinary and zootechnical matters, such as the Diseases of Animals Act 1966.

INTRA-COMMUNITY TRADE IN ANIMAL BREEDING MATERIAL

Bovine semen   The European Communities (Trade in Bovine Breeding Animals, their Semen, Ova and Embryos) Regulations 1993 (SI No. 259) give effect to a number of Directives and Decisions in the area of trade in and approval for breeding animals, their semen, ova and embryos. For discussion of an unusual aspect of the Explanatory Note to the Regulations, see the European Community chapter, 305, below.

Porcine Semen   The European Communities (Trade in Porcine Semen — Animal Health) Regulations 1993 (SI No. 242) implemented Directive 90/429/EEC. They provide for the approval of centres for the collection of pig semen destined for intra-Community trade, and set out the animal health criteria which must be satisfied if pig semen is to be lawfully imported into the State or exported to other Member States of the European Community. As with SI No. 259, above, for discussion of an unusual aspect of the Explanatory Note to the Regulations, see the European Community chapter, 305, below.

MEAT GRADING

Pig carcase   The European Communities (Pig Carcass (Grading)) (Amendment) Regulations 1993 (SI No. 313) and the European Communities (Pig Carcass (Grading)) (Amendment) (No. 2) Regulations 1993 (SI No. 405) amend the 1988 Regulations of the same title and lay down the criteria for testing the lean meat percentage of pig carcasses. They implement Commission Decision 93/320/EEC.

PLANT HEALTH

Cereal seed   The European Communities (Cereal Seed) (Amendment) Regulations 1993 (SI No. 123) amend the Regulations of 1981 of the same title and implement Directive 93/2/EEC by allowing for a minimum germination capacity in the case of a particular variety of oats. The European Communities (Cereal Seed) (Amendment) (No. 2) Regulations 1993 (SI No. 260) further amend the Regulations of 1981 of the same title by revising the fees for cereal crop inspection and certification of cereal seed required under the Regulations.

Feedingstuffs The European Communities (Additives in Feedingstuffs) (Amendment) Regulations 1993 (SI No. 79) amended the 1989 Regulations of the same title and the European Communities (Marketing of Feedingstuffs) (Amendment) Regulations 1993 (SI No. 261) amended 1984 Regulations of the same title to implement a significant number of Directives on the standards associated with the additives approved for, and the actual placing on the market of, animal feedingstuffs. The European Communities (Feedingstuffs) (Method of Analysis) (Amendment) Regulations 1993 (SI No. 370) implemented Directive 92/95/EEC which provided for a new method of analysing feedingstuffs for the purposes of the controls contained in the legislative regime amended by SI Nos. 79 and 261, above. The European Communities (Feedingstuffs) (Tolerances of Undesirable Substances and Products) (Amendment) Regulations 1993 (SI No. 86) amended the 1989 Regulations of the same title and implemented Directive 92/63/EEC, altering the permitted levels for cadmium in phosphates and introduced a maximum permitted level for arsenic in phosphates.

Fertilizers The European Communities (Marketing of Fertilizers) (Amendment) Regulations 1993 (SI No. 110) involved minor amendments to the 1991 Regulations of the same title. On the 1991 Regulations, see the 1991 Review, 202. The European Communities (Sampling and Analysis of Fertilizers) Regulations 1993 (SI No. 257) implemented Directive 93/1/EEC concerning the analysis of fertilizers for trace elements of boron, cobalt, copper, iron, manganese, molybdenum and zinc. See also SI No. 86 above on phosphates.

Fodder plants The European Communities (Seed of Fodder Plants) (Amendment) Regulations 1993 (SI No. 230) prescribed new fees for the certification and testing of fodder plant seed in accordance with the Regulations of 1981 to 1992 of the same title. For earlier Regulations, see the 1992 Review, 15.

Organisms harmful to plants or plant products The European Communities (Introduction of Organisms Harmful to Plants or Plant Products) (Prohibition) (Amendment) Regulations 1993 (SI No. 408) implemented Directives 91/683/EEC, 92/70/EEC, 92/76/EEC, 92/90/EEC, 92/98/EEC, 92/103/EEC, 92/105/EEC, 93/19/EEC, 93/50/EEC and 93/51/EEC, which involved amendments to the Principal Directive in this area, 77/93/EEC. The 1977 Directive was implemented by the 1980 Regulations of the same title.

Pesticide residues   Both the European Communities (Pesticide Residues) (Cereals) (Amendment) Regulations 1993 (SI No. 316) (which amend 1988 Regulations of the same title) and the European Communities (Pesticide Residues) (Foodstuffs of Animal Origin) (Amendment) Regulations 1993 (SI No. 317) (which also amend 1988 Regulations of the same title) implement Directive 93/57/EEC, which laid down further maximum pesticide residue limits for 22 substances contained in cereals and foodstuffs of animal origin, respectively. The term 'foodstuffs' includes beef, pig meat (including sausages), horse meat, milk, cream, butter, cheese, birds' eggs and egg products.

Potato ring rot   The European Communities (Potato Ring Rot) Regulations 1993 (SI No. 346) revoked the 1981 Regulations of the same title and gave effect to Directive 93/85/EEC.

PROPRIETARY PLANT RIGHTS

The Plant Varieties (Proprietary Rights) (Amendment) Regulations 1993 (SI No. 78) extended from 20 to 25 years the period for which plant breeders' rights exist in respect of potatoes under the Plant Varieties (Proprietary Rights) Act 1980. The Plant Varieties (Proprietary Rights) (Amendment) (No. 2) Regulations 1993 (SI No. 332) extended the plant breeders' rights available under the 1980 Act to seven specified genera or species.

RETIREMENT OF FARMERS

The European Communities (Retirement of Farmers) Regulations 1993 (SI No. 204) provided for an increase in the annuity payable to retiring farmers under the terms of the 1974 Regulations of the same title.

Aliens and Immigration

CITIZENSHIP

Fees   The Irish Nationality and Citizenship (Fees) Regulations 1993 (SI No. 89) revoked the 1987 Order of the same title and revised the fees applicable under the Irish Nationality and Citizenship Acts 1956 and 1986.

EC RESIDENCE RIGHTS

The European Communities (Right of Residence for Non-Economically Active Persons) Regulations 1993 (SI No. 109) implemented Directives 90/364/EEC, 90/365/EEC and 90/366/EEC. These Regulations grant a right of residence in the State to nationals of member States of the European Community, over and above the rights granted where such nationals are employed in the State. There are a number of restrictions to the right of residence conferred by the Regulations, such as by reference to the interest of public health or where the person cannot establish a means of support. The Regulations expressly provide that nothing in the Aliens Order 1946, as amended, shall invalidate any provision of the 1993 Regulations but that otherwise the 1946 Order, as amended, shall continue to apply to the persons to whom the 1993 Regulations apply.

VISA REQUIREMENTS

Additional specified States   The Aliens (Amendment) Order 1993 (SI No. 28) amended the Aliens Order 1946 so that a citizen of Moldavia requires a visa in order to enter the State. The Aliens (Amendment) (No. 4) Order 1993 (SI No. 240) imposed a visa requirement for citizens of Uganda. The Aliens (Amendment) (No. 5) Order 1993 (SI No. 271) imposed a visa requirement for citizens of Albania, Montenegro and Serbia (the latter two being the Federal Republic of Yugoslavia). Finally, the Aliens (Amendment) (No. 6) Order 1993 (SI No. 361) imposed a visa requirement for citizens of the Lebanon.

Airline stops   The Aliens (Amendment) (No. 2) Order 1993 (SI No. 90) amended the Aliens Order 1946 by specifying that a transit visa is required for a citizen of a State not referred to in the Sixth Schedule to the 1946 Order where such person is on a flight that has a scheduled transit stop in the State and where the person is not a national of the country in which the airline operating the flight has its head office.

Removal of requirement: Slovenia   The Aliens (Amendment) (No. 3) Order 1993 (SI No. 100) amended the Aliens Order 1946 by adding Slovenia to the list of States in the Sixth Schedule to the 1946 Order. The effect is that a citizen of Slovenia no longer requires a visa to enter the State.

Barristers

DISCIPLINARY PROCEEDINGS

The operation of the non-statutory disciplinary procedure of the Bar of Ireland came to public attention in 1993. The matter arose against the background of the proceedings of the Tribunal of Inquiry into the Beef Industry, established in 1991: see the Administrative Law chapter, 11, above.

A complaint was made to the Council of the Bar of Ireland, the non-statutory regulatory body for barristers in the State, concerning three alleged conversations involving a junior counsel member of the legal team representing the Attorney General at the Tribunal. It was averred that in one of these alleged conversations, the junior counsel had intimated to a senior counsel representing a particular witness before the Tribunal that 'it would not be good' for that senior counsel's career to cross-examine the then Taoiseach, who was, at the time of the alleged conversation, due to give evidence to the Tribunal. On another occasion, again prior to the then Taoiseach giving his evidence to the Tribunal, the junior counsel was alleged to have said that, if the senior counsel were to cross-examine the then Taoiseach, certain people would expose the senior counsel's tax affairs on the same day as any bad publicity might arise from the cross-examination of the then Taoiseach.

In fact, the senior counsel in question did cross-examine the then Taoiseach in relation to his evidence to the Tribunal, but a complaint was submitted by another party alleging that the junior counsel in question had been in breach of the non-statutory Code of Conduct of the Bar of Ireland. On foot of a formal complaint by the Professional Practices Committee of the Council of the bar of Ireland, the matter was initially investigated by the Professional Conduct Tribunal of the Bar of Ireland and statements were requested, on the basis of confidentiality, from the counsel involved in the matter. The statement from the Senior Counsel involved came into the public domain and was published by a newspaper, 'The Sun', which gave rise to a conviction for contempt of court: see *Council of the Bar of Ireland v Sunday Business Post*, High Court, 30 March 1993, discussed in the Criminal Law chapter, 217-9, below.

In March 1993, the Professional Conduct Tribunal found that the conversations in question had occurred and that some of the utterances had been designed to cause some element of unease and disquiet in the mind of the senior counsel in respect of whom the remarks were addressed. However, it determined that there was no sufficient proof of an intention to intimidate, and it noted that the senior counsel in question had proceeded to cross-examine the then Taoiseach at the Tribunal of Inquiry. The Professional Conduct Tribunal concluded that the junior counsel in question had been guilty of conduct unbecoming a barrister and of conduct likely to bring the profession into disrepute, in breach of the Code of Conduct of the Bar of Ireland. For the decision of the Professional Conduct Tribunal, see *Irish Times*, 5 March 1993.

The junior counsel in question appealed against the findings of the Professional Conduct Tribunal to the Professional Conduct Appeals Board, in what was believed to have been the first use of this appeal mechanism, which had been introduced to the Bar's Code of Conduct only a few years before. In July 1993, the Appeal Board affirmed the finding of the Professional Conduct Tribunal that the conversations in question had occurred, but the Board reversed the finding that the junior counsel had been guilty of conduct unbecoming a barrister and of conduct likely to bring the profession into disrepute. The Appeal Board found, instead, that the junior counsel had been guilty of the much lesser matter of breaching proper professional standards, contrary to the Code of Conduct of the Bar of Ireland.

Commercial Law

ARBITRATION

Reasons for decision The circumstances in which an arbitrator is required to give reasons for an award were considered by Barron J in *Manning v Shackleton* [1994] 1 ILRM 346; [1994] 1 IR 397: see the discussion in the Administrative Law chapter, 30, above.

BANKRUPTCY

Set-off against unpaid rates In *In re Casey, a Bankrupt (No. 2)*, High Court, 1 March 1993, the extensive nature of the right of set-off in respect of unpaid rates conferred on a local authority by s. 58 of the Local Government Act 1941 was considered: see the discussion in the Local Government chapter below, 439.

BILLS OF EXCHANGE

The general right to obtain judgment on foot of a bill of exchange, without any stay, was applied by Barron J in *Terex Equipment Ltd v Truck and Machinery Sales Ltd* [1994] 1 ILRM 557.

The plaintiff had sold to the defendant earth-moving equipment consisting of trucks and motorised scrapers which were paid for by the plaintiff accepting bills of exchange drawn by the plaintiff in its favour. Each bill was negotiated as a discount at a bank, and when some of the bills were dishonoured the bank was repaid the discounted sums. The plaintiff then brought proceedings to recover payment on foot of the dishonoured bills. The defendant alleged that the goods were defective and that the plaintiff had fraudulently delivered trucks of a different tonnage capacity to those ordered.

The defendant brought a cross-action in respect of these claims. In resisting the plaintiff's claim the defendant contended that the plaintiff had agreed to regard the bills as no longer subsisting and that they would not sue on them. The plaintiff relied on s. 62(1) of the Bills of Exchange Act 1882 which provides that when the holder of a bill, at or after its maturity, absolutely or unconditionally renounces his rights against the acceptor, the bill is discharged. Such renunciation must be in writing unless the bill is delivered up to the acceptor. Barron J rejected the defendant's arguments and entered judgment in favour of the plaintiff.

He referred to the decision in *Nova (Jersey) Knit Ltd v Kammgarn Spinerei GmbH* [1977] 1 WLR 713 where, he noted, the circumstances were exactly similar to the instant case: the bill had been discounted to the bank for collection, had subsequently been dishonoured and the bank had subsequently been repaid. It was held in that case that the original drawer/payee of the bill was entitled to sue as a holder in due course by reason of the endorsements to the bank and from the bank. However, while not expressing a final view on the matter, Barron J was inclined to the view that where, in modern practice, bills of exchange payable at a later date are always discounted to a bank for collection, this should not benefit a party who was involved in any fraud, as was alleged in the instant case. However, as the alleged fraud (that the plaintiff sought to conceal that the vehicles being delivered were not those which had been ordered) had, it was claimed, occurred after the bills were accepted and was not something which induced the contract, Barron J held that the defendant was not entitled to rely upon any such alleged fraud for the purpose of defeating the validity of the bills.

Finally, Barron J noted that the defendant had alleged that the financial position of the plaintiff was far from secure. He noted that such averments are usually made for the purpose of seeking a stay on any order which may be made against the defendant. In Barron J's view the Supreme Court decision in *Walek & Co. KG v Seafield Gentex Ltd* [1978] IR 167 confirmed that negotiable instruments were the equivalent to cash and that actions on foot of such instruments or judgment in respect thereof could not be stayed to enable the defendant to counterclaim for unliquidated damages. He concluded, therefore, that not only was the plaintiff entitled to judgment for the amount claimed but that the defendant was not entitled to any stay either.

BUSINESS NAMES

The Business Names Regulations 1993 (SI No. 138) amend the 1964 Regulations of the same title by increasing the fees to be paid in connection with certain matters under the Business Names Act 1963 and also to discontinue the requirement to pay such fees by postage stamp.

COMPETITION

Competition Authority: notification of decisions   The Competition Act 1991 (Notice of Licences and Certificates) Regulations 1993 (SI No. 293) revoked the 1992 Regulations of the same title and revised the manner in which the Competition Authority may give notice of its decisions.

European Commission investigations generally   The European Communities (Rules on Competition) Regulations 1993 (SI No. 124) facilitate the full implementation of Council Regulation 17 of 1962 and Council Regulation 4064/89 to enable investigations to be carried out by the European Commission under Article 85 and 86 of the EC Treaty and the 1962 and 1989 Council Regulations. The Irish Regulations also enable officers of the Department of Enterprise and Employment to assist European Commission officials carry out their functions, and in this context confer powers of entry and inspection on Departmental officers. Fines of up to £1,000 and/or imprisonment of 12 months are provided for offences under the Regulations, primarily for obstruction of investigations. See also SI Nos. 386 and 416, below.

Maritime transport   The European Communities (Application of the Rules on Competition to Maritime Transport) Regulations 1993 (SI No. 386) facilitate the full implementation of Council Regulation 4056/86 concerning the application of EC rules on competition to the maritime transport sector. As with SI No. 124, above, and SI No. 416, below, the 1993 Regulations provide, primarily, for enforcement powers for officers of the Minister for Transport, Energy and Communications in carrying out investigations pursuant to the 1986 Council Regulation. Penalties of a maximum fine of £1,000 and/or six months imprisonment are provided for failure to comply with the 1993 Regulations.

Mergers and take-overs: thresholds   The Mergers, Take-overs and Monopolies (Control) Act 1978 (Section 2) Order 1993 (SI No. 135) increased the thresholds contained in s. 2 of the 1978 Act required to trigger the terms of the Act. The 1978 Act now applies where the gross assets of each of two or more of the enterprises involved in a merger or take-over is not less than £10m or the turnover of each of these two or more enterprises is not less than £20m. The previous thresholds were £5m and £10m, respectively, which were contained in the 1985 Order of the same title and which had replaced the original thresholds contained in s. 2 of the 1978 Act as enacted. The 1985 Order was revoked by the 1993 Order. The 1993 Order required a positive resolution by both Houses of the Oireachtas to be confirmed. These were duly made: see 432 *Dáil Debates* cc.555-75 (which involved a full debate on the Order) and 137 *Seanad Debates* cc.570-1 (where no debate of any kind occurred). The new thresholds contained in the 1993 Order had been recommended by the Culliton and Moriarty Task Force Reports: on these Reports see generally the Administrative Law chapter, 8, above.

Rail and road transport   The European Communities (Application of the Rules on Competition to Rail and Road Transport) Regulations 1993 (SI No. 416) gave full effect to the terms of Council Regulation 1017/68, insofar as that Regulation applies to rail and road transport. As with SI Nos. 124 and 386, above, the 1993 Regulations provide, primarily, for enforcement powers for officers of the Minister for Transport, Energy and Communications in carrying out investigations pursuant to the 1968 Council Regulation. Penalties of a maximum fine of £1,000 and/or six months imprisonment are provided for failure to comply with the 1993 Regulations.

CONSUMER PROTECTION

Misleading advertisements   The decision of Keane J in *J. O'Connor (Nenagh) Ltd v Powers Supermarkets Ltd (t/a Quinnsworth Ltd)*, High Court, 15 March 1993 is discussed below, 64-6.

Price indications   The European Communities (Indication of Prices of Foodstuffs and Non-Food Products) (Amendment) Regulations 1993 (SI No. 307) amended the 1991 Regulations of the same title (see the 1991 Review, 202) by requiring the indication of the unit price of foodstuffs and non-food products, as defined in the 1991 Regulations, in written or printed advertisements and catalogues. The 1993 Regulations came into effect on 22 October 1993.

FINANCIAL SERVICES

Moneylenders   The Moneylenders Act 1900 (Section 6(e)) Order 1993 (SI No. 167), made under ss. 6 and 6A of the 1900 Act, as amended by s. 136 of the Central Bank Act 1989, exempts certain financial transactions and institutions from the provisions of the 1900 Act. See on this point the 1989 Review, 38. Article 3 of the 1993 Order revoked the Moneylenders Act 1900 (Section 6) (Exemptions) Order 1992 (see the 1992 Review, 33) as well as an Order of Exemption of 12 September 1989 made under s. 6 of the 1900 Act but which had not been made in statutory form. Certain elements of the 1993 Order were deemed to come into operation on 1 September 1971, in order to be aligned with the exemptions given to banking business carried out under the Central Bank Act 1971.

FINANCIAL TRANSFERS (EXCHANGE CONTROL)

The Financial Transfers (Haiti) Order 1993 (SI No. 351), which came into effect on 30 November 1993, gave effect to UN Security Council Resolution No. 841 of 1993. The Financial Transfers (Libya) Order 1993 1993 (SI No. 410), which came into effect on 23 December 1993, gave effect to UN Security Council Resolution No. 883 of 1993. Both Orders were made under the Financial Transfers Act 1992 (see the 1992 Review, 33-5) and require Central Bank permission to make any financial transfers to nationals of the States in question, in accordance with these UN Security Council resolutions. We note that these statutory instruments, being titled Orders, do not suffer from the apparent defect which we noted in instruments made in 1992 under the 1992 Act: see the 1992 Review, 35.

INSURANCE

Contra proferentem rule   In *Dillon v McGovern (on behalf of Certain Underwriters at Lloyd's)*, High Court, 16 March 1993, Murphy J applied the *contra proferentem* rule in connection with the interpretation of an insurance contract entered into by the plaintiff in the form of a certificate issued by a company, Thoroughbred Insurance Services Ltd, acting effectively as broker or agent for certain underwriters at Lloyd's, represented in the proceedings by the defendant.

The plaintiff was a farmer and the insurance cover concerned a herd of 79 cattle. The insurance documents stated that cover applied where cattle were 'slaughtered under the provisions of the Diseases of Animals Act 1966 . . . following failure to pass the routine brucellosis test.' In the instant case, 15 of the plaintiff's herd of 79 cattle failed the 'routine brucellosis test', but, in accordance with the policy of the Department of Agriculture and Food in the application of the Brucellosis in Cattle (General Provisions) Order 1980, made under the Diseases of Animals Act 1966, the remainder of the herd were 'deemed to be reactors' and the entire herd of 79 cattle was slaughtered. The plaintiff claimed that the insurance policy entitled him to compensation for the loss of the entire herd, while the defendants argued that only the 15 cattle which actually failed the brucellosis test were covered.

The first issue Murphy J addressed was whether the phrase 'failure to pass the routine brucellosis test' was unambiguous. If it was, then parol evidence as to its meaning was inadmissible. He held that the expression 'failure to pass' was 'slightly ambiguous in that it could be held to cover animals which had been tested but had neither failed nor passed the test.' On this basis, he admitted parol evidence to the effect that when the plaintiff took out the policy in 1985, he asked the representative of Thoroughbred Insurance Services Ltd to 'insure my whole herd against brucellosis.' This was confirmed by the Thoroughbred representative.

The plaintiff understood this to mean what Murphy J described as 'depopulation cover'; that is, that the policy would cover the slaughter of an entire herd where this was required by the policy of the Department of Agriculture and Food. However, such 'depopulation' cover was not actually considered by the Thoroughbred representative nor was it in contemplation in the wording used in the contract itself. Nonetheless, Murphy J was prepared to hold that, in view of the plaintiff's intentions and the ambiguity in the wording, the policy did cover the entire herd. While he was prepared to come to this view on general principles, he stated that the *contra proferentem* rule 'greatly strengthens me in the view which I have taken.' In this context, he referred with approval to *dicta* of Kingsmill Moore J in *In re Sweeney and Kennedy Arbitration* [1950] IR 85 on the application of the *contra proferentem* rule in the insurance context. Applying the rule to the instant case, Murphy J stated:

> A farmer, such as the plaintiff, dealing with Thoroughbred would have been entitled to assume that Thoroughbred and its principals undertaking this kind of insurance were aware of the methods by which the provisions of the Diseases of Animals Act 1966 and the Regulations made thereunder were implemented in relation to the eradication of brucellosis. Any such farmer could reasonably expect that, if there was exclusion of liability for depopulation following on a failure of some animals to pass a specific test, this would have been expressly stated in the policy.

Accordingly, Murphy J held that the policy of insurance applied to the entire herd slaughtered and he therefore found in favour of the plaintiff, awarding him £35,180 damages.

Disclosure of information   In *Kelleher v Irish Life Assurance Co. Ltd* [1993] ILRM 643; [1993] 3 IR 393, the Supreme Court again considered the scope of the requirement to disclose material information in an insurance contract.

The plaintiff was the widow of a doctor who, along with the plaintiff, had taken out a policy of health insurance with the defendant insurance company. The policy, described by the defendant as a 'special promotional offer', had been negotiated by the defendant company through an insurance broker, and the defendant company had dispensed with the need for medical examinations of the proposers where they were members of the Irish Medical

Organistion (IMO), of which the plaintiff's husband was one. However, the proposal form required the insured person to answer two questions concerning health: that any absence from work due to illness had been confined to not more than two weeks in the previous three months and, secondly, that the insured had undertaken no medical treatment in the previous six months. In addition, the proposal form contained an undertaking by the deceased doctor and the plaintiff that the information contained in the proposal was true and accurate and formed the basis for the contract of insurance.

The plaintiff's husband had, a number of years previously, been diagnosed as suffering from cancer, and this had recurred shortly before taking out the policy with the defendant company, though the defendant company did not adduce evidence that the deceased had undergone medical treatment within six months of taking out the policy. This information was not disclosed to the company at the time of entering into the contract. The plaintiff's husband died shortly after the contract had been entered into. The company repudiated liability on the basis of the non-disclosure of material information and the plaintiff sought to enforce the agreement.

In the High Court (see the 1988 Review, 56), Costello J held in favour of the defendant company and dismissed the plaintiff's claim. Costello J had referred to the Supreme Court decision in *Aro Road and Land Vehicles Ltd v Insurance Corporation of Ireland Ltd* [1986] IR 403, in which Henchy J had noted that, in certain circumstances, the general obligation to disclose material information could be deemed to have been waived. However, Costello J concluded that, in the instant case, the obligation to disclose material information continued notwithstanding the waiver by the insurance company of the normal obligation to have a medical examination, this being clear, he considered, from the general declaration which the plaintiff and her husband had signed in the proposal. On this basis, therefore, he concluded that the failure by the plaintiff and the husband to disclose the evidence of cancer entitled the company to repudiate the policy.

On appeal, the Supreme Court (Finlay CJ, Blayney and Denham JJ) unanimously reversed the High Court decision. Delivering the Court's decision, Finlay CJ noted that neither party had challenged the general proposition, first stated by Lord Mansfield in *Carter v Boehm* (1776) 3 Burr 1905, concerning the obligation to disclose material information. However, by contrast with Costello J in the High Court, Finlay CJ placed considerable emphasis on the waiver by the defendant company of the requirement to have a medical examination of the plaintiff's deceased husband. In addition to referring with approval to the relevant passage from Henchy J's judgment in *Aro Road and Land Vehicles Ltd v Insurance Corporation of Ireland Ltd* [1986] IR 403, referred to above, Finlay CJ also cited with approval a passage from *MacGillivray and Parkington on Insurance Law*, 8th ed. (1988) and the decision of Woolf J (as he then was) in *Hair v Prudential Assurance Co. Ltd* [1983] 2 Lloyd's Rep 667 dealing with the question of waiver of the disclosure requirement. In particular, Finlay CJ approved the following sentence from *MacGillivray and Parkington* on the question whether an insurer had waived the usual disclosure requirement:

> Whether or not such waiver is present depends on a true construction of the proposal form, the test being would a reasonable man reading the proposal form be justified in thinking that the insurer had restricted his right to receive all material information, and consented to the omission of the particular information in issue?

On this test, Finlay CJ concluded that a reasonable man reading the proposal form would assume that, having truthfully answered the two questions concerning health referred to above and being a member of the IMO, he would be entitled to the insurance. The Chief Justice considered that the case could be decided simply on the basis of this 'true construction' of the contract documents, though he noted that the defendant's 'special promotional offer' constituted:

> a very sound and probable commercial manner in which to attract a very substantial quantity of new business by one single project. That fact constitutes a probable reason why the defendant should significantly limit the disclosure required from proposers for that insurance.

This emphasis on the 'block' nature of the policy in the instant case echoes, of course, the similar situation in *Aro Road and Land Vehicles Ltd v Insurance Corporation of Ireland Ltd* [1986] IR 403. It is also notable that, in the *Kelleher* case, the Court effectively concluded that the general 'basis of contract' undertaking in the proposal form was overridden by the waiver of the disclosure requirement by the defendant company. The decision in *Kelleher* indicates that the *Aro Road and Land Vehicles* case was not a once-off decision, and that the courts will look very closely at the surrounding circumstances of an insurance contract to determine whether full disclosure is required. The excessive breadth of 'basis of contract' clauses, evident from cases such as *Keenan v Shield Insurance Co. Ltd* [1988] IR 89 (see the 1987 Review, 38-9), may be subject to some limitations in the light of the reference in the *Kelleher* case to the commercial context in which policies are targeted at particular sectors.

False and exaggerated claims   In *Fagan v General Accident Fire and Life Assurance Corp plc*, High Court, 19 February 1993, Murphy J permitted the defendant company to repudiate a home fire policy issued to the plaintiff on the ground that the plaintiff's claim had been deliberately over-stated. Murphy J noted that the parties were agreed that the relevant law was correctly stated by Hirst J in *Black King Shipping Corp v Massie* [1985] 1 Lloyd's Rep 437 and in *MacGillivray and Parkington on Insurance*, 8th ed., para.1926, where the connection between the *uberrimae fidei* principle and the obligation not to make a false or exaggerated claim were discussed.

What was in dispute in the *Fagan* case was whether the plaintiff had, in fact, made exaggerated claims. The judgment delivered by Murphy J reviews in depth the evidence given in the case and in particular the claims made by the plaintiff in respect of the losses claimed arising from the fire at his home. Having reviewed this evidence, Murphy J came to the conclusion that the plaintiff's claim had been 'deliberately over-stated' and that the defendant company was thus entitled to repudiate the policy. He came to this conclusion 'with regret' as it was beyond dispute that the plaintiff had a valid policy of insurance which in fact covered a loss of up to approximately £46,000 and that the plaintiff had suffered 'substantial' loss arising from the fire that occurred. Nonetheless, on the basis of the application of the legal principles applicable, Murphy J concluded that the defendant company was entitled to succeed, and he accordingly dismissed the plaintiff's claim for damages.

Illegal act of insured: proof   In *Gray v Hibernian Insurance Co. Ltd*, High Court, 27 May 1993, Barron J rejected a claim by the defendant company that it was entitled to repudiate liability under a contract of fire insurance. The judgment arose against the following protracted background.

The plaintiff's husband had insured his public house, the *Bolton Horse* in Dublin, with the defendant and a fire had occurred in the premises in 1982. The husband instituted a malicious injuries claim against Dublin Corporation and also claimed under the insurance policy. Before the malicious injuries claim was heard, the husband was arrested and charged with being implicated in the fire, and the malicious injuries claim was stayed pending the husband's trial for arson. At his trial in the Circuit Criminal Court, evidence was given by two persons that they had been instructed to set fire to the public house by the husband. The husband gave evidence denying this and he was acquitted by the trial jury.

Proceedings to enforce the insurance policy were then instituted by the husband and, in November 1987, the defendant accepted liability under the policy and later made a payment of £100,000 on account, though the parties could not agree on the full amount to paid under the policy and this was then referred to arbitration. The plaintiff's husband died in September 1988. In February 1989, the defendant's solicitor wrote to the plaintiff indicating they felt prejudiced by the delay in processing the malicious injuries claim, which had been stayed pending the arson charge. They then instituted proceedings seeking to stay the arbitration, but in February 1991 this action was settled on the plaintiff undertaking to pursue the malicious injuries claim and the settlement terms also provided that the defendant 'undertakes unconditionally' that it would not withdraw its agreement to indemnify the plaintiff in respect of her claim under the policy of insurance.

In the malicious injuries application, evidence was given by the same two persons who had alleged in the husband's arson trial that they had been instructed by him to set fire to the public house. The Circuit Court judge found that these two people were probably telling the truth and he dismissed the claim. On the following day, the defendant repudiated liability under the fire policy and the plaintiff then instituted the instant proceedings. As already indicated, Barron J held that the defendant was not entitled to repudiate.

The defendant had argued that the plaintiff was not entitled to succeed because the loss on which she relied was caused by the deliberate act of her husband. Relying on the decision of the House of Lords in *Beresford v Royal Insurance Co. Ltd* [1938] 2 All ER 602, the defendant argued that both as a matter of public policy and of general insurance principles, the plaintiff should not be allowed to succeed. Barron J held that there were two impediments in the instant case which prevented the defendant from asserting that the loss on which the plaintiff relied was caused by the deliberate act of her husband.

First, in November 1987 the defendant had admitted liability under the policy and this was underscored by the terms of the February 1991 settlement of the action in which the defendant undertook 'unconditionally' that it would not withdraw its agreement to indemnify the plaintiff under the policy. Second, in relation to public policy, Barron J was not prepared to hold that the defendant had established that the plaintiff's husband had engaged in an illegal act. He noted that, whereas in the criminal trial the husband had given evidence and an acquittal had resulted, he had died by the time the malicious injuries claim came to hearing and the only evidence heard in the latter proceedings were of the two people who claimed they had been instructed by the husband to set fire to the public house. Barron J concluded that he could not be satisfied 'even on the balance of probabilities' that, if the husband had given evidence in the malicious injuries claim, the court would have dismissed that claim. Since he had been acquitted in the criminal trial at which he gave evidence, Barron J concluded that 'public policy could not require the Court on such evidence to deny to his estate the benefits to which he is entitled by contract.'

One note may be added on the onus of proof required by Barron J in the instant case. Although he held that the defendant had failed to establish illegality 'even on the balance of probabilities', he had also indicated that, although the issue arose in civil proceedings, establishing that the deceased committed a crime 'requires a heavier standard of proof than the balance of probabilities. ' In view of his actual conclusion on evidence, this comment may have been *obiter*. Nonetheless, it would appear to be inconsistent to a degree with the approach taken in *Banco Ambrosiano Spa v Ansbacher & Co. Ltd* [1987] ILRM 669 (see the 1987 Review, 165), in which the Supreme Court had rejected any form of 'intermediate' levels of proof in civil proceedings, even where criminal allegations were involved.

Subrogation In *In re Casey, a Bankrupt (No. 2)*, High Court, 1 March 1993, Hamilton P (as he then was) dealt with certain aspects of the scope and extent of subrogation in the context of a malicious injuries claim. Prior to his adjudication in bankruptcy, Mr Casey had entered into a contract of fire insurance with Guardian Royal Exchange Assurance plc in respect of a house. The house was badly damaged in a fire in October 1977 and, in 1979, Guardian Royal paid to Mr Casey's solicitor the sum of £25,400 in respect of its liability under the policy of insurance. On Guardian Royal's initiative, Mr Casey had also instituted a malicious injuries claim against Cork County Council in respect of the fire in the house and, in December 1979, an award of £31,806 was made in his favour in the Circuit Court. This order was, on appeal, affirmed by the High Court in March 1981. Mr Casey was adjudged bankrupt in July 1981 and, as a consequence, all his property became vested in the Official Assignee in Bankruptcy.

The question then arose as to the destination of the £31,806 malicious injuries award. In 1983, Guardian Royal applied to the High Court to have the entire sum paid to it on the ground that, having paid Mr Casey under the policy of insurance, his rights and remedies in respect of the fire had become subrogated to Guardian Royal. Cork County Council argued that it was entitled to set off from the malicious injuries claim the amount of rates owing to it on the property. In July 1983, Costello J ordered that the proceeds of the malicious injuries claim be paid into court less the amount of rates claimed by the Council, but this order was without prejudice to the claim made by Guardian Royal that it was entitled to the full sum.

The only question which arose, therefore, was the extent of Guardian Royal's subrogation. Hamilton P's judgment states that Guardian Royal's application came on for full hearing 'several months after' Costello J's order. Counsel for Guardian Royal argued that it was entitled to the entire proceeds from the malicious injuries claim, relying on passages from *Goff and Jones on Restitution*, 2nd ed., p. 428, and the authorities cited therein, to the effect that an insurer should not be prejudiced by the bankruptcy of the assured provided that the money in question can be identified in the hands of the assured. In response, the Council referred to s. 58 of the Local Government

Act 1941, which provides:

> Where a sum is due to any person by a local authority and, at
> the time, a sum is due to such local authority by such person in respect
> of rates . . . the former sum may be set-off against the latter either, as
> may be appropriate, in whole or in part.

Hamilton P agreed with the view expressed in Street, *The Law Relating
to Local Government*, that s. 58 was comprehensive in its scope. Turning to
the question of Guardian Royal's claimed subrogation, Hamilton P noted that
in *Orakpo v Manson Investments Ltd* [1977] 1 All ER 666, Buckley LJ had
pointed out that subrogation was in the nature of an equitable right whose
nature and extent may depend on the circumstances in which it is claimed,
and that a feature common to all such claims was that the party subrogated
acquired no greater right or remedy than that of the party to whose position
he is being subrogated. In the instant case, Hamilton P pointed out that, had
Mr Casey initiated the malicious injuries claim in his own right, he would
have been affected by s. 58 of the 1941 Act. He concluded:

> Guardian Royal, standing in the shoes of Mr Casey, as it were, would
> be no less affected by the provisions of that section.

On this basis, he held that the Council were entitled to the set-off under
s. 58, the balance being payable to Guardian Royal on the ground that neither
the bankrupt or his estate had any beneficial interest in the balance.

INTELLECTUAL PROPERTY

Copyright: computer programs   The European Communities (Legal Protection of Computer Programs) Regulations 1993 (SI No. 26) gives effect to
Directive 91/250/EEC on the legal protection of computer programs. Prior
to the 1993 Regulations, it was unclear whether the Copyright Act 1963
extended to computer programs and existing case law indicated that comparable legislation did not provide explicit protection: see Robert Clark's article
(1987) 6 *ILT* 8.
    The 1993 Regulations extend the full range of the protections, and
exemptions, in the 1963 Act to computer programs. This is stated to be
without prejudice to other rights which may exist in law, and while reference
is made in this context in Reg.9(1) of the Regulations to possible rights under
the law of trade marks and patents, we should note that s. 9(2)(c) of the Patents
Act 1992 appears to explicity exclude computer programs from patentability:
see the 1992 Review, 43. The 1993 Regulations are on firmer ground when

referring to trade mark law and also to protections which exist in relation to the topographies of semiconductors: see the European Communities (Protection of Topographies of Semiconductor Products) Regulations 1988 (1988 Review, 210, and below, 58). In addition, the Regulations state that they are also without prejudice to rights connected with unfair competition, trade secrets and pursuant to contract law.

The core provision of the 1993 Regulations is Reg.3 which provides:

(1) Subject to paragraph (2) of this Regulation, copyright shall subsist in a computer program and the Copyright Acts 1963 and 1987 shall apply to every original computer program as if it were a literary work and the legal protection so afforded shall apply to the expression in any form of a computer program.

(2) Without prejudice to the generality of paragraph (1) of this Regulation, a computer program shall be protected if it is original in the sense of being the author's own intellectual creation.

(3) Ideas and principles which underlie any element of a computer program, including those which underlie its interfaces, are not protected by copyright under these Regulations.

While this provision, together with the remainder of the Regulations, provides a clear basis for the protection of computer programs, it is to be regretted that this was effected by means of Regulations rather than an amending Act. Although the decision of the Supreme Court in *Meagher v Minister for Agriculture and Food* [1994] 1 ILRM 1; [1994 1 IR 329 (see the European Community chapter, 299-304, below) may indicate that the Regulations are valid in Irish law, it would appear unfortunate that a signifciant amendment to existing copyright law is found in secondary rather than primary legislation.

The 1993 Regulations were signed by the Minister for Enterprise and Employment on 2 February 1993 but, in order to keep within the requirements laid down in the 1991 Directive, Reg.1(2) provides that the Regulations 'shall be deemed to have come into operation on the 31st day of December 1992.' However, presumably with an eye to Article 15.5 of the Constitution (see the 1992 Review, 68-73 and 383), Reg.1(2) goes on to provide that 'nothing in these Regulations shall have the effect of making or declaring any acts to be unlawful which were not unlawful at the date of their commission.'

Copyright: fees The Copyright (Proceedings Before the Controller) Rules 1964 (Amendment) Rules 1993 (SI No. 218) revised the fees payable in respect of proceedings before the Controller of Patents, Designs and Trade Marks.

Copyright: semiconductor products   The European Communities (Protection of Topographies of Semiconductor Products) (Amendment) Regulations 1993 (SI No. 310) amended the 1988 Regulations of the same title (see the 1988 Review, 210) in order to implement Council Decision 93/16/EEC, as amended by a Council Decision of 27 September 1993, and Council Decision 93/17/EEC. The effect of these Decisions was that the Council recognised that the various countries and territories referred to in them, including the United States, had satisfied the reciprocity requirements of the Directive on semiconductors, 87/54/EEC, which had been implemented in Irish law by the 1988 Regulations. The countries and territories concerned are listed to in the 1993 Regulations.

The 1993 Regulations also inserted two new Regulations, Regs. 12 and 13, into the 1988 Regulations. The new Reg.12 states that the protection afforded by the 1988 Regulations shall extend to persons in respect of whom future Council Decisions provide that they qualify for the protection afforded by Directive 87/54/EEC, but such Decisions must be published in the Official Journal of the European Communities. Similarly, the new Reg.13 states that, where future Council Decisions provide that countries or territories satisfy the reciprocity requirements of Directive 87/54/EEC, notice of such Decisions shall be given in *Iris Oifigiúil*, but again such Decisions must also be published in the Official Journal of the European Communities. The combined effect of the new Regs. 12 and 13 is, as the Explanatory Note to the 1993 Regulations states, that such Decisions 'will have effect in Ireland without the need to draft new S.I.'s [*sic*] to implement these decisions'. While such a result may be welcome to certain people, the effect is to remove some of the transparency one would expect from legislation. Given the lack of an updated index to *Iris Oifigiúil*, the ability of practitioners to determine in the future the true territorial reach of the 1988 Regulations is severely undermined.

Copyright: video piracy   In *Roche v Martin* [1993] ILRM 651, Murphy J approved and applied the decision of O'Hanlon J in *Lennon v Clifford* [1993] ILRM 77; [1992] 1 IR 382 (see the 1992 Review, 270 and 519) in refusing the applicant judicial review of his conviction in the District Court under s. 27 of the Copyright Act 1963, as amended by s. 2(1)(b) of the Copyright (Amendment) Act 1987 (see the 1988 Review, 58). The applicant's main ground on judicial review asserted merely that the evidence adduced at his trial in the District Court was 'not sufficient', and Murphy J considered that such a claim could not result in the applicant's conviction being quashed. The judgment is also of some interest in that it includes the text of the summonses issued against the applicant in respect of the offence under s. 27 of the 1963 Act, as amended, which as Murphy J noted would be described colloquially as video piracy.

Patent application: curing defects In *Schering Corp v Controller of Patents, Designs and Trademarks* [1993] 2 IR 524, Lardner J upheld a decision by the Controller that he had no power to deem good the plaintiff's late international patent application. The case arose in the following way.

On 27 December 1990, the plaintiff, a United States Corporation, had obtained a US patent for an invention concerning disinfecting fluid for contact lenses. The plaintiff then made international patent applications under the 1970 Washington Patent Co-Operation Treaty (PCT) in order to claim priority from the time of the US patent. In connection with the Irish international patent application, the plaintiff by letter of 5 December 1991 wrote to its Irish patent agent instructing them to file the appropriate application, referred to as a convention application, on or before 27 December 1991 and had enclosed the necessary forms to enable the application to be filed. Because of uncertainty with postal deliveries, the letter was sent by DHL Courier Services but unfortunately the bag containing the plaintiff's letter was mislaid and was not delivered to the Irish patent agents until 23 January 1992.

The agents immediately made an application to the Controller on 24 January 1992, but by letter of 17 February 1992 the Controller declined to treat the application as a convention application since it had not been made within 12 months of the US patent from which it claimed priority, as required by Rule 25 of the Patents Rules 1965, made in accordance with s. 63 of the Patents Act 1964. The Controller also indicated in the letter that the applciation would be treated as a non-convention application under the 1964 Act. The plaintiff took no steps to proceed with the application as a non-convention application, but instead appealed to the High Court by way of special summons under s. 75 of the 1964 Act.

The plaintiff argued that the Controller could have deemed the application as having been made on or before 27 December 1991 in exercise of the powers conferred on him by Rule 12 of the Patent Rules 1965, which provides that:

> Any document or drawing . . . and any irregularity in procedure which . . . may be obviated without detriment to the interests of any person may be corrected if and on such terms and in such manner as the Controller thinks fit.

The Controller, on the other hand, pointed to Rule 13 of the 1965 Rules, which provides, *inter alia*:

> The time prescribed by these Rules for doing any act or taking any proceedings thereunder, other than the time prescribed by Rule 25 for

making a convention application, . . . may be extended by the Controller if he thinks fit. . . .

Lardner J commented that, if Rule 12 of the 1965 Rules stood alone, there might be considerable force in the plaintiff's argument that the failure to lodge the convention application in time constituted an 'irregularity in procedure' and could thus be cured. However, he held that Rule 12 'must be construed together with the other Rules' and in particular Rule 13. On this basis, he concluded that Rule 12 could not be construed as permitting something which was expressly not allowed by Rule 13. It may be noted that Lardner J referred, without apparent comment, to the marginal note to Rule 12, which read 'General power of amendment'. While such marginal notes are, under s. 11(g) of the Interpretation Act 1937, inadmissible in the interpretation of legislation it would appear that Lardner J's allusion was in passing and did not affect his textual interpretation of the 1965 Rules. However, for a previous example of using such marginal notes, see the judgment of O'Higgins CJ in *Rowe v Law* [1978] IR 55.

Lardner J also addressed an argument by the plaintiff that, in view of the coming into effect of the Patents Act 1992 on 1 August 1992 (see the 1992 Review, 41-6), the application might now be governed by the 1992 Act. Lardner J dismissed this argument, holding that the various transitional provisions contained in the First Schedule to the 1992 Act had the effect that the 1964 Act continued to apply to the plaintiff's application.

Patent extension In *Application of Smithkline Beecham Corp.*, High Court, 30 September 1993, Costello J declined to exercise the jurisdiction conferred by s. 27 of the Patents Act 1964 (see now the Patents Act 1992) to grant the applicant company an extension of the patent period for its cattle and sheep dose 'albendazole', sold in the State under the name 'Valbazen'. In rejecting the application, Costello J considered that the company's evidence failed to establish that it had been inadequately remunerated for its patent within the meaning of s. 27 of the 1964 Act.

Costello J noted that the onus in this respect had long ago been placed on the applicant for an extension by the Privy Council decision in *Re Saxby's Patent* LR 3 PC 292. Costello J also noted that O.96, r.36(b) of the Rules of the Superior Courts 1986 required that two copies of the balance sheet of expenditure and receipts relating to the patent be filed and provided at the hearing of the petition. While Costello J accepted that the need for filing of accounts had been dispensed with by Murphy J in *Application of Technobiotic Ltd*, High Court, 14 December 1989 (see the 1989 Review, 47-8), Costello J pointed out that there had been particular reasons why the normal filing rule was not applied in that case. In holding that the normal rule should apply in the instant case, Costello J stated:

> The applicant has to show that it has been inadequately remunerated. But nowhere has it shown or even indicated what remuneration it has *in fact* received. Instead, it has presented calculations of what that remuneration *would have been* had it licensed its patent and received a royalty of 5% from its licensee. As Murphy J pointed out in *Technobiotic*, the notional royalty approach is a guide only to the patentee's remuneration. When a patentee asks a Court to adopt this approach it does not obtain an automatic dispensation from its obligation to produce accounts — indeed the obligation may be increased by the adoption of this approach so that the Court can be satisfied (if such be the case) that the accounts do not fairly show the patentee's remuneration and that it would be fairer to apply a notional royalty test.
>
> No satisfactory explanation has been forthcoming as to why accounts were not furnished. The patentee has an Irish subsidiary which exploits the patent in this country and remits profits to its parent company. I can see no reason why the share in those profits earned by Valbazen could not be identified by reference to the proportion which sales of Valbazen bear to the company's total sales. It would, of course, be open to the petitioners to argue that the resulting figures were unfair because, for example, the profits earned included traders profits as well as the profits of the patentee as such. But this argument could be verified by reference to the accounts and the suggested notional royalty tested against them. [emphasis in original]

It can be suggested that this important passage contains an implicit reference to the 'transfer pricing' strategy adopted by many international companies operating in the State. It may be that such companies would not wish to have the full details of the precise arrangements made between the parent and its subsidiaries exposed to the full glare of a public hearing, particularly in view of the approach taken by the Irish courts in recent years to the question of hearings in public: see the discussion of *Irish Press plc v Ingersoll Irish Publications Ltd (No. 1)* [1993] ILRM 747 (SC); [1994] 1 IR 176 (HC & SC) in the Practice and Procedure chapter, 460, below. Whatever the reason, having reviewed the evidence actually offered, Costello J concluded that the applicant had failed to satisfy the onus imposed by s. 27 of the 1964 Act, and he therefore refused to grant the patent extension sought.

Patent: supplementary protection certificate   The European Communities (Supplementary) Protection Certificate) Regulations 1993 (SI No. 125) gives effect to the procedure provided for under Council Regulation 1768/92, by which the named certificate may be applied for in respect of medicinal products. The 1993 Regulations provide that the application shall be made to the Controller of Patents, Designs and Trademarks and also include necessary modifications to the Patents Act 1992 and the Patents Rules 1992 (see the 1992 Review, 41-6) for such purposes. The Regulations, signed on 5 May 1993, were expressed to come into effect on 2 January 1993.

Proprietary plant rights   Two sets of Regulations made in 1993 extended the copyright-like rights which exist under the Plant Varieties (Proprietary Rights) Act 1980: see the Agriculture chapter, 40, above.

INTERNATIONAL TRADE

Abolition of intra-Community border controls   The European Communities (Abolition of Intra- Community Border Controls) Regulations 1993 (SI No. 3) are omnibus-type Regulations which provide that the legislation contained in a series of Schedules to the Regulations are, in effect, amended so as not to restrict the importation of goods into the State from any State in the European Community and, where relevant, the export of goods from this State to any State in the European Community. The effect is that the border inspections provided for under the legislative provisions in question were abolished.

Without purporting to provide the full list of legislation contained in the Schedules, among the provisions affected were: s. 30 of the Sale of Food and Drugs Act 1875, s. 5 of the Customs and Inland Revenue Act 1879 (construed as one with s. 42 of the Customs Consolidation Act 1876), s. 16(1) of the Merchandise Marks Act 1887, s. 1(2) of the Sale of Food and Drugs Act 1889, s. 1 of the Foreign Prison Made Goods Act 1897, s. 3 of the White Phosphorous Matches Prohibition Act 1908, the Copyright Customs Regulations 1964, the Milk and Milk Products (Restriction of Export) Orders 1964 and 1971, the Live Fish (Restriction on Import) Order 1972, the Fish Diseases (Control of Imports) Order 1973 and the European Communities (Food Imitations) (Safety) Regulations 1991 (on which see the 1991 Review, 366).

The 1993 Regulations are expressed to be for the purpose of giving effect to Articles 8A (inserted by the Single European Act) and 30 to 36 of the EEC Treaty (now the EC Treaty in the wake of the Treaty on European Union: see the 1992 Review, 329-30). As already indicated, the Regulations have the effect of abolishing certain border inspections as part of the coming into effect of the Single Market on 1 January 1993. Indeed, although the Regulations were signed on 8 January 1993, they are expressed to come into effect on 1 January 1993.

Contracts with Iraq   The European Communities (Prohibition of Satisfaction of Certain Contractual Claims by Persons in Iraq) Regulations 1993 (SI No. 120) arise from the imposition of international trade sanctions on Iraq. Penalties of a maximum fine of £1,000 and/or 6 months imprisonment for breach are provided for.

Contracts and supply of goods to Libya   The European Communities (Prevention of Supply of Certain Goods and Services to Libya) Regulations 1993 (SI No. 384), which revoke 1992 Regulations of the same title (see the 1992 Review, 41), and the European Communities (Prohibition of Satisfaction of Certain Contractual Claims Arising from Trade Sanctions against Libya) Regulations 1993 (SI No. 385) arise from the imposition of international trade sanctions on Libya. Penalties of a maximum fine of £1,000 and/or 6 months imprisonment for breach are provided for.

Exports to Serbia and Montenegro   The European Communities (Prohibition of Trade with the Federal Republic of Yugoslavia (Serbia and Montenegro)) Regulations 1993 (SI No. 144) gave effect to Council Regulation 990/93, which concern the sanctions imposed in relation to the conflict in former Yugoslavia. The 1993 Regulations revoked, and replaced, the Air Services (Authorisation) (Amendment) (No. 2) Order 1992 (see the 1992 Review, 62) and the European Communities (Prohibition of Trade with the Republics of Serbia and Montenegro) Regulations 1992 (see the 1992 Review, 41).

Import of iron and steel products   The European Communities (Surveillance of Imports of Certain Iron and Steel Products) Regulations 1993 (SI No. 85) implemented the terms of Commission Recommendation 3772/92/ECSC concerning the regime to be applied in respect of imports of specified iron and steel products from non-EC countries (other than EFTA States). For previous Regulations in this area, see the 1992 Review, 41.

Intrastat   The European Communities (Intrastat) Regulations 1993 (SI No. 396) give effect to Council Regulation 3330/91 and Commission Regulations 3046/92, 2256/92 and 3590/92 concerning the Intrastat system and lay down the procedure for traders to transmit the information required under the system to the Revenue Commissioners. Penalties for failure to comply are laid down in the Regulations and prosecutions may be brought by the Revenue Commissioners.

Supply of goods to UNITA   The European Communities (Prohibition of the Supply of Certain Goods to UNITA) Regulations 1993 (SI No. 383) implement Council Regulation 2967/93 in relation to sanctions against UNITA in Angola. Penalties of a maximum fine of £1,000 and/or 6 months imprisonment are provided for contravening the Council Regulation.

Trade with Haiti   The European Communities (Prohibition of Certain Trade with Haiti) Regulations 1993 (SI No. 344) implement Council Regulation 1608/93, as amended by Council Regulation 3028/93 concerning trade sanctions imposed on Haiti. Penalties of a maximum fine of £1,000 and/or 6 months imprisonment are provided for contravening the Council Regulation, as amended.

MISLEADING ADVERTISEMENTS

In *J. O'Connor (Nenagh) Ltd v Powers Supermarkets Ltd (t/a Quinnsworth Ltd)*, High Court, 15 March 1993 Keane J granted an injunction to the plaintiffs pursuant to the European Communities (Misleading Advertisements) Regulations 1988 preventing the defendants from publishing misleading advertisements concerning the prices charged in the plaintiffs' supermarkets.

The 1988 Regulations gave effect in Irish law to the 1984 Directive on Misleading Advertisements, 84/450/EEC: see the 1988 Review, 209. The plaintiffs applied for an injunction pursuant to Regulation 4(1) of the Regulations, which permits 'any person' to injunct misleading advertisements. This is by contrast with the restriction of such power to the Director of Consumer Affairs in the Consumer Information Act 1978. It is notable that the 1988 Regulations do not define the term 'misleading advertisement', but like many other Regulations giving effect to EC Directives they provide, in Regulation 2(2), that any word or expression used in the Regulations which is also used in the 1984 Directive has, unless the contrary intention appears, the same meaning in the Regulations as in the Directive. On this basis, Keane J referred to the following definition of 'misleading advertisement' in Article 2(2) of the 1984 Directive:

> Misleading advertising means any advertising which in any way, including its presentation, deceives or is likely to deceive the persons to whom it is addressed or whom it reaches and which, by reason of its deceptive nature, is likely to affect their economic behaviour or which, for those reasons, injures or is likely to injure a competitor.

The plaintiffs objected to a combination of three matters. The first was an advertisement placed by the defendants in the *Nenagh Guardian*, a local newspaper, which stated:

> You can't buy your family shopping cheaper in Roscrea or Nenagh. We price checked Quinnsworth Roscrea and O'Connors Nenagh and the totals prove it — You can't buy your shopping cheaper than at Quinnsworth, with the widest choice of groceries, the best in fresh foods and friendly service.

The advertisement set out what appeared to be a reproduction of two pay-out slips from the check-outs in the two stores mentioned with the totals stated as 'Quinnsworth Roscrea: £44.13' and 'O'Connors Nenagh: £48.04.' The plaintiffs claimed, *inter alia*, that the advertisement misleadingly suggested that the two pay slips represented an average basket of groceries, whereas they were confined to dry goods and excluded fresh food completely. The defendants denied that there was any such thing as an average shopping basket, asserted that the prices were accurate and that customers would not be deceived by this type of advertising.

The plaintiffs also complained about a hand-out distributed in the Nenagh area by the defendants which made claims similar to those in the newspaper advertisement and which, the plaintiffs asserted, contained five specific mis-statements of prices in the plaintiffs' supermarkets. The defendants denied any mis-statements but also asserted that, if there were discrepancies, the price difference between the plaintiffs' and defendants' goods would be only marginally reduced.

Finally, the plaintiffs also complained in connection with an in-store display of two shopping baskets in the defendants' premises which, in effect, replicated the claims made in the newspaper advertisement and the hand-out.

Keane J accepted that the plaintiffs' angry reaction to the newspaper advertisement was understandable and that, to the casual eye, it could have given a misleading impression bearing in mind the complete absence of fresh food items in what was being put forward as what the average person might buy. However, he added that this on its own might not have justified granting an injunction. Nonetheless, he found that, in relation to the hand-out, the plaintiffs had established that there were five mis-statements of the plaintiffs' prices, and that the price checks made in connection with it must have been 'somewhat perfunctory'. Keane J accepted that this might only have marginally affected the price difference, but he went on:

> However, given the fact that this selection of goods was one to which the plaintiffs could also take legitimate objection as not fairly representing the spread of goods which the average shopper would buy in

either store — fresh goods were again completely omitted — it was incumbent on the defendants to ensure that they stated the prices accurately. If they failed so to do — as I am satisfied they did — the accompanying list of prices could only lend a spurious authenticity to the claims made as to the respective competitive positions of the two businesses in price terms.

Turning to the in-store display of the two shopping baskets, Keane J again stated that, on their own, they might not have justified an injunction but, in conjunction with the other two matters, they reinforced the plaintiffs' claim. On this basis, he granted the injunction sought. However, he finished his judgment by pointing out that the injunction would not restrain legitimate advertising, including price comparisons with a named competitor, provided that they were accurate, 'both in fairness to the competitor and in the public interest.'

PUBLIC SUPPLY AND WORKS CONTRACTS

Further steps in implementing the EC-based requirement that public supply and public works contracts be open to bids from commercial undertakings in all Member States was given effect in 1993. On previous Regulations, see the 1992 Review, 46.

Services   The European Communities (Award of Public Services Contracts) Regulations 1993 (SI No. 173) gave effect to Directive 92/50/EEC on the award of public services contracts. The European Communities (Review Procedure for the Award of Public Supply, Public Works and Public Services Contracts) Regulations 1994 (SI No. 5 of 1994) provide, in accordance with previous Regulations (see the 1992 Review, 46), that the High Court is designated as the review body in respect of these contracts and may quash any contract which has been awarded in breach of the terms of the 1990 Directive.

Water, energy, transport and telecommunications   The European Communities (Award of Contracts by Entities operating in the Water, Energy, Transport and Telecommunications Sectors) Regulations 1993 (SI No. 103) gave effect to Directive 90/531/EEC on the award of public works contracts in the sectors referred to. The European Communities (Review Procedures for the Award of Contracts by Entities operating in the Water, Energy, Transport and Telecommunications Sectors) Regulations 1993 (SI No. 104) provide, in accordance with previous Regulations (see the 1992 Review, 46), that the High Court is designated as the review body in respect of these contracts and may quash any contract which has been awarded in breach of the terms of the 1990 Directive.

Communications

BROADCASTING

Restrictions on broadcasting   Under the Broadcasting Authority Act 1960 (Section 31) Order 1993 (SI No. 1), effective until January 1994, spokespersons for certain named and proscribed organisations, including the Sinn Féin party and organisations proscribed under the Act of the British Parliament entitled the Northern Ireland (Emergency Provisions) Act 1991, were prohibited from broadcasting any material, including party political broadcasts, on Radio Telefís Éireann or stations licenced under the Radio and Television Act 1988. We may note here that, in January 1994, no new Order was made continuing in force these restrictions: see Dr Colum Kenny's article (1994) 12 ILT 50 and Professor Desmond Clarke's article (1994) 12 ILT 53 for a consideration of s. 31 and the effects of the non-renewal of the s. 31 Order. The non-renewal of the Orders under s. 31 may be seen primarily against the background of attempts to bring the Sinn Féin party into the peace process represented most visibly by the December 1993 Downing Street Declaration: see the Constitutional Law chapter, 159, below. In a wider context, it should also be noted that the restrictions under s. 31 were subject to some criticism by the UN Human Rights Committee investigating the State's implementation of the UN Covenant on Civil and Political Rights: see Michael O'Flaherty's article (1993) 11 ILT 225.

During 1993, while the Orders under s. 31 remained in force, the extent of the restrictions imposed by these Orders was considered by the Supreme Court in *O'Toole v Radio Telefís Éireann (No. 2)* [1993] ILRM 458. In the *O'Toole* case, it was held that the s. 31 Orders did not prohibit all forms of interviews with members of the Sinn Féin party, but only with spokespersons for that organisation. Thus, the Court (Finlay CJ, Hederman, O'Flaherty, Egan and Blayney JJ) concluded that Radio Telefís Éireann had acted *ultra vires* the Order when it refused to broadcast an interview with Mr O'Toole, a member of Sinn Féin, who at the time was the designated chairman of a strike committee and where the interview dealt entirely with issues concerning the strike. The Court held that since RTE had effectively operated a complete ban on any interviews with Sinn Féin members, this was more than a mere interpretation of the s. 31 Order and amounted, in effect, to an amendment of its terms. The Court acknowledged the difficulties faced by RTE in implementing the restrictions in the s. 31 Orders, but nonetheless considered that the blanket ban operated by RTE was not acceptable.

In light of the non-renewal of the s. 31 Order in 1994, it may be argued that the precise holding in the *O'Toole* case is largely of historical interest. However, it is notable that the Court drew attention to the fact that, irrespective of Orders under s. 31, s. 18 of the Broadcasting Authority Act 1960, as amended by the Broadcasting Authority (Amendment) Act 1976, imposes a general obligation on RTE to refrain from broadcasting any matter which may reasonably be regarded as being likely to promote or incite to crime or as tending to undermine the authority of the State. In this context, the Court in *O'Toole* noted that, in certain circumstances, RTE might be justified in restricting Sinn Féin members to taped interviews rather than live broadcasts. After the non-renewal of the Orders under s. 31, this remains a matter for the internal management of RTE under the revised guidelines to its employees issued in early 1994: on this point see Dr Colum Kenny's article (1994) 12 ILT 50.

Finally, we may note two further decisions of the High Court in 1993 which also considered the scope of Orders under s. 31. In *Brandon Book Publishers Ltd v Radio Telefís Éireann* [1993] ILRM 806 and *Brandon Book Publishers Ltd v Independent Radio and Television Commission*, High Court, 29 October 1993, the applicant in both cases sought to quash decisions of RTE and the IRTC (whose status is discussed below, 71) which refused to allow advertisements for a collection of short stories written by Gerry Adams, the President of the Sinn Féin party. The proposed advertisements included the voice of Mr Adams, though the text did not advert to Sinn Féin or make any call for support of Sinn Féin. Nonetheless, RTE and the IRTC both concluded that Mr Adams was the public face of Sinn Féin to such an extent that any broadcast by him on any subject would amount to an invitation of support for Sinn Féin, and thus would breach the s. 31 Orders.

On judicial review, Carney J held in both cases that the probable effect of broadcasting particular material was a matter of judgment within the particular expertise of RTE and the IRTC, a view which reflects the deferential approach of courts to decision-making bodies in recent years (see, for example, the 1990 Review, 19-20). In the instant cases, Carney J concluded that the judgments made about the broadcasts were not unreasonable within the meaning of the Supreme Court decision in *The State (Keegan) v Stardust Victims Compensation Tribunal* [1987] ILRM 202; [1986] IR 642. He therefore declined to interfere with the refusal to broadcast the advertisements.

While, as with the *O'Toole* case, it might be said that, with the non-renewal of the s. 31 Orders in January 1994, these decisions are largely of historical interest, they nonetheless highlight the point that since matters of judgment continue to be relevant in connection with s. 18 of the Broadcasting

Authority Act 1960, as amended, the deference of Carney J to the decisions made in the *Brandon Books* cases remains of great importance.

RTE: advertising cap and independent programming   The Broadcasting Authority (Amendment) Act 1993, which came into force on its signature by the President on 30 June 1993, effected two major connected changes to the revenue income of Radio Telefís Éireann (RTE), the State broadcasting authority.

First, ss. 2 and 3 of the Act restored the position that had existed prior to the Broadcasting Act 1990, by which the RTE Authority determines, subject to the approval of the Minister for the Arts, Culture and the Gaeltacht, the total daily times for broadcasting advertisements. S. 3 of the 1990 Act had imposed an 'advertising cap' of 7.5% of daily transmission time. This cap was subject to some criticism, and undertakings had been given at the time the cap was introduced that it would be reviewed. The 1993 Act was the result of this review.

The second, connected, element of the 1993 Act was to provide for increased funding for independent television programmes. S. 4 of the 1993 Act provides that the RTE Authority must open a separate account, called the Independent Television Programme Account, into which sums specified in s. 4 must be placed, rising from £5m in 1994 to £10m in 1998. For subsequent years, s. 4 provides that the sum will amount either to 20% of television programme expenditure or a sum (called 'the appropriate amount') based on a formula related to increases in the consumer price index at the end of 1998, whichever is the greater. S. 5 of the 1993 Act lays down a definition of 'independent television programme', which was intended to ensure that there would be some distance between broadcasters, such as RTE itself, and the makers of the 'independent' programmes. S. 6 of the Act requires the RTE Authority to make an annual report to the Minister on the operation of the independent programme provisions.

RTE Authority: gender balance   In addition to the matters already referred to above, the Broadcasting Authority (Amendment) Act 1993 also provided, in s. 7, for virtually mandatory gender balance in the membership of the RTE Authority. S. 7, which comes into operation on 1 June 1995 amends s. 4 of the Broadcasting Authority Act 1960 by providing that, where the membership of the Authority is seven, not less that three of them shall be men and not less that three of them shall be women; while if the membership of the Authority is eight or nine, not less that four of them shall be men and not less that four of them shall be women. However, it also provides that the Authority may continue to act even if, arising from a vacancy among its members, the provisions of s. 4 of the 1960 Act (as amended by the 1993 Act) are not being complied with.

Television franchise withdrawal   In *TV 3 Television Co. Ltd and Ors v Independent Radio and Television Commission*, High Court, 4 May 1992; Supreme Court, 26 October 1993, the Supreme Court upheld Blayney J's decision in the High Court to quash the withdrawal by the respondent, the Independent Radio and Television Commission (IRTC), of a television franchise which it had granted to the applicants. Blayney J's judgment is discussed in the 1992 Review, 49-50, where the background to the case is also outlined. We should, however, recapitulate the background to the case in order to discuss the Supreme Court decision.

The IRTC had been established by the Radio and Television Act 1988 with a view, *inter alia*, to entering into a contract with some person or persons for the provision of a television programme service. Having examined a number of proposals, the IRTC decided in April 1989 to award the franchise to operate an independent national TV channel to what was known as the Windmill consortium, represented by the applicants. This decision was stated in the IRTC's minutes to be 'subject to suitable contracts being negotiated.' After this decision, the consortium found that technical transmisison problems and the extent of the revenue earning capacity of Radio Telefís Éireann (RTE) placed serious impediments in establishing an effective national TV channel. These were addressed by the Broadcasting Act 1990, which permitted the operators of the independent TV channel to use independent transmission equipment and also placed new advertising limits on RTE. In consequence, the consortium submitted a revised business plan to the IRTC in April 1991.

In June 1991, at a meeting between the consortium and the IRTC, it was agreed that the consortium provide the IRTC by the end of August 1991 with precise information on the identity and extent of the investors in the consortium, whose membership had altered since 1989. After this meeting the consortium became aware that the Department of Communications was undertaking a review of the Broadcasting Act 1990, and that the advertising limits on RTE might be removed. (In fact legislation on this did not materialise until June 1993: see discussion of the Broadcasting Authority (Amendment) Act 1993, above.) The consortium was unable to obtain precise information from the Department, and informed the IRTC that arising from this it was unable to provide the financial information requested in the June meeting. The IRTC deferred any decision on the effect of this, but in October 1991 it communicated to the consortium its decision to withdraw, with immediate effect, what it described as the conditional offer of the TV franchise.

The applicants sought judicial review of this decision, and as we already indicated, Blayney J granted *certiorari* quashing the withdrawal of the franchise and this was upheld by the Supreme Court (O'Flaherty, Egan and

Denham JJ). Delivering the only reasoned judgment, Egan J found, like Blayney J, that it was difficult to describe the precise legal nature of the decision in April 1989 by the IRTC to award, subject to conditions, the franchise to the consortium. Egan J went on:

> I am satisfied that the applicants received a benefit of some description from their selection or acceptance in pursuance of a statutory authorisation. However one might describe it, it was some kind of legal right which no other person or body could claim. It might not ultimately lead to the completion of a final contract containing specific and suitable terms but, quite clearly, there was a right to negotiate with the Commission with such an end in view.

It is unfortunate that Egan J was not prepared to define further the precise nature of the applicants' claim. Two possible descriptions appear to suggest themselves. First, the passage from Egan J's judgment appears to suggest that a legitimate expectation arose in favour of the applicants, albeit conditional: see the discussion of legitimate expectation in the Administrative Law chapter, 23-9 above. An alternative description is that the 'benefit' is similar to the notion of 'a contract to contract', though it must be admitted that this is not a concept particularly favoured in the contract textbooks: see Clark, *Contract Law in Ireland*, 3rd ed., chapter 1 and the discussion in *Bula Ltd and Ors v Tara Mines Ltd and Ors* [1987] IR 95 (see the 1987 Review, 113-4).

Whatever the precise nature of the benefit, the Supreme Court agreed with Blayney J that the unilateral decision of the IRTC to deprive the applicants of the right to continue negotiations, having been made without any notice to the applicants, was invalid. Egan J continued:

> The decision was an administrative one made by a Commission which was created by statute and it was not seriously contended that it could be made without complying with the requirements of natural and constitutional justice. . . .
>
> I emphasise in particular the view taken by the learned trial judge that there should have been a clear warning that the franchsie would be withdrawn if the information required by the Commission was not furnished on the promised day. Natural and constitutional justice would have demanded that this would be a prerequisite.

On this basis, the Court agreed with Blayney J's decision that the decision to withdraw the franchise should be quashed.

DATA PROTECTION

Restriction of access The Data Protection Act 1988 (Section 5(1)(d)) (Specification) Regulations 1993 (SI No. 95) contains a list of persons or bodies, all of whom have statutory functions of preventing financial loss to members of the public, who are entitled by virtue of the Regulations to restrict access to personal data kept by them. The persons and bodies whose functions are referred to are: auditors of companies, the Central Bank of Ireland, the Director of Consumer Affairs and Fair Trade, company examiners, company inspectors, the Irish Stock Exchange, liquidators, the Minister for Enterprise and Employment (though the Regulations refer to the Minister for Industry and Commerce, but see the change of title of the Minister effected in January 1993 in the Administrative Law chapter, 7, above), the Official Assignee in Bankruptcy, receivers, recognised bodies of accountants under the Companies Acts and the Registrar of Friendly Societies.

The scope of the restriction applies only where access to the data would be likely to prejudice the proper performance of the functions in question: see the 1988 Review, 395-6. The 1993 Regulations revoked 1989 Regulations of the same title, which had become obsolete.

FILMS

Censor's office The Censorship of Films (Amendment) Act 1992 (Commencement) Order 1993 (SI No. 237), which brought the 1992 Act into force on 5 August 1993, is discussed in the 1992 Review, 51.

Film Board S. 1 of the Irish Film Board (Amendment) Act 1993 amended s. 10 of the Irish Film Board Act 1980 by increasing substantially the expenditure limit of the Irish Film Board from 4.1m to 15m. This amendment to the 1980 Act masked the fact that the Irish Film Board had, effectively, been defunct since 1987 although the legislation under which it operated had never been formally amended. For criticism of a similar approach to the Farm Tax Act 1985, see *Duggan v An Taoiseach* [1989] ILRM 710, discussed in the 1988 Review, 21-4. The 1993 Act is part of efforts to provide further impetus to the Irish film industry through reforming of the Irish Film Board as well as the use of tax incentives to attract large projects to Ireland. The 1993 Act came into effect on 22 December 1993 on its signature by the President.

INTERCEPTION OF POST AND
TELECOMMUNICATIONS

The Interception of Postal Packets and Telecommunications Messages (Regulation) Act 1993 seeks to lay down a method by which postal and telecommunications messages may be intercepted. Put colloquially, the Act puts in place a system for regulating letter opening and telephone tapping as well as 'fax tapping'. The Act came into effect on its signature by the President on 6 June 1993.

Prior to the 1993 Act, the interception of postal and telecommunications messages were authorised on an administrative, that is non-statutory, basis by means of warrants issued by the Minister for Justice at the request of either the Garda Commissioner or the Chief of Staff of the Defence Forces. This procedure for applying for an interception has been retained in s. 6 of the 1993 Act, but the Act also lays down new independent elements in which senior legal personnel are involved in overviewing the operation of the Act.

The genesis of the 1993 Act can be traced to two developments, one domestic and one European. The domestic background arose in 1982, in the immediate aftermath of a general election which saw a Fine Gael-Labour coalition government elected in succession to a Fianna Fail government. In a highly-publicised press conference the incoming Minister for Justice indicated that the outgoing Minister had not followed the guidelines for the granting of telephone taps on the phones of two journalists, Geraldine Kennedy and Bruce Arnold. As well as revealing this information, the incoming Minister promised that the new government would introduce, as a matter of urgency, legislation placing phone taps on a statutory footing. The circumstances surrounding this press conference gave rise to enormous controversy at the time, and was the subject of a best-selling book: Joyce and Murtagh, *The Boss* (Poolbeg Press, 1984). The incoming government did not publish a Bill to regulate phone tapping until 1985, and by the time of the next general election in 1987, the Bill had not been proceeded with and lapsed. By this time also, the journalists involved in the case had initiated claims for damages for breach of privacy. At the trial of the action in the High Court, no evidence was offered to contravert the plaintiffs' claims that the telephone taps were not required for reasons of national security or in the investigation of crime. Hamilton P (as he then was) found in the plaintiffs' favour: see *Kennedy and Arnold v Ireland* [1987] IR 553 (1987 Review, 99-100).

The European dimension to the 1993 Act can be found in the decision of the European Court of Human Rights in *Malone v United Kingdom* (1983) 7 EHRR 14. In this case the applicant successfully challenged the UK administrative system under which telephone taps were authorised, the Court holding that it constituted a breach of the right of privacy under Article 8 of the European Convention on Human Rights and Fundamental Freedoms. The United Kingdom had argued that the system it operated came within the exception contained in Article 8(2) of the Convention, by which the right of privacy may be regulated 'in accordance with law' if this is 'in the interests of national security [or] for the prevention of disorder or crime.' But the Court held that the absence of any independent safeguards in the system precluded the United Kingdom from relying on this exception. Given that the pre-1993 Irish system was based largely on the UK model, it was clear that legislation was required, regardless of the domestic factors already referred to. Indeed, the 1993 Act maintains the link with the *Malone* case by drawing on the UK Interception of Communications Act 1985 as a model.

S. 2(1) of the 1993 Act provides that the Minister for Justice may give an authorisation for an interception 'but only for the purpose of criminal investigation or in the interests of the security of the State.' S. 2(2) provides that, in ordinary circumstances, the Minister must issue a warrant but that, where the Minister considers that the case is one of 'exceptional urgency', an oral authorisation may be given (whether by telephone or otherwise), to be confirmed 'as soon as may be' by a warrant. S. 2(3) provides that the Minister shall not give an authorisation unless he or she considers that the conditions specified in ss. 4 or 5 of the Act (to which we shall return) have been fulfilled and that there has been no contravention of s. 6 of the Act (to which we will also return). S. 2(4) specifies the material to be included in the warrant and s. 2(5) provides that an authorisation shall ordinarily remain in force for three months. S. 2(6) provides that an authorisation may be extended by the Minister for further periods of three months.

Ss. 4, 5 and 6 of the 1993 Act specify the essential conditions required before an authorisation may be given by the Minister under s. 2 of the Act.

S. 4 deals with the circumstances in which an authorisation may be issued 'for the purpose of criminal investigation'. It applies only where the Gardaí or another public authority are investigating a 'serious offence', defined in s. 1 of the Act as an offence carrying a sentence on conviction of at least five years, the yardstick also used in the detention powers in the Criminal Justice Act 1984. An authorisation can only be issued where there is a 'reasonable prospect' that the use of an interception 'would be of material assistance' in providing either information to show whether an offence is being committed or evidence for the purpose of a criminal prosecution. In addition, s. 4(b) provides that the importance of obtaining the information or evidence must be sufficient to justify the interception, having regard to all the circumstances and notwithstanding the importance of preserving the privacy of postal packets and telecommunications messages. While this section clearly involves the balancing of quite sensitive issues, the general approach taken in

Kennedy and Arnold v Ireland [1987] IR 553 and *Malone v United Kingdom* (1983) 7 EHRR 14 indicates that the courts would, in large part, defer to the Minister in the event of a challenge to the *vires* of an authorisation under s. 2. This is, of course, in line with recent case law in the whole area of judicial review: see, for example, the *Brandon Books* cases, 69, above, and the 1990 Review, 19-20.

S. 5 of the 1993 Act goes on to deal with authorisations 'in the interests of the security of the State.' The conditions here are similar to those in s. 4, except that the focus of an interception under s. 5 is towards 'activities that are endangering or likely to endanger the security of the State' and no express reference is made to the gathering of evidence, but simply to the gathering of information on such activities. Again, in the context of activities likely to endanger the State, the courts have been willing to defer, in large part, to the views of those entrusted with State security: see, for example, *The State (Lynch) v Cooney* [1983] ILRM 89; [1982] IR 337 and *Judge v Director of Public Prosecutions* [1984] ILRM 224, discussed by Byrne (1984) 6 *DULJ (ns)* 177.

S. 6 of the 1993 Act lays down the formalities concerning the application for an authorisation, mirroring the requirements in s. 2 of the Act concerning the form of the warrant to be issued by the Minister. As already indicated, the application may be made by the Garda Commissioner or the Chief of Staff of the Defence Forces only. In the case of the latter, a written recommendation from the Minister for Defence must accompany the application. The application is made, in the first instance, to a 'nominated officer' in the Department of Justice, who then prepares a file for the Minister.

Under s. 7 of the Act, an authorisation will cease to have effect where the Garda Commissioner, or the Chief of Staff of the Defence Forces as the case may be, informs the 'nominated officer' in the Department of Justice that the authorisation is no longer required.

S. 8 of the 1993 act introduces the first element of independent review of the Act: it provides for a High Court judge to be nominated to review the operation of the Act and to ascertain whether its provisions are being complied with. This 'designated judge' may report to the Taoiseach from time to time concerning the operation of the Act and such reports must be laid before the Oireachtas. In addition, the designated judge has the power to investigate the operation of any authorisation issued under the Act, and s. 8(6) provides that if the judge informs the Minister for Justice that such authorisation is not valid, 'the Minister shall, as soon as may be, inform the Minister for Transport, Energy and Communications and shall then cancel the authorisation.' This clearly gives the designated judge a very substantial power to override the issuing of an authorisation.

The second independent element in the 1993 Act is contained in s. 9, which provides for the appointment of a Complaints Referee. The Referee must be either a judge of the Circuit Court or District Court or a practising barrister or solicitor of not less than ten years' standing. The appointment is made by An Taoiseach and the term of office is five years, renewable. The Referee may only be removed from office for 'stated misbehaviour or incapacity and upon resolutions passed by Dáil Éireann and Seanad Éireann calling for his removal.' This gives the Referee, for the term of office, the same tenure as a judge of any of the courts established under the Constitution. Any person who believes that a postal packet or telecommunications message sent to that person has been intercepted after the Act came into force may apply to the Referee to investigate the matter. The Referee has wide powers in such investigation, including the power to quash an authorisation under the Act and to recommend the payment of compensation in appropriate cases. Where the Referee concludes, after complaint, that no breach of the Act has occurred, the Referee is precluded by s. 9(8) from informing the complainant whether there was in fact an authorisation in place: the Referee may only state that there has been no contravention of the Act. This provision was explained in the Oireachtas debate as being required to ensure that those under surveillance are not able, by making a complaint, to discover whether in fact their post or telecommmunications messages are being intercepted, since to reveal this would defeat the purpose of the interception. It may be noted that the first appointee as Complaints Referee was His Honour Judge Esmonde Smyth, judge of the Circuit Court: see (1994) 12 ILT 198.

S. 10 of the 1993 Act complements s. 9(8) of the Act by precluding the institution of criminal or civil proceedings seeking to reveal the existence of an authorisation under the Act. S. 10(1) provides that any private prosecution alleging, *inter alia*, an offence under ss. 84 or 98 the Postal and Telecommunications Services Act 1983, which still regulates the criminal side of interceptions, requires the consent of the Director of Public Prosecutions. S. 10(2) provides that in any similar civil claim an initial assessment must be made by the relevant court as to whether an invalid authoriastion has in fact been made.

It might be noted that both elements of s. 10 should be seen against the background that s. 9(1) of the Act itself states that the operation of the Complaints Referee's powers shall not affect a cause of action for infringement of a constitutional right. It might be argued that, given the very explicit and limited references to particular types of ccriminal and civil claims in s. 10 of the 1993 Act, these also should not be interpreted as affecting a constitutional claim for breach of rights. It remains to be seen whether the courts would adopt a restrictive regime to a constitututional claim as is required by s. 10 of the 1993 Act. However, given the reluctance of the courts in the past to trench on the politically sensitive areas of the investigation of crime and of national security, it seems likely that they would adopt, *mutatis mutandis*, the regime laid down in s. 10 of the Act.

The remainder of the 1993 Act requires that all official documents concerning authorisations be retained for at least three years (s. 11), imposes restrictions on the disclosure of information concerning interceptions (s. 12), amends the Postal and Telecommunications Services Act 1983 to take account of the 1993 Act (s. 13) and repeals s. 18 of the Official Secrets Act 1963, which had contained a reference to the, previously assumed, power of the Minister for Justice to intercept communications.

For further discussion of this area, see Maurice Collins' article, (1993) 3 *Irish Criminal Law Journal* 31 and Hall, *The Electronic Age* (Oak Tree Press, 1994).

JOURNALISTS

Confidentiality of sources   The extent to which the law declines to recognise the journalist's claim to confidentiality of sources was considered in *Kiberd v Mr Justice Hamilton* [1992] ILRM 574; [1992] 2 IR 257, discussed in the Criminal Law chapter, 219-222, below.

Contempt of court   While the issue discussed in the *Kiberd* case emerges against the general background of the law of contempt, a more direct form of contempt, the disregard of a court order, arose in *Council of the Bar of Ireland v Sunday Business Post Ltd*, High Court, 30 March 1993, discussed in the Criminal Law chapter, 217-9, below.

TELECOMMUNICATIONS SERVICES

Conditions of service   In *Ó Cearbhaill and Ors v Bord Telecom Éireann* [1993] ELR 253 (HC); [1994] ELR 54 (SC), the correct interpretation of s. 45(2) of the Postal and Telecommunications Services Act 1983 was considered: see the discussion in the Labour Law chapter, 374-6, below.

General terms and conditions   Various detailed amendments to the Telecommunications Scheme 1992 (see the 1992 Review, 51), which lays down the terms of conditions by which telecommunications services are provided, including charges for telephone use, were effected by the Telecommunications (Amendment) Scheme 1993 (SI No. 33), the Telecommunications (Amendment) (No. 2) Scheme 1993 (SI No. 186), the Telecommunications (Amendment) (No. 3) Scheme 1993 (SI No. 206) and the Telecommunications (Amendment) (No. 4) Scheme 1993 (SI No. 249).

Company Law

Dr David Tomkin and Adam McAuley
of Dublin City University Business School

Construction of Memorandum and Articles of Association   *McAuliffe v Lithographic Group Ltd*, unreported, Supreme Court, 2 November 1993. This case concerns the construction of the memorandum and articles of association of a private company limited by shares. It may assist practitioners in construing similarly worded documentation which requires shareholders on whom the appropriate notice is served to buy out another shareholder's shares.

***Ultra vires* payments to Revenue Commissioners**   *In the Matter of Frederick Inns Ltd (in liquidation), The Rendezvous Ltd (in liquidation), The Graduate Ltd (in liquidation), Motels Ltd (in liquidation) and in the Matter of the Companies Acts 1963 to 1986* [1994] 1 ILRM 387 (Supreme Court, 5 November 1993). Binchy and Byrne point out in the 1990 Annual Review, 124-5, that a solvent company in a group of companies may not lawfully pay tax due by other group companies, unless expressly so permitted by the memorandum of association. This case, though it may not elicit much sympathy from readers for the plight of the Revenue Commissioners, is important. It illustrates the practical importance of the *ultra vires* rule and the difficulties in relying on the modifications contained in s. 8 of the Companies Act 1963 and Article 6 the European Communities (Companies) Regulations 1973.

The facts of this case concerned a number of inter-connected companies in liquidation. Three companies operated licensed public houses. They were wholly owned subsidiaries of a fourth company, Motels Ltd. A liquidator was appointed to the four companies. The liquidator challenged the validity and effect of a series of payments made by the companies to the Revenue Commissioners totalling £1.2 million. These payments had been made in the six months immediately preceding the commencement of the winding-up. They were made out of proceeds from the sale of various licensed premises. This sum was appropriated by the Revenue. It went to pay the tax liabilities of not only the four companies involved in the proceedings, but also of six other subsidiaries of Motels Ltd, in proportion to the individual tax liabilities of each company. The liquidator challenged these payments as being *ultra vires*. They had effected a reduction or alienation of the companies' assets when the companies were insolvent. The actual payments made by three of the companies exceeded their individual tax liabilities. The remainder was set against the tax liabilities of other companies in the group.

In the High Court, Lardner J held that the payments made by the companies who had paid in excess of their individual tax liabilities were *ultra vires*. First, each company in the group was a separate company, and the group could not be treated as a single entity. Such payments were voluntary payments, without consideration, and for the benefit of third parties. Second, the payments made by the insolvent companies constituted a misapplication of assets. The reason that Lardner J so held is that, on insolvency, duties are owed by the directors and the company to the general body of creditors. In this case, the payments were in disregard of these duties. Lardner J directed the Revenue Commissioners to repay to the liquidator sums paid by each particular company in excess of its separate tax debt. No order was made in respect of those companies which had not paid in excess of their individual tax liabilities.

The Revenue Commissioners appealed to the Supreme Court. They contended *inter alia*, that even if the payments were *ultra vires*, they were validated by s. 8 of the Companies Act 1963 or Article 6 of the European Communities (Companies) Regulations 1973. The official liquidator appealed on the issue of how much should be repaid to the Revenue Commissioners. The Supreme Court (Blayney J, O'Flaherty and Denham JJ concurring) dismissed the Revenue Commissioners' appeal and allowed the official liquidator's appeal.

The Supreme Court held that the payments were *ultra vires*. There were two reasons for this. First, the court held that no clause in the memoranda of association of any of the companies, properly construed, gave them power to pay the debts of an associate company. Accordingly, the payments were *ultra vires*. The question then was whether the Revenue had a defence under s. 8 of the Companies Act, 1963 or Article 6 of the European Communities (Companies) Regulations 1973.

The court held that the Revenue Commissioners had not been 'actually aware' that the payments were outside the powers of the four companies. Nevertheless, they could not rely on s. 8 of the 1963 Act to validate them. In any case, the payments could not be described as having been 'lawfully and effectively done' within the meaning of s. 8. The payments were made in total disregard of the directors' duties owed to the companies' creditors. Article 6 of the Regulations of 1973 did not apply because the payments were not made by the Board of Directors in proper form, but were made as a result of agreements reached at meetings between the Revenue Commissioners and accountants acting on behalf of the companies. Secondly, the Supreme Court adverted to the fact that when a winding up order is made, a company ceases to be the beneficial owner of its assets. The directors no longer have the power to dispose of them.

The Supreme Court said that where no winding up has been made, but any creditor could petition to have the company wound up on the grounds of insolvency, the company's beneficial ownership similarly ends. In such a situation, the directors owe a duty to the creditors to preserve the assets to enable them to be applied *pro tanto* in discharge of the company's liabilities. The Supreme Court then considered what should be done with the moneys paid to the Revenue *ultra vires*.

It will be remembered that matters had been so arranged that four companies were discharging the tax liabilities of some ten companies within the group. These four companies did not pay all their own tax liability before discharging some of the tax liabilities of the other six companies. Lardner J decided that the Revenue Commissioners could retain such sum as represented the tax liability of the four companies. Thus the Revenue Commissioners had to repay to each of the four companies everything over and above each of the four companys own individual tax liability.

The Supreme Court held that Lardner J had erred. Blayney J, delivering the judgment of the court, held that the directors, in breaching their duty, had created a constructive trust. The court held further that the Revenue Commissioners were the trustees of the money within this constructive trust. The court had come to this conclusion in reliance on *Belmont Finance Corporation Ltd v Williams Furniture Ltd (No. 2)* [1980] 1 All ER 293. In *Belmont*, it was said that a stranger to the trust who receives the proceeds of the trust cannot retain these proceeds if he has actual or constructive notice of the directors' breach of duty which triggers the constructive trust.

The Supreme Court held in *Re Frederick Inns* that the Revenue had indeed constructive notice of the breach. The reason was that if they had read the memoranda of association of the four companies they would have realised that the payments were *ultra vires*. The Supreme Court therefore ordered the Revenue Commissioners to return all the money without reduction for each of the four individual company's respective remaining tax liabilities. The Revenue Commissioners claimed a right of set-off to overcome this particular difficulty. However, the Supreme Court held that under bankruptcy rules, sums owed to the Revenue by the four companies in their individual capacities could not be offset against sums held by the Revenue as constructive trustees for those individual four companies. Set-off only applies where both parties owe money to each other in the same capacity.

Three points must be made about this judgment. First, practitioners have long understood that the term 'actually aware' in s. 8 of the Companies Act, 1963 is something of a conundrum. However, the Supreme Court have added another complexity to the meaning of s. 8 by according a broad interpretation to the phrase 'lawfully and effectively done'. This phrase now comprehends not merely compliance with the statutory requirements of company law, but adherence to common law duties, from time to time prescribed by judges. If this reading is accepted, it might be taken to require adherence to common law duties not yet invented, articulated or recognised by the judiciary.

Second, the Supreme Court has based the requirement to return the moneys paid by the four companies to the Revenue on the constructive trust doctrine. The judgments refer also to constructive notice. Blayney J says at p. 399 that the Revenue are constructive trustees; had they read the memoranda, they would have known that the directors had breached their fiduciary duty to the company by making *ultra vires* payments. The requirement of any form of notice at all seems superfluous.

We suggest that a point which was not argued directly in the Supreme Court should nevertheless have been considered as it arises out of the equitable considerations in the transaction. It is best demonstrated by three hypothetical examples.

A. The Lardner Formula The first assumes that Lardner J's principles are followed. Assume company A owes £40,000 tax. It proffers £100,000 to settle some of its tax debt and some of the group's tax debt by realising an asset. Company A's own tax debt is reduced by £15,000. The tax debt of the Group (excluding this company's individual tax debt) is reduced by £85,000. The effect of Lardner J's judgment would be to allow the Revenue to keep the £15,000, plus the £25,000 not paid but due on foot of company A's own tax liability; *i.e.*, the Revenue Commissioners would have to return £60,000.

B. The Supreme Court Formula This assumes the Supreme Court judgment's approach is followed. Assume company A owes £40,000 tax. It proffers £100,000 to settle some of its tax debt and some of the group's tax debt by realising an asset. Company A's own tax debt is reduced by £15,000. The tax debt of the Group (excluding this company's individual tax debt) is reduced by £85,000. The effect of the Supreme Court judgment would be to allow the Revenue to keep the £15,000. As the Revenue hold the entire balance (£85,000) on a constructive trust, since it was paid *ultra vires*, the Revenue may not keep the £25,000 not paid but due on foot of company A's own tax liability; *i.e.* the Revenue will have to return £85,000.

C. The Authors' Recommended Formula: The authors submit that there is clear authority that an *ultra vires* payment is void. The entire transaction should be set aside. Assuming this is correct, we would suggest that the position is as follows. Assume company A owes £40,000 tax. It proffers £100,000 to settle some of its tax debt and some of the group's tax debt by realising an asset. This is a transaction *ultra vires*. As such it is void. The transaction may not be partitioned into a valid part and a void part. Company A's own tax debt is not therefore reduced.

As the Revenue hold the entire sum (£100,000) on a constructive trust, the Revenue must return it. They are not unduly penalised by this, as they can claim from the liquidator all sums due and interest.

This decision is noted by H. Linnane (1995) 'Directors Duties to Creditors — The Story So Far', *CLP*, Vol. 2, No. 9, 191 at 201 and ff., and by the same author in *Company Lawyer*, Vol. 16, No. 10, p. 319-320.

Borrowing: charges, their cover of all sums outstanding and future advances *In the Matter of Clare Textiles Ltd (in Liquidation) and in the Matter of the Companies Acts 1963 to 1990*, unreported, High Court, 1 February 1993. There are a few cases in Irish company law, generally to do with borrowing, which illustrate the financial dangers inherent in adopting certain short cuts which every practitioner, from time to time, and through pressure of work, may sometimes adopt: see *Northern Bank Finance Corporation v Quinn* [1979] ILRM 221 and *Welch v Bowmaker* [1980] IR 251. The lucky borrower gains an advantage, and the lending bank has to suffer the consequences of the court's respect for the letter of the law.

In this case Clare Textiles Ltd (Clare) had a loan facility from Ulster Bank Ltd (UBL) of £100,000. The company sought to extend this facility to £150,000. UBL agreed to do this, if the company would create a charge in favour of it for £50,000. This arrangement was confirmed by letter of 11 October 1990. The solicitors for Clare confirmed instructions that the title documents to premises at Station Road, Ennis were to be available to UBL.

Although the charge was for £50,000, it in fact was registered mistakenly as an 'all sums' charge under s. 99 of the 1963 Act. Barron J said that UBL might have been able to rely on this mistake, but it did not do so.

Subsequently, UBL realised that they were exposed by unsecured borrowings of £100,000. Therefore UBL wrote on 20 August 1991 seeking confirmation from Clare's solicitors that their undertaking extended to all outstanding sums. Clare's solicitors replied on 13 September 1991, confirming that they had been instructed by the directors of Clare that title documents were to be held to the order of UBL to secure advances up to an amount of £150,000. Clare subsequently went into liquidation. The liquidator claimed in this application that the letter of 13 September 1991 created a fresh charge which, through lack of registration, was void. UBL submitted that the correspondence varied the term of the charge by extending it from £50,000 to one for £150,000. As s. 99 only relates to the creation of a charge, no further registration was required by its variation.

Barron J agreed with the liquidator. A fresh charge had been created and should have been registered. The judge pointed out that there is nothing special about the term 'charge'. It relates to a contract under the terms of which certain property is available as security to meet the performance of a liability, usually the payment of money. Its creation is dependent upon contract law. The fact that a contract created a charge over property, and subsequent agreement varied the terms of the charge, did not necessarily mean that a new charge had not been created.

The question was whether or not the underlying contract was the same or substantially the same. Barron J held that the fundamental basis of the charge had been altered. It was for £50,000. Later it became one for £150,000.

The rights of borrower and lender, and the value of the property were significantly changed. This was indicative of the creation of a second charge between the same parties. The significance of the fact that the original charge was not a charge for all sums or to secure future advances can be seen from a passage in the judgment of Naish C in *Re O'Byrne's Estate* (1885) 15 LR Ir 373 at 377:

> in reality the security which is acquired in case of a deed to secure future advances, for such future advances, is derived from the deed itself, and when registered the registry act does not detract from its force or efficacy as against persons claiming through the mortgagor, and who cannot prove notice as to affect the conscience of the first mortgagee.

Barron J therefore declared the charge to be limited to the sum of £50,000.

In general, a charge should be drafted to cover not merely sums outstanding at the time of completion of the charge, but all sums that may become due and owing. This is normally the case. Those who act for lenders are of course fully aware of the possible pitfalls of seeking to vary the terms of an existing charge.

Borrowing: lost debenture   *Re Shannonside Holdings Ltd (In Liquidation)*, High Court, 20 May 1993, primarily concerns a lost debenture, whose terms were resurrected by evidence, and whose provisions were enforced, even though they were not on all fours with the Form 47 filed in the Companies Registration Office.

This company went into receivership in 1974, and into liquidation in 1986, and was a party to various complex law suits. This judgment considers the terms and effect of a lost debenture, completed on or about 14 June 1973, in favour of one of the promoters of the company, who had loaned it sizeable sums of money. The promoter had since died. A claim was made by his estate. This application, taken by the liquidator, concerned how the claim should be resolved.

Costello J held that the questions for determination were (a) whether a valid debenture in fact existed, and if it did, what its terms were; (b) whether a claim by on foot of a judgment registered within three months of the initiation of the creditors' voluntary winding up was valid; and (c), what the status was of a second debenture, this time one erroneously unregistered.

Costello J held (a) that the first debenture, though lost, had existed. The evidence of its existence came from the solicitor who prepared it, and who had a draft of the document, from the receiver who had been appointed under it, and from the Statement of Affairs of the liquidation which referred to the debenture. The judge agreed that if the debenture had not come into existence, the lender would have certain equitable rights. However he held that since he had found the debenture had in fact existed, it was not necessary to pursue this point. The judge then had to consider whether the debenture was valid or not. There were a plethora of arguments about its validity. However the judge held that the debenture was valid.

One argument is however of interest. Costello J held that where a company's articles provide that general meetings of the company must be held in the State, the holding of a meeting outside the State does not invalidate the resolution. This is 'provided there is agreement', or if no agreement, evidence of conduct from which an agreement can be inferred. In this case, such agreement could be taken as implied.

According to the evidence of Form 47, the charge was restricted to £200,000. Counsel for the debenture holder argued that the debenture itself covered not only the £200,000 but also interest. Costello J resolved this by holding that where there is a conflict between the terms of the document creating a charge and the form outlining its particulars (Form 47), the court must give effect to the former. Costello J expressly approved *Re Mechanisations (Eaglescliffe) Ltd* [1964] 3 All ER 840 and awarded the promoter's estate interest.

Costello J then considered (b) the validity of the claim on foot of a judgment registered within three months of the initiation of the creditors' voluntary winding up. The judgment creditors argued that the meeting at which the resolution to initiate a creditor's voluntary winding up was passed was invalid, and not *bona fide*, but as a stratagem to defeat the registered judgment. Costello J could find no evidence to substantiate this, nor to evidence the other attempts to impugn the initiation of the liquidation.

Costello J finally discussed (c), the status of the second debenture. This second debenture was erroneously unregistered. For that reason it was void and lost its priority.

There are two matters for reflection from the *dicta* in this case. First, how true is the general proposition which may be inferred from this case, that the articles of association can be overridden by agreement? Second, what are the

equitable remedies that would be available to a borrower whose charge was
defective or completely lost?

Oppression   The *Irish Press plc v Ingersoll Irish Publications Ltd* litigation
involved an application under s. 205 of the Companies Act 1963: the section
dealing with remedies for 'oppression' and 'disregard of . . . interests'. The
s. 205 action was decided by the High Court in 1994, and by the Supreme
Court in 1995. The full facts and commentary on the Supreme Court case
will appear in the 1995 Annual Review. This complex litigation involved
three sets of judgments handed down by the courts in 1993 which we discuss
here.

Oppression: determination of what constitutes oppression   *Irish Press
Plc v Ingersoll Irish Publications Ltd*, High Court, 15 December 1993. Irish
Press Plc (PLC) a well-established Irish company, the proprietor of three
newspapers, required new investment. Ralph Ingersoll agreed to invest £5
million through his Irish company, Ingersoll Irish Publications Ltd, (IIP).
Accordingly PLC and IIP formed two companies in November 1989. The
first was called Irish Press Newspapers Ltd (IPN). The second was called
Irish Press Publications Ltd (IPP). PLC and IIP held 50% of the issued share
capital in both IPN and IPP. Each had the power to appoint a number of
directors to the Board of IPN and IPP.

There were two agreements. The first document provided that IIP could
appoint the chief executive to both IPN and IPP. The second document, a
management agreement, provided that IPN engaged Ingersoll Publications
Ltd (IPL) to conduct the business of IPN for an annual management fee.
Difficulties arose. Mr Ingersoll's other business interests collapsed. The
Ingersoll staff, who were engaged under the management agreement to work
in the Irish Press papers, left. It was claimed that their departure terminated
the management agreement.

Mr Ingersoll himself came to Ireland to look after his interests. Though
many of the managers had left, the directors who were nominees of Mr
Ingersoll's company, still remained. It was alleged that Ingersoll tried to
exercise his powers in order to 'bump up' the value of his 50% shareholding
in the Irish Press Group, so that this could be sold. It was claimed that the
directors who were appointed by the Ingersoll company were not looking
after the interests of the company, but were looking out for Mr Ingersoll's
interests. IIP counter-claimed.

Barron J held that Mr Ingersoll's conduct, and that of the directors, in
advancing the Ingersoll interest rather than that of the company, amounted
to oppression. This oppressism was effected by Mr Ingersoll and his employees, who behaved as if the management agreement was still in place, even

though it had been determined. Barron J held that one of the judicial options open to him was to order the winding up of the company. But the judicial order made should as far as possible be one which restores the oppressed person to his pre-oppression position. Winding up would not achieve this. The requisite order must both bring to an end the oppression, and compensate the petitioners for losses. He therefore ordered that IIP should sell both its shareholdings in IPN and IPP to PLC. IPP was also ordered to pay £6 million to IPN and IPP, and £2.75 million to PLC. PLC was required to pay £2.25 million to IIP for the shares.

There are several problems with this judgment. First, Barron J suggests that Mr Ingersoll's actions in attempting to build the value of his shareholding up, so that he could sell it, was oppression. This is too broad. For a moment, let us disregard the fact that a person in Mr Ingersoll's position must be constrained as to what methods he uses to achieve his objectives. Every director or manager in a quasi-partnership company must at times disregard the interests of others to a greater or lesser degree, when in any dilemma in company management, he adopts a strategy to which the others object.

It could be objected that this would leave a shareholder or director on the other side remediless. Not at all; such a person may remove the directors, or refuse to re-elect them, or convene and hold a general meeting to take the necessary actions. If of course the objector lacks the necessary voting power, he is 'locked in'. But a s. 205 remedy should not be invoked until the petitioner can prove conduct which is 'harsh, burdensome or wrongful'. Barron J held that it would be sufficient in a s. 205 action to show that damage was done either to the company, or to the shareholders in that company. A more conventional reading of the cases might suggest that s. 205 requires the petitioner to show that his interests as a shareholder have been adversely affected, not just that the value of his shares has dropped.

Next, there is the question of the link between the breakdown of a quasi-partnership company and 'oppression'. Barron J held that a dispute in a quasi-partnership company would be decided by reference to the principles of partnership law. This was such a case. Barron J found that there had been a breakdown of the quasi-partnership relationship. Barron J does not indicate why such a breakdown should necessarily be remediable by reference to the principles governing 'oppression' and 'disregard of interests' under s. 205 of the 1963 Act.

There are two conclusions. One is that the quasi-partnership breakdown point is immaterial, and Barron J was basing his judgment on a finding of oppression. The other that in this case, because the quasi-partnership had broken down, there was *ipso facto* oppression. These are alternative conclusions.

The solution to this problem may be simple. A quasi-partnership company of this type is by its nature incapable of surviving a breakdown in confidence between the parties, and should be wound up under s. 213(g), on such terms as will do justice. The mere breakdown is not the relevant consideration; the key finding for a remedy under s. 205 is whether any substantive breaches of company or commercial law took place.

This case was appealed to the Supreme Court on a narrow point. The point was that the court could only make such order(s) under s. 205 as would bring the oppression to an end. It may not make an order for damages. The ironic feature of this case is that although Barron J's judgment has been overruled on this narrow point, it stands as a valid exposition of the law on oppression.

Oppression: discovery *Irish Press Plc v Ingersoll Irish Publications Ltd* [1994] 1 IR 208 (High Court, 17 November 1993; Supreme Court, 19 November 1993) A person claiming a remedy under s.205 is often handicapped by the fact that the evidence which he believes will prove his case is in the possession of others. Thus discovery is important as a mechanism for obtaining the forensic ammunition upon which to build a case. The documents may not be in the possession of the other side to the litigation. They may be in the possession of advisers and agents: 'third parties'.

In this case, the applicant sought third party discovery of solicitors' attendances and inter-office memos. It was claimed that these would throw light on one of the substantive issues which the petitioner would seek to prove in the s. 205 action. The petitioner alleged that Mr Ingersoll's appointees in the company had acted in his interests, rather than in the interests of the companies in which they held their appointments, as they were bound to do. The company solicitors objected to the discovery of these documents. They claimed that these documents were their property. They were essential for the day to day administration of their office, and generated solely for internal private use.

In the High Court, Barron J held that the obligation to discover documents depends on their relevancy to the court proceedings, and not to questions of ownership. Indeed, Barron J suggests that the obligation to discover is not affected by issues of 'privacy'. Barron J ordered the discovery of documents relating exclusively to the issue of whether Mr Ingersoll's appointees in the company had acted in his interests, rather than in the interests of the companies in which they held their appointments. Barron J's judgment does not expressly advert to the distinction between legal professional privilege and privacy, nor how a claim for legal professional privilege would affect such an application.

The Supreme Court decision, given *ex tempore*, does not deal with the substantive issues raised by Barron J in his judgment, but merely reflects, by way of a ruling, that the solicitors only had to discover certain agreed documents. This case may however be useful in providing authority for those seeking discovery in similar circumstances. It may have a wider relevance to the entire area of commercial litigation, where documentary evidence is, as here, in the possession of the other side and/or their advisers. Aspects of this judgment in a wider context are canvassed by N.E. Jackson (1995) *CLP*, Vol 2 No 5 p. 107 at 111.

Oppression: the *in camera* rule   *Irish Press Public Ltd Company v Inger-soll Irish Publications Ltd (No. 1)* [1994] 1 IR 176 (High Court, 27 April 1993; Supreme Court, 14 May 1993), considers the circumstances in which a case taken under s. 205 of the Companies Act 1963 may be heard *in camera*. S. 205 (7) allows for a preliminary application to be made to decide whether the case may be heard in private. Practitioners are well aware that the threat to wash corporate dirty linen in public may be a useful bargaining counter.

In this case, it was the petitioner who opposed the application to have the proceedings heard *in camera*. The petitioner contended as the companies' financial affairs and the disputes among the Irish Press personnel were already in the public domain, there was no reason for the case to be heard *in camera*. However the application was granted by Barron J who held, relying on the Supreme Court decision in *Re R. Ltd* [1989] IR 126, that the person seeking to have the action heard *in camera* must establish two things. First, that the disclosure of information in open court would be seriously prejudicial to the legitimate interests of the company. Secondly, that justice could not be done in the case, were it to be heard in open court.

Barron J found as a matter of fact that indeed certain information was already in the public domain. However, the nature of the claims and counter-claims were such that at the hearing further information would be disclosed. Barron J held that justice could not be done in this case if the proceedings were to be held in public. First, there might be damage as a consequence of the revelation of sensitive secret company plans. Second, the full disclosure of the financial position of the company might prevent any future investment in the company. Third, a public ventilation of the quarrel between the parties might damage their relationships to such an extent as to preclude their being able to work together after the conclusion of litigation.

Barron J held that it was not a relevant consideration that if the case were heard in public, this might diminish the value of the shares. Under s. 205(7) of the 1963 Act, the court is concerned with 'the legitimate interests of the company' not the value of any shareholding. Barron J's grant of the appli-cation was appealed to the Supreme Court.

Finlay CJ analysed the decision in *Re R. Ltd*. His analysis differs from that of Barron J. However, Finlay CJ, with whom the rest of the Supreme

Court agreed, accepted the main points of Barron J's analysis. Finlay CJ saw the judicial process concerned in deciding to hear a s. 205 action otherwise than in public, as a more complicated exercise than Barron J's exegesis might suggest.

First, Finlay CJ points out that there is a condition precedent to the exercise by the court of its discretion under s 205(7). The hearing of the proceedings or part of them in public must involve the disclosure of information which if published, would be 'seriously prejudicial to the legitimate interests of the company'.

Secondly, if the court is of the opinion that this precondition is satisfied, it must go on to balance two competing claims. The one is the fundamental Constitutional right vested in the People to have justice administered in public. The other is whether a public hearing would prevent justice being done. This balancing exercise must be carried out even if the parties consent to an *in camera* hearing.

Thirdly, the court must be satisfied that a public hearing (of all or part of the case) would prevent justice being done. Finlay CJ stressed that the court hearing the application under s. 205(7) had to keep the following consideration in mind: only in special and limited cases was the Oireachtas entitled (under Article 34.1 of the Constitution) to prescribe by law for the administration of justice otherwise than in public.

Finlay CJ lays out three circumstances in which the court may hear the petition *in camera*. One is where the petitioner must disclose information which would frustrate the court's ability to accord a just remedy under s. 205. The second is where the respondent's defence is successful, but an order for costs is insufficient to ameliorate the damages caused by the necessity of a public defence. The third is that either side may refrain from giving full and true evidence for fear that the damage done by disclosure will outweigh the benefits of succeeding in the s. 205 action. The members of the Supreme Court differ in the application of this test to the facts of this case.

Blayney J pointed out that the action could not be heard in private unless a case was made out that a public trial would prejudice the legitimate interests of the company. He held that the respondents had failed to make out the case that there was information additional to that already in the public domain which could so prejudice the companies. Denham, Egan and Hederman JJ expressly agreed with Blayney J on this point.

Finlay CJ seems to have accepted that the respondents had satisfied the court that a public hearing would prejudice the legitimate interests of the company. Rather, he considered the question of whether a public hearing would prevent justice being done. He reviewed the three reasons given by Barron J under this rubric. First, Finlay CJ dismissed the danger that a public hearing would prevent any future investment in the company. A prospective investor, he held, would have to obtain information about the company during negotiations. The s. 205 case would reveal no more information than that which would be available to the hypothetical investor during negotiations.

Second, he considered the damage that could be done to the company by the revelation of confidential business information in the course of the s. 205 proceedings. He pointed out that in *Re R. Ltd* the Supreme Court had considered the sensitivity of such business information, and had decided that nevertheless the hearing should be held in public. In the *Irish Press* case, it had been claimed that publication of confidential business information would cause the companies loss and damage. However, no evidence had been given of the existence of such confidential business information, nor had any evidence been given of specific and identifiable damage that would result from disclosure. Finlay CJ suggested that when such evidence was being considered by the court, this can be done *in camera*.

Thirdly, the public was already aware of detail concerning the companies' management difficulties and internal strife. Additional disclosure could not cause any further harm to the parties' possible future working relationships. For these reasons, Finlay CJ allowed the appeal.

Clearly, this is now the authoritative guide to the judicial principles which must be satisfied before s. 205 cases may be heard *in camera*. Does the judgment apply to a wider set of circumstances than just to s. 205 actions? We believe that the same preconditions must now be satisfied for all similar commercial cases. It is important to note that the allegedly commercially sensitive information which is needed to satisfy the test for an *in camera* hearing may itself be presented to court 'otherwise than in public'. The judge can then determine whether the damage that could be done is sufficient to warrant an *in camera* hearing. Aspects of this case are noted without comment by H. Linnane (1995) 'Oppression of Members: Section 205 Companies Act 1963', *CLP*, Vol. 2, No. 1 p. 3 at pp. 11-12.

Oppression: the rule in *Foss v Harbottle* *O'Neill v Ryan, Ryanair Ltd, Aer Lingus plc, Kennedy, GPA Group Ltd and Transport Analysis Inc* [1993] ILRM 557 (Supreme Court). The distinction between a personal action for damages and an action taken on behalf of the company by a shareholder is well settled in company law. In this case, the distinction between the two sorts of action is explored. As we shall show, the judgments suggest that the courts considered this action was in essence a personal action, though it was brought in the guise of a derivative action. O'Flaherty J states that the basic theme of *Foss v Harbottle* (1843) 2 Hare 461 is that where a wrong has been done to the company it is for the company itself to seek redress for the injury done to it, though in appropriate circumstances a derivative claim may be allowed by a shareholder.

The purpose of a derivative action is to ensure that the company is recompensed for any loss or diminution to its assets. The indirect consequences of a successful derivative action may be that shares are restored to their former value, but it should be stressed that this has nothing to do with the *Foss v Harbottle* action. It is strictly speaking a peripheral benefit.

In this case, the plaintiff, a shareholder and an employee, brought proceedings which are best understood as taking the form of two separate claims. One claim was framed as a personal action. The other was framed as a derivative action, in the name of the company. Both claims related to identical facts and indeed sought redress for the identical grievance. The plaintiff alleged that certain named defendants, who were involved in the management of the company, had so arranged the company's affairs as to allow it to be in breach of Articles 85 and 86 of the Treaty of Rome. This had allegedly caused the company damage. This damage had in its turn diminished the value of the plaintiffs shareholding in the company. The defendants opposed these proceedings. They argued that the plaintiff should not be allowed to take what was essentially a claim on behalf of the company; this was prohibited by the rule in *Foss v Harbottle*.

In the High Court, Lynch J held that the rule in *Foss v Harbottle* dictated that where a company is injured, the company is the proper plaintiff, not any individual shareholder. Lynch J elected to decide that the plaintiff's claim was solely in respect of damage caused to his shareholding, and not to the company.

The plaintiff claimed that the rule in *Foss v Harbottle* did not prevent his taking an action for the breach of the competition law rules contained in Articles 85 and 86 which allegedly caused damaged to the company. He argued that national courts owe a duty to give direct applicability to these provisions. Although agreeing that national courts are under such a duty, Lynch J pointed out that these courts are afforded a discretion. This discretion allows national courts to apply to EU law the same restrictions that they would apply on analogous causes of action under domestic law. There was a proviso. They could not do this if the effect was to nullify or negative the direct applicability of EU provisions.

Lynch J held that the application of the rule in *Foss v Harbottle* constituted a permissible limitation. The company was entitled to bring actions either of its own motion or derivatively. Lynch J accordingly struck out the plaintiff's proceedings, holding that the action as contemplated could only be brought by the company, and not by a shareholder. By the time the appeal was heard, the plaintiff was no longer a shareholder in *Ryanair*. The Supreme Court (O'Flaherty, Blayney JJ, Finlay CJ, Egan and Denham JJ concurring) dismissed the plaintiff's appeal and confirmed the order of the High Court.

The Supreme Court held that it will exercise its jurisdiction to strike out a plaintiff's action where it is established by satisfactory evidence that either the proceedings are frivolous or vexatious or that the claim is clearly unsustainable. The court concluded that the plaintiff's claim was not frivolous or vexatious. The court went on to consider whether the plaintiff's claim was clearly unsustainable. The Supreme Court held that it was.

The Supreme Court held that the plaintiff's main claim was that his shares had fallen in value as a result of the alleged wrongful conduct. But the rule in *Foss v Harbottle* (and its exceptions) requires, as a preliminary matter, that a shareholder aver that a substantial wrong has been done to the company. It may be inferred from this case, that a claim under the exceptions to *Foss* can only be brought where the plaintiff can show that the actions (or inactions) of the directors are responsible for a specific wrong done to the company. The Supreme Court ruled out any personal claim for the diminution of the value of the plaintiff's shares. The Supreme Court upheld Lynch J's finding that European Community law was not contravened by refusal to allow a shareholder to claim for alleged damage to his shareholding as a result of damage to the company.

There are two problems that this case poses. Both the High Court and the Supreme Court held that the plaintiff, while he alleged that his shareholding had been devalued by the alleged wrong done to the company, had failed to plead any alleged wrong was in fact done to the company. The plaintiffs claim (said Blayney J) was not in respect of damage to the company. With respect, damage to the company was specifically pleaded in paragraph 21 of the Statement of Claim.

It is true that both the High and Supreme Courts might have reached the conclusion that the claim was not particularly meritorious, or that the claim in *Foss v Harbottle* disguised an attempt to obtain a personal remedy. Perhaps this judgment should have given clearer guidance as to what circumstances entitle actions to be brought in the name of the company when the directors do not agree to do so. It might have been helpful if the Supreme Court had set out what pleadings should aver, in derivative actions.

The second point relates to the applicability of EU law. It is surprising that more guidance is not offered in this case to the rules which should be applied when a breach of EU law causes a company as distinct from an individual to suffer, and the result is that the individual's shareholding is diminished. See T. Kerr (1995) *IJEL*, Vol. 4, No. 1, p. 107-108.

Receivership: Appointment of receiver may not cease directors' powers
Lascomme Ltd Ballyglass House Hotel v United Dominions Trust (Ireland) Ltd and James Gilligan [1994] 1 ILRM 227 (High Court, 22 October 1993). The appointment of a receiver and manager does not of necessity determine

the appointment of directors; it may however limit — perhaps even effectively extinguish — their powers. This case gives specific guidance about
the exercise of directors' powers in maintaining proceedings against a lender,
when the lender has appointed a receiver and manager over the property of
the company.

From the point of view of a debenture holder, or its advisers, this case
highlights the necessity to provide that all possible management powers
which enure to the directors either in common law or by statute or under the
memorandum and articles of association are either taken away from them
and given to the receiver and manager, or are limited or can only be exercised
subject to the receiver's approval. In addition, the case provides guidance as
to the considerations which must be borne in mind if the directors use their
powers during a receivership.

In December 1989 the plaintiff company borrowed £170,000 from UDT
in order to purchase an hotel costing £237,500. In February 1990 the
company sought a further loan from UDT with a view to improving facilities
at the hotel. No loan was made and the company's financial position
deteriorated. On 10 July 1991 the company commenced proceedings against
UDT for breach of contract and negligence in which it was claimed that UDT
had agreed to lend money to the company or, in the alternative, that it had
made representations which induced the company to believe that a loan
would be made. UDT denied that any such agreement or representations had
been made. On 2 September 1992, (under the terms of the debenture of 21
December 1989) UDT appointed a receiver over the assets and undertaking
of the company.

At this stage there was a deficiency of £122,763 between the assets and
liabilities of the company. The hotel was the company's only asset and it
appeared that its sale would not realise enough to discharge the debt owed
to UDT. The company commenced proceedings against UDT for breach of
contract, negligence and negligent misrepresentation. UDT sought an order
staying these proceedings on the basis that the receiver had not authorised
them. The company sought an order that it was so entitled.

Keane J dismissed UDT's application. He held that the company was
entitled to maintain the proceedings against UDT. The powers of directors
are not terminated on the appointment of a receiver by a debenture holder.
The directors retain the power to maintain and institute proceedings in the
name of the company. He added a qualification: this power is exercisable
where to take such proceedings 'would be in the interests of the company or
its creditors'.

Keane J then pointed out that the directors' residual powers cannot be
used in a manner which interferes with the receiver's ability to deal with or
dispose of the assets charged by the debenture. Nor can they be used in any

way which would adversely affect the debenture holder by threatening or imperilling the assets which are subject to the charge. If a debenture holder's security would be imperilled by a hostile order for costs, that could be a ground for staying the proceedings at the instance of the debenture holder. However, here Keane J held that it was likely that the hotel would be sold and the proceeds paid to UDT well before the company's action against UDT could be finally decided by the High Court.

UDT argued that if it was successful in the action, it would be unable to recover its costs from the company. However, Keane J dismissed this practical commercial consideration, ruling that this was not a ground for staying the proceedings. To do so would mean that the directors of an insolvent company would be unable to maintain a claim against the very persons who were alleged to have brought about the insolvency. The fact that UDT was the debenture holder did not render the action against it by the company an academic exercise. If the company's action was successful UDT would be able to satisfy the balance of its debt out of the proceeds of the action and the surplus, if any, would be available to the other creditors and the company.

Keane J's suggestion is that the Board may initiate proceedings not only on the company's behalf but on behalf of the creditors. This raises the point about the directors' overall duty to creditors. In an insolvency situation, directors' duty to the company is replaced by a duty to creditors. Therefore in some cases, where a receiver is appointed over the assets and undertaking of an insolvent company, the directors duties are not merely subject to the receiver's control or direction as the deed may specify, but are probably subject to the overriding duty to creditors. This may not be entirely within the rule established by *Re Frederick Inns* [1994] 1 ILRM 387 (see 1994 Annual Review) but it may fall within *Parkes v Hong Kong & Shanghai Bank Corp.* [1990] ILRM 341. Further judicial exegesis on this point is necessary.

Examinership: Certification of Costs   *Re Don Bluth Entertainment Ltd* ICLR (1963-1993) 709 (High Court, 24 May 1993), provides guidance for examiners, and those who rely on the powers of the examiners to certify the company's liabilities under ss. 10 and 29 of the Companies (Amendment) Act 1990.

This case was an application under s. 29 of the Companies (Amendment) Act 1990, for sanction by the court of the remuneration, costs and reasonable expenses incurred by the examiner, and s. 10 of the Act, which applies when the company is wound up or a receiver is appointed. The effect of these two sections is that any liabilities necessarily incurred by an examiner to maintain the company as a going concern during court protection, shall be treated as expenses properly incurred, upon certification by the examiner. They must be paid in priority even to secured and preferred creditors in a liquidation or receivership.

An interim examiner, who later had his appointment confirmed, was appointed to the company and its subsidiaries on 7 August 1992. The case was unusual in that the petition was presented by a majority of the directors following a divided board meeting. The examiner reported to the court on 8 October that the company was not capable of surviving as a going concern. One of the reasons was that financiers who had funded the company to $50,000,000 were not prepared to compromise their claim against the company, so new finance could not be raised. The company thereafter was wound up. The examiner sought confirmation for payment of £105,000 approximately for fees, £41,000 for legal fees, and for his certification of a sum of $1,050,000 lent by MKB which the examiner deemed necessary under s. 10 of the Companies (Amendment) Act, 1990.

The High Court judgment discusses the purpose and effect of ss. 10 and 29 and points out that the combined effects of these sections is to ensure that certain creditors of the company will be paid in full, at the expense of preferred or secured creditors, if the insolvent company were to go into liquidation. The judge therefore said that he expected an examiner to exercise great care and professional expertise in the discharge of his function.

Murphy J said that an examiner asked to certify liabilities regarded by the directors as necessary to keep the company as a going concern during the examinership must observe the following procedures. First, the examiner should be given certain proposals from the directors as to the sums they consider necessary to keep the company as a going concern during the protection period. (It is significant that Murphy J views the impetus as coming from the board). Second, these proposals have to satisfy the examiner (a) how the goods or services to be obtained will benefit the company, and (b) in particular, how they will contribute to the survival of the company during the protection period.

In the light of this, Murphy J went on to consider whether the examiner had satisfied these criteria in this case. He first dealt with the legal costs. These costs included a period covering the presentation of the petition and ending with the discharge of the examiner. The petition, as has been mentioned above, was presented not by the entire board, but by three individual directors. Thus there was a question as to whether the costs were those attributable to the company, or (in part at least) were those incurred by the three individual directors personally. Murphy J explained that as the board had validly resolved, by majority vote, to initiate the petition, the petition should have been presented in the name of the company.

Murphy J, reviewing the statement of legal costs, found that most were attributable to the presentation and hearing of the petition. The 1990 Act does not provide any priority for the costs of those petitioning for the appointment of an examiner. Costs cannot be certified until after an examiner has been appointed. Such costs can only relate to the period commencing with the appointment of the examiner, and cannot include either the hearing of the petition or pre-hearing matters. Legal costs relating to the presentation or hearing of the petition are therefore excluded. Murphy J said that this conclusion was not affected by the appointment of an interim examiner. To hold otherwise would be to confer a priority which the legislation had withheld. The judge held that costs relating to the court protection period were admissible.

The High Court then considered a $1,050,000 loan by MKB to the company, made during the examinership. This loan was not documented nor recorded, and its conditions were therefore unclear. The court did not consider whether such sum was certifiable or not, but merely considered the conditions of the loan. Murphy J held that it was implicit in the transaction that the loan should carry interest on the same basis as previous loans between the parties. It was a loan in dollars, and so there was a dispute about the date at which it should be converted to Irish pounds. Murphy J relied on *In Re Lines Bros. Ltd* [1983] Ch 1. This establishes the rules for the conversion of foreign currencies to national legal tender in a liquidation. The judgment directed that the sum be converted as of the date of the commencement of the liquidation of the company.

Murphy J rejected the argument made by the lender, that by fixing the date as he did, they were not 'paid in full' as required by s. 29 (3) of the 1990 Act. Murphy J held that because the debt is converted at a set date, this does not mean that something less than the debt is paid. The lender takes a risk that it may lose or gain between the currency conversion date and the date of payment.

Three points about this case: first, the case sets out clearly what an examiner should consider before issuing a certificate under either s. 10 or s. 29 of the 1990 Act. The use of the words 'great care and professional expertise' would appear to suggest that a claim for negligence could potentially arise against an examiner. Second, any legal costs incurred during the preparation, presentation or hearing of the petition cannot be included in the examiner's costs nor certified as liabilities under these sections. Third, the procedure adopted in this case, as Murphy J noted, overlooked a very obvious point, which is that if a resolution is validly carried at a board meeting, even if there is disagreement, it is nevertheless a valid resolution. It consequently entitles the petition to be brought in the company name.

Examinership: Certification of Costs of Examinership *Re Edenpark Construction Ltd*, ICLR (1963-1993) 721 (High Court, 17 December 1993,

Murphy J) again discusses examiner's costs and the certification of liabilities
under ss. 10 and 29 of the Companies (Amendment) Act. It emphasises the
necessity of what the judgment refers to as 'good housekeeping' with regard
to separation of the remunerations, costs and expenses of examiners from the
certification of liabilities of the company.

The case throws more light on the role of an examiner, and stresses that
though the examiner may need to keep the company a going concern during
the examinership, his function should not be confused with that of the
liquidator, receiver, or the board of directors. But this aspect of the present
decision should be read in the light of the Supreme Court decision in *Re
Holidair* [1994] 1 ILRM 421 (see 1994 Annual Review), and also with *Re
Don Bluth Entertainment Ltd, supra* p.95, and *Re Wogans (Drogheda) Ltd,
infra* 100.

On 11 February and 9 March 1992, petitions were presented for examinership over Edenpark Construction Ltd and Edenpark Homes Ltd The
petitioners in each case were the directors of the companies. The same person
was appointed to both companies as examiner. The examinerships lasted 105
and 77 days respectively. On 25 May 1992 both examinerships were terminated by the examiner by Court application. Both companies were ordered
to be wound up. Allied Irish Banks (AIB) appointed a receiver over the assets
of both companies. The examiner subsequently sought payment of his fees
and expenses. This application was opposed by AIB as a secured creditor
and by the Revenue Commissioners as a preferred creditor.

The sum claimed by the examiner was nearly £242,000. It was comprised
of professional fees payable to the examiner, to his solicitors, and some fees
due to the solicitors for one of the companies. It should be stressed that the
statement of affairs presented by the directors in respect of the first company
showed a deficit of £587,000. Thus from the point of view of the secured and
preferred creditors, the only effect of the examinership was to incur a further
quarter of a million pounds debt over a company whose assets were already
insufficient to meet its liabilities.

Murphy J considered both the claims of the examiner and those opposing
the payments. He considered the combined effect of s. 29 and s. 10 of the
Companies (Amendment) Act 1990. S. 29 allows an examiner to certify costs
and expenses thus according them an extraordinary priority. They rank ahead
of all preferred and secured claims in a liquidation. This is compounded by
the effect of s. 10, which deems certain liabilities of the company itself to be
expenses of the examiner, and accordingly to have the same extraordinary
priority.

Murphy J laid out the conditions that must be satisfied before the
liabilities of the company should be invested with such extraordinary priority.
First, the liability must be certified by the examiner to have been incurred in

circumstances where the survival of the company as a going concern would otherwise be seriously prejudiced. Second, the prejudice must be foreseen as occurring only in the period which commenced with the appointment of the examiner and terminated with the cessation of court protection. Third, the certification by the examiner must take place at the time when these liabilities are incurred.

In this case, the examiner appears to have given some oral certificates. Murphy J said that the Act did not require the certificates to be in writing. Nevertheless he cautioned that it was difficult enough to prove that the three criteria referred to above were satisfied by written certificates. This difficulty might be greater in the case of verbal certificates.

Furthermore, Murphy J pointed out that it would be hard on creditors whose rights were postponed by oral certification to get them to accept that their postponement rested on mere words and then, applying these principles, allow certain of the claims and not others. Some claims were certified as necessary to ensure the survival of the companies during the protection period. Others seemed to have been certified because they were incurred to ensure the survival of the company in general.

The Act permits the examiner to certify liabilities on the basis of his judgment about the company's viability exclusively during the protection period. It does not permit him to certify liabilities incurred on the strength of his belief about the ultimate or long term future of the company. Some of the claims were not certified by the examiner during the currency of the examinership at all. In general terms, Murphy J suggests, first, that an appropriate certification under s. 10 must be made anterior to the provision of the services in question. Second, a distinction must be preserved between the examiner's remuneration, costs and expenses and those liabilities certified by the examiner under s. 10 as being liabilities of the company. In this case, some certificates did not satisfy these tests. The confusion about these certificates raised the question about the examiners role and function.

Murphy J held that examiners have no statutory executive role. Unless the court orders otherwise, their appointment does not dispossess the Board of Directors of its role. The statutory duty of the examiner is to report on the company. Such powers which approximate to executive functions are limited to reviewing liabilities intended to be incurred by the company during this limited protection period at the request of the directors, or a potential investor. This must be done solely with a view to forming an opinion as to whether the survival of the company as a going concern during the protection period will be seriously prejudiced, if such liabilities were not in fact incurred.

Murphy J was faced with the conclusion that the examiner had failed to certify the expenses of the examinership in proper form. He further concluded that the examinership should have determined earlier. For these two reasons, he ordered that the examiner's remuneration should be reduced by 20%. This represented a cut in the time period during which fees were incurred. It did not mean a cut in the hourly rate charged by the examiners.

Murphy J allowed the certified fees of the professional advisers, but disallowed the legal costs of presentation of the petition.

There were some certified costs incurred, appointing the examiner of the first company as examiner to the second company, Murphy J disallowed these, holding that the examiner of the first company could never hold the opinion that a failure to appoint an examiner over the second company could prejudice the existence of the first company as a going concern during the first company's examinership. Directors' emoluments were upheld by Murphy J as proper expenses.

Three final points. First, the case shows how an examiner may be penalised for failure to adopt the 'good housekeeping' principles set out in this judgment. Second, although the Act does not exclude oral certification of liabilities, the *onus probandi* on the examiner requires something more than casually documented parol evidence. Third, the examiner's executive role is strictly limited. See J.L. O'Donnell (1994) *CLP*, Vol. 1, No. 3 at 83-85.

Examinership: Costs *Re Wogans (Drogheda) Ltd (No. 2)* ICLR (1963-1993) 692 (High Court, 9 February, Costello J) highlights the difficulty involved with examinerships, where it transpires that the initial picture presented to court is false. In the 1992 Annual Review, we drew attention to this problem which is inherent in the examinership legislation. See also W. Johnson (1994) 'Bank Finance — Searching for Suitable Security', *CLP*, Vol. 1, No. 1 at 3. This decision should be read in the light of the Supreme Court decision in *Re Holidair* (see 1994 Annual Review), and also with *Re Don Bluth Entertainment Ltd, supra* at 95 and *Re Edenpark Ltd* at 97.

In this case, this company was placed in examinership. However, the court did not approve the proposals formulated by the examiner. The company was wound up and a liquidator appointed. The present application was brought by the examiner, for his remuneration, costs and expenses amounting to over £100,000. The application was strongly resisted both by the Revenue Commissioners, and by a secured creditor. The net position was that the court was being asked to sanction a claim for expenses and fees on foot of an examinership which the judge held was improperly initiated.

Costello J's judgment initially discusses two matters. First, s. 29 of the Companies Act 1990. This accords the court a discretion to determine the extent of the examiner's remuneration. Secondly, Costello J explained the duty owed by an examiner to the court both prior to his appointment and thereafter.

We deal first with the position of the accountant prior to his appointment by the court as examiner. This case was unusual. The company decided that it should be placed in examinership. Its own auditors recommended the directors to an accountant who would act as examiner. This accountant was well-briefed about the company circumstances, and how its business had been conducted. He knew that there were certain irregularities.

On the day the petition was initially presented, the accountant in question was informed of certain 'under the counter' payments to employees. These obviously were not set out in the Statement of Affairs and would effectively distort the sums due to the Revenue Commissioners. This accountant agreed to go forward as the examiner. The company that day applied to have this accountant nominated as 'interim examiner'. The application was unsuccessful.

However, the company and the accountant agreed that notwithstanding the accountant's failure to be appointed interim examiner, the accountant would act as an 'informal examiner' doing such work as he considered necessary preparatory to the court petition. On this basis, it was agreed that the accountant would be paid for his services before the hearing of the examinership proceedings by the High Court. This financial arrangement was entered into in case the petition was unsuccessful. In fact, the petition was granted and the accountant was appointed examiner.

In the High Court, Costello J referred to the principle that directors and their professional advisers are obliged to exercise 'the utmost good faith' in bringing an application for court protection. This principle was set out in *Re Wogans (Drogheda) Ltd (No. 1)*, ICLR (1963-1993) 653. The question was whether this proposed examiner was obliged to act with utmost good faith.

Costello J found that the nominee in this case had carried out professional services for the company prior to the examinership. Notwithstanding, he had allowed his name to go forward as the proposed examiner. He was therefore under an obligation to act with utmost good faith with regard to the presentation of the petition and thereafter. Indeed, the nominee's qualifications and experience, which were considerable, would have an impact on the exercise of this fiduciary obligation.

Costello J examined the evidence. He noted that the accountant had never revealed to the court that he had been employed as an 'informal examiner', and had made arrangements for payment therefor. Costello J was satisfied that the proposed examiner was aware that 'under-the-counter' payments to staff of the company had been made, thus sums due to the Revenue to appear in the petition as 'understated'. In this particular case, the nominee should have taken reasonable steps to ensure that the court was not misled. Costello J stated that the proposed examiner could have achieved this by stating the position with greater frankness to the company's solicitors. In fact, Costello

J opined that had the solicitors known of this, they might not have brought the petition to court.

The examiner was disentitled to be awarded costs and remuneration. This was because of the serious breaches of duty. This would appear to have concluded the matter. But in the judgment, Costello J continued to consider the conduct of the examiner after his appointment, and whether the examiner would be similarly disentitled to be paid in that capacity. In so doing he said that some of the examiner's actions were so flawed as to disentitle him to his fees. Others were not and he should be paid for that part of his work.

Though pressed to make an order for costs against the examiner and the company, Costello J declined to do so, on the grounds that the creditors' costs were not 'debts or other liabilities of the company' within the meaning of s. 297A of the Companies Act 1963. Despite this interpretation of the statute, the judge held that O. 99, r.(I)(1) of the Rules of the Superior Courts gives a general discretion to the court in relation to costs. This could be used to award creditors their costs against the examiner, but only in 'very exceptional' circumstances. These were not very exceptional circumstances.

The case suggests that under the present statutory regime, it is most unwise for a prospective examiner to concern himself with the company's affairs at all. He should rather confine his involvement to a consent or refusal to act. If he becomes aware of any company irregularities, there are two scenarios. If the petition is in the course of preparation, the irregularities must be brought to the attention of the solicitors preparing it. If the petition is already filed, then the court's attention should be drawn to these matters at the hearing. In relation to whether an examiner should be disentitled to receive any or some of his costs, by virtue of his opprobrious conduct after his appointment, the judgment gives no overall guiding principles.

Winding up: debiting current account after commencement of winding up   In the Matter of Ashmark Ltd (in Liquidation and in Receivership) and in the Matter of the Companies Acts 1963 to 1986: Ashmark Ltd v Allied Irish Banks plc [1994] 1 ILRM 223 (High Court, 29 July 1993) clarifies whether the debiting of a current account by a bank is or is not a 'disposition' after the commencement of a winding up.

Ashmark Ltd was the main distributor in Ireland for Zanussi electrical appliances. Following a dispute, Zanussi terminated the distribution agreement and served notice under s. 214 (a) of the Companies Act 1963 demanding payment of a large debt. The company obtained an interim injunction restraining Zanussi from prosecuting winding-up proceedings. A compromise was reached, whereby the company ceased trading on 4 July 1988 and Zanussi presented its petition to wind up the company on 8 July. This petition was not advertised until October 1988. The company was wound up on 27

October 1988 and a liquidator appointed.

The company's current account with the respondent included an over-draft facility. On 8 July 1988 (when the liquidation commenced) the account had a credit balance but interest had accrued from day to day on the overdraft for a period of time after 16 March 1988. These sums were debited by the bank from the account after 8 July 1988. The liquidator claimed that these payments were made after the commencement of the winding-up and were thus void under s. 218 of the Companies Act 1963, as being a disposition made after the commencement of a winding up.

Lardner J refused to grant the liquidator's application because the payments never amounted to 'disposition'. He based this on the English case of *Halesowen Presswork and Assemblies Ltd v Westminster Bank Ltd* [1970] 3 All ER 473. This case establishes that a single banker-customer relationship exists where the banker has accorded the customer an overdraft on his current account. Money paid into the current account becomes the property of the bank.

Applying this to the present case, Lardner J said that the company had incurred liability to its bankers on its overdraft. When the bank was owed money, the company was a debtor of the bank's. When the company was in credit, the bank conversely was a debtor of the company's. For the reason explained in the previous paragraph, such credit was the property not of the company, but of the bank. The debiting of money already in an account is not the abstraction of money from the account holder. It is instead the transfer by the bank of its property. Thus after the liquidation, the debiting of the company's bank account in respect of interest and fees due to the bank did not amount to a disposition from the company for the purposes of s. 218 of the Companies Act 1963. See K. Casey (1995) *Journal of International Banking Law*, Vol 10 No. 1, 11-12.

Winding up: disclaimer   *Re Abbeyford Estates Ltd; Bagnall v Waters*, High Court, 29 October 1993. S. 290 of the Companies Act, 1963 permits the liquidator to disclaim certain of the company's obligations on the grounds that their performance would unduly burden the company. As Dr. M. Forde notes '[p]rovided that the proprietary interest is 'onerous' or the contract is 'unprofitable', it is inherently disclaimable' (*Company Insolvency* (The Round Hall Press, Dublin, 1993 at 225.) This case suggests that there is a distinction between the disclaimer of an onerous and an unprofitable contract, and the disclaimer of an original contract which was not as profitable as one which the liquidator could have subsequently obtained, had he been able to renege on the original contract in question.

This case holds that this section does not allow the liquidator to revisit valid contracts solely on the grounds that while they made reasonable commercial sense when they were made, their terms could now be bettered. Abbeyford Ltd went into liquidation on 16 December 1992. The intending purchaser had validly contracted to buy a property from the company in November 1992. The liquidator could have resold the property for a higher price to another, and sought to disclaim the contract with the intending purchaser, under the provisions of s. 290 of the Companies Act 1963.

The liquidator contended that the contract fell within the s. 290 definition of 'land of any tenure burdened with . . . unprofitable contracts'. Furthermore, he argued that the succeeding category (property . . . not readily saleable by reason of its binding the possessor . . . to the performance of any onerous act) applies to real property specifically and not to other classes of asset mentioned in the section. The intending purchaser argued that s. 290 (modelled as it was on s. 55 of the Bankruptcy Act 1883) was not intended to divest from a purchaser an interest which had already passed to him.

In the High Court, Flood J, adopting the reasoning of Collins LJ in *In Re Bastable, ex parte Trustee* [1901] 2 KB 518, and applying the same reasoning to s. 290, agreed that the intended effect of the section was to allow the liquidator to disclaim onerous contracts, but not to divest a *bona fide* purchaser such as the purchaser here of his interest in the property. The purchaser had fairly obtained a bargain, would have no recourse in damages against the liquidator were this bargain annulled, and the bargain could not consequently be displaced.

Winding up: surplus   *In the Matter of Hibernian Transport Companies Ltd (in Liquidation); Shell International Petroleum Co. Ltd v Gordon and Markham and Murphy (Notice Party)* [1994] 1 ILRM 48 (Supreme Court, 13 May 1993). In the 1992 Annual Review it was pointed out that this insolvent winding-up had commenced in 1970, and that by 1992, there was a surplus, after paying all the company's preferential, secured and unsecured creditors in full. This case raises the extraordinary question, as to whether the liquidation should be governed by the rules of insolvent or solvent windings up. It began as the former, it ended up as the latter. The Supreme Court held that the rules applicable to solvent windings up should apply.

The dispute giving rise to this particular action arose between the unsecured creditors and the shareholders. The unsecured creditors claimed that the surplus should be used to pay interest on their debts up to the time they were discharged by the liquidator. The shareholders claimed that they were entitled to the surplus. Their rights were subject only to the rights of those creditors who were entitled to interest for the period starting with the inception of the winding up and concluding with payment.

In the High Court, Carroll J held that s. 284 of the Companies Act 1963 applies the rules of bankruptcy to insolvent companies. In particular, the respective rights of secured and unsecured creditors are the same, *mutatis mutandis*. The relevant rule is provided in s. 86(1) of the Bankruptcy Act 1988. If the estate of a bankrupt is sufficient to pay his debts in full along with interest at the rate currently payable on judgment debts, the court is required to order that any surplus should be paid to the bankrupt, his personal representatives or assigns.

In the High Court, Carroll J ordered that the unsecured creditors were entitled to interest. Their entitlement ran from the commencement of the liquidation to the date of payment. Those unsecured creditors who had contractual rights to interest were to be paid at the rate specified in their contracts. Those unsecured creditors who did not, were entitled to interest at the rate currently payable on judgment debts. The shareholders appealed against this order.

The Supreme Court allowed their appeal (Blayney J; Finlay CJ, O'Flaherty, Egan and Denham JJ concurring) and held that as the company's liquidation produced a surplus, the liquidation could not be regarded as an insolvent liquidation. It was immaterial whether the surplus arose from a realisation of assets, or from interest earned or in any other way. Consequently, s. 284 was not applicable. Instead, s. 242 applied. This provides that the court may adjust the rights of the contributories among themselves and distribute any surplus among the persons entitled thereto.

Therefore, the Supreme Court ordered that only the unsecured creditors entitled to interest by contract, could claim for interest at the rate specified in the contract. They were so entitled from the date of commencement of the winding up to the date of payment. It was also ordered that any dividends which had been paid to such creditors should be treated as having been applied first to the repayment of interest, thereafter to repayment of capital. Having paid all sums due to the liquidator (and other costs), and paid all sums due to creditors, the shareholders were entitled to the remaining money. See B.H. Giblin, *Irish Tax Reporter* (1995) Vol. 7 No. 11 at 1148-1150.

Winding up: lien *Kelly v Scales (practising under the style and title of Scales and Company)*, High Court, 22 November 1993. A company had one major asset, an hotel. Certain files and documentation relating to the hotel were in the possession of a solicitor, who had done work for the company. Subsequently, the company went into liquidation. The liquidator sought the documents from the company. The solicitor claimed a lien, as she had not been paid. To resolve this, the liquidator brought High Court proceedings.

S. 244A of the Companies Act 1963 was introduced by the 1990 Act. It prohibits any person from withholding from its liquidator, documents belonging to a company. It also prohibits the claim of a lien, except in certain specified circumstances. In this case, the work was done prior to the coming into force of the section. Did the prohibition contained in the Act relate to work done prior to 1990? This raised the question of the possible retrospective effect of the section.

Barron J considered that in relation to the retrospective operation of statutes, two types of situation exist. The first is the enforcement of the terms of the Statute to circumstances in existence at the date of the Statute. If the court so enforces the statute, it is giving the statute retrospective effect. The second is the enforcement of the statute's terms, after the statute has been passed. The court may have regard to the facts and events existing before the statute was passed. New law must not be applied to pre-existing situations, but only to those subsequent to the introduction of the relevant Act.

The liquidator argued that the second situation defined in the previous paragraph applied here. This meant that the court could have regard to the work done by the solicitor and her retention of the documents. But the liquidator argued that no lien arose at that time. He argued that the lien, in order to be successfully claimed, had to be expressly asserted. This had not been done prior to the introduction of the 1990 Act. The relevant time at which the assertion took place was the governing factor in assessing what law should apply. Since the only assertion of the lien took place after the introduction of the 1990 Act, the lien was governed by the provisions of that Act. The solicitor consequently could not claim the benefit of the lien; she was precluded from doing so by the provisions of the 1990 Act.

Barron J could see no merit in suggesting that to deny the validity of the lien, the court was not giving the statute a retrospective effect, but was merely taking into account past events. He said that that can only occur when a statute creates a right, and the past events are permitted to establish the right. That was not the case here. Past events had already created the right.

The work done by the solicitor constituted these past events. The lien claimed arose as soon as the work was done. There was no need to assert the lien to establish the right. Accordingly, if the Act is to take away this right, it must be given retrospective effect. Barron J accordingly rejected the applicant's first submission citing a passage from the judgment of Cave J *In Re Raison* (1891) 63 LT 709 as follows:

> [t]here is an old and well known saying with regard to new laws that you are not by a new law to affect for the worst the position in which a man already finds himself at the time when the law is actually passed.

Nevertheless, where there was a clear intention in the statute itself that it should have retrospective effect, the statute should be so applied. However, in the absence of such clear intention no such effect will be construed: see *Hamilton v Hamilton* [1982] IR 466.

The applicant submitted that the proviso to the section could have distinguished between liens which existed prior to the introduction of the Act and those effected subsequent to it, and applied the provisions only to the latter. Because the draughtsman did not make this distinction, it was necessary to read the statute as if it applied to both: in part retrospectively. Barron J rejected this argument, which, if accepted would require the conventional presumption against retrospectivity to be reversed. He therefore concluded that the respondent was entitled to the lien which she asserted.

Winding up: fraudulent trading and constitutionality   *O'Keeffe v Ferris, Ireland and the Attorney General* [1994] 1 ILRM 425, (High Court, 28 July 1993) concerned an attempt to attack the constitutionality of s. 297 of the Companies Act, under which a person who is a party to the fraudulent trading of a company may be held personally liable for corporate debts. The High Court held that the section is constitutional. The case may be relevant to a consideration of the constitutionality of sections of the Companies Acts 1963-1990 which provide for personal liability for company debts.

The plaintiff had been a director of Aluminium Alloy Refiners Ltd. The company became insolvent. On 15 July 1988 it was resolved that it should be wound up voluntarily and that Mr Ferris should be appointed liquidator. The liquidator subsequently instituted proceedings against the plaintiff and others seeking to impose personal liability for alleged fraudulent trading. The plaintiff sought a declaration that either s. 297(1) or the manner in which the liquidator sought to utilise it was unconstitutional on the grounds that it created a criminal offence which was not minor in nature, and therefore entitled the plaintiff to be tried by jury on indictment.

Murphy J dismissed the plaintiff's claim. He held that s. 297(1) did not contain the necessary indicia of a criminal offence as laid out in the Supreme Court judgment in *Melling v O'Mathghamhna* [1962] IR 1. First, a criminal offence must generally be prosecuted at the instigation of the State. The section allows creditors, contributories or the liquidator of the company to institute proceedings. Secondly, the injured party was not the State, rather each of the creditors of the company who were afforded a right to maintain proceedings. Thirdly, proceedings could only be instituted if the company was in the course of liquidation. If it had been intended that the fraud in question should constitute a criminal offence it was likely that it would have been made punishable irrespective of whether a liquidation was in process or had been completed. Fourthly, the requirement of intention in s. 297(1) did not of itself create a criminal offence. After all, it was equally a requirement of the civil wrong of fraudulent misrepresentation that a mental intention should be present. Finally, unlike s. 297(3), s. 297(1) did not contain terms which one might expect to find in a subsection dealing with a criminal offence, such as 'conviction' or 'imprisonment'.

The plaintiff argued that the redress which the court could impose under s. 297(1) did not conform to the notion of compensation or reparation characteristic of civil proceedings. The court held that proceedings under s. 297(1) were in the nature of a representative or class action which could be taken by the liquidator for the benefit of the creditors as a whole, or by an individual creditor or contributory. The money recovered swells the resources available for distribution amongst those claiming in the liquidation. S. 297(1) gave the court a wide discretion in very special and limited circumstances to impose a burden on the management of a company who had engaged in fraudulent practices.

The plaintiff argued that a judge could use s. 297(1) to impose personal liability on a director irrespective of that directors actions or the consequences of them. This discretion, which was untrammelled, could result in a determination of liability which was so extreme as to be penal, in a criminal sense. Murphy J rejected this argument. He held that the power under this section had to be exercised in a responsible and constitutional manner. The personal liability imposed on the defendants should in general be commensurate with the loss suffered by the plaintiff or the class which he represented. It had to be assumed that the subsection would be so construed and applied. It might be punitive, but it could not be penal.

The plaintiff also claimed that were s. 297(1) to be interpreted as creating merely a civil cause of action, the legislation would have to provide that the civil remedy could not be pursued unless and until the conclusion of criminal proceedings under s. 297(3). After all, it was argued, both proceedings related to the same facts and events. This argument was also rejected. There was no general rule that civil proceedings should be postponed until the conclusion of criminal proceedings relating to the same subject-matter. Likewise, there was no basis for staying a civil action where criminal proceedings were not pending or even threatened.

This decision, which is currently understood to be on appeal to the Supreme Court, has been comprehensively examined by G. Duffy in 'Fraudulent Trading and The Decision in *O'Keeffe v Ferris*' (1994) *CLP*, Vol 1 No. 9 at 255-262.

Winding up: reckless trading *Hefferon Kearns Ltd (No. 2)* [1993] 3 IR 191 (High Court, 14 January 1993) deals with 'reckless trading' originally introduced by s. 33 of the 1990 legislation. The relevant provisions are now contained in s. 297A of the Companies Act, 1963 (as amended). Shortly stated, it would appear as if the concept of reckless trading is in the middle of a somewhat indeterminate path, bounded on one side by a subjective test, and on the other by an objective test. In this judgment, Lynch J clearly inclines to the view that those seeking to prove reckless trading need to incline to the subjective side of the road.

In this case, the company, Hefferon Kearns Ltd was a building company, formed in 1988, which commenced trading in 1989. Its activities were directed in the main to the completion of three building contracts at different sites in Dublin. By June 1989, management accounts showed that the company was trading at a loss. For the year 1990, management accounts were prepared every two months. These showed mounting losses. At the end of June 1990, the directors considered the company's position, and took the view that the company could trade out of these losses. By July 1990, the position had become so serious, that two of the directors borrowed money personally, and used this money to finance the running of the company. In August 1990, the June management accounts were made available to the directors. These management accounts showed a balance sheet deficit of £142,507. By the end of August, the deficit had risen to £411,679.

The directors continued to meet on a regular basis to reassess the situation. By the end of August, the directors appear to have reached the conclusion that the company might have some difficulty in meeting its obligations at the end of the month. At this stage, the directors decided to try to obtain a moratorium on the company's debts from its creditors. Negotiations with creditors were opened, but these did not prove fruitful. An examiner was appointed in October 1990.

One of the creditors was a sub-contractor, who was owed £41,694 for work done. This creditor sought to make the directors personally liable for the debt, on the grounds that they were guilty of reckless trading as defined by s. 33 of the Companies Act 1990. Some of the acts of the directors constituting the alleged reckless trading took place at a time before the 1990 Act had been introduced. The question of retrospectivity had already been addressed in *Re Hefferon Kearns Ltd (No. 1)* [1993] 3 IR 177 where the High Court held that the section did not have this retrospective effect. This meant that the directors could only be held liable for alleged actions of reckless trading which had occurred after the date of coming into force of the Act.

In *Re Hefferon Kearns Ltd (No. 2)* Lynch J said that the previous decision did not preclude him from considering acts done prior to the commencement of the 1990 Act. His consideration of these acts was to see whether what was done after the commencement of the 1990 legislation constituted reckless trading. One could not apply new law to past events, but one could take past events into account in applying the law. Lynch J found that certain facts relevant to a finding under s. 33 (the reckless trading section) were not in dispute: the company's insolvency, the fact that the plaintiff was a creditor, and that the sum owing to him had increased between the end of August and the company's entry into court protection.

Lynch J first dealt with a preliminary issue contained in s. 33(4). This requires the court to have regard to the state of knowledge of a creditor of the company's financial affairs. If a creditor knows of the parlous state of the debtor company's affairs, and nevertheless contracts with the company, the court must take into consideration the creditor's conscious assumption of the risk, before making an order against a director under s. 33(2)(b). Lynch J found that the creditor in this case did not know enough about the company's situation to fall within this category.

Next, Lynch J questioned whether a plaintiff has to prove that each director acted recklessly, or can he simply allege collective responsibility? Lynch J answered this by holding s. 33 does not impose collective responsibility on the Board. It is addressed to individual officers. The plaintiff has to prove each defendant fell within the section. Applying this, Lynch J found that the strongest case lay against the first defendant who appeared to be the *de facto* managing director. The other directors were involved to varying degrees.

Lynch J considered the meaning of 'reckless' in the context of s. 33(1)(a) and then 33(2). Reviewing authority, he concluded that the use of the word 'knowingly' in s. 33(1)(a) requires that the officer in question must know that obvious and serious risk of loss and damage to others. He must either ignore this risk, or be careless or indifferent (or worse) to the consequences. In the instant case, the director Hefferon could not be said to have been careless, indifferent or worse. Lynch J in fact held that Hefferon, so far from being either careless or indifferent, had been diligent in taking what steps he could to render the company viable. His beliefs about the possible turn-around could not be said to be entirely unreasonable, in Lynch J's view.

Lynch J then considered s. 33(2). This provides that if the directors' actions fall within either part (a) or part (b) of this section, the director is automatically deemed to be guilty of reckless trading. S. 33(2)(a) imposes liability where the officer is deemed to have recklessly traded if he ought to have known that his actions or those of the company would cause loss to the creditors or any of them. Lynch J's judgment stresses that this section requires 'knowledge or imputed knowledge' that loss would be caused to the creditors. Worry or uncertainty is not sufficient. Lynch J concluded that Hefferon neither knew nor should have known that his actions or those of the company would cause loss to the creditors, in the period following 29 August 1990, when the Act came into force.

S. 33(2)(b) imposes liability for reckless trading where the officer is party to the contracting of a debt by the company and did not honestly believe on reasonable grounds that the company would be able to pay the debt when it fell due for payment, as well as its other debts. Here Lynch J adverted to the wide-ranging and draconian nature of the section, saying that every insolvent company's director could come within its ambit. He raised the public policy consideration that there is a danger that companies might decide to cease to trade whenever faced with even temporary liquidity problems. Lynch J said that as a consequence of the draconian nature of s. 33(2)(b), the Oireachtas had provided a mitigating section. This is s. 33(6). This gives a 'let out' by permitting the court to excuse all or some liability where a director can establish that he acted honestly and responsibly.

Lynch J considered that Hefferon's activities between 29 August and 27 September were not capable of being impugned under s. 33(2)(b). However between 28 September and 11 October, Hefferon had been party to the company's incurring a new debt. He knew that this debt (and all the other company debts) could not be paid. However, Lynch J held that Hefferon acted 'honestly and responsibly'. He (and two other fellow directors, who were in the same position) were consequently relieved of all liability by Lynch J, who used s. 33(6). No case against the fourth director had been made out.

Lynch J's interpretation of the word 'knowingly' assumes that this word imports some form of intention on the part of the person who it is claimed was responsible for the reckless trading. This interpretation is taken from the fact that in criminal law, the term 'knowingly' usually imports *mens rea*. However, this is not invariably the case: see M. Jefferson *Criminal Law,* Pitman, London, 1992 at 100-101.

As this section is not a criminal section, the intention of the Oireachtas cannot be construed as imposing a requirement of *mens rea* into reckless trading. The authors suggest that s. 33(1) should be read as putting an emphasis, not on the state of mind of the directors, but upon their knowledge of the company's affairs and of the impact on the company's creditors of the decisions reached on its behalf.

Our reading would stress that judicial concentration should rest on the defendant's involvement in the company, in particular his decision making capacity and responsibility, and above all, what he knew about the company's business and its management accounts. Less important is what such a defendant might have believed about which particular creditors might be at risk, and to what extent.

Irrespective of this general point, we would offer two comments on Lynch J's particular analysis of this section. First, Lynch J holds that 'deemed knowledge' for the purposes of s. 33(2)(a) amounts to 'knowledge or imputed knowledge'. We think that trying to ascertain what a director actually knew some years back, is something of a futile exercise. What is important is what the officer in question ought to have known. This is ascertainable by reference to the general knowledge, skill and experience to be expected from a reasonable person in his position.

Second, Lynch J held that s. 33(2)(b) of the Act was 'wide-ranging' and could catch every director of an insolvent company. But it should be noted that to succeed under this section, the plaintiff has to prove that the director in question did not have an honest belief or did not have reasonable grounds to form such a belief. This is self-evidently hard to establish.

It could be argued that it is s. 33(2)(a) which is wide-ranging, since it imports an objective standard of knowledge and care. The remedy for a director who may be judged to merit relief is contained in s. 33(6), which empowers the court to accord such relief, either complete or partial. For an analysis of this case see L. MacCann (1993) 'Reckless Trading Revisited', *ILT*, Volume 11, No.2, February, 31-34.

Business Names Regulations 1993 (SI No. 138 of 1993)   These Regulations increase the fees to be paid in connection with the Business Names Act 1963, and discontinues the requirement to pay such fees by postage stamp.

Companies (Fees) Order 1993 (SI No. 142 of 1993); Companies Fees (No. 2) Order 1993 (SI No. 241 of 1993)   These Regulations increase certain fees payable on filing documents under the Companies Acts 1963-1990.

European Communities (Branch Disclosures) Regulations 1993 (SI No. 395 of 1993)   This Statutory Instrument contains disclosure requirements where companies incorporated outside the State establish a place of business in the State. Part XI of the Companies Act 1963 still applies to 'companies incorporated outside the State establishing a place of business within the State'. The purpose of these regulations is to require these companies to furnish additional information to the Registrar of Companies. The information in question covers a broad spectrum: both financial and non-financial.

Broadly speaking, the regulations require certain information to be disclosed initially. This comprehends the charter or memorandum and articles of association or similar documentation, and also certain details such as the company's name and legal form, its certificate of incorporation, the place of registration of the company and its registration number, a list of authorised representatives of the company, names and addresses of one or more persons resident in the state who are authorised to accept service of proceedings, the address and activities of the branch, and other details. Special details are required for companies which are not registered in the EU.

Again, broadly speaking, the regulations provide that if a change is made to any of the initial details set out in the previous paragraph, such changes must be notified to the Registrar of Companies within 14 days.

There is a further important requirement. Where a company registered outside the State has a branch within the state and is caught by these regulations, it must file accounts, provided the company is obliged to file accounts in the state in which the company is incorporated. Where the company is registered outside the EU, and is not obliged to file accounts under the law of the state of incorporation, it is treated as if it were an Irish company and is obliged to file accounts under the 1986 Act.

Part I of the Regulations provide for commencement, citation and interpretation of the regulations. Part II provides for disclosures by EU Communities First Directive companies (limited companies that establish a branch in the State. Part III provides for disclosures by non-EU Communities companies. Part IV apply to both sorts of companies.

European Communities (Accounts) Regulations 1993 (SI No. 396 of 1993) Parts I and II of this Statutory Instrument came into effect on 1 January 1994. Part III applies to accounts prepared for financial years commencing on or after 1 January 1994. Part IV of these Regulations applies to directors' reports attached to balance sheets for financial years commencing on or after 30 June 1993.

The first function of these Regulations is to amend the limits laid down by the 1986 Act which define 'medium-sized' and 'small' companies. Such companies are entitled to avail of the relevant exemptions in filing full financial details, and may instead file abridged accounting details. Thus to take the principal example, a small company does not have to file a profit and loss account, and a medium-sized company may file an abridged balance sheet. The effect of these regulations will be to allow more companies to avail of the exemptions.

The second function is to extend the requirements by which a company must file accounts, to certain unlimited companies and partnerships; ones where all those shareholders or partners with no limit on their liability are companies limited by shares or by guarantee. Special provision is made to catch EU incorporated or constituted bodies similar to our companies or partnerships, which have an approximately equivalent structure; *i.e.* shareholders or partners with unlimited liability who are limited by shares or guarantee or otherwise.

Such entities must therefore file accounts in the form required by the Companies Act 1983 as amended. Provision is made for special modifications for partnerships. These include but are not limited to requirements that two of the partners must sign the accounts, and that a 'Partners' Report' be annexed instead of a 'Directors' Report'. Such accounts must be audited. The regulations specify that the auditor must have the same qualifications as an auditor for company accounts.

Regulation 23 amends s. 16 of the 1983 Act by extending the power to omit disclosure of subsidiary undertakings where such information is 'of negligible importance only' in the context of preparing a 'true and fair view' of the accounts.

Part I of these regulations amends s. 8 of the Companies Act 1986, by increasing each of the financial limits. Thus s. 8(2)(a) now imposes a limit of £1,500,000, s. 8(2)(b) £3,000,000, s. 8(3)(a) £6,000,000, and s. 8(3)(b) £12,000,000. Part I also provides that financial statements attached to annual returns may submit accounts in European Currency Units as well as in the currency in which the accounts are drawn up. Part III of the Regulations extends the scope of the 1986 Act and the 1992 Group Accounts Regulations to certain types of unlimited companies and partnerships. Part IV applies to disclosure by branches, and requires that their existence must be disclosed in accounts.

New Textbook   Dr M. Forde SC's new work, *The Law of Company Insolvency* (The Round Hall Press, Dublin, 1993) is both a useful commentary and a compendium of relevant statutory provisions.

Conflicts of Law

CONTRACT

In the 1992 Review 270-1, we analysed the decision of *McElroy v Flynn*
[1991] ILRM 294, where Blayney J struck down as champertous an heir-
locator agreement. The subject arose again, in a more complex international
environment, in *Fraser v Buckle* [1994] 1 ILRM 276; [1994] 1 IR 1, analysed
in detail by Eoin O'Dell in the Contract Law chapter, below, 184. The
agreements were between the plaintiffs, a London firm of genealogists and
international probate researchers and the defendants, persons to whom would
be revealed details of inheritance claims they were entitled to make in relation
to a New Jersey estate, for the fee of one third of the value of their shares of
the estate. The contracts were not merely for the provision of information,
however. They contemplated the active participation of the plaintiffs in the
collection of evidence and the presentation of the claims in the New Jersey
courts. The contracts expressly provided that the proper law was to be the
law of England and Wales. Heir-locator contracts, while not constituting a
crime or a tort under the law of New Jersey, were void and unenforceable as
being contrary to public policy. The defendants resisted the plaintiffs' action
for specific performance on the ground that they were unenforceable for
champerty.

The plaintiffs argued that, under English law, the proper law of the
contract, the three contracts were enforceable. The defendants responded
that, *even if this were so*, the court should not enforce them as they were
invalid as being opposed to Irish public policy. They relied, *inter alia*, on the
following principle stated as follows in Binchy's *Irish Conflicts of Law*
(1988), 549:

> We must now consider the final exception to the rule that the proper law
> of a contract determines its validity. This relates to public policy. Under
> the Irish internal law of contract, a contract may be invalid as being
> opposed to public policy. The fact that application of a foreign law
> would be contrary to Irish public policy is a reason for holding it invalid,
> not because it offends against the public policy of some foreign law
> (such as its proper law) but because it offends against *our own*.

Costello J, after a detailed review of the law, concluded that heir-locator

contracts were unenforceable under Irish law because they were champertous. The plaintiffs had vigorously argued that *McElroy v Flynn* and the
influential English decision of *Rees v De Bernardy* [1896] 2 Ch 437 should
not be followed as the court in neither case had been asked to address the
question whether domestic public policy extended to heir-locator agreements
relating to proceedings in a *foreign* jurisdiction. Relying on the concept of
public policy articulated by Steyn LJ in *Sanders v Templar*, CA, 11 January
1993, *The Times*, 13 January 1993, the plaintiffs claimed that Irish public
policy was not and should not be concerned with the integrity of the
administration of justice in New Jersey. It followed, they said, that the
agreements before the Court were not offensive to Irish public policy and,
accordingly, the defendants could not rely on the principle of private international law that they had quoted.

Costello J thought it necessary to recall that the law of champerty
condemned contracts where one party agrees to maintain litigation in which
he or she has no genuine interest in consideration of a promise to receive the
proceeds of the litigation. Echoing Lord Denning MR in *Re Trepca Mines
Ltd (No. 2)* [1963] Ch 199, at 220, he observed that the reason why the law
condemns champertous agreements is because of the dangers associated with
such agreements, namely the temptation that the maintainer might inflame
the damages, suppress evidence or suborn witnesses. These agreements were
contrary to public policy because these associated dangers, if realised, could
compromise the proper administration of justice on account of the unjust
adjudications likely to result. Costello J could see no reason for restricting
the law of champerty in relation to heir-locator agreements to those in respect
of litigation in Ireland, because it seemed to him that the dangers with which
such agreements were associated existed whether the estate to be shared with
the maintainer, and the litigation associated with it, was situated in Ireland
or abroad:

> When such agreements relate to estates situated abroad litigation in
> relation to them may come before the Irish courts when a question on
> the enforceability of the agreement arises. The recognised dangers
> associated with such agreements could lead to unjust adjudications in
> such litigation and it seems to me to be reasonable that in heir-locator
> cases Irish public policy should seek to protect the integrity of public
> justice in this country both in litigation relating to the enforceability of
> the agreements and in litigation determining the persons entitled to share
> in an Irish estate. It follows that Irish public policy should condemn
> heir-locator agreements whether they relate to estates abroad or not.

Perhaps it could be argued that, if the contract is enforceable under its proper law, the concern about the dangers associated with heir-locator contracts loses much of its force. If the estate is situated abroad and Irish law is not the proper law, the connection of the Irish judicial process is arguably insufficient to constitute a public policy basis for interfering with the validity of the expectations of the parties.

Costello J went on the explain *dicta* on which the plaintiff had relied. In the *Trepca Mines* case ([1963] Ch, at 218) Lord Denning had remarked that, if certain champertous agreements (relating to the financing of an appeal in winding-up litigation in the English courts) had concerned French litigation, they might have been lawful 'because I understand champerty is lawful in France.' But Lord Denning had pointed out that this was not the case as they concerned English litigation against an English company to recover sums in England. Costello J observed that Lord Denning had 'not [been] making any reference' to the point of law in the instant case 'as his remarks related to the legal position in France had proceedings taken place in that country.'

Costello J went on to consider two other issues of private international law, which did not arise directly on account of his conclusions on other prior issues. If the enforceability of the agreements had to be decided by the proper law of the contracts, he was satisfied that the proper law of the contract was the law of England and Wales and that the choice of law made by the parties in their contracts had been a *bona fide* one. There had been a dispute between the expert witnesses who gave evidence on English law as to whether or not these agreements were enforceable under that law. Because of that dispute he was required to ascertain what the law of England was. He was satisfied that *Rees v De Bernardy* [1896] 2 Ch 437 had not been over-ruled by any subsequent decisions in England and that he should accept it as establishing the principles of English law relevant to the facts of this case. He was further satisfied that the agreements were contrary to English public policy even though they related to litigation in New Jersey. Costello J therefore concluded that under the proper law of these contracts the agreements were unenforceable.

The plaintiffs had argued that the Irish courts should not enforce the agreements because of the attitude of the law of New Jersey to heir-locator agreements. Costello J rejected this contention. Even if he were to hold that the *lex loci solutionis* of these contracts was New Jersey law the evidence had established not that these agreements were illegal under that law but that they were unenforceable and contrary to public policy. This was not in itself a sufficient reason for refusing to enforce the contracts in this country. Costello J cited *Lemenda Ltd v African Middle East Co.* [1988] 1 QB 448 in support of this holding.

The defendants unsuccessfully appealed Costello J's decision. The Supreme Court delivered its judgment on 5 March 1996: [1996] 2 ILRM 34.

We shall examine that judgment in the 1996 Review. We need here merely note that O'Flaherty J (Hamilton CJ and Barrington J concurring) took the view that the first question to be determined was that of the enforceability of the contracts under their proper law. Holding them unenforceable under that law, he did not have to address the public policy issue, which was central to Costello J's analyses.

JURISDICTION OF COURTS AND ENFORCEMENT OF JUDGMENTS ACTS 1993

In the 1988 Review, 90-104, we analysed the Jurisdiction of Court and Enforcement of Judgments (European Communities) Act 1988, which implemented in Irish law the Brussels Convention of 1968 and the Accession Convention of 1978. The Jurisdiction of Courts and Enforcement of Judgments Act 1993 takes matters further by giving effect to two further Conventions: the San Sebastian Convention of 1989, which enabled Spain and Portugal to accede to the Brussels Convention, and the Lugano Convention of 1988, adopted by the Member States of the European Communities and the six member States of EFTA. For a comprehensive analysis of the 1993 Act, see Gerard Hogan's Annotation in *Irish Current Law Statutes Annotated*.

The Act came into force on 1 December 1993: Jurisdiction of Courts and Enforcement of Judgments Act 1993 (Commencement) Order 1993 (No. 330 of 1993). We shall examine some of its features in detail in the 1994 Review. For commentary of the Lugano Convention, see the papers by Professor Ole Lando, Judge Gustaf Möller, Dr Gerhard Hafner, Professor Paul Volken and Mr Jan Woloniecki in the Irish Centre for European Law's *Creating a European Economic Space: Legal Aspects of EC-EFTA Relations* (eds. Mary Robinson and Jantien Findlater, 1990); James Fawcett, 'The Lugano Convention' (1989) 14 *Eur L Rev* 105; more generally, see Dicey & Morris, *The Confict of Laws*, chapter 11 (12th ed., 1993).

Contract In *Carl Stuart Ltd. v Biotrace Ltd* [1993] ILRM 633, Barron J laid down important principles as to how jurisdiction in contract cases should be determined. Article 5(1) of the 1968 Brussels Convention confers jurisdiction, in matters relating to a contract, on the courts 'of the place of performance of the obligation in question.' In *De Bloos v Bouyer* [1976] ECR 1497, the Court of Justice held that the obligation here envisaged was that which forms the basis of the legal proceedings. Subsequently, in *Shenavai v Kreischer* [1987] ECR 239, the Court recognised that, where the proceedings were based on more than one obligation, the test as formulated in the case of a claim based on one obligation might be difficult to apply. In such circumstances, it said, the courts of the place of performance of the principal obligation should have jurisdiction.

In *Carl Stuart*, the plaintiff company which had been appointed by the defendant, an English registered company, as its exclusive distributor of certain products in Ireland, sought to enforce the distributorship agreement by claiming damages for breach of contract, an injunction restraining the appointment of any other party as exclusive distributor in Ireland and specific performance of the agreement.

Barron J was rightly struck by the difficulty of fixing the place of performance of a negative obligation. So long as the defendant company observed its contractual obligation not to permit any other distributor sell its goods in Ireland, the obligation was 'performed by doing nothing'. A breach of that obligation might occur in a number of ways. The defendant might sell its goods to another within the jurisdiction or it might enter into a written agreement with the foreign parent of an Irish subsidiary. In the former instance, the breach would occur when the goods were delivered; in the latter, when the agreement was executed. But it seemed to Barron J unlikely that the forum for the plaintiff's action should depend upon the place of such breach:

> In the latter instance, suppose the defendant executed a contract in Paris to permit a French company to sell its goods here through a subsidiary, in competition with the plaintiff, would the only forum for the plaintiff's claim be France? It hardly seems likely.

Barron J considered that, in the case of a negative obligation, the court should look to the *right* to which such obligation corresponded and on which the proceedings were based. The place of performance of such obligation would be the place where the right that corresponded to it was 'to be taken'. Barron J found support in one of the definitions of 'Law' contained in the Oxford English Dictionary for this correspondence between right and liability and their equation to obligation.

Applying the principles laid down in *De Bloos v Bouyer* and *Shenavai v Kreischer*, Barron J first sought to consider the substance of the right that the plaintiff was seeking to enforce. Insofar as it sought damages, it was the 'underlying right giving rise to damages' which was relevant. The plaintiff sought to establish the right to continue as exclusive distributor of the defendant's products and the right to a continued supply of these products. The first of these was, in Barron J's view, the principal one, which formed the basis of the proceedings. The principal obligation to which the proceedings related was the obligation to continue the exclusive distributorship.

Continuation of supply was necessary for that continuation but was subsidiary to it. Since jurisdiction depended on the place of performance of this principal obligation, it could only be Ireland.

Counsel for the defendant had argued that the defendant's obligation was to supply goods to the plaintiff; since this obligation was performed by delivery in Wales, jurisdiction should be denied. Barron J made it clear that he would have accepted this submission if the primary obligation had been the obligation to supply. Such would have been the position if the action had been one for damages for the supply of defective goods. Once, however, there were conflicting claims which might result in conflicting jurisdiction, it was clear that only the primary claim governed jurisdiction.

In *Ferndale Films Ltd v Granada Television Ltd* [1993] 3 IR 362, the plaintiff was an Irish company engaged in film production. The defendants were English companies engaged in television and film production and distribution. The parties entered into a production agreement whereby one of the defendants obtained the distribution rights of the film "My Left Foot" for the whole world save for Britain and Ireland and it undertook to use all reasonable endeavours to ensure the proper distribution and exploitation of the film in the distribution territory. In addition it undertook to pay to the plaintiff a certain agreed proportion of the sums it received from this exploitation of the film in the distribution area.

A dispute arose as to whether the defendants had acted reasonably in discharging these obligations. The plaintiff took issue in particular with the terms of an agreement that one of the defendants had entered into with a film company in respect of distribution.

The plaintiff sued the defendants in the High Court, invoking Article 5(1) of the Brussels Convention. The essence of its assertion of jurisdiction was that the defendants were obliged to pay the fruits of global distribution of the film to the plaintiff and that this payment should be regarded as 'the obligation in question' for the purposes of Article 5(1).

Carney J accepted this line of argument. He derived assistance from the Supreme Court decision of *Unidare plc v James Scott Ltd* [1991] 2 IR 88 (discussed in the 1991 Review, 87-8). In that case the defendant had sought to resist jurisdiction on the basis that the defendant's cheque for the payment of goods, when transmitted to the plaintiffs in Dublin, was transmitted by them to an associated company and cashed in England. The Chief Justice rejected this argument; what happened after the delivery of the cheque could not alter the place where the contract provided that the payment was to be performed. Carney J rejected as 'unreal' the defendants' submission that payment was a mere ancillary detail which he could disregard. On the contrary, he found that:

the obligation which arises under the production agreement is the payment of monies to the plaintiff in Ireland and . . . what is mechanical is the collection of the monies and the calculation of its distribution. . . . [T]his is the commercial reality of the transaction between the parties.

The defendants successfully appealed the case to the Supreme Court. Blayney J delivered the only judgment, with which Finlay CJ and Egan J concurred. It seemed to Blayney J that 'the obligation in question' was the obligation to use all reasonable endeavours to ensure the proper distribution and exploitation of the film throughout the distribution territory. The 'main thrust' of the plaintiff's statement of claim had been that the defendants had failed to do this. There was no question that such an obligation was clearly not to be performed in Ireland since Ireland had been specifically excluded from the distribution territory.

It must be said that Blayney J's analysis and conclusion are convincing. There was no doubt that the gravamen of the plaintiff's claim was the alleged improvidence of the agreement the defendants made with the film company in respect of distribution and their alleged failure to administer that contract properly. The payment of the sums generated by the discharge of their distribution obligation was properly regarded as ancillary to the obligation the alleged breach of which inspired the plaintiff's invoking the jurisdiction of the court.

Hanbridge Services Ltd v Aerospace Communications Ltd [1994] 1 ILRM 39, is another Supreme Court case on the subject. The facts were straightforward. The plaintiff, a company registered and domiciled in Ireland, located at Shannon, sought to take proceedings for breach of contract against the defendant company, registered and domiciled in the United Kingdom. The plaintiff claimed that the defendant had agreed to purchase eight thousand computers manufactured by the plaintiff, in accordance with samples it had supplied. The defendant contested the existence of the contract, admitting that it had received samples but contending that negotiations had not been consummated into a completed contract.

More fundamentally, however, the defendant argued that the Irish courts had no jurisdiction to hear the case. Lardner J held in favour of the plaintiff but the Supreme Court reversed.

Finlay CJ delivered the only judgment, with which O'Flaherty, Egan, Blayney and Denham JJ concurred. The Chief Justice was satisfied that the onus was on the plaintiff who sought to have his claim tried in the jurisdiction of a contracting state other than the contracting state in which the defendant was domiciled to establish that the claim 'unequivocally' came within the relevant exception. In the case of a claim for breach of contract, therefore, what the plaintiff had to prove was that the obligation in question in that claim was, by virtue of the terms of contract or by some generally applicable principle of Irish law, an obligation that must be performed in Ireland.

The Chief Justice observed:

> It would follow from this that, where the evidence addressed by the plaintiff seeking to have a claim, for breach of contract tried within the jurisdiction of a contracting state, other than the state of domicile of the defendant, amounts to no greater standard of proof than establishing that the obligation which it claimed was breached could have been performed in such state, he would have failed to establish his entitlement to sue pursuant to article 5.1, the necessary proof being that the obligation which it claimed has been broken by the defendant according to the contract or according to some general principle of law, must be performed in the state concerned.

This is another instance of Finlay CJ's tendency to characterise as a matter of the standard of proof what is in fact a substantive principle of law. The question whether the expression 'the place of performance of the obligation in question' embraces only situations where the place of performance must be in a particular country or whether it extends also to cases where the place of performance may be in a particular country is one of interpretation of the proper scope of paragraph 1 of Article 5.1: it has nothing to do with evidential matters.

In the High Court, Lardner J had identified the placing of orders for computers, in accordance with the alleged contract, as 'the obligation in question'. He considered that this obligation 'is performed by the defendants communicating their order to the plaintiffs at Shannon.' He therefore concluded that the Irish courts had jurisdiction.

On appeal Finlay CJ accepted that the obligation in question was indeed that of placing orders. The problem was that the alleged contract contained no provision for the method of placing an order or for the place where that had to occur. Whilst it was likely, having regard to the value and quantity of the goods concerned in the contract, that an order would be placed in writing, there was no requirement in the contract for it and it was 'not impossible to conceive of a repeat order, for example, communicated by word of mouth'.

The evidence as to negotiations indicated that much of the oral discussion had taken place in Britain and not Ireland. The Chief Justice considered it not unlikely that representatives of the plaintiff company in a commercial transaction of this size and description would regularly attend at the defendant's premises and obtain there, either in writing or verbally, orders for the supply of goods.

Furthermore, Lardner J's conclusion that the obligation was performed by the defendant communicating its order to the plaintiff at Shannon did not necessarily and unambiguously answer the precise question as to whether the obligation to place the orders was an obligation to be performed in Ireland or not. There apparently had been no debate in the High Court as to what the legal situation would be, even if it was unequivocally provided by the contract that the orders were to be placed by a document in writing, executed in Britain and posted or faxed to the plaintiff's premises at Shannon.

Even assuming that Lardner J's conclusion should unequivocally be construed as indicating an act to be performed by the defendant in Ireland in the placing of the orders, there had not been evidence that justified that concession. Such a conclusion could be reached only where the plaintiff had discharged the onus 'to establish with particularity' its entitlement to sue, otherwise than in accordance with 'the primary rule' of the Convention contained in Article 2.

Finlay CJ noted that there was no general proposition of law applicable to the question of placing of orders under a contract such as the one in the instant case which would deem it necessary to be performed in Ireland; an analogy could be made with the general principle of law that a debtor is obliged to pay a creditor where the creditor is residing or domiciled: cf. *Unidare plc v James Scott Ltd* [1991] 2 IR 88, analysed in the 1991 Review, 87-8.

In the circumstances, the Supreme Court allowed the appeal and struck out the proceedings for lack of jurisdiction. It is easy to agree with Gerard Hogan's observation (in his Annotation of the Jurisdiction of Courts and Enforcement of Judgments Act 1993, *ICLSA*, 9-15) that the Chief Justice imposed what 'seems a very heavy onus for the plaintiff to carry. . . .'

In *Devrajan v District Judge Ballagh*, Supreme Court, 11 June 1993 (*ex tempore*), the applicant for judicial review had sought to sue a foreign company in the Irish courts in respect of a contract for services. His case had been dismissed in the District Court and on appeal the Circuit Court on the basis of lack of jurisdiction. His application for judicial review in the High Court failed on the basis that the contract for services had to be carried out outside the State, in the Netherlands. His appeal to the Supreme Court was successful because it transpired that the company had not raised the issue of jurisdiction until a late stage in the proceedings. The Supreme Court in *Campbell International Trading House Ltd v Van Aart* [1992] 2 IR 305 had already held that a party wishing to contest jurisdiction should give the earliest possible notice of the fact to the party asserting jurisdiction: see the 1992 Review, 128-30. In the instant case, the failure to do so was attributable to an oversight; this did not in the view of Finlay CJ (O'Flaherty and Egan JJ concurring) 'go to the justice of the matter. . . .'

The applicant had claimed that there were very restricted limitation periods for contract litigation in the law of the Netherlands. The Chief Justice had no doubt on that point alone that it would be quite unjust for the Court to permit the Company to contest jurisdiction. The Supreme Court accordingly directed that the action should proceed in the District Court.

Unfair dismissal   In *Roche v Sealink Stena Line Ltd* [1993] ELR 89, the Tribunal dealt with a preliminary jurisdictional objection to its hearing an unfair dismissals claim. S. 2(3) of the Unfair Dismissals Act 1977 provides that the legislation is not to apply in relation to the dismissal of an employee who, under the relevant contract of employment, ordinarily worked outside the State, unless:

> (i) he or she was ordinarily resident in the State during the term of the contract, or
> (ii) he or she was domiciled in the State during the term of the contract,

and the employer —

> (i) if an individual, was ordinarily resident in the State during the terms of that contract, or
> (ii) if a body corporate or unincorporate, had its principal place of business in the State during the term of the contract.

In *Roche*, the claimants worked on vessels crossing between Rosslare and Fishguard. They were Irish citizens who lived in the State, two of them owning their own houses here and two living here with their parents. The Tribunal was accordingly satisfied that the claimants fulfilled the jurisdictional requirement of ordinary residence in the State.

The Tribunal had jurisdiction even though the respondent was a British registered company and the employees on board were, as the Tribunal expressed it, 'subject to British law'; the base port for the claimants was Fishguard; their contracts of employment were made in Britain; their wages paid in sterling; they paid British national insurance (though they paid Irish tax); and they received their redundancy entitlements from the British authorities.

One could perhaps criticise the legislation for its insensitivity to the complexity of transnational connections that can affect employment contracts. Some may argue that the court should be given the functions of examining these factors before assuming jurisdiction in unfair dismissals litigation. As against this, it may be replied that there is value in the legislation's prescription of clear jurisdictional criteria. A former employee should not have to face a complicated legal battle before establishing jurisdiction to have his or her case heard by the court. Moreover, the jurisdictional criteria specified in s. 2(3) are reasonable ones: if they are fulfilled, there is a reasonable basis for the application of the Irish unfair dismissals code to the contract of employment.

In *Amstrad plc v Walker*, High Court, 19 July 1993, the applicant in an unfair dismissal case had been employed by an English company to work in Ireland. He initiated claims for unfair dismissal in both England and Ireland. These claims made it clear that he took the position that England was the appropriate forum and that he had invoked Ireland only as a fall-back jurisdiction if problems arose as to the jurisdiction of the English tribunal.

The applicant subsequently vacillated for some considerable time. The Irish Employment Appeals Tribunal accepted jurisdiction, noting the claimant's undertaking to withdraw the English claim provided the company accepted the order. The President of the Circuit Court affirmed the Tribunal's jurisdiction In the meantime the matter came before the English tribunal in the absence of the applicant, who sought unsuccessfully to have it adjourned. The English tribunal found in his favour and then adjourned proceedings for about a fortnight to determine his relief. The applicant again failed to attend; on this occasion it dismissed his application.

On appeal from the Circuit Court, Carney J set aside the President's order. He was satisfied that the company was 'entitled to assert an estoppel by the record both under long- standing principles of private international law and domestic law and also under the provisions of the Brussels Convention and the legislation giving effect to it.'

In setting aside the President's order, Carney J declared that the applicant's claim had been finally and conclusively determined by the English tribunal and that on this account the Employment Appeals Tribunal had no jurisdiction to entertain the matter further.

INTERNATIONAL CHILD ABDUCTION

The Hague Convention   In *P.F. v M.F.*, Supreme Court, 13 January 1993, the mother of children whom she had retained in Ireland in violation of the father's (joint) custody rights under a Massachusetts court order successfully invoked Article 13(b) of the Hague Convention in the Supreme Court, which reversed the High Court order directing the return of the children to the father. The mother's uncontested evidence by affidavit gave a stark picture of gross financial irresponsibility and selfishness on the part of the husband, coupled with acts of violence against her and one of the children.

Finlay CJ (for the Court) stated that, in the light of the evidence, the return of the children would be possible only if the father could disprove the allegations or could establish by very cogent proof that the situation 'was now entirely changed and would be wholly different' if the children were returned.

During the High Court proceedings, the father had expressed a willingness to abide by any conditions that might be imposed, however stringent. The trial judge did not attach any conditions to his order as he had been told that his decision was to be appealed. He indicated that otherwise he would have required advance provision to be made for air fares and maintenance including rent for at least three months.

In the Supreme Court, Finlay CJ said that he was satisfied that:

> it was not sufficient for [the father] to have expressed a willingness in general terms to abide by any orders of the Court to make provisions for his wife and children pending the order of the Massachusetts Court, but that he would have had to prove that he had made the appropriate provisions by producing, for example, money necessary for their maintenance, money necessary for the purchase of the airline tickets for their journey, and evidence that he had established a residence separately from his own for them to which they had a proper title and in respect of which rent in advance had been paid. On the failure of the father to establish any of those facts, in my view, the making of any order for the return of the children, even with the rider that it might be necessary at a later stage to apply conditions to it, was incorrect. . . .

The passage suggests that, if the father *had* established all of these facts, the High Court order returning the children would have been upheld. The lesson for applicants seeking the return of children under the Convention thus is clear: it is not sufficient to indicate a willingness to abide by whatever conditions the Court may impose; it may be essential to put forward a scheme of possible conditions, to establish by credible evidence an ability to comply with these conditions and to convince the Court that this is the best scheme for it to adopt.

In *Wadda v Ireland* [1994] 1 ILRM 128, the facts were as follows. The wife, an Irish citizen married the husband, a citizen of Morocco, in Britain. Both spouses were at all material times habitually resident in Britain. The wife, after 'unhappy differences', returned to Ireland with their daughter and instituted proceedings under the Guardianship of Infants Act 1964. These were stayed when the husband initiated proceedings under the 1991 Act seeking the return of the child under Article 12 of the Hague Convention. Morris J concluded that the husband was entitled to an order returning the child to Britain. He was satisfied that the child had been 'wrongfully removed' from Britain, as Article 3 envisaged, and that the wife had not established that the return of the child would expose the child to a grave risk of harm or otherwise place the child in an intolerable situation, as Article 13 (b) envisaged. Morris J imposed a stay to enable the wife and daughter to challenge the constitutional validity of the 1991 Act.

Keane J heard this challenge, after the Attorney General had been made a party to the proceedings. The plaintiff submitted that the 1991 Act was invalid having regard to Article 40.2.1° of the Constitution, under which the State guarantees in its laws to respect, and as far as practicable, by its laws to defend and vindicate the personal rights of the citizen. They argued that the Act violated this constitutional provision in precluding the Irish courts from determining questions of custody and access under the Guardianship of Infants Act 1964.

Keane J rejected this contention. He considered that Article 13 of the Convention gave a significant margin of discretion to the authorities of the requested state to refuse to order the return of the child where it might not be in the child's interest to do so. That provision of itself presented 'serious obstacles' to the plaintiffs' argument but the provisions of Article 20 put the matter beyond doubt. It was clear that the reference in Article 20 to 'the fundamental principles of the requested state' must refer, in the context of Ireland, to the provisions of the Constitution. Articles 40 to 44 of the Constitution appeared under the heading 'Fundamental Rights' and defined, either expressly or by implication, rights of citizens which could not be modified or abridged by any of the organs of government except to the extent permitted by the Constitution itself:

> These provisions reflect an acknowledgement by the Constitution that there are rights regarded as of such importance in a democratic society such as Ireland as to warrant recognition in this manner by the fundamental law of society, in our case the Constitution. At the international level, rights of this nature are declared in documents such as the European Convention on Human Rights and Fundamental Freedoms, to which Ireland is a party.

In the instant case Keane J thought it unnecessary to reach any conclusion as to whether the court would be entitled to have regard to the provisions of the Convention in a case where Article 20 was invoked. It was sufficient to say that, in the case of Ireland, the 'human rights and fundamental freedoms' which were protected if that Article was invoked included those set out, expressly or by implication, in Articles 40 to 44 of the Constitution. He had no doubt that, if Morris J had been satisfied that those fundamental principles would be infringed by the return of the child, he would not have made the order sought. Keane J was accordingly satisfied that the personal rights of children under 40.2.1° were fully protected and vindicated by the provisions of the Convention, which afforded them an additional machinery for the protection and vindication of their constitutional rights which had not previously been available.

Keane J rejected without ceremony the plaintiff's argument that the Convention violated the constitutional guarantee of fair procedures implicit in 40.2.1°, which had been identified by the courts in decisions such as *State (Healy) v Donoghue* [1976] IR 325: cf. J. Kelly, *The Irish Constitution* (3rd ed., by G. Hogan & G. Whyte, 1994), 350-9, 614-9, G. Hogan & D. Gwynn Morgan, *Administrative Law* (2nd ed., 1991), Chapter 9. This was because the court had power under the Convention to refuse the return of children where to do so would infringe their fundamental human rights, 'which unquestionably include the right to have issues such as custody and access determined in accordance with fair procedures.' He found support for this view in Denham J's judgment in *C.K. v C.K.* [1993] ILRM 534, which we analyse in the 1992 Review, 104-8.

There was perhaps something more to the point about fair procedures than either Keane J or Denham J was willing to recognise. The Hague Convention is based on the judgment that the welfare of children as a group is best served by their fairly automatic return to the state from which they have been taken in breach of a court order or of a custodian's legal right. Undoubtedly this policy, overall, is likely to reduce the incidence of international child abduction, which had become a real problem over the previous decade; it is equally probable that the interests of children, as a group, are better served by this process. Nevertheless, by disdaining detailed enquiry into the welfare of each particular child save in cases where Article 13 or 20 applies, those who drafted the Convention were willing to pay a price. That price was the withdrawal from the abducting parent of the entitlement to demand a full judicial investigation into where the balance of advantage lies from the standpoint of the welfare of the child: only if the abducting parent can raise one of the limited defences under Article 13 or invoke Article 20 will the welfare issue be confronted in the litigation. There is a real argument that the foreclosure of entitlement to a judicial hearing does indeed violate the constitutional guarantee to fair procedures of the abducting parent and, more particularly, of the abducted child.

What is the best reply to this argument? Perhaps it is that the price of dispensing with a fully individual enquiry into the welfare of the particular child before the court is a price that simply has to be paid if abduction is to be discouraged. In other words, the decision to exclude a full enquiry is one that can be justified on the basis that it is for the overall welfare of children. Whether this is a fully satisfactory answer is a matter for discussion. What is involved here is the perennial debate as to the justice of rules that do not allow for exception in individual cases.

At all events, the question of the abducting parent's right to litigate under 40.2.1° might be considered by some to be of less direct significance in the present context, since the primary issue in the welfare of the child. Nevertheless, there is no doubt that an abducting parent has constitutionally protected rights the legal enforcement of which are constitutionally protected. Even parental statutory rights may be enforced by a civil action. Thus in *Cosgrove v Ireland* [1981] ILRM 48, the State had to compensate the plaintiff where it issued passports to the children of the plaintiff and his wife, resulting in her taking them with her to the Netherlands, effectively depriving the plaintiff of the exercise of his right to guardianship under s. 6(1) of the Guardianship of Infants Act 1964. That Act reflects the judicial interpretation of Articles 41 and 42 of the Constitution: cf. *In re Tilson, Infants* [1951] IR 1.

The idea that Article 20 is the sole answer to the uncertainties about the constitutional validity of the 1991 Act is controversial. If there is a constitutional problem with endorsing the philosophy of returning the abducted child, subject to only limited restrictions, without an investigation of the welfare question, that problem would scarcely be resolved by recourse to Article 20, unless that Article were to be regarded as being capable of completely neutralising the application of the Hague Convention's philosophy of displacing the welfare test, subject only to Article 13. That clearly is not how either Denham J in *C.K. v C.K.* or Keane J in *Wadda v Ireland* perceived the scope or implication of Article 20. Both judges regarded Article 20 as envisaging the possibility *in a particular case* of the non-return of a child under a Convention that is otherwise applicable and harmonious with the Constitution.

Keane J went on to reject the plaintiffs' argument that the Convention failed to ensure access to them, as Irish citizens, to the courts established under the Constitution, in breach of Article 40.3 and wrongfully ousted the jurisdiction of those courts in breach of Article 34.1. He accepted that, save in cases where Article 13 or 20 applied, the jurisdiction of the Irish courts under the Guardianship of Infants Act 1964 'and any other relevant laws' was ousted in favour of the jurisdiction of the competent authorities in foreign states. This was established in accordance with the underlying policy of the Convention and in accordance with well established principles of private international law.

Keane J noted that the 'generally recognised principles of international law' to which Article 29.3 of the Constitution referred seemed, at a first reading, to be confined to principles of *public* international law; principles of *private* international law were perceived by Article 50 insofar as they were consistent with the Constitution. Clearly, the rules of private international

law differed from one jurisdiction to another and it might therefore seem that
they had been given no additional force in our law by Article 29.3. Nevertheless, it had also to be borne in mind that the differences that existed
between the private international law rules of states had given rise to injustice
and inconvenience and that one of the principal objectives of the Hague
Conference on Private International Law, which had produced the Child
Abduction Convention, was to eliminate such injustice and inconvenience
to the greatest extent possible. Giving effect in legislation to the provisions
of such Conventions, with their rules relating to jurisdiction, was, in Keane
J's view, clearly in accordance with Ireland's acceptance of the generally
recognised principles of international law and in harmony with one of the
aims of the Constitution, as stated in the Preamble, to establish concord with
other nations. Apart from any consideration flowing from Article 29.3,
Keane J was satisfied in any event that the Oireachtas was entitled to give
effect in domestic law to a convention that conferred jurisdiction in cases
with an international dimension to foreign courts with the object of protecting
the interests of children in Ireland and other countries.

It must be admitted that there is a strong initial attraction in the way in
which Keane J invoked Article 29.3 in aid of a constitutional justification of
ouster of the Irish courts. The day will come, however, when an Irish court
will actually grasp the nettle of addressing the formidable jurisprudential
conundrum of the relationship between constitutionally protected rights and
the rules of Irish private international law. Irish private international law, like
so much of the rest of the corpus of Irish law, is a patchwork of principles,
rules and procedures left over after the demise of British rule in 1922. Almost
all of this patchwork was formed by courts from whose judgments an appeal
lay to the House of Lords. There was, of course, no thought given in the
formulation of this corpus of law to any constitutional implication: the only
Constitution that was considered relevant was the (unwritten) British Constitution. After independence, ad hoc accommodations, such as the Adaptation of Enactments Act 1922, dealt with the obvious challenges raised by the
shift in the *grundnorm* but, even today, the courts and academic commentators have devoted relatively little time to the more subtle, though no less
fundamental, implications of replanting a corpus of foreign-centered law in
an indigenous environment, coupled with the addition of an entirely new
process of legal thought, whereby rights conferred or recognised by the
Constitution are capable of enforcement, not only against the State, but
against any private individual or body who interferes with them: *Meskell v
Coras Iompair Éireann* [1973] IR 121.

When one moves from municipal law to the international context the
position becomes a good deal more complex. To what extent has the
Constitution an international remit? If we take a few sample constitutional

rights — the right to life, the right to one's good name and the right to express freely one's convictions and opinions — to what extent, and in respect of whom, does the Constitution afford these rights protection? If a Kurd whose life is imperilled by Sadam Hussein invokes the protection of the Irish Constitution relative to his or her right to life, what should be the considerations governing the Irish court's response? To what extent can the question be answered in terms of jurisdictional criteria? Would the court require proof of Irish nationality, domicile or habitual residence? Or would mere presence within the jurisdiction suffice?

No Irish court has yet sought to draw a distinction between the exercise of jurisdiction and choice of law in the context of the Irish Constitution. Let us take a case where the Irish High Court is properly exercising jurisdiction over a foreign defendant in a defamation case, for example, where a constitutional issue arises as to the remit of Article 40.6.1.i. It can hardly be argued that, merely because the court is thus exercising jurisdiction, this constitutional provision *necessarily* applies to the foreign defendant. See our discussion in the chapter on Equitable Remedies, 285-7, below, in relation to *Oblique Financial Services Ltd v The Promise Production Co. Ltd* [1994] 1 ILRM 74.

In the context of international child abduction, therefore, the mere fact that the High Court is exercising jurisdiction under the Convention does not necessarily mean that the parties (or, perhaps, one of them) should be entitled to invoke the provision of Articles 40 to 44. It they have strong Irish connections, then the case for invoking these provisions naturally strengthens. There is, of course, a strong argument that Articles 40 and 41 contain a universalist conception of human rights and family rights, rather than an understanding of the rights recognised by these Articles as being limited to Irish citizens. It might be thought that the Supreme Court in the *Abortion Information* reference ([1995] IR 1) dealt a mortal blow to natural law theory. Even if this is so (and we shall examine that decision in detail in the 1995 Review), the question still remains as to the international remit of these Articles. Such attempts as the courts have made to deal with this question have not been entirely successful in clarifying the position.

Luxembourg Convention   In *R.J. v M.R.* [1994] 1 IR 271, the provisions of the Luxembourg Convention, given statutory effect in Ireland by the Child Abduction and Enforcement of Custody Orders Act 1991 (see the 1991 Review 82-6), fell for consideration. The respondent had cohabited in England with the applicant from 1988. Both parties were English. A daughter was born in 1989. A few months later the couple broke up. The child was made a ward of the court; the parties were briefly reconciled and the proceedings were adjourned. The relationship broke down again and the respondent left the applicant, taking the child with her. The English court made an order that the child should remain a ward of court during minority, that she should not be removed from the jurisdiction, that she reside with the respondent and that the applicant should have access at weekends. On *ex parte* application made by the respondent, the court discharged the access provision. In later *ex parte* proceedings, by the applicant, the court restored access entitlements to him. Subsequently, following on the coming into effect of the Children Act 1989, the wardship was translated into the new terminology of the 1989 statute. The respondent disappeared shortly afterwards. The applicant, on *ex parte* application, obtained an order prohibiting the removal of the child from the jurisdiction of the English court. This was served on the respondent's solicitor, her mother and two friends of hers. Further orders, an interim and a full residence order, were sent by post to the respondent at her mother's address.

The respondent was not traced to Ireland for over six months. She had been living here, with her uncle initially, for the previous eight months. She was in receipt of the lone parent's allowance here and had been given accommodation by a local authority.

The applicant sought the return to England of his daughter. He invoked the Luxembourg Convention. He could establish easily that he fell within the scope of Article 1: this defines a decision relating to custody as including a right of access, and defines improper removal as including the removal of a child across an international frontier in breach of a decision relating to custody.

Carroll J was satisfied that the respondent could not successfully invoke Article 9 as grounds for refusing recognition and enforcement. The respondent had been properly served with notice of proceedings; all the parties had been habitually present in England up to the time of the removal of the child. Counsel for the applicant had argued that the respondent and her daughter had changed their habitual residence when they had left the country of origin. Carroll J 'did not accept th[is] submission'; adding that,

> [i]n the context of the Convention, it is my opinion that 'habitual residence' means the ordinary residence up to the time the abduction takes place.

Clearly, there was no difficulty in establishing jurisdiction in the instant case since the facts fell squarely within the competence of the English courts based on 'the last common habitual residence of the child's parents, at least one parent being still habitually resident there.' Once that was established, ground (b) of Article 9 ceased to apply: see clause (ii) of ground (b).

The respondent invoked Article 10 of the Convention, paragraph (a) of which permits the courts of the State addressed not to recognise or enforce a foreign decision 'if it is found that the effects of the decision are manifestly incompatible with the fundamental principles of the law relating to the family and children in the State addressed.' Carroll J held that this paragraph was of no assistance:

> [T]here is nothing manifestly incompatible with the fundamental principles of law relating to the family and children in this country in granting access to the natural father of a child, particularly where the parents have cohabited continuously since the birth of the child and where the child is in no danger from the father.

Paragraph (b) of Article 10 permits the non-return of a child:

> if it is found that by reason of a change in the circumstances including the passage of time not including a mere change in the residence of the child after the improper removal, the effects of the original decision are manifestly no longer in accordance with the welfare of the child. . . .

The respondent argued that the child's welfare required that she remain in Ireland. She had settled in well in her new nursery school and would in due course be attending a Catholic primary school. Her condition of eczema had improved since she came to Ireland. Carroll J did not accept that, after less than nine months here, a child aged four would not adapt back to the environment she had always known. Neither did she accept that the schooling that she would receive in Britain would impede her religious upbringing and education. Nor would health care in England be inadequate to treat the child's eczema. The lapse of time and change of circumstances had not been such that the effects of the original decision were no longer in accordance with the welfare of the child. It was for the child's benefit to have contact with her father: through him she would have contact with his extended family. Carroll J rejected as exaggeration the respondent's claim that the applicant had been guilty of violent and drunken misconduct towards the child.

The respondent appealed unsuccessfully to the Supreme Court. Finlay CJ (Hederman, Egan, Blayney and Denham JJ concurring) first rejected the procedural point that, because the application from the Lord Chancellor's department seeking the return of the child had stated that it was made pursuant to the Hague Convention, no order could be made under the Luxembourg Convention. The High Court clearly had jurisdiction, by virtue of s. 25 of the 1991 Act, which provides that:

> [n]othing in this Part shall prevent a person from applying in the first

instance to the Court under the Luxembourg Convention for the recognition or enforcement of a decision relating to custody made by an authority in a Contracting State, other than the State.

The view of the Chief Justice, s. 25 inevitably had to be construed as giving a clear right to an applicant who had obtained an order relating to the custody of a child in another contracting state to seek as a plaintiff relief from the Irish courts. Any interpretation limiting the jurisdiction of the court to enforce the Luxembourg Convention merely by reason of the form or timing of a request from a Central Authority in respect of the same child would be a completely unjustified ouster of the ordinary jurisdiction of the court.

Turning to the substantive issues, Finlay CJ expressed himself satisfied that the party who invited the court to refuse to grant an order bore the onus of establishing the facts that would justify that refusal. The insertion of the word 'manifestly' in paragraphs (1)(a) and (b) of Article 10 indicated a standard of proof that was 'something more' than the balance of probabilities but less than proof beyond reasonable doubt. (We note here, yet again, Finlay CJ's propensity to translate substantive criteria into matters of the standard of proof: see out discussion of *P.F. v. M.F.*, Supreme Court, 13 January 1993, above, 125). Applying the standard of proof he considered to be the appropriate one, the Chief Justice found that no ease of incompatibility with the fundamental principles of the law relating to the family and children had been made out. Having regard to s. 13 of the Status of Children Act 1987, which gave an unmarried father the entitlement to apply to be made joint guardian of his child, it was quite clear that since 1987, at least, an order by the English court granting access to an unmarried father was in no way inconsistent with these fundamental principles.

As to the mother's argument that the child would be at risk of physical injury if her father was given access, the Supreme Court was bound by Carroll J's findings that the mother's claims of violence and drunkenness had been exaggerated. The women's arguments as to the stability of the situation in which the child had been for the last nine months would be relevant if the order sought to transfer custody to the father or if the father was seeking a right to cohabit with the mother and the child.

The Chief Justice concluded that an order for the return of the child should be made. He thought it appropriate, however, it provide an alternative method which would not involve her being put into the custody of her father, even for that limited purpose. She should instead be returned in the custody of her mother. The mother's solicitor had to inform the relevant authorities of where she intended to go, which had to be in London, so that interim access could be provided, in accordance with the English order, until the English courts could review the matter. The date and method of their travel had also to be communicated to the relevant parties. The mother was required to undertake that she would comply with these terms and would not remove the child from the London area without permission of the English courts.

MAINTENANCE

Costello J's decision in *McC. v McC.* [1994] ILRM 161 represents an important extension of the scope of recognition and enforcement of foreign maintenance orders at common law. In taking this course, Costello J rejected, not merely established English jurisprudence on the subject, but also the considered approach adopted by Finlay P less than a decade previously in *G. v G.* [1984] IR 368.

The central issue related to the *finality and conclusiveness* of the order. The traditional common law attitude, not only in respect of maintenance orders but in regard to all foreign judgments *in personam*, is that recognition should be afforded only to orders that are final and conclusive; if a foreign order recognised and enforced by an Irish court were later to be declared void or retrospectively varied by the courts that made it, this could embarrass the Irish court and occasion injustice in some instances. In the leading English decision, *Nouvion v Freeman*, 15 App Cas 1, at 9 (1989), Lord Herschell expressed the view that:

> it must be shown that in the Court by which [the foreign judgment] was pronounced it conclusively, finally, and for ever established the existence of the debt of which it is sought to be made conclusive evidence in this country, so as to make it *res judicata* between the parties. If it is not conclusive in the same Court which pronounced it, so that notwithstanding such a judgment the existence of the debt may, between the same parties, be afterwards contested in that Court, and upon proper proceedings being taken and such contest being adjudicated upon it, it might be declared that there existed no obligation to pay the debt at all, then I do not think that a judgment which is of that character can be regarded as finally and conclusively evidencing the debt, and so entitling the person who was obtained the judgment to claim a decree from our courts for the payment of that debt.

The Irish decisions at the end of the nineteenth and early part of this century are not easy to reconcile. In *Nunn v Nunn*, 8 LR Ir 292 (1880), the Court of Appeal, affirming the Queen's Bench Division, held that the fact that a foreign maintenance order was interlocutory and subject to subsequent variation did not render it less than final and conclusive. A different view was taken in *Keys v Keys* [1919] 2 IR 160, where the King's Bench Division held that an order for alimony in Irish proceedings for a divorce a *mensa et thoro* lacked the character of finality. *Keys v Keys* had a baneful effect on the same court in *McDonnell v McDonnell* [1921] 2 IR 148, where the members of the court were divided on whether the possibility of subsequent variation of a foreign maintenance order deprived it of the quality of finality: see W. Binchy, *Irish Conflicts of Law*, 306-8 (1988).

In *G. v G.* [1984] IR 368, Finlay P gave a clear analysis of the subject, holding that a foreign maintenance order, which was capable of subsequent variation, was nonetheless final and conclusive. He stressed that, for an order to lack these characteristics, it would have to be subject to *retrospective* variation. He noted that, in *McDonnell v McDonnell*, Pim J, dissenting, had made this distinction between retrospective and subsequent variation.

In *McC. v McC.*, the maintenance order, made by a Hong Kong court as an ancillary order in divorce proceedings, was capable of retrospective variation. Nonetheless Costello J held that it was enforceable, on the basis that it was final and conclusive. He reasoned powerfully as follows:

> The finality and conclusiveness of the order is to be determined by the nature of the proceedings before the foreign court and the effect of the court's orders. If the nature of the proceedings permits an adjudication on all the issues between the parties and if an order is made so that the principle of *res judicata* applies to it then it is clear (a) that the court's order is a 'final and conclusive' one, and this is so even though (b) the order may later be varied or set aside on appeal. When a court is required to determine the right to maintenance and the amount of maintenance and has power to adjudicate on all issues touching on these claims and does so then it is clear (c) that the court's order will estop the parties from litigating those issues again by virtue of the application of the principle of *res judicata*. And this is so even if the law permits the court to vary its earlier order if circumstances change — the court will then be seized with a new issue, that is, whether there has occurred a change in circumstances such as to justify a variation and it will not be reconsidering the issues already determined by the earlier order. The fact that a foreign law may permit a foreign court to vary its orders (as the Spanish law did in the case of the type of 'summary' order which was considered in *Nouvion*) may be evidence that the order is not a final and conclusive one; but it is not conclusive on the point. If it can be shown that the principle of *res judicata* applies to the order then, even though it may be subject to appeal by a higher court or be varied if circumstances change by the same court, ... it is a 'final and conclusive' order which will be enforced.

Costello J considered that English decisions holding maintenance orders subject to retrospective variation not to be final and conclusive had misconstrued the effect of the *Nouvion* decision. He interpreted *Nunn v Nunn* as being 'in conformity with' this approach. This is true only to the extent that nothing was said in *Nunn v Nunn* that was inconsistent with what Costello J said in *McC. v McC.* It would, however, be pressing matters to say that the earlier decision was a definitive authority on the specific issue of the characterisation of awards that are capable of retrospective variation.

Costello J went on to provide a diplomatic explanation for his departure from the approach adopted in Finlay P in *G. v G.*: the President had not been asked to take an approach different from that which had been adopted in the English decisions and he had expressly pointed out that no argument had arisen as to the applicable principles in the case which he was required to decide.

Costello J went on to explain how justice would not be imperilled by recognising a foreign maintenance order that was subject to retrospective variation. The Irish court could exercise its power to stay executions until a pending appeal in the foreign country was determined.

It should be noted that the Maintenance Orders Act 1994 has improved the position of maintenance creditors, who overwhelmingly are wives or children, in the context of international litigation.

TORT

The Irish private international law on tort is in a fluid and uncertain state. No great problem arises as to the question of jurisdiction where there is a European Community dimension: the jurisprudence of the Court of Justice, interpreting Article 5(3) of the Brussels Convention, is reasonably straightforward. Article 5(3) provides that (in addition to the entitlement to sue in the state of the defendant's domicile), an action may be brought in *the place where the tort was committed*. In *Handelswerkerij Bier v Mines de Potasse D'Alsase* [1976] ECR 1735, the Court of Justice held that the place where the tort was committed may be identified as either the place where the wrongful act was done or where the resulting harm occurred.

Once we move outside the European dimension the problems arise. The traditional approach in English law was articulated in *Phillips v Eyre* (1870) LR 6 QB 1, by Willes J:

As a general rule, in order to found a suit in England for a wrong alleged to have been committed abroad, two conditions must be fulfilled. First, the wrong must be of such a character that it would have been actionable if committed in England. Secondly, the act must not have been justifiable by the law of the place where it was done.

In *Chaplin v Boys* [1971] AC 356, the majority of the House of Lords interpreted the latter requirement as to the lack of justifiability as meaning that the wrong should be actionable (rather than simply criminal) under the law of the foreign jurisdiction.

There was very little discussion in Irish courts of the rule in *Phillips v Eyre* until 1986. The matter came before the Supreme Court in a jurisdictional context in *Grehan v Medical Incorporated* [1986] ILRM 627; 1986] IR 528. The plaintiff claimed damages for personal injuries resulting from the disintegration of a heart valve, manufactured by the defendant in America, which had been installed in Ireland. The Supreme Court, affirming Lynch J, held that the plaintiff had established a good jurisdictional ground.

After a detailed review of the authorities, Walsh J (with whom Finlay CJ and Griffin J agreed) concluded that, to fulfill the requirements set out in O. 11, r. 1(f) of the Rules of the Superior Court 1962, it was sufficient if any significant element in the commission of the tort had occurred within the jurisdiction. The court should then examine the circumstances of the case before exercising its discretion to make an order for service out of the jurisdiction. In the instant case, that element had occurred within the jurisdiction, since the plaintiff had been injured here, and thus Lynch J had been entitled to exercise his discretion authorising service out of the jurisdiction.

That was sufficient to dispose of the appeal. However, Walsh J also indicated that, in his view, the High Court in dealing with such applications should have regard to the choice of law implications. He went on to criticise both limbs of the rule in *Phillips v Eyre* and suggested the adoption of a more flexible approach in Ireland. The first limb of the rule was unacceptable because 'it would close the door of the court to every action in tort not recognised by Irish law and would require the application of Irish law even though the case had no connection with Ireland except that the defendant perhaps took refuge there after the tort was committed. It would, moreover, place the victim of a foreign tort in a far worse position than the victim of a breach of contract governed by foreign law, who would only have to prove the breach according to that law.'

As to the second limb of the rule, Willes J's expression, 'not justifiable', had proven to be unsatisfactory on account of its ambiguity and had led to controversial decisions (such as *Machado v Fontes* [1897] 2 QB 231) seeking to interpret it. The rule as a whole had 'nothing to recommend it' because it was capable of producing quite arbitrary decisions and was 'a mixture of parochialism and a vehicle for being, in some cases, unduly generous to the plaintiff and, in others, unduly harsh.'

In *An Bord Trachtála v Waterford Foods plc*, High Court, 25 November 1992, Keane J had to address choice of law issues in relation to the tort of passing off. We analyse the decision in detail in the Torts Chapter, below, 580-2. In the present context, Keane J referred to Walsh J's criticism of the rule in *Phillips v Eyre* in *Grehan v Medical Incorporated Ltd* and noted that Walsh J's remarks (which had not evoked any dissent from the Chief Justice and Griffin J) were entitled to the greatest respect, but were clearly *obiter*. It had also to be borne in mind that *Grehan* was essentially a case raising a jurisdictional rather than a choice of law issue and that the resolution of issues in the latter category on *ex parte* applications in the absence of the proposed defendants presented difficulties. There was, moreover, little agreement among judges and commentators in this and other jurisdictions as to how to rule in *Phillips v Eyre* should best be modified or replaced. Keane J noted that the implications were comprehensively discussed in Binchy, *Irish Conflicts of Law*, 572-580 (1988) and Cheshire and North, *Private International Law* (11th ed., 550-551). He observed that there was much to be said for leaving these complex issues to be resolved by the Oireachtas in the light of the recommendations which would ultimately be made by the Law Reform Commission which was at present examining the entire topic.

In the instant case, counsel had seemed to accept that there was difficulty in applying the rule in *Phillips v Eyre* with the refinement of the second limb proposed by the House of Lords in *Chaplin v Boys*. Both the parties were bodies incorporated under Irish law who would quite reasonably anticipate that their rights and duties would fall to be determined in accordance with Irish law. The application of the first limb thus presented no difficulty. The second limb required the application of the *lex loci delicti* in addition to the *lex fori*, 'thus modifying in part the insularity complained of in the first limb'. Keane J noted that this again should present no problem, although it required evidence as to the applicable foreign law. Keane J reserved for an appropriate case the question as to whether the rule in *Phillips v Eyre* was part of Irish law and, if it was, the modifications, if any, to which it should be subject.

As to the application of the second limb in the instant case, the only evidence as to English law consisted of a letter from an English firm of solicitors in which it was stated that:

> assuming that the Board could establish a reputation and goodwill in England in respect of the Food Ireland logo, a cause of action would be available to the Board under English law.

This 'carefully qualified view' seemed to Keane J, at least for the purposes of the interlocutory application, to mean that the plaintiffs had complied with the second limb of the rule in the case of Britain.

When the Supreme Court revisits the issue of the choice of law in tort, as it surely will be obliged to do in the relatively near future, it will have several possible solutions to choose from, throughout the common law world: see, e.g., *Red Sea Insurance Co. Ltd v Bouygues S.A.* [1995] 1 AC 190 (PC); *Stevens v Head* (1993) 176 CLR 433, analysed by Opeskin (1993) 109 *LQ Rev* 533; *Tolofson v Jensen* (1994) 120 DLR (4th) 299 (Supreme Court of Canada) and the legislative solution adopted in Britain by Part III of the Private International Law (Miscellaneous Provisions) Act 1995, critically analysed by Briggs [1995] *LMCLQ* 519.

Constitutional Law

ADMINISTRATION OF JUSTICE

In *Geoghegan v Institute of Chartered Accountants in Ireland*, High Court, 9 July 1993, Murphy J rejected two arguments challenging the constitutional validity of the mechanism by which the Institute of Chartered Accountants in Ireland conducts a disciplinary hearing into alleged professional misconduct by the applicant, a chartered accountant and member of the Institute. The first point argued concerned the Institute's establishment by Royal Charter. The second was that, in conducting a disciplinary hearing, the Institute was engaged in the exercise of the judicial power under Article 34 of the Constitution. For ease of discussion, we examine both these arguments together. The background to the case was as follows.

The Institute had been incorporated by Royal Charter on 14 May 1888. Under the Charter, the Institute was given power to sue and be sued in its own name and was also given power to make by-laws regulating its affairs, but that such by-laws would not have any effect unless and until they had been submitted to and allowed by the Privy Council in Ireland. A private Act of the Oireachtas, the Institute of Chartered Accountants in Ireland (Charter Amendment) Act 1966, amended the 1888 Charter by providing *inter alia* that any by-laws made by the Institute would not have any effect 'unless and until they have been submitted to and allowed by the Government.' The Act also provided that: '[s]ave as hereby amended the Charter shall be and remain in full force and effect.' On 18 April 1989, the Institute amended its existing by-laws and these were allowed by the Government by an instrument under seal of 12 September 1989.

The amended by-laws provided that if a member was guilty of misconduct in carrying out his or her professional duties they would be liable to disciplinary action. This would take the form of a preliminary investigation by an Investigating Committee, with the possibility of penalties being imposed by means of a decision of a Disciplinary Committee constituted under the by-laws. Penalties envisaged in the by-laws ranged from admonishment to exclusion from membership of the Institute.

As Murphy J pointed out in his judgment, although neither the 1888 Charter or the 1966 Act granted members of the Institute a monopoly in the practice of the profession of accountancy, the Institute was one of the bodies recognised along with a limited number of others for the purposes of auditing of companies under the Companies Acts 1963 to 1990. Murphy J commented that suspension or expulsion from the Institute thus involved not only loss of the auditing recognition but also 'would be likely to have a devastating effect on the professional practice of any of its members.'

In April 1992, the Institute informed the applicant that it had received a complaint concerning auditing procedures for which he was alleged to be responsible. On 2 September 1992, the Institute informed him that the Investigating Committee had formed the opinion that a *prima facie* case of professional misconduct had been established and that a Disciplinary Committee would conduct a hearing into the matter on 14 September 1992. The applicant then sought, by way of judicial review, an order of *certiorari* quashing the convening of the Disciplinary Committee and an order of prohibition restraining the continuation of the disciplinary proceedings. As already indicated, the basis of the applicant's claim was that the Committee would be involved in the unconstitutional exercise of the judicial power which was, under Article 34, exclusively a matter for the courts. As also already indicated, Murphy J rejected this claim.

Before addressing the Article 34 argument, Murphy J dealt with the applicant's suggestion that, as the 1888 Charter under which the Institute was formed had been granted in exercise of the royal prerogative, it had not been carried forward by Article 73 of the 1922 Constitution or Article 50 of the 1937 Constitution. Murphy J accepted that this argument appeared to find support in the decisions of the Supreme Court in *Byrne v Ireland* [1972] IR 241 and *Webb v Ireland* [1988] ILRM 565; [1988] IR 353 (see the 1987 Review, 104-7) to the effect that 'no royal prerogative' had survived the enactment of the 1922 Constitution. Counsel for the Attorney General (a notice party in the instant case) argued that, notwithstanding the *Byrne* and *Webb* cases, certain prerogatives had survived the creation of the Irish Free State in 1922. Using an example close to the hearts of the legal profession, he instanced the patent of precedence granted by the government to senior counsel, a procedure clearly based on the former patent of precedence granted by the monarch to a King's or Queen's Counsel.

Murphy J paraphrased the applicant's argument as being that any body incorporated by royal charter prior to 1922 'withered away or ceased to have the right to exercise the powers conferred upon it by the charter on the coming into operation of the 1922 or 1937 Constitutions.' He commented that no authority was cited for that proposition and went on to reject it for two reasons, contained in this important passage:

> The filtering process provided by Article 73 of the 1922 Constitution (like the comparable provision in the 1937 Constitution) related to the content of the law and not its source. I see no reason why the Institute

and all comparable bodies, whether formed under public or private legislation or incorporated by Royal Charter as part of the royal pre-rogative or residual regal legislative power, should not continue to have a valid and effective existence on the formation of the independent Irish State. Certainly any other result would be chaotic in the extreme. The virtual absurdity of such a situation is illustrated in the present case where the applicant is at the same time claiming to be a member of an incorporated body while asserting that this body had no existence in law.

There is, however, an even clearer answer to the claims by the applicant in this regard. It seems to me that s. 7 of the Chartered Accountants in Ireland (Charter Amendment) Act 1966 puts the matter beyond any debate in using the words . . . 'the Charter shall be and remain in full force and effect.'

Clearly this passage reflects a somewhat pragmatic response to the 'chaotic' vista with which Murphy J was faced in the instant case and is, perhaps, understandable. In referring to 'comparable bodies', Murphy J may have had in mind, for example, the Honourable Society of the King's Inns, the body responsible for the education of future members of the Bar and also founded by royal charter. Nonetheless, whatever the pragmatic benefits of his view, the assertion that the filtering process in Article 73 of the 1992 Constitution related to the 'content of the law and not its source' seems to ignore a fundamental principle underlying the leading decisions of *Byrne* and *Webb*.

Those decisions had clearly established that the 'source' of the preroga-tive powers, not merely their content, was inconsistent in particular with the statement in Article 6 of the 1937 Constitution that the People are the sovereign power. Admittedly, in *Byrne* the prerogative of immunity from suit appeared to focus on 'content', though this was surely the twin of 'source' in that instance. More particularly, in the *Webb* case, the Supreme Court suggested that the 'content' of the former treasure trove prerogative could be reformed, and expanded, to comply with the terms of the 1937 Constitution being transformed into the concept of ownership by the People of all important ancient artefacts, not merely gold artefacts. This approach in *Webb* seems opposed to that of Murphy J in *Geoghegan*. However, it must be acknowledged that, as Murphy J noted, the precise point raised in the instant case had not been raised in either *Byrne* or *Webb* and that the applicant's argument leaves the potential for a 'chaotic' situation.

The second reason given by Murphy J in the passage quoted for dismiss-ing the applicant's claim is somewhat laconic. One could speculate that Murphy J may have had in mind that, since the 1966 Act was now the

statutory basis for the Charter, the arguments concerning the royal prerogative were moot. However, this seems inconsistent with Murphy J's reference
to the 1966 Act as being a 'clearer answer', thus indicating it is linked to his
discussion of prerogative. Alternatively, was he suggesting that, by substituting the government for the Privy Council in Ireland, the 1966 Act was
purging the 1888 Charter of its potentially contaminating links to the royal
prerogative? This possible explanation introduces more problems, since it
might cast doubt over the 'comparable bodies' whose status under Charter
had not been 'validated' by Act of the Oireachtas. Whatever the true
explanation, it seems difficult to see how the 1966 Act was 'an even clearer
answer' to the applicant's claim. The 1966 Act can only have validly carried
over the 1888 Charter on the basis of the conclusion already arrived at by
Murphy J, namely, that, contrary to what seemed to be established by *Byrne*
and *Webb*, the apparent demise of the royal prerogatives in 1922 did not affect
the validity of the 1888 Charter. But it seems difficult to accept that an Act
passed in 1966, some years before the decision of the Supreme Court in
Byrne, could have been intended to be anything more than a relatively simple
substitution of 'government' for 'Privy Council in Ireland', with a proviso
that the remainder of the amended document continued to apply 'without
prejudice' to such changes. One might argue that the 1966 Act thus merely
conforms to good drafting practice, rather than amounting to a sophisticated
form of anticipation of future Surpeme Court decisions.

While there are good reasons why one might breathe a sigh of relief at
the conclusions arrived at in the *Geoghegan* case, another decision subsequent to Murphy J's judgment casts further doubt on the distinction he
drew betweeen 'content' and 'source' in relation to the former royal prerogative. In *Howard v Commissioners of Public Works in Ireland* [1993] ILRM
665; [1994] 1 IR 101 (discussed in the Local Government chapter, 430-2,
below), the Supreme Court again affirmed the decision in *Byrne v Ireland*
[1972] IR 241 by holding that, contrary to the position under the royal
prerogative, there is no general presumption that State bodies are exempt
from legislative requirements. In *Howard*, the Supreme Court held, to use
the terms employed by Murphy J in *Geoghegan*, that both the 'content' and
'source' of the supposed exception were contrary to the Constitution.

But what of the pragmatic argument used by Murphy J that it would be
'chaotic' for all bodies created by Royal Charter to 'wither away'? It may be
that the vista envisaged by Murphy J need not necessarily come to pass. Even
if one accepts that the *Byrne* and *Webb* cases establish that all royal prerogatives are, *ipso facto*, inconsistent with the Constitution, there remains the
possibility that institutions which owe their existence to royal charters might
nonetheless retain their existence through the 'transformation' applied by the
Supreme Court in the *Webb* case. While the Court in *Webb* held that the

treasure trove prerogative disappeared in 1922, it also held that it had been replaced by a new concept in tune with the sovereignty of the People. It might, equally, be possible for a similar transformation process to be recognised for institutions and bodies created prior to 1922. However, this clearly remains for another case.

We may now turn to the second issue raised in the *Geoghegan* case, namely whether the defendant Institute was exercising the judicial power contrary to Article 34 of the Constitution. On this issue, Murphy J drew considerable support from the judgment of Kingsmill Moore J in *In re the Solicitors Act 1954* [1960] IR 239 in order to distinguish the disciplinary powers conferred on the Institute from those purportedly conferred by the 1954 Act on the Law Society of Ireland, and found to have been in violation of Article 34 of the Constitution.

Kingsmill Moore J had noted that the Solicitors Act 1954 had transferred what, historically, had been a matter for the courts to the jurisdiction of the Law Society of Ireland and had purported expressly to confer the powers of the High Court on the Law Society. Such blatant diminution of a traditional aspect of the judicial function was, Murphy J noted, absent in the instant case. Kingsmill Moore J had also emphasised that the Law Society derived its jurisdiction primarily from statute, and he had contrasted this with the situation where members of bodies, such as 'clubs, trades unions, trade and professional associations, chartered or otherwise . . .' could agree that failure by members to abide by the rules of the body would lead to investigation and possible expulsion. Kingsmill Moore J held that such a jurisdistion vested in a domestic tribunal 'is not a diminution or devolution of the judicial power of the State — it rests on contract only.' In the *Geoghegan* case, Murphy J drew particular attention to the inclusion of chartered associations in this list of private bodies which would not fall foul of Article 34. Murphy J continued:

> . . . Kingsmill Moore J had adverted [in the *Solicitors Act* case] to the fact that a domestic tribunal does not cease to be such merely because it is incorporated by Royal Charter. In addition, however, it is clear that the Charter in the present case did not purport to confer on the Institute judicial functions of any description. The judicial functions of the Council of the Institute, such as they are, arise in relation to the rules of professional conduct which the members gave to themselves by a majority vote in general meeting. Their decision in that regard was subject to approval and confirmation by the government but in granting such approval the government merely endorsed the bargain made between the parties and did not purport to grant to the Institute or its constituent committees any of the executive, judicial or legislative powers of government.

With respect, this passage appears to confuse two elements of the decision in the *Solicitors Act* case. It is true that the source of a particular power — statute or contract — is a major factor in determining whether such is in breach of Article 34, and in this respect a statutory power may more closely be identified with the judicial function. In addition, the express conferral of the judicial power in the 1954 Act made the decision to find it in breach of Article 34 rather easy. But the fact that a power is derived from contract and does not expressly purport to confer the power of the High Court on the disciplinary body concerned cannot be a determining factor. The passage quoted from Murphy J's judgment appears to give an excessive priority to 'form over substance' and to place almost no weight on the consequences of expulsion from the Institute. Earlier in his judgment, Murphy J had indeed stated that 'I think it would have to be accepted that the consequences of expulsion, even from a particular accountancy body, might be almost as damaging' as striking off from the roll of solicitors. This factor appeared to recede from view later in his judgment, but it can be argued that a contractual bargain between members of a private body can amount to a breach of constitutional principles even where (perhaps particularly where) those members do not purport to confer unconstitutional powers on their professional organisations. Indeed, it can be argued that private bodies may be more susceptible to falling into an unconstitutionality than the modern Oireachtas, which displays considerable anxiety to avoid falling foul of the Constitution: see for example s. 2(3) of the State Authorities (Amendment) Act 1993, discussed in the Administrative Law chapter, 4-5, above, or s. 5(2) of the European Communities (Amendment) Act 1993, discussed in the European Community chapter, 302, below. It may be said that, in general, private bodies will continue to operate relatively oblivious to the requirements of the Constitution unless and until they are brought before the courts. Nonetheless, where private bodies fail to meet constitutional norms, they are subject to constitutional review and the courts have, in the past, looked primarily to the substantive issue of whether rights have been infringed in this context, rather than the legal genesis from which such bodies derive their powers. This is clear from leading decisions such as those in *Murphy v Stewart* [1973] IR 97 and *Meskell v Coras Iompar Éireann* [1973] IR 121.

Indeed, the confusion suggested here in Murphy J's judgment would appear to be supported by the later part of his judgment in which he concluded that the Institute's powers were not amenable to judicial review under O.84 of the Rules of the Superior Courts 1986. He linked this point to the decision in the *Solicitors Act* case, citing recent decisions such as *Murphy v Turf Club* [1989] IR 171 (see the 1989 Review, 14) and *Beirne v Garda Commissioner* [1993] ILRM 1 (see the 1992 Review, 382-3). While Murphy J undoubtedly had the weight of authority on his side in this aspect of his decision, it may have played an unwarranted role in his earlier conclusion that the Institute's powers were also constitutionally free from invalidity.

COMMUNICATION

The extent to which the right to convey information is protected by the Constitution was discussed by Keane J in *Oblique Financial Services Ltd v The Promise Production Co. Ltd* [1994] 1 ILRM 74: see the Conflict of Laws chapter, 131, above. See also the discussion of the cases concerning Orders under s. 31 of the Broadcasting Authority Act 1960, discussed in the Communications chapter, 68-70, above.

COMPTROLLER AND AUDITOR GENERAL

The Comptroller and Auditor General (Amendment) Act 1993 involves a major legislative attempt to modernise the role of the State's auditor, the Comptroller and Auditor General. While the importance of this office is formally recognised by the fact that it was established by Article 33 of the Constitution, the 1993 Act represents the first time that the role and functions of the Comptroller and Auditor General have been expanded to reflect the enormous impact that the State and, increasingly, State bodies have on the economic life of the State.

Although the 1993 Act is a partial consolidation and modernisation of existing statutory provisions in this area, some of the detail of the Comptroller's functions are still to be found in the Exchequer and Audit Departments Act 1866, as amended by the Exchequer and Audit Departments Act 1921, and the Comptroller and Auditor General Act 1923, as amended, principally by the 1993 Act. The main provisions of the 1993 Act came into effect on various dates between 23 September 1993 and 1 January 1994: see the Comptroller and Auditor General (Amendment) Act 1993 (Commencement) Order 1993 (SI No. 273). The provisions of the 1993 Act concerning remuneration of the Comptroller came into effect on 1 January 1994: see the Comptroller and Auditor General (Amendment) Act 1993 (Commencement) (No. 2) Order 1993 (SI No. 318). While the 1993 Act was thus largely in effect from 1 January 1994, various extensions of the Comptroller's remit provided for under the 1993 Act in relation to the different State bodies referred to in the Schedules to the Act (discussed below) require separate Commencement Orders. Three such Orders were made in 1994 (SI Nos. 196, 197 and 242) and we will return to these in the 1994 Review.

S. 2 of the 1993 Act provides that the Comptroller's first main function is, on receipt of requisitions from the Minister for Finance, to ensure that any government expenditure is in accordance with the requirements of the Central Fund (Permanent Provisions) Act 1965 or, as the case may be, in accordance with any vote by Dáil Éireann. Where the Exchequer's account at the Central Bank is 'operated to a material extent otherwise than in accordance with' s. 2, the Comptroller must, as soon as practicable, draw up a report to this effect and cause the report to be laid before Dáil Éireann.

S. 3 of the 1993 Act deals with the Comptroller's second main function, namely to perform an annual audit of the expenditure of each government Department to ensure that such expenditure has been applied for the purposes intended by the Oireachtas when it made the relevant appropriations. As with s. 2 of the 1993 Act, if the Comptroller finds that the expenditure was not properly made or authorised, then a report of that fact must be drawn up and presented to Dáil Éireann.

S. 4 of the 1993 Act is a new provision which requires the transmission by the Minister for Finance to the Comptroller of the accounts for the preceding financial year not later than 30 June following the end of the financial year to which they relate.

S. 5 of the 1993 Act is another new provision which confers additional audit functions on the Comptroller in relation to the accounts of the organisations specified in the First Schedule to the 1993 Act, which include the Criminal Injuries Compensation Tribunal, the Economic and Social Research Institute, the General Medical Services (Payments) Board, the Institute of Public Administration, the Legal Aid Board, the Shannon Free Airport Development Co. Ltd, St Patrick's College Maynooth, the University of Dublin (Trinity College) as well as bodies established under the Health (Corporate Bodies) Act 1961, such as the Blood Transfusion Service Board. All of these organisations are funded to some extent by the Oireachtas but were not subject to the remit of the Comptroller prior to the 1993 Act. In addition to the organisations specified in the First Schedule, s. 5 of the 1993 Act also extends the Comptroller's functions to include any fund owned, operated or controlled by a Minister or any fund assisted by the Oireachtas as well as the accounts of the transactions in the State of the Guarantee section of the European Guidance and Guarantee Fund established under Article 40 of the EC Treaty. The latter Fund, commonly called FEOGA, is, of course, of enormous significance in the Irish economy as it relates to the disbursement of funds under the EC Common Agricultural Policy.

Ss. 6 and 7 of the 1993 Act, also new, require the Comptroller to audit the accounts of health boards and vocational education committees, respectively, while s. 8 of the Act empowers the Comptroller to inspect the accounts of harbour authorities and the regional tourism organisations specified in the Third Schedule to the Act.

S. 9 of the 1993 Act confers a significant new discretionary power on the Comptroller, namely to carry out such examinations as are considered appropriate for the purpose of ascertaining whether the resources of a government Department or other organisation audited by the Comptroller have been 'used . . . economically and efficiently.' This power, already dubbed the 'value-for-money' audit, extends to determining whether resources which have been acquired or disposed meet the 'economic and efficient' test. However, we should note that there are two significant limits on this power. First, it is not to be applied annually to all audited accounts, but is a matter of discretion and, presumably, dependent on the resources available to the Comptroller. In that sense the audit conducted under s. 3 of the 1993 Act remains the primary function of the Comptroller. The second limit on s. 9 is that a large number of State bodies specified in the Second Schedule to the Act are entirely exempt from its provisions. Those exempted include Aer Lingus, Aer Rianta, ACC Bank, Bord Gáis Éireann, Bord Telecom Éireann, Coras Iompair Éireann, the Electricity Supply Board, ICC Bank, Nitrigín Éireann Teo, An Post, Radio Telefís Éireann, the Voluntary Health Insurance Board as well as all local authorities.

S. 10 of the 1993 Act authorises the Comptroller to obtain information required for the performance of the functions conferred on the office, including computer-held data within the meaning of the Data Protection Act 1988.

S. 11 of the 1993 Act restates existing provisions concerning the reports of the Comptroller prepared for Dáil Éireann, but also includes a provision by which a 'special report' may be made by the Comptroller in connection with any of the powers conferred on the office. This would appear to envisage reports on specific topics rather than the complete annual reports published by the Comptroller prior to the 1993 Act. It may be noted that, in any report by the Comptroller, s. 11 of the 1993 Act provides that 'the Comptroller and Auditor General shall not question, or express an opinion on, the merits of policies or of policy objectives.' A similar injunction applies under s. 19 of the 1993 Act to those public servants, the accounting officers, responsible within government Departments for the preparation of accounts for the Comptroller when required to appear before the Dáil Appropriations Committee.

The remaining provisions of the 1993 Act concern issues within the Office of the Comptroller, including another novel feature of the 1993 Act, the charging of fees by the Comptroller (s. 12), audit of the Comptroller's Office itself (s. 13), remuneration, pension and retirement of the Comptroller at 65, save for the incumbent on the passing of the Act (ss. 14 and 15), delegation of functions (s. 16), provision for the transfer of staff from the local government audit section in the Department of the Environment (s. 17) as well as minor adjustments to ss. 25 and 43 of the Exchequer and Audit Departments Act 1866 (s. 18).

EDUCATION

In *O'Donoghue v Minister for Education and Ors*, High Court, 27 May 1993, O'Hanlon J held that the State had failed to meet its obligation under Article 42 of the Constitution to provide for free primary education for the applicant, an eight year old boy who had contracted Reye's Syndrome.

Education is a subject of much contemporary political debate. At the centre of the controversy are the provisions of Article 42 of the Constitution. These can be understood only in their historical and cultural contexts. The 1922 Constitution had done no more than prescribe a right to free elementary education. Article 42 goes much further, by establishing a complex network of relationships between parents, children and the State. The underlying philosophy is clearly that of Catholic social theory: the family (based on marriage) is the primary unit group of society; parents have the responsibility, and right, to educate their children and to establish the value-system by which they will be reared; the State has a subordinate role, to service these parental needs and to act 'as long stop' when parents neglect their obligations to their children.

It should not be forgotten that, in 1937, this vision of the role of families and parents was controversial: competing philosophies, of Communism and Fascism, regarded the family quite differently and vaunted the State as the primary educator. Article 42, therefore, is very much concerned with stark principles of political philosophy and a good deal less exercised with the detail of pedagogy or school financing and administration.

Much of the litigation involving Article 42 has concerned the troublesome question of the relationship between religious freedom, the rights of parents and children and the entitlement of those who provide education. There is also a substantial body of litigation which essentially relates to family life: see, for example, *In re Article 26 and the Adoption (No. 2) Bill 1987* [1989] ILRM 266; [1989] IR 656, which we analyse in the 1988 Review, 246-52. There have been relatively few cases in which the courts have been called on to address the scope of the obligation resting on the State in relation to the provision of education.

In *Ryan v Attorney General* [1965] IR 294, the plaintiff's constitutional challenge to the introduction of fluoride into the drinking water contained the claim that it compromised her right to provide as she thought fit for the health and welfare of her children, contrary to Article 42. Kenny J considered that:

the terms of the Article show that the word 'education' was not used in this wide sense in the Constitution. Section 1 of the Article recognises the 'right and duty of parents to provide according to their means for the religious and moral, intellectual, physical and social education of their children', but in section 2 it is provided that the parents are free to provide this education in their homes or in schools established or recognised by the State. The education referred to in section 1 must, therefore, be one that can be provided in schools and must, therefore, be one of a scholastic nature.

On appeal, the Supreme Court adopted a somewhat broader definition of the word 'education'. Ó Dálaigh CJ, delivering the judgment of the Court, stated:

> Education essentially is the teaching and training of a child to make the latest possible use of his inherent and potential capacities, physical, mental and moral. To teach a child to minimise the dangers of dental caries by adequate brushing of his teeth is physical education, for it induces him to use his own resources. To give him water of a nature calculated to minimise the danger of dental caries is in no way to educate him physically or otherwise, for it does not develop his resources.' In the High Court case of *Landers v Attorney General* (1975) 109 ILTR I, Finlay J professed to find no inconsistency in the definitions provided by Kenny J and the Supreme Court in *Ryan*.

The matter was revisited in *Crowley v Ireland* [1980] IR 102 The case involved a claim for breach of constitutional rights based on failure to provide education in the plaintiffs' local school during an extended closure brought about by a teachers' strike. The Supreme Court accepted that Article 42.4 conferred on the plaintiffs a right to full primary education, but emphasised the fact that the State's duty was limited to *providing for* such education rather than *providing* it. O'Higgins CJ conceded that the State's duty, thus circumscribed, was one 'of general application to all citizens'.

In *O'Donoghue v Minister for Health*, High Court, 27 May 1993, O'Hanlon J delivered a most significant decision on the subject. His long judgment, of over a hundred pages, has not yet been reported, in spite of its major social implications, its discussion of American judicial authorities and its comprehensive analysis of recent international developments in educational theory.

The plaintiff, aged eight, had contracted Reye's Syndrome when an infant. This resulted in significant physical and mental disability. There were only limited educational facilities in Ireland for children with this significant degree of mental disability, in contrast to considerably better facilities for children who were classified as mildly or moderately mentally handicapped. The plaintiff's mother, on his behalf, sought an order of *mandamus* against the Ministers for Health and Education, to compel them to provide for free primary education for the plaintiff and a declaration that, in failing to do so and in discriminating against him as compared with other children, the defendants had deprived him of constitutional rights under Articles 40 and 42 (in particular Articles 40.1, 40.3.2, 42.3.2 and 42.4). The plaintiff also claimed damages for breach of his constitutional rights.

O'Hanlon J reviewed the evidence that had been adduced in very great detail. It appeared that, whilst a national system of primary education had been part of Irish life for over a century and a half, it was not until the end of the nineteenth century that blind and deaf children received special education. Following the recommendations of the Commission of Inquiry into Mental Handicap in 1965, a network of schools for children with mild and moderate mental handicaps had been established. Ireland was one of the first countries to take this step.

A further Commission, chaired by Sean MacGlennain, in its report (the Blue Report) recommended in 1983 that severely and profoundly mentally and physically handicapped children should receive as much training and education in the broad sense as was possible, with a view to improving the quality of their lives. A pilot scheme was established, but its success was qualified by financial cut-backs. A Review Group, which reported in 1990, lent its support to the 1983 recommendations.

After reviewing the Irish precedents and authorities from the United States, notably *Mills v Board of Education of District of Columbia*, 348 Fed Supp 866 (1972) and *Honig v Doe and Smith* (1988) 484 US 305, O'Hanlon J held in favour of the plaintiff. He reasoned as follows. If, in using the expression 'of a scholastic nature', Kenny J in *Ryan* had had in mind what is traditionally referred to as 'book-learning', one would have to agree that it was virtually certain that education in that narrow sense would never be of benefit to the plaintiff because of his disabilities. In O'Hanlon J's view, Kenny J's real purpose had been to make it clear that 'education' was not wide enough in the context of Article 42 to include rearing and nurturing, as the plaintiff in that case had contended. Ó Dálaigh CJ's more extended definition was 'more useful' and in harmony with the dramatic advances that had since been made in the education of children such as the plaintiff:

> The whole momentum, as evidenced in the Declarations emanating from the Vatican, from the United States, and in the Protocol to the European Convention on Human Rights, has been towards the provision for every individual of such education as will enable him or her – in the words of

the Chief Justice — 'to make the best possible use of his (or her) inherent and potential capacities, physical, mental and moral' — however limited those capacities may be.

O'Hanlon J rejected on the evidence the defendants' assertion that the plaintiff should be regarded as ineducable. Turning to the language of the provisions of Article 42, he referred to Professor W.N. Osborough's article, 'Education in the Irish Law and Constitution' (1978) 13 *Ir Jur (ns)* 145, which provided 'a full consideration of the manner in which the words and phrases used in these constitutional provisions ha[d] been interpreted by the courts. . . .'

O'Hanlon J relying on the Irish text of the Constitution, rejected the idea that the word 'primary' in Article 42, should be treated as synonymous with that word in Article 42.1. The expression 'bun-oideachas' contrasted with 'príomhda' in Article 4.2.1°. O'Hanlon J concluded that:

there is a constitutional obligation imposed on the State by the provisions of Art. 42.4. of the Constitution to provide for free basic elementary education of all children and that this involves giving each child such advice, instruction and teaching as will enable him or her to make the best possible use of his or her inherent and potential capacities, physical, mental and moral, however limited these capacities may be. Or, to borrow the language of the United Nations Convention and Resolution of the General Assembly — 'such education as will be conducive to the child's achieving the fullest possible social integration and individual development; such education as will enable the child to develop his or her capabilities and skills to the maximum and will hasten the process of social integration and reintegration'.

This process will work differently for each child, according to the child's own natural gifts, or lack thereof. In the case of the child who is deaf, dumb, blind, or otherwise physically or mentally handicapped, a completely different programme of education has to be adopted and a completely different rate of progress has to be taken for granted, than would be regarded as appropriate for a child suffering from no such handicap.

The State had hitherto responded generously to its obligations in relation to virtually all of the categories of handicapped children, as had been recognised in several Reports, but had clearly lagged behind many other developed countries in what had been undertaken on behalf of the small but most seriously handicapped group of all: the category to which the plaintiff belonged.

It was admittedly only in the past few decades that research into the problems of the severely and profoundly physically and mentally handicapped had led to positive findings that education in a formal setting, involving schools and teachers, educational equipment of many kinds, and integration as far as possible in the conventional school environment, could be of real benefit to these children. But once that had been established, it appeared to O'Hanlon J that it gave rise to a constitutional obligation on the part of the State to respond to these findings by providing for free primary education for this group of children in as full and positive a manner as it had done for all other children in the community.

O'Hanlon J found support from *Ryan*, where the Supreme Court upheld Kenny J's holding that it had not been demonstrated by the evidence adduced in the case that the introduction of minimal quantities of fluoride into the drinking water of the population presented any danger to health. Ó Dálaigh CJ had gone on to say that if further advances in scientific knowledge in the future should support a contrary conclusion, a claim of the same nature as that put forward by Mrs Ryan would not be foreclosed.

In relation to the instant claim, had it been brought forward even as recently as 1965, when the Commission of Inquiry on Mental Handicap was presenting its Report, a conclusion in line with the findings of that Commission might well have been reached, to the effect that education would do nothing to alleviate the plight of the more severely or profoundly mentally handicapped. Events had moved rapidly since that time, however, and on a world-wide scale, so that the weight of informed opinion had supported the contrary view for many years prior to 1993. The defendants' argument that such education as could be provided for severely or profoundly mentally handicapped did not fall within the scope of 'primary education', as that term was used in the Constitution, was undermined by what had already taken place in relation to education for the mild and moderately handicapped.

The ordinary National School Curriculum had always had a significant 'non-academic' content under such headings of Physical Education, Health and Fitness, Music and Singing, Social and Environmental Education. All that occurred in the special schools for the handicapped was that the emphasis of the educational process was laid on this limited group of subjects, to the exclusion of subjects which would make too great a demand on the intellectual powers of the mentally handicapped.

O'Hanlon J believed that it had now come to be accepted that trained teachers and the school environment could make a major contribution to this process which, with the best will in the world, could not be provided as effectively or as successfully by parents and family in the home. This seemed to him to overcome whatever difficulty might otherwise arise in reconciling the instant claim with the view expressed by Kenny J in *Ryan* that 'education' as used in Article 42 was intended to mean 'education of a kind which could be provided by parents in their homes, or alternatively in schools established or recognised by the State', and therefore 'of a scholastic nature'.

O'Hanlon J therefore concluded that the education to which the plaintiff laid claim, in reliance on rights derived from the provisions of Article 42 could correctly be described as 'primary education' within the meaning of that phrase as used in Article 42.3.4°.

O'Hanlon J rejected the defendants' argument that the plaintiff's claim was a moot one because he had been granted a place at a school established under the pilot scheme for the education of severely and profoundly mentally handicapped children. It was not sufficient for the defendants to grant, as a matter of grace and concession, educational benefits which the plaintiff was entitled to claim as of right. The Second Vatican Council had expressed the principle rather pithily, albeit in a non-legal context:

> The demands of justice must first of all be satisfied; that which is already due in justice is not to be offered as a gift of charity. . . . (*Apostolicam actuositatem*, 8).

Moreover, O'Hanlon J was far from convinced that, notwithstanding the very noble and dedicated work which was being carried out by those engaged in the Pilot Scheme, it could be regarded as meeting the specific obligation imposed on the State by Article 42.4 of the Constitution to provide for free primary education in the case of the plaintiff.

The evidence in the case was sufficient to convince O'Hanlon J that the provision of free primary education for children who were severely or profoundly handicapped, whether mentally or physically, required 'a much greater deployment of resources' than had been thought appropriate even as recently as 1983 when the Blue Report was completed.

Referring to the education which the plaintiff was receiving, O'Hanlon J observed:

> To ask a single teacher to undertake the primary education of 12 severely or profoundly handicapped children, in my opinion, far exceeds the work-load deemed appropriate for a teacher in the ordinary primary school where the pupils do not suffer from mental or physical handicap.

Evidence had been given that the teacher-pupil ratio in Britain was two to five, and in Denmark two qualified teachers and one assistant had responsibility for seven pupils. The evidence also gave rise to 'a strong conviction' on O'Hanlon J's part that primary education for this category of children, to meet their special needs, required a new approach in respect of *three* factors:

(a) *Age of Commencement*: Early intervention and assessment being of vital importance if conditions of mental and physical handicap are not to become intractable.

(b) *Duration of Primary Education*: As this category will, in all probability, never proceed further, and are unlikely to proceed far up the ladder of primary education itself, the process should, ideally, continue as long as the ability for further development is discernible. Professor Hogg suggests that age 18 may not be unrealistic in this context.

(c) *Continuity of Education*: The lengthy holiday breaks which take place in the life of the ordinary primary school appear likely to cause serious loss of ground which may never be recovered, in the case of children with severe or profound handicap. Accordingly, to deal adequately with their needs appears to require that the teaching process should, so far as practicable, be continuous throughout the entire year.

These factors led O'Hanlon J to conclude that the defendants were misled in their belief that the arrangements already made to provide a place for the plaintiff in the pilot scheme were sufficient of themselves to satisfy any claim that might arise in his favour under the provisions of the Constitution to have free primary education provided for his benefit.

Thirdly, O'Hanlon J was satisfied from the evidence in the case that the defendants had failed for some years previously to carry out the duty imposed on them by the Constitution to provide for free primary education for the plaintiff's benefit, and for this breach of his constitutional rights that they were liable in damages for any loss and damage thereby caused to the plaintiff. A very modest claim had been put forward for recoupment of some of the expenses incurred in the effort to make good this default on the part of the defendants. These included journeys to Budapest to obtain help and guidance from the Peto Institute and the hiring of a teacher to come to Cork from Hungary to continue the course of conductive education initiated in Budapest.

Accordingly, O'Hanlon J made an order declaring that the defendants, in failing to provide for free primary education for the plaintiff and in discriminating against him as compared with other children, had deprived him of constitutional rights arising under Article 42 of the Constitution, with particular reference to Articles 42.3.2° and 42.3.4°. He did not find it necessary to deal with the further claims made in reliance on Article 40. He also awarded £7,645.71 by way of damages.

O'Hanlon J noted that, in a case like the instant one, it should normally be sufficient to grant declaratory relief in the expectation that the institutions of the State would respond by taking whatever action was appropriate to vindicate the constitutional rights of the successful plaintiff. He therefore made no further order (save in relation to costs), but he expressly reserved liberty to the plaintiff to apply to the Court again in the future, should it become necessary to do so, for further relief by way of *mandamus*, or otherwise, as might come within the scope of the instant proceedings.

O'Donoghue is an important decision for several reasons. First, its implicit rejection of Kenny J's attempt to limit the concept of education harmonises with modern thinking on the nature and purpose of education. O'Hanlon J throughout his judgment, emphasised the measurable benefits that have been found to flow from the education of severely and profoundly disabled children but in truth the argument in favour of access to education for these children rests ultimately on *a priori* grounds.

Secondly, the case is notable for its lack of emphasis on the practical distinction between an obligation to provide education and an obligation to provide *for* education. As we have seen, the language of Article 42.4 expressly limits the State's obligation to that of providing *for* free primary education, a factor of which much was made by the Supreme Court in *Crowley*. O'Hanlon J interpreted the phrase as requiring the State to give each child such advice, instruction and teaching as will enable him or her to make the best possible use of his or her inherent and potential capacities . . .'. Thus, it is not enough for the State to provide for a *system* of free primary education that, overall, is an excellent one if it fails to deliver the kind of individuated education for every child in the State, however special his or her needs, that O'Hanlon J described. This naturally raises the question of resource implications, about which the judgment is silent. As the editors of Kelly, *The Irish Constitution*, 1059 (3rd. ed., by G. Hogan & G. Whyte, 1994) point out, O'Hanlon J's approach contrasts with that of Costello J in *O'Reilly v Limerick Corporation* [1989] ILRM 181 (noted in the 1988 Review 304-6), who, albeit in a somewhat different context, 'disclaimed any function, as a judge, to adjudicate on the fairness or otherwise of the manner in which other organs of State had administered public resources'.

Thirdly, O'Hanlon J's willingness to set out in detail the ingredients of a constitutionally-adequate system of education for severely and profoundly disabled children is striking. This approach gives substance to abstract entitlements and ensures that constitutional guarantees are not mere rhetoric. It may be contrasted with the Supreme Court's consistent failure to interpret Article 41 as imposing on either the judiciary or the Oireachtas the obligation to develop a meaningful system of family property: *cf.* our observations in the 1991 Review 216-22. One may speculate on the implications of O'Hanlon J's approach in relation to the constitutional right to health. The question of prioritisation criteria in regard to medical resources is one of lively current debate.

ELECTIONS

European Parliament   The European Parliament Elections Act 1993 is discussed in the European Community and Union chapter, 309, below.

Free postage schemes   The Seanad Elections (University Members) Free Postage Scheme 1993 (SI No. 8), the Presidential Elections Free Postage Scheme 1993 (SI No. 311) and the European Elections Free Postage Scheme 1993 (SI No. 312) provide the conditions under which candidates in the elections referred to may avail of the free postage scheme operated by An Post. Previous schemes in relation to each election were revoked by the 1993 Regulations, which were made under the Postal and Telecommunications Services Act 1983. The current postage scheme for Dáil elections is referred to in the 1992 Review, 143. For a successful challenge to restrictions imposed on a candidate for Dáil Éireann in relation to his election literature, see *Dillon v Minister for Posts and Telegraphs*, Supreme Court, 3 June 1981 (from which the leading judgment of Henchy J is extracted in Byrne and McCutcheon, *The Irish Legal System*, 2nd ed. (1989), p. 254).

Presidential   The Presidential Elections Act 1993 revised and consolidated with amendments the arrangements for the holding of presidential elections. As well as repealing and replacing the Presidential Elections Act 1937, the 1993 Act may be seen against the background of the comprehensive overhaul of electoral law in the Electoral Act 1992. On the 1992 Act, see the 1992 Review, 141-4. The 1993 Act provides that the relevant provisions of the 1992 Act are appropriately modified in order to apply to the conduct of the poll for President. The 1993 Act also includes many features unique to the nomination of a candidate for President. This includes the provision by which a retiring President may re-nominate himself or herself. The detailed provisions of the 1993 Act should also be seen against the background of Article 12 of the Constitution, which provides some outline of the procedures to be followed in the nomination and election of the President. The 1993 Act came into effect on 7 December 1993: see the Presidential Elections Act 1993 (Commencement) Order 1993 (SI No. 353).

EQUALITY

In *Lowth and Ors v Minister for Social Welfare and Ors* [1994] 1 ILRM 378, Costello J considered the equality guarantee in Article 40.1 of the Constitution against the background of social welfare legislation: see the discussion in the Social Welfare chapter, 523, below.

EXPRESSION

Aspects of the liberty of expression conferred by Article 40.6.1° of the Constitution are considered in the case law referred to in the Communications chapter, 68, above.

FAIR PROCEDURES

The case law on fair procedures in 1993 is discussed in the Administrative Law chapter, 12-33, above.

FAMILY

The case law on the family in 1993, much of which involves issues centering around Articles 41 and 42 of the Constitution, is discussed in the Family Law chapter, 316, below.

INTERNATIONAL RELATIONS

Downing Street Declaration On 15 December 1993, the then Taoiseach, Albert Reynolds, and the British Prime Minister, John Major, signed a document known as the Downing Street Declaration. The Declaration set out the principles agreed between the British and Irish governments concerning the future of Northern Ireland, including relations between the two governments, relations between Northern Ireland and this State and internal relations between the two communities in Northern Ireland. The governments re-affirmed their commitment to the principles contained in the 1985 Anglo-Irish Agreement, as to which see the Annotation by Prof. Kevin Boyle and Dr. Tom Hadden in 1985 *Irish Current Law Statutes Annotated*. See also *McGimpsey v Ireland* [1989] ILRM 209 (HC); [1990] ILRM 441 (SC); [1988] IR 567 (HC); [1990] 1 IR 110 (SC), discussed in the 1988 Review, 118-20 and the 1990 Review, 170-3. In particular, the 1993 Declaration stated that the right to self-determination was vested in people of Ireland, North and South, and that no change could take place in the status of Northern Ireland as a part of the United Kingdom without the consent of the people of Northern Ireland. For the full text of the Declaration, see *Irish Times*, 16 December 1993 and for analysis, see Prof. Clive Walker's article, (1994) 12 ILT 80.

LEGAL AID

In *Kirwan v Minister for Justice and Ors* [1994] 1 ILRM 444, Lardner J ordered that the applicant was entitled to State-funded legal aid in relation to an appearance before the advisory committee on sentencing review: see the discussion in the Criminal Law chapter, 239-40, below.

LIBERTY

Article 40.4 inquiry   The limits to the range of issues in respect of which the courts will order an inquiry under Article 40.4.2° where a post-conviction complaint is made were discussed in *Hardy v Ireland*, High Court, 10 September 1992; Supreme Court, 18 March 1993 and *Hardy v Ireland (No. 2)*, High Court, 25 June 1993: see below, 172. To the same effect, see *Rock v Governor of St. Patrick's Institution*, Supreme Court, 22 March 1993, discussed in the Criminal Law chapter, 238, below.

Stop and search powers   In *O'Callaghan v Ireland*, High Court, 1 April 1992; [1994] 1 IR 555 (SC), the High Court (Morris J) and, on appeal, the Supreme Court, upheld the constitutional validity of the stop and search powers conferred on Gardaí by s. 23 of the Misuse of Drugs Act 1977, as amended by s. 12 of the Misuse of Drugs Act 1984. The issue of such powers was also considered by the Court in *D.P.P. (Stratford) v Fagan* [1993] 2 IR 95 (HC); [1994] 2 ILRM 349 (SC) in the context of a prosecution under the Road Traffic Acts: see also the Criminal Law chapter, 255, below.

LIFE OF UNBORN

1993 represented the calm after and before the storms on the subject of abortion. The previous year had witnessed the *X.* case and four referenda in which the subject had come before the People. The following two years would see the legislative and judicial sequelae of two of these referenda.

   In *Attorney General, ex rel. The Society for the Protection of Unborn Children (Ireland) Ltd v Open Door Counselling Ltd* [1994] 1 ILRM 256, the second defendant, Dublin Well Woman Centre Ltd, sought in the Supreme Court the discharge of the injunction it had ordered five years previously, restraining the defendants 'from assisting pregnant women within the jurisdiction to travel abroad to obtain abortions by referral to a clinic, by making for them travel arrangements, or by informing them of the identity and location of and the method of communication with a specified clinic or clinic or otherwise': see the 1988 Review, 132. In November 1992, two new provisions had been added to Article 40.3.3° of the Constitution, which since its passage in 1983 had given express constitutional protection to the right to life of the unborn. These provisions were to the following effect:

This subsection shall not limit freedom to travel between the State and another state.

This subsection shall not limit freedom to obtain or make available in the State, subject to such conditions as may be laid down by law, information relating to services lawfully available in another state.

The second defendant argued that, in the light of these provisions, the impugned conduct had become lawful and that accordingly the injunction should be formally discharged.

The majority of the Court showed no interest in becoming entangled with this issue. Invoking *dicta* from earlier decisions which fell well short of resolving the issue raised, Finlay CJ (Hederman, Egan and Blayney JJ concurring) held that it was 'wholly inconsistent with the constitutional obligations and the jurisprudence' of the Supreme Court for it to consider a question of the interpretation of the Constitution by way of motion to vary an order previously made in an appeal finally determined by it which, by inevitable necessity, had never arisen in the High Court. Furthermore, the provisions had not been in force when the appeal was determined.

This plea of judicial impotence is less than convincing. Far more persuasive is Denham J's dissent on the issue. She pointed out that the Supreme Court's jurisdiction was not an exclusively appellate one: Articles 12.3.1° and 26 made this plain. In addition the Court in rare circumstances had an implied jurisdiction to determine an issue not decided by the High Court. *Murphy v Attorney General* [1982] IR 241 was one such decision, where the Court, without legal argument or decision on its jurisdiction, some time after its decision holding certain statutory provisions of the tax code unconstitutional, had, on the initiative of the Attorney General, ruled on the question of the retroactive effect of its decision on the validity of the impugned law. Ó Dálaigh CJ's bold statement in *State (Quinn) v Ryan* [1965] IR 70, at 122 as to the courts' duty to prevent circumvention of the constitutional rights of the citizen, echoed by Walsh J's remarks in *Meskell v C.I.E.* [1973] IR 121, at 132-3, and in *McGee v Attorney General* [1974] IR 284, at 318, added support to Denham J's conclusion that:

[t]he Supreme Court has an inherent jurisdiction to protect constitutional

rights and justice. This jurisdiction must be exercised sparingly in a non-appellate way as the fabric of the administration of justice and the system of courts is best served by a clear hierarchical structure concluding in the Supreme Court. However, in certain circumstances, to protect constitutional rights, or to ensure that justice is upheld, it is appropriate that the Supreme Court exercise such jurisdiction.

There is perhaps a difficulty with an approach that would restrict this appellate function to cases where it is necessary to protect constitutional rights or to ensure that justice is upheld. Unless this function is to be exercised very widely on the mere assertion of the applicant, how is the Court to have any clear knowledge of whether in fact such a necessity arises? Denham J made it plain that the jurisdiction could arise only where the facts are not in issue and there is 'an element of transiency in the time in which this constitutional right can be protected'. Even with these limitations, it is hard to resolve the dilemma of whether the Court should be required to take a preliminary view of the legal merits of the case before it exercises the jurisdiction or must, instead, exercise jurisdiction without any threshold scrutiny of the strength of the case. The latter approach would seem far less prejudicial than the former.

Addressing the merits of the case raised by the second defendant, Denham J interpreted the 'information' amendment (widely referred to as the 14th amendment, but in fact the 13th amendment) as 'clearly' including the names and addresses of lawful abortion clinics abroad. There was a concomitant right and constitutional freedom to make available this information. The Supreme Court in 1995 agreed with this interpretation in *In re the Regulation of Information (Services Outside the State for Termination of Pregnancies) Bill 1995* [1995] 2 ILRM 81. We shall analyse that decision in the 1995 Review.

Denham J rejected the argument that the 'information' amendment was not self-executing and first required legislation by virtue of the phrase 'subject to such conditions as may be laid down by the law'. In her view, the clear meaning of the words was that the right to information existed but was subject to these legislative conditions:

> The absence of legislation does not nullify or postpone the right. Whereas the right to information may in future be subject to conditions in legislation, the legislature is not obliged to set out statutory conditions. It has been given a discretion which it may or may not utilise.

Denham J went on to observe that:

> [c]onstitutional rights are not subordinate to law, or to putative legisla-
> tion. We live in a pluralist society where the Constitution, while acknow-
> ledging God as the ultimate source of all authority, designates the people
> as the rulers of the State who in the final appeal decide all questions of
> national policy according to the requirements of the common good. In
> this instance by the two recent amendments to the constitution the people
> have clarified the position of certain constitutional rights.

The rhetoric here anticipates that of the Supreme Court in the Article 26
reference in 1995. If it seeks to suggest that it is not possible to 'subordinate'
constitutional rights to legislation it would appear mistaken: there is no reason
in principle why a particular constitutional right should not be so delineated,
regardless of whether the legislation is capable of restricting the scope of that
right subsequent to its establishment or even as a precondition to its establishment. Several provisions of the Constitution subject constitutionally
protected rights of legislative restriction. There is no reason in principle why
the Constitution should not provide for the establishment of a particular
constitutional right, subject to its being triggered by the Oireachtas. This is
not to say that Denham J was necessarily mistaken in her conclusion as to
the proper interpretation of this aspect of the 'information' amendment; the
criticism attaches to the chain of reasoning that brought her to that point.

Denham J took the view that the *travel* amendment generated an entitlement to receive information as to the identity and location of abortion services
abroad. She argued as follows. Article 40.3.3° does not limit the freedom to
travel. Therefore the right is 'a full right' to travel:

> The right being an unencumbered right to travel, could assistance given
> to a person exercising this constitutional right be unconstitutional? I am
> satisfied that assistance given to a person exercising their right to travel
> is part and parcel of that right. In arriving at this conclusion I am aided
> by the fact that the [travel] Amendment specifically precludes limitation
> of this right be reference to Article 40.3.3°.

As regards the question of assisting a 'disadvantaged person' (the mother
in this context) to exercise a constitutional right, Denham J observed:

> Assistance would be unnecessary to many persons. The basic informa-
> tion alone will enable the economically and socially advantaged to
> travel. However, assistance may be essential to persons who are eco-
> nomically and socially deprived. A person who has no means and is
> socially deprived or intellectually disadvantaged may be unable to travel
> even if given information. Thus this creates inequality between those

who are not. Restrictions on the provision of assistance to a disadvantaged person may result in their inability to exercise a constitutional
right.

It is a basic tenet of our constitutional law that assistance may be given
to enable the exercise of that constitutional right. Thus legal aid permits
the exercise of the right of access to the courts.

The assistance in this case is of the limited form set out in the order from
the applicant which is a charity which gives non-directive counselling.
The limited assistance, as set out in the order, of a constitutional right
enables the economically and socially disadvantaged, and geographi-
cally distant, pregnant person, to exercise a constitutional right.

This analysis raises several questions. First, as a matter of general
principle, it may be enquired whether every constitutional right is accompanied by the right to be assisted in its exercise or even the entitlement of others
to choose to assist. The right to earn a livelihood does entail the right to insist
that others help out. The right to starve oneself to death (if such a right exists,
rather than the entitlement not to be prevented from doing so) does not
necessarily entail the right on the part of others to provide active assistance.
(We need not here address the question of whether the Supreme Court
decision in *In re a Ward of Court* [1995] 2 ILRM 401 goes so far as to
recognise a right of self-starvation outside the context of a patient refusing
medical treatment.)

Central to Denham J's view of the travel amendment is her understanding
that it involves in essence a constitutionally protected right to have an
abortion abroad. This is not a correct interpretation, as subsequent judicial
analysis has made plain. It is one thing to remove the injunctive power from
those who travel abroad to have an abortion; it is quite another to confer a
substantive constitutional right to have an abortion abroad.

If Denham J's interpretation of the travel amendment were correct, there
would have been no need for the information amendment since, on her view,
the right to travel encompasses a right to be assisted in exercising that right
which in turn involves the right to receive (and impart) information assisting
the exercise of this right to travel by facilitating the having of an abortion
while abroad. Legislation restricting the scope of information that may be
supplied clearly does not offend against the information amendment since
that amendment provides in express terms for such legislative delimitation.
On Denham J's approach, legislation that cuts into the right to information
subverts the *right to* travel, protected under the *travel* amendment. The
Supreme Court decision as to the information legislation, on the Article 26

reference, is contrary to Denham J's analysis. If the travel amendment were interpreted as conferring a constitutionally protected right to have an abortion abroad, and the travel element were regarded as merely the means by which one gave practical effect to that right, then it could be argued that those who, by reason of poverty, for example, were unable to travel abroad, should be entitled to have an abortion within the State. The answer to this argument might seem to be that Article 40.3.3° protects the right to life of the unborn within the State; but, if there were, as Denham J believed, a constitutional right to have an abortion abroad and to travel abroad to exercise that right, then those unable to travel could claim that they should be able to have an abortion within the State because a right to life that is subject to geographical limitation is of so little value and weight that it should give way to the right to abortion.

OIREACHTAS

Privilege for utterances: tribunal of inquiry   In previous Reviews, we have examined a number of cases resulting from the establishment in 1991 of a Tribunal of Inquiry into the Beef Industry, arising from certain allegations made in an ITV 'World in Action' programme and other allegations made in Dáil Éireann: see the 1991 Review, 11-12 and 109-11, and the 1992 Review, 6-7 and 212-17. In this Review, we examine the cases decided in 1993 arising from the Tribunal's deliberations which discussed the nature of the privilege attaching to members of the Oireachtas under Article 15.12 and 15.13 of the Constitution in connection with any utterances made by them in the Oireachtas. A common law privilege was also discussed in these cases, but we will deal with the constitutional issue first.

Article 15.12 provides:

> All official reports and publications of the Oireachtas or of either House thereof and utterances made in either House wherever published shall be privileged.

Article 15.13 provides, *inter alia*:

> The members of each House of the Oireachtas . . . shall not, in respect of any utterance in either House, be amenable to any court or any authority other than the House itself.

In brief, the cases discussed here involved claims by three elected members of Dáil Éireann (Teachta Dáila, or TDs), Dick Spring, Pat Rabbitte and Tomas McGiolla, who had been called to give evidence to the Tribunal, that they were entitled to claim an absolute privilege of confidentiality in respect of the names of persons who had supplied them with certain information. This information formed the basis for some of the allegations concerning the beef industry which they had made in Dáil Éireann and which, in turn, had led to the establishment of the tribunal of inquiry.

The issue of revealing these sources was likely to arise during their cross-examination by counsel appearing for Goodman International and its chief executive, who were, as O'Flaherty J pointed out in *Attorney General v Mr Justice Hamilton (No. 2)* [1993] ILRM 821; [1993] 3 IR 227, discussed below, 'at the receiving end of most of the allegations in the Dáil.' It is of some interest to note that, when the resolutions for the establishment of the tribunal were being debated in Dáil Éireann, the TDs in question recorded that, while willing to co-operate in full with the tribunal, they would not be willing to compromise the confidentiality of their sources.

When this issue was faced at the tribunal itself, the Chairman and Sole Member of the Tribunal, Mr Justice Hamilton, concluded that the TDs were entitled to rely on Article 15.13 in support of their claim to confidentiality. This conclusion was effectively upheld in the various cases under consideration here. We turn now to these cases.

Attorney General v Mr Justice Hamilton (No. 2) [1993] ILRM 821; [1993] 3 IR 227 involved a challenge by the Attorney General to the ruling made by the Tribunal chairman. In the High Court Geoghegan J held that, while complete privilege attached to statements made in the Oireachtas by the TDs called to give evidence to the tribunal, such privilege did not apply in respect of the statements which they had given to the Tribunal. On appeal, the Supreme Court (Finlay CJ, O'Flaherty, Egan and Blayney JJ; Denham J dissenting in part) reversed Geoghegan J's decision in part, restoring in full the ruling made by the Tribunal chairman.

The Court unanimously agreed with Geoghegan J and the Tribunal chairman that the Tribunal was precluded by Article 15.13 of the Constitution from examining a member of either House concerning any utterances made by them in the Oireachtas or indeed from examining them as to the source of information on which such utterances in either House was made.

On the issue of whether such privilege applied in respect of the statements which the TDs had given to the Tribunal, a 4-1 majority in the Court (with Denham J dissenting on this point) agreed with the respondent Chairman that the privilege conferred by Article 15.13 was sufficiently wide to cover the statements made to the Tribunal. However, on the general approach to this issue, the Court was in fact unanimous in acknowledging that Article 15.12 and 15.13 constituted a far-reaching absolute privilege for members of the Oireachtas, a privilege which was more extensive than, for example, the absolute privilege which applies in defamation cases. In this respect, the

Court declined to follow the suggestion of McCarthy J (presumably *obiter*) in *Attorney General v Mr Justice Hamilton* [1993] ILRM 81; [1993] 2 IR 250 (on which case see generally the 1992 Review, 212-7) that Article 15.12 was confined by reference to the defamation privilege. Again, all five judges in the Supreme Court emphasised the importance for democracy that members of the Oireachtas are free to utter statements in either House 'without retribution', (as Denham J stated) which might, in any other arena, leave members open to legal proceedings. In this context also, O'Flaherty J quoted with approval the views of Edmund Burke in 1774 in support of the point that, in addition to being legislators, TDs also perform the important representative function of articulating the views of their constituents.

The only point dividing the majority from the sole dissenter, Denham J, was whether the anticipated cross-examination of the three TDs on their sources would, in effect, amount to making them amenable to an authority other than Dáil Éireann, in breach of Article 15.12 and 15.13. On this point, the majority agreed with the Tribunal that this would be the case. While the statements prepared for the tribunal by the three TDs might have differed in point of detail from the statements made in Dáil Éireann, the substance of the situation was that they would be asked to reveal the sources on which their Dáil statements had been based. Since failure to reveal such sources could attract the criminal sanctions contained in the Tribunals of Inquiry (Evidence) Acts 1921 and 1979, the Court concluded that this was precisely the type of 'amenability' which Article 15.13 prohibited, and on this basis it held that the tribunal was precluded from allowing such a cross-examination of the TDs. (By way of contrast, we note parenthetically here the High Court decision in *Kiberd v Mr Justice Hamilton* [1992] ILRM 574; [1992] 2 IR 257 that a journalist has no constitutional or common law right to claim privilege before a tribunal of inquiry in respect of confidential sources of information. Unlike TDs or Senators, therefore, the journalist remains open to the criminal sanctions for non-disclosure of sources provided for in the 1921 and 1979 Acts: see the discussion of the case in the Criminal Law chapter, 219-20, below.)

We have already noted that *Attorney General v Mr Justice Hamilton (No. 2)* [1993] ILRM 821; [1993] 3 IR 207 arose from the tribunal's ruling that cross-examination of the TDs involved could not extend to seeking to reveal their sources. The second case arising from this ruling, *Goodman International v Mr Justice Hamilton (No. 2)* [1993] 3 IR 307, concerned the impact which this had on the constitutional rights of Goodman International and its chief executive. In particular, it was argued that, in light of the restrictions placed on counsel for the applicants by this ruling, the tribunal would fail to vindicate the applicants' right to their good names under Article 40.3 of the Constitution if it did not immediately exonerate the applicants in full of all

allegations made against them. Counsel argued that it would be of no avail
to the applicants for them to await the final report of the tribunal on this matter
(the publication of which, it transpired, did not occur until September 1994).

Geoghegan J rejected this argument. In doing so, he relied to a large
extent on the decision of the Supreme Court in *Goodman International v Mr
Justice Hamilton* [1992] ILRM 145; [1992] 2 IR 542 (see the 1991 Review,
109-11), in which the Court had analysed in a general way the relationship
between the tribunal and the applicants' constitutional rights. Of especial
importance in this respect in Geoghegan J's view was the Supreme Court's
discussion of the need for the tribunal to respect the applicants' rights by the
adoption of appropriate fair procedures. Geoghegan J concluded that, in the
instant case, there was no indication that the tribunal would fall below the
standards laid down by the Supreme Court, which the tribunal itself had
stated at the outset it would strive to follow. On this basis, Geoghegan J
refused the relief sought by the applicants.

The third, and final, case arising from the tribunal's ruling that any
questioning could not include the sources of the TDs allegations, *Goodman
International v Mr Justice Hamilton (No. 3)* [1993] 3 IR 320, raised an issue
connected with that debated in *Attorney General v Mr Justice Hamilton (No.
2)* [1993] ILRM 821; [1993] 3 IR 227, above. It will be recalled that, in
Attorney General v Mr Justice Hamilton (No. 2), Geoghegan J had concluded
that the Article 15 immunity did not extend to the statements prepared by the
TDs for the tribunal in which they had, to some extent, expanded on their
statements in Dáil Éireann.

As we now know, of course, the Supreme Court held that Article 15
applied to the statements prepared by the TDs for the tribunal and thus they
could not be questioned on the sources for the allegations contained in these
statements. However, the Supreme Court decision in *Attorney General v Mr
Justice Hamilton (No. 2)* was not given until July 1993, and in the immediate
aftermath of the decision of Geoghegan J in the case (in February 1993), the
tribunal of inquiry made another ruling in which it was held that the TDs
were entitled to claim a common law privilege of non-disclosure for their
sources independently of the position under Article 15, as expressed by
Geoghegan J. It was this ruling which was challenged on judicial review in
Goodman International v Mr Justice Hamilton (No. 3) [1993] 3 IR 320. The
matter was again heard by Geoghegan J, who in a judgment delivered in May
1993 upheld the tribunal's decision.

It must be said that, in view of the Supreme Court's decision in July 1993
in *Attorney General v Mr Justice Hamilton (No. 2)*, above, the decision of
Geoghegan J in the instant case appears moot. Nonetheless, his decision is
of some importance, not least for his discussion of the general principles
applicable to the recognition of claims to privilege against disclosure of

information. This is particularly so since he linked his decision that the TDs were entitled to rely on a common law claim to privilege to the case law concerning discovery of documents in civil claims. He expressly approved, with some minor adjustments to take account of Irish case law, the six criteria as to whether disclosure should be ordered laid down by Lord Edmund-Davies in *D. v NSPCC* [1978] AC 171.

Geoghegan J might, perhaps, be criticised in the instant case for not discussing the fact that, in *Attorney General v Mr Justice Hamilton* [1993] ILRM 81; [1993] 2 IR 250 (see the 1992 Review, 212-17), the Supreme Court had rejected the analogy of the 'discovery' cases when it dealt with the question of cabinet confidentiality in connection with the tribunal. It could be argued, of course, that the cabinet confidentiality case was somewhat *sui generis*. Whatever the merits of analysing Geoghegan J's decision from this perspective, there can be no denying that the judgment, being moot (at least with the benefit of hindsight), lacks the status of an authoritative precedent. Nonetheless, whatever its status, the approval by Geoghegan J of the criteria espoused by Lord Edmund-Davies in *D. v NSPCC* is consistent with the decision of Costello J in *Director of Consumer Affairs and Fair Trade v Sugar Distributors Ltd* [1991] ILRM 395 (see the 1990 Review, 434-5) and of Denham J in *Wong v Minister for Justice (No. 2)*, High Court, 16 March 1993 (see the Practice and Procedure chapter, 453, below).

PRESIDENT

Limitations In 1993, the government was reported as having prevented the President, Mrs Robinson, from accepting an invitation to chair a review group concerning the future role of the United Nations Organisation. Professor David Gwynn Morgan considered this governmental decision in the context of the limitations on the role of the Presidency: see *Irish Times*, 20 December 1993, 14.

PROPERTY RIGHTS

The relevance of Article 43 of the Constitution to the assessment of compensation in respect of a compulsory purchase of property was considered by Budd J in *Dublin Corporation v Underwood*, High Court, 12 May 1993: see the Local Government chapter, 418-9, below. See also the reference to property rights in *T. McDonagh & Sons Ltd v Galway Corporation*, Supreme Court, 17 May 1993, also discussed in the Local Government chapter, 425-7, below.

SEPARATION OF POWERS

Political controversies   The reluctance of the courts to become involved in issues of national policy, perceived to be in the political domain, is exemplified by the judgment of Murphy J in *Duff v Minister for Agriculture and Food (No. 2)*, High Court, 10 July 1992: see the Administrative Law chapter, 12, above.

TRIAL OF OFFENCES

Appeal against acquittal   In *Considine v Shannon Regional Fisheries Board and Ors* [1994] 1 ILRM 499, Costello J rejected a challenge to the validity of s. 310 of the Fisheries (Consolidation) Act 1959, which provides for an appeal against an acquittal in a summary prosecution under the Act.

The first named defendant, the Shannon Regional Fisheries Board, had issued a summons against the plaintiff under the Fisheries (Consolidation) Act 1959, alleging various breaches of the 1959 Act. The summons was dismissed in the District Court and the first named defendant appealed to the Circuit Court under the provisions of s. 310 of the 1959 Act, which allows the prosecutor to appeal to the Circuit Court against an acquittal in the District Court of a complaint on a summons. The plaintiff then issued a plenary summons seeking a declaration that s. 310 of the 1959 Act was invalid on the ground that it was in conflict with Article 38.1 of the Constitution which provides that 'no person shall be tried on any criminal charge save in due course of law.' The defendants submitted that s. 310 of the 1959 Act was valid as being in contemplation of Article 34.3.4° of the Constitution, which provides: 'The courts of first instance shall also include courts of local and limited jurisdiction with a right of appeal as determined by law.' They also relied on the Supreme Court decision in *The People v O'Shea* [1983] ILRM 549; [1982] IR 384, and argued that Costello J was bound by that decision.

Costello J discussed the nature of the doctrine of precedent in a paragraph that is worth quoting for its insight and candid admission about the nature of finding the *ratio decidendi* of a case which teachers, students and practitioners alike might do well to remember. Costello J stated:

> The doctrine of judicial precedent provides that a principle of law which is the basis for an actual decision of the Supreme Court must be followed by the lower courts. Like many general principles, the principle of judicial precedent can be easily stated but may be difficult to apply in practice. And undoubtedly there may be instances where the *ratio* of a case is not always easy to discover. Again, the principle is clear. The

ratio of the case is discovered by determining what proposition of law justified the decision in the light of the material facts which the court decided. It is, of course, clear that there may be more than one *ratio* in a decided case.

In relation to the *O'Shea* case, Costello J noted, firstly, that it was concerned with the appellate jurisdiction of the Supreme Court under Article 34.4.3° and not with Article 34.3.4° which deals with appeals from the District Court to the Circuit Court. Secondly, he considered that the *O'Shea* case was dealing with the right of an appeal from a verdict of a jury in a criminal trial in the Central Criminal Court, whereas the instant case concerned an appeal from a summary trial in the District Court.

However, despite these differences, he held that a number of legal principles laid down by the Supreme Court were binding on him. Of these, he focused on two. He pointed out that the defendant in the *O'Shea* case had argued that the appellate jurisdiction of the Supreme Court under Article 34.4.3° must be read subject to the provisions of Article 34.5 relating to trial by jury. Costello J noted that this argument had been rejected by the majority in *O'Shea* which held that Article 38.5 did not qualify the provisions of the earlier Article 34.5. Thus, he concluded, the majority in O'Shea were of the view that Article 38.5 was not a bar to the appellate jurisdiction claimed in the *O'Shea* case.

Second, he noted that the defendant in *O'Shea* had also argued that Article 34.4.3° was to be read not only in conjunction with Article 38.5 but also in conjunction with Article 38.1, which of course was the provision in contention in the Considine case. The submission in the *O'Shea* case that the appellate jurisdiction of the Supreme Court was limited by Article 38.1 had been rejected by the majority in *O'Shea* also. The effect, therefore was that Article 38.1 of the Constitution did not amount to an exception to the right of the appellate jurisdiction of the Supreme Court conferred by Article 34.4.3°.

While Costello J accepted that the Supreme Court was not dealing with Article 34.3.4° in the *O'Shea* case, he concluded that the principle of law established by the decision must apply with equal force to Article 34.3.4°. Accordingly, he dismissed the plaintiff's claim.

The decision in *Considine* is of considerable importance for a wide variety of what is sometimes described as 'regulatory' criminal law, such as the 1959 Act. In recent years, the positive right of appeal against acquittals on summary charges has been included in such legislation: see for example, s. 52 of the Safety, Health and Welfare at Work Act 1989. The outocme in Considine clearly supports such provisions. However, the reliance by Costello J on the *O'Shea* decision is, perhaps, less straightforward than might appear at first, as indeed the passage from his own judgment on the doctrine of precedent anticipated. Costello J was, of course, bound by the Supreme Court decision, but, as he acknowledged, he could only find positive support for his conclusion on Article 38.1 from two judges in *O'Shea*, O'Higgins CJ and Walsh J, Hederman J expressing no view in his concurring judgment (to the same effect see his judgment in *The People v Quilligan and O'Reilly (No. 2)* [1989] ILRM 245; [1989] IR 46, discussed in the 1988 Review, 168-72).

It was of course entirely proper for Costello J to have followed the majority decision in *O'Shea*. Whether the Supreme Court will uphold the rationale of that decision remains to be seen. The *O'Shea* decision could be described as controversial in that it created an appellate jurisdiction which few had anticipated, and its effects were ultimately reversed by s. 11 of the Criminal Procedure Act 1993: see below, 213. By contrast, the appellate jurisdiction created by the 1959 Act has been expressly provided for, and it may be that, in addition to the textual interpretation which pervaded the *O'Shea* case, it could be argued that where the appellate jurisdiction can find support in some overall policy justification confined to summary criminal matters it can be supported on constitutional grounds. Such a rationale may be present in the case of 'regulatory' laws such as the 1959 Act.

Burden of proof *Hardy v Ireland*, High Court, 10 September 1992; Supreme Court, 18 March 1993 was an unsuccessful challenge to the constitutional validity of s. 4 of the Explosive Substances Act 1883.

The applicant had been found in possession of sodium chlorate and of mercury tilt switches and was charged under s. 4 of the 1883 Act. Evidence was given at his trial that these could be used as component parts in what are commonly called car bombs. S. 4 of the 1883 Act provides:

> Any person who makes or knowingly has in his possession or under his control any explosive substance, under such circumstances as to give rise to a reasonable suspicion that he is not making it or does not have it in his possession or under his control for a lawful object, shall, unless he can show that he made it or had it in his possession or under his control for a lawful object, be guilty of a felony. . . .

Applying to the High Court pursuant to an inquiry under Article 40.4.2° of the Constitution, the applicant argued that s. 4 of the 1883 Act invalidly transferred the burden of proof from the prosecution to the defence in respect of the offence of possession of explosives. This was rejected successively by Flood J in the High Court and by the Supreme Court (Hederman, O'Flaherty, Egan, Blayney and Murphy JJ). Regrettably, the judgments in the Supreme Court are especially lacking in any detailed analysis of the issues raised by the applicant's case.

This may, in part, be explained by the fact that, in the applicant's instant claim, he had attempted to include a number of legal claims which had been rejected in previous legal challenges to his conviction: see *Hardy v Special Criminal Court* [1992] 1 IR 204 (discussed in the 1991 Review, 154-5) and *The People v Hardy*, Court of Criminal Appeal, 22 June 1992 (see the 1992 Review, 265-6). The Supreme Court held that the Article 40.4.2° inquiry could not re-open these issues, in particular because, as the applicant had not sought a certificate to appeal from the 1992 Court of Criminal Appeal decision which rejected his appeal against conviction, that decision must be regarded as final under s. 29 of the Courts of Justice Act 1924. In addition, the Court ruled that an Article 40.4 inquiry should not concern itself with some alleged legal error or impropriety in a trial, citing its decision in *The State (McDonagh) v Frawley* [1978] IR 131. For these reasons, the Court confined the applicant to his constitutional point, and perhaps the extent to which the application focused on narrowing the issue may explain the terseness of the judgments in the Supreme Court. Thus, the judgment of Hederman J (with whom O'Flaherty and Blayney JJ agreed) stated that the guarantee under Article 38.1 that trials be conducted in due course of law:

> . . . requires that the prosecution should prove its case beyond all reasonable doubt but it does not prohibit that, in the course of the case, once certain facts are established that [sic] inferences may not be drawn from those facts, and I include in that the entitlement to do this by way even of documentary evidence. What is kept in place, however, is the essential requirement that at the end of the trial and before a verdict can be entered the prosecution must show that it has proved its case beyond all reasonable doubt.

Since Hederman J considered that s. 4 of the 1883 Act fell within the requirement of Article 38.1 that the prosecution must prove its case, he concluded that it was not in breach of the Constitution.

Egan J, in a concurring judgment, equally considered that what he described as the due process clause in the Constitution (see the similar language used by the Supreme Court in *Director of Public Prosecutions v Byrne* [1994] 2 ILRM 91, discussed in the Criminal Law chapter, 223, below) did not prohibit such a 'shifting of an onus in a criminal prosecution.'

However, Egan J's judgment is somewhat more discursive than that of Hederman J on the points raised in the case because he notes (citing *The People v Quinn* [1965] IR 366 and *The People v Dwyer* [1974] IR 416) that, where the question of insanity is raised, it is a matter for the prosecution to negative the defence rather than for the defence to establish insanity. However, Egan J dismissed any analogy with this by pointing out that the Court was dealing in the instant case with a statutory provision, whereas the insanity rule was one of common law origin. The other considered judgment delivered in the Supreme Court was that of Murphy J who concluded that he saw no inconsistency between a trial in due course of law and a statutory provision, such as s. 4 of the 1883 Act, 'which affords to an accused a particular defence of which he can avail if, but only if, he proves the material facts on the balance of probabilities.' We may note that Egan J had also asserted in his judgment that a defence under s. 4 need only be established on the balance of probabilities.

It must be regretted that the Supreme Court in *Hardy* gave such short shrift to the constitutional issue raised in the case. This is in sharp contrast, for example, to the lengthy judgment delivered by Costello J in *O'Leary v Attorney General* [1991] ILRM 454; [1993] 1 IR 102 (see the 1990 Review, 178-82), a case which raised comparable issues. In *O'Leary*, Costello J had drawn the familiar distinction between the burden of proof, which remains on the prosecution, and the evidential burden, which may shift from time to time. Of course this distinction will have been familiar to all the Court members who sat in the *Hardy* case, and it may seem churlish to criticise the judgments for their terseness. Nonetheless, the *Hardy* case presented the first opportunity for the Court to consider the issues which had only previously been considered at first instance in the *O'Leary* case. For that reason, the matters raised might have deserved a more extensive airing.

At least one argument in favour of a more extensive debate appears to arise from the brief reference by Egan J to the insanity defence. In a constitutional claim, it can hardly be an answer that a statutory, as opposed to common law, rule is at issue as a means of dismissing the relevance of a common law rule. Indeed, the existence of a common law rule which, to adapt Murphy J's phrase, 'affords to an accused a particular defence of which he can avail' but which also continues to place an evidential burden on the prosecution to negative that defence might lead one to ask whether this reflects an important principle underlying trial 'in due course of law.' In other words, if the common law, in respect of at least one defence, requires the prosecution to negative that defence, does this reflect a common law principle from which a constitutional principle might be drawn? By way of analogy, the constitutional right to fair procedures has been fashioned from the common law principles of natural justice but, whereas the principles of natural justice may be negatived by statutory provisions to the contrary, the principles of fair procedures by definition must take priority over statutory principles with which they are in conflict. Of course, it may very well be that the nature of the insanity defence is of such an exceptional character that it amounts to an exception to the rule concerning the shift in the evidential burden, but it remains that there is relatively little analysis of these matters, aside altogether from the matters examined in the *O'Leary* case.

In another sequel to the case, we may note that, in *Hardy v Ireland (No. 2)*, High Court, 25 June 1993, Carney J declined to order an inquiry under Article 40.4.2° on the basis that the matters sought to be raised by the applicant were more properly matters for a trial court or the Court of Criminal Appeal rather than an Article 40.4 inquiry. In this respect, Carney J quoted with approval from Hederman J's judgment in the earlier 1993 case concerning the finality of judgments.

Media coverage and fair trials   The effect of media coverage in prejudicing a fair trial was considered by the Supreme Court in *D. v Director of Public Prosecutions* [1994] 1 ILRM 435 and *Z. v Director of Public Prosecutions* [1994] 2 ILRM 481. We allude to these decisions in the Criminal Law chapter, 242, below, but, as noted there, we defer fuller consideration to the 1994 Review.

Speedy trial   The decision in *Director of Public Prosecutions v Byrne* [1993] ILRM 475 (HC); [1994] 2 ILRM 91 (SC) on the nature of the right to a speedy trial, implicit in Article 38.1, is discussed in the Criminal Law chapter, below, 223-6. The Supreme Court decision in *Cahalane v Murphy*, High Court, 13 August 1993; [1994] 2 ILRM 383 (SC), in which the principles in the *Byrne* case were applied, will be discussed in the 1994 Review.

Contract Law

Eoin O'Dell
School of Law, Trinity College Dublin

FORMALITIES

Bills of exchange   By s. 62(1) of the Bills of Exchange Act 1882, 'When the holder of a bill at or after its maturity absolutely and unconditionally renounces his rights against the acceptor the bill is discharged. The renunciation must be in writing, unless the bill is delivered up to the acceptor'.

In *Terex Equipment v Truck and Machinery Sales* [1994] 1 ILRM 557, in a claim to recover payment on foot of dishonoured bills, the defendant submitted that there was an agreement at a meeting that the bills should be waived There was a conflict of evidence as to the nature and purpose of the agreement in writing resulting from this meeting, but it did not expressly refer to the bills and Barron J held that on the facts the existence of an agreement within the meaning of s. 62 had not been established on even a triable basis, and further that '[c]learly there was no such renunciation in writing in the present case'. ([1994] 1 ILRM 557, 559).

FRUSTRATION

In *Sullivan v Southern Health Board High Court*, 29 July 1993, the defendants were in breach of an implied term of the contract that they would appoint a second consultant physician in the plaintiff's hospital by failing to appoint a replacement physician upon the retirement of the incumbent. The defendants pleaded frustration, but Keane J held that contract had not been frustrated. A body such as the defendants cannot enter into contractual obligations with another person in the knowledge that they are dependent on the co- operation of a third party in implementing them and then repudiate responsibility for the consequences to the other contracting party because of the refusal of the third party to co-operate. The contract, its underlying basis and the legal context in which it was entered into all remained the same. In this regard, Keane approved the earlier decision of Lardner J in *Staunton v Sr Laurence's Hospital*, High Court, 21 February 1986.

The difficulty on the facts in *Sullivan* was one of money: due to health service cut backs, the Health Board did not make the necessary second appointment; the narrow view that the common law has taken to frustration does not easily encompass such economic impossibility. This case deserves to be contrasted with the earlier (and, it is submitted, incorrect) *Neville v Guardian Builders* [1990] ILRM 601 (see 1991 Review, 130-131) in which the defendant, who had hired the plaintiff to build houses on a site, successfully resisted an action for specific performance by pleading that his failure to secure an adequate planning permission for the site frustrated the parties' building contract. The doctrine of frustration applies to contracts the performance of which is at one time possible, but *becomes* impossible at some stage in the future. *Neville* is different: performance as envisaged in the contract was never possible, though it was envisaged that it would become possible, but, as matters have turned out, it remained impossible. (Indeed, the Supreme Court on appeal in *Neville* [1995] 1 ILRM 1 overruled. That decision will be considered in the 1994 Review).

GOOD FAITH

Good faith in insurance contracts   A significant feature of contracts of insurance is the duty of good faith, a duty often judicially greeted with scepticism in other areas of the law of contract: see e.g. *Walford v Miles* [1992] 2 AC 128 (HL)). Thus, the insured must act in good faith in disclosing all facts relevant to the risk being insured against by the insurer. In formal terms, this duty is imposed by means of a term to that effect implied by law into the contract (*Carter v Boehm* (1766) 3 Burr 1905; *Chariot Inns v Assicurazioni Generali Spa* [1981] IR 199; [1981] ILRM 173). The duty so imposed is extensive: '[n]ot alone must that person answer to the best of his knowledge any question put to him a proposal form, but, even when there is no proposal form, he is bound to divulge all matters within his knowledge which a reasonable and prudent insurer would consider material in deciding whether to underwrite the risk of to underwrite it on special terms.' (*Aro Road and Land Vehicles v ICI* [1986] IR 403, 408 *per* Henchy J). Nevertheless, the duty does not require the impossible. an insured could not be aware of the condition which he failed to disclose is not in breach of his duty of good faith (*Keating v New Ireland Assurance Co.* [1990] 2 IR 383; [1990] ILRM 110). Again, 'the contract itself may expressly or by necessary implication exclude the requirement of full disclosure.' (*Aro*). The extent to which this implied duty may be so modified by the terms of the contract itself was the issue in *Kelleher v Irish Life Assurance* [1993] 3 IR 393; [1993] ILRM 643. The insured had applied for life assurance on the basis of a special promotion which required only a minimal declaration of health, to which he replied truthfully: in the circumstances, the Supreme Court held that he had discharged his contractual duty, and that the policy was enforceable against the defendants.

Furthermore it is clear that the duty to act in good faith applies not only during negotiations but throughout the currency of the existence of the contract, thus the insured must act in good faith when making his claim. Whether he had in fact done so was the issue in *Fagan v General Accident Fire and Life Assurance Corporation* High Court, 19 February 1993, Murphy J, where it was held that the insured's over-statement of losses sustained constituted a breach of his 'the duty to exercise the utmost good faith (upon which attention is more frequently focused at the stage when the assurance company is considering whether or not to accept the risk offered) [which] continues throughout the relationship up to and including the making of a claim on foot of a policy.'

Kelleher and *Fagan* are analysed from the insurance perspective in the Commercial Law chapter (*supra*, 50-3). From the perspective of the law of Contract, they provoke two observations. First, given that the Courts seem not to find the administration of an explicit good faith standard problematic in the insurance context, is the *Walford* hostility justified? It would seem not. Certainly, *Kelleher* illustrates that it can easily be accommodated within the traditional rules on formation and terms of contracts; and *Fagan* illustrates that it is not beyond the bounds of judicial ability to police a continuing duty of good faith. Indeed, it has been suggested above that the position in *Keating* that an insured who could not be aware of the risk is not in breach of his duty of good faith could be perceived as an incohate application of the good faith standard against the insurance company: it would be in good faith for the insurance company to require the impossible of the insured. Again, it may be that the rule at issue in *Dillon v McGovern* (below) that an insurance contract will be construed *contra proferentem* the insurance company which drafted it is likewise such an incohate application of the good faith standard against the insurance company. That being so, then this year's cases nicely illustrate the reciprocal and continuing nature of the duty of good faith in insurance contracts. Taking these cases at face value, it is clear that if the Irish judiciary were to discover a duty of good faith elsewhere or more generally in the law of contract, they would be able to deal with its complexities (see *e.g.* J.F. O'Connor *Good Faith in English Law* (1990) and J. Beatson and D. Friedmann (eds.), *Good Faith and Fault in Contract Law* (1995).

Second, Clark has observed that there 'is a very significant body of recent jurisprudence on contractual duties of disclosure in insurance contracts, due in the main to the originality and clarity of thought the late Mr Justice McCarthy' (R. Clark, *Contract Law in Ireland* (3rd ed., 1992). These cases demonstrate that this aspect of McCarthy J's legacy has not been lost.

ILLEGALITY

Statutory illegality   Difficult questions relating to illegality were posed this year in *Westpac Banking Corporation v Dempsey* [1993] 3 IR 331. It is trite law that a court will not enforce a contract which is contrary to statute. If a statute expressly prohibits a contract, there is no usually no problem beyond determining whether as a matter of fact a particular contract is in fact caught by the relevant section. Thereafter, problems both of legal and of factual analysis arise.

If the statute expressly prohibits only a course of conduct, and a contract expressly provides for that course of conduct, it is a matter of construction of the statute as to whether only that conduct is thereby prohibited, or whether the statute intended also to render contracts providing for that course of conduct also to be void. The usual enquiry in such circumstances is whether the statutory penalties for the conduct are sufficient, or whether it is necessary to achieve the purpose of the Act by supplementing such penalties with the invalidity of the contract (e.g. *Archbolds v Spanglett* [1961] 1 QB 374; *Hughes v Asset Manager* [1995] 1 All ER 669).

If the statute expressly prohibits only a course of conduct, and a contract, though not expressly providing for its performance by means of that course of conduct, is in fact performed in that manner, then there must again be the above enquiry as to whether the statute intended to render such a contract unenforceable. If not, there is a further enquiry: if both parties at the outset intended that the contract be so performed, it is unenforceable by both, if only one party at the outset intended that it be so performed, it is unenforceable by that party (*St John Shipping v Rank* [1957] 1 QB 267; *cf. Whitecross Potatoes v Coyle* [1978] ILRM 31); presumably, if neither party intended so intended, then the contract is not unenforceable. In all three such cases, though, the transgressing party will be liable to the statutory penalty.

If the statute expressly prohibits only a course of conduct, and a contract expressly provides for that course of conduct, and the statute is construed so as to render the contract unenforceable, a court cannot, of course, grant an order enforcing the contract or requiring the doing of the prohibited course of conduct. However, if the statute is subsequently repealed, and the formerly prohibited course of conduct is no longer prohibited, and if the contract is still in force, there would seem now to be no longer an impediment against granting an order enforcing the contract or requiring the doing of the course of conduct.

If a clause in a contract is unenforceable for any of the above reasons, it is a matter for the court as to whether the remainder of the contract is also unenforceable. Often, a court will distinguish between an illegality which is *malum prohihitum* and one which is *malum in se*, the former being a technical illegality which will not infect the rest the contract, the latter being a serious matter which is in itself wrongful and which will infect the rest of the contract. But such latinisms assume that the relevant illegality will announce itself as technical or serious, and their deployment allows judges to hide judicial discretion behind a veil of principle.

If the statute expressly prohibits only a course of conduct, and the performance of the contract requires, as a matter of fact but only incidentally as a prior matter, the performance of that course of conduct, then it seems that the above considerations should apply, and analysis should therefore proceed as follows: first, is the prohibition on the conduct also necessarily a prohibition on the contract? Second, if not, does the intent of either party or both parties to perform on the basis of that course of conduct render the contract unenforceable ? Third, if the contract is unenforceable for either reason because that course of conduct is prohibited, is the rest of the contract affected ? And, fourth, if the statute is subsequently repealed, is there any impediment to an order enforcing the contract or requiring the doing of the (formerly prohibited) course of conduct. (This fourth enquiry is similar to that in the previous paragraph as to whether the statutory prohibition infects other contractual obligations).

All of these principles, and problems, have been addressed in the context of exchange control regulations, which is the context of *Westpac Banking Corporation v Dempsey*. In the leading English case of *Boissevain v. Weil* [1950] AC 327; [1950] 1 All ER 729, English war-time exchange control regulations prohibited the purchase or borrowing by British nationals of any foreign currency. On three occasions in Monaco during 1944, Boissevain, a Dutch national, made a loan to Weil in French francs and Weil, a British national, agreed to repay the loan later in sterling amounting to £6,000 (calculated at a contractual rate of 160 francs to the pound) plus interest. Boissevain sued on foot of the agreement but failed on the ground that Weil's borrowing was an offence which rendered the contract void. Thus, here the statute expressly prohibited the course of conduct of borrowing, and the contract expressly provided for that course of conduct; according to the House, to achieve the aim of that statutory prohibition on the course of conduct, contracts providing for it also had to be void.

In the leading Irish case of *Namlooze Venootschap de Faam v The Dorset Manufacturing Co.* [1949] IR 203, Dutch sellers had sold goods to Irish purchasers, but Irish exchange control regulations prohibited 'payment' abroad without a licence. The purchasers had a licence for part of the amount, and, after the purchase but before payment, part of that expired and an application for renewal was still pending, and a licence for the remainder was refused. Dixon J held:

I do not find that that the contracts under which the goods were ordered . . . were thereby made either void or illegal . . . the prohibitions . . . related rather to what might be a contemplated or possible sequel to the contract rather than to its essential nature. ([1949] IR 203, 206).

This and *Boissevain* are different. In that case, the contract was a contract for borrowing, and the borrowing itself was illegal, whereas here, the contract was for the sale of good, which is not contrary to statute, but the performance in fact of that contract required a course of conduct which was prohibited by statute, and, indeed, that the prohibition on that course of conduct did not require the prohibition of any contract which, to be performed, required as a prior matter the prohibited course of conduct. *Boissevain* and *Namlooze* would be the same if in *Namlooze* the regulation prohibited the purchase of the goods.

In the event, since to grant an order enforcing the contract would be to grant an order requiring a payment contrary to Irish exchange control regulations, Dixon J refused such an order:

Whatever the terms of the Court's order, the legal effect of it would be to put the plaintiffs in a position to secure payment of the amount in question and it would thus, even if indirectly, compel the defendants to do an act prohibited by the law. . . . Put thus, I feel that it would be improper and contrary to public policy for the Court to give judgment for the plaintiffs on their claim as now framed. (id., *dictum* of Greene MR to that effect in *Stockholms Enskilda Bank Aktiebolag v Schering* [1941] 1 KB 424, 440-441; [1941] 1 All ER 257, 267 approved).

Similarly, in the subsequent *Fibretex v Beleir* (1949) 89 ILTR 141, a Belgian seller sold to a Dublin purchaser, some goods delivered, others ordered, but these were delivered late due to a dock strike in Belgium. The purchasers' licence for the entire amount lapsed during the strike. The sellers' action to enforce the contract was dismissed by Dixon J for the same reasons as he gave in *Namlooze*, and he was upheld on appeal by the Supreme Court.

Furthermore, in *Namlooze*, Dixon J accepted that since the relevant exchange control regulations enabled any of the prohibited acts to be done with the permission of the Minister for Finance, there could be in the contract 'an implied representation that, so far as permission of the Minister might be necessary, such permission existed or would be applied for' ([1949] IR 203, 206). Consequently, 'the existence or terms of the relevant orders would not prevent the plaintiffs maintaining an action for damages for failure to use reasonable diligence to obtain the necessary permission' ([1949] IR 203, 208) but no such claim was there before him.

For this proposition, Dixon J relied upon *Taylor v Landauer* [1940] 4 All
ER 335. There, the appellants, having undertaken to sell beans from Mada-
gascar to the purchasers, argued that a subsequent prohibition on foreign
trade in cereals without licence, meant that they were no longer contractually
obliged to sell. It was held that the sellers' 'duty was to take steps necessary
to enable them to perform the contract, and to take steps envisaged by [the
regulation] . . . namely, to apply in a licence. They did not.' ([1940] 4 All
ER 335, 341 *per* Singleton J). They were not excused from performance and
were in breach. The case in other words is about whether the regulation
effected a frustration, not an illegality. And in *Boissevain* Lord Radcliffe did
not seem impressed with an argument based on such 'a general dispensing
power' ([1950] 1 All ER 729, 735, though this paragraph is opaque).
Nevertheless notwithstanding that Taylor does not seem to support Dixon
J's usage thereof, the technique of finding an implied obligation to seek a
licence, which implied obligation is breached, and for which damages are
available, is a valid one often subsequently deployed by Lord Denning (e.g.
Strongman v Sincock [1955] 3 All ER 90).

The importance of finding that other obligations in the contract are
enforceable means that for Dixon J the contract is one in which the prohibition of a course of conduct necessary for the performance of a contractual
obligation (payment abroad prohibited, but necessary for the performance of
the obligation of payment) did not render the contract itself and other
obligations thereunder unenforceable. Presumably, therefore, if those other
obligations continue to be enforceable, if the prohibition on the course of
conduct (here the payment abroad) is lifted, that obligation too becomes
enforceable, and the plaintiff can have enforcement even of that obligation.
That is the effect of the holding in *Westpac Banking Corporation v Dempsey*
[1993] 3 IR 331. Here, the plaintiff had, in an English court, recovered from
the defendant on foot of a contract by which the defendant guaranteed loans
made by the plaintiff to a third party. Before the Master, the plaintiff obtained
an order enforcing this English judgment in Ireland. On appeal to the High
Court, the defendant contended that the agreement was illegal and void as a
matter of Irish public policy, and that as a consequence, no Irish court could
give aid its enforcement, whether or not it was valid as a matter of English
law. The invalidity of the guarantee was said to flow from the fact that it was
made in contravention of then in force exchange control regulations which
provided that it was an offence for a person 'to make, or commit himself to
make, any payment to . . . any person resident outside the scheduled territories
. . .' (Exchange Control Act 1954, ss. 20 and 5). Counsel for the defendant
relied upon *Boissevain v Weil* and argued that as the contract there was void,
so should the contract here be void. Morris J rejected that submission: the

Act did not render the obligation void, merely unenforceable for so long as the Act remained in force, and when the Act lapsed, the obligation thereupon became enforceable.

As was submitted above, analysis in such a situation should proceed on the basis of the following principles: if the statute expressly prohibits only a course of conduct, and the performance of the contract requires, as a matter of fact but only incidentally as a prior matter, the performance of that course of conduct, then it seems that the above considerations should apply, and analysis should proceed as follows: first, is the prohibition on the conduct also necessarily a prohibition on the contract? Second, if not, does the intent of either party or both parties to perform on the basis of that course of conduct render the contract unenforceable? Third, if thee contract is unenforceable for either reason because that course of conduct is prohibited, is the rest of the contract affected? And, fourth, if the statute is subsequently repealed, is there any impediment to an order enforcing the contract or requiring the doing of the (formerly prohibited) course of conduct.

Here, exchange control regulations expressly prohibited only a course of conduct, the fact of payment *abroad*. The performance of the contract requires, as a matter of fact but only incidentally as a prior matter, the performance of that course of conduct, in that *payment* on foot of the guarantee, the contractual obligation, required as a matter of fact, payment *abroad*. As to the first question whether the prohibition on the conduct also necessarily a prohibition on the contract, Morris J relied upon *Swiss Bank v Lloyd's Bank* [1980] 3 WLR 457; [1980] 2 All ER 419 in which:

> ... Buckley LJ had to consider [a section which] prohibits an authorised depository from parting with a certificate relating to a foreign currency security which is in his custody ... without treasury permission. Buckley LJ had to consider the impact which [a breach of this prohibition] had on a contract: ...

>> ... an act done in contravention of a statute is not necessarily a nullity. Whether it is so must depend upon the terms and effect of the statute, and may depend upon the policy of the statute and the nature of the act itself ... offences under the Act are clearly *mala prohibita*, not *mala in se*; they are not acts the validity of which the law refuses to countenance for any purpose. As such they are not devoid of any effect; they merely expose the culprits to the penalties prescribed by the Act ... ([1980] 3 WLR 457, 473; [1980] 2 All ER 419, 431)

Having regard to the approach of the Supreme Court in *Fibretex*, the views expressed by Buckley LJ are entirely in conformity with Irish law.

Although not adverted to by Morris J, this aspect of the judgment of
Buckley LJ was expressly affirmed on appeal (see [1981] 2 All ER 449, 455
per Lord Wilberforce). Since Morris J accepted that an act done in contravention of a statute is not necessarily a nullity, having regard to decisions in
Fibretex and *Namlooze* he held that a prohibition upon payment abroad does
not render the contract a nullity. Thus, he answered the first point above in
the negative.

As to the second point, whether the intent of either party or both parties
to perform on the basis of that course of conduct renders the contract
unenforceable, he did not address it. But on the application of the *St John
Shipping* test, there would seem to have been no intention on the part of either
party to contravene the exchange control regulations. As to the third point,
whether the rest of the contract is affected, given his approach to *Swiss Bank
v Lloyds Bank*, Morris J clearly considered that the remainder of the contract
remained on foot. However, neither of these two enquiries was relevant, since
the relevant exchange control regulations had been dismantled, the relevant
question was the fourth: given that the prohibition has been repealed, whether
there was any impediment to an order enforcing the contract or requiring the
doing of the (formerly prohibited) course of conduct. If he had concluded
that the effect of the exchange control regulations was such that the prohibition on the payment was also a prohibition on the contract, then the contract
being void when formed, there would have been nothing to embody the
obligation of payment. However, given that *Namlooze*, *Fibretex* and *Swiss
Bank* allowed Morris J to conclude that there was nothing in the prohibition
of the course of conduct which affected the validity of the contract, it
remained on foot; and, since the contract was valid, once the prohibition was
lifted, there was no reason for the payment obligation to remain unenforced.
The Central Bank has been progressively dismantling the exchange control
machinery 'on a gradual basis and from 1 January 1992, all restrictions on
residents in respect of guarantees, bid bonds and performance bonds have
been removed' ([1993] 3 IR 331, 339). Consequently, the plaintiff could
enforce its foreign award.

Finally, therefore, as Morris J observed, to have allowed the defendant
to succeed would have been to 'injure the innocent, benefit the guilty and put
a premium on deceit' ([1993] 3 IR 331, 341, approving *Archbold v Spanglett*
[1961] 1 QB 374, 387).

Champerty It may be said that the decision of Morris J in *Dempsey* (above)
displayed a flexible approach to the question of illegality. On the other hand,
in *Fraser v Buckle* [1994] 1 IR 1; [1994] 1 ILRM 276, another of this year's
cases, Costello J displayed an inflexible approach (which was subsequently
upheld on appeal: 5 March 1996. The decision of the Supreme Court will be

analysed in the 1996 Review). Here, the business of the plaintiffs was the location at their own expense of persons entitled to unclaimed property. When they had traced such persons, they agree to disclose their information and process the claim in return for a fee of one third of the estate The defendants were the heirs to the estate of a New Jersey intestate. Pursuant to a contract with the defendants, the plaintiffs supplied the information and maintained a claim to the estate in New Jersey; it was successful, and the plaintiffs now sought to recover from them the contractual fee of one third of the estate. Costello J held that such heir-locator agreements were champertous and thus unenforceable and void. He further held that Irish law was applied to them whether or not they would have been enforceable under their proper law (and this aspect of the case is considered further in the Conflicts chapter, 115-8 *supra*).

The plaintiff had sought to argue that there was a general emerging liberalisation of public policy, especially in the area of champerty, but Costello J rejected this argument. Lurking in it are two separate arguments: first that there is an emerging liberalisation of public policy; and second, that it extends to the area of champerty. Given that in dealing with this argument, Costello J only considered champerty cases, he can be taken as rejecting only the second of these two points. Whether he was correct in so doing is considered in the the Conflicts chapter, supra. The first point, as to a more general liberalisation of public policy, was unaddressed.

In relation to all claims at private law, whether in tort, in contract, at equity or in restitution, if a plaintiff's claim is founded in an illegality or is contrary to public policy, then a defendant can raise this illegality since the court will not lend its aid to such a claim. (*Holman v Johnson* (1775) 1 Cowp 341). The mere hint of illegality would be sufficient for a court to refuse to lend its aid to a plaintiff — though this could lead, and often did, to injustices as between the parties. Consequently, it was argued that where such a defence was relied upon, the court should look beyond the fact of the illegality to the quality of the illegality relied upon and the proximity of the illegal conduct to the plaintiff's claim, to determine whether there was an illegality of which the court should take notice, and if there was, whether by affording the plaintiff the relief sought, it would affront the public conscience more than by refusing it.

In so far as the law of tort is concerned, Irish law has achieved this position by virtue of s.57(1) of the Civil Liability Act 1961. The Supreme Court of Canada in *Hall v Herbert* [1993] 2 SCR 159 and the High Court of Australia in *Gala v Preston* (1991) 172 CLR 243 have mitigated the common law rules on illegality to arrive at a similar conclusion. As to the English Courts, the above 'public conscience' test first seems to have been articulated by Hutchinson J in the High Court in *Thackwell v Barclays Bank* [1986] 1

All ER 676, where a claim for conversion was dismissed, but only after an enquiry into the substance of the plaintiff's fraud. Likewise, in the Court of Appeal, in *Pitts v Hunt* [1990] 3 All ER 344, the defendant was an unlicensed and uninsured motor cyclist, the plaintiff was his passenger, and was injured in an accident, the Court did not dismiss the plaintiff's claim in limine as being founded in that illegality, rather it again addressed the question of substance of whether the circumstances of the joint illegal enterprise in fact made it impossible to formulate the terms of the duty of care. And in *Saunders v Edwards* [1987] 2 All ER 651, the plaintiff had purchased a lease from the defendant in which the purchase price was understated to reduce stamp duty liability. The contract had been induced by misrepresentation, and the plaintiff sought damages. The defendant pointed to the illegality of defrauding the revenue, but the Court of Appeal expressly disregarded the plaintiff's illegality, because they had an unanswerable claim for fraudulent misrepresentation, the defendant's moral culpability was much the greater, and the illegality in the lease was wholly unconnected with the fraudulent misrepresentation.

As to claims in contract, *Saunders v Edwards* was followed in *Euro-Diam v Bathurst* [1988] 2 All ER 23. Here, the plaintiffs had supplied diamonds to a customer abroad, but in the invoice understated their value so as to reduce the customer's customs liability. However, some of the diamonds were stolen, and the plaintiffs in this action sought to recover from their insurers the value of the theft; the insurers resisted, pointing to the illegality of defrauding customs. The Court of Appeal held in favour of the plaintiffs, since there was no direct and proximate connection between the plaintiffs' claim and the illegality on the invoice, which involved no deception of the insurers, and from which the plaintiffs derived no benefit. And, in *Howard v Shirstar* [1990] 3 All ER 367, the plaintiff had been hired by the defendant to recover aircraft leased in Nigeria. In Lagos, having located a plane, the plaintiff discovered that his life was in danger, and consequently flew it out of Nigeria without obtaining air traffic control clearance, which was a breach of Nigerian law. When he sued for payment, the defendants resisted, pointing to the criminal action he committed in performance of the contract. The Court of Appeal held for the plaintiff, saying that although a court would not normally enforce a contract which would enable a plaintiff to benefit from illegal conduct, since to do would be an affront to public conscience, nevertheless since the plaintiff had committed the crime to escape danger to his life, it would not affront public conscience to hold in his favour.

In Ireland, in *Webb v Ireland* [1988] IR 353 the illegality of the trespass upon which the plaintiffs' claim was founded did not preclude a successful action in estoppel, Finlay CJ in particular sweeping aside objections founded upon the plaintiff's trespass. That authority could illustrate the application of flexibility either in contract (in so far as promissory estoppel is a contractual doctrine) or at equity. As to claims undoubtedly at equity, the Supreme Court in *Curust v Loewe* [1994] 1 IR 450 has taken a flexible of the related 'clean hands' maxim (see especially [1994] 1 IR 450, 467 *per* Finlay CJ; (see Delany (1993) 15 *DULJ (ns)* 228, the 1992 Review, 318-19, 331 and compare the decision of the Supreme Court of Canada in *Hong Kong Bank of Canada v Wheeler* (1993) 100 DLR (4th) 40 (SCC), 52 *per* Sopinka J).

Furthermore, in *Hortensius v Bishop* [1989] ILRM 294 (see the 1989 Review, 129-130) Costello J held that a purchase of loan by the Trustee Savings Bank was *ultra vires* the trustees, but that since what was involved was a statutory provision which prevented a trustee from acting in a certain way rather than a provision which made certain types of contract illegal, the purchase here was not illegal but merely a breach of trust, and the property acquired vested in the trust notwithstanding any breach of trust. Nevertheless, evincing a flexible approach to public policy, he pointed out that 'public policy has never required that trustees should be deprived of their right to enforce proprietary claims over property obtained in breach of trust' ([1989] ILRM 294,302). In the process he approved *Euro-Diam*, in which the 'law relating to a defence based on [illegality] . . . was helpfully summarised by Kerr LJ' (*id.*), which understanding of the defence, as we have seen encompasses the public conscience test Again, the High Court of Australia, in *Nelson v Nelson* (1996) 70 ALJR 47 has rejected the undifferentiated application of the principles of illegality to claims relating to resulting trusts. As to the English Courts, in *Tinsley v Milligan* the plaintiff sought an interest in property in the sole name of the defendant on the grounds of her (the plaintiff's) direct and indirect contributions to the purchase of the property. The defendant resisted on the grounds that the contributions were in part derived from fraudulently obtained welfare payments. The Court of Appeal applied the public conscience test, and decided it would be a greater affront to public conscience to allow the defendant to retain full interest in the property than it would be to allow the plaintiff to succeed in her claim ([1992] Ch 310). The House of Lords also held in favour of the plaintiff, but by a different route, and in the process unanimously rejected the public conscience test as inconsistent with established principles and earlier authority binding on the Court of Appeal ([1994] 1 AC 340). However, this rejection was itself repudiated by the High Court of Australia in *Nelson v Nelson* (1996) 70 ALJR 47. It might nevertheless be said that the fact that result was still the same in the House as in the Court of Appeal is due to an attitude of flexibility, even if that attitude is not expressed in terms of a public conscience test (though cf. the subsequent and difficult *Tribe v Tribe* [1995] 4 All ER 237 (CA)). Certainly, *Webb* is a good example of the Irish courts adopting the more flexible approach; and there is no good reason why Irish law should not adopt the more flexible test, especially since *Euro-Diam* was approved in *Hortentius* and the considerations of precedent in the English Court of Appeal which are at the heart of the rejection of the public conscience test by the House in *Tinsley* are not at all appropriate in Ireland.

Consequently, there is abundant evidence that there is an evolving flexibility of judicial attitudes to illegality, and any understanding of *Frazer* to the contrary ought to be rejected.

Finally, Costello J observed that '[w]hile denying the plaintiff's entitlement to a fee based on their shares of the estate, the defendants accept their entitlement to fees on a *quantum meruit* basis. . . .' ([1994] 1 IR 1, 11; [1994] 1 ILRM 276, 283). It has been argued elsewhere that '[i]f that point had been litigated, it would have run into many formidable obstacles . . . [as a consequence of which] the concession of the quantum meruit was radically misconceived'. ([1995] *Restitution Law Review*, 196-197). For example, in *Bossevain v Weil* (above) the House of Lords held that the plaintiff could not enforce the contract. In the alternative, he sought restitution of the money in fact paid, but the House of Lords held that the policy which denied the claim contract continued on to deny the claim in restitution (*cf. Morgan Ashcroft* [1938] 1 KB 49, 61). Likewise, here, the dangers associated with the possibility of unjust adjudications in the maintained action (here, the New Jersey claim) are such that public policy says that a contract to provide for payment for such maintenance is void. Since the aim of the policy is to discourage the maintenance of actions by precluding payment, that policy should equally be a bar to an action in restitution which is what the *quantum meruit* is).

Illegality and contracts of employment   If the decision in *Fraser v Buckle* is to be seen as the loss of an opportunity to recognise evolving judicial flexibility regarding illegality and establish the public conscience as part of Irish law, *Hayden v Quinn* [1994] ELR 45 (Barry (1994) 12 *ILT (ns)* 32) is a step back to the days before such flexibility. Here, the plaintiff had been hired by the defendant on foot of a contract which provided for a salary and a large sum of non-taxable expenses. The plaintiff had been summarily dismissed, and sued for wrongful dismissal. (This aspect of the case is considered more fully in the Labour law chapter, 379, below). Here, it is important to notice that in the view of Barron J, the large amount of non-taxable expenses was simply a device to reduce income tax, and was thus an attempt to defraud the revenue.

For Barron J, this meant that, although the plaintiff's claim was otherwise well-founded, it was tainted by illegality, and had to be dismissed.

Contracts which have the effect of defrauding the revenue are contrary to public policy, and void (see e.g., *Alexander v Rayson* [1936] 1 KB 169;

Miller v Karlinski (1945) 62 TLR 85). Thus, where an employee is employed on foot of a contract which contains a clause which has the effect of defrauding the revenue, that contract of employment is void, and if he seeks to maintain an action for wrongful or unfair dismissal, he will be met with this illegality (see e.g. *Starling Securities v Woods*, High Court, 24 May 1977, McWilliam J; *Lewis v Squash Ireland* [1983] ILRM 363.) On the other hand, the harshness of the general rules on illegality has led the courts to develop the public conscience test (above) which has been applied even in relation to claims arising from contracts containing clauses the effect of which is defraud the revenue (e.g. *Saunders v Edwards* [1987] 2 All ER 651). And, in the case of employees seeking to rely on employment contracts so tainted, there has been a significant move away from their former rigidity (*Braoders v Kalkare Property Maintenance* [1990] IRLR 421; *O'Dowd v Crowley* [1991] EAT 97 (Barry (1991) 9 *ILT (ns)* 32)). This flexibility could easily be accommodated within the public conscience test. However, none of this was before Barron J in Hayden. According to Barry, '[f]rom the judgment, it does not appear that the employer was making the case that the contract was tainted with illegality'. ((1994) 12 ILT (ns) 32, 33). Equally, it does not appear that Barron J invited argument on the issue. This is regrettable. Had he done so, his attention might have been directed to the public conscience test and to the recent flexibility shown in the employment context. In the absence of such consideration, perhaps this aspect of the case might be regarded as having been decided per incuriam ? Certainly, it is of doubtful validity and ought not to be followed in future cases.

MISTAKE AND *NON EST FACTUM*

A plea of *non est factum* was considered by Flood J in the High Court in *Bank of Ireland v McCabe*, High Court, 25 March 1993, Flood J (overruled on another ground by the Supreme Court; that decision will be analysed in the 1995 Review). Here, a company sought a loan from the bank, and signed a guarantee expressed to cover present and future liabilities. The company subsequently secured a further loan, and, having gone into liquidation, the bank sought to recover from the defendants in respect of this second loan on foot of the guarantee, contending that it was a relevant future liability. The company resisted on the ground that the guarantee was intended only in respect of the single transaction, notwithstanding its reference to future liabilities. Indeed, it was the evidence of the bank manager that the guarantee 'had been created to deal with a particular transaction since successfully accomplished'. Flood J held that the submission amounted to a contention that the company had entered into a transaction essentially different to that which they had intended, which was, in short a plea of non est factum, though it was not pleaded as such. He continued:

> In most cases in which *non est factum* has been successfully pleaded a mistake has been induced by fraud. I am quite satisfied that as far as the bank . . . is concerned, there is no question of fraud.
>
> Even in circumstances where it is clearly established that the person relying on the doctrine did not understand the particular purport of the particular document, such person must establish that they took such precautions as they reasonably could to have the document explained to them and to acquire knowledge of the import of the document. See *Saunders v Anglia Building Society* [1970] 3 All ER 963. There is no such evidence in this case.

As to Flood J's first point here, it is in fact well established that although fraud will exist on the facts in most cases in which *non est factum* has successfully been pleaded, it is not a necessary ingredient of the doctrine. Thus, in *Bank of Ireland v McManamy* [1916] 2 IR 161 Cherry LCJ held that:

> The principle of the cases is not, however, that fraud vitiates consent, but rather that there is an entire absence of consent. That the mind of the party who signs under a fundamental error does not go with the act of signing, and there is consequently no contract at all in fact.

However, even applying this test, it is clear that it could not be said that there was no contract at all in fact between the bank and the borrowers in respect of the first loan. As to Flood J's second point here, it bears comparison with *Norwich and Peterborough Building Society v Steed (No. 2)* [1993] 1 All ER 330 (CA) a recent application by the English Court of Appeal of the House of Lords decision in *Saunders v Anglia BS* [1970] 3 All ER 963; [1971] AC 1004.

> Taken literally, the doctrine of *non est factum* applies where the person sought to be held liable has not, in fact signed the document. . . . But it also covers cases in which a person who has signed a document is none the less allowed to repudiate the document. The authorities all concern cases of the latter sort.
>
> . . . In each of these cases the victim of a fraud had signed a document not understanding what he or she was doing. In each case an innocent

third party had for value acquired rights under the document. In each of these cases the existence of the doctrine of *non est factum* was affirmed, in each the acceptable limits of the plea was discussed, in none was the plea allowed to prevail. It is easy to understand why the plea is unlikely to be successful. A person who signs a document at the request of another puts into circulation a document on which, depending on its contents, others may rely. Where a fraudster has tricked, first, the signer of the document, in order to induce the signature, and then some third party, which of the two victims is the law to prefer? The authorities indicate that the answer is, almost invariably, the latter. ([1993] 1 All ER 330, 336-337 *per* Scott LJ).

Here, the appellant had allowed his mother and his sister and her husband to reside in his house in his absence in the United States. He executed a power of attorney in favour of his mother. Under that power, a document was purportedly executed by which the mother transferred the property to the sister and her husband, who then borrowed from the building society on foot a mortgage over the house. Upon their default, the building society sought possession, and the appellant sought to resist on the grounds that the mother did not know what she was doing when she executed the deed of transfer. This plea of non est factum failed, either because the mother was 'a lady of sufficient understanding an capability to be a suitable donee of the power of appointment . . . [who could therefore] inform herself of the purport and effect of the transfer before signing it', or because, if she was lacking in under-standing, the 'donor of a power of attorney who appoints as his attorney a person incapable of understanding the import of a simple transfer can hardly be allowed . . . to repudiate the transfer on the ground of a lack of under-standing on the part of the donee'. ([1993] 1 All ER 330, 339 *per* Scott LJ).

Again, the decision is unnecessarily predicated upon fraud. But leaving that aside, there is a crucial difference between *Saunders v Anglia* and *Norwich v Steed* on the one hand and *Bank of Ireland v McCabe* on the other, and it is this: in *Saunders* and *Steed*, the court is troubled by the interposition of an innocent third party, and will usually decide in that party's favour, whereas in *McCabe*, the parties to the suit are the original parties to the contract, and it might be thought in such circumstances that the absence of the policy reasons for narrowing the ambit of the plea of *non est factum* which exist when third parties are in the equation might result in a slightly less rigid application of the doctrine. Nevertheless, even in such a two party situation, Flood J's insistence; that the party relying on the doctrine have taken reasonable steps to have the document explained is entirely appropriate.

PRINCIPLES OF INTERPRETATION

Extrinsic evidence and the inadmissibility of parol evidence In the interpretation of written contracts, the courts will usually start from the position that the entire of the contract is embodied in the writing, and that therefore evidence extrinsic to the contract is inadmissible insofar as it is directed to the question of interpretation. Therefore, 'evidence cannot be admitted . . . to add to, vary or contradict a written instrument . . . where a contract has been reduced to writing, neither party can rely on extrinsic evidence of terms alleged to have been agreed' (G. Treitel, *The Law of Contract* (9th ed, 1995, p. 176). Thus, in *In re Wogan's (Drogheda) No. 1)* [1993] 1 IR 157 (see the 1992 Review, 53-56), the Supreme Court held that conduct of the parties subsequent to the making of the contract was inadmissible as a guide to the interpretation of the contract. Nevertheless, it is well settled that if a clause in a contract is ambiguous, the court may, as an exception to the parol evidence rule, adduce evidence extrinsic to the contract to determine the intent of the parties in drafting that clause. It is also well settled that ambiguity in a clause in a contract will often be interpreted strictly and against the interests of the party who inserted that clause. The parol evidence rule was at issue in *Bank of Ireland v. McCabe*, High Court, 25 March 1993, Flood J (above), whilst both principles featured in *Dillon v. McGovern*, High Court, 16 March 1993, Geoghegan J (see the Insurance section in the Commercial Law chapter, *supra*, 49-56). The plaintiff had been insured by the defendant 'in the event of the insured animal(s) being compulsorily slaughtered . . . following failure to pass the routine brucellosis test'. Fifteen cattle failed the test, and the department required that the entire herd of seventy-nine be slaughtered. The plaintiff claimed on foot of the insurance policy in respect of the seventy nine, the insurance company maintained that the clause covered only the fifteen. The plaintiff submitted that the above insurance clause was ambiguous, and sought to rely on the exception to the parol evidence rule and the *contra proferentem* rule.

Geoghegan J found that the clause was 'slightly ambiguous', and thus that it could legitimately be interpreted contra proferentem the insurance company. If a party to a contract chooses 'to adopt ambiguous words it seems to me good sense, as well as established law, that those words should be interpreted in the sense which is adverse to the persons who chose and introduced them. . . .' (*In re Sweeney and Kennedy Arbitration* [1950] IR 85, 98 *per* Kingsmill-Moore J). Geoghegan J held that the plaintiff was entitled to interpret the policy in the way that he did, and since the clause was ambiguous, the defendant must be held bound by that interpretation. This finding greatly strengthened his conclusion in the parol evidence issue.

As to that rule, he held that 'if the words of a clause in a written contract are clear and open to only one meaning 'it would not be permissible to adduce parol evidence to explain or vary the clause.' However he held that such parol evidence was not excluded by the rule and would he admissible in general 'to show the circumstances under which the parties contracted and the general context within which the contract was entered into'. Furthermore, he accepted that if the clause is ambiguous, then parol evidence is admissible to determine:

> the true intention of the parties as well as for the purpose of placing the contract in context. I am satisfied, however that as a matter of law I am entitled to have regard to the parol evidence only for the purpose of helping me to construe the written words in the light of the intention of the parties and the general context and not for the purpose of varying the written agreement.

Here, the parol evidence showed that the plaintiff sought insurance of his 'whole herd against brucellosis' and Geoghegan J was satisfied that he 'would, at all material times, have assumed that he was covered in the event of depopulation of the herd as a consequence of some animals failing the brucellosis test.' The ambiguity in the clause was such that it was open to being so interpreted, thus the plaintiff was entitled to full indemnity on foot thereof.

In *Bank of Ireland v McCabe*, High Court, 25 March 1993, Flood J, a company sought a loan from the bank, and signed a guarantee expressed to cover present and future liabilities, which guarantee the bank sought to apply to subsequent loan. The evidence of the bank manager was to the effect that the guarantee 'had been created to deal with a particular transaction since successfully accomplished', and the company therefore argued that the guarantee was intended to apply only to the single transaction of the first loan. Flood J held that the guarantee was not void for *non est factum* (above 189). However, on the admissibility of the bank manager's evidence, which was after all extrinsic to the written contract, and therefore seemingly excluded by the parol evidence rule, he held that:

> [e]xtrinsic evidence is admissible as stated by Lord Wilberforce in *Rearden Smithline v Hansen-Tangen* [1976] 3 All ER 570, 574 'when it comes to ascertaining whether particular words apply to a factual situation or, if one prefers, whether a factual situation comes within particular words, it is undoubtedly proper and necessary to take evidence as to the factual situation.' In my opinion the evidence of Mr Reid, above quoted, is simply an explanation of the circumstances under which the said written guarantee came into existence. I do not think

however, that the words in question can objectively be held to be
evidence that the said written guarantee was intended to apply to that
transaction, and to that transaction only. In my view, Mr Reid's evidence
is descriptive of the circumstances under which the written guarantee
came into existence and do not relate to the scope of the said guarantee.

Consequently, he gave judgment for the plaintiff bank (though he was
overruled by the Supreme Court: see the 1995 Review). Significantly, both
Goeghegan J in Dillon and Flood J in *McCabe* were prepared to take a broad
view of evidence admissible to explain the context in which the contract was
made. According to Treitel, 'there are obvious grounds of convenience for
the application of the parol evidence rules to contracts: certainty is promoted
by holding that parties who have reduced a contract to writing should be
bound by the writing and by the writing alone.' (pp. 176-177). On the other
hand, the rule is invoked where there is a dispute as to the meaning or totality
of the contract, and if it excludes important material, that certainty is achieved
at the expense of justice. The admission of evidence by way of exception is
justified on this ground. The judgments in *Dillon* and *McCabe* are excellent
illustrations in this context of the perennial judicial need to strike the proper
balance between certainty and justice.

UNDUE INFLUENCE

In *Bank of Ireland v Smyth* [1993] 2 IR 102; [1993] ILRM 790 (HC); [1996]
1 ILRM 241 (SC) the defendant sought to defend an unpaid mortgagee's
claim for possession of a family home on the grounds of undue influence and
s.3 of the Family Home Protection Act 1976. The circumstances of the case
raise profound structural questions not only for Family Law (see *infra*, 328)
and Land Law (see *infra*, 383-8), but also for the law of Contract. In this
volume of the Review, we analyse the High Court judgment; in the 1995
Review, we will consider the approach of the Supreme Court, which affirmed
the result on this different grounds. Similar questions are implicated in the
recent House of Lords decisions of *Barclays Bank v O'Brien* [1994] 1 AC
180 and *CIBC v Pitt* [1994] 1 AC 200 and in the classic cases of *Lloyds Bank
v Bundy* [1974] 3 All ER 757 (CA), *National Westminster Bank v Morgan*
[1985] AC 686 (HL). These cases have in fact done much to obscure rather
than to elucidate the principles involved. Properly to place in context the
defendants' plea of undue influence in such cases and especially in *Smyth*, it
is necessary to return to first principles.

Undue influence   Since a contract is based upon the consent of the parties, if the consent of one or both parties is vitiated, then the contract is invalid. Thus, if one party coerces another into entering into the contract, the consent of that other will be vitiated. At common law, the remedy for such coercion is supplied by the doctrine of duress. In equity, a similar remedy is supplied by the doctrine of actual undue influence.

In relationships where one party has great influence over the other, and the other relies to a great deal on, and reposes much trust and confidence in, the first party, there is a significant risk that the stronger party will take advantage of this inequality and coerce or victimise the weaker party into a disadvantageous transfer. Consequently, where as between parties to such a relationship, the weaker party confers a benefit upon the stronger, equity will raise a presumption that the stronger party obtained that benefit by virtue of the exercise of undue influence (coercion), and it will be for that party to rebut that presumption by showing that the transfer was consensually and voluntarily made. There are certain relationships in which equity will automatically raise this presumption of undue influence, (priest-penitent; doctor-patient), but this category does not include banker-customer or husband-wife (*Bank of Montreal v Stuart* [1911] AC 120; *O'Brien*). In certain other categories of case, the circumstances of a relationship in fact of influence and reliance will be sufficient to raise the presumption (see *Gregg v Kidd* [1956] IR 183), as often happens for example where an older person is entirely reliant upon a younger (see e.g. *McGonigle v Black*, High Court, 14 November 1988, Barr J) and it should be noted that although the banker-customer or husband-wife relationships do not automatically generate the presumption, the circumstances of fact surrounding a particular banker and customer or a particular husband and wife can be such as to generate the presumption. If the presumption is raised and not rebutted, the effect in equity is exactly the same as if P had exercised actual undue influence: the court concludes that D's consent was vitiated and the contract is invalid.

Independent advice   Although anything which has the effect of demonstrating that the transfer was voluntary will rebut the presumption, such voluntariness has often been inferred from the fact that the weaker party was independently legally advised (on the role of such advice, see *Inche Noriah v Shaik Alie Bin Omar* [1929] AC 127 and *Gregg v Kidd* [1956] IR 183). Indeed, where one party has pleaded actual undue influence, the other will often seek to point to independent advice, again to demonstrate that the contract was voluntary. However, it must be remembered that the presence such advice is at best an unreliable guide. There may be no such advice, and yet the contract could be voluntary (in *McCormack v Bennett*, High Court, 2 July 1973, Finlay J held that the independent advice was inadequate but the contract was voluntary). Or, there may be independent advice, and yet the undue influence could be so strong that such advice would be ineffective or ignored. In either such case, a search simply for independent advice would reach a different conclusion to an analysis of whether there was in truth a voluntary consent. Thus, the courts should concentrate primarily on the issue of voluntaries, and on the issue of independent advice only in so far as it advances that primary objective.

Undue influence exercised by a third party who is not a party to the contract These doctrines — duress, actual undue influence, presumed undue influence — and similar equitable doctrines such as improvidence (e.g. *Grealish v Murphy* [1956] IR 35) and unconscionability, all tend to fall to be considered in circumstances where D has entered into a contract with P, P seeks to enforce it, and D resists on the grounds that P coerced him (duress, actual undue influence)t or that the relationship between them was one of influence and reliance (presumed undue influence) or that the transaction was improvident for P or that it would be unconscionable in the circumstances for P to be allowed to rely upon or enforce the contract. Matters are complicated when these doctrines fall to be considered not in the two party contract illustrated so far, but in circumstances in which a third party, T, coerces D into entering into the contract with P. The extent to which the fact that the coercion emanates from T and not from P provides D with a defence on the grounds of duress, actual or presumed undue influence, improvidence or unconscionability is unclear.

Actual undue influence and a third party Assume first, that T has exercised actual coercion — duress or actual undue influence — upon D. At least four strategies present themselves. First, since the enforceability of the contract against D is based upon D's consent, that consent is as much vitiated by P's coercion as by T's, and as a matter of principle it should not matter therefore whether D's consent is vitiated by P or T. In either case, if it is found that actual pressure (whether called duress or actual undue influence) was brought to bear upon D, then the contract should not be enforceable against D. (Let this be the 'coercion *simpliciter*' strategy).

Second, it may be that it can be shown that T is an agent for P. Since the acts of the agent are the acts of the principal, if T has coerced D, in law it is as if P had coerced D. Again, therefore, the contract should not be enforceable against D (this is one reading of *Turnbull v Divall* [1902] AC 429, common in the English Court of Appeal from 1985: see the discussion of these authorities in the decision of Scott LJ in the Court of Appeal in *Barclays Bank v O'Brien* [1993] QB 109; confined in the House of Lords in *O'Brien* 'to cases where, without artificiality, it can properly be held that the husband was acting as the agent of the creditor in procuring the wife to stand as surety.

Such cases will be of very rare occurrence'). (Let this be the 'agency' strategy).

Third, since the exercise of undue influence is an equitable wrong which gives the party coerced, D, an equity to set aside the transaction thereby procured, then a party to the contract with notice of this equity will not be entitled to enforce it. If P exercises this undue influence, of course P has such notice, and thus he cannot enforce the contract. If, as here, T exercises this undue influence, P cannot enforce the contract only if he has notice of T's coercion and thus of D's equity. (Let this be the 'notice' strategy). As Lord Browne-Wilkinson put it (adapted to the nomenclature here) in the House of Lords in *Barclay's Bank v O'Brien* [1994] 1 AC 180:

> [Where D] has been induced to stand as a surety for [T]'s debts by his undue-influence, misrepresentation or some other legal wrong [then D] has an equity against T to set aside that transaction. Under the ordinary principles of equity, D's right to set aside that transaction will be enforceable against third parties (e.g. against a creditor [such as P]) if . . . P had actual or constructive notice of the facts giving rise to D's equity. . . . The key to the problem is to identify the circumstances in which the P will be taken to have had notice of D's equity to set aside the transaction. . . . Therefore, where D has agreed to stand as surety for T's debts as a result of [T's] undue influence or misrepresentation, P will take subject to D's equity to set aside the transaction if the circumstances are such as to put P on inquiry as to the circumstances in which D agreed to stand surety. . . .

> It follows that unless a creditor [P] who is put on inquiry takes reasonable steps to satisfy himself that D's agreement to stand surety has been properly obtained,P will have constructive notice of D's rights ... [the requirement of such reasonable steps will be satisfied if P] insists that T attend a private meeting (in the absence of T) with a representative of the creditor at which D is told of the extent of the liability as surety, warned of the risk D is running and urged to take independent legal advice. . . .

Fourth, a court could simply hold that in all the circumstances of the case, T's coercion made it 'unconscionable' for P to enforce the contract as against D, or the transaction was 'improvident' for D. This is the position urged in Mee, 'Consents, guarantees and the "Badge of Shame"' (1994) 16 *DULJ (ns)* 197. (Let this be the 'unconscionability' strategy).

If a court were to adopt the first (coercion *simpliciter*) strategy, the fact of the coercion would be enough to render the contract unenforceable. If however, a court were to hold that the fact of the coercion is not enough, that something more is required, then it could locate that 'something more' in one of the other three strategies: in the fact that T is an agent for P, or that P had notice of T's coercion? or that there was some 'unconscionability' or 'improvidence' on the facts.

Presumed undue influence and a third party The treatment so far discusses the situation where where T exercises actual coercion: duress or actual undue influence. In relation to the same four strategies, it is necessary also to consider the position where the relationship or circumstances between T and D are such as to raise a presumption of undue influence. Recall that if such a relationship raises such a presumption, and it is not rebutted, then the effect in equity is exactly the same as if T had exercised actual undue influence: the court concludes that D's consent was vitiated and the contract is invalid. Thus, as to the coercion *simpliciter* strategy, if actual coercion is sufficient of itself to render the contract unenforceable, an unrebutted presumption of undue influence between T and I) should likewise be sufficient to render unenforceable the contract between the contract P and D.

Second, as to the agency strategy, where T is agent for P, any relationship or circumstances subsisting between T and D which generate the presumption of undue influence are taken in law subsist between P and D. Therefore, an unrebutted presumption of undue influence between T and D should again be sufficient to render unenforceable the contract between P and D. Third, as to the notice strategy, if P has notice of any exercise of undue influence by T upon D, then P cannot enforce the contract; thus, if P has notice of a relationship or circumstances which give rise to a presumption of undue influence as between T and D, and that presumption is not rebutted, again D will have an equity to set the contract aside, and P will not be able to enforce it against D. Fourth, as to the unconscionability strategy, a court could again simply hold that in all the circumstances of the case, T's coercion made it 'unconscionable' for P to enforce the contract as against D, or the transaction was 'improvident' for D.

If a court were to adopt the first (coercion *simpliciter*) strategy, the fact of the unrebutted presumption would be enough to render the contract unenforceable. If however, a court were to hold that this fact is not enough, that something more is required, then it could locate that 'something more' in one of the other three strategies: in the fact that T is an agent for P, or that P had notice of the relationship or circumstances which give rise to a presumption that T had exercised undue influence upon D, or that there was some 'unconscionability' or 'improvidence' on the facts.

As between these four strategies, as regards undue influence, either actual or presumed, the coercion *simpliciter* strategy is entirely sound in principle, turning as it does upon the consent of D. The agency strategy will often leave the court in the invidious position of enforcing a contract plainly procured by objectionable means, or spuriously finding that T is an agent for P so as to render the contract unenforceable. The notice strategy would seem to have the force of equitable principle behind it, but again it will often leave the court in the invidious position of enforcing a contract plainly procured by objectionable means, or spuriously finding that P had notice either of T's undue influence or of the relationship or circumstances between T and D which generate the presumption of undue influence, so as again to render the contract unenforceable. The unconscionability strategy allows the court to render objectionable contracts unenforceable, but if that result is achieved as a consequence simply of the fact of the (actual or presumed) undue influence, saying that the transaction is thereby unconsionable or improvident adds nothing of substance to the analysis and is not necessary. The agency, notice and unconscionability strategies being unsatisfactory, the law should reject them and adopt the coercion *simpliciter* strategy. Thus, where T coerces D into making a contract with P, that coercion should be regarded as duress or undue influence and give D a defence to an action by P to enforce the contract. Again, where D enters into a contract with P as a consequence of his relationship with T and that relationship or circumstances give rise to the presumption that T had exercised undue influence on D, then if the presumption remains unrebutted, the position is the same as if T had in fact exercised undue influence and D should have a defence to an action by P to enforce the contract.

To complete the above analysis, two further sets of circumstances must be considered. The first concerns transactions involving banks. The second concerns transactions between husbands and wifes.

Banker-customer First, as to banks. In principle, if a bank manager actually coerces a customer into taking a loan or giving a guarantee, then that loan and guarantee are unenforceable by the bank against the customer on the grounds of duress and actual undue influence (in the same way as any contract procured by duress or undue influence is unenforceable). However, the bank manager/customer relationship does not automatically give rise to a presumption of undue influence; and the circumstances in fact will rarely themselves be sufficient to raise the presumption, (though, of course, it can happen, as in *Lloyd's Bank v Bundy* [1974] 3 All ER 757 (CA)). However, let there be a three-party scenario as follows: the bank has given a loan to a customer, secured by way of a guarantee or security granted by a guarantor or surety; the customer defaults; the bank seeks to enforce the guarantee/security. Focussing on the contract of guarantee or security which the bank seeks to enforce, the bank is P, the guarantor/surety is D, and the customer is T. If D (the guarantor/surety) seeks to defend on the grounds either that T coerced him into granting the guarantee or security, or that as between T and D, the relationship itself or the circumstances surrounding it gave rise to the presumption of undue influence, then all four of the above mentioned strategies are available to D. The fact that the parties are bank, its customer, and a guarantor/surety ought to change nothing.

As between the four strategies outlined above, the Court of Appeal in England had adopted and expanded the agency strategy, but the House of Lords has now decided in favour of the notice approach: *O'Brien*, above; and *CIBC v Pitt* [1994] 1 AC 200). Nevertheless, as was submitted above, the fact of actual undue influence or of an unrebutted presumption of undue influence between T and D should in principle be enough.

Husband-wife   As to transactions involving husband and wife, in principle, if a husband actually coerces his wife into entering into a contract with him, then that contract is unenforceable by the husband against the wife on the grounds of duress and actual undue influence (in the same way as any contract procured by duress or undue influence is unenforceable). However, the husband-wife relationship does not automatically give rise to a presumption of undue influence; though the circumstances in fact could themselves be sufficient to raise the presumption. So much for transactions *between* husbands and wives; however, let there be a three-party scenario *involving* husbands and wives, and adding a bank, as follows: the bank has given a loan to a husband, secured by way of a guarantee or security granted by the wife; the husband defaults; the bank seeks to enforce the guarantee/security against the wife. Focussing on the contract of guarantee or security which the bank seeks to enforce, the bank is P, the wife is D, and the husband is T. We have already seen that the fact that the parties are bank, its customer, and a guarantor/surety ought not to affect the outcome in principle. Thus, if D (the wife-guarantor/surety) seeks to defend on the ground that T (her husband) coerced her into granting the guarantee or security, then all four of the above strategies should in principle be open: the duress or actual undue influence exercised by T (the husband) could be held to vitiate her consent to her contract of guarantee or security with P (the bank); or T (the husband) could be held to have been in fact the agent of P (the bank) when he procured by duress or undue influence her consent to the contract; or D could have a defence if P had notice of T's undue influence; or the court could hold the P-D contract unconscionable by virtue of T's coercion.

However, in this special three-party scenario, where a wife is surety for the husband's debts to a creditor/bank/mortgagee, a fifth strategy has been developed. Courts of equity in Australia have been prepared to treat married women differently and more tenderly than other classes of surety, and have therefore developed the theory that vulnerable wives possess a special equity as against creditors to whom they offer security for debts of their husbands. (e.g. *Yerkey v Jones* (1939) 63 CLR 649). (Let this be the 'special equity' strategy). It may be that in the end this could be seen no more than a specific application of the more general doctrines of improvidence and unconscionability, but the treatment here will follow the current understanding that these latter doctrines and the special equity doctrine are independent of and separate from each other.

As a matter of Irish law, the special position of women and mothers secured by Article 41.2 of the Constitution could be deployed in favour of such a special equity strategy. However, the unwillingness of the Supreme Court in *L. v L.* [1992] 2 IR 77; [1992] ILRM 115 (see 1991 Review, 216-22) to rely on the Constitution in the context of trusts of the family home to protect a wife in a similar manner probably makes such a constitutional basis for the special equity theory doubtful; and the emerging right to equality as between spouses (recognised in cases such as *W. v W.* [1993] 2 IR 476; [1993] ILRM 294 and *McKinley v Minister for Defence* [1992] 2 IR 333 (see 1992 Review, 613-618; Hogan (1992) 14 *DULJ (ns)* 115)) even suggests that the special equity strategy would be unconstitutional. Be that as it may, it seems that no Irish case has yet to rule upon it.

In *Barclay's Bank v O'Brien*, faced with a choice between these various strategies, the Court of Appeal adopted this fifth approach, but the House of Lords rejected it, confined the agency strategy to those (rare) situations in which the husband is in fact the bank's agent, and instead adopted the notice strategy outlined above (see also *CIBC v Pitt*). According to Lord Browne-Wilkinson in *O'Brien*, on this approach, the *Yerkey v Jones* tenderness 'is reflected by the fact that voluntary dispositions by the wife in favour of the husband are more likely to be set aside than other dispositions by her', since, on the facts, the circumstances giving rise to a presumption of undue influence are more likely to exist between herself and her husband than between herself and others, because 'in practice, any wives do repose in their husbands trust and confidence in relation to their financial affairs.' Consequently, according to Lord Browne-Wilkinson:

> . . . a creditor is put on inquiry when a wife offers to stand surety for her husband's debts by the combination of two factors: (a) the transaction is on its face not to the financial advantage of the wife; and (b) there is a substantial risk in transactions of that kind that, in procuring the wife to act as surety, the husband has committed a legal or equitable wrong that entitles the wife to set aside the transaction.

On this view, a special equity in favour of wife-sureties is not being created; but the fact of the husband-wife relationship puts the creditor on inquiry, and, as we have seen above, if no steps are taken by the creditor, he will have constructive notice of any equity which the wife may possess to set the transaction aside. Nevertheless, there are significant practical problems with this notice strategy (see e.g. *Swadling* [1993] All ER Rev 367; *Mee* [1995] *CLJ* 536; *O'Hagan* (1996) 47 *NILQ* 174), and it leaves open the possibility of a judicial manipulation of constructive notice on the facts so as to render unenforceable an objectionable contract. Consequently, it is submitted that the coercion *simpliciter* strategy is more in accord with principle, and that the notice approach of the House of Lords ought not to be adopted in Ireland.

So much for actual undue influence. As to the position if D (the wife) seeks to rely on *raising a presumption* of undue influence between her and her husband (T) to defend against the bank (P) seeking to enforce its contract of guarantee against her, it is settled law that the relationship of husband and wife does not of itself generate the presumption of undue influence, though the circumstances between husband and wife may do so. If D raises the presumption based on the circumstances rather than the relationship, then it is for P to rebut it; and if P fails to do so, then the position is in law the same as if D had shown that T had exercised actual undue influence, and analysis proceeds on the basis of whichever of the five strategies outlined and discussed above is chosen.

It is important to notice here that there is nothing in the first four strategies which limits them to situations where a husband coerces a wife to stand surety to the bank. They are not limited to contracts of security but in principle apply to all contracts; furthermore, in principle, they would equally be available if the wife had coerced her husband, or the parties were unmarried but involved — whether in an opposite-sex or same-sex — relationship, or even if there was no connection between D and T except that T coerced D into securing a loan to T from P. Indeed, even as to the fifth approach, which turns primarily on the special tenderness to be shown to wives, in Court of Appeal in *O'Brien*, Scott LJ was prepared to accept that if the notion a specially protected class 'is to continue to be recognised, the class ought, logically, to include all cases in which the relationship between the surety and the debtor is in which influence by the debtor and reliance by the surety on the debtor are natural and probable features of the relationship'.

The Family Home Protection Act 1976 and *Bank of Ireland v Smyth*   In the cases and situations considered so far, the interest possessed by D which is presented to P by way of security is usually a proprietary interest in the family home. In the above situations, nothing of legal substance turns on this, but it becomes important in Ireland in the context of Family Home Protection Act 1976. Here, s. 3(1) requires the consent in writing of one spouse to transactions involving the family home entered into by the other spouse; without such consent, the transaction is void. In practice, then, if the husband wishes to borrow from the bank and grant a mortgage on the family home by way of security, the wife must consent in writing to this transaction. Superficially, there is a similarity of structure between this transaction and that of a wife giving a bank a security over her interest in the family home to secure her husband's borrowing. Yet, there are profound differences. But it is this similarity which is at issue in *Bank of Ireland v Smyth*. Here, the first and second defendants were husband and wife, respectively. The first defendant had charged property (the defendant's house and lands) as security for borrowings advanced by the plaintiff bank. In this action, the plaintiff sought possession of the house and lands pursuant to the terms of the security.

The second defendant resisted on the grounds that her consent for the purposes of s. 3 of the Act 'was not a true consent in that she was not advised to obtain independent legal advice and that she did not have a proper understanding of what she was signing.' Relying on the decision of Scott LJ in *O'Brien*, was submitted on her behalf that:

a consent by a wife under the Family Home Protection Act 1976 to a mortgage or charge in favour the bank is not valid unless the wife understands the nature and consequences of the transaction. She cannot normally be said to have such understanding unless:

(1) She is told of the loan involved, and if the security is to cover future advances she is informed of that.
(2) She is explained the repayment terms.
(3) She is explained the consequences of non-payment and in particular that possession of her family home may be recovered by the bank and may be sold.
(4) She is recommended to obtain independent legal advice.

Goeghegan J seemed to accept this submission: 'Scott LJ delivered the principal. Judgment [in *O'Brien*] and I believe that the views expressed by him; represent Irish law particularly having regard to the line of Irish cases dealing with voluntary deeds'. Consequently, he held that:

It is obvious that [the bank manager] was well aware of the husband and wife relationship and the consequent inherent likelihood of influence and reliance. He was equally well aware that the wife's understanding of the transaction depended essentially on what he told her. He should

have realised that what he told her and what he advised her were
inadequate. He did not take adequate steps to ensure that the second
named defendant fully understood the transaction. In particular he did
not advise her to take independent advice'

and he concluded that:

the bank *via* [the manager] did not adequately explain to Mr Smyth the
potential liabilities secured by the charge and above all did not explain
to her that in the event of default the property *including the matrimonial
home* could be sold. . . . These are vital matters of which Mrs Smyth
should have been made aware before she signed the consent. Furthermore she was not recommended to obtain independent advice.

Consequently, the bank's application was refused (the Supreme Court (at
[1996] 1 ILRM 241) affirmed on different grounds to he discussed in the
1995 Review). Given that *O'Brien* is in terms a case about undue influence,
much of the commentary in the aftermath of this decision perceived *Smyth*
as also being about undue influence (e.g. *Doyle* (1994) *Gazette ICLSI* 187;
Sanfey (1994) 1 *Comm LP* 99; *Reid* (1994) 12 *ILT (ns)* 40; *Mee* (1994) 16
DULJ (ns) 197); (cf. Sanfey (1996) 3 *Com LP* 31 on the decision of the
Supreme Court, likewise discussing undue influence).

It is submitted that this approach of seeking to empty, into the single word
'consent' in s. 3 of the Act, the law of undue influence (as exemplified in
Barclay's Bank v O'Brien), is fundamentally misconceived. In *Barclay's
Bank v O'Brien*, the husband had borrowed from the bank, and the wife had
entered into a contract with the bank by which she granted the bank a security
over her interest in the home to secure her husbands borrowing. In *Bank of
Ireland v Smyth*, the husband had borrowed from the bank, and the wife had
to sigh a consent in writing for the purposes of s. 3 of the Act. Though
structurally superficially similar, the positions are in fact profoundly different. Granted in both *O'Brien* and *Smyth* the husband borrows from the bank,
and in both, the wife is implicated; thereafter the similarities end. Under s. 3
of the Act, the court is concerned with the validity of the contract of loan
between the bank and husband: that contract is valid only if the wife consents
in writing to it. In analysing the consent of the wife, as in *Smyth*, the court is
still determining the validity of the transaction between the husband and the
bank. On the other hand, in *O'Brien* there are two separate transactions, the
contract of loan between the husband and the bank, and contract of guarantee
between the wife and the bank, and in analysing whether the consent of the
wife is vitiated by undue influence, the court is not saying anything about
the validity of the transaction between the husband and the bank, it is

analysing instead the validity of the separate contract between the wife and the bank. In other words, at a very fundamental level, the cases are about two totally different transactions. Thus, s. 3 and *Smyth* deal with the position of the wife in respect of the husband dealing with his interest in the family home. On the other hand, *O'Brien* deals with the position of the wife in respect of her own dealing with her own interest in the family home.

But the differences go deeper. Under the Act, the wife acquires no proprietary interest in the family home, merely a veto over transactions involving it (a veto which may even be dispensed with in certain circumstances — s.4 of the Act — and which may be defeated by registration of a judgment mortgage: *Containercare v Wycherley* [1982] IR 143). Indeed, the rights under the Act are supplementary to any proprietary or other rights or interests which she may have independently of it. S.3 and *Smyth* deal with the valid exercise of this veto by the wife. On the other hand, *O'Brien* is directed to the question of whether the wife has in fact dealt with one of those proprietary or other rights or interests which she may have independently of the statute. Thus, as a matter of structure, on the question of undue influence, *O'Brien* has nothing to say to *Smyth*.

However, *O'Brien* was concerned with the doctrine of undue influence, and, since both that doctrine and s. 3 of the Act are concerned with the validity of consent, it could be argued that on this level, *O'Brien* might have something of relevance to say about the position which presented itself in *Smyth*. This argument, too, is wrong. In *O'Brien*, the coercion of the husband (T) is the reason why it is argued that a separate contract between the bank (P) and the wife (D) ought to be invalid. We have seen that there are five possible strategies for such an argument: coercion *simpliciter*, agency, notice, unconscionability, and the special equity. Each of these arguments turns out to be unworkable, unnecessary or inconsistent with the Act when the are applied to the terms of s. 3 and the facts of *Smyth*.

The best candidate is the first: coercion *simpliciter*. On this approach, where the husband coerces the wife to act as surety, the fact of the coercion (the undue influence) vitiates the security; in *Smyth*, the court seems to say that where the husband coerces the wife to consent to the loan, the fact of that coercion vitiates the consent in writing. However, undue influence is an equitable doctrine, and as such, bars to equitable relief apply. Thus, *laches*, delay, and affirmation, will bar an action based on undue influence (as happened in the leading case of *Allcard v Skinner*). If a bank gives the husband a loan on foot of a security granted by the wife, and all goes well for fifteen years, and then the husband defaults, and the bank seeks to enforce the security as against the wife; it may be that here the wife is barred by the delay from pleading undue influence; whereas there is nothing comparable in s.3 which renders the transaction 'void' (and not voidable as is the case with actual undue influence ∅ and duress). Thus, adding the coercion *simpliciter* approach to 'undue influence' by third parties to the analysis under s.3 adds a whole range of considerations which the Act does not countenance, and is thus statutorily precluded.

As to seeking to apply the agency approach to undue influence to the notion of consent in s. 3 of the Act, it simply will not fit: that approach says that where T coerces D into a contract with P, the (P-D) contract is unenforceable by P *only if T is P's agent*. Whereas, s. 3 says only that if there is no 'consent in writing' by D, the (P-T) transaction is void, and contains nothing that says the P-T transaction is unenforceable where T is P's agent. If it did, it would be a nonsense. And there is no way to adapt the agency approach to fit it within the statutory scheme.

As to seeking to apply the notice approach to undue influence to the notion of consent in s. 3(1) of the Act, it unnecessary by virtue of s. 3(3) of the Act. The notice approach to the exercise of undue influence by third parties provides that where T coerces D into a contract with P, the (P-D) contract is unenforceable by P where P has notice of T's coercion of D. On the other hand, s.3(3) of the Act provides a similar role for notice; by s.3(3)(a), it is provided that no conveyance shall be void by reason only of s.3(1) 'if it is made to a purchaser for full value . . .', and in turn s. 3(6) provides that 'purchaser' means a ... chargeant ... who in good faith acquires an estate or interest in the land'. In *Smyth*, Goeghegan J accepted that the 'Supreme Court in *Somers v W.* [1979] IR 94 has held that the words 'in good faith' import the equitable doctrine of notice.' In this regard, Goeghegan J held that the bank 'had or ought to have had knowledge of the vitiating elements' which the wife asserted rendered her consent invalid. and continued that:

> Since the bank in this case had full notice of all the factors alleged by the defendant to vitiate the consent, it follows that if the consent is invalid by reason of any of those factors, the bank is not a 'purchaser'.

There being a similar role for notice already in s. 3(3), there is no good reason why a different role for it be read into the word 'consent' in s.3(1). In fact, there is a significant difference between the *O'Brien* notice approach and the operation of s. 3. *O'Brien* is predicated upon the husband vitiating the wife's consent by undue influence or some other equitable wrong, and the bank having notice of such a wrong. On the other hand, s. 3(1) is predicated upon an enquiry whether there was any reason why the wife did not in fact consent, and then as to whether the bank had notice of that reason: s. 3(3) and s. 3(6). Thus, as Mee points out, the precise operation of the notice strategy in *O'Brien* would not in fact aid the wife on the facts of *Smyth*: 'Lord

Browne-Wilkinson's approach has the crucial limitation that a mere lack of understanding on the part of the wife will be of no relevance unless it was attributable to some equitable wrong on the part of the husband or the lender' (1994) 16 *DULJ (ns)* 197, 205. There being no such equitable wrong on the facts of *Smyth*, the *O'Brien* approach would not reach the same result as ss. 3(3) and 3(6). Such inconsistencies should not be tolerated, so the *O'Brien* notice approach should not be emptied into s. 3(1).

Finally, as to the unconscionability and special equity approaches (to the extent that they are at bottom different doctrines, and to the extent that they are accepted as a matter of Irish equity) they provide general equitable discretions which apply to the question of the validity of a loan between a bank and a husband without the need for a statutory justification for their exercise. Indeed, these doctrines by their nature look to the totality of the transaction, of which one aspect, but only one, is the circumstance of the wife's consent. Thus, the ambit of the enquiry under the unconscionability and special tenderness approaches to the question of undue influence is not co-extensive with the ambit of the enquiry under s. 3(1) which is simply focussed on consent. Nothing in the statute limits the equitable enquiry, nor should equity expand the statutory enquiry: they are two independent enquiries which can be addressed to the facts of a particular case.

In *Smyth*, the commentators perceive the court as saying that since undue influence vitiates consent, and since s. 3 is concerned with consent, undue influence is relevant to an enquiry under s. 3, a proposition which seems to be derived from *O'Brien*. However, Geoghegan J in *Smyth* nowhere in fact says so. Indeed, the only the only understanding of undue influence by a third party which seems at all compatible with s. 3, the coercion *simpliciter* approach, is not considered at all in *O'Brien*, whilst the approaches adopted in *O'Brien* in the House of Lords (notice) (and even in the Court of Appeal (agency, special tenderness)) are incompatible with the terms of the s. 3.

Thus, both as a consequence of the significant differences in the structures of the transactions at issue in *O'Brien* and *Smyth* and because the doctrine of undue influence by a third party is incompatible with s. 3 of the Act, the emptying of undue influence into s. 3 by reference to *O'Brien* is misconceived.

However, notwithstanding the academic commentary, *Smyth* did not rely on *O'Brien* for the treatment of undue influence, but for the treatment of the issue of independent advice. In *O'Brien*, Scott LJ decided that equity had to be solicitous of the position of vulnerable wives, and, to redress that vulnerability, required that they be furnished with independent advice as to the nature and consequences of the transaction being entered into by them. Those were the probanda set out in the headnote to the decision of the Court of Appeal in *O'Brien* and, upon the submission of counsel for the wife set out above, relied upon by Geoghegan J in *Smyth*. In the context of s. 3, given both that the Act has made a similar policy determination that the position of vulnerable wives needs protection, and that independent advice is the means chosen in equity to ensure that the wife's consent is a valid one, it seems logically to follow that independent advice is a good means to ensure that the wife's consent for the purpose of the Act is a valid one. And in the end, that is all that Geoghegan J in *Smyth* actually says on this issue.

However, there are problems with this almost exclusive reliance on independent advice. A person may not be so advised, and still validly consent; and a person entirely dominated by another can continue to be so, notwithstanding the independent advice of a third party. Thus, 'independent advice' is not some talismanic cure for coercion; it may be an important factor to be taken into account, but it should not be used a proxy for an analysis as whether the wife's consent was a valid one.

In summary, then, the decision of Geoghegan J in *Smyth* is confined to the issue of the validity of a spouse's consent in writing to a conveyance by the other spouse of an interest in the family home as required by s. 3 of the Family Home Protection Act 1976, and, in this regard, so as to ensure that the consenting spouse fully understands the nature and quality of such an action, and fully consents to its the bank should so explain that transaction to the spouse and at least advise that independent legal advice be sought. This requirement of independent advice was derived from the decision of the Court of Appeal in *O'Brien*. The prior question in *O'Brien* of undue influence is irrelevant on the facts of *Smyth* and incompatible with s. 3 of the Act.

Furthermore, s. 3 will have no application in relationships other than marital, and it will have no application to the husband-wife relationship if the husband's borrowing is secured — whether by the husband or the wife — over property other than the family home. In all these situations, however, as was pointed out above, coercion by one party on the other will be capable of being addressed by one of the strategies outlined above to deal with undue influence by a third party not party to the contract: coercion *simpliciter*, agency, notice, or unconscionability. Proof again, if further proof were needed, that the doctrine of undue influence by third parties and the enquiry under s.3 of the Act are entirely separate and distinct.

Finally, two hypotheticals. First, consider from the perspective of s. 3 a situation like *O'Brien* in which a husband seeks to obtain a loan from a bank on foot of a security provided by his wife's interest in the family home. The wife's security is a 'conveyance' for the purposes of s. 3 of the Act, and thus it requires the husbands consent in writing! Since he needs the money, this he will validly give and with alacrity. S. 3 will therefore not render the wife's security void. However, assume that he has by undue influence coerced his wife into giving the security. On the coercion *simpliciter* approach to the validity of contracts procured by undue influence exercised by third parties advocated here, that is sufficient to render the contract of security invalid; on the notice approach advocated by Lord Browne-Wilkinson in *O'Brien*, if the bank has notice of the husband's undue influence, then the contract is invalid. In either case, there is no problem with s. 3 and yet the contract is invalid due to undue influence. Proof again, if further proof were needed, that the doctrine of undue influence by third parties and the enquiry under s. 3 of the Act are entirely separate and distinct.

Second, consider a situation where the spouses jointly own the property and have their own separate interests, and the husband seeks to obtain a loan from a bank on foot of a security over both interests in the family home. If the facts are not within *R. v Murphy* [1979] IR 326, then the granting of such security by each spouse is a conveyance within the terms of s. 3 of the Act requiring the consent in writing of the other. Thus, the husband must consent to the wife's granting of a security, this he will validly give and with alacrity. Assume that the wife grants her security and gives the s. 3 consent to her husband's security as a consequence of her husband's coercion (of which the bank has at least constructive notice). By s. 3 that coercion would render void the grant of the security *by the husband*; whereas, the doctrine of undue influence by a third party would mean that the husband's coercion of his wife would render invalid the grant of the security *by the wife* (notwithstanding, as shown in the above hypothetical, that there is no problem with this security from the perspective of s. 3). Proof again, if further proof were needed, that the doctrine of undue influence by third parties and the enquiry under s. 3 of the Act are entirely separate and distinct.

Criminal Law

1993 saw two fundamental legislative changes in the Irish criminal justice system, each almost a mirror image of the other. One was aimed at the victims of crime, the other at potential victims of miscarriages of justice. The Criminal Justice Act 1993 represents a response to well-publicised cases of crimes of violence, especially rape and other sexual assaults. It provides, *inter alia*, for trial courts to make a 'victim impact assessment' in certain violent offences, for appeals against unduly lenient sentences and for payment of compensation by offenders to the victims of crime. On the other hand, the Criminal Procedure Act 1993 contains the legislative reaction to the fallout from recent well-publicised cases of miscarriages of justice, including the Guildford Four and Birmingham Six cases in Britain and, in Ireland, the Nicky Kelly case. Both Acts are considered in this Chapter, and the breadth of their scope requires that their provisions be discussed under a number of different headings. In combination, however, they have resulted in enormous changes to the Irish criminal justice system and for that reason their significance should not be allowed to pass without comment at the outset of this Chapter.

For ease of reference, we note here the commencement dates for the two Acts. The Criminal Justice Act 1993 came into effect on 3 May 1993, in accordance with s. 14(2) of the Act, one month after its signature by the President. The Criminal Procedure Act 1993 came into effect on 29 December 1993, on its signature by the President.

APPEALS

As already mentioned at the beginning of this Chapter, the Criminal Procedure Act 1993 contains the legislative reaction to the fallout from recent well-publicised cases of miscarriages of justice, including the Guildford Four and Birmingham Six cases in Britain and, in Ireland, the Nicky Kelly case: see the 1990 Review, 240-2 and the 1992 Review, 210. The 1993 Act thus includes highly significant amendments to the criminal appellate jurisdiction of the Court of Criminal Appeal in particular and, to some extent, of the Supreme Court. In addition, the Act introduced the need for a warning in cases where the prosecution relies solely on an uncorroborated confession: this aspect of the Act is considered below, 228.

Court of Criminal Appeal and miscarriages of justice S. 2 of the Criminal Procedure Act 1993 introduced a new mechanism for reviewing a conviction which it is claimed resulted in a miscarriage of justice. S. 2 must be considered against the background of the well-publicised cases of miscarriages of justice, mentioned at the beginning of this chapter, the Guildford Four and Birmingham Six cases in Britain and, in Ireland, the Nicky Kelly case, in which a Presidential pardon was granted: see the 1992 Review, 210.

One defect in the pre-1993 appellate jurisdiction was that there were clear limits to the ability of appellate courts to engage in *de novo* fact finding concerning the basis for a conviction under appeal. And where a convicted person sought, in civil proceedings, to re-open issues determined in a criminal trial, the *res judicata* principle was usually invoked to preclude any challenge to the findings in the criminal trial. On this, see *Breathnach v Ireland and Ors (No. 4)*, High Court, 14 December 1992, discussed in the 1992 Review, 493-4, another case arising from the same prosecution as was involved in the Nicky Kelly case. The Criminal Procedure Act 1993 provides, in effect, for a full hearing in the Court of Criminal Appeal in connection with any conviction on indictment where the convicted person, in the words of s. 2(1)(b):

> alleges that a new or newly-discovered fact shows that there has been a miscarriage of justice in relation to the conviction or that the sentence imposed is excessive.

S. 2 of the 1993 Act provides that an application to the Court of Criminal Appeal may be made by the convicted person and, unlike the review procedure in the United Kingdom first introduced by the UK Criminal Appeal Act 1968, a consideration by the Court is not solely a matter to be determined by the Minister for Justice. Thus, the power of referral is given directly to the convicted person, and a decision on its merits is given to the Court. However, it may be noted that the Minister does have an indirect role under s. 7 of the Act, which we discuss below.

As to the substantive aspect to an appeal under s. 2, s. 3 of the Act confers extensive general powers on the Court of Criminal Appeal to affirm a conviction, quash it without any further order, or quash the conviction and order a re-trial. We deal with s. 3 of the Act below.

S. 7 of the 1993 Act also provides for an alternative mechanism for dealing with such cases. Even where all appellate avenues fail, a convicted person may petition the Minister to set in train inquiries which can lead to the government recomending that the President exercise the pardon power under Article 13.6 of the Constitution. Where the Minister's inquiries reveal that an application to the Court under s. 2 of the 1993 Act is the appropriate course of action, the petitioner must be informed that this is the Minister's opinion and the Minister's role is then at an end, so that any further steps require the petitioner to apply to the Court under s. 2. Similarly, if the Minister is of the opinion that no miscarriage of justice has occurred, the Minister must inform the petitioner that no further action will be taken by the Minister.

However, if the Minister's inquiries reveal that some purpose would be served by a further investigation, the Minister must either recommend to the government that it advises the President to grant a pardon under Article 13.6 of the Constitution or else recommend that the government establish a committee under s. 8 of the Act. Under s. 8, such a committee, if established, would have the powers conferred on a tribunal of inquiry under the Tribunals of Inquiry (Evidence) Acts 1921 and 1979. On these Acts generally, see 167, above, in the Constitutional Law chapter.

We might also note here that the 1993 Act, in providing for both the application to the Court and the mechanism of applying for a pardon diverged from the recommendations contained in the 1990 *Report of the Committee of Inquiry into Criminal Justice*, chaired by Judge Frank Martin, which had been established in the wake of the *Guildford Four* case: see the 1990 Review, 240-1. The Martin Committee had recommended that a revised procedure for seeking pardons would be sufficient to meet the needs of any miscarriages of justice. The Martin Committee had been limited in its terms of reference from recommending any further changes in this area, being precluded from recommending for example that a warning to a jury was required in the case of an uncorroborated confession. The extent to which the policy of the government and the Oireachtas had changed between 1990 and 1993 is indicated by the inclusion in s. 10 of the 1993 Act of such a mandatory warning to juries in such cases: see 228 below.

Court of Criminal Appeal general appellate jurisdiction S. 3 of the Criminal Procedure Act 1993 restates with amendments the jurisdiction of the Court to affirm or quash a conviction, to substitute an alternative verdict and to order a re-trial. In this respect, s. 3 of the Act replaces s. 34 of the Criminal Justice Act 1924 and s. 5 of the Criminal Justice Act 1928, which are repealed by s. 13 of the 1993 Act.

S. 3 of the 1993 Act also confers extensive powers on the Court to order production of documents in relation to appeals. In this respect, it should be noted that s. 3 applies to all appeals and is not confined to 'miscarriage of justice' appeals under s. 2 of the Act.

S. 4 of the 1993 Act provides that, notwithstanding any rule of law, a person who is ordered under the Act to be re-tried for an offence may be again indicted, tried and, if found guilty, sentenced for that offence. This provision must be read subject, however, to the rule concerning delays in bringing a case to trial: see the discussion of the case law in this area, 223-6, below.

Court of Criminal Appeal: summary dismissals S. 5 of the 1993 Act provides for the first time that the Court of Criminal Appeal may, in some circumstances, dispose of an appeal in summary fashion, that is, without the preparation of a transcript of the trial hearing. S. 5(1) envisages that the Registrar of the Court makes an initial determination that an appeal does not disclose any substantial ground of appeal or, in the case of an application under s. 2 of the Act, that the application does not show a *prima facie* case that a miscarriage of justice has occurred. The Registrar would then, without calling for the transcript of the trial, refer the case to the Court for a summary determination, which is empowered to dismiss the case if it considers that the application is 'frivolous or vexatious'. No doubt the case law on abuse of the process of the court will be of importance in guiding the Court in such cases: see for example, the 1992 Review, 469 and the Practice and Procedure chapter, 441, below for references to the 1992 and 1993 case law on this topic. Finally we may note that s. 5(2) provides that this summary jurisdiction may be exercised by one judge of the Court of Criminal Appeal but that a summary dismissal by one judge is subject to appeal to the full Court of three judges.

Supreme Court direct appeal abolished S. 11 of the Criminal Procedure Act 1993 abolished the direct appeal from the Central Criminal Court to the Supreme Court that had first been adverted to in *The People v Conmey* [1975] IR 341. The *Conmey* case had opened up, for the first time in Irish law, the possibility of appeals against acquittals in trials on indictment: see *The People v O'Shea* [1983] ILRM 549; [1982] IR 384. This led to determinations by the Supreme Court as to whether such acquittals had been correct in law. In the first such decision, the Court held that the verdict could not be interfered with: see *The People v O'Shea (No. 2)* [1983] ILRM 589. However, in a further case *The People v Quilligan and O'Reilly* [1987] ILRM 606; [1986] IR 495, the Supreme Court rule that the trial judge in that case had erred in law in directing a jury to enter a not guilty verdict on a murder charge, but the Court subsequently held that a re-trial on this charge should not be ordered: see *The People v Quilligan and O'Reilly (No. 2)* [1989] ILRM 245; [1989] IR 46, discussed in the 1988 Review, 168-72. However, in *The People v Quilligan and O'Reilly (No. 3)* [1993] 2 IR 305, discussed in the 1992 Review, 234-9, the Court upheld the validity of the further prosecution of one of the defendants on a related charge. While this appellate jurisdiction had not, therefore, led to a successful appeal against acquittal followed by a re-trial on the same charge, this may have been more a fortuitous result than one of intention.

It had been indicated in the early 1980s that a provision similar to s. 11 of the 1993 Act was to be included in the Criminal Justice Act 1984, but nothing came of this: see the 1988 Review, 144, 146. S. 11 of the 1993 Act reinstates the former system of appeals from all trials on indictment to the Court of Criminal Appeal, with the further possibility of appeals to the Supreme Court by means of a certificate given under s. 29 of the Courts of Justice Act 1924; it also expressly leaves intact the 'without prejudice' appeal on a point of law under s. 34 of the Criminal Procedure Act 1967, as to which see for example, *The People v Rock (P.)* [1994] 1 ILRM 66, below, 226. On appeals against acquittals in summary cases, see the discussion of *Considine v Shannon Regional Fisheries Board* [1994] 1 ILRM 499, above, 170-2, in the Constitutional Law chapter.

Unduly lenient sentences As indicated at the beginning of this chapter, the Criminal Justice Act 1993 enables appeals to be taken by the prosecution in respect of unduly lenient sentences. This aspect of the 1993 Act is discussed below, 255.

ARREST

Absence of solicitor during interrogation In *The People v Cullen*, Court of Criminal Appeal, 30 March 1993, the Court (Finlay CJ, Morris and Carney JJ) declined to address the issue as to whether a person detained in garda custody had an absolute right to the presence of a solicitor while being interrogated. The Court noted that, in *The People v Healy (P.)* [1990] 2 IR 73; [1990] ILRM 313 (see the 1989 Review, 137-9), the Supreme Court upheld a right of reasonable access, and that the Gardaí had the obligation not to interfere with that right by any conscious or deliberate act. In the *Cullen* case, it was conceded that the Gardaí had made efforts to contact the solicitor to which the defendant sought access, including placing the defendant in telephone contact with the solicitor's office. Ultimately, the efforts to secure the solicitor's attendance proved in vain. The defendant argued that any statements made during garda custody were inadmissible in the absence of his nominated solicitor.

The Court avoided the issue as to whether there was an absolute right to the presence of a solicitor by pointing out that, although such a right had never been considered before in previous case law, it was not contested that it was necessary to show a causative link between any claimed constitutional right concerning access to a solicitor and the evidence impugned in the case. The Court found that, in the particular circumstances of this case, there was no causative connection between the absence of the solicitor and the evidence tendered in court by the prosecution arising from the defendant's interrogation.

While on this basis the Court managed to avoid the more general issue posed in the case, it seems unlikely, on the basis of the *Healy* case, that the courts would be willing to consider an absolute rule in this area. Similarly, the Supreme Court in *The People v Quilligan (No. 3)* [1993] 2 IR 305 (1992 Review, 255-7), albeit by a 3-2 majority, declined to consider the imposition of an aboslute rule concerning warnings on uncorroborated confessions (but see now s. 10 of the Criminal Procedure Act 1993, discussed below, 228).

BAIL

Changed circumstances In *The People v Hannon*, High Court, 20 December 1993, Kinlen J granted the defendant bail for the Christmas period against an unusual background. The defendant's father had been murdered in July 1993. The defendant, a 19-year-old woman, was then charged with murdering a person believed to have been involved in her father's murder. She had been remanded in custody to face trial. The question then arose as to whether she could be released for the Christmas period. Kinlen J's attention was brought to the fact that, pursuant to s. 2 of the Criminal Justice Act 1960, the temporary release (in effect, the parole) of prisoners could only be ordered in respect of convicted prisoners. Prisoners on remand could only be released by means of an application to the High Court for bail.

Kinlen J was unhappy with the situation thus created for those on remand, particularly where compassionate release might be required for a short time. He stated that, although he was prepared to grant bail in appropriate circumstances for those on remand, he considered that this 'could be more effectively controlled by legislation.'

In the instant case, he accepted garda evidence that, if the defendant were released on bail and returned to her home community, there was a real risk that she would not stand trial as she would be under tremendous pressure locally for what was being portrayed as a 'revenge' killing. However, Kinlen J also noted that the defendant's mother and the other children in the family had made definite plans to spend the Christmas period away from the home community. On this basis, Kinlen J considered that the defendant's circumstances had altered since she had been initially refused bail and he granted bail from 21 to 29 December 1993, subject to a number of conditions, in particular that she would not return to her home community.

Kinlen J also added some comments in his judgment concerning the fact that the issue which arose in the instant case had been highlighted in a number of Annual Reports of Prison Visiting Committees. We discuss this aspect in the Prisons chapter, 469, below.

COMPENSATION

As already indicated at the beginning of this chapter, the Criminal Justice Act 1993 and the Criminal Procedure Act 1993 introduced mechanisms for compensating, respectively, the victims of crime and victims of miscarriages of justice.

Compensation orders: victims of crime   S. 6 of the Criminal Justice Act 1993 introduced the first wide-ranging power by which a court may order a convicted person to pay compensation to 'any person . . . who has suffered [any personal] injury or loss' arising from the offence. While s. 6 was intended primarily to compensate the direct victims of crime, it is clear that s. 6 also applies to those who may be indirectly affected by crime, such as relatives of the victim. The amount of compensation involved cannot exceed what the court considers a person would receive in a civil action.

S. 6 applies to any offence and is not limited to those covered by other sections in the 1993 Act (primarily offences involving violence) though clearly personal injury or loss must result for s. 6 to apply. However, s. 6 defines 'loss', in the context of an offence resulting in death, as 'any matter (including mental distress resulting from the death and funeral expenses) for which damages could be awarded in respect of the death by virtue of Part V of the Civil Liability Act 1961.' It remains to be seen whether this definition of 'loss', with its express reference to 'mental distress' in the context of an offence involving death only, excludes a claim for mental distress by a person other than the direct victim in a non-fatal case.

S. 6 of the 1993 Act repeals and replaces the limited compensation order provided for under ss. 9 to 11 of the Criminal Damage Act 1991 (see the 1991 Review, 134-6). While s. 6 thus involves a very wide extension of previous powers to make such awards, its limitations should also be noted. In effect, it allows for compensation awards to the victims of offenders who are of some means, but provides no redress to victims of impecunious offenders. S. 9 is not by any means a statutory criminal injuries compensation scheme. In this context, it may be noted that while a non-statutory criminal injuries compensation scheme has existed in the State since 1972, its paramaters were severely restricted in 1986 (at the same time that the malicious injuries code was statutorily limited by the Malicious Injuries Act 1986). Until 1986, general damages could be claimed from the Criminal Injuries Compensation Tribunal established by the scheme, but since 1986 only special damages may be awarded. The decision of Carroll J in *A.D. v Ireland* [1994] 1 IR 369 (discussed in the 1992 Review, 137-9) was to the effect that this alteration is not in conflict with the right of bodily integrity under Article 40.3 of the Constitution. Thus, the victim of an impecunious offender remains with limited recourse after the 1993 Act. This may be contrasted with the position of the victim of a miscarriage of justice under the Criminal Procedure Act 1993, to which we now turn.

Compensation for miscarriages of justice   S. 9 of the Criminal Procedure Act 1993 provides that, where a conviction has been quashed by the Court of Criminal Appeal under s. 2 of the Act on the basis of a miscarriage of justice or a pardon has been given pursuant to s. 7 of the Act (on both of which see 211, above), the person involved may apply to the Minister for Justice for compensation arising out of such quashed conviction or the convcition on which the pardon was based. While s. 9(4) provides that the compensation shall be 'of such amount as may be determined by the Minister for Justice', s. 9(5) also provides that a person dissatisfied with the amount set by the Minister 'may apply to the High Court to determine the amount which the Minister shall pay under this section'. This would thus appear to envisage a full hearing on the appropriate level of compensation to be given, rather than a mere judicial review of the Minister's decision and thus to involve judicially-imposed levels of compensation, reflecting the level which might be awarded in a civil action.

It is also notable that s. 9(2) of the Act provides that a person may choose between applying for compensation from the Minister or instituting an action for damages. An action for damages would not appear a particularly good choice, for example, if a person were released after spending many years in prison on foot of a conviction which, it emerged, had been obtained by means of perjured evidence given by an impecunious person. In such circumstances, the application under s. 9 of the 1993 Act would appear to be the most advantageous choice for the person seeking compensation. This advantage may be contrasted with the failure by the State in the Criminal Justice Act 1993, discussed above, to provide for the victim of a crime who has suffered loss and injury at the hands of an impecunious person convicted of a criminal offence. The victim of crime is given no redress in such circumstances whereas the victim of a miscarriage of justice is provided State-backed redress.

CONTEMPT OF COURT

Reckless disregard for court order   The title of the judgment in *Council of the Bar of Ireland v Sunday Business Post Ltd*, High Court, 30 March 1993 may be somewhat misleading as it in fact involved a motion for contempt of court brought by the plaintiff Council of the Bar of Ireland against the publishers of *The Sun* newspaper, News Group Newspapers Ltd, its editor and a journalist employed by News Group. However, the motion for contempt arose from proceedings instituted by the Council against the publishers of the newspaper the *Sunday Business Post*, the defendants named in the title to the proceedings.

In November 1992, the Professional Practices Committee of the Council began to investigate a complaint that a junior counsel had acted in breach of the Professional Code of Conduct of the Bar through certain conduct which involved a senior counsel. Both counsel had been retained by different parties who were involved in the Tribunal of Inquiry into the Beef Industry: see the Administrative Law chapter, 11, above. The Committee wrote to the senior counsel involved requesting, in confidence, an account of matters relevant to the investigation. The senior counsel sent by reply a letter of 12 January 1993, enclosing a statement dated 3 January 1993.

The Committee became aware that the *Sunday Business Post* had wrongfully obtained a copy of the letter and, in the absence of an undertaking not to publish, the Bar Council issued a plenary summons claiming, *inter alia*, an injunction restraining publication on the ground of what it claimed was the confidential nature of the letter and its contents. An interlocutory injunction dated 5 March 1993 restrained the proprietors of the *Sunday Business Post* 'and any person having notice of the order' from using the confidential information contained in the letter of 12 January 1993 'or any part thereof' for any purpose and 'from publishing the same or the contents of the same or otherwise from exploiting the said confidential information or any part thereof.'

The motion for contempt of court then arose from an article in *The Sun* of 12 March 1993 which contained extracts from the letter as well as references to some of its contents. In a later article in the issue of *The Sun* of 15 March 1993, the paper claimed that it had hit the headlines 'after revealing details of the letter all Ireland is talking about.'

The motion for contempt was heard by Costello J who commented that it was clear from both articles that 'the author of the articles was well aware of the existence of the court order restraining publication of the letter' and that 'the article [of 12 March] constituted a clear, deliberate and blatant contempt of the court's order of 5 March. . . .'

The respondents to the motion had argued, *inter alia*, that they believed that, because the order of 5 March was not served on 'The Sun', they were not bound by its terms and thus did not knowingly breach its terms and should not be found guilty of criminal contempt. Costello J rejected this defence:

> I am, of course, aware that this application relates to an allegation of criminal contempt of court. But contempt may occur through a reckless failure to ascertain the legal consequences of a court's order just as much

as from a deliberate flouting of it, and I think that such recklessness would have occurred in this case if the respondents had failed to take legal advice on the significance of an order the contents of which they were aware.

In the instant case, Costello J was clearly of the view that the respondents had been reckless in failing to ascertain the significance of the order of 5 March. He categorised the publication as having 'nullified, at least in part' the Bar Council's attempts to protect the confidentiality of the letter of 12 January and it thus constituted a 'most serious interference with the administration of justice.'

In deciding on the penalty to be imposed, Costello J had regard to the fact that other newspapers also had access to the letter but had refrained from publishing it in deference to the court order of 5 March. He commented that it therefore appeared that *The Sun* had gained financially form its wrongful act at the expense of its law-abiding competitors. In order to mark the seriousness of the respondents' wrongful act, the court imposed a fine of £25,000 on *News Group Newspapers Ltd*, a fine of £5,000 on the editor of *The Sun* and a fine of £5,000 on the writer of the article.

For an account of the outcome of the disciplinary proceedings referred to in this case, see the discussion in the Barristers chapter, 43, above.

Suspended sentence *Quinn v Special Criminal Court*, High Court, 30 July 1993 involved an unsuccessful challenge on judicial review to what appeared to be the use of a form of suspended sentence for contempt of court imposed on a reluctant witness: see the discussion of the case below, 234-6.

CONTEMPT OF TRIBUNALS

In *Kiberd v Mr Justice Hamilton* [1992] ILRM 574; [1992] 2 IR 257, the applicant, a journalist, had written an article which appeared in the *Sunday Business Post* newspaper concerning information which was to form the basis for evidence to be given to the Tribunal of Inquiry into the Beef Industry. In the wake of, *inter alia*, allegations contained in an ITV *World in Action* TV programme a Tribunal of Inquiry had been established pursuant to resolutions of both Houses of the Oireachtas and, consequently, was conferred with the powers contained in the Tribunals of Inquiry (Evidence) Acts 1921 and 1979: see the 1992 Review, 6. Included in these Acts are the power to compel attendance of witnesses and the possibility of criminal charges being initiated for impeding the course of the tribunal, that is contempt of the tribunal.

The applicant was called before the Tribunal, but in giving evidence before it, he refused to reveal the sources for the information on which his article had been based. The respondent chairman of the Tribunal ruled that the applicant was required to reveal such sources and that he enjoyed no privilege of non-disclosure in this respect. The applicant applied for judicial review of this ruling, seeking to have it quashed. In the High Court, Geoghegan J refused to quash the respondent's decision.

In his judgment, he did not refer to the decision of the Court of Criminal Appeal delivered by Walsh J in *In re O'Kelly* (1974) 106 ILTR 97. In the *O'Kelly* case the Court had stated that the journalist enjoys no greater immunity in respect of confidential information than any other citizen, the leading decision of the Supreme Court in *Murphy v Dublin Corporation* [1972] IR 215 being cited in support in *O'Kelly*. Geoghegan J concluded in *Kiberd* merely, that the respondent chairman had not acted *ultra vires* and did not expressly address whether the applicant was entitled to rely on any claim to confidentiality in respect of his sources.

At first sight, it might be argued against the *Kiberd* case that it appears to conflict with what are, admittedly, the later decisions of the courts in 1993 in which claims of confidentiality before the Tribunal were upheld in respect of members of the Houses of the Oireachtas, that is TDs and senators: see *Attorney General v Mr Justice Hamilton (No. 2)* [1993] ILRM 821; [1993] 3 IR 227; *Goodman International v Mr Justice Hamilton (No. 2)* [1993] 3 IR 307 and *Goodman International v Mr Justice Hamilton (No. 3)* [1993] 3 IR 320: see the discussion in the Constitutional Law chapter, 165-9, above. However, it must be admitted that the 1993 cases were based in large measure on the acceptance that members of the Houses of the Oireachtas are granted an express privilege by Article 15.13 of the Constitution and that this weighed heavily with the courts in the 1993 cases. For this reason, it may be argued that *Kiberd* remains consistent with the case law which recognises few exceptions to the rule that evidence must be disclosed in order to do justice. Thus, it might be argued that, even if the *Kiberd* case had been brought on appeal to the Supreme Court, the decision of Geoghegan J would have been upheld. Unfortunately, not only was no appeal brought in *Kiberd*, but the 1993 decisions referred to did not involve a discussion of the status of the *Kiberd* decision in the light of these later cases.

However, on the general question, it is true to say that journalistic confidentiality has been the subject of quite conflicting judicial and legislative solutions. It is the case that the United States Supreme Court, in line with most other common law courts of last resort, has declined to recognise a general claim to journalistic privilege. However, a number of States in the United States have enacted what are usually referred to as 'shield' laws in order to protect journalists in certain cases: see generally on this area

McGonagle, *A Textbook on Media Law* (Gill and Macmillan, 1996), 146-7. The UK Contempt of Court Act 1981 also contains a limited form of privilege even in the context of court proceedings which are, arguably, more central to the administration of justice than is a tribunal of inquiry. In that context, it is of interest to note that the applicant in *Kiberd* was not, ultimately, prosecuted under the 1921 and 1979 Acts for contempt of the Tribunal of Inquiry into the Beef Industry. With a twist of some irony, however, the journalist whose *World in Action* programme was instrumental in establishing the Tribunal, Susan O'Keeffe, was charged under s. 5 of the 1921 Act, as amended by the 1979 Act, in respect of her refusal to reveal to the Tribunal the sources of certain information which had formed the basis for allegations contained in that programme.

The trial of these charges, *The People v O'Keeffe*, took place in the Dublin Circuit Criminal Court in January 1995. The opening day of the case was attended by a large amount of publicity, including a picket by Irish members of the National Union of Journalists: *Irish Times*, 27 January 1995, 5. The level of political interest in the case may be guaged from the fact that, on the opening day of the trial, two opposition parties announced the publication of Bills to confer some form of privilege in respect of journalistic confidentiality. Indeed there were indications that the procedure for granting a pardon to the journalist in question under the Criminal Procedure Act 1993 was being actively canvassed and considered in government circles: *Irish Times*, 27 January 1995, 8.

In the event, such speculation became redundant when, on the second day of the trial, the prosecution case collapsed: *Irish Times*, 28 January 1995, 13. The newspaper report of the case would appear to indicate that the collapse centred on the fact that the actual charge against the defendant alleged that she had been in contempt of the tribunal in that she had uttered the words 'Yes. I'm not willing to provide that list.' The trial judge, Judge Lynch, acceded to a defence submission that, under s. 5 of the 1921 Act as amended by the 1979 Act, a charge could not be based on the making of an incriminatory statement. The trial judge then declined a prosecution application to delete the words in question from the charge, and he then directed the jury to enter a not guilty verdict on the charge.

While the precise basis of the trial judge's refusal to alter the charge is not clear from the newspaper report, there were indications from that report that the prosecution had some difficulty in producing the individual stenographer who had taken the note of the relevant portion of the defendant journalist's evidence to the Tribunal in which she had refused to reveal her sources of information. Prosecution counsel is reported as having 'agreed that he could not establish that Ms O'Keeffe had uttered the alleged words' and the newspaper report also refers to the fact that the prosecution then sought to serve additional information on the defence, which the trial judge ruled out, accepting defence counsel's submission that this evidence 'would change the basis of the case.' It may be that this was the basis on which the trial judge declined to allow an amendment of the summons in the case, though in the absence of a transcript of the hearing, this is somewhat speculative.

In any event, it would appear that the outcome of the case was that legislation to provide for confidentiality of journalists' sources may be enacted by the Oireachtas: see *Irish Times*, 28 January 1995, 11. Any such legislation will be discussed in a future Review.

CORPORATE BODIES

In *Truloc Ltd v McMenamin* [1994] 1 ILRM 151, O'Hanlon J dealt, *inter alia*, with the circumstances in which a corporate body may be charged with a criminal offence: see the discussion in the Safety and Health chapter, 472, below.

COURT OF CRIMINAL APPEAL

The different effects of the Criminal Justice Act 1993 and the Criminal Procedure Act 1993 on the jurisdiction of the Court of Criminal Appeal are considered above, 210, and below, 228.

Re-hearing of appeal refused In *The People v Fitzgerald (No. 2)*, Court of Criminal Appeal, 1 February 1993, the Court (O'Flaherty, Keane and Barr JJ), in an *ex tempore* judgment, refused to re-hear an application for leave to appeal against sentence where the applicant sought to adduce new evidence which, he claimed, had not been available at his previous hearing: see *The People v Fitzgerald*, Court of Criminal Appeal, 22 July 1991 (1991 Review, 174, 182). The Court held that such an application would be in breach of s. 29 of the Courts of Justice Act 1924. The Criminal Procedure Act 1993 provides, of course, that such a re-hearing is now possible, though the Court retains a power to decline to hear an application for a re-hearing. It is notable that, in the *Fitzgerald* case, the Court examined the material proffered by the applicant and concluded that it was more appropriate for consideration by the executive in the exercise of the clemency powers rather than for the courts on the application of sentencing principles. It seems unlikely that the operation of the Criminal Procedure Act 1993 would, in the particular circumstances of this case, have led to a much different outcome.

CRIMINAL DAMAGE

Compensation orders The procedure for awarding compensation under ss. 9 to 11 of the Criminal Damage Act 1991 (see the 1991 Review, 135-6) have been repealed and replaced by the wider powers contained in the Criminal Justice Act 1993: see 216, above.

DELAY

Summary trial *Director of Public Prosecutions v Byrne* [1993] ILRM 475 (HC); [1994] 2 ILRM 91 (SC) is a highly important decision concerning delays involved in bringing summary proceedings to hearing.

The defendant had been charged with the drink-driving offence contained in s. 49 of the Road Traffic Act 1961, as amended. Since this was a case concerning delay, it is helpful to use the sequence of dates relevant to the case as set out by Denham J in her judgment in the Supreme Court:

— 19 April 1991, date of alleged offence,

— 27 May 1991, Gardaí applied for summons,

— 19 December 1991, summons issued,

— summons served shortly after and

— 12 February 1992, case came on for hearing.

It appeared that the summonses in cases such as the present are issued by means of computer-generated processes but no specific reason was advanced by the prosecution as to why a delay had occurred in the instant case. At the defendant's trial in the District Court on 12 February 1992, it was argued that the delay of almost 10 months between the date of the alleged offence and the hearing of the case, particularly in the absence of an explanation by the prosecution, was unreasonable and that the summons should be dismissed on that ground. The District Court judge accepted this argument and dismissed the case. The Director of Public Prosecutions applied for a case stated.

In the High Court, Geoghegan J ([1993] ILRM 475) upheld the decision of the District Court judge. He stated that:

the delay in issuing the summons was quite obviously indefensible in the absence of explanation. The onus would have been on the prosecution to produce such explanation. This is not a case where proof by the defendant of actual prejudice would be necessary.

On the issue of requiring the prosecution to produce an explanation for the delay, Geoghegan J followed the approach taken by Barr J in his *ex tempore* judgment delivered in *Director of Public Prosecutions v Burnby*, High Court, 24 July 1989. Geoghegan J noted that certain aspects of the Burnby decision had not been approved by Carroll J in her judgment in *Director of Public Prosecutions v Bouchier Hayes*, High Court, 19 December 1992 (see the 1992 Review, 247-8), but he considered that Barr J's approach amounted to no more than a statement that summonses be issued within a reasonable time after they have been applied for and be served within a reasonable time after issue.

Given that this area has been the subject of a number of High Court judgments (see, for example, the 1992 Review, 246-8), it was not perhaps surprising that the Director of Public Prosecutions chose to appeal Geoghegan J's decision to the Supreme Court. Although the decision of the Court (Finlay CJ, O'Flaherty, Egan, Blayney and Denham JJ) was delivered in March 1994 ([1994] 2 ILRM 91), we discuss it here in view of its importance. In essence, the Court, by a 3-2 majority (O'Flaherty, Blayney and Denham; Finlay CJ and Egan J dissenting) reversed Geoghegan J and rejected the defendant's arguments, and in the process overruled the decision of Barr J in the *Burnby* case.

The Supreme Court judgments in the case can be broken down into three segments. First, the Court examined whether it is for the prosecution or the defence to deal with the question of delay. The second matter addressed was whether the delay in the instant case was so unreasonable as to justify dismissal of the case without proof of actual prejudice to the defendant. Finally, the Court considered the general principles on which cases may be dismissed for delay.

On the first point, the majority held that Barr J had been incorrect in the *Burnby* case in suggesting that the onus was on the prosecution to show that a case has been brought within a reasonable time. On the contrary, the majority considered that, where a valid summons was before a court, it was a matter for the defendant to produce evidence to indicate there was excessive delay or other factors requiring the case to be dismissed. In the instant case the majority considered that the defendant had not discharged the onus on him in this respect.

On the second major point addressed by the Court, the majority was of the view that the delay of ten months between the time of the alleged offence and the hearing of the case was not so unreasonable as to justify its dismissal without proof of prejudice to the defendant. In her judgment, Denham J noted that, whether a summons is issued pursuant to the Petty Sessions (Ireland) Act 1851 or the Courts (No. 3) Act 1986, the statutory scheme envisaged issuing and serving a summons after the application for the summons is made.

Since the summons could be applied for any time within the six month period, she pointed out that the legislation envisaged a time lapse greater than six months. In this, her approach is very similar to that of Carroll J in the *Bouchier Hayes* case, referred to above. On this basis, she concluded that as a general principle the delay in the instant case could not be categorised as so unreasonable as to result in dismissal of the case. However, it might be noted that Denham J sounded a note of warning that may be of relevance in future cases:

> The fact that approximately eight months of the elapsed time in this case occurred as a result of a delay in the court's issuing process is not a matter, or a delay, to be endorsed by this or any court, especially in the absence of an explanation. The fact that it is computer-based should have made it even more efficient. It is highly undesirable that the court process should be as lengthy as in this case. It is a matter to be addressed by the appropriate authorities as a matter of urgency. Further, there may be an issue of statutory duty to be analysed.

This straw in the wind might suggest that, if the appropriate State authorities were to fail to address problems of delay, then a similar case in the future might be approached quite differently.

The third and final issue addressed by the Court was the general approach it should take to delay. On this, the Court unanimously endorsed the view expressed by Powell J, delivering the decision of the US Supreme Court in *Barker v Wingo*, 407 US 514 (1972). All members of the Court noted that the Sixth Amendment to the US Constitution contained a specific right to a speedy trial, an explicit guarantee not contained in the Irish Constitution. However, the judges also took the view that a right to a speedy trial, recognised for example in *The State (O'Connell) v Fawsitt* [1986] ILRM 639; [1986] IR 362, arose by necessary implication from the guarantee to a trial 'in due course of law' contained in Article 38.1, which the judges were prepared to equate to the 'due process' clause in the Fourteenth Amendment to the US Constitution. Denham J noted in this regard: 'An accused is entitled to have a trial free of abuse of process'.

In *Byrne*, the Supreme Court endorsed the view expressed by Powell J in the *Barker* case that it was required to balance the freedom and rights of the individual with the requirements of an ordered society, and that in cases involving delay this was to be done on a case-by-case (*ad hoc*) basis, though by reference to four factors: the length of delay, the reason for delay, the defendant's assertion of his right and prejudice to the defendant. On the question of prejudice, the Supreme Court again agreed with Powell J's list of three interests of the defendant which the right to a speedy trial was designed to protect: to prevent oppressive pre-trial incarceration; to minimise the anxiety and concern of the accused; and to limit the possibility that the defence will be impaired. It is notable that the last matter was regarded as the most serious, as this held the potential of skewing the fairness of the entire system.

While Finlay CJ and Egan J agreed with the majority on the general principles applicable in cases of this kind, they were not prepared to interfere with what they regarded as the District Court judge's exercise of discretion in deciding that the delay in the case had been unreasonble. In addition, the minority would have held that the defendant's right to a speedy trial, applying the principles in the *Barker* case, had been infringed. The majority, on the other hand, applying the same principles, concluded that, in the absence of any specific evidence of prejudice, the delay had not infringed the defendant's rights.

Having regard to the case-by-case (*ad hoc*) approach favoured in the *Barker* case, and endorsed in *Byrne*, it must be said that decisions will continue to be made having regard to the particular circumstances which arise in individual cases. Nonetheless, the decision in *Byrne* allows for future cases to be approached by reference to a clear framework of basic principles.

Trial on indictment   In *Cahalane v Murphy*, High Court, 13 August 1993; [1994] 2 ILRM 383 (SC), the principles enunicated in *The State (O'Connell) v Fawsitt* [1986] ILRM 639; [1986] IR 362 and in *Director of Public Prosecutions v Byrne* [1993] ILRM 475 (HC); [1994] 2 ILRM 91 (SC), above, were applied in the context of a trial on indictment. We will return to the Supreme Court decision in *Cahalane* in the 1994 Review.

DIRECTOR OF PUBLIC PROSECUTIONS

Addition of charges   In *O'Connell v Director of Public Prosecutions*, High Court, 30 July 1993; [1994] 2 ILRM 21 (SC), the High Court and Supreme Court dealt with the power of the Director of Public Prosections to add charges to an indictment after a case has been sent forward for trial. We will discuss the Supreme Court's judgment, delivered in March 1994, in the 1994 Review.

Lesser offence charged   In 1993, the Supreme Court rejected the proposition that the Director of Public Prosecutions is under a general obligation to prosecute an accused person for the most serious offence which the evidence might indicate. In *The People v Rock (P.)* [1994] 1 ILRM 66, the Court held that a charge of simple larceny under s. 2 of the Larceny Act 1916 could validly be brought by the Director even where evidence discloses an aggravated form of larceny for which different penalties are provided for under other provisions of the 1916 Act: see the discussion below, 128-9. To the same effect, see *K.M. v Director of Public Prosecutions*, High Court, 21 June 1993, below, 268.

Prosecutorial discretion In *H. v Director of Public Prosections*, High Court, 26 July 1993; [1994] 2 ILRM 285 (SC), the High Court and Supreme Court declined to compel the Director of Public Prosections to bring criminal charges against two men who, the applicant alleged, had committed various sexual offences against her young son. As the decision of the Supreme Court in this case was delivered in May 1994, we will discuss in the 1994 Review the issues arising in this case concerning review of the prosecutorial discretion vested in the Director.

DISTRICT COURT

Adjournment The review of the discretion of a District Court judge as to whether to adjourn a criminal hearing was considered by the Supreme Court in *O'Callaghan v Clifford* [1993] 3 IR 603 in the context of a revenue prosecution: this will be discussed in the 1994 Review.

Advance furnishing of statements In *Director of Public Prosecutions v Doyle*, High Court, 14 May 1993; [1994] 1 ILRM 529 (SC), Geoghegan J considered the question whether there was an obligation on the prosecution in summary trials to furnish to the defence, in advance of trial, the evidence on which the prosecution intends to proceed. The Supreme Court, in its judgment in 1994 on appeal in this case, held that the obligation could arise in certain circumstances. We will discuss this important decision in full in the 1994 Review. For previous High Court decisions in this area, see the 1990 Review, 197 and the 1991 Review, 145-7.

EVIDENCE

Burden of proof *Hardy v Ireland*, High Court, 10 September 1992; Supreme Court, 18 March 1993 was an unsuccessful challenge to the constitutional validity of s. 4 of the Explosive Substances Act 1883 and concerned the extent to which the evidential burden may be shifted from the prosecution to the defence: see the discussion in the Constitutional Law chapter, 172, above.

Confessions: warning to jury   We have already noted that the Criminal Procedure Act 1993 contains the legislative reaction to the fallout from recent well-publicised cases of miscarriages of justice, including the Guildford Four and Birmingham Six cases in Britain and, in Ireland, the Nicky Kelly case: see 210, above. In addition to changes to the criminal appellate jurisdiction of the Court of Criminal Appeal, which we have already discussed, s. 10 of the 1993 Act introduced a fundamental change in the evidential value of an uncorroborated confession or statement.

It will be recalled that, in the wake of the release of the Guildford Four in 1989, the government established a *Committee of Inquiry into Criminal Procedure*, chaired by Judge Frank Martin. The terms of reference of the Committee were rather narrow, precluding it from recommending whether there was a need for a warning on the dangers involved in convicting a person on the basis of an uncorroborated confession: see the 1990 Review, 240-2. In 1992, the Supreme Court decided, by a majority, that such a warning was not required in all cases: see *The People v Quilligan and O'Reilly (No. 3)* [1993] 2 IR 305 (1992 Review, 255-7). However, despite the terms of reference of the Martin Committee and of the decision in the *Quilligan* case, s. 10 of the 1993 Act now requires such a mandatory warning in trials on indictment.

It is notable that s. 10 expressly uses the word 'confession' in this context, rather than the more traditional phrase 'incriminating statement'. Whether s. 10 will require trial judges to use what might be regarded as the more graphic word 'confession' in the future remains to be seen. The use of the word 'confession' rather than the more neutral 'statement' may indicate to jurors a particular attitude to such admissions. Of course, s. 10(2) provides that it shall not be necessary for a trial judge to use a particular form of words in giving the required warning, and this is similar to that which applies in relation to the visual identification warning required pursuant to *The People v Casey (No. 2)* [1963] IR 33 (as to which see, for example, the 1991 Review, 154, and the 1992 Review, 264). Nonetheless, it would appear difficult to avoid the word 'confession' when giving a warning to juries in the application of s. 10, whatever the form the warning takes. How this will affect juries in the future remains to be seen.

Corroboration: sexual assault   In *The People v D.*, Court of Criminal Appeal, 27 July 1993, the Court (Egan, Lynch and Lavan JJ), in an *ex tempore* judgment, quashed the conviction of the defendant on the ground that the trial judge had erred on a question of what constituted corroboration. The defendant had been charged with indecent assault of his ten year old daughter. The trial judge had correctly defined corroboration for the jury. However, the error occurred when the trial judge dealt with medical evidence that the daughter's hymen had been interfered with. The medical examination in question had occurred a year after the offence was alleged to have been committed and the medical practitioner was unable to state exactly when the interference had occurred. This evidence thus did not amount to corroboration in that it did not directly implicate the defendant in the offence. While the Court noted that the trial judge had stated at the beginning of his charge that corroboration was not absoultely necessary in this case, the Court of Criminal Appeal considered that the danger existed that the jury may have been left with the impression that corroboration did exist in the case. On this basis, the Court quashed the conviction and ordered a re-trial.

Doli incapax In *K.M. v Director of Public Prosecutions*, High Court, 21 June 1993, Morris J dealt, *inter alia*, with the proof required to rebut the presumption of *doli incapax*: see the discussion of the case below, 268.

Video links The Criminal Evidence Act 1992 (Sections 12, 13, 18 and 19) (Commencement) Order 1993 (SI No. 38) and the Criminal Evidence Act 1992 (sections 13, 15(4), 16, 17 and 19) (Commencement) Order 1993 (SI No. 288), which brought into effect certain aspects of the Criminal Evidence Act 1992 concerning video links, were discussed in the 1992 Review, 263-4.

We should also note here that s. 11 of the Criminal Justice Act 1993, which is discussed below, 248, amended s. 7 of the Criminal Procedure Act 1967 so that, in respect respect of evidence given at the preliminary examination, a written deposition is not required.

Visual identification: informal method In *The People v Behan*, Court of Criminal Appeal, 1 February 1993, the Court (O'Flaherty, Keane and Barr JJ), in an *ex tempore* judgment, upheld the conviction of the applicant where the evidence given included an informal identification of the applicant by the victim of the crime. The identification took the form of the victim being brought some days after the commission of the crime to the District (Children's) Court where, in the Court's precincts, she picked out the applicant from a number of other people who were also in the Court's precincts at the time. The Court stressed that the victim had previously known the applicant and reiterated that, where this is not the case, a formal identification parade was the ideal method of providing for identification. The Court also noted that the trial judge had made clear to the jury the dangers of convicting on identification evidence, in accordance with *The People v Casey (No. 2)* [1963] IR 33.

EXPLOSIVE SUBSTANCES

In *Hardy v Ireland*, High Court, 10 September 1992; Supreme Court, 18 March 1993 (discussed in the Constitutional Law chapter, 172, above) the constitutional validity of s. 4 of the Explosive Substances Act 1883 was upheld.

EXTRADITION

Correspondence of offences In *Aamand v Smithwick*, High Court, 21 December 1993; [1995] 1 ILRM 61 (SC), Lavan J rejected the suggestion that the provisions of the Danish Penal Code concerning the possession of cocaine did not correspond to the provisions concerning possession in the Misuse of Drugs Acts 1977 and 1984. He therefore upheld the order made by the respondent judge of the District Court that the applicant be extradited to Denmark. The decision of Lavan J was upheld in July 1994 by the Supreme Court, and we will return to discuss this case in more detail in the 1994 Review.

Political offence The scope of the political offence exception to extradition was further considered by Lynch J in *McGuire v Attorney General* [1994] 2 ILRM 344.

Pursuant to Part II of the Extradition Act 1965, the District Court had ordered the detention of the applicant so that the Minister for Justice might order his extradition to the United States of America. He was charged in the United States with (a) conspiring to violate the Arms Export Control Act, in violation of 18 USC 371, (b) conspiring to injure or destroy property of a foreign government, in violation of 18 USC 956 and (c) being in possession of property in aid of foreign insurgents in violation of 18 USC 957. In ordering extradition, the District Court found that there was correspondence between these charges and offences under Irish law, and that all other formalities required by Part II of the 1965 Act had been complied with. The applicant applied to the High Court seeking an order for his release pursuant to Article 40.4.2° of the Constitution, on the grounds that the alleged offences were political offences or offences connected with political offences. The applicant did not claim a political motive or purpose against the United States, but that anything he might have done in the United States was done with a political motive and for a political purpose against the government of the United Kingdom in relation to its rule and policy in Northern Ireland.

Lynch J refused the application for release. In essence, he followed the majority decision in *Cheng v Governor of Pentonville Prison* [1973] AC 931 to the effect that to constitute a political offence the activity the subject matter of the charge or conviction must have a political motive or purpose against or relating to the requesting State. Since no such claim was made in the instant case, he held that the offences with which the applicant was charged were not political offences.

Third party discovery In *Fusco v O'Dea*, High Court, 21 April 1993; [1994] 2 ILRM 389 (SC), Lynch J refused to make an order for discovery against the government of Great Britain and Northern Ireland under O.31, r.29 of the Rules of the Superior Courts 1986 in the context of an extradition case involving the plaintiff. This decision was upheld by the Supreme Court in July 1994, and we will return to that decision in the 1994 Review.

FIREARMS AND OFFENSIVE WEAPONS

Firearms dealer: records The European Communities (Acquisition and Possession of Weapons and Ammunition) Regulations 1993 (SI No. 362) implemented, *inter alia*, Articles 10 and 11 of Directive 93/15/EEC on the placing on the market and supervision of explosives for civil uses. Articles 10 and 11 of this 1993 Directive deal with ammunition. They also implemented Directive 91/477/EEC on the control of the acquisition and possession of weapons and we deal with this aspect of the Regulations below, 232. Reg.2(3) of the 1993 Regulations provide that they shall be construed as one with the Firearms Acts 1925 to 1990.

In relation to Directive 93/15/EEC, Reg.3 of the Regulations requires a firearms dealer to retain particulars of every transaction in the register kept by the dealer under s. 12 of the Firearms Act 1925 for a period of five years after the date of transaction, even where the dealer ceases to be a firearms dealer. Reg.4 provides that a person under the age of 18 years shall not be entitled to hold a firearms certificate or permit other than for hunting or target shooting.

Intent to endanger life In *The People v Farrell (M.)* [1993] ILRM 743, the Court of Criminal Appeal (Blayney, Lardner and Flood JJ) considered the ingredients of the offence of possession of a firearm with intent to endanger life, as contained in s. 14(a) of the Firearms Act 1925, as amended. The defendant was admittedly part of a group of four men who, armed with shotguns, had robbed a post office. They walked from the post office and were followed by a passing Garda patrol car. Shortly after, one member of the gang fired a shot in the air and then immediately ran towards the Garda car. The Gardaí got out of the patrol car, believing their lives were threatened, and the gang of four then got into the car and drove off. As they did so, the Gardaí moved back towards the car and one of the gang leaned out of one of the squad car's windows and pointed the gun at the Gardaí.

On this evidence, the defendant was convicted in the Special Criminal Court, *inter alia*, of possession of a firearm with intent to endanger life. On appeal, it was argued on his behalf that the evidence did not indicate any specific intent to endanger life, noting in particular that the only occasion on which the gun had been fired was in the air and that the correct construction to put on the gun being aimed at the Gardaí was that it was a threat and no more. The Court of Criminal Appeal rejected this suggestion, noting that the offence under s. 14(a) of the Firearms Act 1925 did not require an intent to kill, but an intent to endanger life. The Court commented:

> A person must be taken to intend the natural and probable consequences of his acts and one of the natural and probable consequences of pointing a loaded gun at someone is that his life is endangered since, altogether apart from any definite intention to fire the gun, there is always the risk of its being discharged accidentally. And this risk was undoubtedly present on both of the occasions on which one of the guns was aimed at the Gardaí.

It therefore upheld the conviction in the trial court, holding that there was ample evidence to support the conclusion of intent to endanger life.

Intra-Community travel   The European Communities (Acquisition and Possession of Weapons and Ammunition) Regulations 1993 (SI No. 362) perform two quite distinct, though connected, functions. First, they implement Directive 91/477/EEC on the control of the acquisition and possession of weapons. Second, they implement Articles 10 and 11 of Directive 93/15/EEC on the placing on the market and supervision of explosives for civil uses. Article 10 and 11 of this latter Directive deal with ammunition. We deal with this aspect of the Regulations above, 231. Reg.2(3) of the 1993 Regulations provide that they shall be construed as one with the Firearms Acts 1925 to 1990.

In relation to Directive 91/477/EEC, the 1993 Regulations provide that the holder of a firearms certificate under the Firearms Acts 1925 to 1990 who wishes to travel to another member State with a firearm is entitled to a European Firearms Pass (in the format contained in the Schedule to the Regulations) which can only be issued by a Garda superintendent. Other provisions concern the procedure by which firearms may be transferred within the Community in accordance with the terms of the 1991 Directive. For these purposes, the Regulations provide that the Firearms Acts 1925 to

1990 are adapted to meet the terms of the 1991 Directive. In addition, Reg.12(1) provides for an explicit amendment to s. 4(1) of the Firearms Act 1964 by the insertion therein of 'or public security' after 'public safety'. S. 4(1) relates to the making of Orders by the Minister requiring the surrender to An Garda Síochána of firearms and weapons and Reg.12(2) provides that any such Orders must in future be notified to the European Commission.

JUDICIAL REVIEW

Discretion to quash: trial not in due course of law In *Duff v Mangan* [1994] 1 ILRM 91, the Supreme Court dealt with a case which related back to its decision in *The State (Clarke) v Roche* [1987] ILRM 309; [1986] IR 619, in which it had held invalid the procedure by which summonses had been issued by District Court clerks.

The applicant had appeared in the District Court in January 1986 to answer a number of summonses under the Road Traffic Act 1961. At the hearing, the applicant's solicitor submitted that the summonses grounding the complaints, having been signed by a District Court clerk, were invalid and the court had no jurisdiction to hear the complaints. The respondent District Court judge refused to accede to the submission and proceeded to convict the defendant. The defendant then lodged an appeal to the Circuit Court. After a number of adjournments, pending the decision in *The State (Clarke) v. Roche*, the appeal was listed for 7 June 1988. However, as the applicant had recieved only four days notice of the appeal, he sought an adjournment which the prosecution resisted and the appeal was later struck out.

On judicial review, Lardner J refused the applicant relief, noting in particular that the appellant had not attended the Circuit Court appeal and that the validity of summonses was a matter for the defence to raise and establish. On appeal, however, the Supreme Court (Finlay CJ, Blayney and Denham JJ) quashed the District Court conviction.

Denham J, in delivering the only judgment, addressed first the core issue raised in the case, namely the validity of the summonses. She concluded that the respondent had erred in law, though within jurisdiction, in determining that he could hear the case without an inquiry as to the whether the complaints and summonses had been validly issued, but that he had exceeded his jurisdiction in then proceeding to hear the case.

The complicating feature of the case was, of course, that the applicant had initiated an appeal to the Circuit Court though, as we saw, this was struck out. As to whether *certiorari* lay in these circumstances, Denham J applied the views of Hederman J in *Sweeney v Brophy* [1993] ILRM 449 (SC); [1993]

2 IR 202 (HC & SC) (1992 Review, 268-70) that *certiorari* could be granted in cases where there had been a fundamental failure to observe due course of law even where the alternative remedy of an appeal had been utilised, as by the applicant in the instant case. Here, Denham J considered that as this case had arisen in the midst of developing law on the making of a complaint and the issuing of a summons, it was appropriate to grant the order of *certiorari* and quash the orders against the applicant.

Insufficiency of evidence   In *Roche v Martin* [1993] ILRM 651 (referred to briefly in the Commercial Law chapter, 58, above) Murphy J approved and applied the decision of O'Hanlon J in *Lennon v Clifford* [1993] ILRM 77; [1992] 1 IR 382 (see the 1992 Review, 270 and 519) in refusing the applicant judicial review of his conviction in the District Court, where the applicant asserted merely that the evidence adduced at his trial in the District Court was 'not sufficient.'

Leave to seek judicial review   In *G. v Director of Public Prosecutions* [1994] 1 IR 374, the Supreme Court reversed the refusal of the High Court (Lavan J) to grant leave to the applicant to seek judicial review of his pending criminal trial. The applicant had been charged on 27 counts of sexual assaults on seven girls, all being under 15 years, the charges relating to dates between the years 1967 and 1981. The book of evidence in the case was served on the applicant in June 1993. The applicant sought an order of prohibition preventing his trial, the main argument being centred on the delay between the offences and the commencement of the trial proceedings. Without expressing any view on whether the applicant was entitled to succeed in prohibiting his trial, the Supreme Court (Finlay CJ, Blayney and Denham JJ) unanimously held that, on the facts as established, the applicant had met what Denham J described as the 'light' burden of proof at the leave to apply stage under O.84, r.20 of the Rules of the Superior Courts 1986. Denham J approved the views of Lord Diplock in *R. v Inland Revenue Commissioners, ex p. National Federation of Self-Employed and Small Businesses Ltd* [1982] AC 617 that the leave to apply stage was a filtering process in which the applicant need prove merely that he has an arguable or *prima facie* case.

Remittal after *certiorari*   In *Dineen v Delap*, High Court, 21 October 1993, Morris J, having quashed a conviction on *certiorari*, declined to remit the case to the District Court under O.84, r.26(4) of the Rules of the Superior Courts 1986: see the discussion below, 246. See also the decision of the Supreme Court in *Duff v Mangan* [1994] 1 ILRM 91, above, 233.

Unitary trial   In *Quinn v Special Criminal Court*, High Court, 30 July

1993, Lynch J declined to grant judicial review to the applicant to prevent his further prosecution in the Special Criminal Court on explosives and firearms charges. In the course of the trial, on 24 March 1993 a witness who had been called by the prosecution refused to testify and he was thereupon sentenced to six months imprisonment for contempt of court. The Court adjourned the applicant's trial to 20 April 1993 and also directed that the witness be brought before the Court on that date to give him an opportunity to purge his contempt. On 20 April 1993, the witness stated that he was now willing to give evidence in the case and the Special Criminal Court accordingly ordered his release. By this time, the applicant had sought judicial review of the orders of 24 March 1993 and also sought to prohibit his further prosecution.

As already indicated, Lynch J declined to grant the relief sought, holding that judicial review was an inappropriate remedy. In effect, Lynch J reflected the commonly-expressed view that a criminal trial, particularly of serious charges, should involve a unitary hearing and should not be subjected to collateral attack while the trial is in progress. Citing the views of O'Higgins CJ in *The State (Abenglen Properties Ltd) v Dublin Corporation* [1981] ILRM 54; [1984] IR 381, Lynch J held that to grant *certiorari* in the instant case would be to debase that great remedy and that the applicant should allow the trial to run its course and, if required, to utilise the appellate jurisdiction of the Court of Criminal Appeal rather than that of judicial review.

While Lynch J's general approach has much to commend it, it may be commented that the procedure adopted by the Special Criminal Court in the instant case brought the application for judicial review out of the ordinary. The reluctant witness in the applicant's trial would appear to have been sentenced on 24 March 1993 to a definite term of six months imprisonment for the criminal offence of contempt of court, and this was not a case where the Court had ordered a person detained for an indefinite period for civil contempt of court (on the distinction, see *Keegan v deBurca* [1973] IR 223). Yet, the order of 24 March 1993 also contained within it elements of civil contempt jurisdiction, because the Special Criminal Court directed that the witness be brought before the Court on 20 April 1993 for the purpose of purging his contempt, that is less that one month into his six month sentence. This appears to resemble a suspended sentence, but its use in the contempt context is open to the objection that the contemnor may suffer less punishment by 'co-operating' with the trial court. If a person is found to be in criminal contempt, they must surely serve that sentence, otherwise the use of the suspended sentence concept leaves the possible impression that their evidence may be less reliable. Giving evidence at the end of the full sentence for criminal contempt is one thing, but in the instant case the sentencing court left open the distinct possibility that less than one sixth of the sentence would be served if the contemnor purged his contempt. Presumably, it was on this basis that the applicant applied for the relief sought in the instant case. While Lynch J had authority on his side, it is to be regretted that this novel form of contempt jurisdiction (at least in the sense that the authors are not aware of a similar such sentence coming before the superior courts prior to this case) was not subjected to some scrutiny.

JURY

Majority verdicts and Constitution   The 1993 decision of the Supreme Court in *O'Callaghan v Attorney General* [1993] ILRM 267 (HC); [1993] ILRM 764 (SC); [1992] 1 IR 538 (HC); [1993] 2 IR 17 (SC), in which the Court rejected a challenge to the constitutionality of the majority jury verdict procedure introduced by s. 25 of the Criminal Justice Act 1984, was discussed in the 1992 Review, 222-26.

LARCENY

Receiving: proof that goods stolen   In *The People v O'Hanlon*, Court of Criminal Appeal, 1 February 1993, the Court (O'Flaherty, Keane and Barr JJ), in an *ex tempore* judgment, held that, in a case of receiving stolen goods contrary to s. 33(1) of the Larceny Act 1916, it was an essential proof that the goods in question be shown to be stolen, but not necessarily to prove from whom. In this instance, the Court was prepared to have regard to circumstantial evidence surrounding the case, citing its own decision in *The People v Gilligan (No. 2)* [1992] ILRM 769; [1993] 1 IR 92 (see the 1991 Review, 163, 167). It may be noted that the offence in this case took place before the entry into force of the Larceny Act 1990, which replaced the offence of receiving stolen goods with that of handling stolen goods: see the 1990 Review, 229. The question dealt with in the *O'Hanlon* case would not, of course, be affected by the 1990 Act.

Simple larceny and other offences   In *The People v Rock (P.)* [1994] 1 ILRM 66, the Supreme Court held, in an important clarification of the law, that a conviction for simple larceny under s. 2 of the Larceny Act 1916 is possible even where the evidence discloses an offence provided for under other provisions of the 1916 Act.

The defendant had been charged with simple larceny contrary to s. 2 of the Larceny Act 1916. At his trial in the Circuit Criminal Court, evidence was given which tended to disclose an offence of larceny from the person contrary to s. 14 of the 1916 Act, or an offence of robbery contrary to s. 23 of the 1916 Act, as inserted by s. 5 of the Criminal Law (Jurisdiction) Act 1976. Counsel for the accused, referring to the decision of the Court of Criminal Appeal in *The People v Mills* (1955) 1 Frewen 153, submitted that it was not open to the court to find the accused guilty of simple larceny contrary to s. 2 of the 1916 Act where the evidence disclosed an offence provided for in the other provisions of the said Act. The trial judge accepted this submission and directed the jury to enter a verdict in favour of the accused.

The Director of Public Prosecutions, in exercise of his power of appeal under s. 34 of the Criminal Procedure Act 1967 without prejudice to the verdict entered, requested the Supreme Court to determine whether this decision was correct in law. The Court (Finlay CJ, O'Flaherty, Egan, Blayney and Denham JJ) held that the trial judge had erred in law but had acted correctly in following the *Mills* decision because at the time it had been binding on him. The Court concluded that the *Mills* decision was incorrect and that it must therefore be overruled. In this context, the Court followed its 1968 decision in *The State (Simmonds) v Governor of Portlaoise Prison* (reproduced as an appendix to the *Rock* case at [1994] 1 ILRM 73) and the decision of Finlay P in *The State (Foley) v Carroll* [1980] IR 150.

Delivering the only judgment, O'Flaherty J stated:

> In my judgment the correct statement of the law is that s. 2 of the Larceny Act 1916 is a reference to what was the common law offence of simple larceny. It follows that it is not an offence created by statute and that, therefore, even if circumstances of aggravated larceny or robbery are forthcoming, the prosecution is not precluded from laying the count in the indictment as contrary to s. 2 of the Act. Therefore, I believe that the Mills case should be overruled in respect of this aspect of the decision reached by the Court of Criminal Appeal. Aside from authority, I would conclude in principle as Finlay P did [in the *Foley* case], that if the State decides not to prosecute a person for some aggravated form of larceny but decides to prosecute for simple larceny only, thus confining the case to a lower maximum sentence, I cannot see that such a course of action should be condemned as in any way contrary to the statute or, otherwise, bad in law.

He concluded by agreeing with Finlay P's comment in the *Foley* case that any other result would lead to the anomalous situation that a person charged with simple larceny could avoid conviction by establishing that the offence was aggravated by being accompanied by force, or carried out by use of a threat or whilst armed with an offensive weapon. We may note that the *Rock* case was followed in *K.M. v Director of Public Prosecutions*, High Court, 21 June 1993, below, 268. The *Foley* case had also been previously approved in another context in *Doolan v Director of Public Prosecutions* [1993] ILRM 387: see the 1992 Review, 286-7.

LEGAL AID

Fees The Criminal Justice (Legal Aid) (Amendment) (No. 1) Regulations 1993 (SI No. 56), which took effect retrospectively from 1 January 1992, provided for a 3% increase in the fees payable to solicitors for attandance in the District Court and for appeals to the Circuit Court, and for an increase to solicitors and counsel in respect of visits to prisons and other custodial centres and for certain bail applications. The Criminal Justice (Legal Aid) (Amendment) (No. 2) Regulations 1993 (SI No. 57), which took effect retrospectively from 1 June 1992, superceded SI No. 56 in respect of work conducted under the criminal legal aid regime after 1 June 1992. SI No. 57 provided for a more comprehensive updating of the different fees chargeable under the statutory scheme created by the Criminal Justice (Legal Aid) Act 1962. Both sets of Regulations amounted to a resolution of a serious dispute between criminal law practitioners and the State in respect of fees chargeable under the regime.

Non-attendance in court In *Rock v Governor of St Patrick's Institution*, Supreme Court, 22 March 1993, the applicant had been summoned to appear in the District Court to answer charges of driving a motor car without a driving licence and driving while uninsured. He failed to appear in Court and was sentenced in his absence to six months detention on both charges, the sentences to run consecutively.

The applicant sought an inquiry into his detention under Article 40.4.2° of the Constitution and in the High Court put forward two grounds: first, that he had not been personally served with the summonses to appear in the District Court and second, that the District Court judge, when he formed the view that he would sentence the applicant to a period of imprisonment, should have issued a warrant for the defendant's arrest or otherwise adjourned the case to enable the applicant appear in court and to consider whether to apply for legal aid pursuant to the Criminal Justice (Legal Aid) Act 1962.

In the High Court, Geoghegan J found, first, that as a matter of fact the applicant had been served with the summonses to appear in court and second, that the District Court judge was not required to adjourn the hearing.

The applicant's appeal to the Supreme Court (O'Flaherty, Egan and Blayney JJ) was unanimously dismissed. Delivering the Court's decision, O'Flaherty J noted that, in view of Geoghegan J's clear finding of fact, the applicant could not raise the issue of service of the summons so that his appeal rested solely on arguing that the District Court judge should have adjourned the case to enable the applicant appear and consider whether to seek legal aid. The Court expressed little sympathy for the applicant's claim.

The Court was prepared to assume for the purposes of the instant case only that, since the applicant was 'young, uneducated and indigent' and had received a custodial sentence, the principles laid down in *The State (Healy) v Donoghue* [1976] IR 325 applied to him. However, the Court also pointed out that, even if that was so, the District Court retained a discretion as to whether to secure the attendance of the applicant or to proceed in his absence. While the judge's decision to proceed might have been subject to review if the applicant had been ill or otherwise unable to attend, this was not the case. The Court noted that the applicant had no excuse for his non-attendance. In addition, it was pointed out that the applicant had not chosen to appeal the District Court decision to the Circuit Court but had instead chosen, on being detained in St Patrick's Institution, to apply to the High Court under Article 40.4.2°. O'Flaherty J quoted with approval the decision of the Court in *The State (McDonagh) v Frawley* [1978] IR 131 to the effect that the Article 40.4.2° procedure was not appropriate for such a case. Accordingly, the Court dismissed the applicant's claim.

This decision does not seem inconsistent with the decision of Denham J in *Cahill v Reilly*, High Court, 24 March 1992, discussed in the 1992 Review, 274-5, where the circumstances were quite different. Both cases indicate that the question as to whether a person is entitled to be informed of the right to legal aid is a matter for discretion and a consideration of the particular circumstances of the case.

Sentence review committee In *Kirwan v Minister for Justice and Ors* [1994] 1 ILRM 444, Lardner J ordered that the applicant was entitled to legal aid concerning a hearing before the sentence review advisory committee. In June 1984, the applicant was found guilty but insane in relation to a charge of murder. The Central Criminal Court directed that he should be detained in the Central Mental Hospital. In 1991 his solicitors obtained a report from the consultant forensic psychiatrist in the hospital which stated that he had formed a view that the applicant might be a suitable candidate for release from detention.

His solicitor applied to the Minister for Justice for a review of the current detention of the applicant. The Department of Justice replied that before the matter could be referred to the sentencing review advisory committee established by the Minister to deal with such cases (see the 1991 Review, 141-2) a detailed statement would be required from the solicitor setting out the grounds on which they were applying for his client's release. The Department told the solicitor that there was no provision for legal aid to enable the applicant to present his application to the advisory committee. The solicitor felt that the presentation of the case would require the assistance of an expert legal team and at least one expert medical witness. Lardner J agreed and made a declaration that the applicant was entitled to such legal aid as was necessary to enable him effectively to present his application and submissions.

Reviewing the Supreme Court's decision in *The People v Gallagher* [1991] ILRM 339; [1991] 2 IR 404 (1990 Review, 164-6), Lardner J noted that from the time of the special verdict the applicant was held pursuant to statute. It was therefore for the executive (in the person of the Minister for Justice or the government) to enquire into all the relevant circumstances of the applicant's continued detention using fair and constitutional means. Since the decision whether to release the applicant was of great importance both for the public and the applicant, an applicant who is without the requisite means to procure the collection of the relevant information and to formulate and present the appropriate submissions is, as a matter of fairness, entitled to legal aid to enable him to do so. In this context, he regarded the Supreme Court decision in *The State (Healy) v Donoghue* [1976] IR 325 as being a particularly persuasive precedent. He also distinguished the instant case from *The State (O.) v Daly* [1977] IR 312, in which the Supreme Court had declined to grant legal aid to the applicant who was detained in the Central Mental Hospital. Lardner J was content to hold that the *O.* case was 'one on the particular facts', and did not bind him to hold against the applicant in the instant case.

The decision of Lardner J in the *Kirwan* case is the first since *The State (Healy) v Donoghue* [1976] IR 325 to extend the concept of fair procedures to encompass a legally enforceable right to legal assistance for those unable to afford legal advice because of their inadequate means. This may be contrasted with the cases in which applicants have sought to argue that the Constitution requires the provision of State-assisted legal aid in civil cases (see the 1990 Review, 144-7). While the *Kirwan* case involves some limited extension of existing decisions, it hardly presages a reversal of those cases involving civil litigation. In *Kirwan*, Lardner J was careful to note the link between the applicant's position and the criminal process to which it was connected.

MANSLAUGHTER

Manslaughter and misadventure The distinction between manslaughter and death by misadventure was adverted to in *The People v Hendley*, Court of Criminal Appeal, 11 June 1993. The defendant had initially been charged with murder arising from the death of his wife following a struggle between the two in their home. The defendant had, on his own admission, grabbed his wife by the neck and held her to the ground in the course of the struggle. He denied lying on top of his wife to hold her to the ground at any stage. This was a crucial point in the case, because the wife did not die from strangulation but rather from the effects of a rupturing of her liver. The defendant stated that he had blacked out at some time during the course of the struggle and came around only when the Gardaí arrived on the scene. The defendant suggested in evidence that his wife's liver had been ruptured when one of the Gardaí stood on her. There was no evidence to support this suggestion.

At the defendant's trial in the Central Criminal Court in May 1991, the trial judge (Barr J) withdrew from the jury the murder charge but left them the charge of manslaughter. His direction indicated that the jury should discount the possibility that the death had occurred through misadventure. He stated that it was sufficient to convict on the manslaughter charge if the jury found that the defendant had been engaged in an unlawful act, namely the assault on his wife, even if the damage to her liver which actually resulted in her death had been inadvertent. The jury convicted the defendant of manslaughter and the defendant was sentenced to five year's imprisonment on foot of this.

On appeal, the Court of Criminal Appeal (O'Flaherty, Barron and Lavan JJ) quashed the conviction. The Court pointed out that the trial judge's direction, in excluding the possibility of death by misadventure, did not conform to the decision of the Court in *The People v Crosbie* [1966] IR 490. In *Crosbie*, the Court had rejected the old law that a killing resulting from an unlawful act was sufficient of itself to constitute manslaughter; what was required was proof that 'the act causing death must be unlawful and dangerous to constitute the offence of manslaughter.' In *Hendley*, the Court stated that it was necessary to separate the struggle between the defendant and his wife from the liver damage which was the actual cause of death. The Court noted that the jury had not been asked to consider whether the liver damage had been caused by:

> a deliberate act of the accused. If it was, it was unlawful and then the further matter to be proved was: had it been demonstrated to be a dangerous act.

Because this two stage approach had not been taken, the Court of Criminal Appeal quashed the conviction. Noting that the defendant had served two years in prison, the Court concluded that this had not resulted in any injustice to him as he was certainly guilty of assault occasioning actual bodily harm and that this would have merited a custodial sentence. However, in all the circumstances, the Court was of opinion that the justice of the case would be met by not ordering a re-trial.

MEDIA COVERAGE AND FAIR TRIALS

The effect of media coverage on pending proceedings, and its potential to prejudice court proceedings, has traditionally been dealt with by means of contempt of court (for a general discussion, see the 1992 Review, 239-45). Contempt of court focuses on the protection by the courts of their own proceedings and on whether the media, usually newspapers or television, should be punished for their contempt. A residual element of the contempt jurisdiction is aimed at protecting litigants from public obloquy: see *Wong for Minister for Justice* [1994] 1 IR 223 (1992 Review, 242-3).

More recently, the point has been made that certain forms of media coverage may have the effect of prejudicing a fair trial, particularly for an accused person in a criminal trial and that, consequently, such trial should be prohibited. This argument is based primarily on the right to a trial in due course of law under Article 38.1 of the Constitution. Such arguments may be made in connection, for example, with pre-trial publicity attending a case that has become a *cause celèbre* or in connection with previous media coverage of a case which, for whatever reason, requires a re-trial. The arguments revolve around whether a person facing a criminal trial, preceded by enormous publicity, can obtain a trial 'in due course of law'.

In *D. v Director of Public Prosecutions* [1994] 1 ILRM 435, the Supreme Court considered this question in detail for the first time and, by a majority, rejected the claim that the publicity involved in the case would prejudice a fair trial. The decision in *D.* was unanimously followed by the Court in 1994 in *Z. v Director of Public Prosecutions* [1994] 2 ILRM 481, a case arising out of *Attorney General v X.* [1992] ILRM 401; [1992] 1 IR 1 (see the 1992 Review, 159-186). Again, the Supreme Court declined to prohibit a trial on sexual assault charges which had been attended by virtually unprecedented media attention. We will return to discuss in detail both the *D.* and *Z.* cases in the 1994 Review, but for a comprehensive discussion, see Gordon Duffy's article, (1994) 4 *Irish Criminal Law Journal* 113.

MISCARRIAGES OF JUSTICE

The Criminal Procedure Act 1993, discussed in different contexts in this chapter, 210, 228, above, and 244, below, sets out a new mechanism by which a miscarriage of justice may be dealt with.

MISUSE OF DRUGS

Illicit drugs trade The European Communities (Monitoring of External Trade in Scheduled Substances) Regulations 1993 (SI No. 6) provide for the administrative measures required to give full effect to Council Regulation 3677/90, as amended by Council Regulation 900/92 and Commission Regulation 3679/92. These lay down measures to be taken to control the international trade in substances known to be used in the illicit manufacuture of narcotic drugs and psychotropic substances. The EC Regulation, as amended, was also intended to give effect to Article 12 of the 1988 UN Convention against Illicit Traffic in Narcotic Drugs and Psychotropic Substances, which deals with traffic outside the European Community. Penalties for breaches of the EC Regulation, as amended, are also provided for in the 1993 Regulations.

Linked to these are the Misuse of Drugs (Scheduled Substances) Regulations 1993 (SI No. 338), which are concerned with traffic inside the European Community. These latter Regulations, made under the Misuse of Drugs Act 1977, give effect to Directive 92/109/EEC (not a Council Regulation as the Explanatory Note states) on the placing on the market of the same substances as are dealt with in Council Regulation 3677/90, as amended. Restrictions are laid down on the production, supply, importation and exportation of the substances concerned, and these controls vary according to the extent to which the substances are likely to be used for the illicit manufacuture of narcotic drugs and psychotropic substances. The Regulations also specify the classes of persons who may possess or supply the substances and the circumstances in which these persons would not be in breach of the Misuse of Drugs Acts 1977 to 1984. Requirements concerning labelling, documentation, record keeping and the furnishing of information to officers authorised by the Minister for Health are also laid down. Finally, we may note that Reg.3 provides that nothing in the 1993 Regulations shall be construed as affecting any provision of the Misuse of Drugs Regulations 1988, the main Regulations concerning the possession and supply of what might be described as licit drugs.

The 1988 Regulations were themselves amended by the Misuse of Drugs (Amendment) Regulations 1993 (SI No. 342) in order to complete the necessary legislative changes to give effect to the 1988 UN Convention against Illicit Traffic in Narcotic Drugs and Psychotropic Substances. The 1988 Regulations were amended to ensure that correct documentation is compiled in respect of the export of controlled drugs to comply with the UN Convention. Other miscellaneous amendments were also effected to the 1988 Regulations.

Scheduled substances   The Misuse of Drugs (Exemption) (Amendment) Order 1993 (SI No. 339) amended the 1988 Order of the same title in order to restrict the possession of certain drugs and to provide exemption for the possession of certain others from the terms of s. 3 of the Misuse of Drugs Act 1977, which deals with unauthorised possession. The Misuse of Drugs (Scheduled Substances) (Exemption) Order 1993 (SI No. 341) involved a similar exemption from the terms of s. 3 of the 1977 Act in respect of the products and substances referred to in the Order. The Misuse of Drugs (Designation) Order 1993 (SI No. 340) revoked and replaced the Misuse of Drugs (Designation) Order 1988 and provides that the drugs specified in the Order shall not be made available for medical purposes. The specified drugs include mescaline and cannabis.

PARDON

Ss. 7 and 8 of the Criminal Procedure Act 1993 lay down for the first time a formal mechanism for seeking a pardon from the President under Article 13.6 of the Constitution: see the discussion above, 211. We may note here that s. 9 of the 1993 Act provides for compensation for a person in respect of whom a pardon has been granted under the 1993 Act, the same section which provides for compensation for a person convicted through a miscarriage of justice: see 217, above.

PROCEDURE

Addition of charges   In *O'Connell v Director of Public Prosecutions*, High Court, 30 July 1993; [1994] 2 ILRM 21 (SC), the High Court and Supreme Court dealt with the power of the Director of Public Prosections to add charges to an indictment after a case has been sent forward for trial. We will discuss the Supreme Court's judgment, delivered in March 1994, in the 1994 Review.

Discretion to prosecute   In *H. v Director of Public Prosections*, High Court, 26 July 1993; [1994] 2 ILRM 285 (SC), the High Court and Supreme Court declined to compel the Director of Public Prosections to bring criminal charges against two men who, the applicant alleged, had committed various sexual offences against her young son. As the decision of the Supreme Court in this case was delivered in May 1994, we will discuss in the 1994 Review the issues arising in this case concerning review of the prosecutorial discretion vested in the Director.

Indictable offence: corporate body as common informer   In *Cumann Luthchleas Gael Teo v Windle (Dublin Corporation, Notice Party)* [1994] 1 IR 525, the Supreme Court rejected the argument that a corporate body could constitute a private prosecutor, or 'common informer', for the purposes of prosecuting an indictable offence under the Fire Services Act 1981: see the discussion in the Safety and Health chapter, 476-9, below.

Indictable offence fit to be tried summarily: presence of accused   In *Lawlor v Hogan* [1993] ILRM 606, Murphy J considered the procedure required to be followed by a judge of the District Court in determining whether an indictable offence can be tried summarily pursuant to s. 2(2) of the Criminal Justice Act 1951, as amended, particularly whether an accused must be present in court when charged with an indictable offence.

The applicant had been convicted by the respondent judge of the District Court of offences contrary to s. 23 of the Larceny Act 1916, as inserted by s. 5 of the Criminal Law (Jurisdiction) Act 1976. The applicant was represented by a solicitor at all times during his trial but was not present in person during any part of the proceedings. The respondent proceeded with the hearing, having rejected a submission made on behalf of the applicant that there was no jurisdiction to hear the matter in the applicant's absence. On judicial review, Murphy J quashed the conviction, not in relation to the absence *per se*, but to the connected matter of trying an indictable offence summarily pursuant to the Criminal Justice Act 1951.

In the High Court, counsel for the applicant, noting that the offences were indictable, drew attention to a passage in Archbold, *Criminal Pleading Evidence and Practice*, 36th ed., para.546, that 'no trial for felony can be had except in the presence of the prisoner'. Authority cited by Archbold included the Irish decision *Ex parte O'Brien Dalton* (1891-92) 28 LR Ir 36, in which Murphy J noted that Palles CB had, at least, not rejected the point argued. A stronger authority was the view of Lord Aitken in *R. v Lawrence* [1933] AC 699 (quoted in *The People v Messitt* [1972] IR 204) which appeared to require continuous presence. However, even though this passage was cited in Ryan and Magee, *The Irish Criminal Process* (Mercier, 1983), Murphy J noted that the authors of that text had referred to certain exceptions to the rule. Approaching the matter from first principles, Murphy J enumerated three propositions to be applied in cases such as this:

(1) That insofar as the judicial process in criminal matters expressly requires matters to be dealt with by or in relation to the individual accused, clearly he must be present to enable these functions to be performed.
(2) The right of an accused to be present and to follow the proceedings

against him is a fundamental constitutional right of the accused which every court would be bound to protect and vindicate.

(3) If a trial judge is satisfied that the accused has consciously decided to absent himself from the trial (at a time when his presence is not essential to enable some particular procedure to be complied with) then the trial judge would be entitled in his discretion to proceed with the trial notwithstanding the absence of the accused.

In the circumstances of the instant case, Murphy J concluded that the trial judge was entitled to exercise his discretion in the manner in which he did and to proceed with the trial notwithstanding the absence of the accused. However, he went on to consider a connected point on which he quashed the conviction, namely whether the requirements of s. 2 of the Criminal Justice Act 1951 had been complied with.

Murphy J noted that the presence of an accused in the District Court is essential to enable the court to inform him of his right to be tried by a jury and to enable him to form a view as to whether he would object to being tried summarily under s. 2 of the 1951 Act. Citing the decision in *The State (Hastings) v Reddin* [1953] IR 134, Murphy J pointed out that this is a condition precedent to the exercise by a District Court judge of jurisdiction in these cases, that this condition had not been fulfilled in the instant case and thus the conviction must be quashed.

Murphy J also opined that the material time for giving or withholding the statutory consent under s. 2 of the 1951 Act is when the accused is informed of his right to be tried by a jury, and not at any other time. He rejected the suggestion by the applicant that the consent issue must be dealt with when the accused is asked for the first time whether he wishes to be tried in the District Court, noting that the power of summary trial and the duty to inform the accused of his right to be tried by jury in s. 2 of the 1951 Act is conferred not on the particular judge by whom the trial is to be conducted but on 'the court' or the 'District Court'.

Finally, Murphy J also considered that as the first-named respondent formed the opinion that the offence alleged was a minor offence only while taking evidence in the course of the trial against the accused, this was not sufficient compliance with the procedural steps laid down for s. 2(2)(a) of the 1951 Act by Butler J in *The State (Nevin) v Tormey* [1976] IR 1.

Judicial interventions creating risk of injustice   The extent to which the courts adopt a rigorous approach to the possible prejudicial effects of judges intervening in a manner which might have the appearance of 'entering the arena' was exemplified in *Dineen v Delap*, High Court, 21 October 1993. The applicant had been charged with a drink-driving offence under s. 49 of the Road Traffic Act 1961, as amended.

At his trial before the respondent judge of the District Court, his counsel objected that the prosecuting garda appeared to be reading a statement of his evidence rather than merely consulting his notes. The respondent indicated that the garda could read from whatever he liked, that there was Supreme Court authority to that effect and that 'the days of the Garda making a slip in the witness box are long gone and if he does make a slip I will recall him.' The garda then stated that he was in fact merely reading his notes, and the respondent then stated to the Garda that he should not bother responding to counsel and that counsel was only trying to trip him up. At the end of the prosecution case, counsel submitted that the case be dismissed on the ground that a particular proof had not been establiahed in the case. The respondent rejected the submission but proceeded to call a garda witness to give evidence on this particular point. The respondent convicted the applicant on the charge under s. 49 of the 1961 Act, as amended.

On judicial review, Morris J held that the procedure adopted by the respondent could not be justified. He described as 'completely unacceptable' and 'an unwarranted interference with counsel performing his duty' the respondent's statement that the garda should not respond to counsel as counsel was only trying to trip him up. He also regarded as improper the suggestion by the respondent that he would recall the garda in the event of him making a slip and, adapting the words of Marguire CJ in *The State (Hegarty) v Winters* [1956] IR 320, concluded that it would:

> . . . cause an impartial observer to recognise that the judge hearing the case was prepared to support the prosecution to the extent of filling gaps which their evidence might leave.

On this basis, Morris J quashed the conviction. In addition, as he considered that the conduct of the applicant's trial had been 'totally unsatis- factory', he declined to remit the case to the District Court under O.84, r.26(4) of the Rules of the Superior Courts 1986, citing in support the *obiter* comments of Hederman J on this in *Sweeney v Brophy* [1993] ILRM 449; [1993] 2 IR 202, discussed in the 1992 Review, 268-70, where the case was decided on different grounds. In the 1992 Review, 270, we noted that the *obiter* comments in *Sweeney* had been made without the apparent knowledge that the Court, in its earlier *ex tempore* decision in *Dawson v Hamill* [1991] 1 IR 213, had actually declined to remit a case under O.84, r.26(4). In the instant case Morris J's attention would not appear to have been drawn to the decision in *Dawson*. Nonetheless, happily his decision was entirely in line with the approach taken in *Dawson*, and thus could not be regarded as being made *per incuriam*, though clearly it was made without knowledge of the

Dawson case. See also the Supreme Court's memory lapse concerning *Dawson* in *Duff v Mangan* [1991] 1 ILRM 91, 233, above.

Lesser offence charged   In *The People v Rock (P.)* [1994] 1 ILRM 66, the Supreme Court held that a conviction for simple larceny under s. 2 of the Larceny Act 1916 is possible even where evidence discloses an aggravated form of larceny for which different penalties are provided for under other provisions of the 1916 Act: see the discussion above, 236-8. To the same effect, see *K.M. v Director of Public Prosecutions*, High Court, 21 June 1993, below, 268.

Preliminary examination: video link   S. 11 of Criminal Justice Act 1993 amended s. 7 of the Criminal Procedure Act 1967 by providing that a written deposition is not required where any part of a preliminary examination is conducted by means of video link evidence in a sexual offence case within the meaning of the Criminal Evidence Act 1992 or a case involving violence or a threat of violence within the meaning of s. 5 of the 1993 Act itself. The amendments to the 1967 Act effected by s. 11 of the 1993 Act have the result that the video link is admissible at the trial of an accused.

Presence of accused   The circumstances in which an accused must be present in court when charged with an indictable offence were considered in *Lawlor v Hogan* [1993] ILRM 606: see 245, above.

Time limits: indictable offences   In *Director of Public Prosecutions v Logan*, High Court, 26 February 1993; [1994] 2 ILRM 229 (SC), the defendant had been charged summarily with indictable assault. At his trial in the District Court the trial judge dismissed the charges on the ground that the prosecution had not been brought within the six month time limit contained in s. 10 of the Petty Sessions (Ireland) Act 1851. On a case stated to the High Court Carney J held that the District Court judge had erred in law, but this decision was reversed on appeal by the Supreme Court in a decision gievn in May 1994. We will return to this decision in the 1994 Review.

ROAD TRAFFIC

Arrest: not necessary in public place   In *Director of Public Prosecutions v Forbes* [1993] ILRM 817, the Supreme Court (Finlay CJ, O'Flaherty, Egan, Blayney and Denham JJ) rejected the suggestion that an arrest on private property invalidates an otherwise valid arrest under s. 49 of the Road Traffic

Act 1961. The Court affirmed that an offence under s. 49 of the 1961 Act must be committed in a public place: see the discussion below, 254, of *Director of Public Prosecutions v Molloy* [1993] ILRM 573 where such a point arose.

However, the Court rejected the *obiter* view of McCarthy J in *Director of Public Prosecutions v McCreesh* [1992] 2 IR 239 (see generally the 1991 Review, 131-2) where he had suggested that the provisions of s. 49 'clearly anticipate an offence committed in a public place and, possibly, also an arrest in such place.'

In the instant case, the garda evidence had been that, while on mobile patrol, he observed a parked car which suddenly took off. The car was followed to the driveway of a private house where the defendant exited the vehicle. The garda caught the defendant as he ran towards the road. Having got the smell of intoxicating liquor from the defendant's breath, the Garda stated he formed the opinion required under s. 49 of the 1961 Act, as amended, and arrested the defendant.

Delivering the only reasoned judgment in the case, O'Flaherty J stated that it was 'axiomatic that any householder gives an implied authority to a member of the garda to come onto the forecourt of his premises to see to the enforcement of the law or prevent a breach thereof.' He noted that such implied authority could be rebutted by contrary evidence. However he held that this was not a case where the issue of trespass arose. He considered that in the circumstances the Gardaí were clearly acting in the exercise of their duties in following the car into the private property and stated that any other view 'would constitute . . . a massive absurdity.'

Arrest for refusing breath specimen: opinion In *Director of Public Prosecutions v Breheny*, Supreme Court, 2 March 1993, the defendant had been charged with two offences under the Road Traffic Acts. First, she was charged that, being in charge of a mechanically propelled vehicle in a public place, she refused to provide a specimen of her breath to a member of the Garda Síochána when requested to do so, contrary to s. 12(2) of the Road Traffic (Amendment) Act 1978, as amended by s. 5 of the Road Traffic (Amendment) Act 1984. Second, she was charged that, being a person arrested under s. 12(3) of the Road Traffic (Amendment) Act 1978 and brought to a Garda station, she refused to permit a designated medical practitioner to take a sample of her blood or to provide a sample of her urine, contrary to s. 13(3) of the Road Traffic (Amendment) Act 1978, as amended by s. 5 of the Road Traffic (Amendment) Act 1984.

The evidence given in the District Court indicated that a member of the Garda Síochána came to the scene of an accident in which the defendant had been involved. The defendant was sitting in her car which, it appeared, could not start at this time. The garda in question formed the opinion that the defendant had consumed intoxicating liquor and required her to exhale into an alcolyser but the defendant refused to do so. The garda then arrested her pursuant to s. 12(3) of the 1978 Act, as amended, and she was brought to a garda station where she refused to permit a designated medical practitioner to take a sample of her blood or to provide a sample of her urine. In the District Court, both charges were dismissed on the ground that it had not been established as a fact that the defendant had, at the material time, been in charge of a mechanically propelled vehicle.

On a case stated to the High Court, Lardner J agreed that this evidential *lacuna* was fatal to the first charge, but not to the second, and on further appeal, the Supreme Court (Finlay CJ, Egan and Denham JJ) upheld Lardner J's view.

Delivering the Court's decision, Egan J pointed out that the ingredients of the offence under s. 12(2) of the 1978 Act were contained in s. 12(1) of the 1978 Act. These were: (a) a person is in charge of a mechanically propelled vehicle; (b) the person is so in charge in a public place; and (c) a garda is of opinion that the person has consumed intoxicating liquor. He agreed that, in the instant case, it had not been established as a matter of fact that the car in which the defendant was sitting at the relevant time was a mechanically propelled vehicle within the meaning of s. 3(2) of the Road Traffic Act 1961. He noted that, in *Director of Public Prosecutions v Joyce* [1985] ILRM 206, the Court had required proof of the 'public place' element of the offence and he was of the view that, equally, proof that the vehicle was a mechanically propelled vehicle was required. Without the three proofs, he concluded, no offence was committed.

Turning to the second charge against the defendant, however, Egan J considered that different considerations arose. He quoted the terms of s. 12(3) of the 1978 Act:

> A member of the Garda Síochána may arrest without warrant a person who in the member's opinion is committing or has committed an offence under this section.

Egan J acknowledged that s. 12(3) when read in conjucntion with s. 12(1) presented a certain anomaly, because whereas in relation to an offence under s. 12 it was required that certain facts be established, the power of arrest under s. 12(3) was dependent only on the Garda's opinion that the three ingredients of the offence under s. 12 were present. Egan J commented:

> If the opinion is genuinely and reasonably held at the time of the making of the request [to inhale into an alcolyser], it seems to me that the literal

terms of [s. 12(3)] have been complied with and it makes no difference that the member's opinion is not proved to be factually correct.

I cannot see any compelling reason why [s. 12(3)] should not be construed strictly in accordance with its wording which only demands an opinion. An arrest under [s. 12(3)] could still be good if the member's opinion regarding the consumption of alcohol was totally wrong and the test at the station proved that not a single drop had been consumed.

On this basis, therefore, the Court concluded that, even though in the instant case it had not been established in evidence that, at the relevant time, the defendant was in charge of a mechanically propelled vehicle, her arrest under s. 12(3) of the 1978 Act was valid and thus the charge under s. 13(3) of the 1978 Act should be remitted to the District Court.

Blood or urine sample: refusal In *Director of Public Prosecutions (Coughlan) v Swan* [1994] 1 ILRM 314, the Supreme Court considered the situation where a person arrested under s. 49 of the Road Traffic Act 1961 opts to provide a urine sample rather than a blood sample but is unable to provide the urine sample.

The defendant was charged with failing to comply with the requirements of a designated registered medical practitioner in relation to the taking of a specimen of urine contrary to s. 13(3)(b) of the Road Traffic (Amendment) Act 1978, following a requirement under s. 13(1)(b) of the 1978 Act.

After the defendant was arrested and brought to a garda station, the registered medical practitioner made the requirement specified in s. 13 of the 1978 Act in relation to the taking of a specimen of blood or, at the option of the defendant, the provision of a specimen of urine. The defendant opted to give a specimen of urine but failed to do so after two attempts. The defendant was informed by a garda of the consequences of refusal or failure to provide a specimen and he was also told that he could change his mind and permit the doctor to take a specimen of blood. The defendant again opted to provide a specimen of his urine, but again failed and indicated that he was unable to do so. At his trial on the charge brought, the garda stated that he could not say that the defendant's failure to provide a sample had been deliberate.

On a case stated from the Circuit Court, the Supreme Court (Finlay CJ, O'Flaherty, Egan, Blayney and Denham JJ) unanimously held that the defendant should be acquitted in the circumstances which had arisen.

Delivering the leading judgment, Egan J (with whom Finlay CJ, O'Flaherty and Denham JJ concurred) reviewed the Court's decision in *Connolly v Salinger* [1982] ILRM 482. He commented:

Connolly v. Salinger, in effect, decided that the declaration of a choice to provide a specimen of urine was not final or irreversible and it is not, in my opinion, a direct authority for the proposition that a person who has declared an election to provide a sample of urine and then finds that he is unable to do so has committed an offence of failing to provide a specimen of urine. In such circumstances there would be a total absence of *mens rea*. Such would appear to be the situation in the instant case as [the arresting garda] agreed in evidence that he could not say that the defendant's failure was a deliberate one.

I go further, however. The obligation under the section is to permit the taking of a specimen of blood but subject, at the option of the person, to provide a specimen of his urine. The word used is 'option'. If the person declares that he wishes to avail of the option but then finds that he is unable to do so, the obligation to permit the taking of a specimen of blood revives and, in such circumstances, a refusal by him to permit the taking of blood is the offence with which he should be charged.

He concluded that, since the defendant in the instant case had been charged and convicted of failing to comply with the requirement of a designated medical practitioner in relation to the taking of a specimen of urine and had not been charged or convicted of any other offence, he should be acquitted.

In a concurring judgment, Blayney J agreed that the defendant should be acquitted. This was on the basis that, since the facts set out in the case stated did not establish that the doctor had made any requirement of the defendant under s. 13(3)(b) of the 1978 Act in relation to the provision of his specimen of urine, the defendant could not be guilty of failing to comply with any such requirement. However, the other members of the Court did not join in this interpretation of the evidence in the case.

Dangerous driving causing death: alcohol consumption   In *The People v Maddock*, Court of Criminal Appeal, 3 May 1993, the Court (Blayney, Lynch and Johnson JJ), in an *ex tempore* judgment, considered whether a trial judge had erred in admitting evidence that the defendant, who had been charged with dangerous driving causing death, had consumed about 12 pints of Guinness between midday and 9.30 p.m. when the offence had occurred. The argument against admitting this evidence was that its prejudicial effect outweighed its probative value. The Court rejected this argument on two grounds. First, the Court pointed out that, on any level, the amount involved was significant and it rejected the suggestion that the effect of alcohol on a particular individual should be considered in determining whether the quantity of alcohol involved was significant. Second, the Court noted that the evidence was that the defendant had veered across to the wrong side of the road and had collided with another car, which was on the correct side of the road at all times. The Court concluded that the jury was entitled to have the evidence on alcohol consumption before it in order to know how the defendant had spent the day prior to the time the offence occurred.

Form of proof of registered medical practitioner The Medical Practitioners (Amendment) Act 1993 is a short Act which provides, in effect, that a computerised print-out of the Register of Medical Practitioners may be produced as evidence in court that a named doctor is registered for the purposes of a prosecution under the Road Traffic Acts. The problem dealt with in the 1993 Act had been identified in, for example, *Director of Public Prosecutions v O'Donoghue* [1991] 1 IR 448: see the 1991 Review, 172. S. 2 of the 1993 Act amends s. 26 of the Medical Practitioners Act 1978 by permitting the Register to be kept in non-legible form, provided it is capable of being converted into a legible form, thus including a computer-retrievable form of Register. S. 2 also provides that a certificate from the Registrar of the Medical Council to the effect that a named person was a registered medical practitioner on a given date will be regarded as evidence of that fact unless the contrary is proved. S. 3 of the 1993 Act amends s. 57 of the Medical Practitioners Act 1978 by providing that the Register of Medical Practitioners can be maintained in a retrievable format. S. 4 of the 1993 Act amends s. 17 of the Road Traffic (Amendment) Act 1978 by providing that failure to comply with a request from a medical practitioner to provide a urine sample is an offence carrying, on summary conviction, a possible sentence of six months and, or alternatively, a fine of £1,000. S. 5 of the 1993 Act introduces consequential changes to s. 23 of the Road Traffic (Amendment) Act 1978 in connection with the presumption as to registration as a medical practitioner.

Furnishing copy of MBRS certificate to defendant In *Hanratty v Kirby*, High Court, 22 July 1993, the applicant unsuccessfully sought to have quashed his conviction under s. 49 of the Road Traffic Act 1961, as amended. When the applicant had given a specimen of his blood while he was in garda custody and it had been divided into two parts under s. 21 of the Road Traffic (Amendment) Act 1978, he had declined to take the part tendered to him under s. 21 of the 1978 Act. In accordance with s. 22 of the 1978 Act, the results of the analysis conducted by the Medical Bureau of Road Safety on the specimen forwarded to it by the Gardaí was sent by registered post to the applicant's address, but the applicant did not collect this letter and it had been returned to the Bureau marked 'not called for'. The prosecution came on for hearing and was adjourned for the purpose of giving the applicant the copy certificate from the Medical Bureau of Road Safety, but in fact it was not furnished to the applicant's advisers until some minutes before the adjourned hearing of the prosecution. In these circumstances, the applicant sought to have the case dismissed. The respondent judge of the District Court offered to adjourn the case for a short time to enable the applicant to consider the certificate, but the applicant declined to accept this offer. The respondent proceeded to hear the case and convicted the applicant.

On judicial review, Keane J declined to quash the conviction. He acknowledged that, in *The State (Walshe) v Murphy* [1981] IR 275, a Divisional High Court had, *inter alia*, held that there was an obligation on the prosecuting authorities to ensure that a person charged under s. 49 is supplied with a copy certificate in good time to enable him to have the specimen he had retained analysed in order to contest the validity or correctness of the certificate. However, he concluded that the *Walshe* case was not relevant to the present case as the applicant had decided not to retain the specimen when it was offered to him in the garda station. Accordingly, he accepted the submission of counsel for the Director of Public Prosecutions that the applicant had suffered no irremediable prejudice and that any possible prejudice could have been remedied by availing of the adjournment offered by the respondent.

Public place: pedestrianised area   In *Director of Public Prosecutions v Molloy* [1993] ILRM 573, Murphy J considered whether the defendant had committed certain offences of which he was charged in a 'public place' within the meaning of s. 2 of the Road Traffic Act 1961.

The defendant had been charged in the District Court on three charges under the Road Traffic Acts, an ingredient of each charge being that it occurred in a 'public place'. The alleged offences took place in Grafton Street, Dublin at 10.35 pm. At the relevant time, the street was closed to traffic generally, pursuant to Part IV of the Dublin Traffic and Parking Temporary Rules 1982. S. 2 of the Road Traffic Act 1961 defines a 'public place' as 'any street or other place to which the public have access with vehicles whether as of right or by permission and whether subject to or free of charge'. The District Court judge held that Grafton Street was not, at the relevant time, a 'public place' within the meaning of s. 3 of the 1961 Act. On a case stated, Murphy J agreed.

Accepting the view of MacDermott LCJ in *Montgomery v Loney* [1959] NI 171 that the words 'public' and 'access' 'have no fixed and inflexible meaning and their true signification must depend on their context and the purpose for which they are used', Murphy J concluded that:

> . . . an essential ingredient in the definition of a public place for the purposes of the Road Traffic Act 1961 is that the public should have access thereto with vehicles so that if and so long as such access is

prohibited by law, that the place in question cannot comply with the statutory definition.

On this basis, Murphy J upheld the decision of the District Court judge to dismiss the charges.

Stopping vehicles: extent of power   In *D.P.P. (Stratford) v Fagan* [1993] 2 IR 95 (HC); [1994] 2 ILRM 349 (SC), the extent of the garda power to stop vehicles was considered by the High Court and Supreme Court in the context of a prosecution under the Road Traffic Acts. The 1994 Supreme Court decision in this case, which upheld the power to establish checkpoints for the purposes of the Road Traffic Acts, will be discussed in the 1994 Review.

SENTENCING

Appeals against unduly lenient sentences   As mentioned at the beginning of this chapter, s. 2 of the Criminal Justice Act 1993 provides that appeals against unduly lenient sentences may be brought by the prosecution. The origins of the 1993 Act, and s. 2 in particular, may be traced to general unease over what was perceived to be the inconsistent application of sentencing principles in certain cases of violent crime, in particular sexual offences. An immediate catalyst was the suspended sentence imposed in *The People v W.C.* [1994] 1 ILRM 321, discussed below, 261-3, a case in which, ironically perhaps, the sentencing judge ultimately laid down in detail the considerations which led him to impose the suspended sentence in that case. Be that as it may, the victim of the crime in this case, Lavinia Kerwick, received substantial praise and media coverage for her decision to allow the shield of anonymity to be removed and to comment on the sentence imposed. Arising from this, the then Minister for Justice supported the introduction of legislation to allow for the prosecution to appeal against unduly lenient sentences, and s. 2 of the 1993 Act was the result of this. For a compehensive account of s. 2 of the 1993 Act, see Tom O'Malley's article, (1993) 11 *ILT* 121.

Consecutive sentencing: remand period   In *Black v Governor of Cork Prison*, High Court, 1 February 1993, the applicant had been sentenced in the District Court to two consecutive terms of 12 months imprisonment, making a total of 24 months. This total appeared to be within the limits conferred on the District Court by ss. 11 and 12 of the Criminal Justice Act 1984. However, the applicant sought an inquiry into his detention under Article 40.4.2° of the Constitution. He pointed out that, in respect of one of the offences for which he was convicted, he had been remanded in custody for five weeks before his trial and that his cumulative detention before and after conviction and sentence amounted to a period of over 25 months. He argued that this was in excess of the powers conferred on the District Court.

Carney J rejected the argument. He noted that, in *The State (Tynan) v Keane* [1968] IR 348, a case dealing with the overhang of a sentence imposed on foot of a conviction quashed by *certiorari* as being void, Ó Dálaigh CJ had indicated that the overhanging sentence could be taken into account if the defendant was charged and convicted afresh. Ó Dálaigh CJ had stated:

> It is to be recommended in this type of case that the court should act on principles of good book-keeping and that the court should state, first, the sentence which the offence warrants in the judgment of the court; that the court should then expressly deduct the imprisonment already served, and then, finally, the court should impose the balance remaining as the court's net sentence.

While Carney J accepted these principles, as he was bound to, he held that they did not apply to the applicant in the instant case, since the *Tynan* case dealt with an overhanging term of imprisonment imposed on foot of a conviction, albeit a void conviction. By contrast, the five week period of imprisonment served by the applicant had not been on foot of a conviction and thus could not be regarded as part of 'any sentence passed' by the District Court within the meaning of ss. 11 and 12 of the Criminal Justice Act 1984. This exclusion of the remand period also seems to be in line with the decision of the Supreme Court in *The People v O'Callaghan* [1966] IR 501, as confirmed in *Ryan v Director of Public Prosecutions* [1989] ILRM 333; [1989] IR 399 (see the 1988 Review, 144-7).

However, while Carney J dismissed the applicant's claim, he also expressed the view that:

> whenever possible the District Court should implement the principles of good book-keeping recommended by Ó Dálaigh CJ and counsel and solicitors should be vigilant to ensure that any pre-trial custody is brought to the court's attention.

While strictly speaking this comment may be regarded as *obiter*, the analogy made by Carney J with the 'book- keeping' recommended in the *Tynan* case would appear to be fully merited.

Incest   S. 12 of the Criminal Justice Act 1993 increased the maximum sentence for incest by a male under s. 1 of the Punishment of Incest Act 1908 from seven years penal servitude to 20 years imprisonment (the distinction between the prison regime for penal servitude and 'ordinary' imprisonment having disappeared between 1908 and 1993).

Law Reform Commission Consultation Paper on Sentencing   The Law Reform Commission's *Consultation Paper on Sentencing*, published in March 1993, presents a comprehensive analysis of the subject, drawing from the work of other law reform agencies throughout the common law world, as well as examining developments in Europe and incorporating the philosophic analysis of the subject, from Plato to Von Hirsh. It is worth noting, however, that the recently appointed President of the Commission, Mr Justice Anthony Hederman, took no part in the preparation of the paper; it will be interesting to see whether, with the benefit of his very extensive experience in the area of criminal law, at the Bar, as Attorney General and on the Bench, the Commission will favour a different approach when it publishes its final Report on the subject.

At the heart of the Consultation Paper, in chapter 4, is the Commissioner's analysis of the values and goals underlying sentencing policy. At present our courts proceed, blithely enough, on the basis of several different philosophies, which can pull against one another: *retribution*, based on a moral assessment of the gravity of what the convicted person has done; *deterrence*, either of would-be offenders or of the convicted person, looking to future conduct, which it seeks to prevent; *rehabilitation*, which also looks to the future, and is designed to achieve the twin goals of moral improvement and reduction in criminal propensity; *incapacitation*, which seeks not to improve the criminal but rather to prevent him or her, by physical restrictions, from committing future crime, at least for some time; and *compensation*, which requires the offender to make reparation to the victim.

It is easy to see how these competing philosophies can render the sentencing process incoherent. Take the case of a twenty-year-old mugger of a pensioner. If he is treated retributively to reflect the seriousness of his crime the appropriate sentence might perhaps be four years' imprisonment. A deterrent approach might indicate a longer period. If his rehabilitation is to be encouraged perhaps the appropriate solution is an indeterminate sentence, with access to medical and social support and guidance. A policy of incapacitation could justify a sentence of ten years or even longer. The legislature can do something to limit the degree of variation in sentencing by prescribing a maximum, as well, perhaps, as a minimum penalty but, within the permitted range, the judges are free to be pulled, consciously or not, by any of these several philosophies.

The Commission reports the bad news about rehabilitation: research for the past three decades has failed to establish its efficacy. Things may be slightly better than the assessment of an influential commentator, Martinson ([1974] Public Interest, 22, at 25) that 'nothing works', but not by a great deal. The Commission sees another difficulty with the rehabilitative philosophy: it can lead to longer or indeterminate sentences.

Deterrence has its own limitations, especially in relation to 'individual deterrence', which is directed to persons who have on a previous occasion been sentenced for an offence:

> Factors such as the high recidivism rate and the 'undeterrability' of compulsive and impulsive offenders have called the success of the goal of individual deterrence into question.

As to 'general deterrence', which is directed at people who have never been sentenced for an offence, the Commission notes that little is known about its efficacy.

A significant problem with incapacitation lies in the difficulty of accurately predicting recidivism: the Floud Report, commissioned by the Howard League for Penal Reform, concedes that the 'false positive' rate for predictions under its scheme of proposals was at least 50% and possibly as high as 66% (cf. (1982) 22 *British J of Criminology* 216). The Commission identifies constitutional doubts about the legitimacy of imprisoning persons on the basis of a judgment about a class of offenders, however accurate, because this denies them of their claim to equal respect as individuals.

Finally, the Commission identifies some practical drawbacks to the compensation philosophy. It is ineffective where the offender lacks means. Not all crimes have readily identifiable victims. Moreover, the compensation theory 'fails to take into account the fact that the criminal law has other concerns such as ensuring that the law is observed'.

In place of these several philosophies, which the Commission regards as discredited to a greater or a lesser extent, the Commission provisionally recommends that the Oireachtas set out by way of statute a clear statement that the sentence to be imposed on an offender be determined by reference to the *just deserts* principle of distribution whereby the severity of sentence is measured in proportion to the seriousness of the offending behaviour. The Commission recommends that this legislative statement should highlight the following concerns:

> (1) The severity of the sentence to be imposed on an offender should be measured in proportion to the seriousness of the offending behaviour;
> (2) the seriousness of offending behaviour should be measured by reference to:

(a) the harm caused or risked by the offender in committing the offence, and

(b) the culpability of the offender in committing the offence.

The Commission goes on to recommend specifically that, in determining the severity of the sentence to be imposed, the sentencer should not have regard to the rehabilitation of the offender, the deterrence of the offender or others from committing further crime or the incapacitation of the offender from committing further crime.

The 'just deserts' philosophy has gained support internationally over the past two decades. It reflects a scepticism about the efficacy of the other, essentially utilitarian, philosophies; it is not based on the notion of vengeance but rather on the principle of objective proportionality, having regard in particular to the elements of harm to the victim and culpability of the offender.

There is a clinical coldness about the 'just deserts' philosophy that makes it repellent to many people. The idea that Irish society should abandon the goals of rehabilitation in its sentencing policy is alarming. It amounts to the despairing, and surely premature, conclusion that rehabilitation can *never* be effective. It is true that the Commission envisages that a sentencer should be permitted to have regard to rehabilitation (as well as deterrence, incapacitation and compensation) when choosing between two sanctions *of equal severity*; in practice this is a very limited function.

The Commission goes on to set out a long list of aggravating and mitigating factors, to provide sentencers with a guiding framework of the factors by reference to which harm and culpability may be assessed. It envisages that this will encourage and facilitate greater consistency in sentencing. The list is not intended to be an exclusive one. The Commission considers that itemising the several common factors that can aggravate or mitigate an offence will have the advantage of 'giv[ing] sentencers a clear indication of the *type* of factors relevant to the question of offence seriousness'. One may perhaps doubt the wisdom of this approach. Its open-endness deprives the list of the certainty that is associated with codification. If the courts are permitted to add their own list of factors, what is served by the prescription in statutory form of factors almost all of which would in any event have affected the judge when deciding the sentence?

Among the more desirable provisional recommendations in the Consultation Paper is the proposal that the Oireachtas should refrain from the introduction of minimum sentences in the future and that those still in force should be abolished. The Commission doubts the deterrent quality of minimum sentences and argues that they can preclude the sentencers from imposing a sentence proportionate to the seriousness of the offending behaviour. This offends against the 'just deserts' philosophy. It is also worth noting that minimum sentences can frustrate the goal of rehabilitation of the offender.

The Commission provisionally recommends the abolition of mandatory sentences for indictable crimes and the examination in more detail of the question of mandatory sentences for minor crimes. The mandatory sentence, in its view, is 'a blunt instrument which could not be tolerated in any sentencing scheme with the slightest sensitivity to a "just deserts" approach.' It accepts that the mandatory sentence has great emotional appeal to the public but suggests that:

> the public need little or no convincing that some murders or rapes are more serious than others. They would or should also be aware of the unreality of the mandatory life sentence for murder in the light of the Minister for Justice's power and practice of earlier release.

It might have been helpful if the Commission had ventured into the troubling area of the rhetorical power, and sociological impact, of legal statements as to the gravity of particular acts. 'Murder' is a word of great potency; that potency is echoed in the sentence for murder, which formerly could not have been more dramatic and even today retains some force. Even if everyone knows that a sentence to life imprisonment does not really 'mean' that, it retains a high degree of rhetorical power. If the sentence for murder ceases to be a mandatory life sentence, does such a change in rhetoric have any measurable sociological impact? The question is not a trivial one and is worth pursuing before embarking on a change in the law.

Preventive detention unknown　In *The People v Jackson*, Court of Criminal Appeal, 26 April 1993, the Court (Hederman, O'Hanlon and Geoghegan JJ), in an *ex tempore* judgment, substituted sentences of 18 and 15 years, respectively, in place of two life sentences imposed for two particular rapes perpetrated by the defendant. The trial judge had stated that the life sentences which he imposed were 'intended to protect women, protect prostitutes [two of whom had been victims of the defendant] but indeed to protect all women against the accused until such time as in the humane judgment of the authorities he is fit to be released.' The Court of Criminal Appeal found this passage unacceptable for two reasons. First, it appeared to contemplate a form of preventive detention, which was unknown in Irish law. A similar view had been taken by the Court in *The People v Carmody* [1988] ILRM 370 (see the 1987 Review, 158-9). Secondly, the Court also noted that the trial judge appeared to be deferring the question of sentence to the executive. The Court considered that:

sentencing and sentencing policy is *exclusively* a matter for the judiciary and not for the executive and, therefore, it is for the courts to impose the appropriate sentence. [emphasis in original]

It may be, of course, that while the Court was perfectly correct to note that the judiciary impose sentences, the trial judge may have reflected another reality, namely, that the executive disposes of them. Given that an 'average' life sentence amounts to about eight years (see O'Mahony, *Crime and Punishment in Ireland*, The Round Hall Press, 1993), the effect of 'reducing' the defendant's sentence to 18 years in the instant case may be more apparent than real. In practice, the executive would, in all probability, determine how long the defendant would remain within a prison environment. However, the decision in *Jackson* may also raise the question as to whether the indeterminate life sentence is an appropriate tool of the criminal justice system or whether it should be replaced by a definite sentence in all cases. On this, see generally O'Mahony, *op. cit.*

Rape: effect of guilty plea   The application of the general principles in *The People v Tiernan* [1989] ILRM 149; [1988] IR 250 (see the 1988 Review, 181-4) was considered in four decisions in 1993, one of the Central Criminal Court, two of the Court of Criminal Appeal and one of the Supreme Court. Of these, the decision of the Central Criminal Court undoubtedly received the most publicity and we discuss it first. On the previous case law in this area, see the 1988 Review, 181-4 and the 1991 Review, 180-1.

In *The People v W.C.* [1994] 1 ILRM 321, the accused, aged 17 at the time of the offence, had pleaded guilty at his arraignment to a charge of raping his girlfriend of five months. The offence had occurred after a New Year's Eve disco which both had attended, though they had not gone there together. The complainant indicated that, having left the disco, they spent some time kissing. They then went to the site of a derelict mill adjacent to a local river where they lay together in a high degree of consensual intimacy for approximately three quarters of an hour. The defendant sought to have sexual intercourse with the complainant, to which the complainant did not consent, but the defendant nonetheless had sexual intercourse without her consent. While it appeared that in the immediate aftermath of the event the accused was neither fully aware, nor appreciated, the wrong he had done, he had admitted his guilt promptly when interviewed by the Gardaí and had made a written admission of the offence thereafter. As already indicated, he also pleaded guilty to the charge of rape at his arraignment.

Against this background, Flood J considered the sentence to be imposed on the defendant. Final sentence had been adjourned in the case for one year at the defendant's arraignment when Flood J had indicated that he might impose a suspended sentence provided certain conditions were met as to probation and attandance by the defendant with a psychiatrist. At the end of that one year period, Flood J reviewed the situation and concluded that a suspended sentence of nine years penal servitude should be imposed. Unusually for a sentence imposed at first instance, and very helpfully, he also delivered a comprehensive reserved judgment in which he analysed the principles applicable to the case.

He referred in his judgment to the general principles applicable to sentencing, beginning with the decision of the Court of Criminal Appeal in *The People v O'Driscoll* (1972) 1 Frewen 351, of the Supreme Court in *The People v Poyning* [1972] IR 402 and of Gannon J in *The State (Stanbridge) v Mahon* [1979] IR 214. From an even broader perspective, he quoted with approval the view of Henchy J in *The State (Healy) v Donoghue* [1976] IR 325 that sentencing should be proportionate not only to the crime but also to the 'relevant personal circumstances' of the defendant. Finally, alluding to the decision in *Cox v Ireland* [1992] 2 IR 503 (1991 Review, 106-7) Flood J concluded that 'the particular punishment to be imposed on an individual offender is subject to the constitutional principle of proportionality.'

In relation to the offence in this case, Flood J accepted the views expressed by the Supreme Court in *The People v Tiernan* [1989] ILRM 149; [1988] IR 250 (see the 1988 Review, 181-4) that the crime of rape *prima facie* requires a custodial sentence. However, he also noted that the Supreme Court had declined to adopt a formulaic or tariff approach to sentencing a convicted person and that there remained exceptional circumstances in which a judge may consider imposing a non-custodial sentence where an accused has pleaded guilty to rape. Acknowledging that such cases would be very rare, as Finlay CJ had noted in the *Tiernan* case, Flood J concluded that the instant case was such a case. He thus imposed the suspended sentence of nine years already referred to.

While it is no doubt the case that the sentencing discretion allows a wide range of manoeuvre for a trial judge, it remains true that the decision of Flood J in this case, which attracted considerable publicity at the time of the original arraignment in July 1992, was much criticised in the media. Indeed, it may be noted that the complainant in the instant case, Lavinia Kerwick, took a ground-breaking decision after the arraignment in July 1992 (and after Flood J had indicated that he was considering imposing a suspended sentence) to lift the veil of her anonymity and to express her personal view that the sentence in the case had not, in her view, been appropriate. It must be said that, at that time, Flood J had not imposed the final sentence in the case, though as it turned out a suspended sentence was in fact imposed. Arising from Lavinia Kerwick's decision, the government committed itself to introduce a mechanism by which the prosecution could appeal against unduly lenient sentences, arising from which the Oireachtas ultimately passed the Criminal Justice Act 1993, discussed above, 210. The sentence imposed in *The People v W.C.* [1994] 1 ILRM 321 could not be seen as the sole reason for the enactment of the Criminal Justice Act 1993 (for an earlier example, see the 1990 Review, 246, but it certainly was the most well-publicised case which led to pressure for the changes contained in the 1993 Act. For an excellent and comprehensive discussion of the principles applied by Flood J in this case, see Tom O'Malley's article (1994) 4 *Irish Criminal Law Journal* 1.

We can now proceed to discuss the other three cases in this area in 1993.

In *The People v Fetherston*, Court of Criminal Appeal, 5 July 1993, the Court (Hederman, Barron and Geoghegan JJ), in an *ex tempore* judgment, substituted a sentence of seven and a half years for one of 10 years in respect of rape. The particular circumstances of the case which the Court took into account were that the defendant had voluntarily given himself up at a Garda station two weeks after the rape had taken place and made, in effect, a full confession immediately. The Court also had regard to the fact that the defendant's victim had made a substantial recovery from the immediate post traumatic stress of the rape.

By way of contrast to the *Fetherston* case, in *The People v Fagan*, Court of Criminal Appeal, 8 November 1993, the Court (Finlay CJ, O'Hanlon and Geoghegan JJ), in an *ex tempore* judgment, declined to interfere with a sentence of 12 years for rape. Here, the defendant had pleaded guilty only after the victim had begun to give evidence at the defendant's trial. There were also aggravating factors such as the youth of the victim (16 years of age) and evidence that the victim had been abducted with a view to committing the rape.

Finally, in *The People v G.*, Supreme Court, 11 November 1993, the trial judge had imposed 12 concurrent sentences of life imprisonment, the maximum sentence for rape. The 12 counts were representative counts arising from what the defendant admitted were approximately 400 different occasions, over a period of six years, on which he had either sexually interfered with or raped three girls when they were between the ages of six and twelve. When one of the victims had informed her parents of the rapes and sexual assaults, the defendant immediately made a full disclosure of the incidents and also indicated at an early stage that he would plead guilty to the offences. The trial judge, in imposing sentence, acknowledged the fullness of the admissions made by the defendant but concluded that, arising from the risk of re-offending, he would impose a life sentence in the knowldege that the defendant would not be released unless the Minister for Justice's advisers were satisfied that the defendant was no longer a risk. The Supreme Court (Finlay CJ, O'Flaherty, Egan, Blayney and Denham JJ) unanimously reversed this decision. Citing the decision in *The People v Tiernan* [1989] ILRM 149; [1988] IR 250 (see the 1988 Review, 181-4), Finlay CJ held that the early admission of guilt by the defendant must, in light of the principles in *Tiernan*, be given weight in virtually all cases. However, the Court accepted that in view of the extremely serious nature of the offences in the instant case, only a very lengthy determinate sentence would be appropriate. The Court therefore reduced the sentence to 15 years, commencing on the date of the trial in the Central Criminal Court.

Victim impact assessment   S. 5 of the Criminal Justice Act 1993, discussed in other contexts above, 213 and 248 and below, 273, provides that, in relation to three categories of offence, a court 'shall' take into account 'any effect whether long-term or otherwise) of the offence on the person in respect of whom the offence was committed.' The three categories are: (a) a sexual offence within the meaning of the Criminal Evidence Act 1992; (b) an offence involving violence or the threat of violence to a person; and (c) an offence consisting of attempting or conspiring to commit, or aiding, abetting, counselling, procuring or inciting the commission of an offence mentioned in (a) or (b). While s. 3 of the Act does not employ the term 'victim impact assessment', this phrase has achieved a certain currency in relation to its provisions. However, s. 3 confers a wide power on a court to receive 'evidence or submissions' concerning the effect of the offence from any person, including (under s. 5(3)), the victim.

SEXUAL OFFENCES

Buggery and gross indecency   Ss. 2 to 5 of the Criminal Law (Sexual Offences) Act 1993 provided for a fundamental change to Irish criminal law concerning buggery, or anal intercourse, and gross indecency. Prior to the 1993 Act, buggery was, under ss. 61 and 62 of the Offences against the Person Act 1861, as adapted by s. 11 of the Criminal Law Amendment Act 1885, a criminal offence in all circumstances, regardless for example of the question of consent. S. 11 of the 1885 Act also dealt with gross indecency on a similar basis.

The most significant changes effected by ss. 2 to 5 of the 1993 Act are that buggery is now an offence in three circumstances only. First, buggery is an offence under s. 3 of the 1993 Act where committed with a person under the age of 17 years, but not where the parties are married. Second, buggery is an offence under s. 5 of the 1993 Act where committed with a person of any age who is mentally impaired. Third, buggery between a human being and an animal remains an offence under ss. 61 and 62 of the Offences against the Person Act 1861. Finally, s. 4 of the 1993 Act replaces s. 11 of the Criminal Law Amendment Act 1885 and, when read in conjunction with s. 5(2) of the Act, provides, in effect, that gross indecency is an offence only when committed either with a person under the age of 17 years or else with a person of any age who is mentally impaired.

This summary of the effects of ss. 2 to 5 of the 1993 Act does not to justice to the enormous degree of public and political debate which preceded the passing of the 1993 Act. In general, ss. 2 to 5 may be described as having 'decriminalsised homesexuality', though clearly this is hardly a precise description of the scope of these sections. Nonetheless, this is largely how the sections have been described and their passage represented the culmination of many years of lobbying for the decriminalistion of sexual acts primarily, though not exclusively, associated with the active homosexual or gay community.

There were two significant pieces of litigation which preceded the 1993 Act. In *Norris v Attorney General* [1984] IR 36, the High Court and, by a majority, the Supreme Court rejected a constitutional challenge to ss. 61 and 62 of the 1861 Act. Subsequently, in *Norris v Ireland* (1988) 13 EHRR 186, the European Court of Human Rights, again by a majority, held that ss. 61 and 62 were in breach of Article 8 of the European Convention on Human Rights and Fundamental Freedoms. Both *Norris* cases provoked sharp debate on what amendments, if any, should be made to ss. 61 and 62 of the 1861 Act. In general, it may be said that successive governments indicated that ss. 61 and 62 would be replaced, though the precise form this would take was left at large nor was the timetable for responding to the 1988 Court of Human Rights a matter of priority for many years.

In the 1990 Review, 247-50, we discussed the Law Reform Commission's *Report on Child Sexual Abuse* and its *Report on Sexual Offences Against the Mentally Handicapped*, in which the Commission had recommended changes along the lines ultimately effected by ss. 2 to 5 of the 1993 Act. We do not propose in the present Review to rehearse the arguments for or against the reform of this area of the law contained in the 1990 Review, though we note that the terms of the 1993 Act have resulted in what might be described as a much more 'liberal' regime in this area than currently applies in the United Kingdom. Nonetheless, it remains the case that, while in the years between 1988 and 1993 there was widespread and heated debate about 'decriminalising homosexuality', the Oireachtas and public debate on ss. 2 to 5 of the 1993 Act were exceptionally muted and faded into the background when compared with the debate surrounding the changes effected to the law concerning prostitution and soliciting which formed the remainder of the 1993 Act. We discuss these provisions below.

Tom O'Malley provides a succinct and full discussion of the background to the 1993 Act and its effects in his Annotation, *Irish Current Law Statutes Annotated.* The 1993 Act came into effect on 7 July 1993 on its signature by the President.

Prostitution and connected offences   Ss. 6 to 12 of the Criminal Law (Sexual Offences) Act 1993 substantially amend the law concerning soliciting or importuning for the purposes of commission of unlawful sexual offences (s. 6), soliciting or importuning for the purposes of prostitution (s. 7), loitering for the purposes of prostitution (s. 8), the organisation of prostitution (s. 9), living on the earnings of a prostitute (s. 10), brothel keeping (s. 11) and searching of brothels (s. 12). As already noted, these provisions provoked much more debate in the Oireachtas and, indeed, much more public criticism during their passage than attended the changes effected by ss. 2 to 5 of the Act, discussed above. For a comprehensive discussion of ss. 6 to 12, see Tom O'Malley's Annotation, *Irish Current Law Statutes Annotated.* The 1993 Act came into effect on 7 July 1993 on its signature by the President. See also s. 23 of the Criminal Justice (Public Order) Act 1994, dealing with advertisement of brothels, which we will discuss in the 1994 Review.

Rape: belief as to consent   In three cases in 1993, the Court of Criminal Appeal considered the effect of s. 2(2) of the Criminal Law (Rape) Act 1981, which provides that if, at a trial for rape, 'the jury has to consider whether a man believed that a woman was consenting to sexual intercourse, the presence or absence of reasonable grounds for such a belief is a matter to which the jury is to have regard, in conjunction with any other relevant matters, in considering whether he so believed.' It will be recalled that, in *The People v Gaffey (No. 2)*, Court of Criminal Appeal, 10 May 1991 (see the 1991 Review, 183), the Court had held that the absence of a specific direction by the trial judge as to the effect of s. 2(2) of the 1981 Act might lead to the quashing of a conviction.

    In the first of the three cases in 1993, *The People v F.*, Court of Criminal Appeal, 27 May 1993, the Court (Finlay CJ, Budd and Geoghegan JJ), in an *ex tempore* judgment, dealt with a case where, unlike *Gaffey*, the trial judge had drawn the jury's attention to s. 2(2) of the 1981 Act by means of a paraphrase of its terms. The Court of Criminal Appeal considered that, while this approach might be acceptable in many instances where the issue arose, it would not be adequate in all cases. The Court adverted to the particular matters which the defendant had raised suggesting that he had reasonable grounds for believing that the complainant in this case had consented to sexual intercourse. In the light of these particular matters, which it is not necessary to repeat in this Review, the Court of Criminal Appeal considered that the trial judge was required to link the general point concerning s. 2(2) with the particular items of evidence which the defence had adverted to in the course of the trial. It should be noted, however, that the Court emphasised that such linkage was not required in all cases in which s. 2(2) of the 1981 Act would arise. Finally, we may also note here that, in this case, the Court did not order a re-trial, on the ground that the complainant had already given evidence in two trials (the instant trial being preceded by a jury disagreement) and the defendant had already served over two and a half years in prison.

The second case involving s. 2(2) of the 1981 Act, *The People v Rock (J.)*, Court of Criminal Appeal, 29 July 1993 involved similar issues to those raised in the *F.* case, above. Here, the Court (Blayney, Keane and Lardner JJ), on this occasion delivering a reserved judgment, expressly followed the approach taken in *F.*, holding that a general discussion of the terms of s. 2(2) of the 1981 Act was insufficient to take account of the defendant's assertion that he believed that the complainant had consented. In the particular circumstances, therefore, the Court ordered a re-trial.

Finally, in *The People v Creighton* [1994] 1 ILRM 551, the Court (Finlay CJ, O'Hanlon and Geoghegan JJ) delivered another considered judgment on the impact of s. 2(2) of the 1981 Act in which it referred approvingly to English authority on the subject. Here, in contrast with the other two cases, there was a direct confrontation in the evidence given by the complainant and the defendant. The complainant's evidence was that, by her words and actions, she had made it unambiguously clear that she did not consent to intercourse. The defendant's account, on the other hand, was that the complainant had expressly agreed to intercourse. In this situation of a direct conflict, the Court of Criminal Appeal considered that:

> whilst a trial judge should state the entire of the statutory provisions applicable to the charge of rape and explain in simple language the constituents involved in it, it is not necessary and might well be confusing for him to leave to a jury directions concerning evidence which did not arise in the particular case but which might arise in another case of reasonable grounds for belief by an accused person of consent.
> . . .

The Court quoted with approval *dicta* to the same effect from the decision of the Court of Appeal (Criminal Division) in *R. v Taylor* (1985) 80 Cr App Rep 327, noting that the definition of rape in the UK Sexual Offences (Amendment) Act 1976 was, in all material respects, identical to that in s. 2 of the Criminal Law (Rape) Act 1981. On this basis, therefore, the Court concluded that the trial judge had not erred in directing the jury and the applicant's conviction was thus upheld.

The effect of these three cases appears to be that, in a situation of direct conflict between the complainant and defendant as to consent, as in the *Creighton* case, the issue of s. 2(2) of the 1981 Act does not arise. However, where, as in the *F.* and *Rock* cases, the particular circumstances give rise to consideration of the issue, the safest course for a trial judge to adopt would appear to be to link the general issue of s. 2(2) to the precise matters relied on by the defence as supporting the suggestion that the defendant believed that consent to intercourse was present. Although the *Gaffey* case had indicated that this was not an invariable requirement, the outcome in the *F.* and *Rock* cases, in which convictions were quashed for the lack of such linkage, would appear to indicate the need for such.

Sexual assault: evidence indicating rape In *K.M. v Director of Public Prosecutions*, High Court, 21 June 1993, the applicant was partly successful in obtaining an order prohibiting his further trial on charges of sexual assault where evidence indicated that he had, in fact, committed rape. The applicant, who was 13 years of age at the time of the alleged offences, was charged with sexual assaults on two named girls, one aged eight years and the second aged 11 years, contrary to s. 2 of the Criminal Law (Rape) (Amendment) Act 1990.

At the applicant's original trial, the 11-year-old girl gave evidence to the effect that the applicant had penetrated her vagina with his penis. Counsel for the defence applied to have the jury discharged on the ground that the evidence given disclosed the offence of rape and that the applicant was thereby prejudiced by this, citing the authority of *The People v Mills* (1955) 1 Frewen 153. Counsel for the prosecution informed the trial judge that medical evidence would be given to the effect that no penetration had occurred. The trial judge discharged the jury, and the applicant then sought an order of prohibition preventing his further trial on the charges. Morris J granted prohibition in respect of the charges concerning the 11 year old girl, but declined to prohibit the applicant's trial on the charges concerning the eight-year-old girl, who had not given evidence at the original trial.

Morris J rejected the general proposition suggested by the applicant that the Director of Public Prosecutions was obliged to charge him with the more serious crime of rape rather than the charge of sexual assault. In support of this, Morris J cited the decision of the Supreme Court in March 1993 in *The People v Rock (P.)* [1994] 1 ILRM 66. It will be recalled (see the discussion of the case, 236, above) that in *Rock* the Supreme Court had overruled the Court of Criminal Appeal decision in *The People v Mills* (1955) 1 Frewen 153, on which the trial judge in the instant case had relied in discharging the jury. The decision in *Rock* was, of course, made after the applicant's trial.

However, the applicant succeeded in part before Morris J on a second point, namely that the conflict between the evidence of the 11 year old girl, which indicated penetration, and the medical evidence to be called by the prosecution, which was to the contrary effect, required that any further proceedings would inevitably involve an acquittal and thus should be prohibited. On this point, Morris J agreed, applying *dicta* of Finlay P (as he then was) in *The State (O'Callaghan) v Ó hUadhaigh* [1977] IR 42, the well-known case concerning the effect of a *nolle prosequi*.

This left the charges against the applicant concerning the eight year old girl. On this aspect of the case, Morris J was not prepared to interfere with the trial process, holding that to do so would be an unwarranted usurpation of the trial judge's function, citing in support the decision of Gannon J in *Clune v Director of Public Prosecutions* [1981] ILRM 17.

Finally, Morris J rejected an argument that there was no evidence to rebut the applicant's presumption of innocence having regard to the fact that he was under 14 at the time of the alleged offences and was therefore *doli incapax*. Morris J accepted as correct the views of Slater J in *R. v Gorrie* (1919) 83 JP 136 on the requirements necessary to rebut the presumption of *doli incapax*, namely that it be shown that the accused knew not merely that what he did was wrong but that he knew it was 'gravely wrong, seriously wrong.' Morris J referred to the transcript of the evidence given by the 11-year-old girl in the first trial, in which she stated that the accused had frightened her by saying that if she said anything he would kill her. From this, he was satisfied that it would be open to a jury to conclude that the accused was aware that his conduct was seriously wrong. Although Morris J acknowledged that this evidence related to the charges which were now being prohibited, he considered that it was capable of being tendered to the court to rebut the presumption of *doli incapax*. This was, however, subject to any rulings which might be made by the trial judge, and Morris J expressly refrained from anticipating such rulings.

Sexual assault: guilty plea indicating absence of consent   In *The People v O'T.*, Court of Criminal Appeal, 18 January 1993, the Court (Hederman, Keane and Flood JJ), in an *ex tempore* judgment, dealt with the effect of a plea of guilty under the Criminal Law (Rape) (Amendment) Act 1990. The applicant had pleaded guilty to sexual assault contrary to s. 2 of the 1990 Act, and the note circulated with the *ex tempore* judgment by the Registrar of the Court of Criminal Appeal states that the applicant had been sentenced to two years detention by the trial judge. The Court of Criminal Appeal was satisfied that this sentence had been correct and that it could not have been less. The Court's judgment noted that a guilty plea under the 1990 Act amounts to a plea of sexual assault without the victim's consent, and that the Criminal Law (Amendment) Act 1935 thus has no application. In a similar case, *The People v W.*, Court of Criminal Appeal, 18 January 1993, the Court

(Hederman, Keane and Flood JJ), also in an *ex tempore* judgment, pointed out that, on a guilty plea in a sexual assault case, there is a duty on the prosecution to ensure that all the facts of the case are established for the trial court and that the condition of the accused and the effects of the offence on the victim should be heard *viva voce* before the trial judge. In this case, a sentence of three years detention was reduced by the Court to two years.

STOP AND SEARCH POWERS

Common law power: road traffic   In *D.P.P. (Stratford) v Fagan* [1993] 2 IR 95 (HC); [1994] 2 ILRM 349 (SC), the extent of the garda power to stop vehicles was considered by the High Court and Supreme Court in the context of a prosecution under the Road Traffic Acts. The Supreme Court decision in this case, which supported the power of the Gardaí to mount roadblocks, will be discussed in the 1994 Review.

Statutory power: drugs   In *O'Callaghan v Ireland*, High Court, 1 April 1992; [1994] 1 IR 555 (SC), the High Court (Morris J) and, on appeal, the Supreme Court, upheld the constitutional validity of the stop and search powers conferred on Gardaí by s. 23 of the Misuse of Drugs Act 1977, as amended by s. 12 of the Misuse of Drugs Act 1984.

In its judgment in the case, the Supreme Court (Finlay CJ, Hederman, Egan, Blayney and Denham JJ) stressed the deference of the courts to the methods used by the Oireachtas to reconcile personal rights with the claims of the common good, quoting the judgment of Kenny J to that effect in the leading case *Ryan v Attorney General* [1965] IR 294. The Court continued:

> It confirms his [Morris J's] conclusion that the potential damage to society from the use and distribution and, therefore, from the possession of controlled drugs, is so great and constitutes such a pernicious evil that the legislature was clearly acting within a reasonable and proper discretion in making lawful such extension of the power of arrest as might be found in the power of search contained in [s. 23].

In an important passage, however, the Court added that the type of procedural protections available to a person arrested and detained in garda custody on foot of arrest powers would also be available, *mutatis mutandis*, to a person in respect of whom the powers conferred by the 1977 Act, as amended, were invoked. On the procedural protections available to such persons, see the quotation from the judgment of Finlay CJ in *The People v Quilligan and O'Reilly (No. 3)* [1993] 2 IR 305 contained in the 1992 Review, 236-7.

SUICIDE (ABOLITION OF CRIME)

The Criminal Law (Suicide) Act 1993 provided for the abolition of the crime of suicide. The Act came into effect on 9 July 1993, one month after its signature by the President: see s. 1(2) of the Act.

S. 2(1) of the Act states, in stark terms: 'Suicide shall cease to be a crime.' Prior to the 1993 Act, suicide was a common law felony. While obviously a completed suicide was beyond the reach of the criminal law, attempted suicide, being an attempt to commit a felony, was a common law misdemeanour and carried a possible sentence of life imprisonment. Although no prosecution for attempted suicide had been initiated in Ireland in recent years, it was felt that the possibility of a criminal prosecution was no longer an appropriate response to a person who attempted suicide.

However, it should be noted that s. 2(2) of the 1993 Act goes on to provide that any person who aids, abets, counsels or procures the suicide, or attempted suicide, of another shall be guilty of an offence carrying a maximum sentence of 14 years imprisonment. S. 2(3) provides that a person charged with murder or manslaughter may, if the circumstances so appear, be found guilty of an offence under subs. (2) rather than the homicide offence. This provision deals with the difficulty of proving homicide in the event of a failed 'suicide pact'. In such circumstances, it will be a matter of fact whether a surviving person in a suicide pact was guilty of, say, murder or of the lesser offence under the 1993 Act of aiding the suicide pact.

S. 3 of the 1993 Act repeals s. 9 of the Summary Jurisdiction (Ireland) Amendment Act 1871, as amended by s. 85 of the Courts of Justice Act 1936, which had dealt with procedural aspects of a trial for attempted suicide. This provision was obsolete by virtue of the 1993 Act.

It may be noted that, while the 1993 Act deals, strictly speaking, only with the criminal aspects of suicide, it has wider implications. Thus, under the Coroners Act 1962, a verdict of suicide was precluded since the 1962 Act prohibited any verdict which imputed criminality to any person: see *Green v McLoughlin*, High Court, 1 December 1989, discussed in the 1990 Review, 189. One result of this had been that inquests were not a reliable source of information as to the level of suicide in the State. However, the change effected by the 1993 Act would clear away this particular problem for inquests. Of course, the verdict arrived at in a post-1993 Act inquest could also have implications in relation, for example, to any insurance policy held by a deceased person.

SUMMARY TRIAL

Advance furnishing of statements In *Director of Public Prosecutions v Doyle*, High Court, 14 May 1993; [1994] 1 ILRM 529 (SC), Geoghegan J considered the question whether there was an obligation on the prosecution in summary trials to furnish to the defence, in advance of trial, the evidence on which the prosecution intends to proceed. The Supreme Court, in its judgment in 1994 on appeal in this case, held that the obligation could arise in certain circumstances. We will discuss this important decision in full in the 1994 Review. For previous High Court decisions in this area, see the 1990 Review, 197 and the 1991 Review, 145-7.

UNINCORPORATED BODIES

In *Director of Public Prosecutions (Barron) v Wexford Farmers' Club* [1994] 2 ILRM 295; [1994] 1 IR 546, O'Hanlon J held that a criminal prosecution for breach of the Intoxicating Liquor Act 1988 could be brought against an unincorporated body, in this case the Wexford Farmers' Club.

S. 45(1) of the Intoxicating Liquor Act 1988 provides that 'a person shall not publish, or cause to be published, any advertisement drawing attention to any function to be held on the premises of a registered club'. S. 45(3) provides that where there is a contravention of s. 45(1), '(a) the registered club, (b) every person entered in the register of clubs as an official or member of the committee of management or governing body of the club at the time the advertisement is published, and (c) any person who published the advertisement or caused it to be published' shall be guilty of an offence. A prosecution was initiated against Wexford Farmers' Club, an unincorporated association, alleging the commission of an offence contrary to the provisions of s. 45(1) of the Intoxicating Liquor Act 1988. The District Court judge before whom the case was tried stated a consultative case to the High Court for a determination as to whether such a charge could properly be brought against an unincorported body such as the club.

O'Hanlon J held in the affirmative. He stated that, while at common law, there could be no question of an unincorporated association committing a criminal offence, criminal liability could be imposed on such a body by statute. Having regard to the definition of 'person' in s. 11(c) of the Interpretation Act 1937, he concluded that the word 'person' in s. 45(1) of the Intoxicating Liquor Act 1988 must be taken to refer to an unincorporated body of persons as well as to an individual.

However, he also drew attention to the 'very draconian' nature of s. 45. Quoting with approval the decision in *Reynolds v Austin & Sons Ltd* [1951] 2 KB 135, O'Hanlon J concluded that, in order to prove an offence under s.

45 of the 1988 Act, active involvement of the club in bringing about the advertisement would have to be proved. On this basis, he remitted the case to the District Court.

VICTIMS

Victim impact assessment   The terms of s. 5 of the Criminal Justice Act 1993 are discussed above, 248 and 264.

YOUNG PERSONS

Commencement of detention   In *Byrne v Director of Trinity House*, High Court, 20 December 1993, Kinlen J expressed disquiet at the manner in which the applicant, a 15 year old boy, had been dealt with by the State authorities having custody of him.

The applicant had been convicted in the District Court on 24 November 1993 on a charge relating to a stolen car. The District Court judge who heard the case had ordered that he be sent to the reformatory school at Trinity House, Dublin for a period of three years beginning on 24 November 1993. However, it appeared that, on that date, there was no place available in the reformatory school for the applicant, and so the judge ordered that, pursuant to s. 63 of the Children's Act 1908, he should be remanded to Trinity House, a place of detention within the 1908 Act, until such time as a place became available for him in Trinity House reformatory school. Trinity House reformatory school and Trinity House place of detention are, in fact, housed in the same building.

The applicant applied for an inquiry into his detention pursuant to Article 40.4.2° of the Constitution and sought his release. During the inquiry, it emerged that the applicant had been been at Trinity House place of detention for a period of three weeks after 24 November 1993 but that, by the time of Kinlen J's judgment, he had been found a place in Trinity House reformatory school. It also emerged that, in so far as Trinity House operated as a place of detention it was under the aegis of the Department of Justice but that, in so far as it operated as a reformatory school, it was under the control of the Department of Education. Kinlen J commented that '[a]t first sight it seemed to me to be an extraordinary administrative quagmire which was quite unnecessary.'

However, Kinlen J rejected the applicant's claim that he was entitled to be released. He accepted that s. 61 of the 1908 Act provides that, where a court orders that a detention order under s. 63 is to be deferred, the court is to have regard to the age or health of a youthful offender. However, Kinlen

J also held that the age or health of the offender was not the sole factor in such cases, and thus the order in the instant case was not invalid for not being based on age or health.

Although he rejected the applicant's claim to be released, Kinlen J stated that it was 'unjust and incredible' that the District Court judge's sentence of detention would not begin until the applicant was moved from one bed to another in the same building, simply because the first bed was under the jurisdiction of the Minister for Justice while the other was under the juris- diction of the Minister for Education. In these circumstances, Kinlen J held that the three year period had begun on 24 November 1993, rather than on the date a place was found in the reformatory school. Kinlen J ended his judgment with a strong criticism of the situation which had arisen and with an analogy and literary reference not often found in the judgments of the courts:

> If [the applicant] is to be left in a place of detention until there is a room for him somewhere else, it would be absurd that credit should not be given for that period of time. Imagine the frustration that Ms Donnelly [counsel for the applicant] refers to of 'planes being stacked at Heathrow Airport not knowing when they were going to land. In other words the prisoner would be in the place of detention and might never know when eventually he or she was going to be released. That is very much the situation inspired by Kafka. I would hope that these Departments would 'get their act together' and that this situation should not arise again.

While these sentiments might very well produce the results hoped for, it is relevant to note here that the applicant's situation not only reflected, albeit less dramatically, the situation in Kafka's *The Trial*, but also mirrored previous failures by the State authorities in this area: see the discussion of *The People v D.E.*, Court of Criminal Appeal, 11 February 1991 and of *G. and McD. v Governor of Mountjoy Prison* [1991] 1 IR 373, discussed in the 1991 Review, 183-5. In this light, it is to be hoped that the views of Kinlen J will find a comprehensive response in the relevant Departments of govern- ment.

Detention in St Patrick's Institution   In *Murray v Clifford and Carroll*, High Court, 17 December 1993, the applicant, then 16 years of age, had been convicted of a number of indictable offences in the District Court by the first and second respondents, both judges of the District Court. He had been sentenced to a total of twelve months detention in St Patrick's Institution in accordance with s. 13 of the Criminal Justice Act 1960. He challenged these sentences on the ground that the respondent judges were precluded by s. 5

of the Summary Jurisdiction Over Children (Ireland) Act 1884 from sentencing him for a period in excess of three months.

As Murphy J pointed out in his judgment, the case arose directly from the decision of the Supreme Court in *Hutch v Governor of Wheatfield Prison and Ors*, High Court, 28 February 1992; Supreme Court, 17 November 1992, discussed in the 1992 Review, 305-6. In *Hutch*, as in the *Murray* case, the applicant had been charged with a number of indictable offences and had been tried summarily in the District Court. He was convicted and sentenced to three terms of one year's imprisonment in respect of three of the charges, two of the terms to run consecutively. The trial judge in *Hutch* had imposed these sentences in purported exercise of powers in s. 2 of the Criminal Justice Act 1951, which empowers the District Court to try summarily certain indictable offences, including the offences with which the applicant was charged. However, the Supreme Court held that s. 5 of the Summary Jurisdiction Over Children (Ireland) Act 1884 limited the District Court to imposing a sentence of three months imprisonment on a young person tried summarily for an indictable offence. The Court noted that s. 5 of the 1884 Act constituted a specific enactment establishing a very definite and important right for young persons and that, since s. 2 of the 1951 Act conferred a general jurisdiction on the District Court without reference to the 1884 Act, the special provision in s. 5 of the 1884 Act had not been impliedly repealed by the general provision in s. 2 of the 1951 Act. The Court thus applied the maxim *generalia specialibus non derogant* in resolving the apparent conflict between the 1884 Act and the 1951 Act.

In the *Murray* case, Murphy J summarised the applicant's case as being that s. 13 of the Criminal Justice Act 1960 should be treated in the same manner as s. 2 of the Criminal Justice Act 1951 had been treated in the *Hutch* case. Murphy J did not see the comparison as being apt. He noted that the 1960 Act did not deal with imprisonment as such, but rather detention of young offenders in St Patrick's Institution. While he acknowledged that imprisonment and detention in St Patrick's Institution both involved 'the same basic element of deprivation of liberty', he cited the decision of the Supreme Court in *The State (Clinch) v Connellan* [1985] IR 597 as authority for the proposition that 'detention cannot be equated for legislative purposes with imprisonment.' He noted that, in *Clinch*, the Supreme Court had held that the restriction imposed on the District Court by s. 5 of the 1951 Act on imposing an aggregate sentence in excess of 12 months imprisonment had no application to the sentencing of a person to detention in St Patrick's Institution under s. 13 of the 1960 Act. On this basis, Murphy J distinguished the *Hutch* case and dismissed the applicant's claim for judicial review.

Defence Forces

COURTS-MARTIAL APPEAL COURT

S. 6 of the Criminal Procedure Act 1993 provides that the changes effected by ss. 2 to 5 and 7 of the 1993 Act to the jurisdiction of the Court of Criminal Appeal shall apply *mutatis mutandis* to the Courts-Martial Appeal Court established by the Courts-Martial Appeal Act 1983. The 1993 Act is considered in detail in the Criminal Law chapter, 210-4, above. S. 2 of the 1993 Act (see 211, above), as adapted by s. 6, provides that the Courts-Martial Appeal Court may review decisions of courts-martial which resulted in a miscarriage of justice or an excessive sentence. S. 3 of the 1993 Act (see 212, above),as adapted by s. 6, extends the appellate jurisdiction of the Courts-Martial Appeal Court. S. 4 of the 1993 Act (see 212, above), as adapted by s. 6, deals with retrials. S. 5 of the 1993 Act (see 213, above), as adapted by s. 6, deals with summary determination of appeals by the Courts-Martial Appeal Court.

MILITARY DISCIPLINE

Judges' Rules: interview by military police In *In re Gunner Buckley*, Courts-Martial Appeal Court, 28 July 1993, the Court (Finlay CJ, Carroll and Barr JJ) held that the requirements of the Judges' Rules apply to an interview conducted by the military police. The appellant in this case had been convicted before a limited court-martial with engaging in conduct prejudicial to good order and discipline, contrary to s. 168(1) of the Defence Act 1954, as amended. The charge concerned smoking cannbis in a military barracks. The main evidence tendered in the case was a written statement by the appellant, later retracted, in which he admitted smoking cannibis. This statement had been written in the course of an interview by the military police. The appellant had not been cautioned prior to the beginning of the interview that he was not obliged to answer any questions.

The crucial point established in the case was that the appellant had been detailed by his commanding officer to make himself available for interview by the military police. The Courts-Martial Appeal Court noted that the result of this was that the appellant would not have been entitled to leave the interview, though he would have been entitled to refuse to answer questions in accordance with the military code. The Court found that this situation, in which the appellant was not entitled to leave the interview, was as near an equivalent as may be to the position of a civilian being interviewed by the Gardaí while in custody. It pointed out that in *The People v Cummins* [1972] IR 312, the Supreme Court had stated that the fact of custody was the essential element in triggering the caution required under Rule 3 of the Judges' Rules.

The Court in *Buckley* therefore held that, while the appellant had presented himself for interview on foot of a lawful military command, nonetheless the appellant should have been cautioned in the manner indicated in Rule 3 before being questioned by the military police. The Court concluded that, while the court-martial would have had a discretion to admit the appellant's statement notwithstanding the failure to issue a warning, on all the facts of the case it was not satisfied that it would have been a proper exercise of that discretion to have admitted the statement. On this basis, the Court quashed the decision of the court-martial. As the appellant's statement was the only evidence tendered against him, and as the military police had obtained the admission by putting the allegation of cannabis smoking to him based on an allegation from a person who was not called as a witness, the Court considered that in the interests of justice this was not a case where a re-trial should be ordered.

Legal aid: fees   The Courts-Martial (Legal Aid) Regulations 1993 (SI No. 309) amended the 1986 Regulations of the same title by providing revised fees for legal aid under the Courts-Martial Appeal Act 1983.

Sentence: desertion   In *In re Private Waters*, Courts-Martial Appeal Court, 15 February 1993, the Court (Blayney, Carroll and Geoghegan JJ), in an *ex tempore* judgment, upheld a court martial sentence discharging the appellant from the Defence Forces for desertion. The desertion, which had been for a period of over 9 years, had initially been the result of the emotional trauma of the appellant seeing his girlfriend desert him for his best friend. While the Court had sympathy for the appellant, it noted that he had given himself up for the purposes of clearing up his position with the army and that he had stated that he could obtain a job with a security firm. In those circumstances, the Court concluded that the sentence of discharge should not be interfered with.

Sentence: effect on ability to be re-engaged   In *In re Corporal Foley*, Courts-Martial Appeal Court, 15 February 1993, the Court (Blayney, Carroll and Geoghegan JJ), in an *ex tempore* judgment, reversed a court martial sentence fining the appellant £300, later reduced to £150 by the appellant's commanding officer. The appellant had pleaded guilty to the civil offence of assault occasioning actual bodily harm, pursuant to s. 169 of the Defence Act 1954, but it had not been made known to the court martial that a fine of £300 would render the appellant's rating in the army unsatisfactory, thus making him ineligible to be considered for re-engagement in the army at the end of his term. In light of the appellant's excellent record in the army over a 21 year period, the Courts-Martial Appeal Court concluded that the fine should be reduced to £50, below the threshold which would render the appellant's rating unsatisfactory.

The principles laid down in *Foley* were approved by the Court (Denham, Barr and Morris JJ) in *In re Corporal McGrath*, Courts-Martial Appeal Court, 21 December 1993.

MISCARRIAGES OF JUSTICE AND PARDON

We noted above, 276, the general effect of s. 6 of the Criminal Procedure Act 1993 (discussed in relation to the Court of Criminal Appeal in the Criminal Law chapter 216-7, above) on the jurisdiction of the Courts-Martial Appeal Court. We noted above that s. 2 of the Act, as adapted by s. 6, provides that the Courts-Martial Appeal Court may review convictions for alleged miscarriages of justice. In addition, s. 7 of the 1993 Act (see 211, above), as adapted by s. 6 and s. 7(5), provides for applications for a pardon to the Minister for Defence in respect of a conviction by a court-martial. Such application may either result in a pardon or no further action by the Minister, in the latter case leaving open the possibility of an application to the Courts-Martial Appeal Court under s. 2, as adapted by s. 5 (see the similar relationship between ss. 2 and 7 in relation to the Court of Criminal Appeal, discussed in the Criminal Law chapter 211-12, above). S. 8 of the 1993 Act provides that, in determining whether a pardon should be granted by the President under Article 13.6 of the Constitution, the government may appoint a committee to inquire into any alleged miscarriage of justice: see 212, above.

Finally, we should note that, in one respect, it would seem that the terms of the Criminal Procedure Act 1993 were not adapted in full to a miscarriage of justice arising from a court-martial. Arising from the quashing of a conviction due to a miscarriage of justice in a civilian court of law or the granting of a pardon under s. 7, an award of compensation may result under s. 9 of the Criminal Procedure Act 1993: see 217, above. However, no express adaptation of the 1993 Act was made in connection with a comparable quashing or pardon arising from a court-martial, the adaptations in s. 6 of the Act being confined to 'sections 2 to 5 and 7' of the Act. However, it must be said that the precise terms of s. 9 of the 1993 Act are somewhat ambigious in this respect, its application to what might be termed the 'military context' being unclear both in relation to miscarriages of justice arising from a court-martial and, perhaps to a lesser extent, in relation to pardons arising from the 'military context'. We will take the latter situation first.

S. 9(1)(b) provides for compensation arising from a conviction for an offence followed by a petition for a pardon under s. 7 of the 1993 Act. This would appear to apply to a petition arising from the 'military context', since s. 7 of the Act was expressly adapted by s. 6 of the 1993 Act. However, this is not altogether free from doubt since the reference in s. 9(1) to a 'conviction' would appear to refer to a conviction in a civilian court, and it may be noted in this context that s. 6(2)(a) of the Act expressly adapts 'conviction' as it appears in s. 2 of the Act to include conviction by a court-martial. Since the adaptations in s. 6(2) are expressly for the purposes of s. 6(1), and since s. 6(1) refers to adaptations of ss. 2 to 5 and 7 of the Act only, it may be that s. 9 does not, after all, apply to petitions under s. 7 concerning the 'military context'.

In relation to whether compensation is payable in respect of a miscarriage of justice arising from a court-martial, s. 9(1)(a) provides for compensation in respect of 'a person [who] has been convicted of an offence' and whose conviction has been quashed by the Court of Criminal Appeal under s. 2 of the Act. Again, there is no adaptation of the word 'conviction' as it appears here nor an adaptation of the reference to the Court of Criminal Appeal.

A further argument for suggesting that the compensation arrangements do not apply in the 'military context' is that, whereas in s. 8 of the Act the usual application for a petition for a pardon to the Minister for Justice is expressly adapted in the 'military context' to an application to the Minister for Defence, no such similar adaptation is made in respect of payment under s. 9 of the Act. While it might be argued that it could have been the intention of the Oireachtas to 'centralise' compensation payments from the Minister for Justice, it seems clear that there are considerable obstacles for a person claiming compensation under s. 9 from the 'military context'. However, given the lack of clarity one way or the other on this point, a clear amendment to the 1993 Act would seem eminently desirable.

PARTICIPATION IN INTERNATIONAL UN FORCES

The Defence (Amendment) Act 1993, which came into force on its signature by the President on 1 July 1993, facilitates the participation by the Irish Defence Forces in International UN Forces, that is, any UN force engaged in peace enforcement as opposed to the more traditional UN role of peace keeping. The statutory basis for Irish participation in UN peace keeping forces is s. 2 of the Defence (Amendment) (No. 2) Act 1960, and the Irish role in such UN Forces, beginning in the Congo and later including many tours of duty in the Lebanon, was confined, in effect, to defensive action. The 1993 Act does not expressly amend s. 2 of the 1960 Act (although its Long Title describes it as an Act 'to amend and extend' the 1960 Act), but s. 2 of the 1993 Act provides for participation in what s. 1 defines as any 'international force or body established by the Security Council or the General Assembly of the United Nations. ' This amounts, in effect, to an extension of the form of UN service for which Irish troops may be dispatched under the 1960 Act. S. 2 of the 1993 Act provides that liability to serve in the form of UN Forces covered by the Act will only apply to those who enlisted in the Defence Forces after the Act came into effect, or, in relation to those who enlisted before the Act only to those who offered to render themselves liable for external service on or after the coming into force of the Act. S. 4 of the 1993 Act requires the Minister for Defence to make an annual report to Dáil Éireann on the operation of s. 2 of the 1960 Act, presumably as amended, in effect, by the 1993 Act. The first operation in which the Defence Forces participated under the terms of the 1993 Act was the, ultimately ill-fated, Second UN Operation in Somalia (UNOSOM II).

PENSIONS

Abatement   In *Ryan v Minister for Defence*, High Court, 23 July 1993, Carroll J declined to quash an abatement of pension made by the Minister under s. 13(2) of the Army Pensions Act 1923, as amended. The abatement occurred in the wake of the landmark award of damages to the applicant arising from injuries sustained while he was on deemed active service in the Lebanon: see *Ryan v Ireland* [1989] IR 177 and *Ryan v Ireland (No. 2)*, High Court, 19 October 1989 (discussed in the 1989 Review, 410-18).

The applicant had sustained injuries to both legs in the incident in the Lebanon, which occurred in 1979, arising from which he had initially been awarded a wound pension under the 1923 Act, as amended. Arising from his claim for damages, the plaintiff was ultimately awarded £223,354, but this figure was not arrived at until 1991, after lengthy litigation including two appeals to the Supreme Court, one on liability and the other on quantum. In May 1991, the applicant was requested to make submissions as to why his wound pension, then standing at £3,150 per annum, should not be abated in full or in part. The applicant submitted that, in view of his service to the country, there should be no abatement at all but that if there had to be the Minister should take into account only that element of the damages award that related to loss of earnings into the future. The Minister, acting on advice, decided that only 40% of the award of damages to the applicant should be taken into account in the abatement of the pension. Accordingly, the Minister decided that an abatement of £8,504, representing 40% of the annualised award to the applicant, would be made. The effect of this was that until the applicant's future pension exceeded £8,504, no pension wouild be payable. Carroll J held that the Minister's decision could not be challenged on any of the grounds contended for by the applicant, whether that the Minister had failed to take into consideration all relevant factors, that it was based on an arbitrary application of a mechanical formula or that there should be a distinction drawn between past and future loss of earnings. In this respect, she concluded that the Minister's decision met all the tests laid down by the Supreme Court in *The State (Thornhill) v Minister for Defence* [1986] IR 1. For another decision in this area, see *Breen v Minister for Defence*, Supreme Court, 20 July 1990 (1990 Review, 265-6).

Education

JUDICIAL REVIEW

The scope of judicial review in relation to third level colleges was discussed in *Rajah v Royal College of Surgeons in Ireland* [1994] 1 ILRM 233; [1994] 1 IR 384: see the Administrative Law chapter, 17, above.

LEGAL EDUCATION

The statutory provisions concerning the Incorporated Law Society's examinations are referred to in the Solicitors chapter, 528, below.

VOCATIONAL EDUCATION

The Vocational Education (Grants for Annual Schemes of Committees) Regulations 1993 (SI No. 418), made under the Vocational Education Act 1930, provided for the grants to Vocational Education Committees for 1993.

Electricity and Energy

GAS

Environmental impact assessment The Gas Act 1976 (Section 40A) (Exemption) Order 1993 (SI No. 166) exempted Bord Gáis Éireann from the environmental impact assessment requirements of s.40A of the 1976 Act, inserted by Reg. 20 of the European Communities (Environmental Impact Assessment) Regulations 1989, in connection with the construction of the gas interconnector pipeline between Ireland and the United Kingdom.

NATURAL RESOURCES

Continental shelf The Continental Shelf (Designated Areas) Order 1993 (SI No. 92) sets out the designation of specified areas in respect of which the State expressed a right in regard to the natural resources of the sea bed and the subsoil of the Continental Shelf, in accordance with the Continental Shelf Act 1968. The 1993 Order revoked the 1989 Order of the same title: see the 1989 Review, 327.

PETROLEUM

Whitegate offtake The Petroleum Oils (Regulation or Control of Acquisition, Supply, Distribution or Marketing) (Continuance) Order 1993 (SI No. 403) continued through 1994 the regime outlined in the 1988 Order of the same title: see the 1988 Review, 198.

Equitable Remedies

INTERLOCUTORY INJUNCTION

Interlocutory injunctions In *Cork Communications Ltd v Dennehy*, High Court, 4 October 1993, the plaintiffs, licensed to engage in broadcasting and re-broadcasting television signals for profit, sought an interlocutory injunction against the defendants who were not licensed and were unlawfully broadcasting and re-broadcasting these signals to the detriment of the plaintiffs' economic interests. Lynch J granted the injunction. He had no doubt that the plaintiffs had established that they had a fair case to be tried and that the balance of convenience lay with them. Serious losses, which the defendants were unlikely to be in a position to make good, would probably be incurred by the plaintiffs if the injunction was refused. No similar consequences followed for the defendants if the injunction was granted.

Lynch J laid some emphasis on the fact that the plaintiffs had given an undertaking as to damages. He quoted from the Supreme Court decision of *Irish Shell v Elm Motors* [1984] IR 200, in which McCarthy J had observed that, unless the material available to the court failed to disclose that the defendant had any real prospect of success at the full hearing, the Court should go on to consider the balance of convenience. In that case the trial judge had taken 'a very decided view' on the complex issues that arose. McCarthy J observed that 'the very positive nature' of his decision and it's finality was marked by the absence from the order of any undertaking as to damages and the awarding of costs to the plaintiffs at the interlocutory stage. McCarthy J whilst reserving the question as to whether or not there are cases in which it is proper for a court to express a concluded view as to factual or legal issues arising at the interlocutory stage, considered that ordinarily:

> the determination of an application for an interlocutory injunction lies, and lies only, in the answers to the two material questions as to there being a fair case to be made and where the balance of convenience lies.

Two issues arise here: the desirability of the courts taking a concluded view of the case at interlocutory stage and the requirement (or otherwise) to make the granting of an interlocutory injunction contingent on the plaintiff's willingness to give an undertaking as to damages. As to the first of these issues, there have been several cases subsequent to *Irish Shell* in which the courts have indeed taken such a concluded view: see the 1989 Review, 194 and the 1992 Review, 319. The second issue has not yet been definitively analysed by an Irish court. The easy answer might appear to be to require the plaintiff to give such an undertaking since, otherwise, if the court on a full hearing took a different view of the case, the defendant's interests would be damaged unnecessarily. But what of a case where an already impecunious plaintiff is the clear victim of a wrong? Is the court to decline to grant an interlocutory injunction on account of the plaintiff's lack of resources? That would seem grossly unjust. Is it to insist on the empty formality of an undertaking as to damages which it and the plaintiff realise has no meaning in reality?

A number of issues of importance arose in *Oblique Financial Services Ltd v The Promise Production Co. Ltd* [1994] 1 ILRM 74: concerning private international law aspects of the injunction remedy and the scope of protection afforded by the Constitution for the disclosure of information. The plaintiff, an English company, engaged in arranging financial support for film productions, invoked s.11 of the Jurisdiction of Courts and Enforcement of Judgments (European Communities) Act 1988 seeking an interlocutory injunction against the third and fourth defendants, the publishers and editor of *The Phoenix* magazine, preventing the publication of information as to the identity of an investor of finance. The first and second defendants were contractually bound to total confidentiality as to the identity of the investor. The plaintiff alleged a breach of this contractual obligation.

It was accepted by counsel for both the applicant and respondent that the substantive proceedings for an injunction, which the plaintiff was taking in England, would be decided in accordance with English law but that proceedings before Keane J, pursuant to s.11 of the 1988 Act, should be determined in accordance with the principles of Irish law applicable to the granting or withholding of interlocutory injunctions. Whilst there was no significant difference between Irish and English law in regard to the principles relating to interlocutory injunctions, counsel agreed that the Irish court, in an application of this nature, could not abridge the rights enjoyed under the Constitution by any of the parties to the action.

In the light of *House of Spring Gardens Ltd v Point Blank Ltd* [1984] IR 611, Keane J had no doubt that the plaintiff had established a serious question to be tried. It was obvious from the case law and was a matter of common sense that the right to confidentiality would be of little value if third parties, to whom the information had been communicated, were free to publish it to others or to the general public. This was the position in both Irish and English law, in Keane J's view.

The third and fourth defendants invoked Article 40.6.1° of the Constitution, contending that an injunction would infringe their rights as an organ of public opinion. Keane J accepted that, if that submission were well founded, then clearly it would be inappropriate for the Court to grant an interlocutory injunction, 'irrespective of what might happen in the proceedings in England'. He rejected this interpretation of the Constitution on misconceived, however, in the light of Costello J's decision in *Attorney General v Paperlink Ltd* [1984] ILRM 373 to the effect that a distinction should be drawn between the right to express freely convictions and opinions, protected in Article 40.6.1°, and the right to communicate information, protected by Article 40.3.1°. The latter right was not an absolute one. As Costello J had observed ([1984] ILRM, at 381), laws 'may restrict the nature of the matter communicated (for example, by prohibiting the communication of confidential information . . .)'.

Applying those principles to the case before him, Keane J observed that:

> The respondents' right to communicate information must be subject to other rights and duties, and in particular to the right of confidentiality . . . alleged to be enjoyed by the plaintiff. Accordingly, while the substantive action remains to be determined by the English cour[t], if that court should find against the respondents it would not be a breach or an infringing of the constitutional rights of the respondents. . . .

The logic of this passage is that it is indeed permissible under the Constitution for a foreign court decree to trench upon constitutional rights. As may readily be appreciated, the implications are significant and difficult to assess with any certainty. To what extent should the exercise in Ireland by an 'Irish-centred' person (or corporate entity) of the right of free speech receive constitutional protection in regard to its impact abroad? Should there be any obligation on a foreign court to give effect to this constitutional protection? If the foreign court is in a situation where it applies Irish law in the exercise of its choice of law function, according to the principles of private international law, a failure on its part to have regard to the constitutional dimension would involve, not the application of Irish law, but its *misapplication*. There is an analogy here with *renvoi* conundrum: if the reference is to the domestic law of the state whose law is to be applied to the case, should the concept of domestic law embrace that state's constitutional law so far as it affects relevant legal rights and, if so, should it also take account of the international remit of the impact of that state's constitutional law on those legal rights? To take a practical example: if, under the choice of law rules of Irish private international law, the law of New York applied to a defamation case, one would expect that the Irish court would not ignore the impact of *New York Times v Sullivan*, 376 US 255 (1964) on New York's law.

In the instant case, Keane J went on to observe that, if the third and fourth defendants failed in the English proceedings it would be open to them to resist any enforcement of the judgment in the Irish High Court on the ground of public policy, based on the infringement of their constitutional rights.

As to the comparative damage that was likely to flow from granting or refusing the interlocutory injunction, Keane J considered that the plaintiff would suffer serious and possibly irreparable damage if the publication went ahead. He conceded that it would be hard to quantify the damage the third and fourth defendants would sustain if the injunction were granted. To accede to their argument, however, would mean that it would, in effect, be impossible for courts to grant interlocutory relief from the breaching of confidentiality, however unjust the consequences, against publishers of magazines or periodicals with a large volume of information and comment other than the impugned evidence.

Keane J thought that in the light of the damage that the plaintiff would suffer in the absence of an injunction, the case was one where interlocutory relief should issue, without considering where the balance of convenience in other aspects might lie. If that factor were to be taken into account, it also supported the granting of an injunction since the whole point of a case like the one before him was to preserve the *status quo* pending the resolution of the action.

In *Kavanagh v Artane Services Ltd*, High Court, 19 November 1993 (1993 No. 4837P), Flood J declined to grant an interlocutory injunction in favour of the plaintiff, whose contract to carry on business on the defendants' behalf had been terminated by the defendants, pursuant to a term in the contract which gave them power to do so on ninety day's notice. The plaintiff claimed that there had been a collateral verbal agreement, whereby the defendants had accepted that this term would be operated only in exceptional circumstances of neglect or failure to run the business properly.

Flood J was satisfied that the plaintiff could establish a *prima facie* case and that the balance of convenience probably was in favour of his retaining possession and continuing management of the service station. He refused to grant the injunction, however, because, if the plaintiff were to succeed in his action, the loss and damage to be sustained by reason of the improper termination of the contract could not adequately be compensated in damages.

In *McEvoy v Prison Officers' Association*, High Court, 28 January 1993, Carney J provided an interesting examination of the issue of the balance of convenience. The plaintiff had been removed from the elected position of presidency of the defendant association by a no-confidence vote of the membership. He challenged this removal on the grounds of unfair procedures and sought an interlocutory injunction against interference in the exercise of his functions as President.

Carney J had no hesitation in refusing to grant the injunction. He did not concern himself with the question as to whether the plaintiff had passed the threshold test laid down in *Campus Oil*. On the question of the balance of convenience he reasoned as follows. The plaintiff, in asserting his entitlement to lead the defendant association must have 'as his primary concern not his own ambition but the promotion and protection of the interests of the membership of the Association.' The primary objective of the association was to improve the conditions and to promote and protect the interests of its members. If the plaintiff were to obtain an interlocutory injunction, there would be uncertainty in relation to the association for a long and indefinite period until the substantive injunction proceedings had been disposed of finally; this might involve an appeal to the Supreme Court. During this period the association would be compromised in its independence by the *de facto* situation of having its leadership imposed on it by court order. Such a situation would be highly inimical to the promotion and protection of the interests of the association and its membership. A refusal to grant an interlocutory injunction would mean that the matter could be resolved democratically by an election for the presidency, for which the plaintiff was eligible to stand as a candidate.

In *DJS Meats Ltd v The Minister for Agriculture and Food*, High Court, 17 February 1993, Lynch J had to deal with a situation where the Minister was claiming from guarantors repayment of European Community export refunds or advances paid to the plaintiff company in respect of the export of beef by the plaintiff to South Africa. The beef had already been exported to South Africa, a qualifying non-European Community country for the purposes of export refunds. The Minister formed the opinion that this export was not genuinely for home use on the South African market but was re-exported to Zimbabwe, a non-qualifying country. He sought repayment of the export refunds on the basis that he had not been supplied with information to which he was entitled under the Export Refund scheme.

Lynch J was satisfied that the plaintiff had established that there was a fair question to be tried. Moreover the balance of convenience tilted in the plaintiff's favour. Its standing with the guarantors would be damaged by their being required to repay substantial sums to the Minister.

One factor weighed against the plaintiff. It had obtained an interim injunction over a year previously, yet the pace of the case had been pedestrian. The application for an interlocutory injunction had taken ten months to present and no pleadings had been delivered subsequent to the plenary summons and appearance. Accordingly, Lynch J continued the interim injunction for a limited period of weeks, conditional on expedition of the proceedings. If due diligence was established, the injunction would crystalise into interlocutory status.

In *Moloney v Laurib Investments Ltd*, High Court, 20 July 1993, Lynch J confronted an important issue of principle regarding the clash of values underlying tort law and company law. For a perceptive analysis of the whole subject, see Thomas Courtney, 'Mareva Injunctions in Personal Injuries Actions' (1995) 9 *Dlí* 107.

The plaintiff, a fifteen year old girl, alleged that she had sustained serious injuries when she fell through an unguarded opening in a floor of the defendant company's unfinished building in Mountjoy Square in Dublin. Lynch J was satisfied that this constituted a statable case of negligence against the defendant. The plaintiff sought a Mareva injunction restraining the defendant from disposing of the premises and from reducing the value of its assets below the sum of one million pounds.

The defendant company had an authorised share capital of £10,000 divided into 10,000 shares of £1 each, with an issued share capital of two pounds, owned by the two directors of the company. It appeared that one of them had lent the company £280,000 to enable it to purchase the premises. Another company of which the director was effectively the owner had advanced £300,000 for the purchase. These debts appeared in the defendant company's accounts. The building was not covered by public liability insurance.

The building had been bought with a view to completing its development so as to make it profitable, whether by way of sale or letting. The original intention had been for it to be an office block. This plan languished for a time; with the passage of the Urban Renewal Act 1986, a new solution appeared attractive: to develop the building into residential apartments within the time limits designated under the legislation. The director of the company who had lent it the money had engaged in discussions with potential partners on the proposed disposal of the unfurnished building to a new entity in consideration of the work to be done and (Lynch J assumed) the wiping out of the company's debts so that thereafter it would have neither assets nor debts. This plan antedated the defendant company's learning of the plaintiff's accident and was designed to realise some profit from a long-term investment rather than to defeat their claim.

On the question of the balance of convenience, Lynch J characterised as 'worthless' the undertaking on the part of the plaintiff as to damages (albeit through no fault on her part). If an interlocutory injuction were granted and the defendants subsequently won the case, they would suffer very serious loss. Moreover, the grant of an injunction would probably prejudice the rights of *bona fide* creditors of the defendant company to repayment of their debts. The 'wholly unliquidated tortious nature of the plaintiff's claim' was also a factor leaning against granting an injunction.

In the Labour Law Chapter, in the section on Trade Disputes, below,

377-8, we analyse *Draycar Ltd v Whelan* [1993] ELR 119, where Lardner J refused to grant an interlocutory injunction against picketing.

In the Torts Chapter below, 579-80, we discuss *Kent Adhesive Products Company t/a Kapco v Ryan*, High Court, 5 November 1993, where Costello J declined to grant an interlocutory injunction against passing off and injurious falsehood, in spite of the fact that the plaintiff had established substantial issues to be tried in respect of both. This was because of the elaborate undertakings which the defendants were willing to give, supplemented by others that Costello J fashioned to meet the needs of the case.

Mandatory injunction   In *McKenna v Commissioner of the Garda Sio-chána* [1993] 3 IR 543, the plaintiff sought a mandatory injunction requiring the return of over a hundred video machines which the defendant had seized at the plaintiff's amusement arcade premises on suspicion that they had been used for unlawful gaming. The statutory authority invoked for the seizure was s. 39 of the Gaming and Lotteries Act 1956.

The crucial issue was whether the entitlement under s. 39(2) to seize 'any gaming instrument' embraced only machines that were objectively proved to be gaming instruments (or were certain to be proved in court to have been used as gaming machines). The Supreme Court rejected this interpretation. O'Flaherty J, (Finlay CJ and Denham J concurring) noted that the entitlement to obtain a search warrant depended on there being a reasonable ground for supposing that an offence against the Act, had been was being or was about to be committed. He added:

> The test is one of reasonableness of belief; not certainty as to outcome. No suggestion of *mala fides* or abuse of statutory power has been advanced against the Gardaí in this case and, therefore, my conclusion is that no arguable ground has been advanced at this stage for suggesting that there has been a breach of the statutory requirement.

One may perhaps question whether the conclusion follows from it's premises. The fact that a *search* may be authorised on the ground of reasonable belief, which clearly is the case under s. 39(1), does not necessarily justify the *seizure* of property based on a reasonable belief as to it's character, unless the statutory provision expressly or impliedly provides such justification. This is precisely what s. 39(2) appears *not* to do, since it authorises seizure of books and documents appearing to relate to gaming or lotteries but does not authorise seizure of instruments that appear to be gaming instruments. The only authorisation for seizure of instruments afforded by s. 39(2) is the seizure of any gaming instrument.

It might be considered that an interpretation of s. 39(2) which excludes authorisation from seizure based on reasonable, though mistaken, belief would be oppressive on the Gardaí, who would be obliged to expose themselves to the risk of civil liability if they seized machines that turned out not to be gaming instruments. As against this, it is worth recalling that private individuals run the risk of civil proceedings for false imprisonment if a suspected shoplifter is acquitted (since frequently, if the suspect cannot be shown to have been guilty of the larceny, no felony will have been established as having been committed by anyone: cf. Ryan & Magee, *The Irish Criminal Process* (1983), at 95). The power of seizure can be an awesome one: in the instant case, the plaintiff claimed a consequent loss of profits of £4,000 per week. The idea that extreme caution should be exercised when deciding whether or not to seize suspected gaming instruments is hardly a fanciful one. This is not to suggest that a legislative provision authorising seizure based on suspicion that a machine is a gaming instrument would not, on balance, be preferable, but it is not the function of the court to amend legislation on the basis of its preference for a social policy that the legislative provision cannot credibly be interpreted as effectuating.

O'Flaherty J went on to explain that, if he had been satisfied that an arguable case had been made out on the construction of s.39, he would not have allowed the fact that the claim was mandatory in form to deter him since he considered that, 'essentially, one would be preserving the *status quo ante* rather than granting a mandatory injunction relief'. He was concerned that civil proceedings should not impede the proper conduct of criminal proceedings. In this regard, the plaintiff's offer to let the Gardaí retain *one* of the machines, are the basis of a written admission by the plaintiff under s.22 of the Criminal Justice Act 1984 that the other machines were similar to the one retained might well have met this concern, in O'Flaherty J's view.

In *Barrington v Bank of Ireland*, High Court, 26 January 1993, Costello J held that the plaintiff customer of the defendant bank was entitled to an interlocutory mandatory injunction requiring the bank to transfer funds from one of the plaintiff's accounts to another bank. The defendant was asserting the right of set-off in respect of a loan that the defendant had made the plaintiff in a separate account, which the plaintiff failed to repay in accordance with the terms of the loan. The terms of the loan, however, amounted, in Costello J's view, to a waiver of the right to set-off. Although the court was slow to grant mandatory relief on an interlocutory application, Costello J considered that the strength of the plaintiff's case justified such an order.

Costello J rejected the defendant's contention that, because the plaintiff was admittedly indebted to it in a substantial sum, it would be inequitable to grant an injunction. If, as was the position, the court concluded that there was a very strong case that the defendant had waived its right to set-off, then equitable considerations did not require the court to allow the defendant until the trial of the action to exercise a right which it appeared to have waived. The balance of convenience favoured granting the injunction with a suitable undertaking as to damages. If no injunction was granted, the evidence established that the plaintiff would suffer a very considerable disadvantage for which he could not be compensated; no corresponding disadvantage would accrue to the bank if an injunction was granted and it was later shown that it should not have been.

Costello J's emphasis on the strength of the plaintiff's case in this context is significant. If an interlocutory injunction of a non-mandatory character had been sought by a plaintiff in breach of the terms of a loan account with a defendant, would the gentler requirement of a *prima facie* case extinguish the defendant's plea that a plaintiff must come to equity with clean hands?

The decision is yet another instance of Costello J's propensity to determine the legal issue at the interlocutory stage: see the 1989 Review, 194.

Permanent injunctions In *Joseph O'Connor (Nenagh) Ltd v Powers Supermarkets Ltd t/a Quinnsworth*, High Court, 15 March 1993, Keane J, having granted an interlocutory judgment in favour of the plaintiff, granted a permanent injunction in its favour, restraining the defendants from publishing in relation to the plaintiff's grocery business at Nenagh any advertisement that was misleading, or likely to mislead, by referring inaccurately to the prices or other terms on which the plaintiff's grocery goods were offered for sale. Keane J in the case was called on to define and to referee the ground rules for 'knocking' advertising. This type of advertising, having proven popular in the United States, not just in the commercial world but also in the realm of politics, has made its way to Ireland. It works on the basis of identifying the enemy by name and establishing that, in a specific area, the enemy is demonstrably deficient, especially in comparison with the advertiser. The discrete references to one's rival as 'another leading brand' have given way to an express identification, followed by a derogatory comparison.

There are, of course, traditional legal controls on this type of warfare. Defamation and injurious falsehood are the most obvious remedies. European law has supplemented them: Article 4(1) of the European Communities (Misleading Advertising) Regulations 1988, implementing the Directive on Misleading Advertisements (No. 84/450/EEC), enables any person to apply to the High Court for an injunction against the publication of misleading advertising. Article 2(2) of the Directive defines misleading advertising as:

> any advertising which in any way, including its presentation, deceives or is likely to deceive the persons to whom it is addressed or whom it reaches and which, by reason of its deceptive nature, is likely to affect

their economic behaviour or which, for those reasons, injures or is likely to injure a competitor.

In the instant case, the defendants had placed an advertisement in the local newspaper which stated boldly:

> You *can't* buy your family shopping cheaper in Roscrea or Nenagh. We price checked Quinnsworth Roscrea and O'Connors Nenagh and the totals prove it — you can't buy your shopping cheaper than at Quinnsworth, with the widest choice of groceries, the best fresh foods and friendly service.

The pricing criteria adopted in this advertisement were different in that they excluded a component of fresh food items, which, as Keane J observed, 'one would expect to find in something that was being put forward as what the average housewife — if such exists — might purchase on her weekly major shopping expedition'.

Keane J would not have been disposed to grant an injunction on the basis of the advertisement. He was moved to do so by a hand-out, distributed in the Nenagh area, which contained a series of errors as to a comparison of prices between the products on offer in the plaintiff's and defendants' premises. These errors did not materially misrepresent the price differences but Keane J took the view that, since they failed to take account of fresh foods, it was incumbent on the defendants to ensure that they stated the prices accurately.

> If they failed to do so . . . the accompanying list of prices could only lend to a spurious authenticity to the claims made as to the respective competitive positions of the two businesses in price terms.

In granting the injunction, Keane J emphasised that it in no sense restrained legitimate advertising by the defendants, even if it took the form of price comparisons with a named competitor's products:

> They are perfectly entitled to mount such comparisons if they wish, but, if they elect to include comparisons with a named competitor, they must ensure that they are accurate, both in fairness to the competitor and in the public interest.

In *Johnston v Horace*, High Court, 26 March 1993, Lavan J granted an injunction and awarded damages in favour of an aunt whose testamentary right of residence was disturbed by her nephew. Lavan J viewed as reprehensible 'any conduct which in this era of homelessness puts a person out of their home'. To suggest that the plaintiff ought to be a burden on the local authority or that she might avail herself of taxation relief was to ignore the reality of the circumstances of the case. The defendant was 'seek[ing] to obtain Court approval to defeat a dead man's well considered intention to properly provide for his children. . . .' Lavan J invoked the maxim that he who comes to equity must come with clean hands.

TRUST

Charitable trusts The Irish courts have contributed several great judgments on charitable trusts. Litigation of this kind has, however, become a rarity. Keane J's decision in *In re the Worth Library* [1994] 1 ILRM 161 is one of the most elegant and urbane to grace our law reports in recent times. For a comprehensive analysis of the decision, see Hilary Delany, 'Charitable Status and *Cy Prés* Jurisdiction: An Examination of Some of the Issues Raised in *In re the Worth Library*' (1994) 45 *NILQ* 364 and James Brady, 'Charities — A Rare Case of *Cy-Pres*' (1994) 16 *DULJ* 153.

The case concerned the fate of the magnificent library of four and a half thousand books bequeathed by Dr Edward Worth in the early eighteenth century for the benefit of the physician, chaplain and surgeon for the time being of Doctor Steeven's Hospital in Dublin. The library, as Keane J noted, was that of 'a man of taste and learning at the flood tide of the Enlightenment'. It included medical books but mostly works on other subjects, particularly English antiquities, astronomy, botany, history, the ancient classics, mathematics, poetry, philosophy, natural history science and travel.

The library in which the collection was housed in the hospital was a room specially designed for the purpose, with glass fronted bookcases. The hospital closed in 1988 and was bought by the Eastern Health Board for use as its headquarters. Pending the ultimate resolution of the fate of the library, the books were sent to Trinity College. The issue confronting Keane J was whether the court had jurisdiction to order a *cy-prés* scheme and, if so, whether the library should remain with Trinity or return to its original home.

Several threshold issues of law required resolution. The first was whether the bequest by Dr Worth of his library was in law charitable. The parties were agreed that it was but Keane J took the view that there was a sufficiently public dimension to the litigation to make it appropriate for him to address the question.

Keane J had no hesitation in rejecting the submission that the bequest was a charitable gift for the advancement of education. Even if it could be said that it was a bequest for educational purposes — which would be difficult, in view of the insignificant proportion of the library devoted to medicine and surgery — there was no public benefit since the beneficiaries were the physician, chaplain and surgeon for the time being of the hospital.

Neither did Keane J consider that the bequest was a charitable gift for the advancement of learning. Keane J was not disposed to accept the narrow prescription of Harmon J, in *In re Shaw, Public Trustee v Day* [1957] 1 WLR 729, that the objective of increasing knowledge be 'combined with teaching or education'. As Wilberforce J had pointed out in *In re Hopkins' Will Trusts, Nais v Francis Bacon Society Inc* [1965] Ch 669, this would exclude from charitable status the promotion of academic research unencumbered by teaching or education. In Keane J's view, the encouragement of pure academic research might reasonably be regarded as being for the public benefit. This is surely a correct conclusion.

The precedents on the charitable status of gifts of libraries were to the effect that these gifts were not charitable *per se* but could be so where there was the necessary public benefit, as, for example where the library was open to the public. (*In re Scowcroft, Ormond v Wilkinson* [1898] 2 Ch 638, at 642) or was part of a university college (*Attorney General v Marchant* (1866) LR 3 Eq 424) or even where there was a fund to purchase a library for an officers' mess, Farwell J considering that this was conducive to increasing the efficiency of the British army (*In re Good, Harrington v Watts* [1905] 2 Ch 60).

In the instant case, Keane J could discern no indication in Dr Worth's will that he had intended the library to be for the benefit of any persons other than the named office holders. He was satisfied therefore that this was not a charitable gift for the advancement of learning within the fourth category of Lord Macnaghten's celebrated classification in *Commissioners for Special Purposes of Income Tax v Pemsel* [1891] AC 531. Counsel for the Eastern Health Board had argued that the gift was for the benefit of the hospital itself, and hence charitable, and that the provision that the gift was for the benefit of the office holders should be treated as precatory. Keane J had no hesitation in rejecting this contention: the bequest was clearly for the benefit of designated individuals and the ancillary directions were equally clearly of a kind that the testator 'wished to be complied with to the letter'. Nevertheless, Keane J held that the gift was indeed one for the benefit of the Hospital:

> While the relatively small number of medical and surgical books in the library would not have rendered it of much practical benefit to the physician and surgeon and the vast number of books devoted to purely secular and profane topics would not have been of any great assistance to the chaplain in his studies of divinity, the library in its beautiful setting would have provided a haven of quiet intellectual relaxation for the beneficiaries. Doctors and surgeons, as we all know, develop a necessary professional detachment from the scenes of death and suffering

which greet them every day in the course of their work. But it is equally obvious that they value the solace of a completely different environment from time to time and I think there can be no doubt that this is what Dr Worth intended to provide. How much more necessary it was in the terrible conditions of the early eighteenth century, when the days of anaesthetics and modern drugs lay far in the future, need not be emphasised.

In addressing the question of the charitable status of the bequest of the library, Keane J's approach may be contrasted with that of O'Hanlon J in *Representative Church Body v Attorney General*, [1988] IR 19; as Hilary Delany points out (*op. cit.*, at 365), O'Hanlon J made a *cy-prés* scheme in relation to a collection of books in the Old Library of St. Canice's Cathedral Kilkenny without raising any question as to the charitable status of the bequest. For analysis of O'Hanlon J's decision see W.N. Osborough, (1989) 24 *Ir Jur* (n.s.) 50, and the 1988 Review 274-6.

In *Worth*, having determined that the bequest was charitable, Keane J turned to the question as to whether circumstances had arisen that justified the invocation of the a *cy-prés* jurisdiction of the court. He found that they had. Applying the criteria specified by Budd J in *In re Royal Kilmainham Hospital* [1966] IR 451, at 469, as modified by s. 47 of the Charities Act 1961, he concluded that whilst there was no 'general charitable intention', in the sense referred to in the authorities, it was quite clear that Dr Worth had intended to make an absolute and perpetual gift of the library to the hospital. Since the hospital had ceased to exist, the original purposes of the charitable gift could not be carried out according to the directions given and to the spirit of the gift. It followed that the court should alter the original purposes to allow the property to be applied a *cy-prés*.

Keane J quoted Meredith J's observations in *Governors of Erasmus Smith Schools v Attorney General* (1932) 66 ILTR 57, at 61, to the effect that to apply without modification a charitable intention that was expressed only in relation to assumed facts and under different conditions from the present was obviously not to carry out the testator's real intention at all. It was on this principle that courts adapted the statement of a charitable intention to suit altered circumstances and conditions with a view to giving effect to the testator's real intention. In the instant case it was 'a futile exercise to transport Dr Worth in one's imagination in some form of time machine to Dublin in 1993'. All that the court could do was to apply the gift as it might be applied by a late twentieth century equivalent of Dr Worth:

> Our hypothetical benefactor should be a medically qualified person with a passionate interest in bibliophilia and of a charitable disposition. It is

also reasonable to credit him with a desire to associate his charitable work with the building in which Steevens' Hospital was housed, since his eighteenth century equivalent wished the hospital to be the object of his benevolence in perpetuity.

Adopting this approach, Keane J thought it brought the court as close as was reasonably possible to what the draftsman of the 1961 Act had called 'the spirit of the gift'. Such a person would have in the forefront of any plan he might devise the paramount necessity of preserving the library in the custody of an appropriate and responsible body:

> He would recognise that the principal value of the library is not the provision of knowledge or intellectual stimulus or excitement to readers of books as books, considered both individually and as a collective library. The typography, paper and bindings, altogether apart from the contents, are of enormous interest to scholars and bibliophiles the world over. Hence, he would be concerned to ensure that such persons had reasonable but supervised access to the library and also the other scholarly tools necessary for making an informed study of the contents of the library, such as a modern computerised catalogue, suitable reference books and other comparable books. Finally, he would consider whether . . . broader aesthetic considerations . . . would point towards preserving the books in Steevens' Hospital or transferring them to Trinity College, the only other institution which has been suggested as a possible repository?

Although it was clear that Trinity possessed the ready availability of conservation techniques that were 'by far the best available' in the State, Keane J held that the library should revert to the Hospital:

> That preserving the Worth library in its original home in Steevens' Hospital will be to 'freeze it in time' is probably true. Many who have visited carefully preserved or restored buildings of historic, architectural or artistic interest in Ireland or abroad will have been conscious of precisely that feeling of moving into long vanished worlds. Far from its being a serious disadvantage, it seems to me . . . one of the chief categories of the treasures of which we are now the custodians. I see no reason why, under careful and responsible management subject to the ultimate control of the court, the Worth Library should not join them, preserving almost exactly as it existed 250 years ago in its original setting the private library of a man of taste and learning at the flood tide of the Enlightenment.

Trusts of pension entitlements   In the 1992 Review, 321-2, we analysed Denham J's judgment in *In re Williams & Co. Ltd: Application of Lynch et al*, High Court, 31 January 1992, relating to the entitlements of particular categories of persons to pensions from a trust. In supplemental proceedings, resulting in judgment on 18 February 1993, Denham J dealt in detail with the applications of several of these persons, applying to each of them the rules of the trust. The case does not involve consideration of any points of general legal interest.

European Community and European Union Law

VALIDITY OF SECONDARY LEGISLATION IMPLEMENTING COMMUNITY DIRECTIVES

The decision of the Supreme Court in *Meagher v Minister for Agriculture and Food* [1994] 1 ILRM 1; [1994] 1 IR 329 is probably the most significant delivered by the Court concerning the *vires* of Irish Regulations implementing EC Directives. In essence, the decision upheld the power asserted in s. 3 of the European Communities Act 1972 that Irish Regulations (secondary legislation) may validly amend Acts (primary legislation) where the Regulations in question implement a Directive which leaves no choice as to the principles to be implemented in the domestic legislation.

The background against which the case was decided was the EC-based legislative code aimed at controlling the use of animal remedies, in particular growth promoters, in the agricultural sector. The most important EC Directives in this area had been implemented by the rather inelegantly titled European Communities (Control of Oestrogenic, Androgenic, Gestagenic and Thyrostatic Substances) Regulations 1988 and the less tongue twisting European Communities (Control of Veterinary Medicinal Products and their Residues) Regulations 1990. Both these Regulations were made by the Minister for Agriculture pursuant to s. 3 of the European Communities Act 1972.

The 1988 Regulations, *inter alia*, provided for search warrants to be issued to authorised officers of the Department of Agriculture and to members of the Garda Síochána to enter lands and other premises with a view to taking samples from animals to ascertain if growth promoters prohibited under the Regulations were being used on such animals. It was pursuant to a warrant issued under the 1988 Regulations that officers entered the applicant's farm and took relevant samples. The applicant was later served with 20 summonses alleging offences under the 1988 and 1990 Regulations. The applicant then launched wide-ranging judicial review proceedings in which he challenged, *inter alia*, the *vires* of the 1988 and 1990 Regulations and, even more significantly, the constitutional validity of s. 3 of the European Communities Act 1972.

The applicant's case centred on the fact that both the 1988 and 1990 Regulations provided that '[n]otwithstanding section 10(4) of the Petty Sessions (Ireland) Act 1851', proceedings for an offence under the Regulations could be instituted at any time within two years after the date of such an offence. S. 10(4) of the 1851 Act provides for a six month time limit on summary prosecutions. While many subsequent Acts provide for different time limits, the applicant's point was that any such alteration to the general rule in the 1851 Act could only be effected by the Oireachtas by means of primary legislation. Since the 1988 and 1990 Regulations purported, in effect, to amend the 1851 Act, it was argued that this was inconsistent with the exclusive law making functions of the Oireachtas under Article 15 of the Constitution.

Of course, the European Communities Act 1972 had expressly envisaged that Regulations made under s. 3 of the 1972 Act could do precisely what the applicant claimed was unconstitutional. S. 3 of the 1972 Act provided that a Minister was empowered to make Regulations to enable effect to be given to acts, such as Directives, adopted by the institutions of the European Communities. S. 3(2) of the 1972 Act goes on to provide:

> Regulations under this section may contain such incidental, supplementary and consequential provisions as appear to the Minister making the Regulations to be necessary for the purposes of the Regulations (including provisions repealing, amending or applying, with or without modification, other law, exclusive of this Act).

In response to the applicant's claim, the respondents argued that s. 3(2) of the 1972 Act was valid on two grounds. First, it was pointed out that Regulations under s. 3 of the 1972 Act were subject to annulment pursuant to resolutions passed by both Houses of the Oireachtas under s. 4 of the 1972 Act, so that in this respect the Oireachtas retained supervision over such Regulations. It was argued that this was analagous to the procedure upheld by the Supreme Court in *McDaid v Sheehy* [1989] ILRM 342 (HC); [1990] ILRM 250 (SC); [1991] 1 IR 1 (HC & SC) (see the 1989 Review, 111-4 and the 1990 Review, 464-5). In response to this, Johnson J noted in the High Court that s. 4 of the 1972 Act, as originally enacted, had required a positive resolution by both Houses as well as a confirming Act in order to validate Regulations made under s. 3 of the 1972 Act, and he accepted that this approximated to the arrangement upheld in *McDaid*. However, he pointed out that s. 1 of the European Communities (Amendment) Act 1973 had amended s. 4 of the 1972 Act and provided that Regulations under s. 3 were to have statutory effect, subject only to invalidation by resolution of both Houses of the Oireachtas, that is a negative resolution mechanism. This was the procedure in place when the 1988 and 1990 Regulations were made. In the absence of the original positive resolution procedure, Johnson J held that Regulations under s. 3 of the 1972 Act did not meet the principles laid down in the *McDaid* case. As we will see below, this point did not arise in the Supreme Court judgments in the case, and so the status of Johnson J's comments remain somewhat doubtful.

The second, and most significant, point argued by the defendant in the *Meagher* case was that s. 3 of the 1972 Act was consistent with European law, as incorporated into Irish law by the amendments effected to Article 29.4 of the Constitution. In particular it was argued that the facility provided for in s. 3(2) of the 1972 Act was 'necessitated by the obligations of membership of the Communities' within what was originally Article 29.4.3° and, since 1992, Article 29.4.5° (see the 1992 Review, 326-7). Attention was drawn in this context to Article 189 of the Treaty establishing the European Community, the EC Treaty (see the 1992 Review, 329-30), which provides that:

> A Directive shall be binding as to the result to be achieved upon each member State to which it is addressed, but shall leave to the national authorities the choice of form and methods.

Therefore, the defendants argued, under Community and (through Article 29.4.3°-6°) Irish law, the amendment of the 1851 Act by the 1988 Regulations was valid as it was open to the national authorities to choose how to give effect to the Directives implemented by the 1988 and 1990 Regulations.

Johnson J rejected this argument in the High Court, holding that, under Article 189 of the EC Treaty, the Minister was obliged to consider the appropriate method by which to implement the Directives in question. Johnson J was of the view that Article 29.4.5° did not confer an absolute discretion in this respect and that, in certain cases, primary legislation (that is an Act) would be the correct choice for the implementation of Directives. Since s. 3 of the 1972 Act conferred what appeared to be an unfettered discretion, Johnson J held it was *ultra vires*. Johnson J's decision cast considerable doubt over the validity of hundreds of Regulations made under s. 3 of the 1972 Act, many of which had included not merely the modification of the Petty Sessions (Ireland) Act 1851 but also even more substantive amendments to primary legislation in the process of implementing Directives. For examples, see the European Communities (Environmental Impact Assessment) Regulations 1989 (1989 Review, 205, 331-2) and the European Communities (Legal Protection of Computer Programs) Regulations 1993 (SI No. 26), discussed in the Commercial Law chapter, 56, above.

The decision of Johnson J was immediately appealed to the Supreme Court and an expedited hearing was granted. However, in the meantime, two statutory responses to the High Court decision were also put in place. In the area of animal remedies and growth promoters, the Animal Remedies Act 1993 provided for a basis in primary legislation on which to continue the EC-based policy: see the discussion of this Act in the Agriculture chapter, 34-7, above. In the wider context of other Regulations which had provided for longer time limits to those contained in s. 10(4) of the Petty Sessions (Ireland) Act 1851, s. 5 of the European Communities (Amendment) Act 1993 purported to meet the two points made by Johnson J. First, s. 5(1) provided that all Regulations made up to the date of the 1993 Act were 'hereby confirmed' from the date on which they purported to come into operation. However, with a view to the then pending Supreme Court appeal, s. 5(2) provided that this confirmation was subject to its being in accordance with the Constitution. Second, s. 5(4) provided that, notwithstanding s. 10(4) of the Petty Sessions (Ireland) Act 1851, prosecutions under Regulations made pursuant to s. 3 of the 1972 Act could be brought at any time within two years of the date of the commission of an offence under such Regulations. As we have already noted, the Supreme Court ultimately upheld the validity of s. 3 of the 1972 Act, so that the confirmation provided for by s. 5 of the European Communities (Amendment) Act 1993 became somewhat moot. However, s. 5(4) remains of some interest because it extends the time limit in respect of those Regulations made under s. 3 of the 1972 Act which had provided, for example, for a 12 month time limit.

We now turn to discuss the basis on which the Supreme Court upheld the validity of s. 3 of the 1972 Act and the 1988 and 1990 Regulations impugned in the *Meagher* case. The Court delivered one judgment on the validity of s. 3, in accordance with Article 34.4.5° of the Constitution. The essence of the judgment can be gathered from this passage, delivered for the Court by Finlay CJ:

> The Court is satisfied that, having regard to the number of Community laws, acts done and measures adopted which either have to be facilitated in their direct application to the law of the State or have to be implemented by appropriate action into the law of the State, the obligation of membership would necessitate facilitating of these activities in some instances at least, and possibly in a great majority of instances, by the making of ministerial Regulations rather than legislation of the Oireachtas.

> The Court is accordingly satisfied that the power to make Regulations in the form in which it is contained in s. 3(2) of the Act of 1972 is necessitated by the obligations of membership by the State of the Communities, and now of the Union, and is therefore by virtue of Article 29.4.3°, 4° and 5° immune from constitutional challenge.

The Court accepted that there might be particular cases where the power conferred by s. 3 of the 1972 Act was not exercised in accordance with the principles of constitutional justice. However, in accordance with the decisions in *East Donegal Co-Op Ltd v Attorney General* [1970] IR 317 and *Harvey v Minister for Social Welfare* [1990] ILRM 185; [1990] 1 IR 232 (see the 1989 Review, 394-5), the Court held that the presumption of constitutionality made it inappropriate to consider this question as a hypothetical matter and that, therefore, each exercise of the s. 3 power should be considered on its own merits. The Court then turned to the 1988 and 1990 Regulations. As these Regulations did not come within the definition of 'law' within the meaning of Article 34.4.5° (which is confined to Acts only), the one-judgment rule under that provision did not apply. Two members of the Court, Blayney and Denham JJ, delivered individual judgments with both of which the other members of the Court, Finlay CJ, O'Flaherty and Egan JJ, concurred.

In his judgment, Blayney J examined the Directives on which the Regulations were based as well as the nature of Community law. He accepted that a fundamental prerequisite of membership was the supremacy of Community law over domestic law and he cited in this context the decision of the Court of Justice in *Marleasing SA v La Comercial Internacional de Alimentacion SA* [1990] ECR I-4135 and the Court's even more ground-breaking decision: *Francovich v Italy* [1991] ECR I-5357. On *Francovich* generally, see Leo Flynn's article, (1995) 13 *ILT* 16.

Turning to Directive 85/358/EEC, one of the Directives implemented by the 1988 Regulations, Blayney J noted that it was mandatory in terms and required member States to make arrangements for the taking of official and random on-the-spot samples on farms in order to detect prohibited substances in farm animals. In his view, this justified the authorisation of searches under the 1988 Regulations. On the question of criminal offences, Blayney J noted that it was accepted on all sides that the 1985 Directive required the creation of offences for breaches of the principles contained in the Directive. As to the time limit for prosecutions, uncontroverted evidence was given on behalf of the Minister that, in view of the complexities involved in taking and analysing samples from a farm, it was necessary to extend the six month time period provided for in s. 10(4) of the Petty Sessions (Ireland) Act 1851. Blayney J concluded that this evidence supported the view that this extension was required in order to ensure that, in accordance with Article 189 of the EC Treaty, effective sanctions were in place to ensure that the Directive was implemented in reality. Blayney J concluded his judgment by accepting that different considerations might apply if the State had not been obliged to implement the 1985 Directive, but that was not the position in the present case. Since the State was obliged to implement the 1985 Directive, he was prepared to uphold the validity of the 1988 Regulations provided that they implemented the requirements of the Directive and, in that sense, the fact that the Regulations also amended an Act was irrelevent. In his view, that question would only arise if the Regulations had gone beyond what was necessitated by the Directive.

This theme was also taken up by Denham J in her judgment. She rejected the argument that an Act of the Oireachtas was required where a Directive lays down a set of rules and principles that must be implemented by the Member States. In an important and direct passage, she stated:

> ... [T]he role of the Oireachtas in such a situation would be sterile. To require the Oireachtas to legislate would be artificial. It would be able solely to have a debate as to what has already been decided, which debate would act as a source of information. Such a sterile debate would take up Dáil and Senate time and act only as a window on Community Directives for the members of the Oireachtas and the nation. That is not a role envisaged for the Oireachtas in the Constitution.

In this passage, Denham J underlined the extent to which law-making authority has been transferred from the Oireachtas to European Community/Union institutions. While, of course, the passage does not apply where a Directive does not lay down mandatory rules and principles there have been relatively few such Directives in recent years. Thus, the effect is that, once a mandatory Directive has been agreed at European level, a Minister is entitled to bypass the Oireachtas entirely and effect substantive change to prior Acts if such is required by the Directive being implemented. In that sense, the Meagher decision amounts to a 'Europeanisation' of the delegation principles laid down by the Court in *Cityview Press Ltd v An Chomhairle Oiliúna* [1980] IR 381. Thus, a Minister implementing a Directive by means of s. 3 of the 1972 Act merely has to show that any changes effected to primary legislation by such s. 3 Regulations are required in order to give full effect to the Directive in question.

As for the role of the Oireachtas, it is clear from *Meagher* that it can only have an effective law-making role where it influences the content of Directives while they are being considered and drafted at European level, that is before they become mandatory texts which can be implemented without further reference to the Oireachtas. In this context, the level of resources provided to the Oireachtas Committee now responsible for European Affairs, the Joint Committee on Foreign Affairs, will be of great importance: see the discussion of the Committee, established by s. 6 of the European Communities (Amendment) Act 1993, below, 310. For trenchant criticism of the reasoning in the *Meagher* case, see Gerard Hogan's article (1994) 3 *IJEL* 190.

DIRECTLY APPLICABLE RULES

The broad effect of the European Communities (Trade in Porcine Semen — Animal Health) Regulations 1993 (SI No. 242), which implemented Directive 90/429/EEC, is outlined in the Agriculture chapter, 38, above. As indicated there, the Regulations provide for the approval of centres for the collection of pig semen destined for intra-Community trade, and set out the animal health criteria which must be satisfied if pig semen is to be lawfully imported into the State or exported to other Member States of the European Community. The Regulations are mentioned in the present context because the Explanatory Note to them, in addition to containing the usual summary of the effect of the Regulations along the lines just mentioned, also contained an additional paragraph of such an unusual nature as to merit quotation here. It reads as follows:

> By virtue of the directly applicable rules of Community Law, these Regulations [i.e. SI No. 242] are now considered to be the only regulatory provisions applicable to the matters dealt with by the Regulations and that any parallel provisions contained in the Livestock (Artificial Insemination) Act 1947 [sic] and Regulations made thereunder are to be regarded as having been disapplied.

We also draw attention here to the Explanatory Note to the European Communities (Trade in Bovine Breeding Animals, their Semen, Ova and Embryos) Regulations 1993 (SI No. 259), also referred to in the Agriculture chapter, 38, above. In the case of SI No. 259, the following appears in the Note:

> These Regulations [i.e. SI No. 259] should now, by virtue of the directly applicable rules of Community Law, be considered to be the only regulatory provisions applicable to the matters dealt with by the Regulations and any parallel provisions contained in other domestic legislation are regarded as having been disapplied. These Regulations will be applied by the Minister for Agriculture, Food and Forestry on this basis.

Although both Explanatory Notes point out, in keeping with practice, that they are not part of the statutory instruments and do not purport to be a legal interpretation, these paragraphs flatly contradict that assertion. Aside from the perplexing reference to 'directly applicable' Community law, it is notable that, for example, Reg.4(3)(f) of the Trade in Porcine Semen Regulations makes express reference to the requirement that pig semen shall not be imported from non-EC States unless it is accompanied by a valid licence issued in accordance with s. 7 of the Livestock Breeding (Artificial Insemination) Act 1947 (the Act's correct title). Of course, it may be argued that what the Note to the Trade in Porcine Semen Regulations indicates is that, where semen is imported from an EC member State, the licensing requirements of the 1947 Act do not apply, but it is extraordinary that this was not expressly stated in the Regulations themselves.

The Note to the Trade in Bovine Breeding Animals etc. Regulations appears open to the further objection that it refers generally to the disapplication of 'domestic legislation' without even identifying such legislation. In addition, there is the additional assertion that '[T]hese Regulations will be applied by the Minister for Agriculture, Food and Forestry on this basis', that is, on the basis expressed in the Explanatory Note, a Note which carries the warning, in italics, that *'This Note is not part of the Instrument and does not purport to be a legal interpretation.'*

There are many examples of Regulations made under s. 3 of the European Communities Act 1972, as these were, which have expressly provided that specified domestic law which appears inconsistent with the EC-based Regulations shall not invalidate anything in the EC-based Regulations. For an example, see the European Communities (Right of Residence for Non-Economically Active Persons) Regulations 1993 (SI No. 109) in the Aliens and Immigration chapter, 41, above. This may be open to some objection in itself in that it may not identify with precision the domestic legislation with which it may be in conflict. However, for such a statement to be relegated to the Explanatory Note is surely inconsistent with one of the basic requirements of the rule of law, namely certainty. One wonders whether the Supreme Court in *Meagher v Minister for Agriculture and Food* [1994] 1 ILRM 1; [1994] 1 IR 329 would have been as deferential to the use of s. 3 of the 1972 Act had they been aware of the method by which primary legislation could be 'regarded as having been disapplied' in this manner.

For a different, though related, complaint in connection with other Regulations made under s. 3 of the 1972 Act, see the discussion of the European Communities (Protection of Topographies of Semiconductor Products) (Amendment) Regulations 1993 (SI No. 310) in the Commercial Law chapter, 57, above.

EUROPEAN COMMUNITY AND UNION

The European Communities (Amendment) Act 1992 (Commencement) Order 1993 (SI No. 304), which gave legislative force in Ireland to the Treaty on European Union (TEU), the Maastricht Treaty, with effect from 1 November 1993, is discussed in full in the 1992 Review, 326-31. As mentioned in the 1992 Review, the commencement of the TEU was made possible when the German government deposited its instrument of ratification in October 1993 after the German Constitutional Court had found that the TEU was consistent with German law. The TEU itself also thus took effect in accordance with its terms on 1 November 1993.

With the coming into force of the TEU, the European Union was established. In addition, the TEU also amended substantially the Treaty Establishing the European Economic Community (EEC) as well as changing its title to 'the Treaty Establishing the European Community.' With the TEU establishing both the European Community and European Union, the title of this chapter reflects this new nomenclature. At the time of writing, the Council of Ministers has altered its title to the 'Council of the European Union' (see the 1992 Review, 329), but no name change has taken place for what remains the Commission of the European Communities and the Court of Justice of the European Communities.

EUROPEAN ECONOMIC AREA

Ss. 2 and 3 of the European Communities (Amendment) Act 1993 provide for legislative effect to be given to the 1992 Agreement on the European Economic Area, the EEA Agreement, as adjusted by the 1993 Protocol to that Agreement. These sections, and the EEA Agreement, came into effect on 1 January 1994: see the European Communities (Amendment) Act 1993 (Commencement) Order 1993 (SI No. 415).

The EEA Agreement was signed between the EC States and the then seven EFTA States (Austria, Finland, Iceland, Liechtenstein, Norway, Sweden and Switzerland). The effect of the EEA Agreement is that, within the EEA, which consists of the EC/EU and EFTA States (apart from Switzerland, which ultimately decided in a referendum not to join the EEA), many of the core elements of European Community law apply as they do in the EC States. For example, the provisions of much of EC law on the 'four freedoms' of persons, services, capital and goods as well as on competition, social policy, the environment, education, research and development were, in effect, extended to the EEA.

The EEA Agreement clearly is not an Accession Treaty, but it does lay down extremely detailed requirements for harmonisation of laws in order to meet the requirements for the extension of existing EC benefits and obligations to the EEA. To that extent, there is a similarity with the type of timetable that might be laid down in an Accession Treaty. We may note, in this context, that in January 1995, three EFTA States, Austria, Finland, and Sweden, became full members of the EC/EU, thus in effect superceding the provisions of the EEA which dealt with these three States.

The most novel institutional change attempted by the EEA Agreement, whose terms clearly are less extensive in geographic scope since January 1995, was the provision of an EEA Court, with compulsory jurisdiction in relation to any disputes on the interpretation and application of the EEA Agreement itself, and whose membership would be drawn from the EFTA States (apart from Switzerland) and the Court of Justice of the Communities. However, the Court of Justice, having been consulted on this aspect of the EEA Agreement, found it inconsistent with the exclusive jurisdiction of the Court itself as an interpreter of EC Law: *Opinion 1/91* [1991] ECR I-6079. The 1993 Protocol to the EEA Agreement provided instead for an EFTA Court to oversee the application of the EEA Agreement in the non-EC States of the EEA. This adjustment was upheld by the Court of Justice: *Opinion 1/92* [1992] ECR I-2821.

The EEA Agreement also established other institutional structures to oversee implementation of the Agreement. These include an EEA Council, an overall body with primarily consultative functions, which includes EC Commissioners, members of the Council of Ministers and representatives of each of the non-EC States. The most significant law-making body is the EEA Joint Committee. This includes representatives from all the non-EC States with the EC Commission representing the EC, and the Joint Committee is empowered, like the EC Council of Ministers, to adopt legislation similar to EC Regulations and Directives. A Joint Parliamentary Committee, with representatives of the European Parliament and the Parliaments of the non-EC States, is also established. Finally, the EEA Surveillance Authority has responsibility with the EC Commission for ensuring that certain aspects of the EEA Agreement are enforced in full, for example, in the area of competition.

In addition to this new institutional structure, the EEA Agreement requires the EC Commission, when preparing legislation relevant to the Agreement, to consult fully with the EFTA States. Thus, any proposed Directives or Regulations relevant to the areas covered by the EEA Agreement are referred to the institutions established by the EEA Agreement. When these are published in the Official Journal of the European Communities, the footnote 'text of EEA relevance' is attached to the document. Given the wide ranging nature of the EEA Agreement, it is not surprising that many such footnotes now adorn the Official Journal.

For an excellent analysis of the background to an effect of the EEA Agreement, see Anthony Whelan's Annotation to the 1993 Act in *Irish Current Law Statutes Annotated.* See also Noel Travers' article, (1993) 3 IJEL 74.

EUROPEAN INVESTMENT FUND

S. 2 of the European Communities (Amendment) Act 1993 gives legislative effect in Irish law to the establishment of the European Investment Fund, an initiative at European level aimed particularly at encouraging growth within the EC States by assisting small and medium sized enterprises (SMEs) and also facilitating infrastructural projects. S. 2 of the 1993 Act came into effect on 5 May 1994: see the European Communities (Amendment) Act 1993 (Section 2) (Commencement) Order 1994 (SI No. 122 of 1994).

EUROPEAN PARLIAMENT ELECTIONS

The European Parliament Elections Act 1993 provided for a number of changes to the procedure for election to the European Parliament, in part arising from the coming into force of the Treaty on European Union (TEU), the Maastricht Treaty, on 1 November 1993: see above, 306. It also altered the representation from two of the four constituences in the State for the purposes of the 1994 election to the European Parliament.

S. 2 of the 1993 Act provided, in accordance with the TEU, that a person who is a national of a member State of the European Union other than Ireland and is ordinarily resident in this State shall not be ineligible as a candidate for election to the Parliament by reason only of not being a citizen of Ireland.

S. 7 of the 1993 Act, which inserted a new s. 15 into the European Assembly Election Act 1977, provides for updated arrangements for the filling of casual vacancies in the European Parliament by means of the 'replacement candidates' list'.

Finally, s. 9 of the 1993 Act laid down the updated allocation of the 15 seats to the European Parliament from the four constituencies in the State. The representation from Leinster and Munster remained unchanged at four seats each, but the Dublin constituency picked up one extra seat, bringing it to four, this being at the expense of Connaught-Ulster, which was reduced to three seats.

The 1993 Act came into effect on 13 December 1993 on its signature by the President, and by its terms it applied to any election to the European Parliament held after 1 January 1993. It thus applied to the elections to the European Parliament held in 1994. The European Elections Free Postage Scheme 1993 (SI No. 312), which applied to the 1994 election, laid down the conditions under which candidates could avail of the free distribution of their election literature.

JOINT COMMITTEE ON FOREIGN AFFAIRS

S. 6(1) of the European Communities (Amendment) Act 1993 provided, in effect, for the transfer to the new Joint Committee on Foreign Affairs of the functions formerly exercised under s. 4 of the European Communities Act 1972 by the Joint Committee on Secondary Legislation of the European Communities. S. 6(1) provided that it could only come into effect on such date as the Minister for Foreign Affairs would by Order appoint, and s. 6(2) of the 1993 Act provided that such an Order could not be made before the establishment by both Houses of the Oireachtas of the new Joint Committee on Foreign Affairs. The relevant resolutions having been passed, the date appointed by Order for s. 6(1) to come into effect was 26 April 1994: see the European Communities (Amendment) Act 1993 (Section 6(1)) Order 1994 (SI No. 91 of 1994). Anthony Whelan's Annotation to the 1993 Act in *Irish Current Law Statutes Annotated* provides an excellent account, in a comparative context, of the limitations imposed on the former Joint Committee on Secondary Legislation of the European Communities. The outcome of the Supreme Court decision in *Meagher v Minister for Agriculture and Food* [1994] 1 ILRM 1; [1994] 1 IR 329, discussed above, 299-304, indicates the importance of stricter scrutiny of EC legislation, particularly where Directives are at proposal stage rather than at the stage where they are being implemented in Irish law.

JURISDICTION OF COURTS

The case law arising from the Jurisdiction of Courts and Enforcement of Judgments Act 1988 is discussed in the Conflict of Laws chapter, 118, above.

LEGISLATIVE IMPLEMENTATION OF EC REQUIREMENTS IN IRISH LAW

The following Regulations and Orders made in 1993 pursuant to the provisions of s. 3 of the European Communities Act 1972, or other statutory powers, involve the implementation of Community obligations.

Air Navigation (Air Operators' Certificate) Order 1993 (SI No. 325): see the Transport chapter, 583, below.

Air Services Authorisation Order 1993 (SI No. 326): see the Transport chapter, 583, below.

European Communities (Abolition of Intra-Community Border Controls)

Regulations 1993 (SI No. 3): see the Commercial Law chapter, 62, above.

European Communities (Accounts) Regulations 1993 (SI No. 396): see the Company Law chapter, 113, above.

European Communities (Acquisition and Possession of Weapons and Ammunition) Regulations 1993 (SI No. 362): see the Criminal Law chapter, 231, above.

European Communities (Additives in Feedingstuffs) (Amendment) Regulations 1993 (SI No. 79): see the Agriculture chapter, 39, above.

European Communities (Application of the Rules on Competition to Maritime Transport) Regulations 1993 (SI No. 386): see the Transport chapter, 586, below.

European Communities (Application of the Rules on Competition to Rail and Road Transport) Regulations 1993 (SI No. 416): see the Transport chapter, 588, below.

European Communities (Award of Contracts by Entities operating in the Water, Energy, Transport and Telecommunications Sectors) Regulations 1993 (SI No. 103): see the Commercial Law chapter, 66, above.

European Communities (Award of Public Services Contracts) Regulations 1993 (SI No. 173): see the Commercial Law chapter, 66, above.

European Communities (Branch Disclosure) Regulations 1993 (SI No. 396): see the Company Law chapter 112, above.

European Communities (Cereal Seed) (Amendment) Regulations 1993 (SI No. 123): see the Agriculture chapter, 38, above.

European Communities (Cereal Seed) (Amendment) (No. 2) Regulations 1993 (SI No. 260): see the Agriculture chapter, 38, above.

European Communities (Equine Stud-Book and Competition) Regulations 1993 (SI No. 305): see the Agriculture chapter, 37, above.

European Communities (Fares and Rates for Air Services) Regulations 1993 (SI No. 256): see the Transport chapter, 583, below.

European Communities (Feedingstuffs) (Method of Analysis) (Amendment) Regulations 1993 (SI No. 370): see the Agriculture chapter, 39, above.

European Communities (Feedingstuffs) (Tolerances of Undesirable Substances) (Amendment) Regulations 1993 (SI No. 86): see the Agriculture chapter, 39, above.

European Communities (Indication of Prices of Foodstuffs and Non-Food Products) (Amendment) Regulations 1993 (SI No. 307): see the Commercial Law chapter, 48, above.

European Communities (Intrastat) Regulations 1993 (SI No. 136): see the Commercial Law chapter, 63, above.

European Communities (Introduction of Organisms Harmful to Plants or

Plant Products) (Prohibition) (Amendment) Regulations 1993 (SI No. 408): see the Agriculture chapter, 39, above.

European Communities (Legal Protection of Computer Programs) Regulations 1993 (SI No. 26): see the Commercial Law chapter, 56, above.

European Communities (Marketing of Feedingstuffs) (Amendment) Regulations 1993 (SI No. 261): see the Agriculture chapter, 39, above.

European Communities (Marketing of Fertilizers) (Amendment) Regulations 1993 (SI No. 110): see the Agriculture chapter, 39, above.

European Communities (Materials and Articles Intended to Come into Contact with Foodstuffs) (Amendment) Regulations 1993 (SI No. 295): see the Safety and Health chapter, 480, below.

European Communities (Mechanically Propelled Vehicle Emission Control) Regulations 1993 (SI No. 363): see the Transport chapter, 590, below.

European Communities (Monitoring of External Trade in Scheduled Substances) Regulations 1993 (SI No. 6): see the Criminal Law chapter, 243, above.

European Communities (Motor Vehicles Type Approval) Regulations 1993 (SI No. 139): see the Transport chapter, 589, below.

European Communities (Mutual Assistance as Regards Correct Application of Legislation on Veterinary and Zootechnical Matters) Regulations 1993 (SI No. 150): see the Agriculture chapter, 37, above.

European Communities (Personal Protective Equipment) Regulations 1993 (SI No. 272): see the Safety and Health chapter, 480, below.

European Communities (Pesticide Residues) (Cereals) (Amendment) Regulations 1993 (SI No. 316): see the Agriculture chapter, 40, above.

European Communities (Pesticide Residues) (Foodstuffs of Animal Origin) (Amendment) Regulations 1993 (SI No. 317): see the Agriculture chapter, 40, above.

European Communities (Pig Carcass (Grading)) (Amendment) Regulations 1993 (SI No. 313): see the Agriculture chapter, 38, above.

European Communities (Pig Carcass (Grading)) (Amendment) (No. 2) Regulations 1993 (SI No. 405): see the Agriculture chapter, 38, above.

European Communities (Potato Ring Rot) Regulations 1993 (SI No. 346): see the Agriculture chapter, 40, above.

European Communities (Prevention of Supply of Certain Goods and Services to Libya) Regulations 1993 (SI No. 384): see the Commercial Law chapter, 63, above.

European Communities (Protection of Topographies of Semiconductor Products) (Amendment) Regulations 1993 (SI No. 310): see the Commercial Law chapter, 58, above.

European Communities (Prohibition of Certain Trade with Haiti) Regulations 1993 (SI No. 344): see the Commercial Law chapter, 64, above.

European Communities (Prohibition of Satisfaction of Certain Contractual Claims Arising from Trade Sanctions against Libya) Regulations 1993 (SI No. 385): see the Commercial Law chapter, 63, above.

European Communities (Prohibition of Satisfaction of Certain Contractual Claims by Persons in Iraq) Regulations 1993 (SI No. 120): see the Commercial Law chapter, 63, above.

European Communities (Prohibition of the Supply of Certain Goods to UNITA) Regulations 1993 (SI No. 383): see the Commercial Law chapter, 64, above.

European Communities (Prohibition of Trade with the Federal Republic of Yugoslavia (Serbia and Montenegro)) Regulations 1993 (SI No. 144): see the Commercial Law chapter, 63, above.

European Communities (Protection of Workers) (Exposure to Asbestos) (Amendment) Regulations 1993 (SI No. 276): see the Safety and Health chapter, 483, below.

European Communities (Radiological Emergency Warning to Public) Regulations 1993 (SI No. 209): see the Safety and Health chapter, 482, below.

European Communities (Restriction of Civil Subsonic Jet Aeroplane Operations) Regulations 1993 (SI No. 130): see the Transport chapter, 584, below.

European Communities (Retirement of Farmers) Regulations 1993 (SI No. 204): see the Agriculture chapter, 40, above.

European Communities (Review Procedures for the Award of Contracts by Entities operating in the Water, Energy, Transport and Telecommunications Sectors) Regulations 1993 (SI No. 104): see the Commercial Law chapter, 66, above.

European Communities (Right of Residence for Non-Economically Active Persons) Regulations 1993 (SI No. 109): see the Aliens and Immigration chapter, 41, above.

European Communities (Rules on Competition) Regulations 1993 (SI No. 124): see the Commercial Law chapter, 47, above.

European Communities (Sampling and Analysis of Fertilizers) Regulations (SI No. 257): see the Agriculture chapter, 39, above.

European Communities (Seed of Fodder Plants) (Amendment) Regulations 1993 (SI No. 230): see the Agriculture chapter, 39, above.

European Communities (Speed Limitation Devices) Regulations 1993 (SI No. 300): see the Transport chapter, 592, below.

European Communities (Supplementary Protection Certificate) Regulations

1993 (SI No. 125): see the Commercial Law chapter, 61, above.

European Communities (Surveillance of Imports of Certain Iron and Steel Products) Regulations 1993 (SI No. 85): see the Commercial Law chapter, 63, above.

European Communities (TIR Carnet and ATA Carnet-Transit) Regulations 1993 (SI No. 61): see the Transport chapter, 586, below.

European Communities (Trade in Bovine Breeding Animals, their Semen, Ova and Embryos) Regulations 1993 (SI No. 259): see the Agriculture chapter, 38, above.

European Communities (Trade in Porcine Semen — Animal Health) Regulations 1993 (SI No. 242): see the Agriculture chapter, 38, above, and 305, above.

European Communities (Value-Added Tax) Regulations 1993 (SI No. 345): this will be discussed in the 1994 Review.

European Elections Free Postage Scheme 1993 (SI No. 312): see 309, above.

Health (Extraction Solvents in Foodstuffs) Regulations 1993 (SI No. 387): see the Safety and Health chapter, 480, below.

Health (Nutrition Labelling for Foodstuffs) Regulations 1993 (SI No. 388): see the Safety and Health chapter, 480, below.

Local Government (Water Pollution) Acts 1977 and 1990 (Control of Aldrin, Dieldrin, Endrin, Isodrin, HCB, HCBD and CHCI3 Discharges) Regulations 1993 (SI No. 348): see the Safety and Health chapter, 475, below.

Medical Preparations (Advertising) Regulations 1993 (SI No. 76): see the Health Services chapter, 344, below.

Medical Preparations (Labelling and Package Leaflets) Regulations 1993 (SI No. 71): see the Health Services chapter, 344, below.

Medical Preparations (Licensing, Advertisment and Sale) (Amendment) Regulations 1993 (SI No. 70): see the Health Services chapter, 345, below.

Medical Preparations (Licensing of Manufacture) Regulations 1993 (SI No. 40): see the Health Services chapter, 344, below.

Medical Preparations (Licensing of Manufacture) Regulations 1993 (Amendment) Regulations 1993 (SI No. 68): see the Health Services chapter, 344-5, below.

Medical Preparations (Prescription and Control of Supply) Regulations 1993 (SI No. 69): see the Health Services chapter, 345, below.

Medical Preparations (Wholesale Licences) Regulations 1993 (SI No. 39): see the Health Services chapter, 345, below.

Misuse of Drugs (Scheduled Substances) Regulations 1993 (SI No. 338): see the Criminal Law chapter, 243, above.

Radiological Protection Act 1991 (General Control of Radioactive Sub-

stances, Nuclear Devices and Irradiating Apparatus) Order 1993 (SI No.
151): see the Safety and Health chapter, 482, below.

Safety, Health and Welfare at Work (Carcinogens) Regulations 1993 (SI No.
80): see the Safety and Health chapter, 482, below.

Safety, Health and Welfare at Work (General Application) Regulations 1993
(SI No. 44): see the Safety and Health chapter, 482, below.

Sea Fisheries (Regulation of Nets) Order 1993 (SI No. 264): see the Fisheries
chapter, 336, below.

In addition to the above, some provisions of primary legislation involved the
implementation of EC Directives, EC-related Conventions or provided
mechanisms for claiming EC assistance and aid. These included the following:

Animal Remedies Act 1993: see the Agriculture chapter 34, above, and
Meagher v Minister for Agriculture and Food [1994] 1 ILRM 1; [1994] 1
IR 329 above, 299-304.

European Communities (Amendment) Act 1993: see 307, 310, above.

European Parliament Elections Act 1993: see 309, above.

Finance Act 1993: see the Revenue Law chapter in the 1994 Review.

Jurisdiction of Courts and Enforcement of Judgments Act 1993: see the
Conflict of Laws chapter, 118, above.

Roads Act 1993: see the Transport chapter, 588-93, below.

Family law

NULLITY OF MARRIAGE

Grounds

Duress and psychological incapacity In *A.M. v T.M.*, High Court, 11 February 1993 O'Hanlon J granted a decree of nullity where the petitioner, an 'immature and naive' pregnant girl of fifteen, married after pressure had been imposed on her by her adoptive parents to choose between marriage and placing her child for adoption. The petitioner had become pregnant when she had gone to a party several miles from home; she had drunk alcohol for the first time; the person who offered to bring her home, a young man of twenty-one, had insisted on having sexual intercourse as a condition of doing so. When she became pregnant, the young man came under similar pressure from his mother to marry her.

The wedding took place in 1985. There was no honeymoon; the parties simply moved into a mobile home at the rear of the petitioner's family home. From the outset the marriage was a failure, with the respondent over the years inflicting much violence on the petitioner and the parties' two children (the second born in 1987). The respondent breached a barring order and was imprisoned; thereafter he disappeared out of the petitioner's life.

In granting the decree, O'Hanlon J laid emphasis on the petitioner's immaturity and her inability to withstand the pressure put on her by her parents to enter the marriage. She could not, in his view, be regarded as having given any real or true consent to the marriage. O'Hanlon J was also willing to hold the marriage void on the basis of the respondent's total incapacity to enter into or maintain a normal marriage relationship by reason of psychological incapacity on his part. This holding is perhaps understandable on the basis that sexual abuse, domestic violence and desertion are profoundly subversive of any marital relationship. Nevertheless the respondent in this case remains a shadowy figure about whom almost nothing was revealed except the external indicia of irresponsibility and cruelty. Of course at some point it becomes entirely legitimate for a court to infer from external conduct an internal incapacity; but could it not be argued that, in the instant case, while the petitioner had clearly established duress, she had only established that the respondent had behaved extremely badly, not that this badness was *necessarily* attributable to incapacity on his part?

Standard of Proof In the 1992 Review 346-7, we considered the question of the standard of proof in nullity proceedings. The courts have yet to reach a settled position on the issue. In *A.B. v E.B.*, High Court, 14 October 1993, after a detailed review of the earlier decisions, Budd J expressed himself 'inclined to the view that the burden of proof is on the balance of probabilities but that the Court must exercise particular caution and scepticism in scrutinising the evidence proffered, bearing in mind that frequently in these cases there has been an irretrievable breakdown of the relationship between the parties and there is no *legitimus contradictor* to the case being made by the petitioner'. He was reinforced in this view by Henchy J's observations in *Banco Ambrosiano v Ansbacher & Co.* [1987] ILRM 669, at 701.

The Supreme Court's affirmation of Budd J's decision, on 31 July 1995, did not address the question of the standard of proof. In this context it is worth noting the view of O'Flaherty J, expressed in *Hanafin v Minister for the Environment*, 12 June 1996, that since the *Banco Ambrosiano* case, it has been 'settled in Irish law that in civil cases the standard of proof is on the balance of probabilities. . . .'

JUDICIAL SEPARATION

Grounds In *M.M v C.M.*, High Court, 6 July 1993, the troublesome question of the conflicting philosophies of the grounds for judicial separation fell for consideration. Grounds (a) to (c) of s. 2 (1) of the Judicial Separation and Family Law Reform Act 1989 are clearly based on the concept of matrimonial fault but, equally clearly, grounds (d) to (f) are not. In this case, the petitioner sought a decree from her husband on two grounds: behaviour (ground (b)) and the absence of a normal marital relationship (ground (f)). The respondent had also claimed a decree on the basis of his wife's adultery (ground (a)) with a priest — which the wife in the instant proceedings admitted.

The evidence in the case presented a picture that O'Hanlon J thought was inconsistent with the 'very demanding vocation' of marriage, which required a large measure of unselfishness and sacrifice on the part of both spouses. The parties' courtship had been characterised by heavy drinking, resort to drugs, pre-marital intercourse and abortion. The wife's unfaithfulness had been 'only one of the rocks on which the marriage foundered'. The husband had abused alcohol and had been extravagant with money. He had failed to develop 'a sense of sturdy independence', since he had been 'baled out repeatedly by his parents from his student days, in relation to his financial problems'.

There were five children of the marriage, one of whom had Down's

Syndrome. The wife had embarked on further academic studies and a
professional career which had taken her away from the family 'to an
inordinate extent just at a time when the children were of an age to need her
presence most around the home — all the more so when she knew that the
husband would do little to make up for the loss of mother-care'. The husband
with his wife's consent, had been sterilized. O'Hanlon J observed that the
spouses were still young people, it was 'not without significance that the
ultimate break-down of the marriage was not long postponed'.

O'Hanlon J quoted at length from a work by Monsignor Cormac Burke,
a Judge of the Roman Rota and member of the Opus Dei Prelature, entitled
Covenanted Happiness-Love and Commitment in Marriage (1990). O'Hanlon J considered that what was quoted "correctly identif[ied] 'the innate
dignity and true meaning of human and spousal sexuality' apart altogther
from the fact that they coincide with the teaching of the Catholic Church on
the moral issues involved". It is somewhat surprising that O'Hanlon J should
have thought that the instant case was a particularly appropriate one in which
to address the question of the possible effect of the practice of contraception
on the quality and stability of spousal relationships, since the parties had five
children, a large family by modern Irish standards.

Monsignor Burke's analysis was as follows:

> Why should the marital act be more significant than any other expres-
> sion of affection between the spouses? Why should it be a more intense
> expression of love and union? Surely because of *what happens* in that
> marital encounter, which is not just a touch, not a mere sensation,
> however intense, but a *communication*, an offer and acceptance, an
> exchange of something that uniquely represents the gift of oneself and
> the union of two selves. . . .

> Therefore, what makes marital intercourse express a *unique* relationship
> and union is not the sharing of a sensation but the sharing of a *power*:
> of an extraordinary life-related, creative physical sexual power. In a true
> conjugal relationship, each spouse says to the other: 'I accept you as
> somebody like no one else in my life. You will be unique to me and I
> to you. You and you alone will be my husband; you alone will be my
> wife; and the proof of your uniqueness to me is the fact that with you
> — and with you alone — am I prepared to share this God-given
> life-orientated power'.

> Now if one deliberately nullifies the life-orientation of the conjugal act,
> *one destroys its essential power to signify union.* Contraception in fact
> turns the marital act *into self-deception or into a lie*: "I love you so much

that with you and with you alone, I am ready to share this most unique power. . . .' But — what unique power? In contraceptive sex, no unique power is being shared, except a power to produce pleasure. But then the uniqueness of the marital act is reduced to pleasure. Its significance is gone. . . .

The anti-life effect of contraception does not stop at the 'no' which it addresses to the possible fruit of love. It tends to take the very life out of love itself. Within the hard logic of contraception, anti-life becomes anti-love. Its devitalizing effect devastates love, threatening it with early ageing and premature death. . . .

The negation that a contraceptive couple are involved in is not directed just towards children, or just towards life, or just towards the world. They address a negation directly towards one another. 'I prefer a sterile you', is equivalent to saying, 'I don't want all you offer me. I have calculated the measure of my love, and it is not big enough for that; it is not able to take all of you. I want a "you" cut down to the size of my love. . . .' The fact that both spouses may concur in accepting a cut-rate version of each other does not save their love or their lives — or their possibilities of happiness — from the effects of such radical human and sexual devaluation.

It is interesting in this context to recall that in *Bravery v Bravery* [1954] 1 WLR 1169, Denning LJ took the view that male sterilization for contraceptive purposes is *a criminal offence*:

When it is done with a man's consent for a just cause, it is quite lawful; as, for instance, when it is done to prevent the transmission of an hereditary disease. But where it is done without just cause or excuse, it is unlawful, even though the man consents to it. Take a case where a sterilization operation is done so as to enable a man to have the pleasure of sexual intercourse, without shouldering the responsibilities attaching to it. The operation then is plainly injurious to the public interest. It is degrading to the man himself. It is injurious to his wife and to any woman whom he may marry, to say nothing of the way it opens to licentiousness; and, unlike contraceptives, it allows no room for a change of mind on either side.

We do not here address the wider issues that arise; it is worth noting that O'Hanlon J did not seek to suggest that a joint decision by spouses to practice contraception gives either of them an entitlement to a decree for judicial separation on that basis: it seems certain that a court would hold that ground

(f) had even established a year after the decision had been put into practice. The unilateral insistence by one spouse that he or she, or the other spouse, practice contraception could indeed constitute a ground for a decree of judicial separation, either on the basis of ground (b) — the 'behaviour' ground — or ground (c), where such conduct could be characterised as constructive desertion on the basis that it effectively drove the other spouse from the home.

In the instant case, O'Hanlon J went on to grant a decree of judicial separation on ground (f) of section 2(1), based on the absence of a normal marriage relationship for a year. He gave the petitioner liberty to apply further in relation to ground (b), on behaviour, should that become necessary at a later stage. He did not seek to apportion blame for the breakdown of the marriage between the parties as he did not consider that it served any useful purpose at that stage to do so and might well exacerbate the feelings of hostility that the spouses had at times felt for each other. There had been from the outset a substantial failure on both sides to face up to the demands of the married state and to work together for the happiness and welfare of all the family; the more recent events had only been 'the culmination of that process and not in reality, a new departure on either side'.

The family home   The problem of how to integrate orders for continuing occupation of the family home with the best use of the economic resources of the family fell for consideration in *L.C. v A.C.*, High Court, 30 March 1993, a Circuit Appeal heard by Murphy J. The Circuit Court judge, on granting a decree of judicial separation, had ordered that the family home remain in the spouses' joint names, that the wife should have the right to occupy the home to the exclusion of the respondent for her life or further order of the court and that the respondent continue to pay the mortgage on the house.

The husband wished to buy a home of his own similar to the existing family home (which was valued at £46,000) 'partly because of his own preference and partly because he was anxious that he would be seen by his son to enjoy accommodation of the same quality as that of his wife'. He sought a capital contribution from his wife to achieve this goal. The equity in the house was around £20,000. The wife indicated that she would be in a position to borrow from members of her own family only £2,000 of the £10,000 that represented her husband's net interest.

Murphy J was of the view that the order of the Circuit Court, insofar as it conferred a right on the wife to reside in the family home for an indefinite period, was unfair to the husband and unsatisfactory for her:

If it is intended that [the wife] should, in fact, have the full and undisputed enjoyment of the existing house, then [the husband]'s investment or equity has no value. If, on the other hand, [the wife] is to have a mere right of residence and not a right of property, her right is limited to the enjoyment of the particular property and if it was desirable for any reason to sell that property her right under the existing order would lapse.

Murphy J was convinced that it was preferable in the interests of both parties that finality should be achieved by a sale by the husband to the wife of his half share in the beneficial interest in the home. The price would have to reflect the wife's right to reside in the home. Alternatively, if sold for the full price, the maintenance payable to her would have to be increased so as to assist her in meeting her additional cost of living.

Murphy J observed that the difficulty of isolating a particular aspect of an order of the court or term of consent was to relate any alteration of that aspect to the other terms of the order. He thought that it was in the wife's interest to become the absolute owner of the home so that, in addition to having a place to reside with her son, she would know that what she paid towards it would be an investment and security for her. The sale would be of benefit to the husband by providing him, in the short term, with additional capital that he required and relieving him from further responsibility in relation to the house. Most of all, it would save him from any speculation as to whether, if at all, he would ever obtain any benefit from his nominal part-ownership of the existing premises.

Murphy J's solution was to adjourn the case with the encouragement to the parties, who, he noted, had displayed 'such wisdom and maturity to date', to arrange for the sale by the husband of his interest in the home to the wife for a reduced price that would reflect her right of residence and 'the somewhat speculative nature of his interest'. He commented that,

[o]bviously whatever price [the wife] paid would increase the amount of the mortgage which she would have to raise as has already been planned but I anticipate that she would welcome the opportunity of determining her rights by such a procedure.

Murphy J stated that the statutory provisions did not give him an express power to implement a scheme of that nature or at any rate in those terms.

The case raises a number of issues of general importance. Marriage law and property law are both in a state of rapid transformation. This can lead to anomalies, where old ideas, which have not yet been rooted out, clash with the new.

If we limit ourselves to the past three decades or so, we see the following pattern emerge. The Victorian system of a separate property regime for spouses has given way, fitfully, and with only grudging assistance from the Supreme Court, to a system where the claims of wives to a share in property (especially the family home) have gained a hearing. A wife who has contributed to the acquisition of property, even if it is in the name of her husband, will be entitled to a share, in proportion to her contribution: see P. Coughlan, *Property Law* (1995) 429-31, H. Delany, *Equity and the Law of Trusts in Ireland* (1996) 143-5.

A wife who devotes herself to rearing the children in the home has no claim to a share of its equity, astoundingly, one might have thought, in view of the underlying philosophy and express terms of Article 41 of the Constitution. Barr J's bold attempt to remedy this judicial failure, in *L. v L.* [1989] ILRM 528 (analysed in the 1988 Review, 213-21 and by Nuala Jackson, (1989) 11 *DULJ (ns)* 158) met with rejection in the Supreme Court: [1992] ILRM 115; [1992] 2 IR 77 (analysed in the 1991 Review, 216-22, by Nuala Jackson (1992) 14 *DULJ (ns)* 153 and by Gerard Hogan and Gerry Whyte in J. Kelly, *The Irish Constitution* (3rd ed., 1994), 1010-12). When the Oireachtas sought to improve the position by introducing a system of joint ownership of the family home, it too received a rebuff from the Supreme Court, which struck the Bill down as violating the constitutionally protected decision-making autonomy of spouses: *In re Matrimonial Home Bill 1993* [1994] 1 ILRM 241; [1994] 1 IR 305. See Coughlan, *op. cit.*, 432, Hogan (1995) 16 *DULJ* (ns) 175.

The Succession Act 1965 gave widows substantial rights in their late husbands' estate, including a fairly wide-ranging entitlement to appropriate the matrimonial home. The Family Home Protection Act 1976 effectively protected wives and children from having the family home sold or mortgaged over their heads by vindictive or feckless husbands but it gave no proprietary interest to women.

The Judicial Separation and Family Law Reform Act 1989 altered the situation by giving the court the power to order the exclusion of a spouse from the home on granting an order for judicial separation, on the basis that it is not possible for the couple to continue living together after a separation decree. Since judicial separation may be sought by the spouse responsible for the marital problem, the judicial power of exclusion alters the perception of the basis of entitlement to live in the family home.

Over the past three decades the role of women has changed radically. Far more married women now work outside the home. Those who stay at home with their children frequently complain that this role has lost all its former status in society. No judge today would feel comfortable, in spite of Article 41.2., in suggesting that the common good is best served by wives' working at home.

Marriage is now seen by an increasing number as a partnership in which spouses have no socially or legally prescribed roles. If this is so, should not family property law stay neutral? Those who favour a neutral position argue that the very notion of 'family home' is premised on assumptions of wifely domesticity and hour- to-hour nurturing relationship with the children which bears no true relationship with modern society.

A second development has affected the position. Thirty years ago marriage in Irish society meant lifelong marriage. Separation was extremely rare: judicial separation (divorce *a mensa et thoro*) was granted in a handful of cases annually, only on the basis of matrimonial wrongdoing. Today, separation is less rare, though still very low by international standards. Decrees of judicial separation are being granted in their thousands for grounds that include 'no fault' criteria. Divorce, of a 'no fault' model, has recently been introduced. All of these changes have profound implications for family property law and its philosophical underpinnings.

If the partnership that marriage involves is not a lifelong irrevocable partnership but rather one that may be terminated unilaterally at any time on giving due notice, then the argument for community of property may seem a good deal less than self-evident. Thus Angelo and Atkin could praise legislation in New Zealand for recognising that, at breakdown of marriage, 'a universal community is not generally acceptable and that the presence and wide use of divorce laws create demands for a regime of separation of property': 'A Conceptual and Structural Overview of the Matrimonial Property Act 1976' (1977), 7 *NZUL Rev* 237, at 258. See also, in this context, Schmidt, 'The Prospective Law of Marriage' (1971) 15 *Scandinavian Studies in Law* 191, at 204-5, 215; Glendon, 'Is There a Future for Separate Property?' (1974) 8 *Family LQ* 315; Deech, 'The Case Against Legal Recognition of Cohabitation' (1980) 29 *Int & Comp LQ* 480, at 483.

If the law treats marriage as revocable rather than lifelong, then those who act altruistically on the assumption that marriage is for life will be punished for their folly. Undoubtedly, sacrificing career prospects by working in the home becomes a foolish decision. Ruth Deech, of the University of Oxford, writing in *The Times*, 14 January 1980, observed that:

> [i]t may be argued that women have a right to be full-time housewives and mothers and that this in fact damages their career prospects permanently. Even if this argument is accepted, the right is not in practice exercisable in conjunction with our easy, no-fault divorce laws.

It is interesting to compare the facts and holding in *L.C. v A.C.* with the argument put forward by the Campaign for Justice in Divorce in England in 1979, in its publication *An Even Better Way Out*, para. 29. The Campaign contended that moving house:

> is part and parcel of normal family life and no one regards it as
> unacceptable. Yet when there's a divorce suddenly all these normal
> events are regarded by the court as something to be avoided. This is the
> main reason why the courts so often endeavour to keep the mother and
> children in the matrimonial home regardless of the hardship this inflicts
> upon the father, who usually is deprived of all this capital. The bitterness
> and resentment this common decision causes is frequently visited upon
> the children and the father's ability to maintain this relationship with
> them is prejudiced or prevented because he has less chance than the
> mother of providing suitable accommodation. This is against the interest
> of the children as well as being grossly unfair to the father. He is
> expected to collect them from the comfortable home, which in all
> probability he provided in the first place, and take them back to his tiny
> flat or bedsit.

The logic of the argument is that, with divorce, it is unjust on the husband
(and indirectly on the children) for the wife to stay in the former family home
with the children. It should, instead, be sold. Of course, Murphy J's judgment
goes nowhere so far, but it scarcely strengthens the wife's prospect of staying
in the home. If a husband is able to 'call in' his equity in the family home
through a formal sale, ordered or encouraged by the court, this will give the
wife extra cash (in the instant case apparently £10,000) but presumably
payment of the mortgage will become her complete responsibility, save to
the extent that this may be dealt with by an increase in the husband's
maintenance obligations to her. In the instant case, if the husband was to fulfil
his wish to buy another home worth about £46,000, on the basis of a
down-payment of £10,000 acquired from his wife, he would have a new
mortgage of £36,000 (plus the costs associated with purchase). The mortgage
appears to have been in the region of £26,000. It seems unlikely that many
separated husbands with an equity base of £10,000 would be able to sustain
two mortgages amounting in total over £60,000 unless they had a good
income. No doubt there will be some cases where the strategy adopted by
Murphy J will work perfectly satisfactorily (and it is quite possible that the
instant case is one such example: the facts stated in the judgment do not
enable a final assessment to be made). There seems a real danger however,
that a widespread practice of permitting such 'buy-outs' would, reduce the
security of wives and children in the home.

SUPPORT OBLIGATIONS

The crucial issue of gender equality in relation to support obligations came before Costello J in *Lowth v Minister for Social Welfare* [1994] 1 ILRM 378. For decades legislation on family maintenance has been gender neutral on its face, while tacitly letting the courts inject into their assessment of what constitutes 'proper' maintenance such value judgments as to gender roles as they wish: cf. Binchy, 'Family Law Reform in Ireland: Some Comparative Aspects', 26 *Int & Comp LQ* 901 at 901-4 (1976).

Social welfare legislation is different: in 1993 it still had not completely shaken off the assumption that women should obtain allowances in cases where men similarly positioned would receive less or nothing. Of course the trend, driven by European initiatives, is to remove any lingering differences in our social welfare code.

Mr Lowth, a deserted husband, challenged the constitutional validity of provisions of the Social Welfare (Consolidation) Act 1981 which gave deserted wives somewhat greater allowances than deserted husbands. He claimed that this offended the equality guarantee contained in Article 40.1 of the Constitution. An undoubted difficulty facing him was the fact that nine years previously Barron J in the decision of *Dennehy v Minister for Social Welfare*, High Court, 26 July 1984 (still unreported, in spite of the crucial constitutional issues involved) had determined the same issue against the claimant.

In Mr Lowth's case, Costello J referred to statistical evidence that established that in 1991 only 30% of married women were in the labour force and of those married women who were working in industrial employment their earnings were only 59.2% of those of male workers similarly employed.

Costello J considered that the Oireachtas 'could reasonably conclude that married women fulfil in Irish society a different social function to married men . . . [and] that married women who were deserted by their husbands require greater income support than married men who were deserted by their wives.' It followed, he thought, that the distinction made in the legislation was based, not on any assumption that husbands deserted by their wives were to be treated 'in some way inferior' to wives deserted by their husbands, but rather on 'a factual assessment by the Oireachtas of the greater needs of deserted wives.' As no reasons had been advanced as to why he should consider this factual assessment was wrong, he concluded that the legislative distinction was not arbitrary, but a reasonable and constitutionally permissible one.

Costello J went on to agree with the views of Barron J in *Dennehy* when he had concluded that, in the light of Article 41.2 of the Constitution which (as Costello J put it) 'recognises the special role of wives and mothers in Irish society', the Oireachtas was not acting unreasonably when it sought to give special financial support to deserted wives who were also mothers.

Costello J's analysis raises a number of observations. The notion of 'the greater needs of deserted wives' needs close examination. It could mean that a deserted wife has, as such, greater financial needs than a deserted husband, as such. The only evidence on this point mentioned in the judgment is that relative to the disparity of earnings between male and female industrial workers. Mr Lowth was not an industrial worker; his employment to look after his two young children and, when they had grown older, found that he could not obtain employment.

The other interpretation of the phrase is that a *greater number* of deserted wives are not in employment outside the home than deserted husbands. The question then arises as to whether this fact warrants the making of a distinction on gender lines than on the basis of financial need without having regard to the gender of the person in need.

In *R.H. v M.H.* [1986] ILRM 352 at 354-5, Finlay CJ observed that, in determining maintenance obligations, the Court:

> must . . . have regard to the somewhat pathetic fact that upon the separation of a husband and wife and particularly a husband and wife with children, it is inevitable that all the parties will suffer a significant diminution in the overall standard of living. The necessity for two residences to be maintained and two separate households to be provided for makes this an inescapable consequence of the separation. Subject to that overriding consideration a court must . . . ascertain the minimum reasonable requirements of . . . the wife and the children for whose upkeep she is responsible: it must then ascertain the income earned or capable of being earned by the wife, apart from the maintenance for which the husband is responsible; its next task is to ascertain the true net take-home pay or income of the husband, and lastly it must ascertain the reasonable expenses of the husband, bearing in mind the general consideration of economy affecting all the parties concerned, but leaving him with a reasonable standard of living.

A crucial issue in this area is that of the wife who has not worked outside the home. In what circumstances should the Court proceed on the basis that her failure to do so in the future should be penalised by a low award of maintenance?

Lynch J had to confront the question in *B.F. v V.F.*, High Court, 20 May 1993 (Circuit Appeal). The husband was a consultant anaesthetist. The wife was providing a home for their three children whose ages ranged from thirteen to seventeen. The husband had obtained a decree of judicial separation in the Circuit Court. The wife appealed against a number of ancillary orders.

Lynch J was satisfied that it was 'reasonable and proper for the wife at the present time not to seek work outside the home'. Her work within the home was 'a full time occupation in itself'. Lynch J agreed with the wife's contention that she should by her presence and availability to the children try to make up for the absence of their father.

The husband's annual earnings were £127,000. The Circuit Court Judge had awarded £20,000 per annum maintenance for the wife and children as well as payment of 'basic' school fees and Voluntary Health Insurance contributions. When the husband's outgoings for tax, maintenance of his wife and children and education and VHI expenses were subtracted from his earnings, he was left with £40,515 to support himself alone.

Lynch J was satisfied that this was an unbalanced situation. He ordered an increase of £13,325 for the wife's maintenance.

The wife had been provided with a two-bedroomed apartment and the husband had agreed to assign to his wife the lump sum payable on his retirement or death. Lynch J considered that, since the wife was 'a capable lady who w[ould] probably be free to obtain employment in eight or nine years' time, if she so wishe[d]', the Circuit Court Judge had acted correctly in extinguishing the statutory succession rights of each spouse in each others' estate.

THE FAMILY HOME

Family home protection legislation In *National Irish Bank Ltd v Graham* [1994] 1 ILRM 372, Costello J was called on to determine an important issue of interpretation of s.2 of the Family Home Protection Act 1976. Section 2 defines 'family home' as meaning, primarily, a dwelling in which a married couple ordinary reside. It goes on to include a dwelling in which a spouse whose protection is in issue ordinarily resides or, if that spouse has left the other spouse, ordinarily resided before so leaving. The fundamental protection afforded by the 1976 Act is s.3, in that it renders void any conveyance of any interest in the family home by one spouse to any person except the other spouse, without the prior consent in writing of the other spouse.

In the instant case, property intended to be family homes had been bought and mortgaged by two husbands *before* they had resided in them with their wives. They sought subsequently to challenge the validity of the mortgages on the basis that the prior consent in writing of their wives had not been obtained. They asserted that their wives had equitable interests in the property and that, if the Act did not include them within its scope, its intended protection would be nullified.

Costello J rejected this contention in clear terms:

> When a husband buys a dwelling for the purpose of residing in it with
> his wife it is by no means unusual, and it was by no means unusual when
> the Act was passed, that the husband would obtain a loan for the purpose
> and mortgage the house to a lending institution before he took up
> occupation. At that point in time the wife has no legal rights in the
> dwelling. But as soon as she and her husband commence to reside
> ordinarily in it then the Act confers rights on her. It then becomes a
> family home and it cannot be alienated without her consent. This is the
> protection which the Act was designed to confer on married women. To
> give this protection I do not think that I am required to construe 'a family
> home' within the meaning the Act not only as a dwelling in which a
> married couple reside but also as a dwelling in which a married woman
> intended to reside on the date of its purchase.

This conclusion is undoubtedly in harmony with the intention of the
legislators when enacting the measure. It is true that the policy of protection
of dependent spouses and children is not advanced by the limitation identified
in the judgment, but it is easy to envisage cases where the expansion sought
by the defendants could yield unjust and uncertain results.

In *Bank of Ireland v Smyth* [1993] 2 IR 102, Geoghegan J held that the
consent of a wife to a mortgage or charge in favour of a bank is not valid for
the purposes of the Family Home Protection Act 1976 unless she understands
the nature of the consequences of the transaction. This should extend to such
matters as the amount of the loan, its repayment terms and the consequences
of non-repayment; the wife should also be recommended to obtain legal
advice. The Supreme Court affirmed Geoghegan J's decision on 15 November 1995.

We shall examine the Supreme Court decision in detail in the 1995
Review. For a detailed analysis of Geoghegan J's decision, see Eoin O'Dell,
above 194 and Paul Coughlan, below, 383-8.

Judicial separation and orders affecting the family home   Earlier in this
chapter, in the Judicial Separation section, above, 320-21, we examine
Murphy J's decision in *L.C. v A.C.*, High Court, 30 March 1993, in relation
to orders in judicial separation proceedings affecting the family home.

SEPARATION AGREEMENTS

In *L.M. v M.*, Supreme Court, 2 March 1993, the question of the validity of
mediated separation agreements fell for consideration. The agreements had

been negotiated by the spouses with the assistance of a mutual long-standing friend, who was a solicitor, not acting as such in this context but rather 'as an honest broker to both parties'. Under the first agreement the husband had agreed *inter alia*, to pay his wife £77,500 in three tranches, the first of which was for £40,000. He failed to pay this in full. The second agreement, two months later, was expressed to be ancillary to the earlier one. In essence, it gave the husband more time to make his payment but otherwise was identical to the first. The husband's execution of this latter agreement was witnessed by his accountant.

The husband failed to comply with its terms. To proceedings for specific performance, the husband responded with the claim that he had been induced to enter the agreement as a result of threats and inducements from the plaintiff. He said that his wife had threatened to expose him to the Revenue Commissioners in respect of certain undisclosed transactions and to give information to suppliers to his company which would have the effect of reducing credit terms on which the company was dependent.

Murphy J found that these threats had indeed been made. He also found that the solicitor mediator 'had warned both parties against being vindictive, and doing anything which might be contrary to their own interests, and he referred to threats of disclosure to the Revenue Commissioners in that context'.

Murphy J rejected the husband's claim of duress and ordered specific performance. The husband was a competent businessman who had availed himself of professional legal advice before negotiating the agreement. He had the advice of the company's accountant and financial adviser after the agreement had been made (and, it seems, subsequent to the financial adviser's witnessing his signature). The husband had entered a second agreement and had allowed several months thereafter to elapse before raising the issue of duress.

On appeal to the Supreme Court, Denham J (Finlay CJ and Egan concurring) invoked McCarthy J's observations in *Hay v O'Grady* [1992] 1 IR 210 at 215-8 as to how the Supreme Court should approach the High Court judge's findings of fact and inferences therefrom: see the 1992 Review, 470-3. In the instant case Murphy J had inferred from the facts that the husband had not been subject to duress. His findings of fact had been supported by credible evidence. He had, moreover, the opportunity of seeing and hearing the witnesses. Denham J saw no grounds on which the Supreme Court should intervene in those findings. Accordingly the appeal was dismissed.

A passage from Denham J's judgment is worthy of particular consideration:

There are two special factors to be considered in this case. First, that the agreement in question is a separation agreement arrived at, which is unfortunately frequently the case, when unhappy differences have occurred between the parties and there is antagonism and hostility in the relationship. Secondly, the inference in question is submitted to be one of duress exercised on the husband, who was a witness, by the wife who was a witness.

Separation agreements relate to special situations. The parties thereto are unfortunately frequently in the midst of varying degrees of disharmony with their spouses which may involve hostilities. The relationship between parties places these contracts in a special category of their own. The human factor is of the utmost importance. The trial judge who hears the oral evidence and sees the witnesses is in a unique position to assess the evidence.

The inference as to the existence or not of duress is an inference based on fact. However, in regard to this specific inference in question the learned trial judge is in a very special position to draw that inference having had the benefit of observing both parties.

In general an appellate court should be slow to intervene in regard to contested agreements by inferring what was in the mind of a party when the learned trial judge has heard the parties and has had the benefit of observing them.

However, in particular in this case, in light of the two factors set out above, an appellate court should be particularly cautious in intervening. It should be slow to intervene in cases relating to proper inferences to be drawn from facts from the oral evidence of a husband and wife in a matrimonial case.

There is merit in the point that assessment of the subtleties of personal relationships is not easy to make at an appellate level, but if this is so it is hard to reconcile with the willingness of the Supreme Court on several occasions in proceedings for nullity of marriage to take a different view of the facts from the trial judge where the ground of duress is invoked.

ADOPTION

Validity of mother's consent   In *G.D. v St. Louise's Adoption Society, An Bord Uchtála and T.M. and P.M.*, High Court, 25, 26 and 30 November 1993, Budd J, in an extensive judgment, held that a mother had validly consented to placing her child for adoption. The test as to the necessary fullness and freedom of consent had been laid down in *S. v Eastern Health Board*, High

Court, 28 February 1979; *G. v An Bord Uchtála* [1980] IR 32; *G.M. v G.M.* [1982] ILRM 103 and *McF. v G. and G., The Sacred Heart Adoption Society* [1983] ILRM 228. In the instant case, the facts were tragic. The mother was living in very poor conditions, with two children as well as the child whose eligibility for adoption was in issue. The mother had a severe drug addiction problem, compounded by anxiety that she might have been infected with HIV by her partner. She had received no independent advice or legal advice.

Budd J considered that:

> the appropriate person to give the natural mother objective and profes-
> sional advice in these delicate matters is the social worker who, by her
> training and experience, is capable of objectivity and who also, by her
> knowledge of the background and indeed problems of the natural
> mother, is able to explain the problems which each option to her will
> involve.

He had no doubt that the social workers in this case had given objective and expert advice. He did not subscribe to the suggestion that the social worker should be a person who was 'independent in the sense of being entirely new and unknown to the natural mother'. He was fortified by Finlay CJ's view, expressed in *In re D.G. and Infant* [1991] 1 IR 491, at 514, that there 'could be . . . no more appropriate person to carry out these two tasks on behalf of the Adoption Society than a professional social worker who has been in constant communication with the mother for a protracted period prior to the time at which the statement is furnished and the form signed'.

There is perhaps cause for concern that at present the Family Home Protection Act 1976 is more stringent than the Adoption Acts in its require-ments for consent. A woman placing her child for adoption need not be legally advised but a woman consenting to a mortgage on the family home must be advised of the need for independent legal advice: *Bank of Ireland v Smith*, Supreme Court November 1995.

Dispensation with consent In *E.F. and F.F. v A Bord Uchtála*, High Court, 23 February 1993, Costello J had to deal with facts which, as he observed, 'like all proceedings in adoption matters [we]re sad and distressing'. The mother of the child whose fate was in issue gave birth to her at the age of thirty two. She had had a long-term relationship with the girl's father, by whom, a year previously, she had another child, a son. She lived, on social welfare, in a local authority house with her mother, her little boy and a twenty-year-old nephew who was mildly handicapped from spina bifida. The father of the children also depended on social welfare but from time to time obtained employment.

The mother put her daughter up for adoption, with the consent of the father. Though the validity of these consents was later challenged, Costello J on the evidence held that they had been freely given. The daughter was placed with a married couple who already had two adopted sons. The husband was in permanent employment, with a good salary. The family lived in a large semi- detached house. Their home was a happy one and the young girl when she went to live with them integrated well and was loved by them and the two boys.

The natural mother sought the return of her daughter She was planning to acquire a house of her own and to marry the father of her children. Not surprisingly the question whether the court should make an order under s. 3 of the Adoption Act 1974 fell for consideration. This section permits the court to authorise An Bord Uchtála to dispense with the consent of the mother to the making of the adoption order in favour of the applicant or applicants for adoption if it is satisfied that it is in the best interests of the child to do so.

Costello J had no hesitation in making this order. The 'overwhelming evidence' in the case was that it was in the young girl's best interests to remain with the applicants. There had been uncontradicted evidence from a highly experienced psychiatrist that to remove her now from the environment where she had been living for the previous three years would have a gravely damaging effect on her. It would represent a major trauma to her and would cause both immediate and long term psychological damage. She was being well looked after both emotionally and physically in her present home.

In *G.D. v St. Louise's Adoption Society, An Bord Uchtála and T.M. and P.M., High Court*, 25, 26 and 30 November, which we have discussed above 330-1 in relation to the question of the mother's consent to placing her child for adoption, Budd J went on to make an order under s. 3 of the 1974 Act authorising An Bord Uchtála to dispense with her consent to the making of an adoption order in favour of a couple with whom the child had been living for nearly two and a half years. It seemed to Budd J, on the basis of a clinical psychologist's report, that the evidence as to the child's best interests was 'very strongly one way in this case'. He added that he believed, not only on the basis of what the clinical psychologist had to say, but also from his 'own knowledge of the type of psychiatric evidence which is given in these cases', that a move at this stage would be traumatic for the child and could damage the child's future capacity to make sound and trusting relationships. We have thus reached the point where, on this issue, judges are proceeding on something akin to judicial notice of the psychological impact of moving young children from an established home environment to a new environment.

Adoptees' access to information as to their origins   The difficult question of an adoptee's right to trace his or her origins arose in *C.R. v An Bord Uchtála*, High Court, 28 June 1993. The applicant for judicial review sought an order of *certiorari* quashing the purported decision of the Adoption Board not to give him details of his parenthood and an order of *mandamus* requiring the Board to carry out its statutory obligations, under s. 22(5) of the Adoption Act 1952 and s. 8 of the Adoption Act 1976, properly to determine the issue of his entitlement to these particulars.

Section 22(5) of the 1952 Act requires the Ard-Chláraitheoir to keep an index to make traceable the connection between each entry in the Adopted Children Register and the corresponding entry in the register of births. It goes on to stipulate that this index is not to be open to public inspection and that no informtion from it is to be given to any person except by order of a court or of the Board. Section 8 of the 1976 Act provides that a court is not to make an order under s. 22(5) unless it is satisfied that it is in the best interests of the child concerned to do so.

In the instant case the applicant had been born in 1941 and had sub-sequently been adopted. His adoptive father, who has been opposed to his wish to find out more about his natural parents, died in 1991. This enabled the applicant to set about making efforts to resolve the mystery. His solicitors wrote to the Board seeking his original birth certificate. The Board declined to provide it, stating that this was for reasons of confidentiality. It referred the applicant to the adoption society through which he had been placed for adoption. In subsequent correspondence the Board stated boldly:

> The Adoption Acts 1952/1991 do not provide for any right of access to birth records by adopted persons. In the circumstances it is not the practice of the Board to furnish such information to adopted persons.

In Morris J's view, this stance amounted to 'clear blanket refusal on the basis of the practice of the Board to furnish this information', and it appeared to him that this practice held good, 'irrespective of the merits.'

In a further letter, the Board referred expressly to its 'practice' in this regard and drew the attention of the applicant to s. 8 of the 1976 Act, presumably as an indication that he was free to apply to the court under that provision. At the time of writing this letter, the Board had made no enquiry as to the merits of the application or the circumstances in which it was made.

Morris J had no doubt that the Board's strategy had involved an invalid determination, without reference to any merits which there might be in the applicant's case. While it would be desirable for the Board, retaining full seisin of the matter, to *seek the assistance and advice* of the adoption society through which the applicant had been placed for adoption, there was no question that it was entitled to *delegate* all functions of decision-making to the adoption society without retaining to itself the ultimate function of making the determination.

Morris J did not consider that the applicant was obliged to proceed with a court application under s. 22(5) rather than by way of judicial review. The Board had available to it all the facilities necessary to make a judgment on the merits of the application with expedition and without undue delay and expense, which, in the circumstances of the applicant's state of health, would be entirely undesirable. In any event, from the standpoint of principle, the applicant was entitled to have his application properly determined by *either* one of the two tribunals identified in the subsection.

Morris J directed that the matter be sent back to the Board with a direction that it determing the application. He observed that, naturally, the result of such determination was a matter exclusively for the Board.

LEGAL AID

The essential issue in *M.F. v Legal Aid Board* [1993] ILRM 797 concerned the manner in which the Legal Aid Board should interpret the general threshold requirements for granting legal aid, contained in the Scheme of Civil Legal Aid and Advice, concerning the applicant's reasonable likelihood of success in the proceedings (paragraph 3.2.3 (4)) and the comparative cost of the participation measured against the likely benefit to the applicant (paragraph 3.2.3 (6)).

In the High Court, O'Hanlon J had observed that in matrimonial proceedings it might be said that in a sense there are no winners and no losers. He did:

> not consider that one can speak of either party being 'reasonably likely to be successful in the proceedings' — yes, perhaps, in the initial stages, if one is seeking judicial separation and the other is resisting it, but not in relation to the ancillary orders which involve the court in the process of working out what arrangements would be reasonable or even necessary in the interest of each spouse, and what should be done in the best interest of any children of the marriage below a certain age, putting the children's welfare ahead of the interest of both spouses at this stage.
>
> In relation to these matters, and particularly in relation to questions as to custody, access to, and maintenance of infant children, once it is established that one or other or both spouses have not the means to be legally represented before the court, I think it would be only in wholly

exceptional circumstances, which I cannot now envisage, and which do not, in my opinion, exist in the present case, that legal aid could be denied in reliance on the matters referred to in paragraph 3.2.3(2) [which requires the applicant to have as a matter of law reasonable grounds for being a party to the proceedings], 3.2.3(4) or 3.2.3(6) of the Scheme.

The Supreme Court narrowed the focus of this approach quite considerably. The case involved questions concerning the guardianship of an infant. Finlay CJ (O'Flaherty, Egan, Blayney and Denham JJ concurring) held that in the context of proceedings of this kind, paragraph 3.2.3(4) should be interpreted by the Board on the basis that, for a person to be 'reasonably likely to be successful in the proceedings' it was only necessary that the Board should conclude that there was a reasonable likelihood that the point of view and submissions of the person concerned, with regard to the welfare, custody and upbringing of the child concerned, should be amongst the material which would be relied upon by the judge in determining the issues concerning the child. In applying the provisions of paragraph 3.2.3.(6), the Board should interpret 'the benefit of the applicant' in a case pursuant to the 1989 Act to be equivalent to the interest of the applicant in the welfare of the child. A similar approach would apply to proceedings involving an application to vary or an appeal from an original hearing.

In *G.D. v St. Louise's Adoption Society, An Bord Uchtála and T.M. and P.M*, High Court, 25, 26 and 30 November 1993, which we have discussed, above, 330-1, Budd J, having held that a mother had freely given her consent to placing her child for adoption and that her consent to the adoption should be dispensed with under s. 3 of the Adoption Act 1974, went on to make a strong recommendation that the Legal Aid Board should look favourably on an application from her solicitor for the appropriate and reasonable costs of the work done in acting for her. When she had originally gone to the Legal Aid Centre near her she had been told that there was a very long waiting list. A solicitor in private practice whom she consulted realised that the case was one in which time was of the essence and had acted on her behalf. Budd J envisaged that, if the State was going to cherish all the children in the State equally it might be necessary for An Bord Uchtála to be given a budget to meet the situation where legal advisers 'take up the running on behalf of an impecunious litigant' in cases where the best interests of a child were at issue.

Fisheries

FISHING NETS

The Sea Fisheries (Regulation of Nets) Order 1993 (SI No. 264) gave effect to Commission Communication 85/C347/05 and regulated the size of certain nets with effect from 1 January 1994.

SAFETY

Musters   The Merchant Shipping (Musters) (Fishing Vessels) Regulations 1993, made under the Merchant Shipping Act 1992 (see the 1992 Review, 625-6), introduced requirements for musters, preparations for emergencies, inspection and maintenance of life saving and fire fighting equipment and the recording of particulars of these in vessels' logbooks.

Gaming and Lotteries

GAMING MACHINE

Definition of slot machine   The *ex tempore* decision of the Supreme Court in *Director of Public Prosecutions v Cafolla*, referred to in the 1992 Review, 380, has now been fully reported: [1994] 1 IR 571.

Search and seizure   In *McKenna and McKenna's Leisure Ltd v Garda Commissioner* [1993] 3 IR 543, the plaintiffs claimed that the seizure of certain machines by the Gardaí on foot of a warrant obtained under s. 39 of the Gaming and Lotteries Act 1956 had been invalid. The circumstances giving rise to the claim were that the plaintiffs operated an amusement arcade in County Donegal. The plaintiffs obtained an amusement arcade permit and amusement machine licences and also paid over £26,000 duty on the video machines installed in the arcade in question. The plaintiffs claimed that the machines in question were amusement machines within the meaning of s. 120 of the Finance Act 1992 and were not gaming machines within the meaning of the 1956 Act. The plaintiffs acknowledged that the machines were capable of being operated as gaming machines in that a money payment could result from a successful playing of the machines. However, the plaintiffs claimed that the machines in question were not gaming machines because, as actually operated, players were only entitled to obtain free plays on the machines rather than a money payment.

The machines in question had been seized by the Gardaí on foot of a warrant granted under s. 39 of the 1956 Act, following from complaints as to alleged offences being committed by the plaintiffs. The plaintiffs argued that a search and seizure warrant granted by a judge of the District Court under s. 39 of the 1956 Act was valid only in respect of machines that are objectively proved to be gaming instruments or which are certain to be proved in court to have been used as gaming machines.

The Supreme Court (Finlay CJ, O'Flaherty and Denham JJ) unanimously rejected this interpretation of s. 39 of the 1956 Act. Delivering the Court's decision, O'Flaherty J stated that such an interpretation 'would render what appears to be its legislative intent quite ineffective.' He interpreted s.39 as requiring that, before a warrant is issued, a District Court judge must be satisfied on the sworn information of a Garda not below the rank of inspector that there is reasonable ground for supposing that an offence against the Act has been, is being, or is about to be committed. He commented: 'The test is one of reasonable belief; not certainty of outcome.' On this basis, the Court refused to order the return of the machines seized in the case.

Finally, the Court noted that the Director of Public Prosecutions had decided to proceed with prosecutions under the 1956 Act. The Court stated that it did not wish in its judgment to in any way pre-empt the outcome of that prosecution but it noted that it was 'concerned that civil proceedings should not impede the proper conduct of criminal proceedings and this applies to the prosecution as well as to the defence.' In this respect, the Court noted that the plaintiffs had offered that, if the Gardaí retained one machine only, they would furnish a written admission under s. 22 of the Criminal Justice Act 1984 that the other machines were similar to the one retained. While the issue did not arise in the instant case, O'Flaherty J seemed to indicate that this course of action might have met the plaintiffs' argument that the seizure of all the machines in question had caused undue hardship to the plaintiffs and to the laying off of their employees.

Garda Síochána

CONCILIATION AND ARBITRATION

In *Garda Representative Association and Ors v Ireland and Ors* [1989] ILRM 1 (HC); [1994] 1 ILRM 81, the Supreme Court rejected a challenge to a decision made by the chairman of a staff relations conciliation council established for the Garda Síochána. The Court thus upheld the decision of Murphy J in the case [1989] ILRM 1; [1989] IR 193: see the 1988 Review, 24-6.

In October 1987, the chairman of the Garda Conciliation Council had ruled that certain proposals contained in two circular letters of that year issued by the Garda Commissioner to incorporate parading time in the ordinary hours of work and to re-roster the 'special services', were not appropriate for consideration by the conciliation council. On judicial review, the plaintiffs sought, *inter alia,* a declaration that the proposals contained in the two circulars fell within the scope of the conciliation scheme. As indicated, this was refused by Murphy J and, on appeal, the Supreme Court (Finlay CJ, Egan and Denham JJ) upheld that decision.

Delivering the only judgment, Finlay CJ repeated the approach he had taken in *O'Keeffe v An Bord Pleanála* [1992] ILRM 237; [1993] 1 IR 39 (1991 Review, 16-8) as to the limits of judicial review. In the instant case, he stated that for the court to give a declaration that the chairman of the Garda Conciliation Council had been incorrect in his interpretation as to whether proposals contained in certain circulars were matters within the scope of the conciliation council, as distinct from declaring that the interpretation was void or invalid, would be to conduct an appeal from that decision rather than engage in judicial review. He went on to state that this well-established limit to judicial review was not merely an artificial restriction imposed by procedural rules of the court, but went to the root of the administrative nature of such tribunals.

He pointed out that the scheme of conciliation and arbitration between the staff and officials of the Gardaí provided that certain decisions should be determined by the chairman of the conciliation council and the parties were deemed to have agreed to that provision. It would not, therefore, be appropriate for the Court to interfere with a decision merely on the basis that it would have raised different inferences and conclusions or that it was satisfied that the case made against a decision was stronger than the case made for it.

Nor did Finlay CJ consider that the chairman's decision was unreasonable within the meaning of the Court's decision in *The State (Keegan) v Stardust Victims Compensation Tribunal* [1987] ILRM 202 [1986] IR 642. In particular the issues of rostering had, it appeared, been accepted as matters particularly within the Commissioner's jurisdiction and outside the terms of the conciliation scheme. On this basis, the relief sought was refused.

DISCIPLINE

Dismissal without inquiry In *O'Shea v Garda Commissioner*, High Court, 25 March 1993, the applicant obtained judicial review of his dismissal which had been made in purported compliance with Regulation 40 of the Garda Síochána (Discipline) Regulations 1989. Regulation 40 empowers the Commissioner, subject to the consent of the Minister for Justice, to dismiss a member of the Garda Síochána where the Commissioner:

> is not in any doubt as to the material facts and the relevant breach of discipline is of such gravity that the Commissioner has decided that the facts and breach merit dismissal and that the holding of an inquiry could not affect his decision.

In the instant case, an allegation came to the attention of the Gardaí that the applicant had entered into an agreement with a prostitute to engage in sex with her for payment. The applicant was interviewed concerning this in the Garda station in which he was stationed. The interviewing Gardaí stated that the applicant had verbally admitted he had agreed a price for sex with the woman in question, but the applicant declined to make a written statement and he denied that the notes of the interview were correct. The notes of the interview were sent to the Garda Commissioner as well as statements from other witnesses.

The Notice of Intention to Dismiss served on the applicant in purported compliance with Regulation 40 of the 1989 Regulations stated that the Commissioner was 'not in any doubt' that the applicant had engaged in discreditable conduct, 'in that you did on 16 April 1992 . . . associate with and enter into an agreement with a known prostitute . . . to engage in sexual activity with her in return for the payment to her of £30.' The Notice ended with a statement to the effect that the applicant was being given an opportunity to advance reasons to the Commissioner against the applicant's proposed dismissal. Solicitors for the applicant replied to the Commissioner requesting the evidence on which the allegation of discreditable conduct was made, to which the Commissioner replied that nothing could be achieved by a meeting with the applicant's legal representatives and that the applicant had made a verbal admission concerning the transaction between the applicant and the woman in question.

Carroll J quashed the dismissal on the ground that it did not comply with fair procedures. She noted that, in *The State (Jordan) v Garda Commissioner* [1987] ILRM 107, O'Hanlon J had upheld the similar power contained in Regulation 34 of the Garda Síochána (Discipline) Regulations 1971, but had stated that the scope for the exercise of such a power must be very limited. O'Hanlon J had suggested in *Jordan* that one of the exceptional cases where the power might be employed would be where there was an admission of guilt of a very serious breach of discipline. Carroll J noted that the applicant argued that the instant case did not fall within O'Hanlon J's comments as there was a dispute as to whether the applicant had made an admission. Although Carroll J did not comment on this aspect of the applicant's case, it must have weighed with her to some extent because she went on immediately in her judgment to decide that the Commissioner had failed to meet the requirements of fair procedures in the instant case.

In connection with the requirements of fair procedures, Carroll J cited with approval passages from the influential judgments of Henchy J in *The State (Gleeson) v Minister for Defence* [1976] IR 280 and *Garvey v Ireland* [1981] IR 75. Applying these to the instant case, Carroll J commented, in finding that the dismissal should be quashed:

> In this case the applicant did not get a summary of the factual background to support the accusation against him. What he was told in the notice was the bare charge. He was entitled to the information his solicitor asked for, namely the evidence on which the allegation was based. . . . He was entitled to a written account of the admissions he was alleged to have made and the factual background to those admissions.

The applicant had claimed that the matter was now beyond retrieval and that the case should not be returned to the Commissioner, as the Commissioner had stated, in accordance with the language of Regulation 40, that he was 'not in any doubt' about the applicant's disreputable conduct (rather than 'beyond doubt' as Carroll J inadvertently describes it in her judgment). However, Carroll J rejected this argument, opining that the Commissioner had merely stated, in effect, that there was a strong *prima facie* case against the applicant and the Court would not assume that the Commissioner would go through a 'token exercise with a closed mind.' On this basis, she returned the matter to the Commissioner for a decision having given the applicant an opportunity to made submissions.

The decision in *O'Shea* indicates that the dismissal procedure under Article 40 of the 1989 Regulations is likely to remain the exception, as opposed to the more usual procedure of an inquiry under the 1989 Regulations. This is even more so since the courts insist that, even though Article 40 appeared to envisage a virtually summary dismissal, the application of fair procedures requires some form of hearing (albeit falling short of an inquiry under the Regulations) before dismissal can take place.

Effect of acquittal   In *Gallagher v Garda Commissioner*, High Court, 30 March 1993, Murphy J applied the decision of the Supreme Court in *McGrath v Garda Commissioner* [1990] ILRM 5 (HC); [1989] IR 241 (HC); [1990] ILRM 817 (SC); [1991] 1 IR 69 (SC) (see the 1989 Review, 275-6 and the 1990 Review, 330-1) in declining to prohibit a disciplinary inquiry against the applicant. In the instant case, the applicant had been acquitted on a number of charges under the Road Traffic Acts and the Forgery Act 1913.

The disciplinary proceedings against him, under the Garda Síochána (Discipline) Regulations 1989, involved some overlap with the matters concerned in the criminal charges on which the applicant had been acquitted. However, Murphy J noted that, for example, the applicant's acquittal on one of the charges under the Forgery Act 1913 was on the basis that the documents alleged to have been forged were not 'official documents' within the meaning of s. 3(3) of the Forgery Act 1913. The disciplinary charges against the applicant, which concerned the same documents, could not therefore be regarded as identical to the criminal charges. On this basis, Murphy J concluded, on the authority of the *McGrath* case, that since the disciplinary charges were not identical to those in the criminal trial, the disciplinary proceedings could not be prohibited.

For other cases applying the *McGrath* case, see the 1992 Review, 383-6.

GARDA SÍOCHÁNA COMPLAINTS BOARD

Discovery of documents   In *Skeffington v Rooney and Ors*, High Court, 27 May 1993, Barr J ordered discovery of certain documents which had been compiled in a complaint under the Garda Síochána (Complaints) Act 1986: see the discussion in the Practice and Procedure chapter, 457, below.

PROMOTION

The Garda Síochána (Promotion) (Amendment) Regulations 1993 (SI No. 27) amended the Garda Síochána (Promotion) Regulations 1987 in order to introduce amended procedures for competitive interviewing of candidates for promotion to the ranks of sergeant, inspector, superintendent and chief superintendent.

Health Services

CONTRACEPTION

The Health (Family Planning) (Amendment) Act 1993 was considered and discussed in the 1992 Review, 388-91, in conjunction with the terms of the Health (Family Planning) (Amendment) Act 1992.

ELIGIBILITY

In-patient charges   The Health (In-Patient Charges) (Amendment) Regulations 1993 (SI No. 50) amended the 1987 Regulations of the same title by raising the daily charge for in-patient hospital services from £15 to £20 and by raising the maximum amount payable in any period of 12 consecutive months from £150 to £200. The Regulations came into effect on 1 March 1993. On this area generally, see the 1991 Review, 258.

Out-patient charges   The Health (Out-Patient Charges) (Amendment) Regulations 1993 (SI No. 51) provided that, in place of the £10 charge for out-patient services introduced by the 1987 Regulations of the same title, a charge of £6 per visit was introduced subject to a limitation of £42 in any period of 12 consecutive months from 1 March 1993, when the Regulations came into effect. The Health Services (Out-Patient) Regulations 1993 (SI No. 178) provided for the manner in which a person may avail of entitlement to consultant out-patient services under s. 56 of the Health Act 1970 and also provided for the first time for charges for 'private patients' who avail of this entitlement. The 1993 Regulations revoked the 1991 Regulations of the same title (see the 1991 Review, 258) which had not provided for charges to private patients.

HEALTH BOARD

Failure to comply with common contract   In *Sullivan v Southern Health Board*, High Court, 29 July 1993, Keane J found that the defendant Board had failed to fulfil its contractual obligations to the plaintiff under the 'common contract' with consultant physicians: see the discussion of the case in the Contract chapter, 176-7, above.

MAINTENANCE ALLOWANCES

Disability The Disabled Persons (Maintenance Allowance) Regulations 1993 (SI No. 211), made under s. 5 of the Health Act 1947, provided for an increased maintenance allowance for persons with a disability and amended the 1991 Regulations of the same title.

Infectious diseases The Infectious Diseases (Maintenance) Regulations 1993 (SI No. 212), made under ss. 5 and 44 of the Health Act 1947, made improved provision for those with specified infectious diseases who are receiving hospital treatment for those diseases. The 1993 Regulations revoked the 1992 Regulations of the same title.

MEDICAL PREPARATIONS

1993 saw a substantial updating of the statutory regime for the manufacture, wholesaling, advertising, labelling and retail supply of medical preparations intended for human use in accordance with the Health Act 1947 and the Misuse of Drugs Act 1977. The Regulations discussed below give effect to various EC Directives on the subjects in question. In addition, a number of Regulations made in 1993 under the Misuse of Drugs Act 1977 are of relevance to the possession, authorised and unauthorised, of certain medical preparations: these Regulations are discussed in the Criminal Law chapter, 243-4, above.

Advertising The Medical Preparations (Advertising) Regulations 1993 (SI No. 76) consolidated the statutory controls concerning the advertising of medical preparations intended for human use and superceded the provisions on advertsing contained in a number of previous Regulations. Advertisements in the media, such as press and TV, are strictly regulated as are the provision of hospitality and of samples to health professionals.

Labelling and package leaflets The Medical Preparations (Labelling and Package Leaflets) Regulations 1993 (SI No. 71) amended the Medical Preparations (Advertisement and Sale) Regulations 1958 and updated the statutory controls concerning the labelling of, and package leaflets contained in, medical preparations intended for human use.

Licensing of manufacture The Medical Preparations (Licensing of Manufacture) Regulations 1993 (SI No. 40) and the Medical Preparations (Licensing of Manufacture) (Amendment) Regulations 1993 (SI No. 68) consolidated the statutory controls concerning the licensing of manufacturers of medical preparations intended for human use and revoked the 1974 Regulations of the same title. The 1993 Regulations take account of the requirements of Directive 75/319/EEC, as amended by Directive 91/356/EEC.

Prescription and control of supply   The Medical Preparations (Prescription and Control of Supply) Regulations 1993 (SI No. 69) deal in general with the limits on the sale of medicinal products by pharmacists. The Regulations prescribe the classes of medicines which may only be supplied on prescription, the form which a prescription must take, the detailed labelling requirements imposed on pharmacists in respect of medicines supplied to the public on foot of a prescription, as well as the records required to be kept of prescriptions dispensed. While a manual prescription book record may be used for this purpose, the Regulations also provide that, where prescription labels are prepared with the aid of a computerised data base, as is the case in many pharmacies, a daily computer printout or a prescription book containing adhesive labels from the computer which generated the prescription labels will suffice. In relation to non-prescription medicines, the Regulations amended the range of medicinal products available for over-the-counter sale by pharmacists and which were previously prescription-only medicinces. The Regulations revoked the Medical Preparations (Control of Supply) Regulations 1987.

Summary of product characteristics   The Medical Preparations (Licensing, Advertisment and Sale) (Amendment) Regulations 1993 (SI No. 70) amended the 1984 Regulations of the same title in order to further define the summary of a product's characteristics for the purposes of obtaining a licence for a medical preparation intended for human use.

Wholesale licensing   The Medical Preparations (Wholesale Licences) Regulations 1993 (SI No. 39) consolidated the statutory controls concerning the licensing of wholesalers of medical preparations intended for human use and revoked the 1974 Regulations of the same title.

MISUSE OF DRUGS

Declaration of scheduled substances   A number of Regulations made in 1993 updated the legislative code concerning possession of substances under the Misuse of Drugs Act 1977. These are discussed in the Criminal Law chapter, 243-4, above.

International drugs trade   The European Communities (Monitoring of External Trade in Scheduled Substances) Regulations 1993 (SI No. 6) and the Misuse of Drugs (Scheduled Substances) Regulations 1993 (SI No. 338) are referred to in the Criminal Law chapter, 243, above.

NURSING HOMES

The Health (Nursing Homes) Act 1990 (Commencement) Order 1993 (SI No. 222) brought the 1990 Act into effect from 1 September 1993. In consequence, a number of Regulations were made which lay down detailed requirements concerning the operation of the 1990 Act, as to which see the 1990 Review, 340.

Detailed care and accomodation provisions   Of these Regulations, the most important and detailed are the Nursing Homes (Care and Welfare) Regulations 1993 (SI No. 226) as amended by the Nursing Homes (Care and Welfare) (Amendment) Regulations 1993 (SI No. 379), which lay down detailed requirements to ensure that adequate and suitable care and accommodation are provided for 'dependent persons' in nursing homes. They came into force on 1 September 1993. Reg.5 lays down general duties concerning nursing care and facilities, including privacy and facilities to practice religion as well as encouraging contact with persons outside the nursing home. Reg.7 requires that a 'contract of care' be executed with each dependent person in the nursing home. Reg.8 deals with facilities for personal possessions. Reg.9 requires that 14 days notice be given of an intention to discharge a person. Reg.10 requires that there be a person in charge of a nursing home, generally a full-time position, and that a fully-qualified nurse is on duty at all times. Reg.11 lays down requirements for accommodation and facilities such as bedrooms and day spaces, including minimum heating standards of 65 degrees F (18 degrees C) in bedroom areas and 70 degrees F (21 degrees C) in day areas. Reg.12 requires that precautions be taken against the risk of accidents in the design of a nursing home, for example in relation to handrails. Regs. 13 to 15 detail requirements concerning kitchen facilities and hygiene and sanitary facilities generally. Reg.16 lays down general standards concerning the food served in a nursing home. Reg.17 requires that a brochure on the nursing home be prepared, while Reg.18 requires that a bound register be maintained in the nursing home, with specific requirements being laid down on the contents of the register. Reg.20 requires confidentiality concerning records. Reg.21 requires that records be kept of staff employed in the nursing home. Reg.22 requires that notice of the death of a dependent person in the nursing home be sent to the Medical Officer of Health for the area. Reg.23 (as amended by SI No. 379, above) authorises designated officers of the local health board to inspect nursing homes and grants them powers to interview staff and other persons. Reg.24 requires that inspections be made at least every six months. Reg.25 empowers a designated officer to inspect a premises which the officer reasonably believes is a nursing home, albeit not registered under the 1990 Act. Reg.26 provides for complaints to the health board by a dependent person in a nursing home. Regs. 27 and 28 lay down detailed requirements concerning fire precautions and records, including the requirement to obtain a certificate of compliance with the Regulations from a 'competent person', defined in Reg.4 (as amended by SI No. 379, above) as either a chartered engineer or a properly and suitably qualified architect with experience in fire safety design and management. Reg.29 requires that adequate arrangements be made for the administration of drugs and medicines, while Reg.30 deals with other treatment required by a dependent person. Reg.31 authorises health boards to provide facilities to a nursing home at the request of the proprietor, and Reg.32 authorises the health board to provide training facilities for nursing home staff, both subject to such charges as may be made by the health board. Reg.33 requires that the current registration certificate for the nursing home is prominently displayed. Reg.34 requires the registered proprietor to ensure that dependent persons are adequately insured against injury while being maintained in the nursing home. Finally, Reg.35 provides that the Regulations 'shall be enforced and executed' by the chief executive officer or deputy chief executive officer of the local health board. SI No. 226 revoked the Homes for Incapacitated Persons Regulations 1985.

Fees The Nursing Homes (Fees) Regulations 1993 (SI No. 223) prescribe the fees for a declaration and registration required under the 1990 Act.

In-patient and boarding out services The Health (In-Patient Services) Regulations 1993 (SI No. 224) prescribe that in-patient services provided by a health board under s. 52 of the Health Act 1970 in a nursing home registered under the 1990 Act must comply with the 1990 Act and the Regulations made under it. Similarly, the Boarding Out Regulations 1993 (SI No. 225) provide that boarding out arrangements made under the 1990 Act must comply with certain requirements.

Subvention   The Nursing Homes (Subvention) Regulations 1993 (SI No. 227) and the Nursing Homes (Subvention) (Amendment) Regulations 1993 (SI No. 378) prescribe the conditions under which a subvention may be paid to persons in need of nursing home care who are without means to avail of such care. The Regulations provide for six monthly reviews of subventions.

PHARMACY

On this area, see the Regulations discussed under the Medical Preparations heading, above, 344, and the Regulations made under the Misuse of Drugs Act 1977 in the Criminal Law chapter, 243-4, above.

REGISTRATION OF BIRTHS AND DEATHS

Amalgamation of Registrars' Districts   In 1993, a series of 18 statutory instruments were made which amalgamated certain Superintendent Registrars' Districts and, where applicable, Registrars' Districts in different administrative counties so as to reduce the number of such districts in each county. The first of these was the Registration of Births and Deaths (Ireland) Act 1863 (Section 17 and 18) (Monaghan) Order 1993 (SI No. 87). The remainder, which all bore similar titles, were: SI No. 88 (Tipperary North), SI No. 159 (Longford), SI No. 160 (Offaly), SI No. 161 (Sligo), SI No. 162 (Kildare), SI No. 163 (Westmeath), SI No. 164 (Wicklow), SI No. 165 (Laoighis), SI No. 279 (Kerry), SI No. 280 (Cork), SI No. 281 (Cavan), SI No. 357 (Roscommon), SI No. 358 (Tipperary South), SI No. 359 (Mayo), SI No. 360 (Galway), SI No. 371 (Limerick) and SI No. 372 (Carlow). Further such Orders were made in 1994, to which reference will be made in the 1994 Review.

Labour Law

EMPLOYMENT EQUALITY

Adoptive leave   The subject of adoptive leave raises difficult issues in the area of employment equality. To what extent does adoptive leave echo leave based on childbirth? To what extent (if any) is the law entitled to have regard to practical differences in socially prescribed functions of parenting between mothers and fathers? May the law reflect present inequalities or must it provide a lead for the future? These issues have come before various tribunals in the past few years. In *Aer Rianta v Irish Distributive and Administrative Trade Union* (DEE 3/1990), the Labour Court held that Aer Rianta had not been in breach of the Employment Equality Act 1977 in granting special leave to adoptive mothers while denying a similar entitlement to adoptive fathers. The essence of the Court's reasoning is contained in the following passage from its determination:

> The Court considers that the six weeks optimal leave within the statutory period of fourteen weeks when taken after the birth is related to the broader aspects of maternity such as the bonding process between mother and child . . . [S. 16 of the 1977 Act], where it refers to 'childbirth', can properly be interpreted in a broad rather than restrictive sense. . . . It follows that the permissible protection allowed by s. 16 must apply to the mother who has the material task of caring for the child even if the mother is the adoptive rather than the natural mother. If one adopts that wider meaning of 'childbirth', which the Court does, then the favoured treatment by the company of an adopting mother is justified. . . .

This broad approach echoes that adopted by the Court of Justice in *EC Commission v Italian Republic* (Case 163/82) and *Hofmann v Barmer Ersatzkasse* (184/83).

In *Doolan v City of Dublin Vocational Education Committee* [1993] ELR 193, the Equality Officer genuflected to the precedential hierarchy in following the Labour Court and rejecting the claimant's argument that he was the victim of discrimination on the basis of sex by being refused adoptive leave. It seems clear, however, that the Equality Officer, if not thus constrained, would have held in favour of the claimant.

The argument centred around the extent to which s. 16 of the 1977 Act should be affected by Article 2(3) of EC Directive 76/207. The Employment Equality Agency, which had referred the case to the Labour Court under the 1977 Act, argued that there was no requirement to rely on Article 2(3) to clarify s. 16 and that therefore there was no need to refer to the two decisions of the Court of Justice. S. 16 provides that nothing in the Act makes it unlawful for an employer to arrange for or to provide special treatment to women 'in connection with pregnancy or childbirth'. The Agency argued that this exception was more specific and narrower in scope than Article 2(3), which refers more broadly to the 'protection of women particularly as regards pregnancy and maternity.' S. 16 referred to a specific biological function that solely affected women; adoption was something different. Adoptive leave based on stereotyped assumptions about the respective parental functions of women and men could not be justified on the basis of a derogation such as s. 16 or Article 2(3). There was nothing improper about a statutory derogation that was narrower than that and there was no justification in interpreting s. 16 expansively so as to give it the same breadth as Article 2(3).

In the 1994 and 1995 Reviews, we shall discuss the judicial and legislative sequelae to *Doolan*. We shall analyse *O'Grady v Telecom Éireann*, 5 December 1994, where the Labour Court took a different view from that favoured in *Doolan*, and the Adoptive Leave Act 1995, which extended the entitlements to adoptive fathers in very limited circumstances. For a perceptive commentary on the Act, see Marguerite Bolger's analysis (1995) 13 *ILT* 218.

Married women in the Civil Service In *A Worker v Department of Finance* [1993] ELR 129, the Labour Court had to deal with the grotesque statutory and regulatory framework relating to employment of married women in the Civil Service. This had resulted from successive accretions of rules over decades, modifying an essentially sexist original policy, each accretion being less sexist than its predecessor but nonetheless creating new, entirely indefensible, anomalies.

S. 10 of the Civil Service Regulation Act 1956 had required women to retire on marriage. Re-admission to the civil service was permitted, *for widows only*, by s. 11. The Civil Service (Employment of Married Women) Act 1973 repealed the requirement to retire on marriage. S. 4 of the 1973 Act extended the scope of s. 11 of the 1956 Act. It permitted all women who had resigned (voluntarily or compulsorily) from the civil service for the purpose of marriage to be re-admitted, subject, in the case of married women, to the requirement that they satisfied the Minister for Finance that they were not being supported by their husbands. Women civil servants who had resigned for any reason other than marriage were treated identically with men who had resigned for any reason: their re-admission could be achieved only by way of open competition conducted by the Civil Service Commissioners.

In the instant case, the claimant was a married women employed by the Revenue Commissioners until 1969, when she had been required to resign to get married. In 1990 she sought re-instatement. She challenged the requirement under s. 4 of the 1973 Act that she should establish that she was not being supported, claiming that it amounted to discrimination by the Revenue Commissioners against her, contrary to s. 2(b) and (c) of the Employment Equality Act 1977 and claiming that the Minister for Finance had contravened s. 9 of that Act, which prohibits procuring or attempting to procure discrimination.

The Equality Officer found in her favour under s. 2(b) and s. 9 (the claim under s. 2(c) thus not requiring resolution). The Labour Court, on appeal, took the same view. The Labour Court was satisfied that s. 11 of the 1956 Act, as amended by s. 4 of the 1973 Act, discriminated *in favour of* a particular category of women, namely those who left the civil service to marry. In doing so, it discriminated against all others, male and female, who left the civil service for other reasons, and included males who left to get married.

Within the 'favoured' group of women, certain of them — those who had married and were not widowed — had to establish to the Minister's satisfaction that they were not being supported by their husbands in order to be re-instated. It was for the very reason that they were married that the support question arose; no such questions arose if they were single or widowed. It was because of their marital status that the requirement of supply of information relating to support arose. The form sent by the Revenue Commission requiring a statement of financial means and personal circumstances treated married women less favourably than single or widowed women, who were not subjected to this investigation. There was a violation of s. 2(b) of the Act since it was the case that because of her marital status, the claimant had been 'treated less favourably than another person of the same sex.'

The Labour Court did not think it right to decide the case only by looking within, 'the narrow confines of a 'favoured' group of women.' It was satisfied that the whole scheme for the re-instatement of some women in the civil service was discriminatory and contrary to the principle of equal treatment, and that the proper solution was to recommend the repeal of s. 11 of the 1956 Act. It seemed to the Labour Court that the situation with regard to the employment of women had changed so fundamentally since 1973 that there was now no justification in having a special provision to enable some women to be re-admitted to the civil service through exceptional procedures. All recruitment should be by open competition, including the re-recruitment of former civil servants who had resigned for whatever reason. The Court concluded that,

> [i]n other words, . . . while the claimant suffered discrimination by the
> operation of the 1956 and 1973 Acts, those Acts themselves offended
> the principle of equal treatment, and the offending parts should be
> repealed.

The Labour Court noted that, under the Equal Treatment Directive
(Council Directive 72/207/EEC), and in applying the principle to the conditions for access to jobs or posts, member states were required to ensure that
laws, regulations and administrative provisions contrary to the principle of
equal treatment be abolished. Article 3.2(c) of the Directive called for the
revision of these laws 'where the concern for protection which originally
inspired them is no longer well founded.' The Court observed that:

> [n]owadays concern for the protection of access to employment is a
> concern which applies to both sexes and to all marital situations.
> Everyone, therefore, should have an equal chance to compete for
> situations for which they are qualified.

The Court went on to hold that the Minister for Finance, in his directions
to the Revenue Commissioners to require information as to the financial
means and personal circumstances of the claimant, over and above the simple
question as to whether she was being supported by her husband, had gone
outside the statutory authority afforded by s. 4 of the 1973 Act and had thus
attempted to procure discrimination in seeking details from the claimant only
because she was a married woman.

In exercising its powers under s. 22 of the 1977 Act the Labour Court
decided that payment of compensation was inappropriate as the claimant's
'right' to compensation arose only in circumstances that offended the principle of equal treatment. It recommended that that Minister for Finance, with
a view to establishing equality of opportunity for both men and women in
relation to access to employment in the civil service, should introduce 'at the
earliest opportunity' the appropriate legislation to repeal s. 11 of the 1956
Act as amended by s. 4 of the 1973 Act.

Sexual harassment   Sexual harassment in the workplace has come into
focus over the past decade: see Adam McAuley, 'Sexual Harassment in
Ireland' (1995) 10 *JISLL* 215. In *An Employee v An Employer* [1993] ELR
75, the Equality Officer found that the respondent company had discriminated against the claimant on the basis of her sex where it had taken
inadequate steps to prevent sexual harassment. There had been two incidents

involving a vanman employed by the respondent. As to the first, the Equality Officer found it difficult to ascertain what exactly had happened but she accepted that the vanman's behaviour had caused great distress to the claimant. The claimant had described what would amount to a serious sexual assault upon her; the vanman had claimed that he had engaged in no more than gestures of reassurance. The background to the incident was consistent with the toleration of 'a certain amount of horseplay' but nonetheless the vanman had overstepped the boundaries of acceptable behaviour on his part and upset the claimant to such an extent that she was totally unable to fraternise with him again.

After the first incident, which the respondent company had investigated, the vanman was instructed not to approach the claimant. Four months later, the vanman attempted to scratch the claimant's back. The Equality Officer considered that, whilst this 'm[ight] be minor in itself', it was gravely offensive and intimidating to the claimant and it was an indication that the vanman had not taken seriously the instructions that management had given him.

The Equality Officer observed:

> The company had argued that it took steps to ensure that there would not be a repeat of the first incident but it is evident that, although the vanman was instructed not to approach the claimant again or to touch her, he did so. Consequently the steps taken by the company in this case proved to be insufficient to prevent her from feeling insecure.

These remarks could be interpreted as amounting to the proposition that attempts by an employer to prevent harassment must be characterised as unreasonable merely because they prove ineffective. That argument is less than convincing, since the law of negligence accepts that conduct that is entirely reasonable may in some circumstances have unhappy consequences. Perhaps a better interpretation of the remarks is that they are seeking to incorporate strict liability rather than a negligence test.

Sexual orientation In *A Worker v Brookfield Leisure Ltd* [1994] ELR 79, the Labour Court held that unfair treatment arising from an employee's sexual orientation, as opposed to any attribute of her sex, did not amount to discrimination within the meaning of the Employment Equality Act 1977. The claimant, employed as a lifeguard/fitness instructor, was dismissed after the respondent had informed her that it had received some complaints that she had been seen kissing another woman in the changing rooms at the leisure centre. The Court considered that this treatment was arbitrary and unfair. The claimant had been given no opportunity to respond to the complaints, and no opportunity to alter her behaviour if they had been substantiated. Even if they had been substantiated, they did not appear to the court to constitute so serious a matter as to justify immediate dismissal:

> The worker should at the very least have been given another chance to conform to behaviour which was deemed acceptable in the employment in which she was engaged.

The Court denied relief because it was satisfied that the unfair treatment arose from the claimant's sexual orientation rather than any attribute of her sex and that, in all probability, a man would have suffered the same treatment for a similar display of his sexual orientation.

In a trenchant critique of the Labour Court's holding, Leo Flynn argues that '[c]ompulsory heterosexuality is a matter of sex stereotyping, and sex stereotyping in employment is clearly forbidden in Irish law': 'Employment Law "No Gay People Need Apply",' 16 *DULJ* 180, at 184 (1994).

Protection of employees' personal security   In *Field v Irish Carton Printers* [1994] ELR 129, the respondent provided the facility of a taxi home on completion of their night shift to female employees who had no transport of their own. The claimant, a male employee, contended that this constituted remuneration under the Anti-Discrimination (Pay) Act 1974 which was not protected from the charge of discrimination by reason of an asserted justification that the different rate of remuneration was based on 'grounds other than sex', under s 2(3) of the Act. The respondent replied that it had introduced the facility in response to pressure from a union of female employees rather than because it considered that women employees were more in need of such transport than their male colleagues.

The Equality Officer concluded that the facility did indeed constitute remuneration. Relying on the precedents of *Male Employees v Educational Building Society* (EP9/1987), *127 Catering Assistants v British Home Stores (Dublin) Ltd* (EP1/1988) and *Primark, t/a Penneys v 42 Claimants* (ET8/1993), the Equality Officer considered that the facility constituted a benefit in kind and therefore formed part of the contractual consideration that was given by the employer to the employees benefiting from the facility.

Having regard to the evidence, the Equality Officer held that the respondent, in providing the facility, had acted on the perception that, because of their sex, women were more at risk of assault than men, rather than merely responding to pressure from the women's union. While this concern for the well-being of women might be laudable, the Equality Officer did not consider that it was justifiable within the provisions of the relevant legislation. The only instance where special treatment of women was permitted by equality legislation was contained in s. 16 of the Unfair Dismissal Act 1977, which permits employers 'to arrange for or provide special treatment to women in connection with pregnancy or childbirth.' The Equality Officer considered that s. 16 was 'clearly intended to protect a woman's biological condition and the special relationship which exists between a mother and her child.' Special treatment of women based on the opinion that they are more at risk than men was not therefore permitted by either the 1974 or 1977 legislation.

Child-minding responsibilities In *Corrib Airport Ltd v A Worker* [1995] ELR 81, the Labour Court concluded that the failure to offer the claimant a position was largely determined by the perception that her work availability had limitations because of her child-minding responsibilities. The person conducting the interview had engaged in persistent questioning on this theme and had required the claimant's baby-sitter to telephone him.

The Court was satisfied that the child-minding factor would not have arisen in the case of a male applicant, married or otherwise. In view of this conclusion and in the absence of objective assessment criteria for candidates and having regard to the respective merits of the CVs of the claimant and the successful candidate, the Court was satisfied that the decision not to offer the position to the claimant constituted discrimination on grounds of sex, contrary to s. 2(a) of the Employment Equality Act 1977.

The decision also offended s. 2(b) of the Act in so far as other questions asked by the managing director concerning the claimant's husband's attitude to her decision to seek a job and concerning his availability to share child-minding responsibilities while she worked, would not have been asked of a female applicant of single status. For a comprehensive statement of the subject of discriminatory questions in job interviews, see Leo Flynn (1993) 11 *ILT (ns)* 221.

Job-sharing In *Hill v The Revenue Commissioners* [1994] ELR 65, the Equality Officer had to adjudicate upon a claim by women who had engaged in job-sharing that they were the victims of discrimination on the basis of sex and marital status where two years' job-sharing service was equated to one year's full-time service for the purposes of progression on the increment scale. The Court of Justice in *Nimz v Freie und Hansestadt Hamburg* (Case No. 184/89) had held that Article 119 of the EEC Treaty should be interpreted as precluding a collective agreement from providing for the services of full-time workers to be fully taken into account for reclassification to a higher salary grade, where only one half of such was taken into account in the case of part-time workers, who comprised a considerably smaller percentage of men than women, unless the employer could prove that the provision was objectively justified by the relationship between the nature of the duties performed and experience afforded by the performance of those duties after a certain number of working hours had been worked.

In the instant case, the overwhelming majority of job-sharers was female. The Equality Officer saw no reason why the principles set out in *Nimz* should not be applied. There was no reason to distinguish between promotion and progression on the increment scale. While it was true that an increment system could be justified on the basis that it encouraged motivation and commitment, in this case it was the difference in the application of the reward system that was in dispute and not the reward system itself.

Interview procedures   S. 2(d)(1) of the Employment Equality Act 1977 provides that it is discrimination to penalise a person for having in good faith made a reference of a dispute under s. 7 of the Anti-Discrimination (Pay) Act 1974. In *SIPTU v Dunne* [1993] ELR 65, the claimant had made such a reference when, as an employee of ITGWU (the predecessor of SIPTU), she had in 1982 been actively involved in an equal pay case against her employer. In 1990 she applied for one of two positions of personal secretary to assistant general secretaries of SIPTU. Although interviewed, she failed to be appointed to either of the positions. She brought proceedings under s. 2(d)(1).

The Equality Officer proceeded on the basis that, in proceedings of this kind, two principles applied. The onus lay on the claimant to produce evidence in support of the allegation of discrimination. Where, however, the employer had treated a person in an unfavourable manner after that person had referred a dispute with the employer under s. 7 of the 1974 Act, it was 'reasonable to expect that employer to show that there was no relationship between the reference and this treatment of the person concerned'.

In the instant case, although the advertisement for the positions had stated that first class speeds in shorthand were essential, one of the applicants, who had no shorthand at all, had been allowed to compete. The claimant's shorthand was excellent. One of those who were appointed, however, was not of that standard since she had not used shorthand for some time and her speeds were low. The selection committee 'felt that all she required was a refresher course to achieve her former skills again.'

The Equality Officer considered that a candidate who did not have skills to the standard required and who was successful over a candidate who did should at least rate higher in relation to other qualifications or assessment criteria. Whereas the Union had referred to such fundamental and universally accepted criteria as punctuality, level of judgment and interpersonal skills, no evidence had been given as to how the selection committee had applied these criteria in assessing the candidates for interview. The interview board had based its decision on a 'totally subjective' assessment of the candidates' performance. No effort had been made to assess objectively each of the candidates under specific factor headings and the final selection had been based on an overall impression that the two successful candidates were more suitable. The Equality Officer noted that:

[i]t is widely recognised that a subjective decision, not based on any predetermined criteria, can facilitate unintentional discrimination.

The Equality Officer accordingly held in favour of the claimant.

Comparison criteria for determining 'like work' In *Irish Crown Cork Co. Ltd v Desmond* [1993] ELR 180, Lynch J had the thankless task of seeking to unravel an obscure decision of the Labour Court on the issue of equal pay. He remitted the case to the Labour Court to reconsider the matter so far as it arose under s. 2(3) of the Anti-Discrimination (Pay) Act 1974 which provides that nothing in the Act prevents an employer from paying to his or her employees who are employed on like work in the same place different rates of remuneration on grounds other than sex.

The case concerned the duties of a comparator who was being paid on a higher grade than the claimants. Most of these duties, which involved work as a general cleaner, were less demanding than that performed by the claimants but he also performed relief duties as a skilled multi-die machine operator, which were more demanding than those of the claimants. Lynch J held that the correct approach was to compare the former set of duties with those of the claimants rather than to make an overall comparison of the combination of these two sets of duties with the duties of the claimants.

Reasons for decision In *Faulkner v Minister for Industry and Commerce* [1993] ELR 187, the claimant, an executive officer, applied unsuccessfully for promotion. A male competitor was appointed. The claimant's employers contended that she had had a problem with her writing. The Equality Officer found that there was not such a problem and held that she was the victim of sexual discrimination. The Labour Court held against her, however. It expressed its judgment on the substantive issue in one laconic sentence:

Having examined in detail the claimant's assessment records, the Court is satisfied that the Department had reasonable grounds other than sex or marital status for her non-promotion in April 1989.

The plaintiff appealed to the High Court on a point of law, pursuant to s. 21 (4) of the Employment Equality Act 1977. She contended, first, that the Labour Court had failed to specify the basis of its conclusion or to give any adequate reasons for it. She invoked the statement of Finlay CJ in *North*

Western Health Board v Martyn [1987] IR 565, at 579, stressing the desirability of the Labour Court's articulation, 'in an unambiguous fashion, of the facts that it has found and the evidence on which it has found them'.

Murphy J emphasised the Chief Justice's use of the word 'desirable' in this context:

> He was not concluding as a matter of law (whether *obiter* or otherwise) that the judgments or conclusions of [the Labour Court] were required to be formulated in the manner which he indicated.

It was unfortunate that the Labour Court had not expanded further on the reasons for its decision. The pithy conclusion contrasted with the full recitals in the judgment, the lengthy submissions and the very detailed analysis contained in the Equality Officer's report. Nevertheless, when all the documents were read together, there was no ambiguity about the matter. The fact that the Labour Court had expressed its satisfaction to rely on the claimant's assessment records, in conjunction with the Equality Officer's acceptance that a difficulty with writing, if established, would defeat the claim meant that the Labour Court should be interpreted as having rejected the claim on the basis that it was prepared to operate on the claimant's assessment records where the Equality Officer was not. The failure to have spelt out in detail, as recommended by the Chief Justice in *Martyn's* case, did not invalidate the Labour Court's order and gave no ground for appeal under s. 21.

The claimant's second argument, that no administrative body could reasonably or fairly have come to the conclusion at which the Labour Court arrived, was rejected summarily by Murphy J. Following the judgment of Finlay CJ in *O'Keeffe v An Bord Pleanála* [1992] ILRM 237, at 262 (noted in the 1991 Review, 16-8), Murphy J was satisfied that there was indeed 'relevant material' that would support the Labour Court's decision. It was undisputed that the plaintiff's immediate supervisors had commented adversely from time to time on the plaintiff's 'written expression'.

Personal appearance and dress code   In *Pantry Franchise (Ireland) Ltd v A Worker* [1994] ELR 8, the Labour Court gave important guidance on how requirements as to personal appearance or dress code which distinguish between males and females should be assessed from the standpoint of employment equality. The claimant, a male employee at a McDonalds hamburger outlet, had been constructively dismissed for wearing his hair longer than company policy permitted. He wore a hair net at work. Female employees with long hair who wore a hair net were permitted to exceed the hair length requirements, but not male employees.

The Court accepted the company's claim that it was entitled to set standards of dress and appearance for its employees which projected the commercial image that it sought and ensured that the necessary levels of hygiene were maintained. Whilst the requirements for such standards should be the same for male and female employees, they might 'differ in some respects between men and women for business reasons allied to public perception.' These differences did not necessarily retain their justification over time:

> Fashions of dress and appearance and their public acceptability are constantly changing. For example, the wearing of trousers by women would not have been acceptable in past times but now the company has an identical uniform for male and female employees consisting of trousers and shirt.

The Court considered that the styles and length of men's hair were also in the realm of changing fashion and, crucially, that in these circumstances the company's insistence on different hair-lengths for its male and female employees had 'little justification and would not reflect the hair-fashion of the company's customers.' The company was satisfied that its regulations concerning women employees' hair-style, which had no length limitations, did not contravene its hygiene requirements. There was no case, therefore, to justify more restrictive rules for males; accordingly the Court found that there had been discrimination against the claimant contrary to s. 3(4) of the 1977 Act.

Leo Flynn strongly criticises the Court's approach: 'Boys Wear Blue: Dress Codes as a Form of Sex Discrimination' (1994) 12 *ILT (ns)* 286, at 288-9. He argues that different rules for the two sexes in this context amounts to direct discrimination, in relation to which 'reasonable requirements' have no relevance.

UNFAIR DISMISSAL

Who is an employee?   In tort law the crucial element in the distinction between an employee and an independent contractor, for the purposes of determining vicarious liability, is *control*: *Moynihan v Moynihan* [1975] IR 192. This same element determines which of two employers is to be vicariously responsible for the tort of an employee who is 'loaned' by a general employer to another employer to perform a specific service: *Lynch v Palgrave Murphy Ltd* [1964] IR 150.

In *McCurdey v Bayer Diagnostics Manufacturing Ltd* [1994] ELR 83, in proceedings for unfair dismissal taken by a doctor working in industrial

medicine with the respondent company, the Tribunal held that the relationship was that of employment rather than one for services. The contract
required the claimant to work for at least eight hours a week for the
respondent, to attend the company's premises in the morning and thereafter
to be on call for medical emergencies at the Company's premises. The
Tribunal accepted that the claimant had a significant element of autonomy
in discharging his duties under the contract but observed that:

> [h]aving regard to the degree of skill involved on the part of a doctor,
> we would expect a manufacturing company's control of such a person
> to be less than that which they would exercise over their other employ-
> ees.

The fact that the claimant was not paying income tax under the PAYE
system was not, of itself, a bar to his being an employee.

In *Young v Bounty Services (Ireland) Ltd* [1993] ELR 224, the Tribunal
held that the claimant, who worked as field supervisor for the distribution of
the respondent's products to maternity hospitals, was its employee rather than
an independent contractor, even though she had responsibility for paying her
own tax and PRSI. The Tribunal had regard to several factors pointing in
favour of a characterisation of her position as that of employee: the claimant
had had a three-month trial period in her position; she could not undertake
any other business or occupation without the previous written consent of the
respondent; she was paid an hourly rate of pay and received holiday pay, as
well as payment during periods of illness; the respondent had provided the
claimant with an office since 1992; and she was at all times answerable to
the board of the company, whose publications suggested that she was a
member of management. The Tribunal awarded the claimant compensation
for unfair dismissal since the respondent had not established that a redundancy situation justified the termination of her contract.

What constitutes dismissal?   In *North Bowl Ltd t/a Strand Bowl v Maxwell*
[1993] ELR 228, the respondent had been employed by the appellant
company as a maintenance mechanic at its bowling premises. On a day off,
he was participating in a competition at the bowling alley in which the
operations manager of the company was also participating. When one of the
lanes stopped working, the operations manager asked him to repair the
machine, but he refused twice to do so. The operations manager told him that
if he did not fix the machine he need not come back to work on the following
day. The respondent again refused and on his way out of the premises told
the operations manager to have his P45 ready the next day. The operations
manager made no attempt to tell him that he was not dismissed.

In the Circuit Court, Spain P held that the respondent had been dismissed and that the dismissal was unfair. He considered that it would be unreasonable to take any other meaning out of the words spoken by the operations manager. If he had not meant them to act as a dismissal 'he would have sought out the respondent later to explain properly.'

Constructive dismissal In *Pantry Franchise (Ireland) Ltd. v A Worker* [1994] 4 ELR 8, which we consider, above, 358-9, in relation to the issue of employment equality, the claimant, a male worker at a McDonalds hamburger outlet, wore his hair longer than shoulder-length, contrary to company policy. He had practice of wearing a hair-net (which was all that was asked of female employees with long hair). Ultimately, after several earlier requests by management to have his hair cut, he was advised by management that he could not work the shift unless he obtained a regulation haircut to company standard. The claimant treated this as a constructive dismissal and, having left the premises, did not return.

The Labour Court held in favour of the claimant. It was clear to the Court from the evidence that the company had not been prepared to allow the claimant to work again until he had his hair cut to standard. It was also clear to the Court that, 'as the claimant did not intend to have his hair cut in the fashion required by the company, it was not unreasonable for him to regard the manager's edict as a dismissal.'

The dismissal was unfair because it offended the provisions against discrimination contained in s. 3(4) of the Employment Equality Act 1977. The Court considered, however, that the claimant had contributed to his own dismissal. He had had the reasonable option of retaining his employment while accepting the company's requirement under protest, and processing a claim of discrimination under the Act. He would not have been at any permanent disadvantage, stated the Court, 'as his hair would have grown again'. The Court awarded the plaintiff £200, stating that it had regard to the contributory element of the claimant in making its order.

In *McCloskey v Dillon Bros.* [1993] ELR 232 the Tribunal held that an employee of eleven years' standing had been constructively dismissed when she ceased to continue her employment after an incident in which her employer remonstrated with her about her failure to remove boxes from a stairway. There was a severe conflict of evidence in the case. The claimant asserted that the respondent had used obscenities and had scared her by using his fists at her. She claimed, moreover, that her work shift was over at the time of the incident. The respondent claimed that the incident occurred during the claimant's work shift. He said that the claimant had been abusive and offensive to him and that he had not used obscenities, though he admitted to having employed the term 'bucking'.

The Tribunal stated its conclusion, as unfortunately is so often its practice, in a way that makes it difficult to discern how it resolved the specifics of the matters in conflict. It was satisfied on the balance of probability, that 'whatever was said during the incident between the two parties was sufficient to entitle the claimant to walk out as she did.' The Tribunal bore in mind that the claimant had been a good employee for the previous eleven years, in relation to whom there had been no cause previously for the respondent to issue any warnings to her about her work.

Redundancy In *Roche v Sealink Stena Line Ltd* [1993] ELR 89, the claimants, who had been dismissed by reason of redundancy, argued that the employer's selection of who should be declared redundant was unfair because it was not based on the 'last in, first out' principle. S. 6(3)(b) of the 1977 Act provides that the dismissal of an employee by reason of redundancy is deemed to be an unfair dismissal if the employee:

> was selected for dismissal in contravention of a procedure (being a procedure that has been agreed upon by or on behalf of the employer and by the employee or a trade union . . . representing him or has been established by the custom and practice of the employment concerned) relating to redundancy and there were no special reasons justifying a departure from that procedure.

There had been no compulsory redundancies previous to those involving the claimants; therefore, the 'last-in, first-out' rule had not been established by custom and practice *in that company*. A shipping branch organiser for the claimants' union told the Tribunal that *throughout the trade* the normal practice in redundancy situations was for this rule to apply.

The Tribunal found that there was 'no evidence of any agreement or custom and practice relating to redundancy which would show that the 'last-in, first-out' rule should have applied'. This suggests that the Tribunal's understanding of the remit of the phrase 'the custom and practice of the employment concerned' was that only the custom and practice of the *particular company* could be considered. This is a surprising interpretation. It leaves employees of new companies (or at all events companies with no previous record of compulsory redundancy) in the invidious position of being excluded from the entitlement to invoke the custom and practice of other companies in the same trade, industry or business, where those other companies have had to address the question already.

The Tribunal went on to hold that s. 6(3)(b) of the Act 'is the only section which deals with the question of selection and there is no provision in this section which allows the Tribunal to consider the fairness of the assessments used.' While that is undoubtedly true, there is no reason why an unfair selection procedure should not in some circumstances be capable of being characterised as unfair, under s. 6(1). S. 6(3) does not deal with a case where there is no *agreed* procedure or procedure *established by the custom and practice of the employment concerned* (as the latter notion was narrowly interpreted by the Tribunal). The idea that an employer in such a case should be free to adopt an unfair procedure with impunity is so violative of basic principles of justice as to require the rejection of an interpretation which has that result.

In *Murphy v Marine Port and General Workers' Union* [1994] ELR 15, the Tribunal held that the claimants had not been unfairly selected for redundancy since the 'last in, first out' principle, which applied to them, reflected the policy of their employer. Accordingly their dismissal was not unfair.

In *Wall v Northamber plc* [1993] 5 ELR 223, the Tribunal held that the claimant had been unfairly dismissed where the company that employed her as sales manager ceased trading and she was made redundant; the functions of that company were taken over immediately by the respondent company, which did not re-engage her but instead employed another person to do a job that was the same as she had done.

Misconduct In *Fitzpatrick v Polygram Records Ltd* [1994] ELR 24, the Tribunal held that there had not been substantial grounds justifying the dismissal of the claimant from her position as a product manager in the respondent company where the managing director had conveyed to her his anger about the quality of market plan she produced and she had mouthed an obscene response, following which she walked out of the meeting with him. The Tribunal appears to have accepted the claimant's evidence that the managing director had mistakenly underestimated the amount of work that she had done. The Tribunal held that, although the dismissal was unfair, the managing director had had 'reason for dissatisfaction' with the claimant's marketing plans and that, by her past performance in this area, she had contributed to her dismissal. This was reflected in the Tribunal's choice of compensation as the most appropriate form of redress and in the quantum awarded.

In *Treacy v Kilkenny Textile Mills BV* [1994] ELR 12, the Tribunal held that an assault by the claimant on a co-worker constituted gross misconduct, warranting his dismissal, even though there might have been 'a slight element of provocation'. The claimant said that the co-employee had tampered with his locker by tying it up with string and moving it about.

Leave outside holiday period   In *Costello v Gerard F. May Roofing Ltd*
[1994] ELR 19, the claimants had been dismissed for having taken their
holidays outside the agreed period of the first two weeks of August. A circular
in April had, in stark terms, made it plain that '[a]ny employee who does not
arrive for work on Monday morning, 27 June 1992 due to holidays which
were not taken at the agreed time is automatically on two weeks notice and
can collect their P45 and back week when our office re-opens on Tuesday
18 August 1992'. There had been discussions early in 1992 between the
employer organisation and trade unions about the possibility of moving the
annual holiday period to the last two weeks of July and the respondent had
circulated a notice about this possible development to its employees; but on
31 July it had issued another circular confirming that for 1992 there would
be no change. This had been re-iterated in yet another circular in April.

The claimants had booked their holidays in January. They could have
cancelled them with no loss of deposit up to eight weeks prior to the date of
departure or varied the date (subject to availability) for a charge of £15. They
admitted receiving the April circular but said that they had not paid much
heed to it 'because they received so many notices about various things.'

The text of the Tribunal's determination does not state when precisely
the claimants took their holidays. If it was not in fact the last two weeks of
July, it is hard to see how the uncertainty in January was in any way relevant.
At all events the Tribunal dismissed the claim on the basis that, whether or
not the claimants had received the circular of 31 January 1992, they were
aware of the position with regard to the taking of holidays. They had
disregarded the April notice. They were therefore the authors of their own
misfortune.

Illness   In *Cummings v Jurys Hotel Group plc* [1994] ELR 21, the claimant,
who had been employed by the respondent as a house assistant since 1981,
suffered from asthma which led to absences in 1986 and 1987. After an
accident at work in 1988, she again went on sick leave and, after a brief return,
collapsed, resulting in her continuing absence on sick leave. Her asthmatic
condition was compounded by lower back pain. After several medical
examinations, the doctor to whom the respondent had referred the claimant,
formed the view that it would be unrealistic to expect that she would be fit
to work again; if she returned to work, he thought that she 'would be exposed
to conditions which m[ight] precipitate her problem and the situation could
end in tragedy.' Acting on this medical report, the respondent discharged the
claimant in January 1992. The Tribunal held that, having regard in particular
to the medical evidence, the decision to terminate the claimant's employment
had not been unfair.

Role of the Rights Commissioner   S. 8(10) of the Unfair Dismissals Act prohibits the reference to a Rights Commissioner under s. 13(2) of the Industrial Relations Act 1969 of a dispute in relation to a dismissal that is an unfair dismissal. In *Furey v Clarke* [1994] ELR 41, a Rights Commissioner had dealt with a situation where the trade union of two employees who had received dismissal notices from their employer had picketed the employer's premises, resulting in the withdrawal of the dismissal notices, on the basis that the dispute would be referred to a Rights Commissioner, under the 1969 Act, with the employees being placed on suspension with full pay while the Rights Commissioner was dealing with the case. The Rights Commissioner, in his recommendation, recorded that he believed that 'the evidence just is not there to warrant the dismissal' of the two employees, whose immediate re-instatement he recommended. The employer, having unsuccessfully appealed this recommendation pursuant to s. 13(9) of the 1969 Act, sought to challenge it in proceedings for judicial review on the basis of the Rights Commissioner's lack of jurisdiction to deal with a dispute in relation to an unfair dismissal.

O'Hanlon J rejected this assault on the Rights Commissioner's competence to hear the case. He had not been called on to investigate a claim based on wrongful dismissal since the dismissals had been rescinded and the *status quo* in this respect restored before the dispute between the parties had been referred to him for consideration. The two employees had been re- instated, albeit temporarily suspended on full pay pending the resolution of the dispute. The dispute at that stage was as to whether the circumstances were such as to justify the employer in going ahead with its previously announced decision to dismiss the employees or whether the suspensions should be lifted. This, in O'Hanlon J's view, placed the dispute within the definition of a 'trade dispute' under s. 3 of the Industrial Relations Act 1946, which was the relevant definition for the purposes of the 1969 Act. S. 8(10) of the 1977 Act clearly contemplated a situation where a dismissal had taken place and the employee *remained dismissed from the employment.*

O'Hanlon J would in any event have dismissed the claim for judicial review on the basis of estoppel by virtue of the employer's participation in the Labour Court appeal. He left to another day the question whether *certiorari* lies against a determination of the Rights Commissioner or the Labour Court; the employees had contented that it does not, on the basis that such a determination does not impose liability or affect rights.

Assessment of compensation   In *North Bowl Ltd t/a Strand Bowl v Maxwell* [1993] ELR 288, discussed above, 360-1, Spain P held that, in calculating the claimant's salary loss, the Court, '[i]n fairness', should deduct the social welfare payments he had received. This approach may be contrasted with that of s. 6 of the Unfair Dismissals (Amendment) Act 1993, discussed below, 368.

Appeal procedure   In *Brady v An Post*, High Court, 20 April 1993, the plaintiff, who had been dismissed from his employment with the defendant, sought a mandatory injunction compelling his re-engagement. He had been employed by the defendant for eleven years. He was charged with, and pleaded guilty to, assault in November 1990. The sentence was six months' imprisonment. Four months later, the defendant dismissed him. The Tribunal held in December 1991 that he had been unfairly dismissed, though he had by his actions contributed to his own dismissal. It ordered that he be re-engaged within fourteen days. In the meantime, the plaintiff had appealed unsuccessfully against the sentence of imprisonment which was affirmed in November 1991. He was released from prison in May 1992.

Although the defendant appealed the Tribunal's determination in January 1992, it served notice of discontinuance in January 1993. In July 1992, it brought proceedings by way of judicial review. Barron J, in November 1992, ruled the application inappropriate as being moot until such time as the plaintiff sought to rely on the Tribunal's order.

Morris J accepted that, since the plaintiff was seeking mandatory relief, he had to establish that there was 'a high probability' that he would succeed in his action, rather than merely having to raise a *prima facie* case. He rejected three arguments put forward by the defendant against granting the injunction. The first was that s. 10 of the Unfair Dismissals Act 1977 prescribed a procedure available to the Minister to enforce a determination of the Tribunal in the event of the defendant's failure to comply with it; such a procedure, contended the defendant, precluded the plaintiff from seeking the injunction. Morris J was satisfied that the power given to the Minister under s. 10 of the Act was 'no more than any power which m[ight] already be vested in the plaintiff to enforce the order' and was not an ouster of the plaintiff's constitutional right to seek to vindicate his rights.

The defendant argued, secondly, that the plaintiff's failure to be re-employed within fourteen days of the Tribunal's determination had resulted from the fact that he was in prison during that period and that no further obligation remained on the defendant to re-employ him. Morris J held that the plaintiff had 'a strong case to make' that this argument should not be accepted. To construe the determination in the way suggested 'would result in the extraordinary circumstance that all the defendant has to do is to avoid re-employing the plaintiff for a period of fourteen days and he may then disregard the determination.' With respect, this ignores the element of self-induced impossibility that arose in the case. A far more convincing basis for rejecting the defendant's argument was, as Morris J held, that the determination imposed on the defendant an onus actively to re-engage the plaintiff.

The third argument put forward by the defendant was that it had never been the practice for the courts to order a reluctant employer to employ a reluctant employee and that the mandatory relief sought was inappropriate. Morris J rejected it on the basis that what was sought was no more than the type of order that could be expected of the Circuit Court if the Minister were to move under s. 10 of the 1977 Act. The plaintiff had made a strong case that it was equally open for the High Court in injunction proceedings to make an order to the same effect.

Morris J did not consider that granting an order would disturb the *status quo*. The plaintiff having been in the defendant's employment for eleven years and the defendant having discontinued its appeal, the *status quo* was that the plaintiff was in the defendant's employment rather than unemployed. The balance of hardship lay in favour of granting the injunction. The plaintiff had already been out of work for a significant period and it was well accepted that the longer one remains out of work the harder it is to become re-employed.

Limitation period   In *Amber Ltd v Donnelly* [1993] ELR 170, the Tribunal on 29 June 1992 had made an award in favour of the respondent for unfair dismissal. The appellant, who had failed to participate in the hearing, sought to appeal the award. S. 10(4) of the 1977 Act prescribed a six week time limit. Although a written communication of the Tribunal's determination was sent by registered post from the Tribunal offices on 22 July 1992, the appellant did not post its notice of appeal to the respondent's solicitor until 4 September. The appellant claimed that it first received notification of the Tribunal's decision on 27 July 1992, thus bringing its notice of appeal within the six week period.

Spain P held, on the evidence that, on the balance of probabilities, the letter was received on 23 July 1992, thus placing the appellant's appeal out of time. We should note that s. 7 of the Unfair Dismissals (Amendment) Act 1993 permits the extension of the limitation period for claims for unfair dismissals from six months to up to twelve months in 'exceptional circumstances.' See below, 369.

Unfair Dismissals (Amendment) Act 1993   This Act contains a miscellany of important reforms of the unfair dismissals legislative code. For an analysis of the Act, see Gary Byrne's article in (1990-1993) 9 *JISLL* 100, and his lecture on 25 November 1993 (Law Society of Ireland's Continuing Legal Education series) and Tony Kerr's Annotation of the Act (*ICLSA*).

S. 2 is a largely technical provision, amending the definitions of 'trade unions' and 'the Tribunal' in the 1977 Act. It also provides that, where, on the date of an award of re-instatement, the terms or conditions on which other employees are employed in similar positions are more favourable to the employees than they were at the date of the dismissal, the re-instated employee is to benefit from this improvement.

Among the more important changes is that relating to fixed term and fixed purpose contracts. S. 2(2) of the 1977 Act excludes these from the protection of the Act in certain circumstances. Employers used to seek to side-step the provisions of the Act by entering into a sequence of fixed term contracts, sometimes broken by a short gap between contracts. S. 3 of the 1993 Act amends s. 2(2) of the 1977 Act. It deals with cases where there is a re-employment of an employee within three months of the employee's dismissal under an earlier contract by reason of its expiry (or the cesser of its purpose), and the nature of the new employment is 'the same or similar' to that of the employment under the earlier contract. If, in the opinion of the Rights Commissioner, the Tribunal or the Circuit Court, the entry by the employer into the later contract was 'wholly or partly for or was connected with' the purpose of avoidance of liability under the 1977 Act, then that Act is to apply to the dismissal and the term of the prior contract and of any antecedent contracts is to be added to that of the subsequent contract for the purpose of ascertaining the period of service of the employee. The period so ascertained is deemed to be one of continuous service.

S. 4 amends s. 5 of the 1977 Act so as to streamline the approach of the 1977 Act and paragraph 2 of the First Schedule to the Minimum Notice and Terms of Employment Act 1973, so far as lock-outs, dismissal and reinstatement are concerned.

S. 5 amends s. 6 of the 1977 Act by rendering a dismissal unfair if it results wholly or mainly from the sexual orientation of the employee, the age of the employee or the employee's membership of the travelling community. It also contains an amendment to s. 6(7) designed to ensure that the Rights Commissioner, Tribunal or Circuit Court may have regard to the reasonableness (or otherwise) of the employee in relation to the dismissal and the compliance (or otherwise) by the employer with required dismissal procedures or codes of practice, in determining whether the dismissal was unfair.

S. 6 extends the circumstances in which the payment of compensation to the employee is permitted. It is no longer limited to compensating the employee for financial loss: if there has been no such loss the employee is still entitled to up to four weeks' remuneration. In calculating the appropriate compensation, regard is to be had to the extent of the employer's compliance (or non-compliance) with dismissal procedures and codes of practice and the extent to which the employee's conduct may have contributed to the dismissal. S. 6 also provides that, in calculating the employee's loss, regard is not to be had to social welfare payments or payments under the income tax legislation received by the employee. Cf. *North Bowl Ltd t/a Strand Bowl v Maxwell* [1993] ELR 288, noted above, 360. Whether the social welfare or revenue authorities should be entitled to *recoup* monies paid is another matter: see Kerr, *op. cit.*, General Note to s. 6.

S. 7 deals, *inter alia*, with certain kinds of illegal contracts. Previously, an employee who had been dismissed unfairly would have the proceedings dismissed if the employer established that the contract contravened the revenue or social welfare statutory code. S. 7(d) amends s. 8 of the 1977 Act by inserting two provisions. First, the employee in such cases, notwithstanding the contravention, will be entitled to redress under the Act in respect of the dismissal. Secondly, where a contravention of this kind is established, the Rights Commissioner, the Tribunal or the Circuit Court must notify the Revenue Commissioners or Minister for Social Welfare of the matter.

S. 7 contains some other important provisions. It requires the decision maker (the Rights Commissioner, Tribunal or Circuit Court) when giving one form of redress, to specify why it did not award other forms of redress in favour of the employee. It extends the limitation period for claims of unfair dismissal from six to twelve months after dismissal where the Rights Commissioner or the Tribunal is satisfied that 'exceptional circumstances' prevented compliance with the six-month period. Gary Byrne (*op. cit.*, p. 12 of his lecture) questions the wisdom of this approach:

> It is asking too much of [the Tribunal] to have the right of excluding employees from the provisions of the legislation. It is the legislation that should make such provisions and leave the application to the Tribunal.

S. 7 also imposes on an employer a time-limit of twenty-one days of receiving notice of an employee's application to a Rights Commissioner if the employer intends to block the claim. The section amends s. 8(4) of the 1977 Act by enabling the Tribunal to issue a determination confirming the recommendation of a Rights Commissioner, at the instance of the employee, *without* hearing the employer. It also effectively overrules O'Hanlon J's decision in *Sutcliffe v McCarthy* [1993] ELR 53 (noted in the 1992 Review, 400) by prohibiting the processing of a claim under *both* the 1977 Act and the Industrial Relations Acts 1946 and 1969.

S. 9 of the 1977 Act required the appellant from a Rights Commissioner's recommendation to provide a copy of the notice of appeal to the other party within the six-month period allowed for an appeal. As Tony Kerr (*op. cit.*, General Note to s. 8) points out, this could lead to practical difficulties where (as often was the case) appeals were lodged at the last minute. Section 8 of the 1993 Act changes the position by placing responsibility on the Tribunal, 'as soon as may be' after the receipt by it of the notice to appeal, to serve a copy on the other party.

S. 9 introduces minor technical amendments to s. 14 of the 1977 Act, which deals with the furnishing to new employees of details of the employer's dismissal procedure and the entitlement to take into account grounds for dismissal other than those furnished to the employee by the employer.

S. 10 deals with the employee's dilemma of whether to proceed for *unfair* or *wrongful* dismissal. Under s. 15 of the 1977 Act, once a claim for unfair dismissal had been initiated, the employee was prevented from taking proceedings for wrongful dismissal. S. 10 delays the fateful moment. The employee's options remain open up to the time the Rights Commissioner makes a recommendation in respect of a claim for redress under the 1977 Act or the Tribunal has commenced hearing of an unfair dismissals claim or the Circuit Court has commenced hearing of proceedings for wrongful dismissal.

S. 11 deals with the troublesome question of appeals to the Circuit Court. It entirely repeals and replaces s. 10 of the 1977 Act. Most importantly, it permits an employee or, 'if he considers it appropriate to make the application having regard to all the circumstances, the Minister', to appeal to the Circuit Court against the failure by an employer to carry out a determination of the Tribunal within six weeks of its being communicated to the parties. The Circuit Court, *without hearing the employer* or any evidence, is required to make the necessary order directing the employer to carry out the recommendation. The section thus overrules Judge Clarke's decision in *Minister for Labour v We Frame It Ltd*, Circuit Court, (1987) 5 *ILT (ns)* 185, noted in the 1987 Review, 221-2.

S. 11 permits the Circuit Court to award interest and to alter the nature of the award from re-engagement or re-instatement to financial compensation under s. 7(1)(c) of the 1977 Act. Tony Kerr (*op. cit.*, General Note to s. 11). points out that however '[w]elcome these changes may be, the section does not address the position of the High Court to which a full appeal still lies. . . .'

S. 12 provides that a document signed by the chairman or a vice-chairman of the Tribunal stating that a named person failed to give evidence or to produce a significant document is to be evidence of the matter so stated, without further proof, in a prosecution under s. 39(17)(c) of the Redundancy Payments Act 1967.

Prior to the 1993 legislation people who were placed with an employer through an employment agency fell outside the protection of the 1977 Act: see Gary Byrne's article (*op. cit.* at 107), citing *Minister for Labour v PMPA Insurance Co.* (1986) 5 *JISLL* 215. S. 13 of the 1993 Act extends the protection of the 1977 Act to employees placed by employment agencies within the meaning of the Employment Agency Act 1971 in the course of that business.

S. 14 makes it clear that employees without one year's service who are dismissed for trade union membership or activity are protected by the 1977 Act.

S. 15 of the Act amends the First Schedule of the Minimum Notice and Terms of Employment Act 1973, by which continuity of service is reckoned for the purposes of the 1977 Act. Henceforth, the transfer of a business operates to break continuity of service where 'the employee received and retained redundancy payments from the transferor at the time and by reason of the transfer.'

This change has been widely criticised. Tony Kerr (General Note to s. 15, *ICLSA*) observes that some doubts must exist as to whether it is compatible with the provisions of the European Communities (Safeguarding of Employee's Rights on the Transfer of Undertakings) Regulations 1980 (SI No. 306 of 1980). Gary Byrne (*op. cit.*, 20) considers that the amendment is 'most unsatisfactory'. He points out that frequently employees believe in ignorance that they are entitled to a redundancy payment simply because a business changes hands, even though they might remain working with the new employer:

It seems though that the new employer can now dismiss with impunity because the employee does not have continuity of service for the required one year to claim under the 1977 Act.

He identifies another difficulty, of a drafting nature, with s. 15. This section substitutes a new paragraph (7) for that which was inserted by the 1977 Act into the First Schedule of the 1973 Act. The new paragraph 7 provides that, on transfer, the service of an employee with the old employer 'shall be reckoned as part of the service of the employee' with the new employer *unless* the employee received and retained a redundancy payment from the old employer as indicated above. Gary Byrne points out that paragraph 6 of the First Schedule provides that continuity is not broken by a dismissal when it is followed by immediate re-employment. Which is to prevail?

RESTRAINT OF TRADE

In *Apex Fire Protection Ltd v Murtagh* [1993] ELR 201, the Competition Authority gave an important decision in relation to restraint of trade. The applicant was a company involved in the provision of fire protection and detection products and related services throughout the State. It employed over fifty persons, with an annual staff turnover of around 50%. It had a customer base of several thousand, of whom about two thousand lived in the Dublin area. Mr Murtagh had formerly been engaged as a sales/service representative of the company. After promotion to field training supervisor, he had left its employment in October 1992 and set up his own company. The applicant had obtained an injunction against him, enforcing the provisions in his contract of employment which restrained him from soliciting certain customers and former customers of his employers for a stated period. The applicant later sought a licence from the Competition Authority under s. 4(2) of the Competition Act 1991 for the arrangements contained in this contract of employment.

The clause in question provided as follows:

> On the termination of this agreement howsoever occasioned, the representative shall not for the period of two years next after such termination within the district of which he has operated during the course of this agreement solicit any of the persons who were customers of the employer within two years immediately preceding the date of such termination and shall not divulge or disclose to any other party any information gained as a result of employment with the employer.

The first issue requiring resolution was whether Mr Murtagh was 'an undertaking'; if he was not then, of course, the 1991 Act would have no application. S. 3(1) of the Act defines an undertaking as 'a person being an individual, a body corporate or an unincorporated body of persons engaged for gain in the production, supply or distribution of goods or the provision of a service.' The Competition Authority held that Mr Murtagh, who owned and controlled his own new business, was an undertaking. Its earlier decision in *Budget Travel v Phil Fortune*, Decision No. 9. 14 September 1992 and the Commission's decision in *Nutricia v De Rooij* 83/670/EEC, OJL 376, 31 supported that conclusion.

The Authority then turned to consider the terms of clause 15 of the contract. In a notice entitled 'Employee Agreements and the Competition Act', *Iris Oifigiúil*, No. 75, 18 September 1992, 32-3, the Authority had stated as follows:

> If the former employer were to seek to enforce a non-competition clause in an employment contract in respect of an employee who had left and was seeking to establish his or her own business, the Authority believes that this would represent a restriction on competition within the meaning of s. 4(1). While such an agreement between one individual and an

employer may not have a substantial impact on competition, the existence of such agreements in many sectors of the economy means that
their combined effect would be to greatly restrict competition. The
Authority therefore believes that in these circumstances such agreements would offend against s. 4(1) of the Competition Act. The Authority also believes that it would be difficult for such an agreement to satisfy
the requirements specified for the grant of a licence in s. 4(2) of the Act.

A *total* restriction seeking to prevent a former employee from entering
the market as a competitor would thus offend against s. 4(1). There was,
however, a difference between such a restriction and one that sought only to
protect the proprietary interests of the employer in its own business. It was
essential to employment relationships that an individual should not be able
to take up employment solely for the purpose of gaining an introduction to
the employer's customers in order to solicit these customers. A restriction on
soliciting the former employer's customers might therefore be regarded as
essential both to protect the employer's proprietary interest in the goodwill
of his business and to normal employment relationships. Such a restriction
should not exceed what was absolutely necessary to protect the employer's
interests; if it did so, it would be regarded as an attempt to prevent competition
by the ex-employee.

The Authority took the view that, insofar as the applicant company was
arguing that the non-solicitation clause was necessary to protect the public
from the provision of unsatisfactory goods or services, this function was 'not
one for private firms' and could not afford any justification for the imposition
of clauses of the kind under consideration.

The Authority had no objection to the scope of the *restricted activities*.
The clause applied only to soliciting certain customers. It did not prevent
either general advertising such as in the Yellow Pages, or passive sales
resulting from an approach by the customer to the former employee. Neither
did the Authority have a difficulty with the scope of the provision by
reference to *customers and area*.

It was the *duration* of the prohibition that proved to offend against s. 4(1).
A one-year period of protection, in the view of the Authority, would provide
the company with ample opportunity to confirm its business connection and
goodwill with its existing customers before facing competition for those
customers from Mr Murtagh. Two years was, however, too long. In reaching
this conclusion the Authority took account of several factors. Insofar as the
purpose of the restriction was to protect the company's goodwill, only some
of that goodwill was exclusively attributable to Mr Murtagh. Whereas a
two-year period of protection was normally necessary to protect the goodwill
of a business that is sold, since the purchaser normally possessed none of the

goodwill at the start, the position was different with employment contracts, where the employer retained most of the goodwill.

Notwithstanding his previous employment with the applicant company, Mr Murtagh was in a position somewhat akin to a new entrant into the market since he had to convince customers that his products and services were at least as good as the competition. The applicant company was one of the leading firms in that market. While there was obviously some degree of technical expertise involved in the provision of the services concerned, that degree was not such as to justify a lengthy period of protection.

The Authority did not consider that the period of eighteen months, which the applicant company had proposed was necessary to protect its legitimate commercial interests. As the restriction on soliciting exceeded what was required for those interests, it could not be considered to be 'indispensable' within the meaning of s. 4(2).

It is interesting to note what the Authority had to say on the restriction on divulging information which clause 15 contained. The tenor of its observations is clearly supportive in principle of restrictions of this kind, provided that they are not used as a means of preventing or impeding a party from re-entering the market after the expiry of a non-competition clause:

> Unless confidentiality can be ensured, employer/employee relationships, and many others, just could not occur. This is relevant during the term of an agreement, and afterwards. It is akin to the goodwill being transferred as part of the sale of a business, but is probably even more important. It is hard to see how an employer would be prepared to give confidential information to employees if they were allowed to use this or disclose it to competitors when employment ceased. At the same time, it often has to be disclosed to employees for them to be able to do their job. Confidentiality may therefore be seen as ancillary in the sense of being fundamentally necessary for such relationships.

COLLECTIVE AGREEMENTS

In *Ó Cearbhaill v Bord Telecom Éireann* [1994] ELR 54, the Supreme Court had a rare opportunity to consider the law relating to collective agreements. The plaintiffs were officers and technicians who had worked for the Department of Posts and Telegraphs and who continued to be employees of Bord Telecom Éireann when the Department was split into two limited companies by the Postal and Telecommunications Act 1983. S. 45(2) of the Act provides that, '[s]ave in accordance with a collective agreement negotiated with any recognised trade union or staff association concerned, employees of the former regime transferred to the new company are not to receive a lesser scale of conditions of service than the former scale of pay and the former conditions of service'.

The plaintiffs were on a panel from which engineering superintendents were appointed when vacancies arose. As a result of the restricting of various grades in 1991, this particular grade was abolished, thus damaging the plaintiffs' promotion prospects. The plaintiffs claimed that their employment prospects were a condition of service and that the defendant company had breached s. 45(2). Their claim succeeded in the High Court, where Lardner J held them entitled to damages. Lardner J accepted that there had been a collective agreement between the defendant and the plaintiffs' union but that the union had required the authority of the plaintiffs before they could make a collective agreement, and they had not this authority because the information given to them as to the effect of the agreement was misleading.

The defendant appealed successfully to the Supreme Court. Blayney J (Finlay CJ and Egan J concurring) considered that Lardner J had been incorrect in holding that the specific consent of union members was required:

> S. 45(2) clearly envisages collective agreements negotiated with a recognised trade union as affecting the position of individual employees, but there is nothing in the subsection from which it could be implied that before entering into such an agreement the union required the specific assent of its members. The legislature no doubt took the view that trade unions, in entering into collective agreements, could be relied upon to protect fully the interests of their members.

There had in his view been nothing misleading or relevant to the grade of engineering superintendent in the information given by the union originally to its members.

The latter agreement, in 1991, which clearly did relate to this grade, was valid and effective even though it had not received the approval of the plaintiffs and brought them to less beneficial conditions of service.

Blayney quoted a passage from Von Prondzynski & McCarthy's *Employment Law in Ireland* (2nd ed., 1989), 24, which pointed to one of the essential elements of a collective agreement:

> The outstanding fact about a collective agreement is that there is a collectivity at work at least on the part of the workers. A collectivity for our purposes here is not a unitary group, such as a board of directors, but a widely dispersed group the members of which by definition cannot have a direct involvement in the bargain but at best an indirect one.

Blayney J rejected with 'no hesitation' the argument of counsel for the plaintiffs that, even if there was a valid collective agreement, it would not prevent an individual coming to court to enforce his rights. He had no doubt that the effect of s. 45(2) was that the rights of individual employees could be affected by a collective agreement.

This was sufficient to dispose of the case; but Blayney J went on to consider whether in any event a term dealing with an employee's prospect of promotion came within the category of 'conditions of service'. He concluded that it did not. It did not concern 'the immediate relationship' between the employer and employee, as would, for example, the rate of pay, hours of work, length of holidays, sick leave and pension rights. It related rather to the general manner in which the employer's business was structured and managed:

> If an employer were to make it the subject of the contract of employment of individual employees, he would be unable to change it without the consent of each of them. No employer would be prepared to restrict his freedom in this way. For this reason it would be wholly inappropriate to include a prospect of promotion in a contract of employment and so it could not be considered as being a condition of service. It is simply an incident of a person's employment depending entirely on how the employer's business is structured and subject to change since the employer is under no obligation not to alter the structure of his business.

Finally, Blayney J rejected the plaintiffs' argument that there had been a breach of their legitimate expectation that their prospects of promotion would not be changed without prior consultation. It was not necessary to consider whether the plaintiffs had such a legitimate expectation because, even if they had, it had not been infringed on account of the requirements in s. 45(2) and (3) for prior consultation with the trade unions and staff associations. One may perhaps wonder whether this statutory procedure for consultation was *necessarily* sufficient: the plaintiffs had not been personally consulted and the essence of their complaint was that they were not satisfied with the fruits of consultation with others.

PENSIONS

In *Turner v Hospitals Trust (1940) Ltd* [1994] ELR 35, Geoghegan J held that employees of the defendant company, which had gone into liquidation, were entitled to full (albeit very modest) pensions even though the company had informed them, at the time it ceased operations, that it was ceasing to pay the *ex gratia* element of their pensions. Geoghegan J held that, in the light of earlier communications between the company and the employees, the employees had 'quite reasonably understood that they had a contractual right to the entirety of the pension.' He did not enlarge of this analysis but it appears from remarks earlier in his judgment that this holding amounts to one that there was a contractual obligation to pay the entirety of each pension rather than that the employees' claim was properly grounded on some equitable principle of detrimental reliance or legitimate expectation.

Geoghegan J held that damages should be assessed as of the date of the winding up of the company rather than the date of the hearing of the action. The general tenor of the judgments in *Re Haughton Main Colliery Company Ltd* [1956] 3 All ER 300 and *Re Dynamics Corporation of America* [1976] 2 All ER 300 supported this conclusion and the plaintiffs' counsel had admitted 'that he could not draw much comfort' from the Supreme Court judgment in *In re Hibernian Transport Companies Ltd* [1994] 1 ILRM 48, noted in the Company Law Chapter, above, 104-5.

Geoghegan J considered that, although the Court had power to award interest under the Courts Act 1981, it would not be proper in the circumstances to do so since it would create an inequality of benefit between those pensioners named as plaintiffs in what was essentially a test case and other pensioners of the company in an identical position. Delay was also a factor encouraging him to take this course.

TRADE DISPUTES

In *Draycar Ltd v Whelan* [1993] ELR 119, Lardner J had to deal with the application of the provisions relating to picketing in the Industrial Relations Act 1990 to a situation where a single company in the fashion wholesale business, with two boutiques, was re-organised corporately so as to become a number of companies, one of which carried on business in one of the boutiques and another of which carried on business in the other. After this re-organisation, a number of employees were made redundant by their new employer. The defendants picketed the premises of that company and the plaintiff sought an interlocutory injunction.

The defendants contended that the corporate re-organisation had not been matched by any change in practice in the real world. They argued that the two boutiques shared facilities, staff and stock — a claim denied by the plaintiff. The contended that the trade dispute was with their employer on the basis that the status of employer had not been disturbed by the corporate re-organisation.

Lardner J considered that the defendants had raised a fair *question* to be tried on this matter. If the defendants' employer was running the business of both boutiques and if the employees in the boutique that was picketed were under the same management as to the employees of the other boutique, the defendants would be entitled, under s. 11(1) of the Act, to picket the former boutique. If, however, the defendants were 'in truth and in fact' not employed by the same employer as the employees of that boutique, their entitlement to picket it would depend on whether they could establish, as s. 11(2) required, that their secondary picketing was inspired by a reasonable belief on their part that the employer they were picketing had directly assisted the employer who was a party to the trade dispute 'for the purpose of frustrating the strike or other industrial action. . . .'

Having regard to the evidence of a common trade name and letterheading and the considerable sharing between the business of staff, stock and the fact of payments from a single bank account, it seemed to Lardner J that there was a body of evidence from which the defendants might reasonably have come to that belief.

As to balance of convenience, the defendants' bargaining position would undoubtedly be weakened if an injunction was granted, on account of the fact that the plenary hearing would be unlikely to be heard for more than twelve months; in contrast, the plaintiff's allegation that its business would be irreparably damaged if picketing continued was unsupported by any facts on which the question could be said to be based. Lardner J accordingly refused to grant an interlocutory injunction.

TRADE UNION

In the Chapter on Equitable Remedies, above, 287-8, we examine *McEvoy v Prison Officers' Association*, High Court, 28 January 1993, where Carney J decided to grant an interlocutory injunction against interference with the plaintiff's exercise of his functions as President of the defendant association. The balance of convenience lay against imposing by court order on the association its leadership: the matter could be resolved democratically by an election for the presidency, for which the plaintiff was eligible to stand as a candidate.

PAYMENT OF WAGES

What can an employer do if an employee gives shorter notice than the contract provides? Dock the wages when paying the final cheque? No, said the Tribunal, in *Curust Hardware Ltd v Dalton* [1993] ELR 10. In that case, the employee gave two weeks' notice rather than the month that her contract provided. The Tribunal noted that the contract had no express condition authorising deduction from wages for failure to give notice. It added that '[s]ince, therefore, this provision is not expressed it cannot be implied.' With respect, this is a curious and unsustainable proposition. Perhaps the Tribunal meant no more than to say that, in the particular context and in the absence of an express provision, it considered it inappropriate to imply one.

The Tribunal went on to hold that the deduction contravened s. 5 of the Payment of Wages Act 1991: see the 1991 Review, 269. It found that the remedy for default on a term of a contract 'lies in contract law and such remedy would have its basis in compensation rather than penalty.' In the Minimum Notice and Terms of Employment Acts 1973 to 1991 there was no provision for a penalty to be imposed on either the employee or employer for failure to comply with the Act. There was, however, a provision for payment of compensation by an employer to an employee for any loss sustained by the employee as a result of the employer's failure to give notice.

WRONGFUL DISMISSAL

In *Hayden v Sean Quinn Properties Ltd* [1994] ELR 45, Barron J held that the plaintiff, the general manager of the respondent's hotel, had been wrongfully dismissed on a pretext but that nonetheless his claim should fail because it was founded on an illegal contract. The plaintiff had been entitled under the contract to £6,000 non-taxable allowance expenses, when both parties knew that there would be none. This provision was designed to give the plaintiff the same after-tax salary as he had received when working in the hotel business in England.

Barron J relied on the English decision of *Napier v National Business Agency Ltd* [1951] 2 All ER 264 where Sir Raymond Evershed had stigmatised agreements to defeat the proper claims of the Inland Revenue as being contrary to public policy. Notwithstanding 'the very great changes' that had occurred in Irish society since then, Barron J did not believe that public policy on this issue would have changed in any way. Accordingly he dismissed the claim.

There is now an anomaly between claims for *wrongful* dismissal, on the one hand, and, on the other, certain claims for *unfair* dismissal, which by virtue of s. 7 of the Unfair Dismissal (Amendment) Act 1993, will not be dismissed on the basis of their invocation of an illegal contract: see above, 369: see Éilis Barry, 'Illegal Contracts of Employment' (1994) 12 *ILT (ns)* 32, at 33.

FAIR PROCEDURES

In *Ó Scanaill v Minister for Agriculture and Food* [1993] ELR 176, Lynch
J, in proceedings for judicial review, held that the respondent had failed to
comply with fair procedures when he summoned the applicant, a veterinary
surgeon, to an interview at the Department, the purpose of which was to
determine whether ministerial permission to participate in the bovine tuber-
culosis eradication scheme should be revoked; the letters summoning him to
the Department had referred to certain incidents of alleged irregularities
involving the applicant, but they had not made it clear that, in the light of
these instances, the Minister was contemplating revoking permission under
s. 25 of the Diseases of Animals Act 1966.

Lynch J was satisfied that the applicant had not been made aware that his
authority to test, 'and therefore, to a significant extent, his likelihood', were
at stake when he went to the meeting. Lynch J could not see why he had not
been told in advance in plain language what the Minister was considering. It
was not possible to know what difference, if any, such a plain intimation
would have made but, in its absence, the applicant had been 'at a disadvantage
and the unannounced conversion of the interview into a hearing involved a
procedure which did not comply with legal requisites.' Accordingly the
application for judicial review was unsuccessful.

Land Law

Paul Coughlan, School of Law, Trinity College

ADVERSE POSSESSION

Acts necessary in order to give rise to adverse possession *Hickson v Boylan*, 25 February 1993, is yet another case which demonstrates that presence without permission on another person's land may not necessarily constitute adverse possession. The plaintiffs claimed to be entitled to 155 acres of bogland adjoining a farm known as 'Haggard Farm'. The defendants were the trustees under a 1906 deed of trust which provided for the distribution of bogland amongst the tenants of a particular estate who had bought out their landlord's interest under the Land Act 1903. The plaintiffs sued the defendants for trespass and the latter counterclaimed that they were entitled to the land.

The plaintiffs purchased Haggard Farm and 168 acres of bog from C in 1956. C had bought the farm from D in 1952 who in turn had acquired it from B in 1950. The contract of sale between the plaintiffs and C provided that the root of title to the bog was a statutory declaration made by B in 1952 at the request of C and which stated that a portion of the bog adjoining the farm had been given to a predecessor in title of his and that he had occupied that strip of bog without interference. It also stated that the boundaries of the strip were marked by a lockspit (*i.e.* a shallow trench dug into the surface of the bog). Carroll J held that the statutory declaration made by B showed that he did not claim to be entitled to the entire bog, but only the strip. At no stage did B expressly convey the strip to D, nor did he join in a confirmatory conveyance of it to C. However, while this meant that the legal title to the strip remained in B, this title was extinguished by the running of time. Furthermore, as B had made the statutory declaration for the convenience of C, he had to be taken as acquiescing in the vesting of the beneficial interest in the strip in C. In purporting to convey the entire bog, and not just the strip, to the plaintiffs in 1956 C did not supply a statutory declaration indicating that she had been in possession of the bog.

In support of their claim to the bog, the plaintiffs pointed to the fact that over the years they had paid rates and taxes in respect of the land. However, Carroll J pointed out that such activity could not confer title. Accordingly, Carroll J concluded that when they acquired the farm the only part of the bog which vested in them was the strip. Carroll J held that the trustees had a good paper title to the bog and so the question which arose was whether that title had been ousted in respect of all or part of the bog. Carroll J rejected the plaintiffs' claim that they had acquired a title to the bog through adverse possession because their actions in walking, shooting and raising pheasants on it did not constitute unequivocal acts of possession. Similarly, while D had cut turf from the bog, the decision of Black J in *Convey v Regan* [1952] IR 56 established that this was not an act of ownership. The plaintiffs never erected fencing or demarcated the boundary of the bog which they claimed. According to Carroll J, they would have had to do something as radical as that in order to claim a title to the land. The courts usually look for such actions by squatters where the land claimed cannot be occupied or utilised in a normal fashion. All of this left the plaintiffs with the strip and the defendants with the remainder of the bog. Carroll J felt that while it should be possible to identify the strip on the map, in default of agreement between the parties she could delineate the boundary.

The plaintiffs' also claimed that the defendants were estopped from asserting a title to the land. The plaintiffs pointed to the fact that in 1955 and 1961 they had advertised the bogland as being for sale in various national newspapers and that no one had come forward to dispute their right to do so. Carroll J held that regardless of the legal niceties of whether the plea of estoppel was being used as a shield or a sword, the acts relied upon by the plaintiffs did not give rise to an estoppel. Furthermore, it transpired that when the plaintiffs' predecessor in title advertised the land in 1955 the trustees wrote to her solicitor indicating that the land was vested in them.

Transferring land acquired through adverse possession   In *Creavin v Donnelly*, 25 June 1993, the plaintiffs purchased a bungalow in 1988. The land on which the bungalow was built was held under a sub-lease dated 14 December 1964 that was derived from a head lease dated 4 July 1949. The defendants, who were the trustees of the Kilmacud Crokes G.A.A. Club, held land under a sub-lease dated 27 January 1965 which was also derived from the 1949 head lease. A dispute arose as to the ownership of a strip of land which was occupied by the plaintiffs along with their bungalow. The plaintiffs claimed that they had a title to the strip by virtue of adverse possession. They claimed that because of an error in a map annexed to the head lease, on the grant of the subleases the lessee under the head lease retained possession of the strip and that such encroachment on to the strip as had been carried out by the plaintiffs' predecessors in title had constituted adverse possession against the lessee's title and not as against that of the defendants. However, Costello J accepted the defendants' submission that there was no error in the map. Accordingly, he concluded that the land which formed the subject-matter of the sublease dated 27 January 1965 made in favour of the trustees was contiguous to the site of the bungalow and therefore the disputed plot constituted an encroachment onto the land held by the trustees.

The defendants argued that while their right to possession of the strip had been extinguished by the Statute of Limitations, the plaintiffs had no right to it because the possessory rights obtained by their predecessors in title had not been conveyed to them. However, Costello J rejected this argument on the grounds that s. 6(1) of the Conveyancing Act 1881 made it unnecessary to mention those rights in the conveyance which transferred the bungalow to the plaintiffs. According to Costello J, s. 6 operated to convey all rights appertaining to the land or enjoyed with the land. This would seem to suggest that if a person conveys a particular piece of land, in the absence of an indication to the contrary the conveyance will, by virtue of s. 6(1), transfer his title to adjoining land which he has hitherto enjoyed along with the land which is being conveyed expressly. This is a startling proposition. The traditional view of s. 6 of the Conveyancing Act 1881 is that it is a word-saving provision which avoids the need to mention rights over the land of others, such as easements and profits a prendre, which hitherto have been enjoyed along with the land which is being conveyed. The law regards a squatter as having a title to the land which he possesses which is good against all the world except someone with a better title. This is a right of ownership in respect of the land and is not to be confused with a right which one has over the land of another. Accordingly it would not seem to fall within the class of rights which pass automatically by virtue of s. 6.

FAMILY HOME PROTECTION ACT 1976

The need for informed consent *Bank of Ireland v Smyth* [1993] 2 IR 102; [1993] ILRM 790 is undoubtedly one of the most important cases to have been decided under the Family Home Protection Act 1976. The first named defendant was the registered owner of a farm in County Tipperary which included the family home of himself and his wife, the second named defendant. By a deed of charge dated the 25 May 1978 the first defendant charged the house and land as security for all present and future liabilities owed to the plaintiffs. The second named defendant signed a consent form contained in the deed of charge which was stated to be for the purposes of the Family Home Protection Act 1976. The employee of the plaintiffs handling the transaction did not explain to the second named defendant that she would lose her home if payments were not made, nor did he suggest to the second named defendant that she should get independent advice before consenting to the creation of the charge. In signing the consent form the second named defendant believed that the charge did not affect the family home because the house had been built with the aid of a loan from another financial institution which was secured by means of a mortgage over the farm. On 19 June 1978 the charge was registered as a burden on the lands. The first named defendant defaulted in making repayments and the plaintiffs sought possession of the house and land pursuant to s. 62(7) of the Registration of Title Act 1964.

In a judgment delivered on 26 March 1993 (reported at [1993] 2 IR 102; [1993] ILRM 790) Geoghegan J held that the second named defendant had not given an appropriate consent to the charge for the purposes of the Family Home Protection Act 1976 and dismissed the plaintiffs' claim. Given the bank's awareness of the inherent likelihood of influence and reliance in the relationship of husband and wife, it had failed to take adequate steps to ensure that the wife fully understood the transaction and that the property could be sold if the loan secured by the charge was not repaid. In particular, it should have advised her to obtain independent advice before signing the consent. It is significant that Geoghegan J made no finding that the husband had in fact exerted any improper pressure or influence over the wife. On its own the mere failure of the bank to give the appropriate warning was fatal.

Geoghegan J placed considerable reliance on the decision of the English Court of Appeal in *Barclay's Bank plc v O'Brien* [1993] QB 109 which concerned the position where a wife is persuaded to use her property as security for her husband's debts. It was held that equity afforded special protection where the relationship between the debtor and surety was such that influence by the debtor over the surety, and reliance by the surety on the debtor, were natural features of the relationship. The surety's obligations could be avoided if the creditor was aware of the relationship between the surety and the debtor, the surety's consent was obtained without an adequate understanding of the nature and effect of the transaction, and the creditor failed to take reasonable steps to ensure that the surety had given a true and informed consent. The House of Lords subsequently rejected this expansive approach ([1994] 1 AC 180) and held that the fact that a wife did not fully understand a transaction does not invalidate it. However, where the husband induces his wife to act as surety through some form of legal wrong, such as duress, misrepresentation or undue influence, she has a right to have the transaction set aside unless the creditor can establish that he had no notice of the husband's wrongdoing. As the transaction was not to the financial advantage of the wife and there was a substantial risk that the husband had wrongfully procured his wife to act as surety, the creditor had to be regarded as having been put on inquiry as to the possibility of pressure. But by warning the wife of the risks and advising her to obtain independent advice, the creditor would be able to avoid being fixed with constructive notice of any claim to have the transaction set aside which she might subsequently assert. On the other hand, in *C.I.B.C. Mortgages plc v Pitt* [1994] 1 AC 200 monies advanced to a husband and wife were secured by a mortgage over their family home. The mortgagee was informed that the loan would be used to purchase a holiday home, but in fact the husband purchased shares with it. Although the husband had procured his wife's concurrence through the exercise of undue influence, it was held by the House of Lords that this did not affect the mortgagee as it had no notice. There was nothing to indicate that this was anything other than a normal advance to a husband and wife for their joint benefit. It followed that here there had been no need for the mortgagee to ensure that the wife was independently appraised of the nature and effect of the transaction.

The plaintiffs in *Bank of Ireland v Smyth* appealed to the Supreme Court and argued, inter alia, that if the second named defendant's consent to the creation of the charge was invalid, this did not affect the validity of the charge relating to that portion of the land which was not a family home and thus did not fall within the scope of s. 3 of the 1976 Act. In a judgment delivered on 15 November 1995 (reported at [1996] 1 ILRM 241), Blayney J (with whom Hamilton CJ and Egan J concurred) dismissed the appeal. No reference was made to the divergent approaches adopted by the Court of Appeal and House of Lords in *Barclay's Bank v O'Brien*. Instead, Blayney J turned to the policy behind the 1976 Act and the way in which the legislation sought to fulfill that policy. The validity of the charge was an essential proof in the assertion by the plaintiffs of a right to take possession of the land and the onus of establishing that the consent given by the first named defendant was sufficient for the purposes of the 1976 Act lay on the plaintiffs. A consent for the purposes of s. 3(1) of the 1976 Act must be a fully informed consent. In particular, the spouse giving the consent must know to what his or her consent pertains. Here Blayney J drew support from cases dealing with the sort of consent which must be forthcoming before a valid adoption (*G. v An Bord Uchtála* [1980] IR 32) or a valid marriage can take place (*N. v K.* [1985] IR 733).

As the second named defendant believed that the charge affected only the land and not the family home, it followed that her consent was not a fully informed one and was thus invalid. It was irrelevant whether the employee of the plaintiffs who handled the execution of the charge did not know what was in the second named defendant's mind as the validity of the consent depended solely on whether the second named defendant had full knowledge of what she was doing. Furthermore, by virtue of s. 3 of the Conveyancing Act 1882, the plaintiffs had constructive notice of the second named defendant's lack of knowledge. If the plaintiffs' employee had enquired as to the knowledge of the second named defendant, he would have discovered that she believed that it did not apply to the family home. Consequently, s. 3 of the 1882 Act deemed the plaintiffs' employee to have constructive notice of this as it would have been reasonable for him in the circumstances to make such an enquiry. There was no discussion as to whether the second named defendant's belief that the family home did not fall within the scope of the charge was objectively justifiable notwithstanding the fact that the consent form was headed 'Family Home Protection Act.' Blayney J was careful to point out that the plaintiffs did not owe a duty to the second named defendant to explain the charge fully to her or to suggest to her that she should get independent advice. The only reason why the plaintiffs should have taken such steps was to ensure that their own interests were protected and that the consent would not be open to challenge.

As to the plaintiffs' submission that the charge could be severed so that the portion of the land which did not constitute the family home remained as security for the debt notwithstanding the absence of the second named defendant's consent, Blayney J held that as this point had not been raised in the High Court it could not be argued on appeal. Nevertheless, Blayney J went on to consider the merits of the argument. The unreported decision of Johnson J in *Bank of Ireland v Slevin* (16 February 1989) suggested that if there was evidence indicating the line of demarcation as between the family home and the other property forming the subject matter of the conveyance, the court could effect a severance and treat the conveyance as void in relation the family home and valid as regards the remainder of the land. However, Blayney J preferred the view expressed by Costello J in the earlier case of *Hamilton v Hamilton* [1982] IR 466 that something which was executed as a single conveyance could be partially effective. If any aspect of a convey- ance was rendered void by s. 3(1) of the 1976 Act the entire transaction was avoided. In any event, there was no evidence in *Bank of Ireland v Smyth* as to what would constitute the boundaries of the family home and so severance could not be ordered even if the court had a jurisdiction to do so.

The first and most obvious question which comes to mind in the light of the Supreme Court's decision in *Bank of Ireland v Smyth* concerns how many other conveyances of family homes are now open to question because the purchaser did not take sufficient steps to ensure that a non-disposing spouse's consent was a fully informed one. In this sense the decision is reminiscent of that in *Somers v W* [1979] IR 94 where it was held that the enquiries fell short of the standard necessary to put the person acquiring the family home in the position of a purchaser in good faith so that a clear title could be obtained notwithstanding the absence of the non-disposing spouse's consent. The legal profession responded to this decision by adopting a more rigorous approach to the requirements of the 1976 Act. Nevertheless, there remained many properties where the chain of title consisted of a conveyance which now appeared to be of questionable validity. This problem does not arise where registered land has been transferred as the register is conclusive as to the registered owner's title (see *Guckian v Brennan* [1981] IR 478). In an effort to bring certainty to titles which consist of a conveyance which might be open to challenge because of the absence of a spouse's consent, s. 3(8) was inserted into the Family Home Protection Act 1976 by s. 54(1) of the Family Law Act 1995. This provides that a conveyance will not be deemed to be void by reason of s. 3(1) unless a court has declared it to be void or, subject to the rights of any other person concerned, the parties to the conveyance or their successors in title make a written statement that it is void before the expiration of six years from the date of the conveyance. It is further provided that proceedings to have a conveyance declared void by reason only of s. 3(1) cannot be instituted after the expiration of six years from the date of the conveyance. There is no requirement that the person who takes the land under the conveyance and in whose favour time runs should have provided any consideration for the disposition. The limitation period does not apply to proceedings instituted by a spouse who has been in actual occupation of the land concerned from immediately before the expiration of six years from the date of the conveyance until the institution of the proceedings. In practice, the only situations in which it is usual for a spouse to remain in occupation following a conveyance of the family home is where the property is mortgaged or a contract of sale has been agreed. If the family home is transferred outright to a third party and the spouse who did not consent to the conveyance leaves the property, he or she will have only six years within which to challenge the conveyance.

While s. 3(8) may limit the retrospective effects of *Bank of Ireland v Smyth*, it will provide little comfort for lending institutions seeking to enforce their rights under mortgages and charges where the spouse whose apparent consent is now being impugned has remained in the family home throughout the life of the security. As regards the future, it is evident that conveyancing practice will have to adapt so as to take on board the further refinements concerning the 1976 Act. There may be an understandable sense of frustration on the part of financial institutions that the courts have criticised their procedures for failing to measure up to standards which are not explicitly laid down in the Family Home Protection Act 1976. In recent years legislation in a variety of contexts has started to contain the requirement that a person cannot waive or abrogate rights existing in his favour unless he has obtained independent legal advice beforehand. The Landlord and Tenant (Amendment) Act 1994 lays down such a prequisite where one is contracting out of the right to a new tenancy of an office. More significantly in the present context, s. 7 of the abortive Matrimonial Home Bill 1993 allowed a spouse to forego the statutory right of joint ownership after having obtained inde-

pendent legal advice. Given *Bank of Ireland v Smyth*, it might have been in
the interests of all concerned if the Family Law Act 1995 had contained a
similar provision in respect of the giving of the consent under the Family
Home Protection Act 1976. Of course there is the inevitable argument that
this would increase conveyancing costs, but at the end of the day it would
promote certainty and serve to further the policy of the 1976 Act.

When does a house become a family home?   Where a property is being
purchased in the name of one spouse with the aid of a loan secured by a
mortgage, it is commonplace for the mortgagee to require the consent of the
non-owning spouse to the mortgage even though the married couple have
not yet taken possession of the property. Prior to its amendment by s. 54(1)(a)
of the Family Law Act 1995, s. 2(1) of the Family Home Protection Act 1976
provided that the term 'family home' meant:

> primarily, a dwelling in which a married couple ordinarily reside. The
> expression comprises, in addition, a dwelling in which a spouse whose
> protection is in issue ordinarily resides, or if that spouse has left the
> other spouse, ordinarily resided before so leaving.

In *National Irish Bank Ltd. v Graham* [1994] 1 ILRM 372 Costello J was
called upon to decide whether premises can constitute a family home within
the meaning of s. 2(1) at a point in time before a married couple begin to
reside there.

On 29 August 1989 the first, third and fifth named defendants purchased
a large estate of approximately 3,000 acres with the aid of a loan granted by
the plaintiff. The loan was secured by a deed of mortgage dated 9 August
1989 which had been executed by the first, second, third and fifth named
defendants, along with their solicitor who had purchased the property in trust
for them. At this time the first and second named defendants were married
to each other, the third and fourth named defendants were married to each
other and the fifth named defendant was unmarried. However, the latter got
married on 17 November 1990. None of the mortgagors obtained possession
of the land until after completion of the purchase and execution of the
mortgage. On 21 February 1991 the mortgagors, with the consent of the
plaintiff, transferred some of the land between themselves and executed three
further mortgages in favour of the plaintiff. The mortgagors defaulted in
repayment of the loan and the plaintiff sought an order of possession so that
it could exercise its power of sale under the first mortgage. An affidavit filed
on behalf of the plaintiff stated that the third and fourth named defendants
had been in possession of the land prior to 9 August 1989 and that the fourth
named defendant had given her prior consent to the mortgage. This statement

was subsequently corrected by means of later affidavits which averred that the third and fourth named defendants had not been in occupation before that date and that the fourth named defendant had not given any prior consent to the mortgage. The defendants claimed that the four mortgages were void under s. 3 of the 1976 Act.

In a judgment delivered on 8 November 1993 Costello J made an order of possession in favour of the plaintiff which excluded certain parts of the land which were already subject to contracts of sale which had been entered into with the plaintiff's consent. According to Costello J, a house becomes a family home within the meaning of s. 2 only when a married couple take up residence. There was no basis for interpreting the definition as including a dwelling in which a married woman intended to reside at the date of its purchase. At the time when the first mortgage was executed four of the mortgagors were spouses within the meaning of s. 3. However, as none of the mortgagors were in possession of the land when they executed this mortgage none of them could be regarded as having conveyed an interest in a family home by means of this deed. Thus there was no need for the prior consent in writing of any of their spouses and the mortgage was not void under s. 3. Furthermore, the equitable interest of a purchaser which arises prior to completion by virtue of a contract for the sale of land could not be regarded as having transformed any dwelling on the land into the family home of either the third or fifth named defendant so as to confer rights on their wives before the taking of possession.

The defendants appealed to the Supreme Court which dismissed their appeal on 4 May 1994 (reported at [1994] 2 ILRM 109). Finlay CJ (with whom Egan and Blayney JJ concurred) held that the use of the word 'primarily' in the first sentence of s. 2(1) meant that the definition of a family home as a dwelling in which a married couple ordinarily reside was in the first place the appropriate definition under the 1976 Act. The second sentence, which refers to a dwelling in which a spouse whose protection is in issue ordinarily resides, provided an additional or subsidiary definition. Both definitions were expressed in complete terms and so left no room for the addition of any other subsidiary definition by means of judicial interpretation.

Finlay CJ concluded his judgment by observing that in reality a joint conveyancing transaction had taken place whereby the land was conveyed to the purchasers who immediately executed a mortgage in favour of the bank which had advanced a substantial portion of the purchase money. By virtue of this transaction the purchasers acquired an equity of redemption. It would be inconsistent with both the purposes and the provisions of the 1976 Act if the consent of the wife to the mortgage which was part of this transaction was required. Finlay CJ was careful to point out that different considerations would apply where land was acquired under a conveyance and was then, within a short time, subsequently mortgaged so as to provide the purchase price which up to then had been supplied by means of a bridging loan. The substantive approach taken by Finlay CJ echoes that adopted by the House of Lords in *Abbey National Building Society v Cann* [1991] 1 AC 56. The purchaser acquires nothing more than an equity of redemption because from the outset the property is bound by the mortgage securing the loan without which it would not have been transferred in the first place. Insofar as it concentrates on what is perceived as the substance of the successive transactions rather than the legal form which they have to adopt, it may be explained as an attempt to protect mortgagees who have, by insisting on execution of the mortgage at the same time as the conveyance in favour of the mortgagor, done all in their power to prevent the creation of intervening rights or interests.

LANDLORD AND TENANT

Distinction between a lease and a licence   In *Governors of the National Maternity Hospital, Dublin v McGouran* [1994] 1 ILRM 521 Morris J was faced with the familiar dispute as to whether a transaction under which one person acquired a right to occupy and use the land of another gave rise to a lease or a licence. In May 1986 negotiations commenced between the secretary manager of the plaintiff hospital and the defendant with a view to the latter operating a shop within the hospital. During these discussions references were made to the 'lease' or 'tenancy' which the defendant would obtain and the consideration was described as 'rent.' Despite warnings from the hospital's solicitors as to the statutory rights which the creation of the relationship of landlord and tenant could generate, draft leases were prepared. In June 1986 the defendant and her husband signed a caretaker's agreement and started trading in the shop. In 1988 the defendant was granted a franchise in respect of a coffee shop within the hospital. Once again during negotiations reference was made to the proposed 'lease' and the 'rent' which would be payable. Notwithstanding further warnings from the hospital's solicitors as to possible statutory rights draft leases were prepared, but they were not signed. At the same time the shop was moved to another location within the hospital.

A new secretary manager who had been appointed by the hospital then sought to clarify the basis on which the defendant operated the shop and coffee shop. During a meeting at which the hospital's solicitor was present it was made clear to the defendant that the hospital was not prepared to grant her a lease in respect of the shops but only a licence. She was then presented with draft licence agreements. The defendant consulted her solicitor in relation to these agreements and they were executed by the parties on 9

August 1989. Both agreements were expressed to run for one year from dates in 1988. They defined the term 'licensee' as including 'successors and assigns,' and contained covenants prohibiting assignment and obliging the licensee to insure against public liability, effect repairs and pay the rates. Clause 2B provided that the licence was granted on a non-exclusive basis and that the licensee was entitled to use the premises in common with the licensor. Clause 3 provided that the agreement created only a licence, that the hospital retained possession subject to the rights granted by the agreement and that nothing in the agreement was intended to confer any tenancy on the licensee. Clause 6 gave the hospital the right at any time while the agreement was in force and on giving reasonable notice to substitute for the premises any other premises within the hospital which were reasonably equivalent. After these agreements came into operation the hospital required the defendant to provide a price list for customers of the coffee shop, fitted safety catches to the windows and added fans to the smoke extractor unit which had been fitted by the defendant. The defendant did not sign further licence agreements which were sent to her, but continued to run the shops while paying the increased amounts mentioned therein. On 3 March 1993 the hospital informed the defendant that the franchise was being put out to tender and she replied that she was a tenant. The hospital denied that this was the case and on 23 March 1993 required the defendant to remove her equipment and vacate the premises.

In a judgment delivered on 3 November 1993 Morris J made an order of possession in favour of the plaintiffs subject to a stay of six months so as to enable the defendant to remove her equipment. In identifying the nature of the agreement Morris J disregarded any representations made by the plaintiffs to the defendant as to her status when she entered the original caretaker's agreement in 1986 because that agreement related to a part of the hospital which did not constitute the location of the existing shop and coffee shop. Morris J concluded that the defendant was a licensee because clauses 2B and 3 of the agreements prevented her from having a right to exclusive possession. The inclusion of these terms constituted an acknowledgment by the defendant that the plaintiffs had the right to use the premises irrespective of whether they sought to exercise that right or not. The fact that the defendant was the sole key-holder of the shops was irrelevant. The plaintiffs' actions in requiring price lists and effecting improvements demonstrated that they continued to exercise dominion over the premises. Even if the plaintiffs had not exercised dominion this would not have detracted from their right to do so by virtue of clause 2B of the agreements. Furthermore, Morris J regarded the plaintiffs' right under clause 6 to switch the location of the shops to other premises within the hospital as a provision which could not be found in a lease.

Extension of time for serving notice claiming relief In *O'Callaghan v Ballincollig Holdings Ltd*, unreported, 31 March 1993, the plaintiffs failed to serve a notice of intention to claim relief within the time limit specified in s. 20 of the Landlord and Tenant Act 1980. Pursuant to s. 83 of the 1980 Act they sought an extension of the time within which they could serve the notice, but this was refused by the Circuit Court. They appealed to the High Court where Blayney J noted that the plaintiffs' failure to serve the notice within the time limit laid down by s. 20 was not due to a mistake on their part, but because they had instituted separate proceedings in which they claimed that they had acquired a title to the house by adverse possession (see the discussion under Proprietary Estoppel below). If these proceedings had been decided in favour of the plaintiffs it would have disposed of any need for relief under the 1980 Act. According to Blayney J, while the basic principle under s. 83 is that time should be extended when it is just to do so, the primary test to be applied in deciding what is just is whether injustice would be caused to the landlord. If the court was satisfied that injustice would not be caused, the time should be extended provided that one of the grounds for doing so set out in s. 83 could be established. It followed that if there was some reasonable cause for not serving the notice at the appropriate time, the court had to extend time unless injustice would be caused to the landlord. On the facts of this case, the existence of the separate proceedings in which the plaintiffs claimed a title based on adverse possession made it reasonable for them to refrain from serving a notice of intention to claim relief under the 1980 Act. After all, the assertion that one has a right to land by virtue of the extinguishment of the freeholder's title is inconsistent with a claim that one is entitled to relief under the 1980 Act as the tenant of that freeholder. The desire to avoid asserting two wholly inconsistent claims at the same time made it reasonable for the plaintiffs to delay serving the notice of intention to claim relief. Blayney J concluded that no injustice would be done to the defendant if time was extended and so the appeal was allowed and the plaintiffs were given one week from the date of the judgment to serve the notice.

Sporting leases The decision of Barr J in *Brittas Fly-Fishing Club Ltd v Aimsitheoir Deantoreacht Teo*, unreported, 30 March 1993, provides useful guidance as to the sort of rights which a sports club must enjoy in respect of land before it can qualify for a sporting lease pursuant to s. 2 of the Landlord and Tenant (Amendment) Act 1971. Here the applicant claimed a sporting lease in respect of the Brittas Reservoir which consists of two adjacent ponds. The original purpose of the reservoir was to supply water to certain paper mills in Dublin. However, the last of the mills closed in 1987 and was purchased by the respondent for development purposes. While the applicant company was formed by members of the Brittas Fly Fishing Club in 1990, the club itself had been founded in 1881. In 1936 an agreement was entered into between the then owner of the reservoir and the club which referred to the parties as 'the lessor' and 'the lessees' and went on to give the lessees, *inter alia*, the sole right to stock and fish the reservoirs for a term of 25 years in return for a yearly rent. On the determination of the 25-year term successive agreements were concluded which referred to the parties as 'the lessor' and 'the lessees'. However, in 1982 the agreements began to use the terms 'licensor' and 'licensees'. The respondent resisted the application for a sporting lease on the grounds that the land in question had not been held by the club for the purpose of carrying on a sport for a period of not less than 21 years as required by s. 2 of the 1971 Act.

Barr J accepted that the reservoir had been used by the club for in excess of 21 years. However, the key issue was whether the land was held under a lease or a licence, in which case the club would be entitled to a lease, or whether the rights of the club in respect of the reservoir and its curtilage were no more than an incorporeal hereditament. The respondent argued that the latter was the case and so no rights under the 1971 Act accrued to the applicant. Both parties accepted that apart from minor amendments and changes in terminology, the contractual relationship between the parties had not changed since the 1936 agreement. Barr J concluded that the terms of the agreement fell to be construed in the light of the realities prevailing at that time. It was clear that the reservoir had been constructed to provide water for the paper mills and that this had remained its primary purpose until the last of the mills closed in 1987. It followed that while it had been intended that the club should receive the right to fish and stock the reservoir for a fixed period of time, there had been no intention to confer an interest in land on the club. The terms of the 1936 agreement supported this finding in that they consistently referred to the 'rights and privileges hereby granted' and not to 'land' as one would expect to find in a lease or licence. Furthermore, while a right of access in favour of the lessor as regards the reservoir, dams, canals and sluices would have been essential while the reservoir was operational, no such provision appeared in the agreement. Barr J concluded that the absence of such a term was due to the recognition by the parties that it was not required given that the agreement demised only a right to fish and shoot game. Likewise, in 1986 the club had sought permission for the building of a car park. If an interest in land had been granted the club would have been entitled to exclusive possession, the lessor would not have been able to object to the building of the car park and it would have required an express clause entitling it to enter the property in order to effect maintenance.

Of course the absence of an express right of entry is not inconsistent with the existence of a licence to occupy land (see *Irish Shell & B.P. Ltd v John Costello Ltd* [1981] ILRM 66) and by virtue of s. 3(5) of the 1971 Act a sports club that holds land otherwise than under a lease is entitled to apply for a sporting lease. Nevertheless, the decisive factor here was that the applicant could not be regarded as having any right which entitled it hold land. An incorporeal hereditament which entitled a club to use land was insufficient. It was argued by the applicant that an incorporeal hereditament fell within the definition of 'land' and so s. 2 of the 1971 Act applied. However, Barr J pointed out that by virtue of s. 12(2) of the 1971 Act, it fell to be construed along with the Landlord and Tenant Acts 1931-1967 and none of these statutes contained a definition of land. In these circumstances the court had to fall back upon the definition of 'land' in the schedule to the Interpretation Act 1937 which provides that land includes 'messuages, tenements and hereditaments, houses and buildings, of any tenure'. Barr J regarded it as significant that this definition could be contrasted with that contained in s. 1 of the Landlord and Tenant Law Amendment Act, Ireland, 1860 (Deasy's Act) which includes incorporeal hereditaments within the definition of land. Barr J distinguished the decision of O'Keeffe P. in *Smiths (Harcourt Street) Ltd v Harwick Ltd* (unreported, 30 July 1971), where it was held that a fee simple estate in an incorporeal hereditament (here a right of way) could be acquired under the Landlord and Tenant (Ground Rents) Act 1967, on two grounds. First, it dealt with an incorporeal hereditament enjoyed as an adjunct to a lessee's right to occupy land. Secondly, O'Keeffe P. had not adverted to the difference between the definition of land given in Deasy's Act and that which applied to the Landlord and Tenant Acts 1931-1967 by virtue of the Interpretation Act 1937. In any event, according to Barr J the narrower definition of the term 'land' as used in the Landlord and Tenant Acts 1931-1971, coupled with the other provisions of the 1971 Act, and in particular s. 2(2) which referred to 'holding land', demonstrated that the Oireachtas did not intend that a club with a mere right to fish should be in a position to claim a sporting lease. If the Oireachtas had intended to do so the 1971 Act would have referred to land 'occupied or used' by the club.

MORTGAGES

Financing the acquisition of co-owned property The decision of the Supreme Court in *O'Keeffe v Russell* [1994] 1 ILRM 137 demonstrates the need to ensure that loans made to finance the acquisition of property are recoverable from all owners of that property and that the entire property constitutes the security for the debt. Here the plaintiff and her husband had been joint tenants of a farm in Cork. In 1978 they decided to sell this property and acquire a larger farm which would also be in their joint names. They entered into a contract of sale in respect of a farm in Limerick for £700,000 after the second named defendant, Allied Irish Banks plc, agreed to lend Mr O'Keeffe the requisite deposit. On 29 November 1978 the first named defendants, who were the couple's solicitors, wrote to the bank and informed it that the plaintiff and her husband were purchasing the Limerick farm in their joint names and that on completion the solicitors would hold the land certificate pertaining to that property in trust for the bank. They also undertook to lodge the net proceeds realised from the sale of the Cork farm to the credit of an account in the couple's joint names which would be opened by the bank. In a letter to the bank dated 4 April 1979 the solicitors indicated that the plaintiff and her husband were completing the purchase of the Limerick farm and issuing a cheque for the balance of the purchase price. They also confirmed that they would hold the title deeds on trust for the bank and lodge them as soon as completion occurred. The proceeds of sale of the Cork farm were not paid into a joint account but into one in Mr OKeeffe's sole name. No joint loan account was ever opened and, instead of lending the couple the balance of the monies necessary to finance the purchase, the bank made the loan to Mr O'Keeffe alone and opened a loan account in his sole name. The balance of the purchase price was paid to the vendor by bank draft and not by means of a cheque issued by the plaintiff and her husband as contemplated in the letter of 4 April. Mr O'Keeffe subsequently failed to make repayments in accordance with the loan contract and the debt owed to the bank grew considerably. The bank attempted to get the plaintiff to accept joint responsibility for the debt owed by her husband but she refused to do so. The plaintiff left her husband in April 1980 and instructed the solicitors not to lodge the land certificate with the bank. However, they maintained that they were bound by the undertaking of 29 November 1978 and accordingly lodged the certificate with the bank on 8 July 1980. The Limerick farm was sold in April 1982 and the bank applied most of the proceeds towards satisfaction of the debt owed by the plaintiff's husband.

In proceedings entitled *O'Keeffe v O'Flynn Exhams & Partners and Allied Irish Banks plc*, the plaintiff sued the solicitors for negligence and breach of contract and sought a declaration that the bank did not have an equitable charge over her share in the Limerick farm. In an unreported judgment delivered on 31 July 1992, Costello J held that the bank had not obtained a mortgage or charge over the plaintiff's share and ordered that it should pay to her the sum of £282,530.52, together with interest and costs, by way of her share of the proceeds of sale. He also held that the solicitors had not been negligent because they had instructed the bank to lodge the proceeds of sale in a joint account and informed it that the purchase was to be a joint one. The bank appealed and in the Supreme Court argued, *inter alia*, that it had a charge over the plaintiff's share through a right of subrogation to the lien which the vendor of the farm would have had if the purchase money had not been paid to him. In essence the bank argued that the only reason why the vendor was not asserting a lien was because money advanced by the bank to the plaintiff's husband had been used to pay the purchase price in respect of both the plaintiff's share and the share of her husband.

The Supreme Court unanimously dismissed the bank's appeal. Finlay CJ (with whom Blayney and Denham JJ concurred) held that the plaintiff had not been a party to any loan contract with the bank regarding the purchase of the Limerick farm. Accordingly, no equitable charge operated in respect of the plaintiff's half-interest. The letter of 29 November, even as confirmed by the letter of 4 April 1979, did not constitute an agreement by the plaintiff to create an equitable charge over her share as security for a loan advanced solely to her husband. Her proposal to charge the lands was clearly confined to a transaction in which a joint loan was granted and joint accounts were created in order to implement it. As to the subrogation argument, Finlay CJ concluded that it was not appropriate for the Supreme Court to consider this point because it had not been raised in the pleadings or in the grounds of appeal. As a matter of general principle a claim to a lien must be specifically and specially pleaded.

It would be have been instructive to hear the Supreme Court's views on this interesting submission. The argument undoubtedly has a certain superficial attractiveness given the respective merits of the parties. At the end of the day the plaintiff received a windfall in that she was left with the proceeds of a share in property which could not have been acquired without the loan made by the bank. But while it may be tempting to draw an analogy with what happens when trust monies come into the hands of a volunteer, or the presumed resulting trust which can arise where one person provides the purchase money for land which is put into the name of another, personal and proprietary rights should not be confused. There was no question of fraud in this case and what did occur was due to a lack of care on the part of the bank. Quite simply the bank advanced monies to the plaintiff's husband while taking inadequate security. The money became the property of the husband, while the bank was left with a chose in action against him. By purchasing the farm in joint names the husband made a gift of a half share in the property in favour of his wife. He owned the money which he used to acquire that half share and owed the bank a debt which was secured by a mortgage over the half share which vested in him. As the bank had no rights in respect of the money that the husband used to acquire the farm, there would appear to have been no basis on which the bank could have become subrogated to the lien which would have been enjoyed by the vendor of the farm if the purchase price had not been paid.

Possession proceedings in the case of registered land   Because mortgages of registered land operate by way of charge, the mortgagee does not have an immediate right to take possession of the land by virtue of the security. Instead, he must apply to the court for an order for possession under s. 62(7) of the Registration of Title Act 1964 which provides:

> When repayment of the principal money secured by the instrument of charge has become due, the registered owner of the charge or his personal representative may apply to the court in a summary manner for possession of the land or any part of the land, and on the application the court may, if it thinks so proper, order possession of the land or the said part thereof to be delivered to the applicant, and the applicant, upon obtaining possession of the land or the said part thereof, shall be deemed to be a mortgagee in possession.

In *Bank of Ireland v Smyth* [1993] 2 IR 102; [1993] ILRM 790 Geoghegan J rejected the notion that this provision confers a wide discretion on the court which enables it to refuse an application for possession on the grounds of sympathy. According to Geoghegan J, the words 'may, if it so thinks proper' simply mean that the court should apply equitable principles in considering the application for possession and thus ensure that the application is made bona fide with a view to realising the security.

Mortgagee as *bona fide* purchaser for value of a legal estate without notice   In *Hibernian Life Association Ltd v Gibbs*, unreported, 23 July 1993, the leasehold estate in a house arising under a 300-year lease dated 5 April 1962 was assigned to Mr Gibbs on 7 March 1973. On 1 December 1982 Mr Gibbs executed a mortgage by sub-demise in favour of the plaintiff as security for a loan of £25,000. Mrs Gibbs gave her consent to the mortgage as required by s. 3 of the Family Home Protection Act 1976 and executed a joint statutory declaration with her husband which stated that he was the owner of the leasehold estate. The mortgage was expressed to be subject to a prior mortgage in favour of the Educational Building Society. Mr Gibbs defaulted in repaying the loan owed to the plaintiff and it instituted proceedings against him which resulted in the making of a well charging order on 18 April 1988. Bank of Ireland also instituted proceedings against Mr and Mrs Gibbs in respect of monies which they owed to it and registered a judgment mortgage against the property. An order for sale was made on foot of the judgment mortgage and the plaintiff asserted its rights over the property in the course of those proceedings. On 18 January 1989 Mrs Gibbs instituted proceedings under the Married Women's Status Act 1957 in which she claimed a beneficial interest in the house. The plaintiff was not a party to these proceedings. By virtue of an order dated 18 January 1989, McKenzie J declared that Mrs Gibbs was entitled to the entire beneficial interest in the leasehold estate. In the light of this decision, Mr Gibbs applied to have the well charging order of 18 April 1988 discharged.

Costello J held that the declaration that Mrs Gibbs was beneficially entitled to the entire leasehold estate did not affect the validity of the mortgage created by Mr Gibbs in favour of the plaintiff on 1 December 1982. It followed that the charging order granted on 18 April 1988 was valid and the plaintiff could proceed to seek a sale of the property in order to recover the monies owed to it. The plaintiff was a purchaser for value without actual or constructive notice of Mrs Gibbs' interest in the land. There was nothing in the circumstances surrounding the transaction which would cause a prudent purchaser to enquire whether Mrs Gibbs had an equitable interest in the land. Indeed, the manner in which Mr and Mrs Gibbs dealt with the transaction indicated that Mr Gibbs claimed to own the land beneficially and that Mrs Gibbs accepted that this was the case. Accordingly, the plaintiff was entitled to have the debt owed to it discharged out of the proceeds of sale in priority to Mrs Gibbs' interest. Given this finding, it was unnecessary for Costello J to express any view in relation to the argument that given her consent to the mortgage and the contents of her statutory declaration, Mrs Gibbs was estopped from asserting her equitable interest in priority to the rights of the plaintiff (see *Doherty v Doherty* [1991] 2 IR 458).

PROPRIETARY ESTOPPEL

Improvement of land while under mistaken belief as to rights insufficient The decision of Blayney J in *O'Callaghan v Ballincollig Holdings Ltd*, unreported, 31 March 1993, demonstrates that a person who effects improvements to the land of another under the misapprehension that he has or will acquire a title to that land cannot acquire rights through the doctrine of proprietary estoppel unless the landowner was in a position to prevent the carrying out of those improvements. The plaintiffs became the tenants of a house in 1959. The defendant became the owner of the reversion in 1974. In the 1970s' the plaintiffs ceased paying rent and claimed that they had acquired a title to the house through adverse possession. As a result the defendant served a notice to quit upon them. The Circuit Court rejected the plaintiffs' claim to a title and granted an order for possession to the defendant. The plaintiffs then claimed that by virtue of the doctrine of proprietary estoppel they had a lien over the house in respect of monies which they had spent in reinstating and repairing the house after fires in 1981 and 1983. They argued that the doctrine applied here because the defendant had stood by while they had spent money on the house. However, Blayney J held that the inaction on the part of the defendant could not give rise to an equity in favour of the plaintiffs. At the time when the plaintiffs spent money on the house they were tenants of the property and enjoyed an exclusive right to possession as against the defendant who was their lessor. Because the plaintiffs were entitled to possession at the relevant times the defendant could do nothing to stop them spending money on the house and so its inaction could not give rise to rights against it. This would seem to suggest that Blayney J regarded a failure to assert title against the improver, as opposed to a failure to disabuse the improver as to the true legal position, as being an essential element. Blayney J went on to find that the plaintiffs knew that they held the house as the tenants of the defendant and that when their tenancy came to an end the defendant as landlord would be entitled to recover possession of the house with the benefit of all improvements. Blayney J accepted that when the plaintiffs stopped paying rent they might have been under the misapprehension that they had become the owners of the house, or that they would become the owners. This misapprehension might have been a factor which led them to spend their own money on reinstating the house. Nevertheless, the defendant had not been responsible for this misapprehension and so the plaintiffs could not be regarded as having acquired any rights over the house by reason of their expenditure.

RESTRICTIVE COVENANTS

Construction of restrictive covenants   In *St. Luke and St. Anne's Hospital Board v Mahon*, unreported, 18 June 1993, Murphy J was called upon to construe the following covenant which was contained in a deed of conveyance dated 12 March 1889:

> The Scottish Provident Institution hereby covenant for themselves their successors and assigns with the said Charles Elliot Tisdall his heirs and assigns that their successors and assigns will not permit or suffer any building to be erected on the ground adjoining the premises hereby conveyed on the western side thereof save a good substantial and well built dwellinghouse of the same character and class as the buildings now erected on the premises known as Sunbury Gardens and that such dwellinghouse shall not project beyond the line of the dwellinghouse hereby conveyed in the front and will not permit or suffer the ornamental ground in front of the said premises or of the other premises known as

Sunbury Gardens or any part thereof to be built upon or used for any
purpose other than in accordance with such scheme or plan as the said
Scottish Provident Institution shall hereafter settle. . . .

The applicants were the successors in title of the Scottish Provident
Institution and the respondents were the successors in title of Charles Elliot
Tisdall who had been the purchaser of 7 Sunbury Gardens, the property
conveyed by the deed dated 12 March 1889. It was accepted by the parties
that the covenant was negative in nature and bound the applicants, as the
successors in title of the Scottish Provident Institution, and was for the benefit
of the respondents, as the successors in title of Charles Elliot Tisdall. The
applicants planned to build 41 houses on an area of land measuring between
three and four acres which was to the west of 7 Sunbury Gardens. The
respondents objected to this and pointed out that it would involve the erection
of 12 houses to the acre while the original development of Sunbury Gardens
in the 1880s or earlier had involved on average the development of one house
per quarter of an acre. While conceding that they were bound by the
restrictive covenant, the applicants argued that the words 'on the ground
adjoining the premises hereby conveyed' should be read so that the operation
of the covenant was confined to an area having approximately the same
dimensions as 7 Sunbury Gardens with the result that the covenant would
have no effect in relation to any other land belonging to them, regardless of
whether it was to the west of Sunbury Gardens or otherwise. It was also
accepted by the applicants that the covenant should be construed *contra
proferentem* and thus any ambiguities would have to be read against them as
the successors in title of the Scottish Provident Institution which had conceded the restriction. The respondents argued that the words were appropriate
to describe all of the land to the west of Sunbury Gardens which was owned
or held by the applicants and originally by the Scottish Provident Institution
under the same title as 7 Sunbury Gardens.

Murphy J rejected the assertion by the applicants that the covenant should
not be given a wide construction as to do so would sterilise their land. He
observed (at p. 5 of the transcript):

I would hesitate to accept that argument as it seems to me that it depends
upon applying current commercial values to the nineteenth century.
What would be regarded today as the obvious facts of property development might have been, and I believe were, very different even fifty
years ago, perhaps more so a hundred years ago. The potential for
developing land and the value of land for development purposes was
certainly very different up to the early 1950s than the manner in which
such a problem would be approached today.

Having said this, Murphy J concluded that the covenant had to be read as bearing the limited operation contended for by the applicants. In his view the most decisive factor was the provision that any building which might be erected 'shall not project beyond the line of the dwellinghouse hereby conveyed in the front.' This demonstrated that the covenant could only apply to a house which was erected close to 7 Sunbury Gardens. It was designed to ensure consistency of style and character and the need for such consistency would make no sense if it applied to an area of approximately 3.5 acres on which only one house could be erected. If the original parties to the covenant had intended that only one house should be placed on the retained land one would have expected to find the phrase 'one good and substantial dwelling house only' being used.

RIGHTS OF RESIDENCE

Legal nature of rights of residence   S. 81 of the Registration of Title Act 1964 provides:

> A right of residence in or on registered land, whether a general right of residence on the land or an exclusive right of residence in or on part of the land, shall be deemed to be personal to the person beneficially entitled thereto and to be a right in the nature of a lien for money's worth in or over the land and shall not operate to create any equitable estate in the land.

While it would appear that this provision denies rights of residence the status of estates in land in order to prevent persons entitled thereto from being able to exercise the powers of a tenant for life under the Settled Land Acts 1882-90, the courts have given little practical guidance on the consequences of such a right being in the nature of a lien for money's worth. In *Bank of Ireland v Smyth* [1993] 2 IR 102; [1993] ILRM 790 the issue was to a large extent moot. Here it was argued that possession proceedings brought by a mortgagee were defective because they had not been served on the mortgagor's mother who had a right of residence in respect of the mortgaged premises. O. 9, r. 9 of the Rules of the Superior Courts 1986 provides that in actions for the recovery of land other than for non- payment of rent or overholding, it is necessary for the summons to be served on every person in actual possession, or in receipt of the rents and profits, of the lands or any part thereof unless the court directs otherwise. Geoghegan J held that by virtue of s. 81 the right enjoyed by the mortgagor's mother constituted a lien for money's worth. The entitlement to that right or a right of support did not make her a person in possession or in receipt of the rents and profits of the land within the meaning of O. 9, r. 9. In fact the mother had died by the time of the court hearing and Geoghegan J took the view that even if the special summons should have been served on her, because she was dead he could now dispense with any requirement that she should be served. It is interesting to note that Geoghegan J expressly left open the question as to whether the mother, if she was still alive, could have been required to vacate the premises in favour of the mortgagee. If her right had been registered as a burden against the land under s. 69(1)(q) of the 1964 Act it would have been binding on any person who acquired rights in the land. However, the consequences which would flow from such a right being binding are another matter which were explored in more detail by Lavan J in *Johnston v Horace* [1993] ILRM 594.

Here the plaintiff's father, who died in 1956, left his entire estate to B, the plaintiff's sister, subject to rights of residence in respect of the family home in favour of the plaintiff, her disabled brother and her daughter. The plaintiff's right of residence was registered as a burden on the folio pertaining to the house under s. 69(1)(q). B died subsequently and the house vested absolutely in her son, the defendant, subject to the rights of residence. Following the death of the plaintiff's brother, relations between the parties deteriorated and the defendant deliberately embarked upon a course of conduct which made life in the house intolerable. In particular, he attempted to confine the plaintiff to the use of one bedroom. Eventually the plaintiff was forced to leave and initiate legal proceedings with a view to obtaining an injunction restraining the defendant from interfering with her right of residence.

Lavan J held that the plaintiff enjoyed a right to share with others the use and occupation of the premises and, although no exclusive rights had been conferred, she had the personal use of one bedroom in the three bedroomed house. It was thus reasonable to say that her proportionate interest in the use and occupation of the premises was one third. But as she had not contributed towards the improvement of the premises, Lavan J felt that the value of the right should be determined on the assumption that the premises had not been improved. One possible approach to valuation was to look at the rental value of similar premises. Here one would have to ascertain what would represent a third of the rental value of the house in its unimproved condition or of a similar property of similar character in a similar area. An alternative but less precise method of valuation would be to determine a sum which one would reasonably expect a residing relative to contribute to a household in respect of the right to reside, but excluding contributions in respect of household expenses. However, Lavan J warned against valuing the right in terms of the cost of acquiring alternative accommodation, because this leaned away from valuing the right of residence and towards determining compensation for its loss. Irrespective of the method of valuation actually adopted, Lavan J felt that given the limited nature and extent of the right, care should be taken to avoid reaching an unrealistically high valuation. After all, the intention of the Oireachtas in enacting s. 81 was to avoid the holder of a right of residence having a tenant for life's power of sale. It was thus implicit in s. 81 that any valuation should be such that it did not unduly force a sale of the property so as to destroy other interests therein.

Evidence of rental values was adduced so as to show how much it would cost to provide the plaintiff with a similar form of accommodation. On the basis of a figure of £25 per week, Lavan J accepted a capital sum of £13,875 as representing the plaintiff's future loss if she was not restored to her right of residence. However, it did not automatically follow that the plaintiff should be awarded such an amount instead of an injunction as had been argued by the defendant. Like Geoghegan J in *Bank of Ireland v Smyth*, Lavan J was of the opinion that by virtue of s. 81 the plaintiff had a lien for money's worth in or over the land. But the general understanding of a lien is that it is security for a liquidated amount and here, as is usually the case, the will did not stipulate a financial equivalent for the right of residence. A liberal process of construction could support the view that the holder of a right of residence has a lien on the property for such capital sum as may be determined by the court to be the value of the right of residence. However, Lavan J rejected this method of valuation except where the land which was subject to the right was being sold. Instead, as the right was of an 'ongoing nature', he concluded that it should be measured by reference to some reasonable periodic amount depending on the circumstances of the parties. The period could be monthly, quarterly or yearly. Lavan J observed ([1993] ILRM 594, 600):

> In so far as the court has to arrive at a valuation, that valuation should be measured as a periodic sum. The periodic sum should not be capitalised. It is only in circumstances where such periodic sums are not being paid or that the property is being disposed of that the lien becomes a lien secured or enforceable by way of additional security in the form of a capitalised sum if necessary. To capitalise the money's worth of the right is akin to giving the beneficiary the equivalent of the statutory rights of a tenant for life. To capitalise assumes the ability of the owner of the property to pay or raise a capital sum or in the alternative becomes punitive on the owner in that the cost of sale of the premises has to be borne and the additional cost of repurchasing another property at some later date.

This might read a little too much into s. 81. For a start, prior to its enactment, the possibility of powers under the Settled Land Acts 1882-90 being exercised in this context only arose where there was an exclusive right of residence. These powers could only facilitate a disposition of that part of the holding which was subject to the right of residence and thereby settled land. This was not a problem with a general right of residence because, despite the uncertainty as to its exact nature, it did not give rise to a life estate. Furthermore, it is questionable whether recognising the holder of a right of residence as having the right to insist upon capitalisation is tantamount to conferring the powers of a tenant for life. Whilst the exercise of these powers is totally at the discretion of the tenant for life, the holder of the right of residence could hardly insist on the sale of the premises if the owner was able and willing to pay him its financial equivalent.

One questionable facet of Lavan's J's approach is the fact that in the absence of specific statutory provisions such as those pertaining to maintenance for spouses and children, courts do not have the power to award periodic sums. Even if the court regards a periodic sum as the correct measure of compensation, at most all it can do is award a capital sum which, if invested, would produce a return equal to the appropriate periodic payment. Having said this, the approach advanced by Lavan J could be implemented if the court merely identified a periodic sum which should be paid and, without ordering payment, indicated that if the owner chose not to pay this sum the holder of the right of residence would be at liberty to re-apply to the court for a determination of its capital value and a declaration that this debt was well charged on the property. In any event the issue of valuation did not arise as Lavan J held that the plaintiff was entitled to damages of £7,500 and an injunction restraining future interference with her rights.

SUCCESSION

Property falling within scope of application under s. 117   In *Reidy v McGreevy*, unreported, 19 March 1993, the deceased left his entire estate to his widow. At the time of his death he was the donee of a special power of appointment in relation to certain land. The objects of the power were his six children and in default of appointment the land was to vest in all of the children as tenants in common. The plaintiff was a son of the deceased who claimed that he had worked on the deceased's land as a result of promises by his father that if he did so the special power of appointment would be exercised in his favour. In fact the power was exercised in favour of the plaintiff's three sisters. The plaintiff instituted proceedings under s. 117 of the Succession Act 1965 claiming that the court could make provision for him out of the land which was subject to the special power of appointment.

By virtue of s. 117(3) no order could be made affecting the testamentary gift in favour of the plaintiff's mother. He argued that the land formed part of the deceased's estate because the only objects were the deceased's children. Barron J rejected this contention because the estate which can be made liable to a claim under s. 117 is defined in s. 109(2) and property subject to a special power of appointment clearly fell outside the scope of this provision which refers to:

> ... all estate to which he was beneficially entitled for an estate or interest not ceasing on death and remaining after payment of all expenses, debts, liabilities (other than estate duty) properly payable thereout.

Law Reform

In 1993, the Law Reform Commission published two Consultation Papers on sentencing and on occupiers' liability. We briefly examine the *Consultation Paper on Sentencing* in the Criminal Law Chapter, above, 257-40. The *Consultation Paper on Occupiers' Liability* was in turn followed by the Commission's final Report on the subject, published in 1994. This ultimately resulted in the Occupiers' Liability Act 1995, which departed from the Commission's approach and made concessions to lobbyists that are hard to justify. The 1995 legislation is analysed by Dr Eamon Hall (1995) 89 Law Society of Ir Gazette 189, O'Doherty, Annotation, *ICLSA*, Walsh, *Agriculture and the Law*, chapter 12 (1996) and Binchy, 'The Occupiers' Liability Act 1995', Law Society Continuing Legal Education lecture, 13 March 1996.

Legislation in 1993 gave substantial effect to some earlier recommendations of the Law Reform Commission in relation to criminal law. Ss. 2 to 4 of the Criminal Law (Sexual Offences) Act 1993 reflect the proposals of the Commission in respect of homosexual offences against children contained in its *Report on Child Sexual Abuse* (LRC 32-1990). S. 5 of the Act substantially implements a number of recommendations of the Commission in its *Report on Sexual Offences against the Mentally Handicapped* (LRC 11-1985). For consideration of the Act, see the Criminal Law Chapter, above, 264-70.

The Criminal Justice Act 1993, considered in the Criminal Law Chapter, gives effect to recommendations as to compensation of victims made by the Law Reform Commission, as a recurring theme, in its *Report on Receiving Stolen Property* (LRC 23-1987), *Report on Rape and Allied Offences* (LRC 24-1988) and *Report on Malicious Damage* (LRC 26-1988).

Licensing

INTOXICATING LIQUOR

Beer production and warehousing The Beer Regulations 1993 (SI No.285), which came into effect on 2 October 1993, govern the brewing, production, importation and warehousing of beer for the purposes of securing and collecting the excise duty payable on beer. The Regulations were made under the Finance Act 1992. On the power of entry to beer warehouses given to the Revenue Commissioners by the 1992 Act, see the 1992 Review, 506-7.

Clubs: prosecution In *Director of Public Prosecutions (Barron) v Wexford Farmers' Club* [1994] 2 ILRM 295; [1994] 1 IR 546, O'Hanlon J held that a criminal prosecution for breach of the Intoxicating Liquor Act 1988 could be brought against an unincorporated body, in this case the Wexford Farmers' Club: see the discussion in the Criminal Law chapter, 222, above.

Immediate vicinity The issue as to whether it can be established that a premises is in the 'immediate vicinity' of an existing licence within the meaning of s. 14 of the Intoxicating Liquor Act 1960 arose in *Perfect Pies Ltd v Doran* [1993] ILRM 737. In holding that the premises under consideration in the instant case fell within s. 14, Lynch J applied the principles laid down by Butler J in *In re Irish Cinemas Ltd* (1967) 106 ILTR 17. For previous cases on this topic, see the 1987 Review, 240 and the 1992 Review, 428-9.

Theatre and place of public entertainment The issue as to what constitutes a theatre or place of public entertainment arose in *Point Exhibition Co. Ltd v Revenue Commissioners* [1993] ILRM 621; [1993] 2 IR 551.

The applicant had applied to the Revenue Commissioners for a retail liquor licence under s. 7 of the Excise Act 1835, in respect of the well-known premises *The Point*, Dublin. S. 7 of the 1835 Act provides, in somewhat quaint terms, that the Commissioners may grant a retail liquor licence to 'any theatre or other place of public entertainment licensed by the Lord Chamberlain or by Justices of the Peace'. The applicant argued that since *The Point* was a place of entertainment in respect of which there had been granted a licence under s. 51 of the Public Health Acts Amendment Act 1890 to use *The Point* for public music, singing or other public entertainment and a licence for public dancing under the Public Dance Halls Act 1935, it fell within the description 'other place of public entertainment licensed by Justices of the Peace' in s. 7 of the 1835 Act.

The respondents were concerned as to their legal entitlement to grant the licence and had informed the applicant that the matter was still under consideration. The applicant sought *mandamus* directing the granting of the licence or, in the alternative, a declaration that it was entitled to the licence. Geoghegan J granted the declaration sought.

While he appreciated that the issue presented was one of difficulty, he nonetheless considered that the applicant was entitled to a decision one way or the other within a reasonable time and as the respondents had not made such decision within any time span which could be regarded as reasonable, the applicant was entitled to treat the delay as a refusal and to seek judicial review.

As to whether it was entitled as a matter of law to the licence sought, the most difficult issue which arose in this context was whether s. 7 of the 1835 Act had been impliedly repealed by s. 72 of the Licensing Act 1872. The 1872 Act provided that a liquor licence could not, in general, be issued to premises which did not possess an excise licence. An exception to this was a 'theatre'. The High Court decision *R. v Commissioners of Inland Revenue* (1888) 21 QBD 569 was to the effect that, since the 1872 Act had specifically exempted 'theatres', the previous exemption in s. 7 of the 1835 Act for 'any theatre or other place of public entertainment' had been impliedly repealed. Geoghegan J did not find this reasoning particularly persuasive, but in any event he noted that, in argument in that case, the then Solicitor General had accepted that s. 77 of the 1872 Act had the effect of keeping the 1835 Act in force in Ireland. And Geoghegan J noted that this view was reinforced by the references to s. 7 of the 1835 Act in s. 7 of the Licensing (Ireland) Act 1874 and in the definition of 'theatre' in the Intoxicating Liquor Act 1927. On this basis, he concluded that s. 7 of the 1835 Act continued in being.

The second issue was whether *The Point* was a place of public entertainment. Geoghegan J concluded that, having regard to the range of diverse entertainments carried on there as well as in the context of what could have been contemplated in the phrase 'other place of entertainment' in 1835, *The Point* was clearly within the definition.

The third issue was whether *The Point* was licensed as a place of public entertainment by the District Court as successors to the Justices of the Peace. He concluded that the ambiguous expression 'licensed . . . by Justices of the Peace' in s. 7 of the 1835 Act had to be construed as meaning a licence under any enactment whether before or after the 1835 Act. In this respect, he held that a licence under s. 51 of the Public Health Acts Amendment Act 1890 in respect of a place of public entertainment within the meaning of s. 7 of the 1835 Act constitutes a licensing by the District Court within the meaning of

s. 7 of the 1835 Act and thus the applicant was entitled to succeed.

Like many other cases on the licensing code considered in previous Reviews, the *Point* case surely illustrates the pressing need for a modern codification of the intoxicating liquor legislation.

Limitation of Actions

COUNTERCLAIM

S. 6 of the Statute of Limitations 1957 provides that, for the purposes of the Act, any claim by way of set-off or counterclaim is deemed to be a separate action and to have been commenced on the same date as the action in which the set-off or counterclaim is pleaded. O. 21, r. 10 of the Rules of the Superior Courts 1986 permits a defendant by his or her defence to set up a counterclaim raising questions as between the defendant and the plaintiff along with other persons. O. 21, r. 11 provides that those other persons, if not already parties to the action, are to be summoned to appear by being served with a copy of the defence. They must then appear thereto as if they had been served with a summons to appear in an action (r. 12) and may deliver a reply within the time within which they might deliver a defence if it were a statement of claim (r. 13).

In *Strick v Treacy, Ireland and the Attorney General*, High Court, 10 June 1993, the first defendant, in proceedings against her initiated in January 1989, resulting from an accident in 1988, issued a counterclaim in December 1992, joining the Minister for Finance as a party to the proceedings for the first time. The Minister for Finance contended that the first defendant's claim was statute-barred as the alleged cause of action had arisen more than three years before the delivery of the counterclaim.

O'Hanlon J accepted that it might seem inequitable that a claim against a party who was not a party to the original proceedings, and perhaps knew nothing about them, should, if it was interceded by way of counterclaim, be regarded as having been commenced on the same date as the action in which the counterclaim was pleaded. In the absence of any authority to the contrary, however, he felt bound to give the words of the statute their plain meaning and to hold that the counterclaim was not statute-barred.

ESTOPPEL

In *Curran v Carolan & Boyle Ltd*, High Court, 26 February 1993, Johnson J was required to determine whether proceedings for negligence, issued admittedly eleven weeks after the three-year limitation period had expired, could nonetheless be maintained on the basis of estoppel. The plaintiff, a painter employed by the defendant, had fallen off a ladder. He instructed a solicitor nearly two years later. The solicitor had been in contact almost immediately with the defendant and its insurer. During the next several months correspondence had taken place. The defendant had resisted nominating a solicitor and sought to obtain from the plaintiff details of the alleged negligence rather than to have them presented by way of statement of claim. The plaintiff's solicitor responded that the proceedings had been drafted and that he was intending to serve them on the defendant's insurers; he refrained from doing so as they said that they were continuing to investigate the matter. At their request, and to facilitate them, he sent them a plain copy of the summons and statement of claim, stating that he was not prepared to defer the issuing of these proceedings any further as they would be likely to become statute-barred.

The insurers failed to respond. A further threat by the plaintiff's solicitor to issue proceedings on account of the time limit involved was met by a request not to issue proceedings as the insurers were still attempting to clarify matters to their own satisfaction. The plaintiff's solicitor later wrote a letter to the insurers indicating that, unless he had a reply within fourteen days, proceedings would issue. Two further attempts by telephone to reach the key person involved with the case in the insurers' office met with failure. The limitation period expired more than four months after the final letter from the plaintiff's solicitor.

Johnson J held that the defendant was estopped from pleading the statute. The defendant's insurers' two requests to the plaintiff's solicitor not to issue proceedings, in conjunction with the fact that he had expressed his concern about the statute at an early stage, had supplied them with plain copies of the proceedings and had sought thereafter to contact them to continue negotiations, led Johnson J to conclude that these requests had had a material effect on the plaintiff's solicitor and amounted to conduct that would legitimately lead him to conclude that the statute would not be pleaded against his client. This took the case 'outside the uncompromising judgment' of Henchy J in *Doran v Thompson* [1978] IR 223.

PERSONAL INJURIES

In the 1991 Review, 299-302, we examined the Statute of Limitations (Amendment) Act 1991, which modifies the stark approach of the 1957 legislation, whereby a plaintiff might lose the right to take an action before he or she could reasonably have become aware that such a right existed. Under the 1991 Act, in personal injuries (and fatal accidents) litigation, the clock starts to tick against the injured person (or personal representative or dependent) only where he or she might reasonably have acquired knowledge of the injury, of the fact that it was significant, of the fact that it was attributable to the act or omission alleged to constitute the wrong and of the identity of the defendant. The Act is retrospective in its operation. It contains detailed provisions dealing with the role of expert advice and the extent to which the plaintiff's case should be affected by the quality or timing of that advice.

In *Boylan v Motor Distributors Ltd and Daimler Benz A.G.*, High Court, 9 June 1993, Lynch J gave a clear judgment relating to several provisions of the 1991 Act, which will be considerable help to the legal profession. The plaintiff was injured on 6 May 1986 when unloading goods from a van which had been driven by a customer to her family firm to have chrome plating added to it. It was not entirely clear how the accident occurred: the plaintiff's finger got caught as she was closing the door, resulting in the amputation of the top joining.

The plaintiff consulted her solicitor later that month. High Court proceedings for negligence and breach of statutory duty were issued in January 1987 against the customer, with the statement of claim following a month later. The plaintiff was not in a position to provide her solicitor with a financial retainer. The customer's response to the proceedings was a full defence, which gave no prospect of a settlement.

During a consultation with senior counsel in December 1987, the senior counsel advised that the van should be inspected by an engineer, from whom a report should be obtained. It proved difficult for the plaintiff's solicitor to establish the identity of the van and to obtain permission for its examination. An engineering firm was recruited in May 1988 and after some further delays and reminders an inspection was carried out in August of that year. Thereafter, in spite of reminders from the solicitor to the engineer, there was delay in receiving the report from the engineer, who was keeping a look out for other similar vans. In December 1988, the engineer noticed a newer van of a similar type, which had a variation in the door hinge mechanism. On 18 January 1989 he delivered his report to the plaintiff's solicitor, which included references to this variation. Up to then it had not occurred to the plaintiff's solicitor that there could be any defendant to the plaintiff's claim other than the customer who owned the van.

The desirability of joining Motor Distributors and Daimler Benz, the distributor and manufacturer of the van, was overlooked until after 7 May 1989; thereafter any cause of action against those parties was barred by s. 11(2)(b) of the Statute of Limitations 1957. The enactment of the 1991 Act re-opened matters; as has been already indicated, the Act applies to all causes of action whether accruing before or after its passing and to proceedings pending at its passing.

Consideration of the possibility of maintaining a claim against those parties does not appear to have been undertaken until the end of 1991, when the plaintiff's solicitor and junior counsel formed the view that this might be sustainable. The proceedings against them were commenced on 14 January 1992. Motor Distributors and Daimler Benz resisted the proceedings on a number of grounds. The first was that the words '(if later)' in s. 3(1) of the 1991 Act should be interpreted as meaning after the expiration of the three year period. Section 3(1) provides as follows:

> An action, other than one to which section 6 of the Act applies, claiming damages in respect of personal injuries to a person caused by negligence, nuisance or breach of duty . . . shall not be brought after the expiration of three years from the date on which the cause of action accrued or the date of knowledge (if later) of the person injured.

Counsel for the defendants contrasted ss. 4 and 6 of the Act, which used the unambiguous phrase 'which ever is the later'.

Counsel for the plaintiff pointed out that, if counsel for the defendants was right in his interpretation, a plaintiff might acquire knowledge for the first time a day or even a few hours before the three year period expired and thus might lose his or her cause of action virtually before he or she could know that it existed; this was the precise evil that the 1991 Act had been enacted to alleviate.

Lynch J held that counsel for the plaintiff's interpretation was correct:

> There is no doubt that the words '(if later)' are not as clear as they ought to be whereas if the words were '(which ever is the later)' the subsection would be crystal clear. The words '(if later)' could mean either, as submitted by the defendant, later than 'three years from the date on which the cause of action accrued' or, as submitted by the plaintiff, later than 'the date on which the cause of action accrued'. I find that they mean the latter.

This is surely the better interpretation. The other interpretation would lead to anomalies and injustice.

The next question concerned the time at which the plaintiff should be considered to have sufficient knowledge to activate the clock against her. Lynch J approached the matter as follows. The plaintiff could not reasonably be expected to know that her injury might have been caused by a design defect in the hinge mechanism of the door of the van; under the Act, however, the plaintiff would be fixed with knowledge that her solicitor had or ought to have had at the time when he had or ought to have had that knowledge.

The plaintiff's solicitor could not reasonably be expected to have gleaned such knowledge from the plaintiff's instructions. Accepting that he did in fact acquire that knowledge as late as January 1989, the only question was whether or not he should have acquired it earlier.

Counsel for the defendants argued that the solicitor ought to have obtained an engineer's report before delivering the statement of claim to the owner of the van, especially as the plaintiff's instructions as to the precise cause of the accident were vague. Moreover, the allegations in those proceedings that the van was defective and in contravention of the Road Traffic (Construction, Equipment and Use of Vehicles) Regulations 1963 (SI No. 190 of 1963) should have been verified by such an early examination.

Lynch J rejected this argument. A general rule that an engineer's report should be obtained before the delivery of the statement of claim in every case 'would add quite unreasonably to the costs in very many cases: indeed probably in the majority of cases because the majority of cases are settled at a relatively early stage of the proceedings'. Here it was reasonable for the plaintiff's solicitor not to have requested an inspection and report by an engineer until requested to do so by senior counsel. Lynch J did not attach much weight to the defendants' argument based on allegations relating to contravention of the Road Traffic Regulations:

> [T]hese allegations of defects in the van are of a stock or formal nature very vague in themselves and the reference to Regulation 34 of the 1963 Regulations adds nothing to the particularity of the allegations.

Lynch J was satisfied that, once the decision to have an inspection had been made, the plaintiff's solicitor had taken all reasonable steps in arranging the inspection and obtaining the report. The engineer had not been at fault in regard to the delay in producing the report since after his inspection he had 'kept a lookout for similar type vans as a result of which he found a later model with a variation in hinge mechanism which he photographed and such information and photograph may be of assistance to the plaintiff in this case'. Accordingly, Lynch J held that the plaintiff's action against these two defendants was not statute-barred as the plaintiff's date of knowledge was not earlier than 18 January 1989.

Practitioners will welcome the commonsense that underlies Lynch J's judgment: to require, as an inflexible rule, that engineers' reports must precede the institution of proceedings would be an intolerable addition to the expense of litigation, for no great advantage. Nevertheless, it may be debated whether, for the purposes of the 1991 Act, a delay of close on three years before obtaining an engineer's report is reasonable. The notion of suing the manufacturer of a product that causes injury for negligence in its design is scarcely an esoteric one. Here the plaintiff's injury in her encounter with the door of the van must have had some explanation. That explanation might of course be found in her own default, the default of the owner of the van or in some cause reflecting no fault on any party: but the possibility of a design fault is one that might perhaps occur to an engineer and to a lawyer at an early stage. Having said this, it is easy to be wise after the event. A striking feature of Irish (and British) litigation, in contrast to that of the United States of America, is the paucity of cases on product liability in general and design issues in particular.

In *Clerkin v Irwin Pharmacy Ltd*, High Court, 30 April 1993, the plaintiff bought waterproof mascara from a pharmacy on 12 April 1986. She used it three days later. When she tried to remove it, her eyelashes were affected and fell out. Her solicitor wrote to the supplier on 22 April 1986, saying that it appeared the mascara was not suitable for the purpose in which it was intended and offering a sample for analysis. The plenary summons was issued on 28 April 1989. The crucial question thus was when the three-year limitation period began to run.

The plaintiff argued that the clock did not start ticking until she had received from her solicitor a copy of a letter sent to the supplier, dated 30 May 1986, from those who had carried out an analysis of the mascara. This letter indicated that the mascara should have been removed with a particular kind of wipe-off pads. The plaintiff, invoking the test laid down by Finlay CJ in *Hegarty v O'Loughran* [1990] 1 IR 148, at 157, argued that until she received this letter, she had not had a 'provable personal injury capable of attracting damages'. The letter had shown that her attempt to remove the mascara could have caused damage and it established also that other complaints had been received. Until she knew these facts, she had not known that he injury was one that would attract damages.

Carroll J rejected this argument:

> The cause of action is not postponed until the plaintiff knows whether she can prove negligence. It occurs where the personal injury is provable. In this case the damage occurred on the one and only occasion when she used the mascara and her eyelashes fell out. When that damage was caused, the cause of action accrued.

Constructive trust In *Reidy v McGreevy*, High Court, 19 March 1993, the plaintiff claimed that he had worked on his father's lands as a result of promises by his father that he would exercise a special power of appointment by will, in favour of the plaintiff. The father failed to do this and the plaintiff sought a declaration that the lands subject to the power were held on a constructive trust for his benefit. Lynch J held that time ran from the date of the father's death. The claim could not have been maintained before then because it could not have been ascertained until then that he had failed to honour his promise. Lynch J noted that an *inter vivos* claim could have arisen if the father had *repudiated* his promise during his lifetime.

Dismissal for want of prosecution In *Hogan v Jones*, High Court, 12 December 1993, Murphy J declined to dismiss for want of prosecution proceedings for negligence in relation to the construction of a stand at Lansdowne Road rugby grounds. The contract was made in 1977. Work was completed the following year. Defects became apparent shortly afterwards. A plenary summons was issued in 1982; a statement of claim came two years later. The defendants tarried and produced a defence in 1988 after a motion for judgment in default. The subsequent interlocutory stages relating to discovery and particulars dragged on for a further five years. The case was eventually listed to fix a date for hearing in July 1993.

Murphy J was guided primarily by Finlay P's criteria laid down in *Rainsford v Limerick Corporation*, High Court, 31 July 1979. A factor in the instant case was the defendants' lethargy in delivering a defence in the case and, more particularly, in putting pressure on the plaintiff to expedite proceedings. A difference in approach has arisen in this context between the courts of England and Australia. In England the courts take the view that a defendant should not be penalised for failing to put pressure on the plaintiff to expedite proceedings. In Australia, in *Calvert v Stollznow* [1982] NSW LR 749 (AC., affirming High Court, Cross J), Cross J favoured the opposite approach. His analysis is so convincing that it merits extended quotation:

> [T]he defendant in such a case is not blameless. I realise that Lord Salmon has at least twice said that the defendant is entitled to let a sleeping dog lie in the hope that it will expire. Yes he is. But in my respectful opinion the defendant cannot or should not have it both ways. A defendant faced with litigation which the plaintiff is not actively pursuing has an election. He can either press the plaintiff to get on with the action; i.e. he may cause a letter to be sent to the plaintiff's solicitors to that effect or he may approach the court in a proper case — and if it is a proper case he can do so at no cost to himself — for an order that the plaintiff take the necessary procedural steps reasonably quickly; or he may allow the matter to lie. But if he chooses silently to acquiesce in the delay in the hope that it will eventually result in his financial advantage in the sense that the matter will 'die' i.e. if he seeks and hopes to advantage himself by that delay, is he then entitled to point to that delay, which he could have taken steps to prevent, as prejudicial to him — though in some fashion not prejudicial to the plaintiff — and seek

to achieve by a court order striking the matter out what he hoped, wrongly as it turned out, to achieve by deliberately lying silent himself? In my opinion, no. Considerations of justice transcend all other considerations in these matters. Of course justice is best done if an action is brought on while the memory of the witnesses is fresh. But surely imperfect justice is better than no justice at all.

Murphy J expressed no final preference for either approach but the tenor of his judgment seems clearly to lean towards Cross J's approach. He stressed that the draconian penalty of dismissing proceedings was not made with a view to punishing a party for dilatoriness but rather to protect the legitimate interests of the party sued and in particular his or her constitutional right to a trial in accordance with fair procedures. In the instant case the defendants had failed to exercise their right at an earlier stage to apply for a dismissal; this was an ingredient in the exercise of the court's discretion on the issue. If the defendant's concern about the unavailability or death of key witnesses had been exercising them strongly, this would have influenced them to expedite proceedings. The constitutional right to fair procedures was protected, in Murphy J's view, not only by the court's power of dismissal for want of prosecution but also by the other interlocutory procedures that protected either party from undue delay by the other.

Rainsford v Limerick Corporation was also endorsed by the Supreme Court, in *Celtic Ceramics Ltd v Industrial Development Authority*, 4 February 1993 (*ex tempore*), affirming [1993] ILRM 248 (High Court, O'Hanlon J.) The plaintiffs, having delayed nine months in serving the plenary summons, which was issued just before the expiration of the six-year limitation period, had also been tardy in delivering the statement of claim and in replying to the notice for particulars, more than two years after receipt of the notice. In dismissing the proceedings for want of prosecution, Finlay CJ (O'Flaherty and Blayney JJ concurring) stressed that a plenary summons should, 'in the ordinary way', be served within days or weeks of its issue. The defendants established that they would suffer prejudice if the case went on: two of their witnesses had died and the passage of time had inevitably dulled recollection of the facts at issue.

Local Government

BUILDING CONTROL

Farm buildings: fire certificate The Building Control (Amendment) Regulations 1993 (SI No. 190) exempted certain farm buildings from the requirement to obtain a fire safety certificate under the Building Control Regulations 1991 (as to which see the 1991 Review, 307).

COMPULSORY PURCHASE

In *Dublin Corporation v Underwood*, High Court, 12 May 1993, Budd J overturned some elements of established practice in relation to the award of compensation under the Acquisition of Land (Assessment of Compensation) Act 1919 on foot of a compulsory purchase order. The defendant was the owner of two houses in New Street, Dublin, in respect of which a compulsory purchase notice to treat had been served by Dublin Corporation as part of a road widening scheme. The defendant was not an owner/occupier of the houses but had purchased them for investment purposes. The issue raised in the case was whether the defendant was entitled, as part of his compensation for the compulsory purchase, to any reinvestment costs incurred by him if he reinvested in equivalent property. The property arbitrator in the case held that he was so entitled, and the Corporation then sought a special case stated to the High Court on this issue. The Corporation argued that, as the defendant was not an owner/occupier, he was not entitled to any reinvestment costs. In the instant case, the sum awarded for compulsory purchase of the two houses without reinvestment costs was £94,000, and the property arbitrator had measured the reinvestment costs as being an additional sum of £7,990.

In his judgment, Budd J embarked on a long and exhaustive discussion of the case law in this area. He also approved the views expressed on the question of compensation in McDermott and Woulfe, *Compulsory Purchase and Compensation: Law and Practice in Ireland* (1992), at 245. It may be noted that the first-named author of this text was also the highly experienced property arbitrator in the instant case. In approaching in general terms the question of compensation Budd J stated:

. . . in a State where the Constitution recognises the ideal of private ownership subject to the principles of social justice, and where Article 43 of the Constitution provides that the State guarantees to pass no law attempting to abolish the right of private ownership, it seems to me that one should strive for the construction of the law which most nearly accords with exactly equivalent reinstatement in pecuniary terms when it comes to the assessment of compensation.

In relation to the case law, Budd J accepted that certain *dicta*, including those of Denning LJ in *Harvey v Crawley Development Corp* [1957] 1 QB 485, leaned in favour of the view expressed by the Corporation that only owner/occupiers were entitled to reinvestment compensation and that this view had been accepted in practice to some extent in assessing compensation under the 1919 Act. However, Budd J did not consider that this view was consistent either with the general approach expressed by him in the passage set out above or by the views expressed in cases such as *Horn v Sunderland Corporation* [1941] 2 KB 26 or *Gunning v Dublin Corporation* [1983] ILRM 66. On the basis of these latter authorities, Budd J held that the defendant was entitled to reinvestment compensation. He continued:

As for the argument that the disallowance of reinvestment costs is a practice hallowed by time, I take the view that the true principle of equivalence together with an overriding need for reasonableness with regard to the reinvestment costs may well require the cost of reinvestment to be an aspect of the compensation in particular cases, depending on the circumstances. The existing practice seems to me to be manifestly unjust, illogical and at times out of line with the true principle of equivalence. . . .

On this basis, Budd J found that the property arbitrator had been correct in awarding a sum for reinvestment costs in the instant case. As he indicated at the end of his judgment, this decision will be one of great interest both to property arbitrators and local authorities. It is also of interest to note that the views expressed on the topic in McDermott and Woulfe, *Compulsory Purchase and Compensation: Law and Practice in Ireland* (1992) have been so speedily endorsed by the High Court.

DERELICT SITES

The Derelict Sites (Urban Areas) Regulations 1993 (SI No. 392) prescribe certain areas in Cavan and Louth to be urban areas for the purposes of the Derelict Sites Act 1990. On the Act, see the 1990 Review, 410-11 and the 1991 Review, 309.

DUBLIN COUNTY REORGANISATION

The Local Government (Dublin) Act 1993 provided, as its Long Title indicated, for the reorganisation of the administrative county of Dublin into three administrative counties, namely, South Dublin, Fingal and Dun Laoghaire-Rathdown. These three councils replaced Dublin County Council and the Corporation of Dun Laoghaire, which were abolished on the coming into force of the 1993 Act.

The Act is essentially administrative in nature, in that no substantive changes to local government law were occasioned by it. Thus, for example, s. 12 of the 1993 Act provides that the South Dublin Council shall consist of 26 members, the Fingal Council 24 members and the Dun Laoghaire-Rathdown Council 28 members.

The changes effected by the 1993 Act were originally envisaged in the Local Government (Reorganisation) Act 1985, and the Second Schedule to the 1985 Act was acccordingly adapted to the terms of the 1993 Act. A basis for putting in place the administrative arrangements for the new Councils was established by the Local Government Act 1991 (on the 1991 Act in general, see the 1991 Review, 310-13). The First Schedule to the 1993 Act contains the list of legislation repealed consequent on the changes effected by the 1993 Act: these largely involve now redundant references to Dublin County Council and the Corporation of Dun Laoghaire in a wide range of legislation.

The administrative preparations for the establishment of the three new Councils were contained in the Dublin (Preparations for Reorganisation) Regulations 1993 (SI No. 52), made under the Local Government Act 1991. Pursuant to the Local Government (Dublin) Act 1993 (Commencement) Order 1993 (SI No. 400), certain provisions of the 1993 Act came into effect on 22 December 1993, the remainder on 1 January 1994. The new Councils came into being on 1 January 1994, that being the establishment day provided for in the Local Government (Dublin) Act 1993 (Establishment Day) Order 1993 (SI No. 401), made under s. 7 of the 1993 Act.

Finally, it may be useful to note here that the area comprising the administrative county of Dublin excluded the area for which Dublin Corporation has responsibility and so the functions and powers of Dublin Corporation were unaffected by the 1993 Act.

HOUSING

Grants: disabled persons and essential repairs   The Housing (Disabled Persons and Essential Repairs Grants) Regulations 1993 (SI No. 262) amended the Housing Regulations 1980 and provided for schemes of grants for the adaptation of houses for disabled persons as well as those for essential repairs.

Grants: new houses The Housing (New House Grants etc.) Regulations 1980 (Amendment) Regulations 1993 (SI No. 350) provided for increased grants under the 1980 Regulations referred to in the title.

Homeless persons The Housing (Miscellaneous Provisions) Regulations 1988 (Amendment) Regulations 1993 (SI No. 157) increased the level of recoupment by the Department of the Environment to 90% of certain payments made by local authorities concerning the accommodation of homeless persons under s. 10(1) of the Housing Act 1988. On the 1988 Act generally, see the 1988 Review, 302-6.

Mortgage allowance The Housing (Mortgage Allowance) Regulations 1993 (SI No. 32) provided for a mortgage allowance for tenants and tenant purchasers of local authority houses who surrender their houses to the authority and provide another house for their own occupation with the assistance of a mortgage loan of not less than £10,000. The allowance is paid to the agency making the loan and is credited towards the borrowers's loan charges during the first five years of the loan.

Refusal to rehouse In *Carton v Dublin Corporation* [1993] ILRM 467, Geoghegan J declined to quash a refusal by the Corporation to re-house the applicant, who had sought accommodation for herself, her sister and her father. The factual background was that the applicant's father had been a tenant of Dublin Corporation in 37 different corporation dwellings, having moved from dwelling to dwelling and, in the Corporation's veiw, having breached his tenancy agreements in many respects in these different dwellings. The Corporation had decided not to accede to a further request by the applicant's father for new accommodation.

In so refusing, the Corporation invoked a 'good estate management' clause in the scheme of priorities for housing accommodation it had drawn up pursuant to s. 11 of the Housing Act 1988, which had replaced s. 60 of the Housing Act 1966 (see the 1988 Review, 305). When the applicant sought accommodation from the Corporation, and included her sister and father in the request, the Corporation treated this as a ploy to get around its refusal to rehouse the father. It took into account the father's alleged past breaches of tenancy agreements in declining the applicant's request.

As already indicated, Geoghegan J declined to quash this refusal. Citing the decisions of the Supreme Court in *The State (Keegan) v Stardust Victims*

Compensation Tribunal [1987] ILRM 202; [1986] IR 642 and *O'Keeffe v An Bord Pleanála* [1992] ILRM 237; [1993] 1 IR 39 (see the 1991 Review, 16-18), he noted that, whatever sympathy the Court might have for the applicant, it could only interfere with a decision of the Corporation, as housing authority, if the decision flew in the face of reason, was defective for failure to observe the rules of natural justice, was illegal, or was otherwise *ultra vires*. In the instant case, Geoghegan J accepted that there was 'ample evidence' to justify the view that the use of the applicant's name in the request for re-housing was a ploy to get around the Corporation's refusal to re-house the applicant's father. He concluded that the Corporation was entitled to look at the entire history surrounding the application, in particular because the applicant had specifically requested that her father be housed with her.

Rent books S. 17 of the Housing (Miscellaneous Provisions) Act 1992 for the first time enabled the Minister for the Environment to make Regulations requiring a landlord to provide a tenant with a rent book, a requirement confined until now under s. 25 of the Housing (Private Rented Dwellings) Act 1982 to the former rent-controlled sector. The 1992 Act applies to all lettings. On the detailed contents of such rent books see the Housing (Rent Books) Regulations 1993 (SI No. 146), which came into effect on 1 September 1993. On the 1992 Act generally, see the 1992 Review, 441-4.

Sale of houses by housing authority The Housing (Sale of Dwellings) Regulations 1993 (SI No. 267), made under s. 26 of the Housing (Miscellaneous Provisions) Act 1992 (see the 1992 Review, 444), lay down the detailed requirements for the sale by housing authorities of dwellings to local authority tenants.

Standards for rented houses The Housing (Miscellaneous Provisions) Act 1992 (Commencement) Order 1993 (SI No. 145) brought s. 37 of the Housing (Miscellaneous Provisions) Act 1992, concerning standards for rented houses, into effect on 1 September 1993. On the details of these standards, which came into effect on 1 January 1994 for private dwellings but will not come into effect until 1 January 1998 for local authority dwellings, see the Housing (Standards for Rented Houses) Regulations 1993 (SI No. 147). On the 1992 Act generally, see the 1992 Review, 441-4.

LOCAL AUTHORITY NAME CHANGE

Kells UDC The Local Government (Change of Name of Urban Council) Order 1993 (SI No. 156), made under s. 76 of the Local Government Act

1946, changed the name of the urban council of Ceanannus Mór in County Meath to Kells.

LOCAL AUTHORITY PROCEDURE

Estimates The Public Bodies (Amendment) Order 1993 (SI No. 275) in effect revoked the 1992 Order of the same title (see the 1992 Review, 444) and inserted an amended Article 53 into the Public Bodies Order 1946 in order to specify the period for preparation of the estimates of expenses and the holding of estimates meetings by local authorities. Special arrangements were included in the 1993 Order in relation to the new councils established by the Local Government (Dublin) Act 1993: see 420, above.

Expenses The Local Government (Expenses of Local Authority Members) Regulations 1993 (SI No. 391) lay down revised expenses for local authority members with effect from 1 January 1994. The Local Government Act 1991 (Commencement) Order 1993 (SI No. 390) brought into effect connected provisions of the 1991 Act on 1 January 1994.

Galway The County and City Management (Galway) Order 1993 (SI No. 258) provided that the county and county borough of Galway must have their own separate managers. The Order, in effect, terminated the operation in Galway of s. 7(5) of the Local Government (Reorganisation) Act 1985.

LOCAL GOVERNMENT REFORM

The Local Government Act 1991 (Removal of Controls) Order 1993 (SI No. 172) removed the need for local authorities to obtain certain consents, approvals and confirmations from the Minister for Environment across a wide range of functions. These relate to certain land disposals, delegation of functions by city and county managers, local authority contributions to certain bodies, local authority superannuations, car parks, certain local authority meetings, and other miscellaneous matters. Without attempting to provide a complete list of the legislative provisions affected, they include the following:

— the City and County Management (Amendment) Act 1955: consent under s. 15(1) and approval to delegate to an approved officer under s. 17(1)(a);

— the Local Government (Planning and Development) Act 1963: fixing of limits and conditions under s. 15(1); consent under s. 74(1); consent under s. 75(2)(b);

— the Local Government (Financial Provisions) Act 1978: sanction under s. 11;

— the Casual Trading Act 1980: requirement to inform the Minister under ss. 7(5) and 9(4)(a)(i); approval under s. 9(2); and

— the Derelict Sites Act 1990: consent under s. 31.

PLANNING

Access to information   The Access to Information on the Environment Regulations 1993 (SI No. 133) are referred to in the Safety and Health chapter, 475, below.

Bord Pleanála chair   The Local Government (Planning and Development) Act 1983 (Section 5) Order 1993 (SI No. 343) provides for amendments to the selection committee for the position of chair of An Bord Pleanála. The chair of the Council for the Status of Women was added to the selection committee by the 1993 Order.

Compensation: s. 13 notice   In *Browne v Cashel UDC*, High Court, 26 March 1993, the applicant had been refused planning permission on grounds which entitled her to claim compensation for refusal of permission pursuant to the Local Government (Planning and Development) Act 1990 (on which see generally the 1990 Review, 415-6). The applicant then made her claim for compensation pursuant to s. 11 of the 1990 Act. In response, the respondent Council served a notice on the applicant purportedly made under s. 13 of the 1990 Act indicating that, in the Council's opinion, the land in question was capable of other development which was specified in the notice. However, the notice also stated that, since such other development would constitute a material contravention of the Council's development plan, permission for it would be subject to the passing of an appropriate resolution by the elected members of the Council.

The applicant applied to have the appropriate resolution passed by the elected members, but this was refused, apparently on the basis that the applicant's proposed development did not conform with the suggestion contained in the notice purportedly made under s. 13 of the 1990 Act. In those circumstances, the applicant returned to claiming compensation in respect of her original planning application. The Council argued that, since the applicant had not taken advantage of the Council's s. 13 notice, she was no longer entitled to compensation under the 1990 Act. The applicant argued that the s. 13 notice was invalid since it purported to suggest the applicant seek permission for a development which was outside the Council's own development plan. The property arbitrator appointed to determine the level of compensation payable to the applicant stated a case for the High Court as to whether the notice from the Council had been valid.

Geoghegan J stated that he 'had no difficulty at all' in holding that the notice served by the Council in this case was not a valid notice for the purposes of s. 13 of the 1990 Act. He held that if the permission suggested in the notice is clearly one which at the time of its service could not lawfully be granted then the notice is invalid. In the present case, he concluded that the Council could not get around this by purporting to make the effectiveness of the notice conditional on a resolution being passed by the elected members of the Council. Geoghegan J referred to a number of provisions of the Local Government (Planning and Development) Act 1963, from which he concluded that the scheme of the Act is to make the planning auhtority bound by the development plan, and thus any notice served by the Council purporting to go outside the terms of the plan was *ultra vires* the Council. Nor, finally, did he consider that the applicant was estopped, by her attempt to apply for the other development referred to in the Council's notice to her, from challenging the notice itself. In any event, he noted that the issue of estoppel had not been raised by the Council at the arbitration hearing.

Conditions: specificity In *Houlihan v An Bord Pleanála*, High Court, 4 October 1993, Murphy J accepted that An Bord Pleanála was empowered to include in a decision to grant planning permission a large range of conditions which might require approval between the developer and the planning authority. However, in a particular instance in the permission under review, he concluded that a condition had lacked sufficient specificity. Accordingly he quashed the permission granted, but remitted the matter to An Bord Pleanála in order to allow it clarify any ambiguity in the condition in question.

Contribution by local authority to excess works In *T. McDonagh & Sons Ltd v Galway Corporation*, Supreme Court, 17 May 1993, the Supreme Court considered the correct interpretation of s. 26(7) of the Local Government (Planning and Development) Act 1963. S. 26(7) of the 1963 Act provides that where a planning authority imposes a condition under s. 26(2) of the Act for requiring 'roads, open spaces, car parks, sewers, water mains or drains in excess of the immediate needs' of the proposed development, then:

> . . . a contribution towards such of the relevant roads, open spaces, car parks, sewers, water mains or drains as are constructed shall be made by the local authority, who shall be responsible for their maintenance. . . .

In the instant case, the applicants had sought permission from the respondent Corporation to build a complex consisting of a 126-bedroom hotel, some retail outlets and a three-storey car park with 158 spaces. In a further application lodged simultaneously, the applicants proposed to build a five-storey car park on top of the three-storey car park, but that this would not be built until such time as they were satisfied it would be viable. Both applications were granted by the Corporation, subject to a condition that building of the five-storey car park begin before the hotel or retail outlets were opened for business and that it would be completed within 12 months of the building commencement. The Corporation stated that the reason for adding this condition was that the area in question had been zoned by the Corporation for a public car park and that, therefore, the construction of the hotel and retail outlets would not be in accordance with the proper planning and development of the area unless they formed part of an integrated development which ensured that the five storey car park was constructed with the hotel and retail outlet development.

The two main questions which arose in the case were, first, whether this condition was one 'in excess of the immediate needs' of the proposed development and, secondly, whether the Corporation were required to make a contribution towards the building costs in accordance with s. 26(7) of the 1963 Act. In the High Court, Blayney J had held in favour of the applicants on both questions, but on appeal by the Corporation to the Supreme Court (Finlay CJ, Hederman, O'Flaherty, Egan and Denham JJ) the Court unanimously held in favour of the Corporation on the second crucial question.

Delivering the Court's decision, Finlay CJ agreed with Blayney J's finding that a 158 car park facility would have been perfectly adequate for the proposed hotel and retail outlets planned by the applicants and that the condition attached by the Corporation was 'in excess of the immediate needs' of the proposed development. However, he disagreed with Blayney J's interpretation of s. 26(7) of the 1963 Act that the Corporation was required to make a contribution to the development costs of the five-storey car park.

Finlay CJ acknowledged that there were considerable difficulties in finding an all-embracing interpretation for the wording of s. 26(7) of the 1963 Act. However, he rejected the interpretation arrived at by Blayney J that it obliged a local authority to make a contribution where, as in the instant case, the local authority would not be responsible for the maintenance of the property in question as it would remain in the hands of a private developer.

As to what s. 26(7) meant (as opposed to what it did not mean), Finlay CJ did lean to some extent in the direction of the Corporation's argument that s. 26(7) would require a contribution where, for example, the local authority would eventually take in charge the works in question, as might occur with some roads, sewers, water mains or drains. He also accepted that the refusal of a contribution would appear justifiable under s. 26(7) where the works involved, as here, 'a commercial undertaking capable of yielding a profit'. But, in relation to the reference to 'open spaces' in s. 26(7), Finlay CJ was fearful that a developer could be 'left with something from which no profit could be derived, for which he would get no help in maintenance and in respect of which he would have got no contribution.' In arriving at a possible *via medium* on this thorny issue, Finlay CJ suggested the following:

> It is possible that a condition imposed under s. 26(2)(f) which required a developer to construct works in excess of the immediate needs of the development in respect of which he could neither derive a profit from his ownership or occupation of them, nor impose a responsibility for their maintenance upon a local authority and therefore obtain a contribution for them, would be an unjust condition and one which could be set aside either on appeal to An Bord Pleanála, or if its injustice was an invasion of the constitutional right to protection of property rights, by judicial review.

However, he concluded that such a course was not open in the instant case and therefore he allowed the appeal by the Corporation on this aspect of the High Court decision. Nonetheless, the comments on the scope of s. 26(7) of the 1963 Act will undoubtedly prove of great benefit to any future claims in this area.

Development plan: revision In *Huntsgrove Developments Ltd v Meath County Council* [1994] 2 ILRM 36, Lardner J rejected the applicant's claim to quash a decision by the respondent Council to revise a development plan.

The applicant, Huntsgrove Developments Ltd, had acquired a large site in the centre of Ashbourne, Co. Meath, and obtained planning permission in 1989 to develop a shopping centre comprising 4,000 square metres at a cost of £4,000,000. It understood at the time of its application for planning permission that substantial vacant areas in the immediate vicinity of the site were zoned for agricultural purposes under the Ashbourne development plan adopted by the respondent Council in 1989. On the basis of this plan it believed that these vacant areas were unlikely to be developed by any commercial competitor within the remainder of the five year life of the development plan.

The Council was approached by a third party, Ladgrove Stores Ltd, in November 1989 for pre-planning discussions with regard to a proposed shopping, leisure and residential development in the centre of Ashbourne. The Council was agreeable in principle to the concept but indicated, *inter alia*, that financial constraints prevented them from undertaking a review of the development plan. At the request of Ladgrove Stores Ltd, the Council then carried out a costing of the work which would be involved in a review of the development plan and Ladgrove subsequently forwarded a cheque for £20,000. The review was then initiated and it was resolved by the Council in February 1992 that the draft plan for the Ashbourne area should be put on public display. The applicant sought judicial review, but Lardner J refused the reliefs sought.

He held that the Council was not obliged to consult parties likely to be affected by a revision of the development plan before making their decision to initiate a review, because s. 21 of the Local Government (Planning and Development) Act 1963 afforded an ample opportunity for the making of objections and representations at a later stage before any decision to adopt a revised plan was made. He characterised the decision to initiate a review of the development plan as an administrative one. Applying the decision of the Supreme Court in *O'Brien v Bord na Móna* [1983] ILRM 314; [1983] IR 255, he stated that in invoking the requirements of constitutional justice it was incumbent on the applicant to establish as a matter of probability that in deciding to exhibit the proposed revision of the development plan in public the respondents acted with an indirect or improper motive, and that there was a real likelihood of actual bias.

On the question of bias, he held that the acceptance by the respondents of a contribution of £20,000 to help fund the preparatory work for the review of the development plan did not establish as a matter of probability that in making their decision the respondents acted with an indirect or improper motive or that there was a real likelihood of actual bias. This was supported, in his view, by a consideration of the draft plan as a whole. In particular, he noted that the draft plan differed in important respects from the proposals made by the party that had contributed to the costs of the review. Nor did he consider that the acceptance by the respondents of a contribution, which was in effect a gift, was not unlawful or *ultra vires* merely because it was received by them in their capacity as the planning authority without specific statutory authority. On the *ultra vires* doctrine generally, see the 1991 Review, 311.

Finally, Lardner J rejected a suggestion that the applicant had a legitimate expectation to be consulted. In this respect he expressly followed the principles laid down by Costello J in *Tara Prospecting Ltd v Minister for Energy* [1993] ILRM 771: see the Administrtaive Law chapter, 25-8, above.

Environmental impact assessment: exemption The Gas Act 1976 (Section 40A) (Exemption) Order 1993 (SI No. 166) exempted Bord Gáis Éireann from the environmental impact assessment requirements of s. 40A of the 1976 Act, inserted by Reg.20 of the European Communities (Environmental Impact Assessment) Regulations 1989, in connection with the construction of the gas interconnector pipeline between Ireland and the United Kingdom.

Extension of permission   In *Garden Village Construction Ltd v Wicklow County Council* [1994] 1 ILRM 354 (HC); [1994] 2 ILRM 527, the issue arose as to whether the applicant company had carried out 'substantial works' on foot of a permission which would entitle it to an extension of time pursuant to s. 4 of the Local Government (Planning and Development) Act 1982. As the 1993 decision of Geoghegan J in this case was reversed by the Supreme Court in 1994, we will discuss the decision in detail in the 1994 Review. Suffice it to note at present that the Supreme Court held that works effected outside the boundaries of the planning permission could not be regarded as 'substantial works' for the purposes of s. 4 of the 1982 Act.

Fees   The Local Government (Planning and Development) (Fees) (Amendment) Regulations 1993 (SI No. 349) amended the 1984 Regulations of the same title to provide with effect from 1 February 1994 the revised fees for planning applications.

Mining ban   The decision of Costello J in *Tara Prospecting Ltd v Minister for Energy* [1993] ILRM 771 is discussed in the Administrative Law chapter, 25-8, above.

Permission subject to existing property right   S. 26(11) of the Local Government (Planning and Development) Act 1963 provides that a person shall not be entitled solely by reason of the grant of planning permission to carry out a development. This provision provides, in effect, that a developer may not interfere with existing property rights, such as rights of way, merely on the ground that planning permission for a development had been granted. The effect of this provision was considered by Keane J in *Doolan v Murray and Ors*, High Court, 21 December 1993.

Proper planning and development   In *Healy and O'Neill v Dublin County Council*, High Court, 29 April 1993, Barron J declined to grant judicial review of a permission granted by the Council and, on appeal, by An Bord Pleanála, which the applicants alleged was in breach of the relevant development plan. Barron J held that, since the Council and An Bord Pleanála had the statutory function of determining the issue of whether there was, in fact, a breach of the development plan, the Court would be reluctant to interfere with the decision arrived at and in the instant case he would decline to grant judicial review on that ground alone. In addition, he stated that, since the applicants had not appealed the permission granted by the Council to An Bord Pleanála, he would have regarded them as being estopped from seeking judicial review.

State bodies   The applicability of the planning code to State bodies was considered by Lynch J in *Byrne v Commissioners of Public Works in Ireland* [1994] 1 IR 91 and by Costello J and the Supreme Court in *Howard v Commissioners of Public Works in Ireland* [1993] ILRM 665 (SC); [1994] 1 IR 101 (HC & SC) (an interlocutory judgment of O'Hanlon J in *Howard v Commissioners of Public Works in Ireland*, High Court, 3 December 1992 had also considered the issue).

Both *Byrne* and *Howard* involved challenges to the proposed development of interpretive centres by the Commissioners of Public Works, commonly called the Office of Public Works or OPW. The *Byrne* case concerned a proposed interpretive centre at Luggala, Co. Wicklow, while the *Howard* case concerned a centre at Mullaghmore, Co. Clare.

In the *Howard* case, Costello J held, firstly, that the Commissioners of Public Works lacked a general power to develop and manage public buildings and, secondly, that in any event the Commissioners were required to seek planning permission for the development of the interpretive centre at Mullaghmore. On the first issue, the High Court decision in the *Howard* case was immediately followed by the enactment of the State Authorities (Development and Management) Act 1993: see the Administrative Law chapter, 4, above.

On the planning question, the *Byrne* and *Howard* cases were consolidated into one appeal for the Supreme Court. In May 1993, the Supreme Court (Finlay CJ, O'Flaherty, Egan, Blayney and Denham JJ) upheld the decision of Costello J that the Commissioners came within the planning code: *Howard v Commissioners of Public Works in Ireland* [1993] ILRM 665 (SC); [1994] 1 IR 101 (HC & SC). The essence of the Supreme Court decision can be divided into two elements, one being an argument on what the planning code did not state, the other being about an interpretation of what the planning legislation did state.

On the first point, the argument had been made that the Commissioners, as an emanation of the State, were entitled to rely on a form of prerogative exemption from the planning code, and that when the Local Government (Planning and Development) Act 1963 was passed by the Oireachtas it was assumed that the State was simply not bound by legislation unless express provision was made for this. This argument was rejected by a majority of the Court (Finlay CJ, Egan, Blayney and Denham JJ; O'Flaherty J dissenting) primarily on the ground that the Court's decision in *Byrne v Ireland* [1972] IR 241 had rejected the same argument and had ruled, in effect, that such a prerogative exemption was inconsistent with the Constitution. In addition, the Court found persuasive the similar views expressed by the Indian Supreme Court in *State of West Bengal v Corporation of Calcutta* [1967] All IR (SC) 997. However, the Court also accepted that there could be no hard and fast rule and that each piece of legislation would turn on its own interpretation, in the absence of an express provision. In dissent, O'Flaherty J found persuasive the views expressed by Diplock LJ in *British Broadcasting Corporation v Johns* [1965] Ch 32 (as approved by the House of Lords in *Lord Advocate v Dumbarton DC* [1990] 2 AC 580) where the question of certainty had been emphasised in support of the continued operation of the old rule presuming non-application to the State.

The second argument considered by the Court in *Howard* was whether s. 84 of the Local Government (Planning and Development) Act 1963 indicated a positive intention that the Commissioners were not required to comply fully with all elements of the planning code. S.84 of the 1963 Act provides that, before undertaking the construction or extension of a building, a State authority 'shall consult with the planning authority to such extent as may be determined by the Minister [for the Environment]'. Such consultation had taken place in relation to both the Luggala and Mullaghmore interpretive centres, and it was suggested that the Commissioners had thus complied with all relevant planning requirements. On this point, however, a differently constituted, bare majority (Finlay CJ, Blayney and Denham JJ; O'Flaherty and Egan JJ dissenting) held that, on the true construction of s. 84 and the 1963 Act as a whole, the Commissioners were required to apply for planning permission from the relevant planning authority.

On this second point, Blayney J for the majority referred first to general principles of statutory interpretation found in the leading English textbooks, *Craies on Statute Law*, 7th ed., at 65 and *Maxwell on the Interpretation of Statutes*, 12th ed., at 28. These relate primarily to concentration on the words actually used by parliament to indicate its intention. He then approached s. 24 of the 1963 Act, the provision which sets down the general requirement that planning permission is required in respect of any development of land, unless it is exempted development under s. 4 of the 1963 Act, or occurred before the appointed day, 1 October 1964, when the Act came into force. Blayney J's view was that s. 24 clearly applied to the Commissioners. He noted also that this result could have been avoided if s. 4 had provided that development by the Commissioners should be exempted development, but that this had not been done.

Blayney J then turned to s. 84 of the 1963 Act. Blayney J rejected the submission that it would lead to a pointless situation to interpret the Act as requiring the Commissioners to have to consult with the planning authority, as required by s. 84, if subsequently they had to apply for planning permission in the normal way. Again citing a passage from *Craies on Statute Law*, 7th ed., at 109, Blayney J held that such 'interpretation by implication' was only permissible if the statutory words were not plain and unambiguous. In the present case, he considered the statutory language was 'perfectly plain' and continued:

> In the first place, it is provided [in s. 24] that permission is required for any development which is not exempted development, and secondly, it is provided in s. 84 that where a statutory authority wishes to undertake the construction or extension of any building it must comply with the terms of that section. What is being suggested is that it is a necessary implication from the terms of s. 84 that the Commissioners should be relieved from complying with s. 24. But this conclusion does not result from any difficulty in interpreting s. 84. It results from forming a conclusion as to why s. 84 was included in the Act. In other words, it results from coming to a conclusion as to the intention of the legislature without that intention being expressed in the section itself. It seems to me that this amounts to speculation, particularly as, if it had been intended to exempt statutory authorities from having to apply for planning permission for the construction or extension of any building, it would have been a simple matter to provide that development by them should be exempted development.

He also considered that the enforcement of both sections did not create an absurd situation. As a result of consulting under s. 84 with the planning authority (Blayney J inadvertently referring here to consultation with the 'local authority'), he considered that the Commissioners would obtain information as to whether their application for planning permission would or would not be likely to be successful. Thus, compliance with s. 84 might in fact be of benefit to the Commissioners in enabling them to assess in advance whether it would be worthwhile seeking planning permission for a particular development. Of course, the minority on this point (O'Flaherty and Egan JJ) considered that this interpretation of s. 84, in the words of Egan J, 'makes little sense' if, at the end of the consultation period under s. 84, the Commissioners were still required to apply for planning permission. The minority regarded s. 84 as containing the entire planning code for State authorities, while the majority concluded that, since it did not contain an express exemption from s. 24, State authorities were required to seek such permission. Clearly, in terms of the prior understanding of the 1963 Act, the minority view would have been regarded as conforming to practice. Nevertheless, a different view prevailed.

As was the case in the wake of the decision in the High Court in *Howard* that the Commissioners lacked a general power to develop and manage public buildings (see above), the legislative reaction to the planning element in *Howard* was swift. Within a month of the Supreme Court decision, the Local Government (Planning and Development) Act 1993 was enacted to regularise the situation and to provide for certain express exemptions from the planning code for certain State developments.

S. 2(1) of the 1993 Act provides that the Minister for the Environment may, by means of Regulations, specify that the Local Government (Planning and Development) Acts 1963 to 1993 shall not apply to certain classes of development by a 'State authority', defined in s. 1 of the Act as either a Minister of the Government or the Commissioners of Public Works, that is, the same definition as is contained in the State Authorities (Development and Management) Act 1993: see the Administrative Law chapter, 4, above. In particular s. 2(1)(a) provides that such Regulations would apply where, in the Minister's opinion 'such development is . . . in connection with or for the purposes of public safety or order, the administration of justice or national security or defence.' The wording here envisaged that the building of Garda stations, prisons, courthouses or military installations would be given exemption from the planning code, as was ultimately provided in the Local Government (Planning and Development) Regulations 1994 (SI No. 86 of 1994), which also revoke and replace the Local Government (Planning and Development) Regulations 1977. We will discuss the 1994 Regulations in the 1994 Review.

S. 2(1)(b) of the 1993 Act also provides that the Minister may by Regulations deal with matters such as consultation with the planning authority (a provision which supercedes s. 84 of the 1963 Act, repealed by s. 5 of the 1993 Act), the inspection of documents (as to which, see generally the Access to Information on the Environment Regulations 1993 (SI No. 133), below in the Safety and Health chapter, 475) and the preparation of an environmental impact statement. In addition, s. 2(2) provides that, where a development by a State authority is required by reason of 'an accident or emergency', the Minister for Finance may, by Order, exempt the development from the planning code.

S. 3 of the 1993 Act amends s. 78 of the 1963 Act in respect of the consultation mechanism required for local authority developments (local authorities also being, under the planning code, planning authorities), while s. 4 of the 1993 Act provides for a general validation of all developments undertaken prior to the decision of the Supreme Court in the *Howard* case, except for pending proceedings such as the *Byrne* and *Howard* cases themselves. This saver for pending proceedings is, of course, to ensure that the Oireachtas does not interfere with the exercise of the judicial power, a concept which can be traced back to the Sinn Féin Funds case, *Buckley and Ors v Attorney General* [1950] IR 67. The result of this saver is that planning permissions were required for the Luggala and Mullaghmore interpretive centres.

We may note here that a previous example of the type of exemption found in s. 4 of the 1993 Act had some unexpected consequences. In *The State (Pine Valley Developments Ltd) v Minister for the Environment* [1984] IR 407, the Supreme Court held that a purported planning permission to Pine Valley had been *ultra vires*. The Local Government (Planning and Development) Act 1982 was then passed to validate all such planning permissions, except for the permission to Pine Valley itself. In *Pine Valley Developments Ltd v Minister for the Environment* [1987] ILRM 747; [1987] IR 23 (1985 Review, 24), the Supreme Court held that the 1982 Act was, in terms of Irish constitutional law, entirely correct and the company was not entitled to any compensation for the loss of its planning permission. Subsequently, in *Pine Valley Developments Ltd v Ireland* (1991) 14 EHRR 319, the European Court of Human Rights held that the 1982 Act constituted a violation of the company's property rights under Article 14 of the European Convention on Human Rights and Fundamental Freedoms, and the Court subsequently ordered the Irish government to pay £1.5m compensation to the company: *Pine Valley Developments Ltd v Ireland (No. 2)* (1993) 16 EHRR 373.

While the Luggala and Mullaghmore cases are quite different to *Pine Valley*, since a State body is involved as opposed to a private company, nonetheless the *Pine Valley* litigation is a reminder that legislative retrospective validation with an eye to respect for the judicial power, does not always provide a neat solution to a particular problem.

Finally, the 1993 Act, apart from s. 5, came into effect on 15 June 1993, while s. 5 (which repealed s. 84 of the 1963 Act) came into effect on 15 June 1994: see the Local Government (Planning and Development) Act 1993 (Commencement) Order 1993 (SI No. 152).

Urban renewal: designation   The Urban Renewal Act 1986 (Designated Areas) Order 1993 (SI No. 228), the Urban Renewal Act 1986 (Remission of Rates) Scheme 1993 (SI No. 229), in conjunction with the Finance Act 1987 (Designation of Urban Renewal Areas) Order 1993 (SI No. 244), the Finance Act 1987 (Designation of Urban Renewal Areas) (No. 2) Order 1993 (SI No. 245), the Finance Act 1987 (Designation of Urban Renewal Areas) (No. 3) Order 1993 (SI No. 246) and the Finance Act 1987 (Designation of Urban Renewal Areas) (No. 4) Order 1993 (SI No. 292) conferred urban renewal status, with the connected taxation reliefs associated with such status, on a number of different areas. On the urban renewal regime generally, see the 1992 Review, 461-3.

REGIONAL AUTHORITIES

The Local Government Act 1991 (Regional Authorities) (Establishment) Order 1993 (SI No. 394), which came into operation on 1 January 1994, provided for the establishment of eight regional authorities in accordance with s. 43 of the 1991 Act: see the 1991 Review, 313. The Order also prescribes the general procedures applicable to the regional authorities. S. 43 of the 1991 Act had been brought into effect by the Local Government Act 1991 (Commencement) Order 1993 (SI No. 390).

RESERVED FUNCTIONS

The Local Government Act 1991 (Reserved Functions) Order 1993 (SI No. 37) declared that various local authority functions, listed in the Schedule to the Order, were to be reserved functions within the City and County Management Acts, thus requiring a vote by the elected members of the local authority. The matters referred to in the Schedule are: the making of a contribution under s. 40 of the Local Government (Sanitary Services) Act 1948; the making of arrangements under s. 96(1) of the Road Traffic Act 1961; requesting the Minister for the Environment to extend the period for complying with s. 20(1) of the Local Government (Planning and Development) Act 1963; entering into an agreement under s. 7 of the Local Authorities (Traffic Wardens) Act 1975; the making of a contribution under s. 29 of the Local Government (Water Pollution) Act 1977; the making of a waste plan under article 4 of the European Communities (Waste) Regulations 1979; the making of a scheme under s. 279(5) of the Social Welfare (Consolidation) Act 1981 (see now the Social Welfare (Consolidation) Act 1993, discussed in the Social Welfare chapter, 507, below); the making of a special waste plan under article 4 of the European Communities (Toxic and Dangerous Waste) Regulations 1982; entry into arrangements under s. 15(2) or 15(3) of the Control of Dogs Act 1986 and the granting of assistance (other than the provision of services of staff) under s. 15(4) of the 1986 Act; the making of a decision to provide a public abattoir under s. 19(1) of the Abattoirs Act 1988; and the consideration of a request under s. 30(3) of the Local Government Act 1991. The 1993 Order came into operation on 1 March 1993.

SANITARY SERVICES

Notice to connect to public water supply   In *Keogh v Harnett and Arklow UDC*, High Court, 19 March 1993, the applicants were the owners and occupiers of two premises in Arklow, both of which were connected to the public water supply system. However, it appeared that, when a nearby premises took a branch connection between the applicants' premises and the main, the supply to the applicants' premises was adversely affected. The second respondent, the Council, served a notice on the applicants purportedly pursuant to s. 8(2) of the Local Government (Sanitary Services) Act 1962 requiring them to make individual water connections to the two premises which they owned. S. 8(2) of the 1962 Act empowers a sanitary authority to serve a notice on the owner of premises requiring the execution of specified works for the purpose of securing the service of the premises by the public water supply system. S. 8(2) provides that such a notice may be served where, in the opinion of the sanitary authority any premises are:

(i) not provided with a satisfactory supply of water, and
(ii) capable of being served by the public water supply system by means of a connection not exceeding one hundred feet in length. . . .

The applicants appealed the notice served on them to the District Court, the hearing being before the first respondent. The first respondent confirmed the notice made by the Council. The applicants then sought judicial review of the first respondents' decision and also of the notice served by the Council. Johnson J granted the relief sought.

In relation to the decision of the first respondent, the applicants argued that he had failed to comply with principles of fair procedures in not permitting evidence to be adduced as to the history of the water connection to the applicants' premises. Johnson J agreed that *certiorari* lay to quash the decision on the ground that it was relevant to hear evidence as to the fact that the nearby premises had taken a branch connection between the applicants' premises and the main, thereby affecting the supply to the applicants' premises.

On the notice issued by the Council, Johnson J also considered that the correct interpretation of s. 8 of the Local Government (Sanitary Services) Act 1962 was that it did not apply to premises which were already connected to a public water supply. Thus, a notice could not be served on the applicants, since they were already connected to the public supply. In addition, Johnson J cast some doubt on another aspect of the notice, namely that it did not state, as specified in s. 8(3) of the 1962 Act, what portion of the works required by the notice were to be undertaken by the Council itself as sanitary authority.

SERVICE CHARGES

In *O'Leary v Cork County Council* [1994] 1 IR 59, O'Hanlon J considered the scope of s. 2(1) of the Local Government (Financial Provisions) (No. 2) Act 1983, which conferred on local authorities a general power to charge for services.

In the instant case, the applicant challenged the Council's imposition of a £25 fee to register him as a 'dairyman' under the Milk and Dairies Act 1935. S. 21 of the 1935 Act requires every sanitary authority to keep a register of dairymen who are operating in the authority's functional area. S. 22 provides that a person who proposes to carry on the business of dairyman may apply to be registered with the authority. S. 23 provides that the authority may refuse registration if satisfied that the applicant or the premises sought to be registered are not suitable. S. 24 of the 1935 Act provides that it is an offence to carry on the business of dairyman unless the person concerned and their premises are registered in the authority's register. Finally, by virtue of s. 49(2) of the Abattoirs Act 1988, the functions to be carried out by an authority under the 1935 Act are to be regarded as being carried out in its capacity as local authority rather than as sanitary authority.

The applicant had been registered as a dairyman since 1958 and, until 1991, no fee had been imposed by the Council for such registration. When the £25 fee was imposed in 1991, the applicant paid the sum under protest and initiated judicial review proceedings. The Council argued that it was entitled to impose the fee under s. 2(1) of the Local Government (Financial Provisions) (No. 2) Act 1983. S. 2(1) of the 1983 Act provides that:

> Subject to section 4 of this Act, any existing enactment which requires or enables a local authority to provide a service but which, apart from this subsection, does not empower the authority to charge for the provision of the service shall be deemed so to empower that authority.

Of some importance in the instant case, s. 1(1) of the 1983 Act defines 'service' as follows:

> 'service' means any service, facility, licence, permit, certificate, approval or other thing which a local authority may render, supply, grant, issue or otherwise provide in the performance or exercice of any of its functions, powers or duties to any person or in respect of any premises and includes the processing of an application for such a licence, permit, certificate or approval.

Given the breadth of these two provisions in the 1983 Act, O'Hanlon J

commented that 'the present claim for relief is an important one, notwithstanding the smallness of the amount of the charge which is being disputed
by the applicant.'

O'Hanlon J agreed with the applicant's argument that the Council was
not providing a service 'within the ordinary meaning of that expression' since
the registration system under the 1935 Act was a facet of the curtailment, in
the public interest, of the rights of people to carry on the business of
dairyman. Nonetheless, he concluded that, in view of what he described as
the 'rather artificial and extended' meaning of service contained in s. 1(1) of
the 1983 Act, the Council had acted *intra vires*. Relying in particular on the
decision of Gannon J in *Ballybay Meat Exports Ltd v Monaghan County
Council* [1990] ILRM 864 (see the 1990 Review, 406-7), the applicant had
argued that s. 2(1) of the 1983 Act should be restricted to the provision of a
discretionary service of a commercial nature, such as the provision of car
parks, but not to matters of obligation such as the provision of sewers.

O'Hanlon J declined to limit s. 2(1) of the 1983 Act in this way, pointing
out that s. 2(1) referred to any existing enactment 'which requires or enables
a local authority to *provide* a service' (emphasis added by O'Hanlon J). This
conclusion by O'Hanlon J indicates the potential scope of the power conferred by s. 2(1) of the 1983 Act. Whether s. 2(1) will be used in the future
as a means of raising further revenue directly by local authorities remains to
be seen. As we noted in the 1991 Review, the Local Government Act 1991
also provides for the conferring of additional powers and functions on local
authorities, and it seems more likely that additional revenue-raising functions
will arise from the use of the 1991 Act rather than the 1983 Act. We may
note that, in the present context, the registration system under the 1935 Act
had originally been under the control of the 'sanitary authority', but that, by
virtue of what O'Hanlon J described as 'an obscure provision' in s. 49(2) of
the Abattoirs Act 1988, this had been altered to 'local authority'. It was for
this reason that s. 2(1) of the 1983 Act became applicable in the instant case.
Given that many powers in existing legislation have been conferred on local
authorities acting as sanitary authorities, this provides some limits to the
decision in the instant case.

VALUATION (RATING)

Plant inducing process of change   In *Caribmolasses Co. Ltd v Commissioner of Valuation*, Supreme Court, 25 May 1993, the company owned and
operated two large tanks at Dublin Docks. Crude molasses was pumped into
the tanks from ships, and hot water was later added to different shipments of
the molasses, after it left the tanks, to achieve a standardised consistency for

the company's customers. The Commissioner of Valuation determined that the tanks were rateable hereditaments under the valuation code. The company appealed to the Valuation Tribunal which held that the tanks were non-rateable in accordance with ss. 7 and 8 of the Valuation Act 1986, which, by means of amendments to the Valuation (Ireland) Act 1852 and the Valuation (Ireland) Act 1860, excluded from rating plant designed or used primarily to induce a process of change in the substance contained or transmitted. On a case stated, Gannon J [1991] ILRM had upheld the decision of the Tribunal: see the 1990 Review, 424-6. On further appeal, the Supreme Court (Egan, Blayney and Denham JJ) reversed Gannon J's decision and held that the original decision of the Commissioner had been correct.

Delivering the Court's decision, Blayney J held that the tanks were rateable under s. 8 of the 1986 Act for the simple reason that the evidence indicated that 'no process of change is induced. The molasses remains molasses.' Insofar as any change occured by means of the blending of the different shipments, this occurred outside the tanks in which the molasses was held. Blayney J rejected a suggested analogy with the Court's decision in *Beamish & Crawford Ltd v Commissioner of Valuation* [1980] ILRM 149, noting that whereas that case was concerned with the issue of whether tanks used in brewing constituted machinery, that question did not arise in the instant case at all.

Set-off against unpaid rates In *In re Casey, a Bankrupt (No. 2)*, High Court, 1 March 1993, the extensive nature of the right of set-off in respect of unpaid rates conferred on a local authority by s. 58 of the Local Government Act 1941 was considered: see the discussion in the Commercial Law chapter, 45, above.

WATER POLLUTION

Regulations concerning water pollution are referred to in the Safety and Health chapter, 475, below.

Practice and Procedure

ABUSE OF PROCESS

A number of cases in 1993 considered whether an action should be dismissed as an abuse of process under O.19, r.28 of the Rules of the Superior Courts 1986: see *Kelly v McCarthy and Ors*, High Court, 14 January 1993, *per* Morris J and *LAC Minerals Ltd v Chevron Mineral Corp of Ireland*, High Court, 6 August 1993, *per* Keane J. The decision of the Supreme Court in *O'Neill v Ryan and Ors (No. 1)* [1993] ILRM 557 is discussed in the Company Law chapter, 91-3, above.

APPELLATE COURT FUNCTION

Variance of court order   The power of the Supreme Court to vary court orders was discussed in *Belville Holdings Ltd v Revenue Commissioners* [1994] 1 ILRM 29 (to be discussed in the Revenue Law chapter in the 1994 Review) and in *Attorney General (SPUC Ltd) v Open Door Counselling Ltd (No. 2)* [1994] 1 ILRM 256 (see the Constitutional Law chapter, 160-5, above).

COSTS

Counsel's brief fees: reasonableness   In *McGahon v Independent Newspapers Ltd*, High Court, 20 October 1993, Kinlen J upheld a taxation of costs made by the Taxing Master in respect of brief fees settled by senior and junior counsel in a complex defamation action. Kinlen J's judgment was *ex tempore* and a newspaper account only of his judgment was available to the authors, though the account appears quite comprehensive: *Irish Times*, 21 October 1993, p. 2.

The plaintiff, an elected member of Dáil Éireann, or Teachta Dála (TD), had instituted defamataion proceedings against the defendants arising out of two articles published in two of their newspapers in 1987 and 1988. The defendants pleaded in their defence, *inter alia*, fair comment on a matter of public interest. The plaintiff retained two senior counsel and one junior counsel for the case. The plaintiff's solicitor agreed a brief fee of £7,350 for each of the senior counsel and a brief fee of £4,900 for the junior counsel, and the plaintiff agreed to these fees. Senior counsel had explained that the matter was complex, involving the plea of fair comment, and also concerned two separate articles and the solicitor stated that this was the most complicated defamation action he had come across in practice. When the case came on for hearing in 1992, it was settled for £25,000 without admission of liability.

When the plaintiff's bill of costs was later produced, the defendants sought to have them taxed. The defendants pointed to the disparity between the fees for the plaintiff's counsel and those for the defendants', whose senior counsel had settled a brief fee of £2,100, the brief fee for their junior counsel being £1,400. However, the Taxing Master upheld the brief fees, concluding that the plaintiff's solicitor was entitled to have regard to his experience as a solicitor without being required to make further enquiries as to the level of fees charged in defamation actions. In essence, this view was upheld by Kinlen J on appeal to the High Court. He is reported as having said:

> As it stands, the law is what the market will bear. . . . It doesn't matter if the court may feel the fees are too high, if they are the fees the market will bear.

Kinlen J is also reported as having commented that, if one wanted an expert in any field one asked the expert what the fee was, and that if the fee was outrageous the person might choose another expert. He is reported as having noted that, in this instance, the fees had been fixed with the plaintiff's approval.

For a more extensive consideration of the issue of disparities between the fees charged by plaintiff's and defendant's counsel, see *Crotty v An Taoiseach (No. 2)* [1990] ILRM 617 discussed in the 1989 Review, 346-7.

Security for costs In *Fares v Wiley* [1994] 1 ILRM 465, the Supreme Court applied the decision of Finlay P, as he then was, in *Collins v Doyle* [1982] ILRM 495 in granting the defendant security for costs in respect of his personal injuries action against the defendant.

The plaintiff, a resident of Libya, had instituted a personal injuries action against the defendant arising from a traffic accident involving the defendant's car. The defendant denied liability and brought an application for security for costs. This was refused by MacKenzie J on the ground that it would be open to the trial judge to find both parties at fault and that to grant the application would be to deny the plaintiff his right of action simply because he lived in another country. The defendant appealed and the Supreme Court

(O'Flaherty, Egan and Blayney JJ) unanimously allowed the defendant's appeal in an *ex tempore* judgment delivered by O'Flaherty J.

O'Flaherty J referred with approval to the following propositions contained in Finlay P's judgment in the *Collins* case:

(1) *Prima facie* a defendant establishing a *prima facie* defence to a claim made by a plaintiff residing outside the jurisdiction has a right to an order for security for costs.

(2) This is not an absolute right and the court must exercise a discretion based on the facts of each individual case.

(3) Poverty on the part of the plaintiff making it impossible for him to comply with an order for security for costs is not even when *prima facie* established, of itself, automatically a reason for refusing the order.

(4) Amongst the matters to which a court may have regard in exercising a discretion against ordering security is if a *prima facie* case has been made by the plaintiff to the effect that his inability to give security flows from the wrong committed by the defendant.

Of these four principles, O'Flaherty J considered that the first seemed to apply in the instant case. In relation to the discretion to be exercised by the Court, O'Flaherty J noted that points (3) and (4) were not in issue in the instant case and that, indeed, the plaintiff was a man of some means so that there could be no question of poverty. In those circumstances, he ordered that the plaintiff should give security for costs.

O'Flaherty J added that, having read the papers in the case, he considered it was a case that would call for a rather modest sum to be fixed by way of security.

Standby fees   In *Aspell v O'Brien* [1992] ILRM 278 (HC); [1993] ILRM 590 (SC); [1991] 2 IR 416 (HC); [1993] 3 IR 516 (SC), the Supreme Court held that the payment of standy fees to professional witnesses were proper disbursements and were thus appropriate items for taxation under O.99, r.37 of the Rules of the Superior Courts 1986, thus reversing the decision of Costello J in the High Court (1991 Review, 332-3).

The plaintiff's personal injury action against the defendant had been listed for 30 and 31 May 1990. Evidence was heard on 30 May but the action was settled on 31 May. Counsel for the plaintiff had directed the attendance of four doctors, but only one had given evidence when the case was settled. All four doctors had charged standby fees for 30 May, and the plaintiff's solicitor discharged these fees. It was a long-standing practice that such standby fees were not allowed on taxation by the Taxing Master, but the Law Society of Ireland recommended that such fees be discharged. It was argued that such fees should be allowed on taxation, but the Taxing Master declined to allow them. On appeal, Costello J affirmed the Taxing Master's decision but, as indicated, this was reversed by the Supreme Court (Finlay CJ, O'Flaherty and Denham JJ).

Delivering the Court's unanimous decision, O'Flaherty J concluded that the practice which had developed amongst solicitors of paying 'standby fees' to witnesses to secure their attendance was a reasonable one so that such payments were proper disbursements within the meaning of O.99, r.37 of the 1986 Rules and could not be regarded as 'special charges or expenses' within the meaning of O.99, r.37(18). O'Flaherty J pointed to the approval of the practice by the Law Society and also to the acceptance of such fees by insurance companies involved in personal injuries litigation. He thus concluded that such payments would lead to a reduction of costs in such actions as a full attendance fee would not be charged by the professional on 'standby'. On the other policy issues raised by the case, concerning the acceptance in evidence of written medical reports, see the 1991 Review, 333. See also generally on hearsay in civil cases the 1990 Review, 440.

COURTHOUSES

Failure to maintain Circuit Court courthouses As we noted in the 1992 Review, 478, the Civil Bill Courts (Ireland) Act 1851 (Adaptation) (No. 2) Order 1992 (SI No. 174 of 1992) was made to enable the government to exercise the functions formerly exercisable by the Lord Lieutenant under s. 31 of the 1851 Act and in purported exercise of the powers conferred on the Minister for Justice by s. 22(4)(b) of the Courts (Supplemental Provisions) Act 1961. We also noted that the Civil Bill Courts (Ireland) Act 1851 (Adaptation) Order 1992 (SI No. 193 of 1992) was made for precisely the same purpose as SI No. 174 of 1992. However, SI No. 193 of 1992 was made in purported exercise of the powers conferred on the government by s. 12 of the Adaptation of Enactments Act 1922 and s. 5 of the Constitution (Consequential Provisions) Act 1937. Both these Orders under the 1851 Act were made on 23 June 1992, despite appearances to the contrary arising from the gap in the SI numbers allocated to them.

We pointed out in the 1992 Review that the purpose of these Orders was to allow the government to determine that a particular courthouse was no longer required for sittings of the Circuit Court. The validity of these Orders was successfully challenged in *Hoey v Minister for Justice* [1994] 1 ILRM 334. We now turn to discuss that decision.

The background was as follows. Sittings of the Circuit Court at the courthouse in Drogheda ceased in 1964 due to its state of disrepair. In 1972 the High Court ordered the Minister for Justice to perform the duties imposed on him by s. 6 of the Courthouses (Provision and Maintenance) Act 1935. Repairs were carried out in compliance with this order and sittings recommenced in 1974. The Circuit Court sittings at Drogheda continued until July 1991 when Drogheda Corporation served a dangerous buildings notice on Louth County Council and the sittings were transferred to Dundalk. On 11 July 1991 the President of the Circuit Court made an order pursuant to s. 10 of Courts of Justice Act 1947 specifying the venues at which the court should sit in the Eastern Circuit. This order omitted Drogheda.

The applicants, who were solicitors practising in the town of Drogheda, wrote to Louth County Council and the Minister calling upon them to perform their duties under the 1935 Act. In a letter dated 19 June 1992 the Minister indicated that, pursuant to s. 3 of the 1935 Act, the County Council was not required by the Minister to provide courthouse accommodation in Drogheda for sittings of the Circuit Court and that the sittings would be fully accommodated by the courthouse in Dundalk, and that accordingly the Council was not required to repair the courthouse or provide a replacement building.

The applicants were unaware that the Minister had already written to the Council on 8 January 1992 stating that he did not require the provision of courthouse accommodation in Drogheda for the Circuit Court sittings and that sittings would be accommodated by the continued provision and maintenance of the courthouse in Dundalk. On 23 June 1992 the government and the Minister for Justice made the two Orders already referred to, SI No. 193 of 1992 and SI No. 174 of 1992, purportedly pursuant to s. 31 of the Civil Bill Courts (Ireland) Act 1851. These Orders purported to allow the government and the Minister for Justice to provide that the courthouse in Drogheda should be discontinued as a Circuit Court venue with effect from that date. This discontinuation was purportedly effected by another Order entitled the Circuit Court (Drogheda) Amendment Order 1992, which was not promulgated as a statutory instrument.

The applicants challenged these Orders and sought an order of *mandamus* compelling the respondent to perform the duties imposed by s. 6 of the 1935 Act. Lynch J granted the order of *mandamus* requiring the Minister to direct the County Council to provide accommodation for the Circuit Court in Drogheda, though he put a stay on the order until 1 December 1993, with liberty to both parties to apply for further relief.

In relation to the statutory provisions applicable to the case, Lynch J pointed out that s. 3(1) of the Courthouses (Provision and Maintenance) Act 1935 states that every Council shall provide and maintain in their functional area courthouse accommodation for the sittings of any court which are held in their functional area as the Minister shall direct either generally or in any particular case. He considered that, by virtue of s. 3(2), it was clear that the courthouse in Drogheda must be deemed to have been provided by the Council in pursuance of the 1935 Act. It followed that *prima facie* an obligation rested on the Council to repair and maintain the courthouse and on the Minister under s. 6 to ensure that the Council complied with their obligations.

Lynch J accepted that the executive could agree to indemnify the local authority against the cost of observing the requirements of the 1935 Act, but such an agreement could not in any way limit or reduce the statutory obligations of local authorities or the Minister. Thus, budgetary and financial constraints could not afford an answer to the present proceedings. He opined that if the executive wished to limit or reduce its obligations it would have to seek the enactment of appropriate legislation by the Oireachtas.

As to the two Orders made in 1992, Lynch J held that s. 31 of the Civil Bill Courts (Ireland) Act 1851, as adapted, did not apply to the present Circuit Court. He accepted the argument by the applicants that it had been impliedly repealed, first of all by the creation of the Circuit Court under the Courts of Justice Act 1924, and subsequently by the Courts (Establishment and Con-stitution) Act 1961. He accepted the point adumbrated in cases such as *The People v Bell* [1969] IR 24 that the 1924 and 1961 Acts established wholly new courts and they were not merely a continuation of the former courts. Thus, the two Orders purporting to adapt s. 31 of the 1851 Act and the Order purporting to delete Drogheda as a Circuit Court venue were of no effect. In any event, Lynch J concluded that these Orders had not been made to regulate the sittings of the Circuit Court but merely to provide a defence to the present proceedings and for that reason they were void.

However, Lynch J also made clear that, while the County Council were obliged under s. 3 of the 1935 Act to provide suitable accommodation as directed by the Minister, they were not bound to maintain the same court-house building and were entitled to abandon an old or dilapidated building provided that they made available suitable alternative accommodation for the sittings of the Circuit Court.

Finally, we may note for the sake of completeness that two similar challenges to those in the *Hoey* case were made in respect of courthouses in Carrick-on-Shannon and in Clonmel. Judgments in these two cases, *Keane v Minister for Justice*, High Court, 3 September 1993 and *Reilly and Morris v Minister for Justice*, High Court, 3 September 1993 were also delivered by Lynch J on the same date as in the *Hoey* case. The essential approach of Lynch J in both cases was identical to that in the *Hoey* case, though the details of these cases differed in some respects.

Thus, in the *Keane* case, Lynch J held that s. 16 of the Courts of Justice Act 1953 and s. 3 of the Courts of Justice Act 1964 had the effect of requiring the Minister for Justice to ensure that the full range of circuit court business, civil and criminal, must be capable of being conducted in every county of the eight circuits in the State. Thus, the provision of a courthouse in Manorhamilton which was unsuitable for criminal work did not meet the requirements of the 1935 Act.

And in the *Reilly and Morris* case, no order of *mandamus* issued as remedial work was in train in relation to the Clonmel courthouse, but otherwise Lynch J would have granted the relief sought.

COURT ORDER

The circumstances in which a court may alter or amend a final court order were considered in two Supreme Court decisions in 1993. In *Belville Holdings Ltd v Revenue Commissioners* [1994] 1 ILRM 29, the Court was prepared to amend a final order. However, in *Attorney General (SPUC Ltd) v Open Door Counselling Ltd (No. 2)* [1994] 1 ILRM 256, discussed in the Constitutional Law chapter, 160-5, above, the Court declined to interfere with a final order of the Court itself. In both cases, the Court accepted the general principles stated in *Ainsworth v Wilding* [1896] 1 Ch 673. However, in the *Open Door* case, Denham J in dissent emphasised that, pursuant to Article 34 of the Constitution, the Supreme Court had a greater inherent power to vary orders than the majority was prepared to concede.

DELAY

Delay in processing claims   The case law on delay in processing criminal proceedings is discussed in the Criminal Law chapter, 223-6, above.

Delay in delivering judgment   In *O'Donoghue v Minister for Health and Ors*, High Court, 27 May 1993 (discussed in the Constitutional Law chapter, 151-7, above), O'Hanlon J apologised to the parties for a delay of ten months between the conclusion of the hearing of what was a complex constitutional action and the delivery of his judgment in the case. He stated that:

> . . . this is an inevitable consequence of a situation where the number of judges appointed to the High Court is not sufficient to enable the ordinary work of the Court to continue while judges who have to prepare reserved judgments are allowed time off to complete their work. I hope

that this problem, which has now become a serious one, can be addressed, otherwise justice delayed will continue to be justice denied.

This very worrying comment from O'Hanlon J no doubt reflects a view which others would share. It might be said that, in relation to the complexities of the case with which he was dealing, the delay involved would have been understandable in any event. And no doubt, practitioners might be able to cite even longer gaps between the reserving of judgments by other members of the High Court in less complex cases. While the appointment of more judges to the High Court would not cure all the problems reflected in the passage from O'Hanlon J's judgment, his views reflect a real need.

DISCOVERY

General continuing obligation to discover rejected In *Bula Ltd and Ors v Tara Mines Ltd and Ors (No. 7)* [1994] 1 IR 487 (for previous judgments see the 1987 Review, 282-3, the 1990 Review, 432-4; the 1991 Review, 336 and 240 and below, 452-3) Murphy J and, on appeal, the Supreme Court rejected the suggestion that parties to litigation were under a continuing obligation to 'top up' affidavits of discovery. However, the Supreme Court indicated that, in highly exceptional circumstances, there may be an obligation to discover documents which come into existence after the initial affidavit of discovery is sworn.

The moving plaintiffs had applied for further and better discovery of the 'records to date and not already discovered of communications between the . . . defendants . . . and with any others, including their advisers.' The defendants resisted the application on the grounds that, firstly, the documents in question were priviliged and, secondly, the communications between the defendants and their advisers were not in existence, still less in their possession, at the time when the original affidavit of discovery was made by them.

Counsel for the moving plaintiffs asserted that there was a continuing obligation to place on record any documents which might come into existence after the affidavit of discovery is filed, and relied on passages from the 1988 edition of the English *Supreme Court Practice* (the 'White Book'), dealing with O.24, rr.1/2 of the English Rules of the Supreme Court, and also a passage in another English text, Mathews, Malek and Bradfield, *Discovery*, p.103. Researches by counsel into the cases cited by these textbooks revealed that they did not support what Murphy J had described in the High Court as a 'surprising proposition'.

Murphy J accepted that if, subsequent to filing an affidavit of discovery, the deponent traced a document which was in existence at the time the affidavit was filed, the deponent would be required to rectify the error. But he was not convinced that there was a continuing obligation under O.31, r.12 of the Rules of the Superior Courts 1986 to make further affidavits of discovery to detail documents which come into existence subsequent to the date of the original affidavit.

On appeal, this general view was upheld by the Supreme Court (Finlay CJ, Egan and Denham JJ). In the only reasoned judgment delivered, Finlay CJ noted that a continuing obligation to discover documents would impose an almost impossible burden on the party against whom discovery was initially ordered. He also took the view that such an obligation could lead to the absurd situation where such a party would only communicate verbally with their advisers or other persons once the original affidavit of discovery was sworn. Finlay CJ continued:

> Such a situation, in my view, would not only lead to a patent absurdity but would be demonstrably invidious as far as the due and proper administration of justice and trial of actions is concerned. I therefore conclude that there is no question of any principle of a continuing automatic obligation for discovery of documents created and brought into existence after the filing of an affidavit of discovery.

However, the Court also dealt with an alternative contention that discovery should be ordered in cases such as the present where the substantive action consists of claims for continuing wrongs in conspiracy and trespass (see the description of the claim in the instant case in the 1987 Review, 282) and where the plaintiffs have, *prima facie*, established the existence of such documents. The plaintiffs relied on the general power in O.31, r.20(3) of the Rules of the Superior Courts 1986 to order a party to state whether a particular document or documents 'is or are . . . in his possession or power.' It was argued that this covered the possibility of ordering discovery of documents created after the original affidavit of discovery.

Finlay CJ noted that there was no authority of which counsel was aware where any such order for discovery had been made under 0.31, r.20(3), nor was he aware from his own experience of any such order. Nonetheless, he was prepared to conclude 'with some hesitation and on the basis of principle only' that, having regard to the importance of the discovery of documents, as confirmed by the Court in *Smurfit Paribas Bank Ltd v AAB Export Finance Ltd* [1990] ILRM 588; [1990] 1 IR 469 (see the 1990 Review, 435-6):

> . . . it would not be correct to say that there may not be cases and instances where a court would, in the interests of justice, direct the discovery and

production of a specified document, at the request of a party, even though it had come into existence after the filing of an earlier affidavit of discovery.

The tentative and negative manner in which Finlay CJ stated this rule indicates the exceptional nature of the power being acknowledged in the Court's decision. Finlay CJ stated that the jurisdiction would be 'very sparingly used and only in accordance with very limited and restricted conditions.' Without purporting to lay down a comprehensive set of such conditions, he referred to four factors which were relevant to the instant case. First, the moving party would be required to specify particular documents and not merely indicate the possibility of a type or range of documents. Second, where the documents are created after proceedings have been initiated and would thus be *prima facie* privileged, discovery would only be ordered where the court is satisfied that for some 'special reason' the privilege should be lifted. Third, the moving party must show that the document cannot be obtained in any other way. Finally, Finlay CJ stated that the moving party would be required to prove 'not only a general probability of relevance but a significant important relevance of a specified or identifiable kind.' Whatever the exact meaning of the latter condition, it is clear that the Court was imposing a high standard of proof on the moving party.

The difficult task facing a moving party was illustrated by the fact that, in the instant case, the Court concluded that the plaintiffs had failed to meet the criteria laid down. Finlay CJ concluded that most of the documents sought by the plaintiffs, being communications between the defendants concerning the plaintiffs, were manifestly privileged and that no useful function would be served by ordering discovery. Other documents, while potentially relevant to the plaintiffs' action, failed to meet the strict criteria for this exceptional type of discovery order. In those circumstances, the Supreme Court upheld the order of Murphy J in the High Court, though on different grounds.

Legal professional privilege: attendances   In *Irish Press plc v Ingersoll Irish Publications Ltd (No. 2)* [1994] 1 IR 208, Barron J and the Supreme Court ordered third party discovery of certain attendance notes and other office memoranda prepared by a firm of solicitors which were regarded as being relevant to the issues in the case. For discussion of whether the case should be held in public, see *Irish Press plc v Ingersoll Irish Publications Ltd (No. 1)* [1993] ILRM 747; [1994] 1 IR 176, below, 460.

Legal professional privilege: moral turpitude   In the 1992 Review, 480-2, we discussed the decision of Costello J in *Murphy v Kirwan*, High Court,

9 April 1992; [1994] 1 ILRM 293 (SC); [1993] 3 IR 501 (SC), in which he
ordered discovery by the plaintiff of correspondence, notes and memoranda
between the plaintiff and his legal advisers and between those legal advisers.
We noted there that in July 1993 the Supreme Court had upheld this decision
and that the case thus constitutes an exception to the normal privilege
attached to communications with legal advisers. We now return to discuss
the Supreme Court decision in the case. To do so, we should briefly
recapitulate the background.

The plaintiff had instituted the instant proceedings for specific performance claiming the existence of an enforceable agreement to assign certain
shares in a company to the plaintiff. These shares related to ownership of a
number of properties. The defendant at all times denied the existence of this
alleged agreement and sought to have the claim dismissed by the High Court
as vexatious and an abuse of the processes of the court. This application was
refused, and the defendant then entered a full defence to the claim and also
entered a counterclaim claiming damages on the ground that by the institution
of the proceedings, the plaintiff had deliberately endeavoured to forestall the
sale by the defendant to a third party of the properties connected with the
shares involved in the litigation, and he claimed that the proceedings were
frivolous, vexatious and brought without reasonable cause and were an abuse
of the processes of the court.

On the hearing of the plaintiff's claim, the trial judge non-suited the
plaintiff after hearing his evidence and dismissed his claim with costs. The
defendant's counterclaim was then deferred and it was in this context that
the defendant then sought discovery of the communications between the
plaintiff and his legal advisers and between the plaintiff's legal advisers. The
plaintiff sought to resist discovery on the basis of the usual privilege attaching
to such matters. As already indicated, Costello J considered that the instant
case fell within the narrow category of exceptional circumstances in which
discovery should be ordered and the Supreme Court (Finlay CJ, O'Flaherty
and Egan JJ) upheld this view. While the Court was in agreement on the
principles to be applied, Egan J dissented from the conclusion that discovery
should be ordered.

Delivering the leading judgment, Finlay CJ traced the origin of the
exemption from privilege to *R. v Cox* (1884) 14 QBD 153, which dealt with
the furtherance of a criminal purpose. However, Finlay CJ accepted Costello
J's description of the extension of the exemption to include all forms of fraud
and dishonesty, such as fraudulent breach of trust, fraudulent conspiracy,
trickery and sham contrivances. Finlay CJ commented:

> I am satisfied that these extensions of the application of the exemption
> flow logically and consistently from the principle laid down in *Cox's*

case for the real reason for the introduction of the exemption in the first place, and that the essence of the matter is that professional privilege cannot and must not be applied so as to be injurious to the interests of justice and to those in the administration of justice where persons have been guilty of conduct of moral turpitude or of dishonest conduct, even though it may not be fraud.

Nothing could be more injurious to the administration of justice nor to the interests of justice than that a person should falsely and maliciously bring an action, and should abuse for an ulterior or improper purpose the processes of the court.

He thus concurred with Costello J's description of the legal position. He then went on to consider whether the defendant has given sufficient evidence of a plausible or viable case to support his claim for discovery. It was on this point that the the Court divided, Finlay CJ and O'Flaherty J (the latter with 'a degree of scepticism') holding that the order should be made while Egan J concluded that a case had not been made out by the defendant. Finlay CJ was prepared to place some reliance on the fact that the plaintiff had at no stage filed an affidavit to dispute the defendant's claim that the plaintiff had lacked *bona fides* in instituting the original action which had been non-suited. While emphasising that this in no way determined the matter, he concluded that this supported a plausible or viable case in favour of the motion for discovery.

While the *Murphy* case is of great importance in indicating circumstances where the courts will order discovery of communications with legal advisers which are clearly in contemplation of legal proceedings, it must be concluded that the general privilege remains intact. However, the courts have clearly indicated that this privilege will not be extended, a point noted in the 1990 Review, 435-6, and that it is not an automatic entitlement.

The limits to the decision in *Murphy v Kirwan* were quickly illustrated by the decision of the Court less than three months later in *Bula Ltd and Ors v Crowley and Ors (No. 4)* [1994] 1 ILRM 495. Here the Court refused to order discovery of communications between the first defendant, an accountant, and his legal advisers. The plaintiffs claimed that the defendant had neglected to follow the legal advice he had been given and that, as a result, the plaintiffs had suffered loss.

However, the Supreme Court (Finlay CJ, Egan and Denham JJ) distinguished this from the situation in *Murphy v Kirwan*, in which it had been alleged that a criminal act had been committed. The Court was not prepared to extend this to a situation where it was being alleged that the defendant had acted negligently and in that sense had been involved in committing a tort. The Court concluded that such an extension of the principle accepted in

Murphy v Kirwan would involve a 'massive undermining' of the privilege between legal advisers and their clients and which the Court said 'is considered in all the authorities to be a major contributor to the proper admninistration of justice.' The Court went on to hold that the suggestion that it should examine the documents in question in order to determine whether they be discovered also suffered from the same attempt to undermine the lawyer-client privilege and it declined to examine them.

Professional advisers   In *Bula Ltd and Ors v Tara Mines Ltd and Ors (No. 8)* [1994] 1 ILRM 111 (SC) and Supreme Court, 11 October 1993 (for previous judgments see the 1987 Review, 282-3, the 1990 Review 432-4, the 1991 Review, 336 and 340 and above, 447), the Supreme Court, in judgments delivered in June and October 1993 (the latter being *ex tempore*) ordered discovery of certain documents in the possession of professional advisers to the Minister for Energy, a defendant in the proceedings.

The case centred on the scope of O.31, r.12(1) of the Rules of the Superior Courts 1986, the general provision concerning discovery, and in particular whether the documents were 'in [the] possession or power' of the Minister. The plaintiffs' discovery motion sought that the Minister should request from those professional advisers (Arthur Cox & Co, solicitors, Coopers & Lybrand, accountants and ICC Bank) all documents in the possession or procurement of the professional advisers which related to the issues in the proceedings (other than internal memoranda or drafts prepared by the professional advisers for their own purposes as distinct from final drafts or advice prepared for the Minister) and that the Minister should then discover such documents.

In the High Court, Murphy J had refused the order, holding that the issue should be more appropriately dealt with under the third-party discovery procedure in O.31, r.29 of the 1986 Rules. On appeal by the plaintiffs, the Supreme Court (Finlay CJ, O'Flaherty and Egan JJ) unanimously reversed and granted the order sought.

Delivering the Court's decision, O'Flaherty J referred with approval to the Court of Appeal decision in *Leicestershire County Council v Michael Faraday and Partners Ltd* [1941] 2 KB 205 on the question of what constituted being 'within the power' of a party for the purposes of the 1986 Rules. He concluded that final documents, approved by the professional adviser for sight by the Minister, were documents within the 'power' of the Minister and were discoverable under O.31, r.12. This was because the Minister had an enforceable legal right to obtain these documents without the need to obtain the consent of anyone else. However, all other documents held by the advisers were preparatory and personal to the professional adviser and not discoverable under O.31, r.12.

In its later *ex tempore* judgment in October 1993 on this matter, the Court concluded that the Minister had made all efforts to comply with the order for discovery and that the case should proceed to hearing. The Court had examined a particular document which the plaintiffs claimed had not been discovered on foot of the Court's earlier order. However, the Court concluded that this document was in fact a draft of a later document which had been discovered. As this was a draft prepared by the adviser in question, it was not discoverable under the terms of the earlier judgment.

Public interest: confidentiality In *Goodman International v Mr Justice Hamilton (No. 3)* [1993] 3 IR 320, Geoghegan J approved the criteria laid down by Lord Edmund-Davies in *D. v NSPCC* [1978] AC 171 in connection with the disclosure or non-disclosure of material in respect of which a confidentiality is claimed: see the discussion in the Constitutional Law chapter, 168, above.

A similar approach was taken in two other judgments delivered in 1993, that of Denham J in *Wong v Minister for Justice (No. 2)*, High Court, 16 March 1993 and of Costello J in *Buckley v Incorporated Law Society of Ireland*, High Court, 2 November 1993.

In a third case, *Burke v Central Independent Television plc* [1994] 2 ILRM 161 (HC & SC), which involved very unusual circumstances indeed, a High Court decision that discovery should be restricted by allowing sight of documents to lawyers only was reversed on appeal by the Supreme Court in judgments delivered in 1994. We will consider the *Wong* and *Buckley* cases first and then proceed to discuss the High Court judgment in the *Burke* case.

In *Wong v Minister for Justice (No. 2)*, High Court, 16 March 1993 the applicant had instituted judicial review proceedings seeking to quash a decision made by the Minister for Justice under the Aliens Acts 1935 to 1970 refusing him permission to remain in Ireland. In 1992, an issue arose as to whether media coverage of the initial stages of the case amounted to contempt of court: see *Wong v Minister for Justice* [1994] 1 IR 223, discussed in the 1992 Review, 242-3. The judgment under discussion here concerned a discovery motion by the applicant.

The applicant's case rested, in part, on the question whether a stamp affixed to the applicant's passport by a member of the Garda Síochána working in the Aliens Registration Office had been validly made. An official in the Department of Justice deposed on affidavit that the Garda in question had been moved from the Aliens Registration Office and was the subject of an investigation into the circumstances in which the stamp had been applied. The Minister's defence to the applicant's judicial review was based, in part, on an assertion that the stamp had been invalidly affixed to the applicant's passport and that, consequently, the applicant did not meet the residency requirements to be considered for naturalisation.

The applicant sought to discover a number of documents, some of which concerned the affixing of the stamp to the applicant's passport and some of which related to what Denham J described as the wider aspects of the applicant's case. The Minister sought to claim privilege in respect of the documents. Having examined the documents, Denham J ordered discovery of a limited number of them.

In approaching the documents in question, Denham J accepted the general principles laid down in *Murphy v Dublin Corporation* [1972] IR 215 and *Ambiorix Ltd v Minister for the Environment* [1992] ILRM 209; [1992] 1 IR 277 (see the 1991 Review, 338-9) that it was a matter for the courts to determine the conflict between the public interest involved in production and the public interest in the confidentiality of documents concerning the executive. Some of the documents which she examined concerned the possible initiation of criminal proceedings as well as certain information from a third party concerning the applicant.

On the question of privilege in respect of what amounts to information from police informers, Denham J quoted with approval the views of the House of Lords in *D. v NSPCC* [1978] AC 171 as well as those of Costello J in *Director of Consumer Affairs and Fair Trade v Sugar Distributors Ltd* [1991] ILRM 395; [1991] 1 IR 225 (see the 1990 Review, 434-5). In respect of the more general question of information and files collected by the authorities in the course of a criminal investigation or in a matter of some sensitivity to the security of the State, Denham J also quoted with approval the views of Murphy J in *Gormley v Ireland* [1993] 2 IR 75 (see the 1991 Review, 339-40).

In relation both to the statement of a third party (who Denham J described as an 'informant') concerning the applicant and also the Garda minute forwarding the statement to the Department of Justice, Denham J noted that these two items did not relate to the affixing of the stamp to the applicant's passport but were of relevance to the applicant's general position. However, she concluded that, on balance, the identity of the informant should not be revealed and she refused discovery of these documents. Denham J ordered discovery of portions of certain other documents which, although again not directly related to the question of the affixing of the stamp to the applicant's passport, she none the less considered contained 'some paragraphs [which] relate to issues which it would be unfair and unreasonable to conceal from the applicant.'

Finally, we may note that Denham J followed the approach taken by Murphy J in the *Gormley* case, above, by reminding the parties that discovered documents were to be used solely for the purposes of the litigation, and with that in mind the documents would be made available to the applicants' legal advisers alone.

The second case in 1993 which raised the issue of discovery of confidential material was *Buckley v Incorporated Law Society of Ireland*, High Court, 2 November 1993. Here, the plaintiff had instructed a solicitor to institute proceedings against his employer for damages arising from injuries sustained in an accident at work. Due to the negligence of the solicitor, the plaintiff's claim became statute barred. He then instituted the present proceedings against the defendant Law Society, claiming that the Society's negligence in failing to strike off the solicitor arising from previous complaints against the solicitor had caused the plaintiff to suffer loss. The defendant denied liability. The plaintiff applied for discovery of the Society's files concerning their investigations into previous complaints against the solicitor.

Costello J held that the Society could not claim privilege in respect of these files. He held that legal privilege did not attach to them since any replies given by the solicitor to the Law Society in the course of an investigation did not form part of the advice given by the solicitor to his clients. In addition, applying the principles Costello J had himself stated in *Director of Consumer Affairs and Fair Trade v Sugar Distributors Ltd* [1991] ILRM 395; [1991] 1 IR 225 (see the 1991 Review, 434-5), he concluded that, despite the confidentiality of the investigations conducted by the Law Society, they should not be immune from discovery.

The third case dealing with questions of confidentiality was *Burke v Central Independent Television plc* [1994] 2 ILRM 161 (HC & SC). Here, the plaintiffs had instituted libel proceedings arising from an edition of the TV series 'The Cook Report'. The plaintiffs claimed that the programme had falsely alleged that they had close connections with the Provisional IRA. The plaintiffs applied for discovery of certain documents, and an order for discovery was made on consent. The affidavit of discovery filed for the defendants claimed privilege in respect of a notebook and other documents in the possession of a journalist who had been involved in making the programme involved in the case. It was claimed that, as these documents contained the names of those people who had supplied information to the programme makers and as these people had done so on the undertaking that their identity would not be revealed, the court should not order discovery. In addition, the defendants argued that discovery should be refused on the ground that the lives of the people involved would be at risk in the event of disclosure.

Citing the decision of the House of Lords in *D. v NSPCC* [1978] AC 171 and of the Court of Criminal Appeal in *In re O'Kelly* (1974) 108 ILTR 97, Murphy J firstly rejected the suggestion that discovery could be resisted solely on the ground that a promise of confidentiality had been made. Second, again citing the *O'Kelly* case, Murphy J stated that journalists do not enjoy any privilege against non-disclosure. He might also have cited in this context the decision in *Kiberd v Mr Justice Hamilton* [1992] ILRM 574; [1992] 2 IR 257: see the Constitutional Law chapter, 167, above.

As to the proposition that discovery could be refused on the ground that lives might be at risk, Murphy J noted that there was no authority to support this point. Indeed, counsel for the defendants had expressly argued that the existing categories of privilege should be extended for this purpose, pointing to the acceptance of such extensions in *D. v NSPCC* [1978] AC 171 and in *Director of Consumer Affairs and Fair Trade v Sugar Distributors Ltd* [1991] ILRM 395; [1991] 1 IR 225 (see the 1990 Review, 434-5). However, Murphy J stated that the extensions in those cases from the 'police informer' privilege to those connected with investigating bodies created by Charter or statute indicated that any extension must be closely related to existing categories. He went on:

> However serious the risk to life may be as a result of the production of the documents in question and however desirable it may be that such production should be avoided I think it must be recognised that the recognition of such a ground of privilege from production would be in no sense an extension or extrapolation of any existing known ground of privilege but the creation of an entirely new ground.

In addition to rejecting the claim to privilege, Murphy J also held inapplicable the rule that news organisations should not be required to identify their sources of information in advance of the hearing of an action whether by means of discovery or interrogatories, a rule examined in the judgment of Dixon J in the High Court of Australia in *McGuinness v Attorney General of Victoria* (1940) 63 CLR 73. Murphy J showed little enthusiasm for what he described as this 'somewhat anomalous rule of practice' but in any event he stated that, in the instant case, it had no application as the defendants did not seek to limit discovery nor were the plaintiffs expressly seeking the identification of sources. As the defendants had conceded the relevance of the documents being sought by the plaintiffs, Murphy J felt that the rule should not apply.

However, in keeping with his own judgment in *Gormley v Ireland* [1993] 2 IR 75 (see the 1991 Review, 337, 339-400), which he noted had been cited with approval by Denham J in *Wong v Minister for Justice (No. 2)*, High Court, 16 March 1993, above, Murphy J ordered that the documents in question should only be seen by the lawyers for the plaintiffs and not by the plaintiffs themselves. He stated that if, at some future date, the lawyers would need to consult the plaintiffs on the contents of the documents then that would be brought to the attention of the court. In this way, it may be said that Murphy

J ensured that, to a large extent, the confidentiality of the names involved was maintained even though discovery was ordered.

As already indicated, the decision of Murphy J in the *Burke* case was reversed on appeal by the Supreme Court in judgments delivered in 1994: [1994] 2 ILRM 161. We will consider the Supreme Court decision in full in the 1994 Review, but we note here that the Court held that, in the circumstances which arose, the right to life and to bodily integrity took precedence over the right to the protection and vindication of the plaintiff's good name. In those circumstances, discovery was refused, but the Court also struck out the defendant's plea of fair comment but with liberty to amend its defence to plead justification.

Third party discovery: diplomatic immunity In *Fusco v O'Dea*, High Court, 21 April 1993; [1994] 2 ILRM 389 (SC), Lynch J refused to make an order for discovery against the government of Great Britain and Northern Ireland under O.31, r.29 of the Rules of the Superior Courts 1986 in the context of an extradition case involving the plaintiff. This decision was upheld by the Supreme Court in 1994, and we will return to that decision in the 1994 Review.

Third party discovery: Garda Síochána Complaints Board In *Skeffington v Rooney and Ors* [1994] 1 IR 480, Barr J ordered discovery of certain documents which had been compiled in a complaint under the Garda Síochána (Complaints) Act 1986.

The plaintiff had instituted a claim for damages in assault, alleging that the first and second named defendants, members of An Garda Síochána, had assualted him. After the alleged assault occurred, the plaintiff had made a complaint concerning the assault and this had been transmitted to the Garda Síochána Complaints Board under the terms of the 1986 Act. An investigating officer enquired into the matter on behalf of the Board, and written statements were obtained from, *inter alia*, the first two defendants in the instant proceedings. Having considered the matter the Board referred the case to the Director of Public Prosecutions who directed that no criminal charges were warranted. Under s. 7(8) of the 1986 Act, the Board thereupon decided that no further action would be taken and communicated this to the parties involved.

After the plaintiff had instituted the instant proceedings, his solicitor applied to the Board to furnish him with the details of the responses of the first two defendants to the plaintiff's complaint under the 1986 Act. The Board declined to do so, and the plaintiff then applied by motion for discovery of the statements made pursuant to O.31, r.29 of the Rules of the Superior Courts 1986. At the hearing in the High Court, the Board referred to s. 12 of the 1986 Act which prohibits members of the Board from disclosing confidential information obtained while performing functions as members of the Board, unless duly authorised to do so as well as the concern of the Board to ensure confidentiality in all its dealings in order to ensure that people involved in complaints will freely assist the Board in its functions.

Barr J noted that, in the instant case, it was not disputed that the documents being sought by the plaintiff were relevant to his claim. He went on to quote from the judgment of Finlay CJ in *Ambiorix Ltd v Minister for the Environment* [1992] ILRM 209; [1992] 1 IR 277 (see the 1991 Review, 338-9) in describing the general principles applicable to discovery. He accepted that, in certain cases, people might only be willing to co-operate with the Board on the basis of confidentiality, but he noted that, in the instant case, there did not appear to be anything in the documents which he had examined which involved any confidential material. Thus he ordered discovery of the statements in question and, indeed, added that the plaintiff would be entitled, on application, to obtain any documents obtained by the Board in its investigation of the plaintiff's complaint under the 1986 Act.

Barr J ended his judgment by stating that he did not consider his decision in the instant case to be in conflict with the decision of Costello J in *Director of Consumer Affairs and Fair Trade v Sugar Distributors Ltd* [1991] ILRM 395; [1991] 1 IR 225 (see the 1990 Review, 434-5). Nonetheless, given the broad nature of Barr J's decision, it would seem that the decision might give some pause for thought. Whether or not it is appealed, it might be argued that the absence of a more detailed analysis of the 'police informer' cases, such as the *Sugar Distributor* case, makes the decision of Barr J open to some doubt. See, by contrast, the more restrictive approach adopted by Denham J in *Wong v Minister for Justice (No. 2)*, High Court, 16 March 1993, above, 453.

LEGAL AID

Civil Legal aid: family cases   In the 1992 Review, 487-8, we discussed the decision of O'Hanlon J in *M.F. v Legal Aid Board*, High Court, 4 November 1992; [1993] ILRM 797 (SC), in which he had quashed a refusal by the Legal Aid Board to grant the applicant civil legal aid in connection with judicial separation proceedings instituted by her husband under the Judicial Separation and Family Law Reform Act 1989. We had also noted in the 1992 Review that the Supreme Court (Finlay CJ, O'Flaherty, Egan, Blayney and Denham JJ), in a decision delivered in March 1993, had affirmed O'Hanlon J's decision, though varying his order in the case, and we now return to the Supreme Court decision.

It will be recalled that the Board had considered that the applicant did not come within the requirement of paragraph 3.2.3(4) of the non-statutory Scheme of Civil Legal Aid and Advice (1979) that she was 'reasonably likely to be successful in the proceedings. ' O'Hanlon J held that this provision could not be applied directly to the context of judicial separation proceedings, where, he pointed out, there were no real winners or losers.

We may also note here that this approach by O'Hanlon J was approved and applied by Lardner J in *R.S. v Landy and Ors*, High Court, 10 February 1993, in relation to an application to the Board for civil legal aid concerning wardship proceedings. It may thus be said that the views of the Supreme Court in *M.F. v Legal Aid Board* will prove of great importance in connection with applications concerning proceedings which do not fall into the category of litigation *inter partes*.

Delivering the only reasoned judgment, Finlay CJ stated that two legal principles appeared to be applicable in the instant case:

1. In the case of an application for civil legal aid by a person who is a party or intended party to proceedings under the Act of 1989 which involve questions of the custody, guardianship and welfare of an infant of the marriage, the provisions of paragraph 3.2.3(4) of the Scheme should be interpreted and implemented by the Board on the basis that for a person to be 'reasonably likely to be successful in the proceedings,' it is only necessary that the Board should conclude that there is a reasonable likelihood that the point of view and submissions of the person concerned, with regard to the welfare, custody and upbringing of the child concerned, should be amongst the material which would be relied upon by the judge in determining the issues concerning the child.
2. In applying the provisions of paragraph 3.2.3(6) of the Scheme, the Board should interpret 'the benefit of the applicant' in a case pursuant to the Act of 1989 to be equivalent to the interest of the applicant in the welfare of the child.

While the Supreme Court varied the order of O'Hanlon J in minor respects, it also acknowledged that judicial separation proceedings were in a *sui generis* category. Clearly, the Court held that the 'likelihood of success' test in the Civil Legal Aid Scheme should be interpreted as meaning that a person be granted legal aid if there was a reasonable likelihood that the point of view of the applicant for legal aid would be amongst the material to be taken into account in a decision concerning, for example, the welfare of the children of a marriage.

Criminal legal aid On this area, see the Criminal Law chapter, 238, above.

LODGMENT

In the 1992 Review, 488, we discussed *Brennan v Iarnród Éireann and Ors* [1993] ILRM 134; [1992] 2 IR 167, a case on late lodgments. Amendments to the lodgment rules were made by the Rules of the Superior Courts Rules (No. 2) 1993 (SI No. 265): see below, 465.

PRECEDENT

Court of Criminal Appeal decision In *The People v Rock (P.)* [1994] 1 ILRM 66, the Supreme Court overruled the Court of Criminal Appeal decision in *The People v Mills* (1955) 1 Frewen 153. However, in so doing, the Court also stated that the Circuit Court judge who had followed that decision in the instant case had acted correctly as the *Mills* decision had been a binding authority until overruled by the Supreme Court: see the discussion of the case in the Criminal Law chapter, 236-8, above.

Ratio decidendi   The perennial problem of trying to find the *ratio decidendi* of a case was adverted to by Costello J in *Considine v Shannon Regional Fisheries Board and Ors* [1994] 1 ILRM 499: see the Constitutional Law chapter, 170-2, above.

PRELIMINARY ISSUE OF LAW

In *Duffy v News Group Newspapers Ltd and Ors (No. 2)* [1994] 1 ILRM 364, the Supreme Court declined to order that a preliminary issue of law be set down pursuant to O.25, r.1 of the Rules of the Superior Courts 1986 in a defamation action: see the discussion in the Torts chapter, 567, below.

PUBLIC HEARING

In *Irish Press plc v Ingersoll Irish Publications Ltd (No. 1)* [1993] ILRM 747 (SC); [1994] 1 IR 176 (HC & SC), the Supreme Court applied its decision in *In re R. Ltd* [1989] IR 169; [1989] ILRM 757 (1989 Review, 55-8. 96. 351-2), by confirming that the circumstances in which cases may be heard otherwise than in public are extremely limited.

The petitioner and respondent in the case were both 50% shareholders in Irish Press Newspapers Ltd and Irish Press Publications Ltd, to which we will refer as the companies. They had entered into agreements regulating the relationship between them and the management of the companies. The petitioner brought proceedings alleging oppression and misconduct by the respondent concerning this management agreement and sought a variety of reliefs. The respondent's defence contained counter allegations of breach of the agreement and claimed relief by way of counterclaim. The respondent sought an order pursuant to s. 205(7) of the Companies Act 1963 that the petition be heard otherwise than in public. The petitioner contended that knowledge of the companies' financial affairs and of disputes between the parties was already in the public domain and opposed the application. Numerous newspaper articles concerning the companies' financial affairs were put in evidence as was the fact that much of this had also been published in audited accounts.

The application for an *in camera* hearing was granted by Barron J, but, on the petitioner's appeal, the Supreme Court (Finlay CJ, Hederman, Egan, Blayney and Denham JJ) unanimously held that the hearing should be in public.

Finlay CJ delivered a judgment, with which the other Court members agreed, laying down the principles to be applied to these cases in light of the decision in *In re R. Ltd* [1989] IR 169; [1989] ILRM 757 (1989 Review, 55-8), and it may be useful to quote here his summary of these principles:

1. The court cannot even begin to exercise a discretion under s. 205(7) unless it is of opinion that the hearing of the proceedings or some particular part of the proceedings would involve the disclosure of information the publication of which would be seriously prejudicial to the legitimate interests of the company.

2. If it is of opinion that such a situation exists the court may then enter upon an investigation as to whether it should exercise its discretion under s. 205(7) to hold the case *in camera*. In doing so, it will however, be involved in considering a fundamental constitutional right vested in the public, namely, the administration of justice in public, and it cannot, therefore, make an order under s. 205(7) merely on the consent of all the parties concerned in the petition before it.

3. The additional matter which a court would have to be satisfied of in order to direct a hearing of the whole or part of the petition otherwise than in public would be that a public hearing of the whole or of that part of the proceedings would prevent justice being done.

4. In reaching a conclusion as to whether this test has been satisfied in any particular case, it would be appropriate for the court, having regard to the terms of the provisions of Article 34.1 of the Constitution, to construe s. 205(7) bearing in mind that the entitlement of the Oireachtas pursuant to Article 34.1 to prescribe by law for the administration of justice otherwise than in public is confined to special and limited cases.

Delivering the other main judgment in the case, Blayney J pointed out that, in view of the publicity which had attended the companies' financial problems, the public was already aware of so much detail concerning the companies' financial affairs that additional disclosure would not seriously prejudice the legitimate interests of the companies within the meaning of s. 205(7) of the 1963 Act. On this basis, the Court ordered the hearing to be held in public.

REMITTAL OF ACTIONS

In *O'Shea v Mallow UDC and Ors* [1993] ILRM 884, Morris J considered the power to remit a High Court action to the Circuit Court under s. 24 of the Courts of Justice Act 1924.

The plaintiff brought an application seeking an order that his personal injuries action be remitted to the Circuit Court on the basis that the injuries which he had sustained were not as serious as had initially been thought at the time that High Court proceedings against the defendants had been initiated. At the time of the application for the remittal, it was considered that any damages would not exceed the jurisdiction of the Circuit Court.

Counsel for the second named defendants, Cork County Council, who opposed the application on a point concerning costs (see below), did not dispute any of the facts grounding the application, but submitted that the High Court's jurisdiction to remit under s. 24 of the 1924 Act was limited by s. 11(2)(a) of the Courts of Justice Act 1936. S. 11(2)(a) of the 1936 Act provides that an action commenced in the High Court:

> shall not be remitted [to the Circuit Court] if the High Court is satisfied that, having regard to all the circumstances, and notwithstanding that such action could have been commenced in the Circuit Court, it was reasonable that such action should have been commenced in the High Court.

Counsel submitted that the correct interpretation of s. 11(2)(a) of the 1936 Act was that the court might only transfer and remit an action to the Circuit Court where it was not reasonable that the action should have been commenced in the High Court. He argued that that it would follow that any order remitting the action to the Circuit Court must therefore contain an express finding that it was not reasonable to have commenced the action in the High Court, the corollary being that no award in excess of Circuit Court jurisdiction could be made.

Morris J rejected this argument and granted the plaintiff's application. In relation to s. 11(2)(a) of the 1936 Act, he stated:

> The subsection removes from the High Court the obligation to transfer
> an action simply because the subject matter fell within the Circuit Court
> jurisdiction. . . . It does not logically follow that, simply because the
> court makes an order transmitting the action for hearing to the Circuit
> Court, it must follow that it was unreasonable to commence the pro-
> ceedings in the High Court.

Indeed, Morris J concluded that he was confirmed in this view by s. 20
of the 1936 Act, which provides that in actions remitted to the Circuit Court
there may be an award in excess of the normal Circuit Court jurisdiction. On
this basis, he acceded to the plaintiff's application.

RES JUDICATA

The manner in which the *res judicata* principle imposes restrictions on the
circumstances in which a criminal conviction may be challenged in civil
proceedings arose again in the judgment of Murphy J in *Pringle v Ireland*
[1994] 1 ILRM 467. In finding that the plaintiff was estopped from challenging in civil proceedings the validity of the convictions recorded against him,
Murphy J followed the long line of authority established in this and other
jurisdictions. He also followed his own judgment in *Tassan Din v Banco
Ambrosiano SPA* [1991] 1 IR 569 and of the Supreme Court in *Hardy v
Ireland*, Supreme Court, 18 March 1993 (see above, 172). In addition, we
may refer to the various decisions in what became known as the Sallins Mail
Train case: *Kelly v Ireland* [1986] ILRM 318, to which Murphy J also
referred, and also the other cases in that saga to which Murphy J did not refer:
see *Breathnach v Ireland* [1989] IR 489 (1989 Review, 358-61) and culmi-
nating in *Breathnach v Ireland (No. 4)*, High Court, 14 December 1992 (1992
Review, 493-4). What these cases established is that convicted persons
attempting to challenge their convictions after exhausting their appellate
remedies were left with an immensely uphill battle arising from the *res
judicata* principle.

However, we may note that, just over one month after the judgment of
Murphy J in the *Pringle* case, the Criminal Procedure Act 1993 came into
force. As we note above, 211, the 1993 Act provides for a new mechanism
by which alleged miscarriages of justice may be re-examined by the Court
of Criminal Appeal notwithstanding the exhaustion of previous appellate
remedies. The applicant in the *Pringle* case availed of this procedure: see *The
People v Pringle*, Court of Criminal Appeal, 16 May 1995, which we will

discuss in the 1995 Review. It would thus seem that the tortuous efforts required to re-open criminal convictions through civil proceedings may be more expeditiously pursued under the 1993 Act.

RULES OF COURT

The following Rules of Court were made in 1993.

Appeal: Court of Criminal Appeal   The Rules of the Superior Courts (No. 2) 1993 (SI No. 265), which came into effect on 9 September 1993, *inter alia*, amended O.86, r.5 of the Rules of the Superior Courts 1986 by requiring that notice of appeals to the Court of Criminal Appeal be served within 21 days from the date of the grant of a refusal of leave to appeal.

Company voluntary winding-up: declaration of solvency   The Rules of the Superior Courts (No. 2) 1993 (SI No. 265), which came into effect on 9 September 1993, *inter alia*, inserted a new O.74, r.139 and Form No. 47 of Appendix M into the Rules of the Superior Courts 1986, amending the declaration of solvency which is required to be filed pursuant to s. 256 of the Companies Act 1963.

Court Sittings: District Court   The District Court Areas (Alteration of Place) Order 1993 (SI No. 114) amended the 1961 Order of the same title by providing that Carrick-on-Shannon District hearings may be held in Drum-shambo instead of Carrick-on-Shannon.

Discovery   The Rules of the Superior Courts (No. 2) 1993 (SI No. 265), which came into effect on 9 September 1993, *inter alia*, amended O.31 of the Rules of the Superior Courts 1986 by inserting a new O.31, r.12(4), which emphasises the need to seek voluntary discovery prior to applying for an order for discovery.

Notaries   The Rules of the Superior Courts (No. 2) 1993 (SI No. 265), which came into effect on 9 September 1993, *inter alia*, inserted a new O.127 into the Rules of the Superior Courts 1986 concerning the appointment of notaries public by the Chief Justice. The newly-inserted O.127 provides that the Chief Justice may make rules and regulations or give practice directions as to the form and mode of appointment or application to be appointed as a notary public, including requirements that applicants satisfy the Chief Justice in advance they they have the requisite and appropriate knowledge of notarial practice and procedure. For discussion on this this area, see *In re McCarthy* [1990] ILRM 84.

Payments out: infant cases   The Rules of the Superior Courts (No. 2) 1993 (SI No. 265), which came into effect on 9 September 1993, *inter alia*, amended O.63 of the Rules of the Superior Courts 1986 in relation to payments out in infant cases by inserting a new O.63, r.12.

Payment into court   The Rules of the Superior Courts (No. 2) 1993 (SI No. 265), which came into effect on 9 September 1993, *inter alia*, amended O.22 of the Rules of the Superior Courts 1986 in relation to payments into court without leave.

Public works contracts: High Court   On the effect of the European Communities (Review Procedures for the Award of Contracts by Entities operating in the Water, Energy, Transport and Telecommunications Sectors) Regulations 1993 (SI No. 104) see the Commercial Law chapter, 66, above.

Solicitors' Acts cases   The Rules of the Superior Courts (No. 1) 1993 (SI No. 238), which came into effect on 5 August 1993, amended O.53, r.7(2) of the Rules of the Superior Courts 1986 by providing that the Registrar of Solicitors (as well as the Secretary of the Incorporated Law Society of Ireland) may swear the affidavit referred to in O.53, r.7(2), which verifies the petition of the Disciplinary Committee to the High Court pursuant to the Solicitors (Amendment) Act 1960.

Small claims procedure   The District Court (Small Claims Procedure) Rules 1993 (SI No. 356) are referred to below, 466.

Taxation of costs   The Rules of the Superior Courts (No. 2) 1993 (SI No. 265), which came into effect on 9 September 1993, *inter alia*, amended O.99 of the Rules of the Superior Courts 1986 in relation to taxation of costs by providing that, where a notice of taxation specifies a particular item as being subject to appeal, the Taxing Master shall have power to tax that item only.

SETTING DOWN

Adjournment of date fixed for hearing   In *Bula Ltd and Ors v Tara Mines Ltd and Ors (No. 6)*, Supreme Court, 11 October 1993, the Supreme Court (Finlay CJ, Egan and Denham JJ), in an *ex tempore* judgment, reversed a refusal in the High Court to grant an adjournment of a complex case (see the judgments dealing with discovery above, 447-58) which had been fixed to begin on 2 November 1993. The Supreme Court, stating that it was 'with considerable reluctance and slowness' that it would interfere with the decision of a High Court judge fixing a date for hearing, adjourned the hearing until the first available Tuesday in December 1993, taking account of unspecified difficulties which counsel for the plaintiffs had with the November date. In fact, the case was at hearing for only a short time in December 1993 when it was adjourned, apparently with a view to possible settlement: see *Irish Times*, 8 December 1993. The case ultimately recommenced, with a reduced number of plaintiffs, in November 1994: see *Irish Times*, 24 November 1994.

SMALL CLAIMS PROCEDURE

The small claims procedure for processing certain claims in the District Court other than through a civil process, first introduced on a pilot basis by the District Court (Small Claims Procedure) Rules 1991 (1991 Review, 343), was extended to the entire State by the District Court (Small Claims Procedure) Rules 1993 (SI No. 356), which came into effect on 8 December 1993.

The Rules provide for an initial application to a clerk of the District Court who is empowered to attempt to reach a compromise between the parties in dispute, described as the claimant and respondent. A fee of £5 for the entire procedure is laid down in the Rules. In the event of continued dispute, the matter can be referred to a judge of the District Court for resolution.

In general terms, a 'small claim' is defined in Rule 4 of the 1993 Rules as one involving a claim not exceeding £500 which comes within the three categories mentioned in that Rule. The first category concerns consumer contracts (consumer being defined in identical terms to the definition in s. 3 of the Sale of Goods and Supply of Services Act 1980), but excluding any claim 'under the Hire Purchase Acts 1946 and 1960' (the 1993 Rules do not to allude to the changes effected to the 1946 Act by the Sale of Goods and Supply of Services Act 1980) or arising from an alleged breach of a leasing agreement. The second category included is a 'minor' property damage claim in tort ('minor' not being further defined, but obviously subject to the £500 overall limitation) provided the claimant is not a body corporate and excluding personal injury claims. The third category included in a claim by a tenant for the return of rent deposit or any sum known as 'key money'.

The 1993 Rules revoked the District Court (Small Claims Procedure) Rules 1991 (1991 Review, 343), as amended in 1992 (1992 Review, 495).

SUPREME COURT

Stay of execution pending appeal   In *O'Toole v Radio Telefís Éireann (No. 1)* [1993] ILRM 454, the Supreme Court (Finlay CJ, Hederman, O'Flaherty, Egan and Blayney JJ) granted a stay of execution on a High Court decision that Radio Telefís Éireann had acted *ultra vires* the ban contained in Orders made under s. 31 of the Broadcasting Authority Act 1960, as amended, on interviews with spokespersons for the Sinn Féin party. The Court concluded that, on balance, the High Court order should be stayed because the Court had arranged an early appeal in the case. As we discuss in the Communications chapter, 68-9, above, the Court ultimately upheld the decision of the High Court: *O'Toole v Radio Telefís Éireann (No. 2)* [1993] ILRM 458.

Prisons

DISCIPLINE

In *Dumbrell and Ors v Governor of Limerick Prison*, Supreme Court, 20 December 1993, the Supreme Court quashed a disciplinary punishment imposed on the applicants by the respondent governor pursuant to the Rules for the Government of Prisons 1947. The case arose in the following way.

A cloth on a snooker table in the prison's recreation hall had been damaged and the applicants were the only prisoners who had been in the recreation hall at the relevant time. The applicants were reported to the Governor under the 1947 Rules charged with the offence of 'acting contrary to the good order and discipline of the prison by damaging prison property.' Each case was heard separately by the Governor and all three applicants denied the charge or that they were playing snooker. The Governor convicted all three applicants and imposed the same punishment on each, namely, to forfeit recreation for one month and to pay for one third of the damage to the snooker cloth, the total cost of repair being £390.

On judicial review, the applicants claimed that the Governor's decision should be quashed for unreasonableness, within the meaning of the Supreme Court decision in *The State (Keegan) v Stardust Victims Compensation Tribunal* [1987] ILRM 202; [1986] IR 642. The Governor argued that, as the applicants were in the recreation hall at the relevant time and had given untruthful accounts to him of their movements, his finding that all three were involved in the damage to the cloth on the table could not be challenged as being unreasonable. This argument was accepted in the High Court, but, on appeal, the Supreme Court (O'Flaherty, Blayney and Denham JJ) unanimously held in favour of the applicants.

Delivering the Court's decision, Blayney J concluded that the Governor's decision failed the test of reasonableness or rationality laid down in the *Keegan* case. He commented:

> There was no evidence that all three [applicants] had been seen damaging the snooker table, nor was there evidence that the damage was such that it must have been caused by all three. Accordingly, it was not reasonable to find all three guilty of having damaged the table. And while it was reasonable to conclude . . . that one of the [applicants] had damaged it, it was not reasonable to find all three guilty simply because

all three denied the charge and were uncooperative.

Blayney J expressed some sympathy for the Governor in his concern to maintain good order and discipline within the prison. He indicated, indeed, that if the applicants had been charged with having offended against good order and discipline in any other way than they had, for example, by standing by and allowing destruction to happen, they could have been found to be in breach of the 1947 Rules. This suggestion must, of course, have been *obiter* and might be open to the objection that while it could capture two of the applicants rather than one, there would still be some lacuna in proof, namely who stood by and who actually destroyed?

On a wider level, the decision in *Dumbrell* reiterates the point that, in Irish law, the courts are prepared to review decisions of prison governers which, under English authority, might be regarded as unreviewable: see *Leech v Governor of Parkhurst Prison* [1988] AC 533 and Hogan and Morgan, *Administrative Law in Ireland*, 2nd ed., 553

TRANSFER FROM ST PATRICK'S INSTITUTION TO PRISON

S. 7 of the Prisons Act 1970 empowers the authorities in St Patrick's Institution (the detention centre for convicted male juveniles between the ages of 17 and 19, formerly borstal) to transfer any excess population to prison. The Prisons Act 1970 (Section 7) Order 1993 (SI No. 219) continued s. 7 of the 1970 Act in operation for a two year period from 28 June 1993. The previous 1991 Order had also involved a two year period (1991 Review, 356), though prior extensions (see the 1990 Review, 457; the 1989 Review, 364; and the 1988 Review, 353) had involved periods of one year only.

VISITING COMMITTEE REPORTS

Media access   In *The People v Hannon*, High Court, 20 December 1993, the defendant, remanded in custody on a murder charge, was granted bail for the Christmas period by Kinlen J. The case is discussed in the Criminal Law chapter, 215, above. Towards the end of his judgment, Kinlen J added some comments concerning the attitude of the media to the Annual Reports of Prison Visiting Committees. He commented:

This problem in prison [which arose in the instant case] is just one of the many highlighted in the annual reports of the Visiting Committees. Unfortunately the media and other interested persons do not bother going to the Department of Justice for these reports. Under s. 3 of the Visiting Committees Act 1925 everyone is entitled to go to the Department and ask for the reports free. Unfortunately the media seem to think they have to wait until they are printed. This may be years later. The media then regard the reports as too ancient to be news. In fact visiting reports very frequently sound alarms on the same theme year in and year out. My colleague, Mr Justice Carney, has already decided that the rights of the media and the public to know is not confined to the annual report but they are entitled to see any other report sent to the Minister, including the minutes of their meetings.

There are a number of points worth commenting on in this passage. It is of interest to note firstly that Kinlen J was a long-established and distinguished member of the Mountjoy Prison Visiting Committee prior to his appointment to the High Court, and is thus particularly qualified to comment on the actvities of Visting Committees. It is also true to say that, in recent years, Visiting Committees have drawn attention to problems in prison conditions, a practice which contrasted with the rather more staid approach of some years ago.

As to Kinlen J's comments on access to unpublished annual reports, the history of this might be somewhat more complex than suggested. It has been the case for a number of years that the Visting Committee reports are published by the Department of Justice substantially in arrears. This led certain 'interested parties' to seek access to the unpublished reports from the Department of Justice which, in spite of the terms of s. 3 of the 1925 Act to which Kinlen J referred, brought a less than forthcoming response from the Department. It was against that background that judicial review proceedings were initiated and which produced the decision of Carney J to which Kinlen J also referred. Whether the Department of Justice will, in the future, make the unpublished reports available on request remains to be seen.

In relation to whether the reports, when published, are regarded by the media as being 'too ancient to be news', it is of interest to note that Kinlen J's comments came just days before the Department of Justice published the Annual Reports on Prisons for the years 1989, 1990 and 1991. It has been suggested by Dr. Paul O'Mahony, in his article on the release of these Reports, (1994) 12 ILT 6 that the timing of the publication, coupled with the delay in their release, indicates that the Department does not place a high priority on ensuring public debate of issues arising in the prison context. Given that it is the statutory duty of the Minister for Justice to publish the Visiting Committee Reports, it must surely be that the onus remains with the Department rather than the media to stimulate interest in relation to prisons.

Finally, it is notable that the release of the Reports for 1989 to 1991 was accompanied by statements from the Minister for Justice criticising certain comments made in the reports of the Visiting Committee to Mountjoy Prison. Given this public disassociation by the Minister from the comments of Committees appointed by the Minister under the 1925 Act, it is not surprising that this particular series of Visiting Committee Reports, albeit published substantially in arrears, received more media attention than Kinlen J could have imagined in his judgment in the *Hannon* case.

Revenue

This will be discussed in the 1994 Annual Review.

Safety and Health

ENVIRONMENTAL SAFETY

Air pollution: criminal offences against corporate bodies   In *Truloc Ltd v McMenamin* [1994] 1 ILRM 151, O'Hanlon J rejected a number of challenges to criminal prosecutions brought against the applicant company under the Air Pollution Act 1987. In particular, O'Hanlon J examined the situation at common law prior to the 1987 Act and also the circumstances in which a corporate body may be charged with a criminal offence.

The applicant carried on an adhesive manufacturing plant in premises located in Donegal. Donegal County Council had prosecuted the company under the 1987 Act, alleging various acts of nuisance contrary to s. 24(2) of the Act by reason of emissions from their premises. The respondent judge of the District Court convicted the applicant in respect of seven charges and a fine of £300 was imposed in relation to each of them. The applicant was also ordered to pay sums of £2,000 for costs and £2,000 for witnesses' expenses. During the hearing of the charges evidence was taken from ten witnesses called in support of the prosecution, including an executive chemist and a chemical technician. No evidence was given on behalf of the applicant.

The applicant did not seek to appeal to the Circuit Court, but instead applied for judicial review.

Many of the grounds raised related to the quality of the evidence adduced and whether such was sufficient to ground a conviction. But O'Hanlon J made the point that on an application for judicial review, it was not appropriate for the High Court to examine in detail the evidence tendered in support of a prosecution in the District Court for the purpose of assessing whether, in the opinion of the High Court judge, that evidence was sufficient to support the conviction which has been entered against a defendant. In this context, he cited in support the Supreme Court decisions in *The State (Keegan) v Stardust Victims' Compensation Tribunal* [1987] ILRM 202; [1986] IR 642, *O'Keeffe v An Bord Pleanála* [1992] ILRM 237; [1993] 1 IR 39 (1991 Review, 16-8) and *Garda Representative Association v Ireland* [1994] 1 ILRM 81 (see the Garda Síochána chapter, 339, above).

Having said that, he added that he had been given no reason to believe that the evidence in the present case was insufficient to sustain the conviction of the applicant on the charges referred to in the present application. He pointed out also that, prior to the 1987 Act, it was a criminal offence at common law to commit a public nuisance. Citing Archbold, *Criminal Pleadings, Evidence and Practice*, 35th ed., paras. 3821-3 and *Attorney General v Keymer Brick and Tile Co. Ltd* (1903) 67 JP 434 in support, he continued:

> Such an offence is committed by every person who (a) does an act not warranted by law, or (b) omits to discharge a legal duty, if the effect of the act or omission is to endanger the life, health, property, morals or comfort of the public, or to obstruct the public in the exercise or enjoyment of rights common to all. . . . It is immaterial whether the annoyance arises from noise, stench, unwholesomeness or interference with public health or convenience.

In the instant case, he held that there was evidence which satisfied the requirements of s. 4 of the 1987 Act if accepted by the respondent District Court judge, and he noted that no rebutting evidence had been offered on behalf of the applicant.

The next major point raised was that where a charge under the 1987 Act is brought against a body corporate it is necessary to join in the prosecution some officer of the company. O'Hanlon J rejected this argument. First, he pointed out that s. 2 of the Interpretation Act 1889 defined the word 'person' as including a body corporate. We might note here that, in the context of the 1987 Act, it might have been more apt to refer to the virtually identical definition of 'person' in s. 11 of the Interpretation Act 1937, which applies to Acts passed by the Oireachtas, whereas the 1889 Act does not. Indeed, O'Hanlon J adverted to this point himself in the judgment he delivered later in 1993 in *Director of Public Prosecutions (Barron) v Wexford Farmers' Club* [1994] 2 ILRM 295; [1994] 1 IR 546: see the Criminal Law chapter, 272-3, above. However, the reference to the 1889 does not affect the substance of the point made by O'Hanlon J in *Truloc*, as the 1937 Act contains an identical provision.

He went on to note in *Truloc* that a corporation is exempt from prosecution for offences which can only be committed by a human person, such as perjury or bigamy, or for which death or imprisonment are the only punishments, but that the modern view was that a corporation could even be convicted of the crime of manslaughter, which can be punished by the imposition of a fine. He cited in this context *Halsbury's Laws of England*, 4th ed., Vol. 11(1), para.35 and *R. v ICR Haulage Ltd* [1944] KB 551. He might also have added the more recent decision in *R. v P & O European Ferries (Dover) Ltd* (1990) 93 Cr App R 72, the (ultimately unsuccessful) manslaughter prosecution arising from the 1988 Herald of Free Enterprise disaster at Zeebrugge.

In relation to the instant case, O'Hanlon J noted that s. 11(2) of the 1987 Act expressly recognises that an offence under the Act may be committed by a body corporate, and he could find nothing in the Act to suggest that it was necessary to join an officer of the company in any such prosecution, or for the purpose of imposing a penalty by way of fine under s. 12 of the Act.

As already noted, O'Hanlon J also rejected a number of other points raised by the applicant concerning the quality of the evidence tendered in the District Court and he thus concluded that the application for *certiorari* should be refused.

Coal: Cork   The Air Pollution Act 1987 (Marketing, Sale and Distribution of Fuels) (Cork) Regulations 1993 (SI No. 294), which came into effect on 18 October 1993, require retailers of coal in most of the Cork city area to have a supply of one or more specified smokeless or low-smoke solid fuels for retail sale. The Regulations also prohibited bituminous slack in the same area. For more rigorous requirements and prohibitions in the Dublin city area, see the 1990 Review, 470 and the 1992 Review, 534, and immediately below.

Coal: Dublin   The Air Pollution Act 1987 (Marketing, Sale and Distribution of Fuels) Regulations 1992 (SI No. 297) amended the 1990 Regulations of the same title (1990 Review, 470) by providing that any necessary tests under the Regulations are to be conducted by Eolas, the Irish Science and Technology Agency. Similar arrangements are contained in SI No. 294, above.

Emissions from vehicles   The European Communities (Mechanically Propelled Vehicle Emission Control) Regulations 1993 (SI No. 363) are referred to in the the Transport chapter, 590, below.

Environmental Protection Agency (EPA)   In the 1992 Review, 529-34, we dealt with the following Regulations and Orders in the context of our discussion of the Environmental Protection Agency Act 1992: the Environmental Protection Agency (Advisory Committee) Regulations 1993 (SI No. 43), which concerned the procedure for establishing the EPA; the Environmental Protection Agency (Establishment) Order 1993 (SI No. 213), by which the Environmental Protection Agency was established on 26 July 1993; the Environmental Protection Agency Act 1992 (Dissolution of An Foras Forbatha Teoranta) Order 1993 (SI No. 215), by which An Foras Forbatha Teo., the National Institute for Physical Planning and Construction Research Ltd, was dissolved and its staff transferred to the EPA on 1 August 1993 in the wake of the establishment of the EPA itself; and the Environmental Protection Agency Act 1992 (Commencement) Order 1993 (SI No.

235), which brought into effect on 10 August 1993 s. 104 of the 1992 Act, empowering the EPA to conduct reports and investigations into the causes of any incident causing environmental pollution. As we noted in the 1992 Review, 533, this latter Order was made in the immediate wake of incidents in the Ringaskiddy area of Cork which led to calls for an investigation by the EPA, and the s. 104 power was brought into force for that purpose. The more formal power to conduct an inquiry pursuant to s. 105 of the 1992 Act had not been brought into force at the time of writing (June 1996).

Municipal waste   The Air Pollution Act 1987 (Municipal Waste Incineration) Regulations 1993 (SI No. 347) gave effect to Directive 89/369/EEC concerning emission levels from municipal waste incineration and the best practicable means for limiting such emissions.

Public access to information   S. 110 of the Environmental Protection Agency Act 1992 required, in mandatory language, that the Minister for the Environment make Regulations requiring public authorities to make available to the public information concerning the environment. This was expressly stated to be for the purpose of giving effect to Council Directive 90/313/EEC. The relevant Regulations are the Access to Information on the Environment Regulations 1993 (SI No. 133). For a comprehensive analysis of the background to the Directive and the Regulations, as well as criticism of the manner of implementation of the Directive, see David Meehan's two-part article, (1994) 12 ILT 85, 114 and Conor Mullany's article, (1994) 12 ILT 138.

Water discharges: control Regulations   While one might criticise the length of the title of the Local Government (Water Pollution) Acts 1977 and 1990 (Control of Aldrin, Dieldrin, Endrin, Isodrin, HCB, HCBD and CHCl3 Discharges) Regulations 1993 (SI No. 348), few can be in any doubt about their general purpose. The 1993 Regulations, made under the Local Government (Water Pollution) Acts 1977 and 1990, laid down limit values and quality objectives in respect of the discharge of the substances referred to in the title of the Regulations. They implemented Directive 88/347/EEC, a Directive made under the terms of the general 'Framework' Directive in this area, 76/464/EEC.

Water discharges: effect of licence   In *Simunovich v An Bord Pleanála*, High Court, 23 April 1993 the applicant unsuccessfuly sought to quash a decision by An Bord Pleanála, on appeal from Meath County Council, to grant, under s. 4 of the Local Government (Water Pollution) Act 1977, a licence to Irish Cement Ltd to discharge effluent from a shale quarry into the local water system. The applicant maintained that the licence was *ultra vires* An Bord Pleanála as it purported to licence discharges into water in the applicant's ownership. Irish Cement Ltd, a notice party in the proceedings, argued that the water was in its ownership. However, Hamilton P held that this dispute as to ownership was irrelevent to the question whether An Bord Pleanála had acted *ultra vires*. He pointed out that s. 4(12) of the 1977 Act provides that a person shall not be entitled solely by reason of the granting of a licence under the section to discharge effluent into waters. He concluded:

> The granting of such licence does not interfere with the rights of the owners of the waters because the granting of such licence does not of itself permit the discharge into their waters. . . . If the applicant is, as he alleges, the owner of the stream at the point at which discharge is licensed, it is open to him to apply, in appropriate proceedings, for an order restraining such discharge and the mere fact that such disharge has been licensed is not sufficient to defeat his claim.

On this basis, Hamilton P concluded that an order of *certiorari* should not be granted to the applicant.

FIRE SAFETY

Nursing homes The fire safety provisions of the Nursing Homes (Care and Welfare) Regulations 1993 (SI No. 226) are referred to in the Health Services chapter, 347, above.

Prosecution of indictable offence In *Cumann Luthchleas Gael Teo v Windle (Dublin Corporation, Notice Party)* [1994] 1 IR 525, the Supreme Court rejected the argument that a fire authority could constitute a private prosecutor, or 'common informer', for the purposes of initiating a prosecution for an indictable offence under the Fire Services Act 1981.

Dublin Corporation initiated a prosecution by way of summons against the applicant, Cumann Luthchleas Gael Teo, known in the English language as the Gaelic Athletic Association (GAA). The summons alleged that, on 4 September 1988 at Croke Park in Dublin, being a stadium and place of assembly, the applicant failed to ensure that all escape routes were unobstructed and immediately available for use and that all doors and gates were kept secured in such a manner that they could easily and immediately be opened by persons in Croke Park. The summons continued that this was '[i]n breach of Regulation 4(i) and (ii) of the Fire Safety in Places of Assembly (Ease of Escape) Regulations 1985, as provided under section 37 and contrary to ss. 4 and 5 of the Fire Services Act 1981.' The occasion in respect of which the summons had been brought was the 1988 All-Ireland hurling final in Croke Park.

When the case came before the respondent judge of the District Court, having heard the submissions of counsel for the Corporation opening the facts of the case and setting out the allegations against the applicant, he announced his conclusion that the offences charged were indictable offences and that he was not satisfied to try them summarily. He therefore directed that a 'book of evidence' be served on the applicant under the Criminal Procedure Act 1967. At a later hearing, the respondent sent the applicant forward for trial to the Circuit Criminal Court. The applicant sought to have this order quashed on judicial review. In the High Court, O'Hanlon J declined to quash the order and indicated that, in his view, the Corporation had brought the prosecution in its capacity as common informer. The applicant appealed this decision, and the Supreme Court (Finlay CJ, O'Flaherty, Egan, Blayney and Denham JJ) unanimously reversed O'Hanlon J's decision and quashed the order sending the applicant forward for trial.

To understand fully the arguments discussed by the Supreme Court, it is necessary to outline the statutory provisions applicable to the prosecution brought by the Corporation. The 1985 Regulations referred to in the summons were made by the Minister for the Environment in exercise of the powers conferred by s. 37 of the Fire Services Act 1981. S. 4 of the 1981 Act provides, *inter alia*, that a person 'who contravenes . . . any Regulations under this Act . . . shall be guilty of an offence.' S. 5(1) of the 1981 Act provides that a person guilty of an offence under the Act, other than an offence to which s. 5(2) of the Act applies, shall be liable on summary conviction to a fine of £500 and/or six months imprisonment. S. 5(2) of the 1981 Act provides that a person guilty of 'an offence by reason of a contravention of s. 18(2), 20 or 37' of the Act shall be liable on conviction on indictment to a fine of £10,000 and/or two years imprisonment. S. 5(3) of the 1981 Act provides that a judge of the District Court has jurisdiction to try summarily an offence to which s. 5(2) applies if, *inter alia*, the judge is of opinion that the facts proved or alleged in a case constitute a minor offence fit to be tried summarily, and s. 5(3) goes on to provide in such event for penalties of a fine of £500 and/or six months imprisonment. Finally, s. 6(1) of the 1981 Act provides that summary proceedings for an offence to which s. 5(1) of the Act applies may be brought by a 'fire authority . . . or by any other person.'

It may be noted, for the purposes of the instant case, that while s. 6(1) expressly confers the right to prosecute on a fire authority, such as Dublin Corporation, in respect of offences to which s. 5(1) of the 1981 Act applies, it is silent on the position of a fire authority in relation to offences to which s. 5(2) applies. As can be seen, the prosecution in the instant case alleged a failure to comply with the 1985 Regulations which had been made under s. 37 of the 1981 Act, a case to which s. 5(2) applies. Thus, the key issue arising in the case was whether the Corporation was lawfully entitled to bring a prosecution in the first place.

Delivering a judgment with which all other members of the Court agreed, Finlay CJ disposed of two preliminary points raised by the applicant.

First, it was argued that s. 5(2) of the 1981 Act was defective in that it referred to 'an offence by reason of a contravention of section . . . 37' of the Act. The applicant argued that there was no such thing as a contravention of s. 37, since s. 37 merely provided for the Regulation-making power of the Minister for the Environment. Finlay CJ accepted that if s. 5(2), in referring to s. 37, had purported to create a criminal offence, then the ambiguity in s. 5(2) might render it open to question. However, he pointed out that s. 5(2) merely involved a description of an offence created by s. 4 of the Act. Using a more generous method of interpretation than that advocated by the applicant, Finlay CJ was thus prepared to conclude that s. 5(2) should be read, in effect, as a reference to 'an offence by reason of a contravention of [any Regulation made under] section . . . 37' of the 1981 Act.

The second preliminary point raised by the applicant was that the respondent judge had erred in concluding, in accordance with s. 5(3) of the 1981 Act, that the offence charged was not fit to be tried summarily. Finlay CJ noted that, in this connection, a court on judicial review would only interfere with such a decision if it was irrational or was unsupported by the evidence. The use of the word 'irrational' here is, of course, an allusion to the concept of reasonableness explained by the Court in decisions such as *The State (Keegan) v Stardust Victims Compensation Tribunal* [1987] ILRM 202; [1986] IR 642 (on which, see for example the 1991 Review, 16-19 and the Administrative Law chapter, 30, above). In the instant case, Finlay CJ noted that the respondent had before him an allegation that the acts or omissions involved occurred on the day that the All-Ireland hurling final was being played in Croke Park, for which a very large number of people would be in the stadium. In those circumstances, Finlay CJ could not see how the decision reached by the respondent could be challenged.

Finlay CJ then turned to the issue on which the case ultimately turned. He noted that s. 6(1) conferred a right of prosecution on the Corporation to bring summary prosecutions for an offence to which s. 5(1) of the 1981 Act applies. However, by contrast:

> No provision is contained in any part of the Act giving a specific power to any person or body to bring and prosecute proceedings for offences to which s. 5(2) applies.

In the context of this *lacuna* or silence in the Act, the question arose as to whether the Corporation could prosecute as a private prosecutor or 'common informer.' Finlay CJ, on behalf of the Supreme Court, concluded it could not. He cited the Court's decision in *The State (Ennis) v Farrell* [1966] IR 107 as authority for the proposition that a private individual has the right to prosecute an indictable offence up to the stage of a return for trial, but noted that no previous decision had examined whether such a right was vested in a juristic person, such as a corporation. Finlay CJ considered that legislation might expressly provide that the right of private prosecution identified in *Ennis* could be exercised by a corporate body, but he added:

> I am satisfied, however, that a body corporate cannot be seen as a member of the public and that, in a case such as this where a liability to criminal prosecution is involved, there are no grounds for implying a right in a body corporate to institute proceedings for an indictable offence by way of common informer.

In the absence of an express provision in the 1981 Act empowering a fire authority to prosecute an indictable offence up to the stage of a return for trial, Finlay CJ concluded that the return for trial in the instant case was invalid.

The decision in this case clearly identifies a significant *lacuna* in the procedure for bringing prosecutions on indictment in respect of offences to which s. 5(2) of the 1981 Act applies. Finlay CJ suggested that 'a member of the fire brigade or an official of the Corporation who was an authorised officer' within the meaning of the 1981 Act could, like any other individual person, institute proceedings for an indictable offence. We would note that while this suggestion is an obvious attempt to fill the gap in the 1981 Act identified by the Court's decision, it may prove to be an impractical solution. One reason for this is that a member of the fire brigade or an authorised officer, by contrast with a member of the Garda Síochána (see *Dillane v Attorney General* [1980] ILRM 167), would face the daunting prospect of potential liability for the costs involved in any unsuccessful prosecution. This problem could, of course, be remedied on the basis that the individual's employer could indemnify them against any such costs, though whether such an arrangement would be legally enforceable must be open to question on grounds of public policy: but see the 1990 Review, 431. It would therefore seem that, on a long term basis, a specific amendment to the 1981 Act is required to deal with the problem identified in the instant case.

FOOD SAFETY

Extraction solvents in foodstuffs The Health (Extraction Solvents in Foodstuffs) Regulations 1993 (SI No. 387) implemented Directive 88/344EEC, as amended by Directive 92/115/EEC concerning the levels of extraction solvents permitted in foodstuffs.

Materials in contact with foodstuffs The European Communities (Materials and Articles Intended to Come into Contact with Foodstuffs) (Amendment) Regulations 1993 (SI No. 295) amended the 1991 Regulations of the same title (see the 1991 Review, 202, 366) in order to implement Directive 92/39/EEC which prescribes further precautionary measures concerning plastics materials and articles intended to come into contact with foodstuffs.

Nutrition labelling for foodstuffs The Health (Nutrition Labelling for Foodstuffs) Regulations 1993 (SI No. 388) implemented Directive 90/496/ EEC laying down the requirements for nutrition labelling, namely precise information concerning energy values (kJ and kcal) and nutrients, such as protein, carbohydrate, fat, fibre, sodium and vitamins and minerals.

Tin in food The Health (Tin in Food) Regulations 1993 (SI No. 389) prohibit the sale and importation of any food intended for human consumption which contains more than 200 milligrams of tin per kilogram of food.

MANUFACTURING STANDARDS IN THE EC

In the 1991 Review, 368, and the 1992 Review, 538, we noted the increased number of EC 'New Approach' or 'Approximation' Directives which establish minimum safety and health criteria for various products and which are linked to detailed technical standards, or European Norms (EN), developed by the European Standards bodies such as CEN and CENELEC. Relevant Regulations implementing such Directives in 1993 were as follows.

Motor vehicles The Regulations governing the type of approval for motor vehicles are referred to in the Transport chapter, 589, below.

Personal Protective Equipment The European Communities (Personal Protective Equipment) Regulations 1993 (SI No. 272), which came into effect on 22 September 1993 on their signing by the Minister for Enterprise and Employment, implemented the 1989 Directive on Personal Protective Equipment (89/686/EEC). In general terms, the Directive and Regulations apply to equipment which may be used to provide protection against injury or ill-health for an individual, such as 'hard hats', goggles, ear muffs, respiratory protection, gloves, overalls, safety boots and so forth. However, certain items are excluded from the scope of the Directive and Regulations, including defensive equipment used by the emergency services, such as shields used by the police in a riot situation. These excluded items will be covered, it is envisaged, by other EC Directives. We may note here that the 1993 Regulations were amended in January 1994 by the European Communities (Personal Protective Equipment) (Amendment) Regulations 1994 (SI No. 13 of 1994) in order to implement Directive 93/95/EEC, which had amended the 1989 Directive after a number of member States had found difficulty with the implementation of the original 1989 Directive. The 1994 Regulations provide that PPE may continue to be placed on the market and brought into service until 1 July 1995 provided it conforms with the law of the State which was in force on 30 June 1992. In addition, helmets and visors intended for users of two or three-wheeled motor vehicles were added to the list of matters excluded from the terms of the 1993 Regulations. On the standards for motor cycle helmets, see the Road Traffic (Construction, Equipment and Use of Vehicles) (Amendment) (No. 2) Regulations 1993 (SI No. 322) in the Transport chapter, 590, below. On the connection between the European Communities (Personal Protective Equipment) Regulations 1993 (SI No. 272) and the Regulations requiring employers to provide personal protective equipment to employees, see 496, below.

OCCUPATIONAL SAFETY (GENERAL)

Employer's liability The case law from 1993 on employer's liability is discussed in the Torts chapter, 538, below.

Merchant shipping The Regulations made in 1993 under the Merchant Shipping Acts are discussed in the Transport chapter, 586-8, below.

Noise In *Barry v Nitrigín Éireann Teo* [1994] 2 ILRM 522, Costello J held that the defendants had been in breach of their statutory duty to the plaintiff under the Factories (Noise) Regulations 1975, in respect of the exposure to noise suffered by the plaintiff while an employee of the defendants between 1979 and 1985. The case is discussed in the Torts chapter, 538, below. As the note to the law report indicates, the 1975 Regulations which applied between the dates in question have since been revoked and replaced by the European Communities (Protection of Workers) (Exposure to Noise) Regulations 1990: see the 1990 Review, 474-5.

Nursing homes   The safety provisions of the Nursing Homes (Care and Welfare) Regulations 1993 (SI No. 226) are referred to in the Health Services chapter, 346, above. These primarily concern the safety of dependent persons in a nursing home, rather than the employees. We may note here that, in addition to laying down preventive measures, the Regulations impose express requirements concerning adequate insurance cover in the event of an accident to a dependent person.

Radiation   The Regulations made in 1993 concerning radiological safety are discussed below.

Safety, Health and Welfare at Work Regulations 1993   Because of the wide scope of their application, the Safety, Health and Welfare at Work (General Application) Regulations 1993 (SI No. 44) are discussed below, 483-506, under a separate heading. We also discuss there the more limited Safety, Health and Welfare at Work (Carcinogens) Regulations 1993 (SI No. 80) and the European Communities (Protection of Workers) (Exposure to Asbestos) (Amendment) Regulations 1993 (SI No. 276).

RADIOLOGICAL SAFETY

Emergency warning to public   In the 1991 Review, 375, we noted that the European Communities (Ionising Radiation) Regulations 1991 had implemented those parts of Directive 80/836/Euratom, as amended by Directive 84/467/Euratom, that applied to protecting workers. Further elements of the 1980 and 1984 Directives were implemented by the European Communities (Radiological Emergency Warning to Public) Regulations 1993 (SI No. 209). These Regulations, as their title implies, concern procedures required for the protection of the public in the event of a radiological emergency.

Licensing and control of material   The rather awkwardly titled Radiological Protection Act 1991 (General Control of Radioactive Substances, Nuclear Devices and Irradiating Apparatus) Order 1993 (SI No. 151), involved yet further implementation in Irish law of Directive 80/836/Euratom, as amended by Directive 84/467/Euratom, referred to above. The Order, made under s. 30 of the 1991 Act, empowers the Radiological Protection Institute of Ireland (RPII) to licence and control radioactive substances, nuclear devices and irradiating apparatus referred to in the Order and the Schedules thereto. The general scope of the Order may be gauged from Article 3(1), which provides:

The custody, transportation, handling, holding, storage, use, manufacture, production, processing, importation, distribution, exportation or other disposal of [radioactive substances, nuclear devices and irradiating apparatus] is prohibited save under a licence issued by the Institute.

This comprehensive licensing system reflects the intention of s. 8 of the 1991 Act: see the 1991 Review, 373. The 1993 Order also revoked the more limited licensing system contained in the Nuclear Energy (General Control of Fissile Fuels, Radioactive Substances and Irradiating Apparatus) Order 1977 (1991 Review, 373), which had been made under the Nuclear Energy Act 1971. The 1993 Order came into effect on 1 July 1993.

Finally, we may note here for the sake of completeness that the remaining elements of the two Euratom Directives referred to were implemented by the European Communities (Protection of Outside Workers from Ionising Radiation) Regulations 1994 (SI No. 144 of 1994), to which we shall return in the 1994 Review.

SAFETY, HEALTH AND WELFARE AT WORK REGULATIONS 1993

Regulations of application to virtually all places of work   In 1993, nine highly significant EC Directives on safety and health at work were implemented by the Safety, Health and Welfare at Work (General Application) Regulations 1993 (SI No. 44), the Safety, Health and Welfare at Work (Carcinogens) Regulations 1993 (SI No. 80) and the European Communities (Protection of Workers) (Exposure to Asbestos) (Amendment) Regulations 1993 (SI No. 276). Of these nine Directives, seven were implemented by the General Application Regulations 1993. As we will see below, the General Application Regulations also introduced new statutory requirements on three topics not directly concerned with the implementation of EC Directives.

The General Application Regulations 1993 have introduced a legislative revolution in the potential scope for breach of statutory duty claims arising from accidents and ill-health at work. Where previous legislation on safety and health was limited in scope, the 1993 Regulations apply to virtually all places of work, whether factories, shops, offices, schools, mines, colleges, forests or farms. We will focus here primarily on the General Application Regulations and will then proceed to discuss the Carcinogens Regulations (SI No. 80) and the Asbestos Regulations (SI No. 276).

The General Application Regulations 1993, which came into effect on 22 February 1993, were made by the Minister for Enterprise and Employment in exercise of powers conferred by the Safety, Health and Welfare at Work

Act 1989. As we noted in the 1989 Review, 379-93, the 1989 Act was the first piece of Irish legislation in this area to apply to all places of work, by contrast with previous legislation, such as the Factories Act 1955 (as amended by the Safety in Industry Act 1980), the Office Premises Act 1958, the Mines and Quarries Act 1965 and the Safety, Health and Welfare (Offshore Installations) Act 1987. The 1989 Act aimed to lay down a common set of standards for all places of work, not just those which had previously been covered by legislative codes but also those never subjected to statutory regulation. The sectors which had not been regulated prior to the 1989 Act included agriculture, forestry, schools and colleges and smaller offices. The 1989 Act also established a National Authority for Occupational Safety and Health, commonly called the Health and Safety Authority, with responsibility for inspecting places of work and enforcement of the statutory regime.

It is notable that the 1989 Act differed from its statutory predecessors in that it laid down general principles rather than prescriptive codes. However, the Act also conferred a wide-ranging Regulation-making power on the Minister for Labour, now the Minister for Enterprise and Employment (see the Administrative Law chapter, 7, above), as well as the power to repeal by Order all previous legislation in this area, whether Acts or Regulations. The ultimate mission of the 1989 Act was to replace pre-1989 legislation with the 1989 Act and subsidiary Regulations made under the Act. It should be clear from the following pages that, to a large extent, the General Application Regulations 1993 have achieved this general mission.

British and European dimension As we also pointed out in the 1989 Review, the 1989 Act largely reflected the terms of the British Health and Safety at Work Act 1974, with some important additions resulting from the passage of time between 1974 and 1989. In following the British model, the 1989 Act reflected a history of following the lead of our nearest neighbour in this area of law. Those elements of the General Application Regulations 1993 which are not simply an implementation of EC Directives can also be compared very closely with British Regulations made under the 1974 Act.

The second influence on the shape of the 1989 Act, and more particularly the 1993 Regulations, emerges from the increasing importance of EC initiatives in this area. In the 1970s and 1980s, a number of Directives were agreed at EC level in this area and these were implemented in Irish law by various Regulations: see the 1989 Review, 378, the 1990 Review, 474-5 and the 1991 Review, 370. However, it was not until the Single European Act inserted a specific provision on occupational safety and health, Article 118a, into what is now the EC Treaty that major initiatives were proposed. In 1989, the Council of Ministers, acting on a major Programme from the Commission, embarked on an ambitious plan to lay down a comprehensive set of common rules for all member States, as part of the Social Dimension to the Single Market. A general, or Framework, Directive on the safety and health of workers (89/391/EEC) was first agreed, followed by a series of Individual Directives, whose number continues to grow. The Safety, Health and Welfare at Work (General Application) Regulations 1993 implemented the first six of these individual Directives, together with a 1991 Directive concerning fixed duration and temporary employees.

Even before the 1989 Framework Directive and the Individual Directives that followed, the pre-SEA EC Directives in this area had already required the revocation of domestic Regulations where these were not sufficiently comprehensive in application. Thus, the 1986 EC Directive on Noise (86/188/EEC) required the replacement of the Factories (Noise) Regulations 1975 by the European Communities (Protection of Workers) (Exposure to Noise) Regulations 1990, which apply to virtually all places of work: see the 1990 Review, 474-5. It will be apparent from the title of these 1990 Regulations that they were made under the general power conferred by s. 3 of the European Communities Act 1972. By late 1991, the 1989 Act had begun to be the vehicle for the implementation of EC Directives in this area. Thus the Safety, Health and Welfare at Work Act 1989 (Control of Specific Substances and Activities) Regulations 1991, implementing a 1988 Directive controlling certain substances (88/364/EEC), revoked the Factories (Carcinogenic Substances) (Processes) Regulations 1972: see the 1991 Review, 370. However, s. 3 of the 1972 Act continues to be used as the basis for implementing amendments to older Directives: see the European Communities (Protection of Workers) (Exposure to Asbestos) (Amendment) Regulations 1993 (SI No. 276), below, 505.

Effect on previous safety legislation of 1993 Regulations It is notable that the General Application Regulations 1993 do not, by their terms, repeal or revoke any previous Acts or Regulations on safety and health at work. This may be contrasted with the situation in Great Britain where, when the same EC Directives on which these Regulations are based were implemented in 1992, the implementing Regulations, made under the British Health and Safety at Work Act 1974, provided for what can only be described as wholesale repeal and revocation of primary and secondary legislation, including large portions of the British Factories Act 1961, the model for the Factories Act 1955 (as amended by the Safety in Industry Act 1980). For a helpful analysis of the British Regulations, see Smith, Goddard and Randall, *Health and Safety: The New Legal Framework* (Butterworths, 1993) and for a comprehensive discussion of British Law, see Redgrave, Fife and Machin, *Health and Safety*, 2nd ed. (Butterworths, 1993).

Given the similarity between the Irish and British legislative codes in this area, it is greatly to be regretted that a similar 'pruning' was not effected in this jurisdiction. It will be apparent from the discussion below of the General Application Regulations that such pruning would highlight the significance of the new provisions contained in them as well as preparing practitioners for the need to be 'weaned' from the older legislation. However, it was not until December 1995 that a Safety, Health and Welfare at Work (Repeals and Revocations) Order 1995 (SI No. 357 of 1995) was made under the 1989 Act to effect the pruning implicitly required by the 1993 Regulations.

Layout of the General Application Regulations   It might be more accurate to describe the Safety, Health and Welfare at Work (General Application) Regulations 1993 as ten separate sets of Regulations rather than a single set of Regulations. The reason for this is that the General Application Regulations, as the explanatory note to them indicates, implement seven EC Directives on safety and health and also introduce new requirements on three other topics.

Part II of the Regulations (which has the heading General Provisions) implemented those parts of the 1989 'Framework' Directive (89/391/EEC) which were not already part of domestic law by virtue of the Safety, Health and Welfare at Work Act 1989. Part II also implemented the 1991 Directive concerning the safety and health of fixed duration and temporary employees (91/383/EEC).

Part III of the General Application Regulations (with the heading Workplace) implemented (with one exception, which we discuss below) the 1989 Directive on the Workplace (89/654/EEC), the 1st Individual Directive under the 1989 Framework. Part IV of the Regulations (headed Use of Work Equipment) implemented the 1989 Directive on Work Equipment (89/655/EEC), the 2nd Individual Directive under the 1989 Framework. Part V of the Regulations (Personal Protective Equipment) implemented the 1989 Directive on Personal Protective Equipment (89/656/EEC), the 3rd Individual Directive under the 1989 Framework. Part VI of the Regulations (Handling of Loads) implemented the 1990 Directive on Handling of Loads (89/269/EEC), the 4th Individual Directive under the 1989 Framework. Part VII of the Regulations (Visual Display Screens) implemented the 1990 Directive on Visual Display Screens (90/270/EEC), the 5th Individual Directive under the 1989 Framework.

Part VIII of the General Application Regulations 1993 introduced new requirements concerning the use of electricity at work. Part IX of the Regulations concern the provision of first-aid at work. Finally, Part X of the Regulations require the notification of certain accidents and dangerous occurrences to the National Authority for Occupational Safety and Health (commonly called the Health and Safety Authority), which was established by the 1989 Act.

It may be noted that the General Application Regulations are also distinguished (it might be argued, are disfigured) by no less than 12 Schedules in which in many respects the detailed requirements of the Regulations are contained. Thus, while Part III of the Regulations, the Workplace Regulations, comprise Regulations 16 and 17 only, the substance of these Regulations is to be found in the 2nd, 3rd and 4th Schedules which, between them, lay down requirements concerning issues such as ventilation and temperature, stability of floors, the control of pedestrians and internal traffic control and the provision of sanitary facilities. This use of Schedules may be explained by reference to the format used in the Directives on which much of the Regulations are based (Schedules in the Regulations replacing the Annexes to Directives). However, this has a tendency to make the Regulations somewhat difficult to follow and may be contrasted with the equivalent British Regulations in which the use of Schedules was largely avoided.

Limited non-application of safety legislation to Defence Forces Before proceeding to a general discussion of the 1993 Regulations, brief mention should be made of Part I of the 1993 Regulations. As the heading to Part I, 'Interpretation and General', indicates it is primarily concerned with providing some definitions and other general interpretative information for the remainder of the Regulations. However, it also contains one important substantive provision. Regulation 3 provides:

> The relevant statutory provisions shall apply to members of the Defence Forces except when they are:
> (a) On active service as defined in section 5 of the Defence Act 1954 . . . or deemed to be on active service, as defined in Section 4(1) of the Defence (Amendment) (No. 2) Act 1960 . . .;
> (b) Engaged in action in the course of operational duties at sea;
> (c) Engaged in operations in Aid of the Civil Power; or
> (d) Engaged in training directly associated with any of the above mentioned activities.

It is to be noted, firstly, that this Regulation provides for the application, in general, of the 'relevant statutory provisions' to the Defence Forces, but that the 'relevant statutory provisions' will not apply in the four situations mentioned. The phrase 'relevant statutory provisions' is not defined in the 1993 Regulations, but is defined in s. 2(1) of the Safety, Health and Welfare at Work Act 1989 as including, *inter alia*, the 1989 Act as well as any Regulations made under the Act. Thus, Regulation 3 does not merely provide

for the non-application of the 1993 Regulations to the Defence Forces when
they are engaged in the four activities mentioned, but also provides that the
1989 Act itself does not apply in these situations. The possibility of such
non-application of, or exemption from, the 'relevant statutory provisions'
was anticipated in s. 28(6) of the 1989 Act, subject to the proviso that the
Minister is 'satisfied that the application of such provisions is unnecessary
or impracticable.' The preamble to the 1993 Regulations expressly records
the Minister as 'being satisfied, in relation to Regulation 3, that the application of the relevant statutory provisions mentioned in that Regulation is
impracticable. . . .'

However, subject to the limited exemption granted by Regulation 3, the
1989 Act and the Regulations made under it apply to the Defence Forces. In
addition, of course, we may note that the common law principles developed
by the courts as a consequence of the Supreme Court decision in *Ryan v
Ireland* [1989] IR 177 (see the 1989 Review, 410-18) are fully applicable
across the range of activities in respect of which partial exemption from the
statutory provisions was granted by Regulation 3. It will be recalled that, in
the *Ryan* case, the Supreme Court held that the State owed a duty of care to
the plaintiff in that case notwithstanding that he was deemed to be on active
service (in the Lebanon) within the meaning of the Defence (Amendment)
(No. 2) Act 1960. For criticism of the form of the exemption contained in
Regulation 3, see 136 *Seanad Debates* cc.1527-35.

The nature of the obligations created by the Regulations   The scope of
the General Application Regulations is such that the basis for claiming breach
of statutory duty in work-related accidents has now greatly increased.
Whereas in the past, breach of statutory duty was confined to what were
generally described as 'industrial accidents' the potential scope for such
claims can now encompass the 'service' sector, whether offices, shops,
schools, agriculture and whether in the private or public sector. It is important
not to over-emphasise this point as the common law principles of employer's
liability had always extended to those areas not already regulated by a
statutory code. Nonetheless, the extension of the statutory regime has two
important consequences.

First, the extent to which contributory negligence may be raised is likely
to be affected, since in the past the courts have been reluctant to ascribe
contributory negligence to an employee where the employer has been in
breach of a statutory duty: see *Kennedy v East Cork Foods Ltd* [1973] IR
244.

Secondly, a particular feature of the General Application Regulations is
that, virtually without exception, they appear to create strict, and sometimes
absolute, duties.

By *strict* duties, we mean the kind of obligation where it is stated that '[t]here shall be provided and maintained suitable and sufficient sanitary and washing facilities' (2nd Schedule, point 11). The phrase 'shall be provided' indicates that some type of facilities must be present, whereas if the obligation was subject to the limit 'so far as in reasonably practicable' (a phrase that appears throughout the 1989 Act under which these Regulations were made), then in certain cases it could be argued that, for example, the small number of employees or the cost factors involved justified no facilities. This would be consistent with the most frequently cited judicial exposition of the phrase 'reasonably practicable', that of Asquith LJ in *Edwards v National Coal Board* [1949] 1 KB 704.

By *absolute* duties, we have in mind the well-known provisions of ss. 21 and 23 of the Factories Act 1955 that 'dangerous parts of machinery . . . shall be securely fenced'. This type of duty has been repeated, though in updated language, in the 5th Schedule to the 1993 Regulations, connected to the Work Equipment Regulations.

The 1993 Regulations, as Dr White has noted in his monumental work *Civil Liability for Industrial Accidents* (Oak Tree Press, 1994), contain none of the familiar statutory limitations, such as 'so far as is reasonably practicable' or 'so far as is practicable'. Instead, phrases such as 'suitable and sufficient', 'as far as possible', 'as soon as possible' and 'if necessary' appear in the 1993 regulations. These unfamiliar phrases can be explained by the fact that the Regulations have remained faithful to the letter of the Directives from which they derive. By contrast, the British Regulations implementing the same Directives have departed from the exact text of the Directives to align the Regulations with previously familiar legislative terms of art, such as 'reasonably practicable'.

It may thus become necessary in the future to determine whether the absence of phrases such as 'reasonably practicable' and the use of phrases such as 'as far as possible' and 'if necessary' create a greater level of obligation than the corresponding British Regulations implementing the same Directives. A number of points might arise in that context. For example, it may be noted that Article 118a of the EC Treaty, which is the legal basis for the Directives implemented by the 1993 Regulations, states that such Directives must lay down 'minimum requirements' only. On this basis, it seems unlikely that the courts would regard laws setting down minimum standards as creating absolute liability, though clearly an argument for strict liability in some cases could be made. In addition, the Directives on which the Regulations are based also use the language of 'minimum requirements', though the implementing Irish Regulations adopt an inconsistent approach on this, occasionally stating that 'minimum requirements' are being laid down (see Regulation 20 concerning work equipment and Regulation 31 concerning display screen equipment) but at other times simply stating that particular matters are 'requirements' without any epithet (see Regulation 17 concerning workplaces).

Of course, it may be argued that the Irish Regulations, being creatures of the 1989 Act and not entirely dependent on EC law, may have gone beyond the minimum requirements of the Directives in question, as indeed Article 118a and the Directives themselves also envisage. On this argument, the Irish Regulations stand alone and are to be interpreted in their own right. However, given the reverential adherence to the 'Euro-language' of the Directives in question, this does not appear to be a very strong argument. And since the 1989 Act itself is hallmarked by the limiting phrase 'so far as is reasonably practicable', it would be difficult to argue that Regulations made under the Act which, without exception, created absolute duties could be *intra vires*. For these reasons, it seems sensible to suggest that the duties created by the 1993 Regulations, though in many ways creating strict liability in the sense used here, do not create absolute liability in all cases.

We can now turn to a discussion of the 1993 Regulations. However, given their scope and breadth, it is possible to give merely a brief outline of their contents. For a somewhat more expansive discussion, see Byrne, *A Guide to Safety, Health and Welfare at Work Regulations* (NIFAST, 1995). In the discussion that follows, we will use the headings contained in the different parts of the Regulations.

General Provisions Regulations   The General Provisions Regulations are contained in Part II of the General Application Regulations. The equivalent British Regulations are the Management of Health and Safety at Work Regulations 1992, a title that perhaps more accurately reflects the purpose of Part II and the 1989 EC Framework Directive on which its terms are based. Part II is relatively general in tone, and lacks the specifics of later Parts of the General Application Regulations. In that respect, Part II resembles a statutory manifestation of the common law principles of employer's liability, albeit expressed in a more extensive manner. It is notable that the British Management of Health and Safety at Work Regulations 1992 may not be used to found a civil claim for damages, an exclusion made under the terms of s. 47(2) of the British Health and Safety at Work Act 1974. No such exclusion is made in respect of Part II of the General Application Regulations under the equivalent provision in s. 60 of the Safety, Health and Welfare at Work Act 1989. Thus, practitioners are free to base a claim on the somewhat general duties laid down in Part II.

By way of introduction to these general duties, we should note that s. 12 of the Safety, Health and Welfare at Work Act 1989 expressly required all organisations to prepare a safety statement, a document which must identify hazards and assess the risks in a place of work as well as put in place the organisational measures to deal with those hazards and risks. This requirement to combat hazards and risks was, indeed, based on a draft of the 1989 EC Framework Directive (89/391/EEC) and, to that extent, it may be said that the 1989 Act had already implemented some elements of the Framework Directive. A similar point may be made in respect of the Directive's requirements on consultation of employees: see s. 13 of the 1989 Act.

Significant other elements of the Framework Directive remained to be implemented by means of Part II of the Regulations. Among the provisions included in Part II of the 1993 Regulations is the requirement that risk assessments be in writing (Regulation 10(1)), a point perhaps only implicit in s. 12 of the 1989 Act. In addition, such risks as are identified by the employer must be 'periodically evaluated' to take account of 'changing circumstances' (Regulation 5). Lastly on this point, organisations are required to integrate the measures to protect employees into all the work activities under the control of the employer and at all levels of responsibility in the organisation. While this appears quite general in nature, it again reflects the types of concerns expressed in common law principles. Similarly, the requirement in Regulation 8 that the employer must ensure that any personnel designated with safety functions are 'competent' finds resonances in the 'competent staff' element of the common law duty of care of employers.

It is also significant that Part II requires organisations to 'take account' of the General Principles of Prevention contained in the First Schedule to the 1993 Regulations. These Principles, nine in all and, in effect, amounting to a hierarchy of controls which might be more familiar to students of management theory than of law, have been taken directly from the 1989 Framework Directive. Again, while quite general in tone, these Priniciples may prove of interest in future litigation where a particular issue is not covered by a specific statutory provision.

Part II of the Regulations also contains some provisions which, again, make explicit what might merely have been implicit in the Safety, Health and Welfare at Work Act 1989. Thus Regulation 7 provides that, subject to some specified exceptions, measures related to safety, health and welfare cannot involve financial cost to an employee. Similarly, Regulation 9 states that employers must take the measures necessary to ensure that employees can be evacuated safely in the event of an emergency. Appropriate instructions must also be given to employees to enable them to stop work and/or immediately leave the place of work and proceed to a place of safety in the event of 'serious, imminent and unavoidable danger'. There is partial exemption from this Regulation for members of the Defence Forces or the Garda Síochána, fire fighters or the civil defence services. This exception is based on the 1989 Framework Directive and is different in kind from the partial exemption, limited to the Defence Forces, contained in Regulation 3: see above, 487.

Regulation 15 provides that employers must have in place appropriate health surveillance for employees. This general requirement should be seen against the background of the specific Regulations on health surveillance which have been implemented in recent years: see the Noise Regulations 1990 (1990 Review, 474-5), the Display Screen Regulations, the Carcinogens Regulations and the Asbestos Regulations, the latter three discussed below.

As already mentioned, Part II of the Regulations also implemented the 1991 Directive on fixed-term and temporary employees. Regulation 11 states that, where such employees have been taken on through an employment agency, the employer must inform the agency what, if any, occupational qualifications are needed for the job as well as the specific features of the task for which the employee is required. The employer must also inform the employee, in advance of taking up the job, of the risks the employee may face as well as the skills needed for the job. Regulation 4(2) of the Regulations also provides that any duty imposed on an employer by the Regulations shall apply in respect of fixed-term and temporary employees.

Workplace Regulations   Part III of the General Application Regulations 1993 implemented, with the exception of one area, the 1989 Directive on Workplaces, the first 'Individual' Directive under the 1989 'Framework' Directive (89/391/EEC) referred to in Part I of this article. The one area not implemented in Part III concerned the provisions of the Directive on fire safety. This aspect of the Workplace Directive was due to have been implemented by means of legislation emanating from the Department of the Environment. At the time of writing (June 1996) no such legislation had been promulgated, though this element of the Directive, as with all others, was due to have been implemented by 31 December 1992. It is expected that some legislative amendments will be effected in this area, though this may await legislative action in other Member States, many of whom (including the United Kingdom) have expressed difficulty in implementing the relevant provisions of the Workplace Directive.

The main focus of the Workplace Regulations, as laid down in the 2nd, 3rd and 4th Schedules to the Regulations, is on setting out requirements for what might be described as the physical layout of places of work under 17 headings.

It is virtually impossible to describe here the extensive nature of the Workplace Regulations except to state that they include such diverse matters as: lighting, heating, ventilation, room dimensions, preventing slips on floors, access to confined and dangerous areas, internal traffic control, loading bays and ramps, rest areas (including the issue of smoking in rest areas), sanitary facilities (an issue in respect of which 14 separate points are referred to), a requirement that 'pregnant women' and breastfeeding mothers ('nursing mothers' as they are politely called) must be able to 'lie down to rest in appropriate conditions' and a general requirement to arrange places of work to take account of employees with disabilities.

Some of these (but certainly not all) were matters which featured in legislation such as the Factories Act 1955 (as amended by the Safety in Industry Act 1980) or the Office Premises Act 1958. Indeed, as already mentioned, the equivalent British Regulations, the Workplace (Health, Safety and Welfare) Regulations 1992, provided for repeal of equivalent older legislation which overlapped with the new provisions. Indeed, when the Repeals and Revocations Order 1995 eventually emerged in December 1995, the Office Premises Act 1958 was repealed *in toto* and many provisions of the Factories Act 1995 were also repealed. We will discuss this in greater detail in the 1995 Review.

However, it is also important to bear in mind that the 1993 Regulations not only apply to those premises covered by the older legislation, they also apply to many other premises never previously subject to statutory controls. The Workplace Regulations 1993 cover virtually all 'indoor' places of work, including factories, offices, shops, warehouses, schools and universities. It may be noted, however, that they do not apply to cars, trucks and other means of transport, construction sites, mines and quarries and other extractive industries, fishing boats and fields or woods related to agricultural and forestry work. Detailed requirements for these places of work will be set out in separate Regulations implementing other EC Directives on those topics, such as the 1992 Directive on Temporary or Mobile Construction Sites (92/57/EEC).

As can be seen from the list of matters referred to, the terms of the Workplace Regulations are extremely extensive, but equally it may be noted that the Regulations do not provide the type of specific information common to previous Regulations on these topics. For example, on the question of temperature, the Regulations state merely that it must be 'adequate for human beings, having regard to the working methods being used and the physical demands placed on the employees' (2nd Schedule, point 3(1)). The lack of specificity in this provision can be explained by the fact that the 1993 Regulations, unlike their predecessors which applied to a narrow range of places of work, apply to many diverse places of work, including school-rooms, factories and some cold stores. In Britain, the difficulties associated with such non-specific provisions have been eased somewhat through the publication of an Approved Code of Practice (ACoP) by the UK Health and Safety Executive. Similar guidelines were published by the Health and Safety

Authority in Ireland in December 1995.

Finally, it may be noted that the Workplace Regulations lay down different requirements for what are termed 'new' and 'existing' places of work. 'Existing' places of work are those already in use on 1 January 1993. 'New' places of work are those places used for the first time on or after 1 January 1993. Perhaps it is not surprising that the Regulations impose greater obligations on 'new' places of work. New places of work must comply immediately with all the requirements laid down in the 2nd and 3rd Schedule to the 1993 Regulations. Modifications, extensions or conversions to all places of work undertaken after 1 January 1993 must also comply with the 2nd and 3rd Schedules. This is similar to the approach taken in the Building Regulations 1991, made under the Building Control Act 1990 (see the 1991 Review, 307-8). For places of work already in use on 1 January 1993, only the requirements contained in the 2nd Schedule to the 1993 Regulations came into force on 22 February 1993. The remaining requirements for existing places of work, contained in the 4th Schedule to the Regulations, must be complied with by 1 January 1996. Some requirements in the 4th Scehdule are identical to those in the 3rd Schedule, such as those concerning sanitary facilities, so that by 1996 all places of work will be required to reach the same standard in this area. However, other elements of the 3rd Schedule are not repeated in the 4th Schedule, such as in relation to certain aspects of windows and skylights. Thus, even by 1996 there will be some different standards in operation for pre-1993 and post-1993 places of work in this respect.

Work Equipment Regulations   Part IV of the General Application Regulations 1993 implements the 1989 Directive on Work Equipment, the 2nd Directive under the 1989 Framework Directive. The scope of the Regulations may be gauged from Regulation 2 of the 1993 Regulations which defines work equipment as 'any machine, apparatus, tool or installation used at work'. Clearly, this covers mechanical 'workshop' equipment such as abrasive wheels, lathes, power presses and saws, which would be classified as 'machinery' having 'dangerous parts' within the meaning of s. 23 of the Factories Act 1955. But the 1993 Regulations differ in a number of ways from the older legislation. First, they apply to all places of work, so that saws in supermarkets are captured by their terms, whereas the 1955 Act did not apply to a shop. Second, the Work Equipment Regulations also apply to other 'work equipment', not just the 'machines' with 'dangerous parts' of the 1955 Act. Thus, check-out machines, filing cabinets, hammers, ladders, personal computers, road tankers and x-ray machines are brought within a legislative framework for the first time. Third, the Workplace Regulations are quite systematic in the approach to the problems posed by work equipment.

Thus, while the issue of 'dangerous parts' is still addressed, this is done within the context of requiring employers to examine many other issues, whether it is the transport, repair, modification, maintenance and servicing, or cleaning of equipment (Regulation 18). In addition, the employer must ensure that work equipment is suitable for the work to be carried out or is properly adapted for that purpose and may be used by employees without risk to their safety or health and that they receive appropriate training and instruction (Regulation 19). The employer must also ensure that work equipment complies with relevent European technical standards Directives (Regulation 20). One of the most important standards Directive in this area was implemented by the European Communities (Machinery) Regulations 1992: see the 1992 Review, 539. We might note that these 1992 Regulations have since been superceded by the European Communities (Machinery) Regulations 1994 (SI No. 406 of 1994), to which we will revert in the 1994 Review.

While Regulations 18, 19 and 20 address all work equipment, the admittedly more complex problems posed by mechanical equipment in particular are also dealt with in Regulation 19 by reference to the 5th Schedule to the Regulations. This contains some detailed requirements, some of which will be familiar to practitioners accustomed to the language of the Factories Act 1955. However, the 5th Schedule also contains many other matters which reflect the modern tone of the 1993 Regulations and, by contrast, the 19th Century tone of the Factories Act 1955. The 5th Schedule includes requirements on: control devices and systems; stabilising and clamping of equipment; guarding and protective devices (the point most clearly similar to sections of the Factories Act 1955); lighting; temperature; warning signs; maintenance, isolation and access; and the protection of employees against fire, explosion, overheating and discharges. Many of these headings are, in turn, referable to technical standards on machinery, both national and European, which would no doubt form the basis for any litigation arising from a prosecution under the Regulations or a claim for breach of statutory duty arising from an accident at work.

In relation to the standing of certain precedents on the issue of what constitutes a 'dangerous part' of machinery, the emphasis in the 1993 Regulations on protection against rupture must surely consign to history certain English precedents which made the dubious point that the Factories Act was intended only to prevent the worker coming into contact with the moving part but did not extend to protecting the worker if a piece of a machine disintegrated and struck the worker. In any event, as Dr White has correctly pointed out in his *Civil Liability for Industrial Accidents, op. cit.*, such precedents were of doubtful standing in Ireland. Of course, it should be pointed out again that the scope of the 1993 Regulations requires practitioners to have in mind the issue of breach of statutory duty in relation to accidents in all places of work, not merely those which were previously covered by the Factories Act 1955.

We may also note here that, as with the Workplace Regulations, above, the Work Equipment Regulations cry out for the repeal of the relevant provisions of the Factories Act 1955, in particular ss. 21 to 25 of the 1955 Act. This is all the more so because the 1993 Regulations replicate provisions on dangerous parts of machinery, including familiar phrases from s. 23 of the 1955 Act relating to any 'stock-bar which projects beyond the head-stock of a lathe' (see the 5th Schedule, paragraph 8(c)). Again, it is notable that the equivalent British Regulations, the Provision and Use of Work Equipment Regulations 1992, provided for the repeal of ss. 12 to 16 of the UK Factories Act 1961, the equivalent of ss. 21 to 25 of the 1955 Act. Curiously, while the Repeals and Revocations Order 1995 (493, above) repealed some elements of the Factories Act 1995, s. 23 was retained on the statute books. We will return to this anomaly in the 1995 Review.

It is of some interest, however, that the British Regulations provide for the full implementation of the terms of the Work Equipment Directive only on 1 January 1997 in respect of work equipment supplied for use before 1 January 1993, what might be termed 'old' work equipment. This 'phasing in' period for older equipment was envisaged in the 1989 Work Equipment Directive itself. By way of contrast, the Irish Regulations did not take advantage of this 'phasing in' period, so that the onerous terms of the 1993 Regulations apply to all equipment, old and new. Thus, the terms of the Irish Factories Act 1955 could have been repealed in 1993 when the General Application Regulations were made. Practitioners are thus left with the task, even after the Repeals and Revocations Order 1995, in the case of a factory accident, of pleading both the 1955 Act and the relevant provisions of the 1993 Regulations. Of course, where an 'equipment' accident occurs in a non-factory premises, this overlap problem does not exist as only the 1993 Regulations apply.

Personal Protective Equipment Regulations   Part V of the General Application Regulations 1993 implements the 1989 Directive on Personal Protective Equipment (PPE), the 3rd Directive under the 1989 'Framework' Directive. Regulation 2 of the 1993 Regulations defines PPE as all equipment designed to be worn or held by an employee for protection against hazards likely to endanger the employee's safety and health at work, and includes any addition or accessory designed to meet this objective. However, the following are excluded: (a) ordinary working clothes and uniforms not specifically designed to protect employees; (b) PPE for road transport; (c) sports equipment; (d) self-defence equipment or deterrent equipment; (e) portable devices for detecting and signalling risks and nuisances. Despite these exclusions, it is clear that the 1993 Regulations have a very wide scope. Again, as with other Parts of the 1993 Regulations, the Personal Protective Equipment Regulations apply to all places of work, including factories, offices, shops, hospitals and schools. Many of these places of work were not previously regulated by such a detailed set of requirements on PPE.

Regulation 22 of the 1993 Regulations requires employers to engage in an analysis and assessment of risks to determine whether they can be avoided or otherwise limited by technical means which would avoid the need to provide employees with PPE. In other words, in a well-worn cliche, PPE is regarded as the last line of defence where other means are not available. However, if it is clear that PPE is the only method of providing protection, Regulation 21(1) states that employers 'shall' provide PPE for use by employees. Regulation 24 states that the employer must ensure that PPE is maintained at all times in good working order and in a satisfactory hygienic condition, by means of any necessary storage, maintenance, repair or replacement. Regulation 7 states that PPE must be provided free of charge where used exclusively at the place of work. Where PPE is not used exclusively at the place of work, the employer can request a contribution in proportion to the cost to the employer of its use outside work.

Regulation 21(3) states that, in providing PPE, employers must take account of the Guide List of Activities and Sectors for which PPE may be required, contained in the 6th Schedule to the Regulations. The 6th Schedule attempts to match many activities with general types of PPE. Thus, building work under scaffolding is connected with head protection, whereas boning and cutting work is connected with pierce-proof aprons. The 6th Schedule is described as a non-exhaustive list, so it is not a comprehensive list of activities for which PPE is required. And where other Regulations require particular types of PPE, as with the Noise Regulations 1990 (see the 1990 Review, 285, 474-5), these must also be complied with. The 6th Schedule to the Regulations approaches the issue of what activities require PPE by listing the activities under eleven different headings of PPE, including head protection, foot protection, eye or face protection and body, arm and hand protection, with the activities listed under these headings. In relation to some headings, such as foot protection, a number of different sub-headings are used, differentiating between activities which require 'safety shoes with puncture-proof soles' (e.g. scaffolding and roof work) and those which require 'protective shoes with insulated soles' (work with and on very hot or very cold materials). Regulation 21(3) also states that, in providing PPE, employers must take account of the guide list of items of PPE, contained in the 7th Schedule to the Regulations. Again, this is not a comprehensive list of PPE, but employers must at the least comply with its requirements. As with work equipment (see above), Regulation 21(4) states that the employer

must ensure that PPE complies with any relevant European technical standards Directives on PPE. The relevant EC Directive in this context was
implemented in Ireland by the European Communities (Personal Protective
Equipment) Regulations 1993 (SI No. 272): see 481, above.

On the question of training and instruction, Regulation 26 states that
employers must, in relation to PPE: (a) inform the employee of the risks
against which the PPE protects; (b) provide the employee with adequate
information on PPE; (c) provide instruction on the use of PPE; and (d) arrange
for training and, if appropriate, organise demonstrations in the wearing of
the PPE. Finally, Regulation 14 of the 1993 Regulations states that, where
employees are provided with PPE, they must, taking inito account the
training and instruction given to them: (a) make full and proper use of the
PPE; (b) use the PPE in accordance with the instructions given under
Regulation 26; and (c) take all reasonable steps to ensure that PPE is returned
to storage after use.

One issue which is not explicit in the 1993 Regulations but which has
been a feature of litigation in this area is to what extent the employer must
ensure that employees actually wear PPE provided by the employer. The
equivalent British Regulations, the Personal Protective Equipment at Work
Regulations 1992, make explicit this obligation on the employer, but it might
also be argued that the same obligation follows from the extensive obligations placed on the employer concerning selection and suitability. It seems
to flow also from the extent to which the employer must pay attention to
whether PPE is maintained in a condition that provides the appropriate level
of protection originally intended.

Manual Handling of Loads Regulations   Part VI of the 1993 Regulations
implements the 1990 Directive on Manual Handling of Loads, the 4th
Directive agreed under the 1989 Framework Directive. Regulation 27 of the
1993 Regulations gives a wide definition of the term 'manual handling of
loads', namely, 'any transporting or supporting of a load, by one or more
employees, and includes lifting, putting down, pushing, pulling, carrying, or
moving a load which, by reason of its characteristics or of unfavourable
ergonomic conditions, involves risk, particularly of back injury, to employees.'

The Regulations are, in common with the other provisions based on EC
Directives, very systematic in approach. Thus, Regulation 28 first requires
an employer to take appropriate organisational measures, or use appropriate
means, in particular mechanical equipment, in order to avoid the need for
manual handling of loads by employees. Only where the need for manual
handling cannot be avoided do the Regulations permit an employer to take
appropriate measures to reduce the risk involved in the manual handling of

loads. The employer must do so having regard to the factors specified in the 8th Schedule to the 1993 Regulations. The 8th Schedule lists four factors in this context, with particular points of detail relevant to each. The factors are: the characteristics of the load, the physical effort required, the characteristics of the working environment and the requirements of the activity.

Regulation 13 of the 1993 Regulations states that, in relation to the appropriate training and information required by employees, an employer must take into account the individual risk factors set out in the 9th Schedule to the 1993 Regulations. These include whether an employee is physically suited to carry out the task in question, is wearing suitable clothing, footwear or other personal effects, has adequate or appropriate knowledge or training. On the question of training, see *Dunleavy v Glen Abbey Ltd* [1992] ILRM 1 (1991 Review, 369, 406-9).

It is notable that the 9th Schedule is gender neutral in relation to these 'individual' risk factors. Thus, it does not lay down any maximum weights for different categories of employees, by way of contrast with the approach taken in the Factories Act 1955 (Manual Handling) (Maximum Weights and Transport) Regulations 1972. Under the 1972 Regulations, maximum weights were specified for employees on gender lines. The maximum weight for a male employee over 18 years was 55kg (121lb), while for a female employee over 18 years it was 16kg (35.2lb). The 1993 Regulations differ from the 1972 Regulations in two respects. First, they contain no absolute limit to what can be lifted and, secondly, they are clearly gender neutral.

Regulation 28(d) states that the employer must ensure that employees involved in manual handling must receive general indications and, where possible, precise information on: the weight of each load, and the centre of gravity of the heaviest side when a package is 'eccentrically loaded', a phrase which appears in the EC Directive, but which was 'translated' in the equivalent British Regulations, the Manual Handling Operations Regulations 1992, as a load 'whose centre of gravity in not positioned centrally.'

One matter which the Regulations does not define is the word 'load'. An area in which this may prove a difficulty is whether 'load' includes human beings, an issue particularly important in the context of whether the Regulations impose an obligation to provide training in 'patient handling' for health sector employees. It is notable that the British Regulations expressly provide that '"load" includes any person and any animal.' It may be that no such definition is required, though the detailed provisions of the Irish Regulations may prove troublesome in this context. Thus one might wonder whether the following references to 'loads' in the 8th Schedule to the Regulations do or do not have relevance to human beings: 'unstable or has contents likely to shift'; 'positioned in a manner requiring it to be held or manipulated at a distance from the trunk'; 'likely, because of its contours or consistency (or both), to result in injury to employees, particularly in the event of a collision'. While employers in the health sector would be well advised to conclude that patient handling comes within the terms of the Regulations, since the common law would require proper systems in any event, the language of the Regulations remains oblique on this point.

Display Screen Equipment Regulations   Part VII of the General Appli-cation Regulations 1993 implements the 1990 European Directive on Dis-play Screen Equipment, the 5th Directive agreed under the 1989 Framework Directive. The Display Screen Directive is colloquially referred to as the VDU Directive, and while it applies to computer screens, it also applies to other forms of display screens, such as microfilms and microfiche. In addition, while not directly relevant, the issues addressed in Part VII are also relevant, for example, to the repetitive strain injury (RSI) problems associ-ated with 'old-technology' typing work.

The Regulations apply to 'users', that is an employee who 'habitually' uses 'display screen equipment' and to the 'workstations' connected to the display screen. Regulation 29 defines 'display screen equipment' as any alphanumeric or graphic display screen, regardless of the display process involved, thus including microfilm and microfiche display screens. Regula-tion 29 defines the 'workstation' as including the screen and keyboard (or other input device) which comprises the interface between the operator and the screen, as well as optional accessories such as diskette drive, telephone, modem, printer, document holder, work chair and work desk and the imme-diate work environment of the equipment.

Regulation 30 states that Part VII of the Regulations do not apply to: (a) drivers' cabs or control cabs for vehicles or machinery; (b) computer systems on board a means of transport; (c) computer systems mainly intended for public use; (d) portable display screen equipment not in prolonged use at a workstation; (e) calculators, cash registers and any equipment having a small data or measurement display required for direct use of the equipment; and (f) typewriters of the kind commonly known as 'typewriter with window'.

While the 1993 Regulations clearly exclude certain equipment in the general display screen 'family', it should also be borne in mind that many of the issues addressed by the Regulations also arise with, for example, work on traditional typrewriters. While the extensive obligations imposed on employers by the 1993 Regulations clearly do not apply to the excluded categories of equipment, it might be noted here that common law duties would be relevant to a claim by, for example, a typist claiming that they had deveopled musculo-skeletal problems arising from poor 'worstation' design, such as poor design of seat. Indeed, many of the original repetitive strain injury (RSI) claims arose from pre-VDU typing pools.

Regulation 29 states that Part VII applies to an employee who 'habitually uses display screen equipment as a significant part' of their normal work. While 'habituallly uses' is not further defined, the Health and Safety Authority has indicated in published guidance that this includes employees who work on a screen for a continuous period of one hour or more during the normal course of their duties. This is in line with the comprehensive Guidance Notes issued by the Health and Safety Executive in connection with the equivalent British Regulations, the Health and Safety (Display Screen Equipment) Regulations 1992.

Regulation 31 of the 1993 Regulations states that employers must: (a) perform an analysis of display screen workstations in order to evaluate the safety and health conditions to which they give rise for employees, 'particularly as regards possible risks to eyesight, physical problems and problems of mental stress'; and (b) take appropriate measures to remedy any risks found on the basis of the evaluation conducted, taking into account the minimum requirements laid down in the 10th and 11th Schedules to the Regulations. Different requirements are laid down in the 10th and 11th Schedules depending on whether the equipment was first put into service before or after 31 December 1992.

Regulation 31 also requires that the employers must plan the activities of users in such a way that daily work on a screen is periodically interrupted by breaks or changes of activity that reduce workload at the screen. Regulation 31 also states that the employer must: (a) provide users with information on the measures taken by the employer to comply with the Regulations; and (b) provide training to users before commencing work on display screens and whenever the organisation of the workstation is substantially modified.

Regulation 32 of the 1993 Regulations states that the employer must ensure (taking account of any State entitlement of the user to eye tests or to glasses): (a) that an appropriate eye and eyesight test, carried out by a competent person, is made available to every user: (i) before the user commences work on screens; and (ii) at regular intervals thereafter; but in any event (iii) if an employee experiences visual difficulties that may be due to work with display screens; (b) that if the results of an eye and eyesight test show that it is necessary, an ophthalmological examination is carried out on the user; and (c) that where the results of a test or examination show it is necessary, and if ordinary prescription glasses cannot be used, the user is provided with special corrective appliances appropriate to the work.

It should be noted that Regulation 32 does not make eye tests mandatory; what is mandatory is that the employer make them available to employees. However, as with the Noise Regulations 1990 (see the 1990 Review, 285, 474-5) some employers may decide to provide eye tests in order to provide the highest level of protection for their employees and to protect against any future problems.

It may be noted that the Display Screen Regulations do not overtly address the question of reproductive problems posed in connection with the use of VDU screens in particular. There are general references to the safety and health conditions associated with display screen equipment, but the issue of reproductive risks is not specified. This may reflect the lack of any concrete evidence to link VDU use with such problems, but the Regulations are written in such a manner as to allow for such issues to be addressed if any clear evidence were to emerge in the future. It seems, however, that best practice indicates that employers are well advised to adopt a cautious approach, particularly in relation to pregnant employees.

Use of Electricity Regulations   Part VIII of the General Application Regulations 1993, unlike the previous Parts of the 1993 Regulations, does not involve the overt implementation of the terms of an EC Directive. Rather, it imposes new requirements on safe use of electricity for all places of work. While the 1989 Workplace Directive did make brief reference to electrical installations, the scope of Part VIII owes more to the British Electricity at Work Regulations 1989 than to European initiatives. Part VIII is also distinguished by the absence of any accompanying Schedule: the Electricity Regulations run from Regulations 33 to 53 of the 1993 Regulations. By way of contrast, Part III of the Regulations, the Workplace Regulations cover merely two Regulations (16 and 17) but are of much wider scope (the detailed provisions are, of course, contained in the 2nd, 3rd and 4th Schedules).

Part VIII of the 1993 Regulations involves new requirements on safe use of electricity in almost all places of work, but Regulation 34 specifically excludes mines and quarries within the meaning of the Mines and Quarries Act 1965, to which specific Regulations already apply.

By this single exclusion, therefore, Part VIII of the 1993 Regulations apply to factories and other premises regulated by the Factories Act 1955 (as amended by the Safety in Industry Act 1980). This created a problem of overlap, since the Factories (Electricity) Regulations 1972 and 1979, made under the 1955 Act, were not expressly revoked by the 1993 Regulations. This overlap with existing legislation was, as we have noted, a problem with the entire text of the 1993 Regulations, but was particularly clear with Part VIII (and the remaining two Parts of the Regulations: see below). This is especially so because Part VIII of the 1993 Regulations (in line with the approach taken in the British Electricity at Work Regulations 1989) are much less prescriptive that previous Regulations on this area, such as the 1972 and 1989 Regulations. However, this anomaly was resolved by the revocation of the 1972 and 1979 Regulations by the Repeals and Revocations Order 1995. While the essential principles are contained in Part VIII, reference is also made, where necessary, to relevant standards and codes on electrical equipment in order to avoid the kind of excessive detail which characterised previous Regulations.

First-Aid Regulations Like Part VIII, Part IX of the General Application Regulations 1993 involves new requirements on first-aid for all places of work. Again, previous Regulations, the most wide-ranging being the First-Aid in Factories Regulations 1975, were relatively limited in their application. In common with most other Parts of the 1993 Regulations, Part IX applies to all places of work. Part IX of the Regulations are quite laconic and provide relatively little detail in terms, for example, of the number of trained first-aid personnel in a place of work or the number of first aid boxes per employee in a shop, factory, office or school. However, in July 1994 the Irish Health and Safety Authority published *Guidelines on First-Aid at Places of Work*, which provide very detailed information on the general terms of Part IX. We may note here also that the Repeals and Revocations Order 1995 formally revoked previous Regulations in this area.

Notification of Accidents and Dangerous Occurrences Regulations Part X of the 1993 Regulations expands considerably the obligation to report accidents and dangerous occurrences to the Health and Safety Authority. Previous Regulations requiring such reporting were confined to factories, mines and quarries and offshore installations. The 1993 Regulations bring all other places of work within the ambit of a legal obligation to report. Fatal accidents are reportable within the Regulations, as well as accidents in which a person is prevented from performing their 'normal work for more than three consecutive days, excluding the day of the accident'. This 'three day accident' base for reporting purposes is in line with European norms. In addition to such accidents, the Regulations also specify a number of dangerous occurrences, including explosions and failure of certain equipment such as certain wire ropes, which must be reported regardless of whether any personal injury results.

An Approved Form for Reporting such accidents or dangerous occurrences has been issued by the Health and Safety Authority. Again, it is notable that, while Part X applies to factories, the Safety in Industry (Notification of Accidents) Regulations 1956 and 1981, which dealt with the notification of accidents in factories and other premises covered by the Factories Act 1955 (as amended by the Safety in Industry Act 1980) were not revoked by the 1993 Regulations. They were, however, revoked by the Repeals and Revocations Order 1995.

It may also be noted that Part X does not apply to occupational ill-health, such as dermatitis or cancer-like illnesses (in the language of the past, 'industrial diseases'). It is understood that Regulations on this topic will be promulgated at some time in the future.

Carcinogens   The Safety, Health and Welfare at Work (Carcinogens) Regulations 1993 (SI No. 80) implemented the 1990 Carcinogens Directive, the 6th Individual Directive under the 1989 Framework. As we have already seen, the General Application Regulations 1993 implemented the first five Directives under the 1989 Framework, and the Carcinogens Regulations follows the same pattern as the other European Directives on safety and health at work.

In general terms, the Carciongens Regulations 1993 apply to all chemicals that are labelled 'may cause cancer', which is the European 'risk phrase', R-45, for carcinogenic chemicals. This covers a large number of chemicals, but unfortunately the Regulations do not provide a list. The Health and Safety Authority's Approved Code of Practice (ACoP) for the Safety, Health and Welfare at Work (Chemical Agents) Regulations 1994 (SI No. 446 of 1994) (to which we will return in the 1994 Review) contains the most recent listing of such chemicals. The list of chemicals which carry the 'may cause cancer' phrase is subject to change as scientific knowledge changes, but the HSA ACoP is a very helpful starting point.

In addition to the 'R-45' chemicals to which the Regulations apply, they also apply to certain activities specified in the First Schedule to the Regulations, including: the manufacture of auramine; work involving exposure to artomatic polycyclic hydrocarbons present in coal soot, tar, pitch, fumes or dust; work involving exposure to dusts, fumes and sprays produced during the roasting and electro-refining of cupro-nickel mattes; and strong acid process in the manufacture of isopropyl alcohol.

Regulation 4 of the Regulations requires employers to assess the risk to the health or safety of employees exposed to carcinogens at work and to take the appropriate measures to protect employees. This is in line with the obligation to prepare a safety statement in accordance with s. 12 of the Safety, Health and Welfare at Work Act 1989. In addition, Regulation 4 also requires employers to take the precautionary measures specified in the 2nd Schedule to the Regulations. These precautions reflect the type of approach contained in the General Principles of Prevention referred to above, 490, in the context of Part II of the General Application Regulations. These include the following: limitation of the quantities of a carcinogen at a place of work; keeping as low as possible the number of employees exposed or likely to be exposed to a carcinogen; the use of appropriate systems for the extraction of carcinogens at source; the use of both collective protection measures and individual protection measures where exposure cannot be avoided by other means; the use of hygiene measures, in particular regular cleaning of floors, walls and other surfaces; the marking of risk areas and the use of adeuqate warning and safety signs, including 'no smoking' signs; drawing up plans to deal with emergencies likely to result in abnormally high exposure; and the means for safe storage, handling and transportation of carcinogens and carcinogenic waste, in particular by using sealed containers that are clearly and visibly labelled.

Under Regulation 10 of the Regulations, employers are required to inform employees of the particular risks connected with exposure to carcinogens at work, including, for example, the additional risks due to smoking cigarettes. In addition, the need to wear appropriate personal protective equipment (PPE) is highlighted.

Finally, Regulation 12 of the Regulations require employers to make provision for relevant health surveillance for those employees for whom the results of the risk assessment carried out under Regulation 4 reveal a risk to their health or safety. If possible, this health surveillance should occur before exposure to a carcinogen. It must be carried out under the responsibility of a registered medical practitioner. Records of health surveillance must be kept for 40 years, either by the employer or the Health and Safety Authority. Clearly, such records, or their absence, will have a bearing on future claims in this area.

Asbestos The European Communities (Protection of Workers) (Exposure to Asbestos) (Amendment) Regulations 1993 (SI No. 276), which came into effect on 1 October 1993, amended the 1989 Regulations of the same title (see the 1989 Review, 378) in order to implement Directive 91/382/EEC, which had amended the main Directive on asbestos, 83/477/EEC, implemented by the 1989 Regulations. Although these Regulations were made under s. 3 of the European Communities Act 1972, they apply to virtually all places of work, as do the other 1993 Regulations on safety and health at work discussed above. Thus, they apply to garages where employees may be engaged in cleaning the brake lining of motor vehicles as well as to employees in the construction industry, where demolition of insulation in older buildings (the Berlaymont Building in Brussels being one of the most famous examples of this) may also involve exposure to asbestos fibres. The Regulations amend the precautions to be taken against exposure to airborne asbestos fibres laid down in the 1989 Regulations and, in particular, lower the levels of airborne asbestos fibres in relation to which preventive measures must be taken.

Conclusion It should be clear from a review of the General Application Regulations in particular that, since they came into effect on 22 February 1993, the scope for claiming breach of statutory duty in work-related accidents has been greatly increased. While it might have been preferable for the Regulations to provide for simultaneous repeal and revocation of those previous legislative provisions with which they overlap rather than delaying this process for almost three years when the Safety, Health and Welfare at Work (Repeals and Revocations) Order 1995 (SI No. 347 of 1995) eventually emerged, this should not cloud the fact that the Regulations have transformed the existing statutory landscape. It can hardly be doubted that, in the years to come, the General Application Regulations will become even more frequently pleaded in personal injuries actions for work-related accidents than had been the case with the Factories Act, and the Regulations made under it.

Social Welfare

G.W. Whyte, School of Law, Trinity College Dublin

SOCIAL WELFARE ACTS OF 1993

In all, three Social Welfare Acts were passed during the period under review. The Social Welfare Act 1993, which is annotated by Robert Clark at 1993 ICLSA 5-01, gave effect to the changes in welfare rates announced in the 1993 Budget and also made a number of substantive changes to the welfare code. Thus Part IV (ss. 16-21) provided for the introduction of a PRSI Exemption Scheme for employers who take on new employees from the Live Register and made a number of other changes relating to the payment and collection of social insurance contributions. Anticipating the subsequent enactment of the Social Welfare (Consolidation) Act 1993, Part VI (ss. 27 to 41), which was brought into effect by the Social Welfare (Consolidation) Act 1993 (Commencement) Order 1993 (SI No. 174 of 1993) provided for the amendment, consolidation and alignment of existing provisions relating to claims and payments, the powers of inspectors, offences, the effect of decisions, the suspension of payments and the recovery of overpayments. In relation to this last topic, the opportunity was taken to enhance the power of the Department to recover overpaid welfare received by claimants who were not guilty of any fraudulent behaviour. (See further discussion of this topic, in the context of the administration of estates, by Whyte in (1993) ILSI Gazette, 175-7.) As a *quid pro quo*, as it were, s. 31 provided, *inter alia*, regulatory powers for the introduction of a Code of Practice as to how to deal with overpayments. These powers have not yet been exercised however. Parts III and V effected a range of changes to various aspects of the welfare code, of which perhaps the most controversial was the restriction of entitlement of people in full-time education to Unemployment Assistance or Supplementary Welfare Allowance in respect of vacation periods — s. 14. S. 8 addressed the entitlement of returned volunteer development workers to maternity benefit (see SI No. 201 of 1993) while s. 9 extended entitlement to invalidity pension in certain circumstances to persons who are incapacitated for less than one year — see SI No. 132 of 1993. S. 10 increased the amount of 'after death payments' payable to a person in receipt of Carer's Allowance in respect of his or her spouse and whose spouse has died. The definition of 'adult dependant' was amended by s. 11 to ensure that cohabiting couples are treated in the same way as married couples for all social welfare payments while s. 12 dealt with the rather technical matter of the linking of various disability benefit claims for the purpose of determining when entitlement has been exhausted. S. 13 provided for regulatory powers to prescribe amounts to be disregarded in assessing income from employment when means-testing for unemployment assistance (see SI No. 99 of 1993) while s. 15 provided statutory authorisation for the administrative practice of limiting the amount of pre-retirement allowance payable to a claimant whose spouse/partner is in receipt of a social insurance payment or pre-retirement allowance or the old age (non-contributory) pension. S. 22 empowered a deciding officer to disqualify a claimant, discovered making a fraudulent claim for welfare, from any welfare payment administered by the Department of Social Welfare for a period of up to 9 weeks and further restricted the person's entitlement to supplementary welfare allowance during such period of disqualification. S. 23 provided that the Minister may allocate and issue personal social services numbers while s. 24 clarified the basis for the assessment of non-cash benefits as means for the purpose of Lone Parent's Allowance. Penultimately, s. 25 abolished the requirement that the sex of a person be taken into account in determining, for the purpose of determining entitlement to unemployment assistance and benefit, whether or not a person was unable to obtain suitable employment and s. 26 provided that people participating in certain prescribed training courses would be insurable for occupational injuries payments — see SI Nos. 177 and 203 of 1993. Finally, Part VII (ss. 42 to 52) effected certain amendments to the Pensions Act 1990.

Unquestionably the most welcome enactment of the year for social welfare lawyers was the Social Welfare (Consolidation) Act 1993, consolidating the Social Welfare (Consolidation) Act 1981 and all of the amending Acts enacted from 1981 to 1993 inclusive. (For commentary on the Social Welfare Acts 1993 to 1995, see Clark, *Annotated Guide to Social Welfare Law* (London, 1995). That the Social Welfare Acts had to be consolidated for the second time in twelve years is eloquent testimony to the pace of change in this area of the law and the Department of Social Welfare is to be commended for its efforts in consolidating both the primary legislation and some of the accompanying regulations.

Hardly was the ink on the Consolidation Act dry when it, in turn, was amended by the Social Welfare (No. 2) Act 1993. (See annotation by Clark at 1993 *ICLSA* 32-01). Part II of this Act established a new category of optional contributor for social insurance purposes for persons engaged in share fishing. It will be recalled that in *Minister for Social Welfare v Griffiths* [1992] ILRM 667; [1992] 1 IR 103, Blayney J held that share fishermen were not covered by social insurance — see the 1992 Review, 547-8 and see also the decision of Costello J in *Director of Public Prosecutions v McLaughlin* [1986] IR 355. Under the 1993 Act, workers with an annual income of £2,500 or more and whose principal means of livelihood is derived from share fishing may opt to pay 5% of that income up to the PRSI earnings ceiling, subject to a minimum annual contribution of £250. In return, optional contributors may qualify for disability benefit for a maximum continuous period of one year (after which they will have to requalify by paying contributions in respect of the income tax year following the calendar year in which they exhaust their entitlement) and unemployment benefit for up to 13 weeks in any calendar year. In the case of either benefit, where an optional contributor fails to qualify because his earnings are below the prescribed amount, provision is made for the payment of reduced rate benefit related to the level of actual earnings. (The implementing Regulations for this Part of the Act are the Social Welfare (No. 2) Act 1993 (Part II) (Commencement) Order 1994 (SI No. 52 of 1994) and the Social Welfare (Optional Contributions) Regulations 1994 (SI No. 53 of 1994).)

The reasoning in *Griffiths*, namely that the obligation to pay employment contributions necessarily presupposed the existence of an employer/employee relationship, arguably has implications for another category of worker, student nurses and midwives, currently treated as insurable but to date this matter has not been addressed in legislation.

Part III effects two miscellaneous amendments to the welfare code. Ss. 11 to 13 extend the disability benefit and unemployment benefit schemes to volunteer development workers returning from overseas by removing the requirement of having minimum reckonable earnings for claims made in the calendar year in which the claimant returns from overseas or the next succeeding calendar year. S. 14 provides for regulatory powers under which specified employers and contractors may be required to keep certain records relating to employees and persons engaged by them under a contract for service. The section also provides that the regulations may specify the place at which such records must be kept and that failure to keep such records is an offence. (The relevant Regulations are the Social Welfare (Maintenance of Records) Regulations 1994 (SI No. 24 of 1994).)

Finally, s. 15 amends s. 62 of the Pensions Act 1990 relating to the selection by members of funded schemes of persons for appointment as trustees. (See further Occupational Pensions Schemes (Member Participation in the Selection of Persons for Appointment as Trustees) (No. 2) Regulations 1993 (SI No. 399 of 1993).)

REGULATIONS

The following Regulations were made in 1993 in relation to social welfare. Social Welfare (Old Age (Contributory) Pension and Retirement Pension) Regulations 1993 (SI No. 9). These Regulations provide entitlement to the old age (contributory) pension and the retirement pension, on a *pro rata* basis, to persons with an insurance record based on work in both the private and public sectors.

Social Welfare (Miscellaneous Social Insurance Provisions) Regulations 1993 (SI No. 82). These Regulations define 'substantial loss of employment' for the purposes of qualifying for unemployment benefit as the loss of at least one day of insurable employment in any week.

Social Welfare (Disability Benefit) Regulations 1993 (SI No. 83). These Regulations deal with the requirement of having recent involvement in the labour force in order to qualify for disability benefit.

Social Welfare (Treatment Benefit) (Amendment) Regulations 1993 (SI No. 84). These Regulations, *inter alia*, raise the upper earnings limit for eligibility for treatment benefit to £30,000 p.a. for a single claimant.

Social Welfare (Unemployment Assistance) Regulations 1993 (SI No. 99). These Regulations provide for an earnings disregard in assessing income from insurable employment for the purpose of qualifying for unemployment assistance.

Social Welfare (Invalidity Pension) Regulations 1993 (SI No. 132). These Regulations relax the definition of 'permanent incapacity for work' for the purposes of qualifying for invalidity pension and also consolidate the earlier regulations governing this benefit.

Social Welfare (Miscellaneous Provisions for Self-Employed Contributors) (Amendment) Regulations 1993 (SI No. 137). These Regulations set the minimum social insurance contributions for certain categories of self-employed contributor.

Social Welfare (Adult Dependant) (Amendment) Regulations 1993 (SI No. 154). These Regulations raise the income limit used to determine whether a person is to be regarded as an adult dependant for welfare purposes to £60 per week.

Social Welfare Act 1993 (Part VI) (Commencement) Order 1993 (SI No. 174). This Order brought Part VI of the 1993 Act, aligning and consolidating the provisions relating to general administrative arrangements, powers and duties of social welfare inspectors and offences, into effect from 25 June 1993. It has, of course, been overtaken by the subsequent enactment of the 1993 Consolidation Act.

Social Welfare (Insurable (Occupational Injuries) Employment) (Amendment) Regulations 1993 (SI No. 177). These Regulations provide that courses approved by FÁS, Teagasc and CERT and projects approved by the Department of Enterprise and Employment under certain EC initiatives are insurable employments for the purposes of Occupational Injuries Benefit.

Social Welfare (Lone Parent's Allowance and other Analogous Payments) (Amendment) Regulations 1993 (SI No. 179), Social Welfare (Old Age and Blind Pension) Regulations 1993 (SI No. 180) and Social Welfare Act 1992 (Section 13) (Commencement) Order 1993 (SI No. 181). These Regulations provided for the disregard of up to £75,000 from the proceeds of sale of the claimant's principal residence in the means test for various social assistance payments. They were subsequently overtaken by SI No. 364 of 1993, mentioned below.

Social Welfare (Claims and Payments) Regulations 1993 (SI No. 189). These Regulations consolidate existing provisions governing the making of claims and payments.

Social Welfare (Household Budgeting) Regulations 1993 (SI No. 196). These Regulations regulate the making of deductions from social welfare payments for the purpose of the administration of the Household Budgeting Scheme by An Post.

Social Welfare (Maternity Allowance) (Amendment) Regulations 1993 (SI No. 201). These Regulations set out the conditions of eligibility for maternity allowance which have to be satisfied by volunteer development workers and also increase the weekly minimum and maximum payments of this allowance.

Social Welfare Act 1993 (Section 8(2)) (Commencement) Order 1993 (SI No. 202). These Regulations activated s. 8(2) of the 1993 Act, dealing with the calculation of reckonable earnings for the purpose of determining the weekly rate of maternity allowance. They were subsequently overtaken by the bringing into effect of the 1993 Consolidation Act.

Social Welfare (Modifications of Insurance) (Amendment) Regulations 1993 (SI No. 203). These Regulations provide that people participating in certain EC initiatives are insurable for Occupational Injuries Benefits only.

Social Welfare (Waiver of Interest and Penalties) Regulations 1993 (SI No. 208). These Regulations provide for the waiving of interest and penalties on PRSI arrears as part of the general tax amnesty in 1993.

Social Welfare (Amendment of Miscellaneous Social Insurance Provisions) Regulations 1993 (SI No. 231), Social Welfare (Miscellaneous Social Insurance Provisions) (No. 2) Regulations 1993 (SI No. 232) and Social Welfare (Deserted Wife's Benefit) Regulations 1993 (SI No. 233). These Regulations provide for increases in the reduced rates of various insurance payments.

Social Welfare (Rent Allowance) (Amendment) Regulations 1993 (SI No. 234). These Regulations provide for increases in the amount of means disregarded for the purposes of the rent allowance scheme and also for an increase in the minimum rent payable by the claimant.

Social Welfare (Agreement with the United States of America on Social Security) Order 1993 (SI No. 243). This Order gives effect to the Bilateral Agreement on Social Security made between Ireland and the USA which came into effect on 1 September 1993.

Maintenance Allowances (Increased Payment) Regulations 1993 (SI No. 331) and Social Welfare (Temporary Provisions) Regulations 1993 (SI No. 354). These Regulations provide for the payment of a Christmas bonus to welfare claimants.

Social Welfare (Consolidation) Act, 1993 (Commencement) Order 1993 (SI No. 335). This Order brought the 1993 Act into effect from 16 November 1993.

Social Welfare (Social Assistance) Regulations 1993 (SI No. 364). These Regulations consolidate previous regulations relating to social assistance schemes, other than supplementary welfare allowance.

See also the Disabled Persons (Maintenance Allowance) Regulations 1993 (SI No. 211) and the Infectious Diseases (Maintenance Allowance) Regulations 1993 (SI No. 213) made under the Health Act 1970 and the Health Act 1947 respectively.

EQUAL TREATMENT

The implementation (or more accurately, in some respects, non-implementation) of Directive 79/7/EEC on equal treatment for men and women in respect of certain aspects of social security was one of the most controversial episodes in the history of Irish social welfare law. However, there are signs now that this episode may be drawing to a close. On 12 April 1994, the Free Legal Advice Centres Ltd. announced that an action which it had taken on behalf of approximately 1,800 married women had been settled on the basis of the payment of all arrears for the period 1984 to 1992, together with a compromise sum in respect of interest. In February 1995, Carroll J handed down her decision in a case challenging the failure of the European Communities (Social Welfare) Regulations 1992 (S.I. No. 152) to make proper provision for retrospective payments of social welfare arrears pursuant to the Directive — *Tate v Minister for Social Welfare* [1995] ILRM 507.

In order to understand fully the present state of affairs and the implication of *Tate*, it is necessary to provide an overview of the main characteristics of Directive 79/7/EEC, together with an account of its reception in Ireland.

Directive 79/7/EEC Directive 79/7/EEC on the progressive implementation of the principle of equal treatment of men and women in matters of social security is the third in a series of EC directives which address the issue of sex discrimination. This Directive, which had its roots in Directive 76/207/ EEC on equal treatment of men and women in employment and vocational training, focuses specifically on certain aspects of social security and provides that, in relation to those schemes covered by the Directive, there shall be no discrimination between men and women whatsoever on grounds of sex, either directly or indirectly by reference, in particular, to marital or family status. The Directive was adopted in 1978 and the member states of the EC were required to comply with its terms by 23 December 1984.

Scope of Directive: *ratione materiae*   The scope of Directive 79/7/EEC is restricted by reference both to the type of social security scheme affected and to the categories of individual who can rely on the Directive.

Article 3(1) provides that the Directive shall apply to:

(a) statutory schemes which provide protection against the following risks: sickness, invalidity, old age, accidents at work and occupational diseases, unemployment

(b) social assistance, in so far as it is intended to supplement or replace the schemes referred to in (a).

Article 3(2) provides that the Directive shall not apply to survivors' benefits or family benefits. Thus the schemes covered by the Directive are all work-related social security schemes, reflecting the ultimate origins of this Directive in Directive 76/207/EEC on equal treatment in employment and vocational training.

The material scope of Directive 79/7/EEC has been considered by the Court of Justice in a series of cases coming from the UK. In *Drake v Chief Adjudication Officer* [1986] ECR 1995; [1986] 3 CMLR 43, the Court held that, in order to fall within the scope of the Directive, a benefit must constitute the whole or part of a statutory scheme providing protection against one of the risks specified in article 3. In this case, the Court ruled that the Directive applied to a carer's allowance payable to a person looking after an invalid, as the carer's allowance was considered to be part of the overall statutory protection against the risk of invalidity. The Court indicated that, in order to ensure harmonious interpretation of the principle of equal treatment throughout the Community, article 3(1) must be interpreted as including any benefit which in a broad sense forms part of one of the social security schemes to which it refers; otherwise it would be possible, by making formal changes to existing benefits covered by the Directive, to remove them from its scope. Furthermore, the fact that the allowance was paid to a third party was not relevant since a situation of invalidity was a pre-condition for its payment and since disabled persons derived an economic advantage from its payment to their carers.

In contrast to *Drake* is the decision of the Court of Justice in *R. v Secretary of State for Social Security, ex parte Smithson* [1992] 1 CMLR 1061; [1992] 3 All ER 577. Here the claimant applied to have a higher pensioner premium included in the calculation of her needs for the purpose of her claim to housing benefit. Because of the differential state pension age for men and women, she was not entitled to claim this premium and so she invoked Directive 79/7/EEC. The Court held that schemes of allowances to meet housing costs were not referred to in article 3 and consequently did not come within the scope of the Directive. The fact that the age and invalidity of the beneficiary were two of the criteria applied to determine the amount of such an allowance was not sufficient to bring that allowance within the scope of the Directive. By emphasising the mode of payment in determining the scope of the Directive, the Court would appear to have departed from its earlier approach in *Drake*. The new test for inclusion of a benefit within the scope of Directive 79/7/EEC would appear to be that benefits are covered by the Directive where they are directly and effectively linked to the protection provided against one of the risks specified in article 3(1).

This test was subsequently applied by the Court in *Jackson and Cresswell v Chief Adjudication Officer* [1993] 1 QB 367; [1993] 3 All ER 265; [1992] 3 CMLR 389. At issue here was whether the Directive applied to a welfare payment which may be granted in a variety of personal situations to persons whose means are insufficient to meet their needs as defined by statute. The Court held that it did not, pointing out that article 3 did not refer to a statutory scheme which, on certain conditions, provides persons with means below a legally defined limit with a special benefit designed to enable them to meet their needs. The amount of theoretical needs in such cases was calculated independently of any consideration relating to the existence of any of the risks listed in article 3(1). Furthermore, the schemes at issue exempted claimants from the obligation to be available for work and consequently could not be regarded as being linked to protection against unemployment. In coming to its conclusion on this matter, the Court also indicated that such conclusion was not affected by the circumstance that the recipient of the benefit is in fact in one of the situations covered by article 3(1).

In the Irish context, counsel for the plaintiff in *Lowth v Minister for Social Welfare* [1994] 1 ILRM 378, was forced to concede, in the light of these decisions of the Court of Justice, that deserted wives' payments did not fall within the scope of the Directive, a concession of which Costello J expressly approved.

Luckhaus has commented that, in applying the test formulated in *Smith-*

son and *Jackson*, it would appear that the Court will seek to ascertain the intention or purpose of the scheme and that such intention or purpose will be deduced from the design of the scheme and the policy-makers' stated views on its purpose, rather than from the effect of the scheme in practice, see (1992) ILJ 315. See also the critical comment by Vousden in (1993) JSWFL 224 and Cousins in (1994) EL Rev 123.

Scope of Directive: *ratione personae*   By virtue of article 2, only members of the working population, retired or invalided workers and self-employed persons can invoke the Directive. In *Achterberg te Riele and Ors v Sociale Verzekeringsbank* [1989] ECR 1963 the Court held that the Directive did not apply to persons who have not had an occupation and are not seeking work or to persons who have had an occupation which was not interrupted by one of the risks set out in article 3(1)(a) and are not seeking work. In this case, therefore, the applicants, all of whom were housewives, were not entitled to rely on the terms of the Directive.

In *Johnson v Chief Adjudication officer* [1991] ECR I-1155 the Court had to consider the position of a person who had left work for a reason not covered by article 3 — child-minding — but who was now prevented from resuming work by one of the risks specified in that article — sickness. The Court held that such a person is covered by the Directive, provided she can prove that she was seeking work at the time when the risk materialised.

Finally, in *Verholen and Ors v Sociale Verzekeringsbank* [1991] ECR I-3757, the Court ruled that a person who did not come within the terms of article 2 could not rely on the Directive merely because that person came under a national scheme which was within the material scope of the Directive. At the same time, a person not covered by the Directive could invoke the Directive on behalf of another person who was so covered.

For a useful comment on the scope of the Directive, see Cousins (1992) 17 EL Rev 55.

Transposing Article 4(1) into domestic law   Article 4(1) provides:

> The principle of equal treatment means that there shall be no discrimination whatsoever on ground of sex either directly, or indirectly by reference in particular to marital or family status, in particular as concerns:
>
> — the scope of the schemes and the conditions of access thereto,
> — the obligation to contribute and the calculation of contributions,
> — the calculation of benefits including increases due in respect of a spouse and for dependants and the conditions governing the duration and retention of entitlement to benefits.

The deadline for implementation of the Directive was 23 December 1984 and the Court of Justice has held on two occasions that article 4(1) has had direct effect since that date, i.e. it gives rise to rights which are enforceable by individuals in the national courts even in the absence of implementing domestic legislation — see *Netherlands v FNV* [1986] ECR 3855; [1987] 3 CMLR 767 and *McDermott and Cotter v Minister for Social Welfare* [1987] ECR 1453; [1987] 2 CMLR 607. Moreover, where discriminatory provisions have been continued in effect after the deadline, the only manner in which the principle of equal treatment may be implemented retrospectively is by extending the benefit of such provisions to the disadvantaged sex, i.e. by levelling up. However where one is talking of prospective application of the principle, the national authorities have the option of either levelling up or levelling down — see comments of Advocate General Darmon in *Roks v Bestuur van de Bedrijfsvereniging voor Detailhandel, Ambachten en Huis-vrouwen and Ors*, 8 December 1993.

In *Emmott v Minister for Social Welfare* [1991] ECR I-4269; [1991] 3 CMLR 894 the Court went further to hold that member States could not rely on national procedural rules — in this case, time-limits — to defeat claims taken under the Directive for so long as the Directive had not been properly transposed into national law. Furthermore the earlier rulings of the Court, that article 4(1) had direct effect, did not amount to proper transposition for this purpose. However in *Steenhorst-Neerings v Bestuur van de Bedrijfsver-eniging voor Detailhandel, Ambachten en Huisvrouwen*, 27 October 1993, the Court drew a distinction between a procedural rule precluding the initiation of judicial proceedings alleging infringement of the Directive and a rule restricting the back-payment of claims for benefits, holding that the latter is not precluded by the Directive as it serves to ensure sound admini-stration and also reflects the need to preserve financial balance in a scheme in which claims submitted by insured persons in the course of a year must in principle be covered by contributions collected during that same year. This distinction undermines to a certain extent the *Emmott* decision which has been described as a 'very strong decision in favour of the enforcement of individual rights where directives had not been properly implemented in national law': Cousins, (1994) *EL Rev* 123

In a number of cases, the Court held that, not only must the member States have repealed any national provisions inconsistent with the Directive by 23 December 1984, they cannot continue the effect of such provisions beyond that deadline. Thus in *Clarke v Chief Adjudication Officer* [1987] ECR 2865; [1987] 3 CMLR 277, the UK had replaced a welfare scheme discriminating in favour of men, the non-contributory invalidity pension, with a new scheme, severe disablement allowance, which contained no such discrimi-nation. However as a transitional measure, entitlement to SDA was extended to those men who had previously been in receipt of NCIP. According to the Court, this was contrary to the Directive as entitlement to SDA had to be on the same terms for both men and women. Similarly in *Johnson*, the Court held that by requiring women to have applied for NCIP in order to be able to claim SDA, UK legislation maintained the discrimination against women which had existed in relation to NCIP. In *Verholen*, the Court indicated that one could not calculate pension rights by reference to facts which took place prior to 23 December 1984 if that would result in discrimination against either sex. See also *Dik v College van Burgemeester en Wethouders* [1988] ECR 1601, [1989] 2 CMLR 936 and *MA Roks v Bestuur van de Bedrijfsvereniging voor Detailhandel Ambachten en Huisvrouwen and Ors.*, 24 February 1994.

Penultimately, in *McDermott and Cotter v Minister for Social Welfare (No. 2)* [1991] ECR I-1155; [1990] 2 CMLR 10, the Court of Justice rejected the argument of the Irish Government that article 4 did not apply to supplements payable on the basis of notional, as opposed to actual, dependancy. The Court also rejected the further argument that the national authorities could rely on principles of law prohibiting unjust enrichment in order to defeat claims taken under the Directive, holding that to permit reliance on such prohibition would enable the authorities to use their own unlawful conduct as a ground for depriving article 4(1) of its full effect. See note by Whyte and O'Dell, (1991) 20 ILJ 220.

Two final points are worth noting in this context. First, in *Verholen*, the Court of Justice held that a national court could consider, of its own motion, the conformity of a national provision with the precise and unconditional provisions of a Directive where the period for implementation of the Directive had expired, even if the parties to the litigation had not themselves invoked the Directive. (See also the decision of the Court in *Van Gemert-Derks v Bestuur van de Nieuwe Industriele Bedrijfsvereniging*, 27 October 1993, wherein it stated that, in the absence of adequate national measures transposing article 4(1) into national law, it was for the national courts to apply such procedures of domestic law as would guarantee women the benefit of the same rules as those applicable to men in the same situation.) Second, the decision of the Court of Justice in *Marshall v Southampton and South West Hampshire Area Health Authority (No. 2)*, 2 August 1993, that the payment of interest as part of an award of damages was an essential component of full compensation, for the purposes of article 6 of Directive 76/207, clearly has implications for Directive 79/7/EEC, article 6 of which is framed in identical terms to its counterpart in the earlier Directive.

Direct discrimination Direct discrimination occurs where a provision applies to one sex only — for example, a rule excluding married women from eligibility for unemployment payments. Such a provision is, subject to article

7(1), completely prohibited by article 4(1) of the Directive. In *Van Gemert-Derks v Bestuur van de Nieuwe Industriele Bedrijfsvereniging*, 27 October 1993, the Court ruled that article 4(1) precluded the withdrawal of a benefit from a woman merely because she subsequently became entitled to a benefit — here, survivor's benefit — which falls outside the scope of the Directive. While, traditionally, discrimination in social security has worked to the detriment of women, one can encounter provisions which discriminate against men. Such provisions are equally prohibited by the Directive, see *Caisse d'Assurances Sociales pour Travailleurs Independents 'Integrity' v Rouvroy* [1990] ECR 1-4243. Here special concessions in Belgian law given to married women, widows and students in respect of contributions on self-employed income were declared to be contrary to the Directive because men were not entitled to the same concessions. This decision has been criticised on the ground that it reflects a view of equality as neutrality between the sexes, whereas one could argue that an equality policy is intended to remove the disadvantage suffered by one group and that an element of reverse discrimination is necessary to achieve that end.

The prohibition of discrimination in relation to the persons and schemes covered by Directive 79/7/EEC is not absolute, however. Article 7(1) allows member States to exclude certain matters from the scope of the Directive, namely:

> the determination of pensionable age for the purposes of granting old age and retirement pensions and the possible consequences thereof for other benefits;
>
> advantages in respect of old age pension schemes granted to persons who have brought up children and the acquisition of benefit entitlements following periods of interruption of employment due to the bringing up of children;
>
> the granting of old age or invalidity entitlements by virtue of the derived entitlements of a wife;
>
> the granting of increases of long-term invalidity, old age, accidents at work and occupational disease benefits for a dependent wife;
>
> the consequences of the exercise, before the adoption of this Directive, of a right of option not to acquire or incur obligations under a statutory scheme.

The Irish welfare code has not had to rely on any of these derogations, prior to the conclusion of the period under review.

Indirect discrimination   Directive 79/7/EEC proscribes not only direct sex discrimination but also indirect sex discrimination, i.e. provisions which, on their face, apply to both sexes equally but which, in practice, affect one sex more than the other. In *Teuling v Bestuur van de Bedrijsvereniging voor de Chemische Industrie* [1987] ECR 2497; [1988] 3 CMLR 789, the Court indicated that a person who complains of indirect discrimination must shoulder the initial burden of establishing that the impugned provision had a disproportionate impact on one sex by comparison with the other. The burden of proof then shifts to the party defending the provision to show that the provision can be objectively justified by reference to factors other than sex. If this defence is made out, the complainant will only succeed if she can show either that the provision is not effective to achieve its purpose or that an alternative provision could accomplish the purpose with less discriminatory impact. In this case, a provision in Dutch law for the payment of adult dependant allowances, which, it was found, benefitted men more so than women, was nonetheless upheld because it was objectively justified as being necessary to tackle household poverty. In *Commission v Belgium* [1991] ECR I-2205, the Belgian system of pre-determined rates for claimants of unemployment and invalidity payments was successfully defended on the same ground. This case involved replacement income, albeit payable at minimum levels. Thus the distinction between contributory and minimum level benefits, which had survived *Teuling*, was blurred. In the case of *Molenbroek v Sociale Verzekeringsbank* [1992] ECR I-5943, the Court of Justice similarly upheld the Dutch system of dependency additions to contributory old age pensions. These three cases emphasise the Member States' discretion in relation to social policy and social security matters — the Member States can decide how to secure minimum levels of income (whether contributory or non-contributory) for households, even if this discriminates indirectly against women.

Finally on the topic of indirect discrimination, and in contrast to the cases on dependancy payments, the exclusion of part-time workers from the scope of a Dutch disability allowance was held by the Court of Justice to be contrary to the Directive because it affected women more than men and the Dutch authorities were unable to show any objective justification for this exclusion: *Ruzius-Wilbrink v Bestuur van de Bedrijfsvereniging voor Overheidsdiensten* [1989] ECR 4311; [1991] 2 CMLR 216. But even on this topic of the scope of social protection, recent decisions of the Court have been more deferential to national interests, for in Case C-371/1993, *Nolte v Landesversicherungsanstalt Hannover*, 14 December 1995, it held that the exclusion of some minimal employment (regularly consisting of fewer than 15 hours' work a week and regularly attracting remuneration of up to one-seventh of the average monthly salary) from old age insurance corresponded to 'a structural principle of the German social security scheme' and so was not contrary to Directive 79/7/EEC. A similar decision was reached in Case

C-444/1993, *Megner v Innungskranken-Kasse Vorderpfalz*, 14 December 1995, concerning the exclusion of minor or short-term employment from certain insurance schemes.

Reception of the Directive in Ireland   Prior to the adoption of Directive 79/7/EEC, the household model used for determination of welfare entitlements was that of the male breadwinner with the stay-at-home wife looking after the domestic responsibilities of the family. Accordingly, a married woman living with her husband was not entitled to unemployment assistance (a means-tested payment). Furthermore, she was automatically considered to be her husband's dependant for the purpose of his welfare entitlements, irrespective of her actual economic status, whereas he would be treated as her adult dependant only where, by virtue of some physical or mental disability, he was incapable of supporting himself. Even where a 'working outside the home' wife could claim insurance benefits, based on her own social insurance contributions, she received lower rates of unemployment, disability, disablement and injury benefit, invalidity pension and unemployability supplement than a man and, in the case of unemployment benefit, for a shorter period of time (maximum 12 months as opposed to 15 months in the case of a man). In addition, she could not claim any dependency increase in respect of her husband or her children unless her husband was, because of a physical or mental disability, incapable of supporting himself.

Directive 79/7/EEC required Ireland to address these various forms of discrimination and the Department of Social Welfare set about implementing the Directive in three stages. Stage I occurred in May 1986, when reduced rates of welfare for married women were abolished and the maximum duration of payment of unemployment benefit to married women was increased to 15 months. These reforms were achieved through a process of 'levelling-up'.

Stage II followed six months later, when a sex-neutral definition of 'adult dependant' was introduced, governing entitlement to both adult dependant and child dependant allowances, and married women became eligible for unemployment assistance. On this occasion, however, equality was achieved through a process of 'levelling down'. In the first place, 'adult dependant' was more narrowly defined as a person earning less than (by 1993) £60 per week and not in receipt of welfare (other than disablement benefit, orphan's death benefit or orphan's pension or allowance) in his or her own right. This change was very controversial because it resulted in a significant reduction, in some cases by as much as £50 per week, in the level of welfare payments to many families, where the husband lost his adult dependant allowance and half of the child dependancy allowance.

In order to soften the blow for such families, a system of transitional weekly payments was introduced, which remained in place until 1992.

Second, a limitation was placed on the amount of unemployment assistance payable to a married person living with a spouse on welfare so that the total amount of welfare received by that household would not exceed the amount payable to the spouse claiming for an adult dependant. The effect of this 'cap' was to reduce the amount of unemployment assistance to a level lower than that payable to a single claimant and because the limitation did not apply to cohabiting couples, this gave rise to constitutional difficulties which were eventually resolved, following the Supreme Court decision in *Hyland v Minister for Social Welfare* [1989] IR 624; [1990] ILRM 213, by extending the limitation to cohabiting couples — Social Welfare (No. 2) Act 1989 (see now s. 122 of the Social Welfare (Consolidation) Act 1993).

Legal defects in Stages I and II of implementation process Stages I and II of this implementation process suffered from a number of legal defects. In particular, the process began 18 months behind schedule, in that article 4(1) of Directive 79/7/EEC became directly effective on 23 December 1984. This gave rise to claims for arrears of welfare payments covering the period from that date until May 1986, during which time married women continued to receive lower rates of certain welfare payments than their male counterparts (and in the case of unemployment benefit for a shorter period of time) and dependency allowances were payable on a discriminatory basis. Following three references to the Court of Justice — *Cotter and McDermott v Minister for Social Welfare (No. 1)* [1987] ECR 1453, *Cotter and McDermott v Minister for Social Welfare (No. 2)* [1991] ECR I-1155 and *Emmott v Minister for Social Welfare* [1991] ECR I-4269, the Government eventually accepted that it had to pay such arrears, introducing, in Stage III of the implementation process, the European Communities (Social Welfare) Regulations 1992 (SI No. 152 of 1992) for this purpose.

Legal defects in Stage III of implementation process These Regulations provided for the payment of the arrears (referred to as 'household supplement') on a phased basis over three years starting in 1992. However, it is arguable that they were legally defective in a number of respects. It is worth recalling that the Court of Justice had held, in both *The Netherlands v FNV* [1986] ECR 3855 and *McDermott and Cotter v Minister for Social Welfare (No. 1)* [1987] ECR 1453 that retrospective implementation of the principle of equal treatment could be achieved only through a process of 'levelling up'. However, in determining entitlement to arrears of dependency allowance, the Regulations provided for the application to the period between December 1984 and November 1986 of the new (and more restrictive) definition of 'adult dependant'. It follows that married women were not being treated in exactly the same way as married men in respect of this period — the men had the benefit of the older, sexist definition during this time — and consequently the principle of equal treatment was infringed. A similar point may be made with regard to the calculation of arrears of unemployment assistance, where both the reformed means test for that payment, together with the limitation on the amount of such assistance payable to married claimants, were applied retrospectively to the arrears claim. Again neither provision applied to male claimants of unemployment assistance during the period December 1984 to November 1986.

A particular difficulty existed with regard to the payment of transitional payments. It will be recalled that such payments were made between November 1986 and April 1992 to families affected by the restriction in the payments of dependency allowances in November 1986. Such families were, by definition, those in which the husband was claiming welfare; households in which the wife was claiming welfare in November 1986 did not qualify. In *Cotter and McDermott (No. 2)* [1991] ECR I-1155, the Court of Justice held that married women were entitled to these transitional payments but this matter was not addressed at all in the Regulations. Finally, the Regulations made no provision for the loss in the value of the benefits in the eight years or more since 1984, a problem exacerbated by the fact that the Regulations deferred complete satisfaction of the claims for arrears until July 1994 in some cases. However, one could reasonably infer from the decision of the Court of Justice in *Marshall (No. 2)*, 2 August 1993 that the payment of interest was an essential aspect of full satisfaction of claims taken under Directive 79/7/EEC.

In *Tate v Minister for Social Welfare* [1995] ILRM 507, Carroll J clarified many aspects of the law governing entitlement to arrears under Directive 79/7/EEC. First, she confirmed that the payment of transitional payments between November 1986 and July 1992 constituted a breach of the Directive and that, having regard to *Marshall (No. 2)*, Case 271/91, 2 August 1993, the amount of arrears payable to any claimant would have to be adjusted in line with the Consumer Price Index in order fully to compensate for delay. She also held that the failure of the State to comply with the Directive was neither a breach of constitutional rights, a breach of statutory duty nor a breach of duty of care but was rather a wrong under Community law which approximated to a breach of constitutional duty. The word 'tort' in the Statute of Limitations was sufficiently wide to cover this breach of the State's obligations under Community Law so that the limitation period of six years in s.11(2) of the Statute was applicable. The 1992 Regulations created a new cause of action insofar as they failed fully to implement the Directive with regard to entitlement to dependancy allowances and arrears of unemployment assistance so that, with regard to these claims, the time limit started to run from June 1992. However, insofar as the Regulations never addressed the issue of transitional payments at all, there was no new cause of action here. Moreover, having regard to the effect, in practice, of s.11(2) in cases of continuing breach of duty (i.e. it limited the amount of arrears payable but did not preclude the initiation of any action), that section could be relied on by the State in the light of the *Steenhorst-Neerings* case. The judge also found that there was no evidence to support the claim that the State was estopped from relying on the Statute of Limitations. Finally, she held that it was not necessary to declare the 1992 Regulations to be null and void but that the State could not rely on any portion thereof which had the effect of not fully recognising the plaintiffs' rights under the Directive.

Outstanding issues in relation to Directive 79/7/EEC Apart from the foregoing, there are at least two other possible instances of unlawful discrimination contrary to Directive 79/7/EEC which have never been addressed by the authorities at any stage in the implementation process. These are the conditions of eligibility for occupational death benefit, which vary according to whether the claimant is a widow or bereaved mother on the one hand, or a widower or bereaved father on the other and the fact that the periods over which a claimant may average his or her contributions, for the purpose of qualifying for the old age (contributory) pension and the retirement pension, differ for male and female workers who were insurable between 1953 and 1979, see ss. 83(2) and 88(3) of the 1993 Consolidation Act.

Discrimination against deserted husbands As we have already noted above, a claim of unlawful discrimination was raised by the plaintiff in *Lowth v Minister for Social Welfare* [1994] 1 ILRM 378, though reliance on Directive 79/7/EEC was ultimately foregone on the ground that that the Directive was inapplicable to the welfare payments in question here, namely, deserted wives' payments. The legislative background to this case, briefly, was that in 1989, discrimination against deserted husbands *vis-à-vis* deserted wives under the welfare code was significantly reduced, though not entirely eliminated. Whereas deserted husbands and deserted wives with dependant children were now treated alike for the purpose of the means-tested lone parent's allowance, deserted wives over the age of forty with no dependant children qualified for a means-tested deserted wile's allowance, whereas there was no comparable payment for similarly situated husbands. Moreover, and perhaps more significantly, the insurance-based deserted wife's benefit continued to be payable to women only. As a result, the plaintiff in the instant case, a deserted husband with two children receiving lone parent's allowance, received £6.20 per week less than a similarly situated deserted wife in receipt of deserted wife's benefit. He argued that this was contrary to the guarantee of equality in Article 40.1 of the Constitution.

Dismissing this claim, Costello J made two points in relation to Article 40.1. First, he pointed out that this article did not guarantee that all citizens would be treated equally in all circumstances. Rather it was 'a guarantee against inequalities grounded upon an assumption that one individual or class of individuals by reason of their human attributes or their racial, social or religious backgrounds are to be treated as the inferior of, or the superior of, other individuals in the community'. This ruling constitutes an interesting refinement of the so-called 'human personality' doctrine which for so long has inhibited judicial development of the guarantee of equality by insisting that Article 40.1 could apply only where the essential attributes of the human person were affected. The basis for the original, very restrictive under-standing of this doctrine was, arguably, a refusal to differentiate between the grounds of the discrimination and the context in which it operated, so that both had to implicate the essential attributes of the human personality if Article 40.1 was to apply. Thus, in *Murtagh Properties Ltd v Cleary* [1972] IR 330, for example, a sex-based discrimination, clearly involving an essen-tial attribute of the human personality, was held not to come within the remit of Article 40.1 because it operated in the context of trading activities and conditions of employment where those attributes were, allegedly, not impli-cated. There is some evidence that, in recent times, the Irish courts are quietly abandoning this 'human personality' doctrine, or at any rate, the original, restrictive version of the doctrine — see J.M. Kelly, *The Irish Constitution* (3rd ed.), 723-4. Costello J's decision adds to this body of evidence inasmuch as he appears to be suggesting that the doctrine applies only in relation to the basis for the impugned discrimination and not in respect of the context of its application. For if the working environment has nothing to do with the essential attributes of the human person, how can they possibly be implicated by welfare entitlements? In refining the doctrine in this way, one could argue that Costello J is implicitly endorsing a similar approach by Barrington J in *Brennan v Attorney General* [1983] ILRM 449, wherein he said:

> There may be differences and distinctions made between individuals in society in the course of their trading activities or otherwise which are not based upon an assumption that those individuals are superior or inferior to other people. With such distinctions Art. 40.1 is not normally concerned. But a law can be based upon an assumption that some individuals are inferior to others as human persons and yet manifest itself, in the social or economic sphere, in some superficially trivial regulation, such as who may or may not sit on a park bench; who may or may not own a horse worth more than five pounds; or who may or may not serve drink in a public bar.

Unfortunately the Supreme Court, on appeal in *Brennan*, did not take up this hint, preferring instead to re-affirm the original version of the doctrine. It is to be hoped, however, that perhaps Costello J's more recent initiative will fare somewhat better.

Costello J's second point in relation to Article 40.1 was that inequalities may be tolerated if they were based on a difference of capacity, physical or moral, or a difference of social function. 'The court will consider the legislative inequality in suit and will not set it aside as being repugnant to the Constitution if any state of facts exist which may reasonably justify it'. In the instant case, Costello J was persuaded by the statistics adduced to the court about lower participation rates of married women in the labour force in comparison to married men, and the lower average industrial earnings of women in comparison to men that the Oireachtas could reasonably conclude that deserted wives required greater income support than deserted husbands. While no one could take issue with Costello J's formulation on the applicable legal principle, one might query the relevance of the statistics relied on by the judge in coming to his conclusion. The plaintiff in the instant case complained of a difference in treatment between a deserted husband and a deserted wife, *neither of whom are in employment because of their family circumstances consequent on the desertion.* The statistics referred to do not appear to justify any discrimination in these particular circumstances, though, no doubt, they would justify a statutory requirement that a claimant would only get a deserted spouse's payment where they were unable to work because of family commitments. (In passing, one might ask whether the introduction of an insurance-based widower's pension in 1994, complementing the widow's (contributory) pension, undermines the State's position in relation to its refusal to provide a similar type of payment to deserted husbands.)

Costello J concluded his judgment by agreeing with Barron J's remarks in the earlier case of *Dennehy v Minister for Social Welfare*, High Court, 26 July 1984, that Article 41.2, recognising the special position of women within the home, offered some support for the distinction drawn by the Oireachtas between deserted wives and deserted husbands for social welfare purposes. A minor quibble here is that, while Article 41.2.1° refers generally to the position of women in the home, the 'imperfect obligation' imposed on the State by Article 41.2.2° is directed towards mothers only, and while many claimants of deserted wives' payments are mothers, some are not.

One issue not considered in this case, though it might have been, is the troublesome matter of whether the courts may review a legislative failure to act, for one imagines that the essence of the plaintiffs' complaint was not so much that the Social Welfare Acts made provision for deserted wives as that they failed to make similar provision for deserted husbands.

SOCIAL WELFARE APPEALS AND ADMINISTRATION

The decision of Keane J in *Lundy v Minister for Social Welfare* [1993] 3 IR 406 highlighted a detect in s. 300(1) of the Social Welfare (Consolidation) Act 1981 relating to the revision of decisions by deciding officers which was quickly corrected by the Oireachtas (see also the companion case of *O'Connor v Minister for Social Welfare*, High Court, 30 April 1993). According to the judge, s. 300(1) empowered a deciding officer to revise earlier decisions of other deciding officers — it did not empower such an officer to revise an earlier decision of an appeals officer. S. 31 of the Social Welfare Act 1993, the Bill for which had been introduced in the Dáil some seven weeks before the decision in *Lundy* was handed down, removed this limitation on the power of a deciding officer to revise earlier decisions — see now s. 248 of the Social Welfare (Consolidation) Act 1993. In the course of his judgment, Keane J also ruled that the power to revise earlier decisions, conferred by s. 300(1) of the 1981 Act, was not a power of a judicial nature such that it could only be exercised by courts established under the Constitution. According to the judge, a revised decision made under s. 300(1) that a lower rate of welfare should have been paid to a claimant would not have prevented such claimant challenging a decision of the Minister, pursuant to s. 172(2) of the 1981 Act, that any overpaid welfare should be repaid to the Department. In coming to this conclusion, Keane J would appear to be implicitly relying on that part of Kenny J's decision in *McDonald v Bord na gCon (No. 2)* [1965] IR 217, wherein he held that one of the characteristic features of an administration of justice was the final determination (subject to appeal) of legal rights or liabilities or the imposition of penalties. S. 172(2) has since been repealed (by s. 32 of the Social Welfare Act 1993) and revised and reformulated powers of the welfare authorities to recover overpaid welfare are now set out in Part VIII of the 1993 Consolidation Act. However, Keane J's ruling on this point continues to offer constitutional protection to s. 248 of the latter Act.

PENSIONS

Finally, it is worth noting that the Final Report of the National Pensions Board, *Developing the National Pension System* (Pl. 9979), published in December 1993, makes many important recommendations in relation to the future development of public and occupational pension schemes. In particular, it recommends the retention of a flat-rate social welfare pension (with social assistance payments complementing social insurance pensions) as the basis for development of the public system while, by a majority, rejecting the need for a universal pension scheme. In addition, certain limited proposals are advanced for amending public pension schemes in the interests of providing for flexible retirement, while the Report also suggests increases in the level of contributions required for eligibility to public pensions. Significantly, a majority of the Board reject, for both principled and pragmatic reasons, arrangements for contracting-out of public pensions in favour of private pensions. Recommendations that social insurance cover for various pensions be extended to new entrants to public sector employment, widowers and homemakers were subsequently acted on, to varying degrees, in 1994 and will be examined in the 1994 Review.

Solicitors

APPRENTICESHIP

Arrangements   The Solicitors Acts 1954 and 1960 (Apprenticeship and Education) (Amendment) Regulations 1993 (SI No. 320) amend the 1991 Regulations of the same title (1991 Review, 381) and provide for the circumstances in which the holder of an LL.B. degree from University College Galway may be exempted from the Final Examination — First Part (the Entrance Examination) in the Law Society's School in Blackhall Place, Dublin.

Fees   The Solicitors Acts 1954 and 1960 (Apprentices' Fees) (Amendment) Regulations 1993 (SI No.250), which revoked the Solicitors Acts 1954 and 1960 (Apprentices' Fees) (Amendment) (No. 2) Regulations 1992 (see the 1992 Review, 549) prescribed revised examination fees at the Law Society's School in Blackhall Place, Dublin.

NEGLIGENCE

Cases involving solicitors' liability in negligence are discussed in the Torts chapter, 552-4, below.

PRACTISING CERTIFICATES

The Solicitors Acts 1954 and 1960 (Fees) Regulations 1993 (SI No. 2) prescribed revised fees for obtaining practising certificates.

Statutory Interpretation

Ambiguity and implication   In *Howard v Commissioners of Public Works in Ireland* [1993] ILRM 665 (HC); [1994] 1 IR 101 (HC & SC), the Supreme Court discussed the extent to which a court may interpret legislation by reference to an implied understanding of its purpose: see the Local Government chapter, 430, above.

Explanatory notes   For two unusual explanatory notes, see the discussion of the European Communities (Trade in Porcine Semen — Animal Health) Regulations 1993 (SI No. 242) and the European Communities (Trade in Bovine Breeding Animals, their Semen, Ova and Embryos) Regulations 1993 (SI No. 259) in the European Community chapter, 305, above.

Feminine and masculine: gender balance   The Interpretation (Amendment) Act 1993 is an extremely short, but significant, Act intended to introduce a sense of gender balance into statutory language. The Act may be seen against the background of the creation for the first time of a Department of Equality and Law Reform in 1993: see the Administrative Law chapter, 7, above.

The Long Title to the 1993 Act provides that it is an 'Act to amend the Interpretation Act 1937', though the 1993 Act does not amend in the usual sense of substituting any new wording into the 1937 Act. Instead, s. 1 of the 1993 Act, which is the only substantive provision in the Act, provides:

> In every Act of the Oireachtas passed on or after the date of the passing of this Act and in every instrument made wholly or partly under any such Act, every word importing the feminine gender shall, unless the contrary intention appears, be construed as if it also imported the masculine gender.

This may be contrasted with s. 11(b) of the Interpretation Act 1937, which provides:

> The following provisions shall apply and have effect in relation to the construction of every Act of the Oireachtas and of every instrument made wholly or partly under any such Act, that is to say:
> (b) Every word importing the masculine gender shall, unless the con-

trary intention appears, be construed as if it also imported the feminine gender.

For an example of s.11(b) of the 1937 Act in operation, see *The State (Neville) v Limerick County Council*, 105 ILTR 1.

Clearly, the terms of s. 1 of the 1993 Act are prospective in effect only. The 1993 Act came into effect on its signature by the President on 22 December 1993, so this is the relevant date for the purposes of s.1. The 1993 Act provides, in effect, for the future 'gender proofing' of Irish legislation, and in particular the removal of constant reference to 'he' in primary and secondary legislation.

At the time of writing (June 1996), the authors have been unable to find any instances where 'she' has replaced 'he' in Irish primary or secondary legislation ('s/he' being, presumably, an inadmissible hermaphrodite under s. 1 of the 1993 Act, though clearly very common in contemporary writing).

However, there are indications that some primary legislation enacted in 1994 attempted to take account of the intention behind the 1993 Act. Thus, in s. 3 of the Industrial Training (Apprenticeship Levy) Act 1994, where 'the Minister' is referred to on a number of occasions, there would appear to be a conscious effort to avoid 'he'. Thus, this Act could be classified as gender-neutral. By way of contrast, s. 2(1) of the Irish Shipping Limited (Payment to Former Employees) Act 1994 refers to 'his or her personal representative'. However, a number of sections in the Criminal Justice (Public Order) Act 1994 revert to the use of 'he', thus indicating that not all post-1993 primary legislation has been 'gender-proofed'. In 1995, the general pattern developed of using 'he or she' and 'his or her'.

In the case of secondary legislation, an example of what appears to be consciously gender-neutral language is that contained in the Nursing Homes (Care and Welfare) Regulations 1993 (SI No. 226) (on which, see generally, but not on this point, the Health Services chapter, 346-8, above). Indeed, it may be noted that these Regulations preceded the coming into effect of the Interpretation (Amendment) Act 1993. However, in 1994 the record on gender-proofing in secondary legislation appears less effective than with primary legislation. This will no doubt continue to be a source of difficulty for some time into the future.

Person: corporate body   The meaning given to the word 'person' in s. 11 of the Interpretation Act 1937, so as to include corporate bodies, was at issue in *Truloc Ltd v McMenamin* [1994] 1 ILRM 151 (see the Safety and Health chapter, 472, above) and *Director of Public Prosecutions (Barron) v Wexford Farmers' Club* [1994] 2 ILRM 295; [1994] 1 IR 546 (see the Criminal Law chapter, 272-3, above).

Torts

THE DUTY OF CARE

In *Madden v The Irish Turf Club*, High Court, 2 April 1993, Morris J had to determine an important issue as to the proper scope of the duty of care. The Irish Turf Club administers flat racing in Ireland. The Irish National Hunt Steeple Chase Committee (another of the defendants) has a similar function in relation to steeple chasing. They share facilities and employees. The plaintiff attended a race meeting at Punchestown and placed a bet on the totalisator which would have yielded a jackpot win for him of over £18,000 if his selection on the final race had come first. In fact it came second, behind a horse called 'Dell of Gold'. The rules of the totalisator, operated by the Racing Board under a licence, were that payment of winnings was made after the 'alright' had been declared. No subsequent disqualification or irregularity would affect this procedure.

It later transpired that 'Dell of Gold' had not the necessary qualifications to compete in the race. The defendants disqualified the horse and awarded the race to 'Lucky Bucket', the plaintiff's selection in the race. The plaintiff, unable to obtain the jackpot retrospectively under the totalisator rules, sued the defendant for negligence, arguing that the defendants had not used reasonable care in permitting 'Dell of Gold' to be entered for the race.

Morris J held in favour of the plaintiff. The horse had run in England. The defendants had argued that it would be too difficult to monitor the forms of thousands of foreign-trained horses. Morris J rejected this contention because the evidence had established that less than two hundred foreign-trained horses come to race in Ireland each year. When 'Dell of Gold' had been imported into Ireland from England, an application was made to the defendants to train the horse here. As a result of that application, the defendants would have known that the horse had come from abroad. Morris J was satisfied that 'the defendants needed only to have made a simple reference to the English Form Book' in order to discover the facts; indeed, this was what they had done when they received a complaint after the race. He observed:

> Given that the administration of racing in Ireland is entrusted to [the defendants] and that it is commoncase that this is a multi-million pound industry and one of the country's major industries, I am of the view that

they did not, at the relevant time, comply with their obligations by taking no steps in the matter. It might well be that in any given case an error will emerge in the racing performance of a horse imported from a country where unsatisfactory records are kept. All that is required of the defendants is that they take reasonable care. To make no effort does not meet the required standard of care.

Counsel for the defendants had argued that, given the position of the parties, the defendants had owed no duty to the plaintiff on the *Donoghue v Stevenson* principle ([1932] AC 562, at 580) because there was a lack of the relationship of proximity. During the argument it was suggested that such proximity could arise only where there existed what could be broadly described as a semi-formal relationship between the parties. Morris J did not accept that this was the case. *Purtill v Athlone Urban District Council* [1968] IR 205 and *McNamara v E.S.B.* [1975] IR 226 were well known examples where there had been no formal or semi-formal relationship between the parties and where the necessary proximity to impose a duty was nonetheless found to exist. Having considered all the circumstances in the case, he had:

> no hesitation in holding that where the running of a totalisator, managed by the Racing Board, is dependent upon the proper supervision and management of the runners, in the sense that their qualifications to run in any given race are correctly checked and confirmed, then the person carrying out that check and confirmation is proximate, not only to the Racing Board but also to persons wagering on the totalisator. Moreover, it is clear to my mind that it should have been clearly foreseen that a failure on the part of such person to exercise reasonable care in the carrying out of such functions would be likely to cause injury, loss and damage to the Racing Board or such person wagering.

The defendants had argued that, even if there was such negligence, it had not caused the plaintiff any loss or damage because it was always open to him to back 'Dell of Gold' and, since it was declared 'alright', its subsequent disqualification under the rules of racing had not prejudiced his status as a winner so far as the jackpot was concerned. Morris J considered that this argument would be valid if the plaintiff was making a claim against the Racing Board to be paid as the true winner of the jackpot by reason of 'Dell of Gold's being disqualified. That was not the case he made before the Court. His case was that 'Dell of Gold' should never have started the race and would not have done so but for the defendants' negligence.

Morris J was prepared to hold that, if 'Dell of Gold' had not been in the race, then, on the balance of probabilities, 'Lucky Bucket' would have won the race in view of the fact that he had come second to 'Dell of Gold'. Since the plaintiff was the only person who would have nominated all four winning horses he would have been entitled to be paid the winning jackpot. That sum represented the damages that flowed from the defendants' negligence.

Madden is an interesting case because it permits a plaintiff, not in a direct contractual relationship with the defendant, to succeed in an action for negligently occasioned pure economic loss. Against a traditional background of judicial hostility to the contractual enforceability of wagers, or of attempts to evade the principle of unenforceability (see *Coral v Kleyman* [1951] 1 All ER 518; cf. *O'Donnell v O'Connell* (1923) 57 ILTR 92, criticised by Raymond Friel, *The Law of Contract* (1995), p. 255) the decision may seem difficult to rationalise. Undoubtedly Morris J was swayed by the fact that racing is one of the country's major industries. The idea that those in charge of the administration of this industry should be permitted to shelter behind the old philosophy must have seemed to him to be unjust. *Madden* therefore is scarcely an authority for a general enforcement through tort law of wagering contracts.

It could perhaps be argued that recovery in this case should have been denied on the basis of s. 36(2) of the Gaming and Lotteries Act 1956, which provides that '[n]o action is to lie for the recovery of any money or thing which is alleged to be won or to have been paid upon a wager. . . .' To this it could be replied that the plaintiff was not here seeking *recovery* of what he had actually won but rather damages to compensate him for what he had not won. At the end of the day it is hard to see how the case can be understood except in terms of a selective non-application of the non-enforceability rule; for could it not be said that the loss of an entitlement that cannot legally be enforced is really no loss at all?

In *Gorey v Gorey and P.H. Gorey & Sons Ltd*, High Court, 10 June 1993 the plaintiff, who was the director of the second defendant, was injured when he went to the assistance of the first defendant, his brother, whom the second defendant employed to drive a tipper truck. The truck had broken down on the highway. An airlock had developed on the fuel line between the tank and the pump. The plaintiff, when passing it, noticed that it was in difficulties. His brother was working a hand primer pump on the outside to the driver's side with a fellow employee. The plaintiff climbed on the fuel tank to obtain a clear view of the fuel lines. When, on his suggestion, the starter was pressed, the body of the truck came down on his neck, injuring him severely.

The expert evidence was that the only absolutely safe method of working under a partially lowered body of a hydraulically operated truck was to have it wedged or to lock the rams in position. Flood J held that the first defendant had been negligent in failing to do this. A duty of care arose, on the basis of legal proximity, to any person who had legitimate occasion to come in proximity to the truck. The plaintiff's presence was reasonably foreseeable and there was nothing to negate or reduce the scope of the duty or the class of person to whom it was owed. Flood J here had no apparent hesitation in following the lead of McCarthy J in *Ward v McMaster* [1988] IR 337, at 347, following Lord Wilberforce's famous, and controversial, 'two-step' test for determining the duty of care in *Anns v Merton London Borough* [1978] AC 728, at 751-2. This was so in spite of the eclipse of that test in later British decisions. It seems that in Ireland, as in Canada, Australia and New Zealand, there is not longer any presumption that the latest opinions dominating the House of Lords should necessarily be endorsed. Cf. *Invercargill City Council v Hamlin* [1996] 1 All ER 756.

In recognising the foreseeability and proximity of the plaintiff, Flood J was adopting an approach similar to that favoured by the Supreme Court in *Philips v Durgan* [1991] ILRM 321: see our observations in the 1990 Review, 493-500. It might seem overdramatic to characterise the plaintiff in the instant case as a rescuer but he was at least a person whose intervention was clearly foreseeable and the foreseeability was enhanced by the fact that employers can own affirmative duties to their employees: cf. *Smith v Howdens Ltd* [1953] NI 131.

TRAFFIC ACCIDENTS

Child pedestrians	In *Mulcahy v Lynch and Butler*, Supreme Court, 25 March 1993, an eight year old boy who ran out from behind a school bus, from which he had alighted, into the path of an oncoming car which was travelling at between five and ten miles per hour in second gear, succeeded in an action for negligence against the driver of the car. In the High Court, Lynch J dismissed the claim, but the Supreme Court reversed.

Blayney J (Finlay CJ and Egan J concurring) held that the driver's failure to sound the horn constituted negligence. Invoking Budd J's observations in *McDonald v Coras Iompair Éireann* 105 ILTR 13, at 20 (Supreme Court 1968) (as to which see McMahon & Binchy, *Irish Law of Torts* (2nd ed., 1990, 284-5), Blayney J went on to say:

> Where a driver is approaching a school bus which has stopped to let children out, one of the obvious things that must be anticipated is that one of the children will want to cross the road and may do so by running out suddenly from behind the bus. The approaching driver should be aware that the approach of his car is obscured from view by the presence of the bus so that the only way that he can give warning of his approach is by blowing the horn. In such circumstances it seems to me that the

heavy responsibility referred to by Budd J can only be satisfied by not only driving slowly and keeping a careful look out but also by blowing the horn. This is a case in which giving warning of her presence by doing this was of major importance.

The plaintiff had also sued the driver of the school bus alleging that he had been negligent in not having insisted that children who intended to cross the road after leaving the bus should always wait until the bus had gone. He contended that the driver should have established a safety code containing such a prescription. The Supreme Court affirmed Lynch J's dismissal of this claim. The driver's duty, said Blayney J, was confined to transporting the children safely from the place of where he picked them up to the place where he left them off:

> His function was to drive the bus. So his primary duty was to drive the bus carefully with a view to ensuring that it was not involved in any accident. In addition, he had to keep order amongst the children while they were on the bus. And finally, in picking up the children, or letting them off, he had to choose a place where this could be done safely without exposing the children to any risk. These were of themselves duties requiring considerable attention and concentration, and it seems to me that it would be unreasonable to impose any additional duty on [the driver] once the children had left his bus. Once they had left the bus, by reason of his being the driver of the bus and no more, I consider that he ceased to have any duty of care in regard to them.

The decision is worthy of comment for a number of reasons. First, there are dangers in turning judgments of fact in negligence litigation into rules of law. We have already seen this in Ireland where the courts formerly laid down, as a rule of law, that one must stop one's vehicle in all cases when one's vision is occluded, even where the source of the occlusion is the light coming from the headlights of an oncoming vehicle. The lack of wisdom of such an all-embracing rule of law was eventually appreciated by the Supreme Court. Cf. McMahon & Binchy, *op. cit.*, 285-6.

A second issue in the case concerns the duties of drivers of school buses. The Supreme Court was surely right in the particular circumstances of the case not to impose liability of the driver but it is another proposition entirely that all drivers of school buses should have no duty of care to the children under their charge once they have left the vehicle. It is easy to envisage some cases where a duty might indeed arise, as, for example, where a very young child had to be left off at a place that the driver knows is completely new to the child, who will be obliged to cross a busy highway to reach his or her destination. If we make the hypothetical case still more demanding by assuming that the child had temporarily suffered an injury to both eyes, eventually we reach a situation where no one could deny that the duty of care falling upon the bus driver is not fully discharged at the moment of the child's departure from the bus.

A broader area of uncertainty concerns the relationship, so far as the law of negligence is concerned, between the school's duties and the school bus driver's duties. As *Mulcahy* makes plain, it is impossible to draw a clear line between the school bus driver's duty as bus driver and his or her duty as superviser of school children. Of course every bus driver has a supervisory duty relative to his or her passengers, regardless of whether they are children or adults; clearly a bus driver has a duty to supervise a group of school children who happen, by chance, to board the bus. But it is equally clear that, in cases where school bus transport is organised on an ongoing basis, with consultation between the school, the Department of Education and the driver, the driver's duty must reflect the fact that his or her role is part of a larger transaction. If there is a flaw in the system, which unreasonably exposes school children to the risk of injury, there is at least some plausibility in the argument that, since transport is integral to the provision of the educational service by the school, an obligation falls on the school to concern itself with the nature and quality of the transportation service and to ensure that all aspects of the provision of that service are delivered with due care. This was not, perhaps, fully reflected in the Supreme Court decision of *Dolan v Keohane and Cunningham*, 8 February 1994, which we analysed in the 1992 Review, 579-81, but the facts of the case did not require the Court to confront the question starkly.

In *Byrne v C.P.I. Ltd*, High Court, 3 February 1993, the plaintiff, a fifteen-year-old schoolboy, was struck by an articulated tanker lorry which was turning left from the road into an entrance of an industrial premises. The accident happened when the vehicle was actually on the footpath on its way into the entrance. The driver testified that he was observing two cyclists in his mirrors: one was passing on each side of the lorry at the time. He had seen no one on the pavement.

Budd J, in imposing liability, noted that the plaintiff must have been clearly visible on the footpath as he approached the entrance. The driver's attention must have been diverted by the cyclists. There was a heavy onus to take care on the driver of a lorry when there was a 'blind spot' in front of the left side of the cab especially when the truck had to traverse a footpath. Vigilance was even more necessary 'at a time of day when school children may be "creeping like snails unwillingly to school" . . .'. The case, he considered, brought out 'the need for all large trucks to have a front view mirror of the type now usually fitted to the driver's side wing mirror attachment'.

Duty to cyclists   In *Van Keep v Surface Dressing Contractors Ltd*, High Court, 11 June 1993, the facts were somewhat similar to those in *Byrne v C.P.I. Ltd*, above, Budd J imposed liability on the driver of a large articulated lorry which, when making a left turn at traffic lights, crushed the plaintiff cyclist who had stopped close to the rear wheel and became trapped between the vehicle and the high kerb. The driver had either failed to have his mirrors properly adjusted so that he could see the plaintiff or else had failed to use the mirrors. Budd J held that the plaintiff's damages should be reduced by 10% to take account of her contributory negligence in failing to have adverted to the indicator on the front left of the cab, which had started flashing before she reached the rear of the vehicle.

Emergency Vehicles   In *Strick v Treacy*, High Court, 10 June 1993, the problem of how the law should treat emergency vehicles fell for consideration. The plaintiff, driving her car on the Tallaght by-pass highway, approaching a junction controlled by traffic lights that were in her favour, found that first a Garda car with flashing lights emerged from the road to her left, against the traffic lights, and halted close to the centre of the highway and then a yellow Civil Defence fire tender, travelling 'some considerable distance' behind the Garda car, also emerged from the same road, with its own flashing lights, still against the traffic lights. She collided with the fire tender and was injured. Some of the cars in the outside lane of the highway had come to a halt in response to the Garda car's activity, but traffic in the slow lane had continued to flow.

It transpired that the Garda car was escorting the fire tender which was in action because of a strike in the ordinary fire services. The two vehicles were on their way to attend a fire that had broken out in a local school. O'Hanlon J held that all three drivers were at fault. He reduced the plaintiff's damages by 50% on account of her contributory negligence. The driver of the fire tender had been negligent because he had had a clear unobstructed view for a long distance to his right when he neared the junction. He ought to have ensured that the plaintiff had seen what was happening and was yielding to him the right of way before he drove into her path at a time when the lights were in her favour. The Garda car driver had been unreasonable in proceeding on the basis that it could clear a path for itself through all the traffic on the way to the fire, leaving the fire tender 'to solve its own problems. . . .' He should have done more to halt the traffic, particularly having regard to the large gap that had opened up between him and the fire tender. The plaintiff should have been alerted by the presence of the Garda car on the highway and the halting of the traffic to her right, notwithstanding that it had the lights in its favour. She should have been 'doubly cautious' when she saw the large yellow fire tender approaching from her left with its lights flashing. Moreover, her failure to wear a seat belt had 'contributed significantly to the seriousness of her injuries'. (She had suffered injuries to her chin, neck, and knee.)

It is well established that, is assessing the question of negligence of emergency vehicles, the court should take into account the positive social utility of rescue, even if this means that the price of encouraging this desirable policy is paid by innocent people who have the misfortune to be struck by vehicles on missions of mercy: see *Daborn v Bath Tramways Motor Co. Ltd* [1946] 2 All ER 353, *Watt v Hertfordshire County Council* [1954] 2 All ER 368. Nonetheless, there is no question of these vehicles having an *immunity* from the duty of care. As Denning LJ observed in *Watt*:

> I quite agree that fire engines, ambulances and doctors' cars should not shoot past the traffic lights when they show a red light. That is because the risk is too great to warrant the incurring of the danger. It is always a question of balancing the risk against the end.

Some may feel that the 50% reduction of damages was harsh on the plaintiff for her failure to have responded more effectively to the high drama in which she was forced to play a part.

EMPLOYER'S LIABILITY

At the beginning of this section, we should note the publication of Dr John White's monumental treatise, *Civil Liability for Industrial Accidents*, published in 1993. The work, of well over 3,000 pages, comprehensively analyses all aspects of the subject, at common law and arising from breach of statute. It helpfully extracts the relevant statutory provisions and the regulations made under them.

Exposure to noise   In *Barry v Nitrigin Éireann Teo* [1994] 2 ILRM 522, Costello J addressed the important question of the scope of liability at common law and for breach of statute in respect of exposure of an employee to the risk of injury from noise. We address the statutory dimension later in the chapter, below, 563-4.

The plaintiff during his period of employment with the defendants had been provided with earmuffs. In the early part of his employment, there was a defect in the earmuffs. The spring that was meant to keep them tight to his ears wore out, thus loosening the earmuffs and rendering them less effective. The employers also supplied glasses to the plaintiff which, because of the tightness of their wings, decreased further the effectiveness of the earmuffs.

In order to communicate by radio to the communication centre in the plant, the plaintiff found that he had to remove his earmuffs, exposing himself from time to time to very high levels of noise. These several problems were in Costello J's view attributable to the unreasonable failure by the employer to provide a safe system of work. The plaintiff was accordingly entitled to recover damages for permanent hearing loss attributable to this failure.

The case is a good example of how it often does not matter whether the negligence is characterised in terms of an *unsafe system* or of the failure to provide proper *equipment* to the employee to enable the employee to do the work safely.

Duty to provide training for employee In *Muldoon v Brittas Plastics Ltd*, High Court, 18 March 1993, Morris J dismissed proceedings for negligence where the plaintiff, when operating a forklift truck, drove it so that its mast struck a beam over the entrance door of a shed. The plaintiff argued that the failure of his employers to instruct him adequately in how to drive the truck properly caused his injuries. Morris thought not. If there had been training, it would have been to the effect that the mast should be kept lower than the doorway lintel. This was something of which the plaintiff was fully aware: thus the question of lack of training had no relevance to the particular accident.

In *McGowan v Wicklow County Council*, High Court, 27 May 1993, the plaintiff, who was employed by the defendant council as a labourer working on the installation of pipes on a road, was struck by a JCB digger operated by the employee of an independent contractor: see our discussion of the status of the independent contractor below 566-7. The plaintiff sought to impose liability on the Council on the basis that it had failed to instruct the workmen where to position themselves in relation to moving machinery when it was in use. Morris J rejected the claim. He accepted the evidence of the engineer in charge of the project that the work force on site at the time were all highly experienced and fully aware of any dangers that might arise from machinery such as JCB diggers. It would have been superfluous in these circumstances for the Council to have issued any directions such as the plaintiff claimed ought to have been issued.

Foreseeability of injury In *Sammon v Flemming GMbH*, High Court, 23 November 1993, the plaintiff was employed in the immunology department of the defendant's factory to fill and cap small phials used in various diagnostic kits. She developed the painful condition known as 'tennis elbow', for which she received cortisone injections. Once her supervisor had been informed by a doctor some time later that her condition was attributable to the nature of her employment, he 'protected the plaintiff from screw capping as best he could.' The pain nevertheless continued.

The plaintiff sued her employer for negligence. She argued that the defendant ought to have known that work of the kind she was doing carried with it the risk of repetitive strain injury and should have warned her to report any pain sustained in the course of her work.

Barron J dismissed her claim on the basis that the injury could not reasonably have been foreseen. No other employee doing similar work had suffered such an injury. The plaintiff had not submitted that the actual use of the hand was one that a prudent and careful employer would consider might cause injury. It was not sufficient for her to establish merely that she had suffered a repetitive strain injury. An expert witness called by the defendant had explained that this injury was brought about by the use of the hand when the muscles of the forearm were tired.

Barron J observed:

> Any engine which is worked beyond its designed capacity is liable to break down. Similarly, any part of the body which is used beyond its capacity is likewise liable to break down. The use which causes such breakdown is in reality an abuse of the particular part of the body concerned. What the plaintiff is therefore submitting is that the abuse to which the plaintiff's muscles in her forearm were subjected was an abuse which should have been recognised by the defendant. In my view there is nothing in the evidence to support such a submission. In fact [the supervisor] showed concern for the plaintiff once he realised that she had a problem and he did what he could to protect her from screw capping.
>
> In my view the defendant acted reasonably and could not reasonably be expected to have anticipated that the particular work which the plaintiff was doing would lead to such an abuse of the muscles of her forearm that she would sustain an injury.

One aspect of the case is of particular interest. Barron J observed that there might have been factors predisposing the plaintiff to contract tennis elbow:

> She may for example habitually tighten caps and the like with more force than is necessary. However, [an expert witness] did not suggest that her work could not have caused her injury. I am satisfied that it played a part. The defendants must accept the plaintiff as they find her and accordingly, in my view, causation has been established.

The notion of taking the plaintiff as you find him or her is characteristically associated with the 'eggshell skull' doctrine, whereby an admittedly negligent defendant may not hide behind the reasonable foreseeability limitations established by *The Wagon Mound (No. 1)* [1961] AC 288 if the plaintiff sustains unforeseeable enhanced injury by reason of a particular physical weakness of constitution: cf. *Smith v Leech Brain & Co.* [1962] 2 QB 405. In the instant case the defendants were not guilty of any negligence to the plaintiff in that they had not unreasonably subjected her to the risk of foreseeable injury. If as a matter of fact she sustained injury by reason of her unusually susceptible physical condition, that might satisfy the requirement of establishing physical causation (though it might be argued that the causation should be attributed to her own condition, rather than to the activity in which she had engaged); but clearly the 'eggshell skull' doctrine could have no application since the threshold requirement of establishing negligence on the part of the defendants had not been fulfilled.

Duty to protect employee from criminal act In the Supreme Court decision of *Bradley v CIE* [1976] IR 217, at 223, Henchy J observed that, 'even where a certain precaution is obviously wanted in the interests of the safety of the workman, there may be countervailing factors which would justify the employer is not taking that precaution'. A succession of recent decisions, notably *Heeney v Dublin Corporation*, High Court, 16 May 1991, analysed in the 1991 Review, 398-9, *Dowdall v Minister for Defence, Ireland and the Attorney General*, High Court, 23 July 1992, analysed in the 1991 Review, 571-2 and *Walsh v Securicor (Ireland) Ltd* [1993] 2 IR 507 make Henchy J's observations seem echoes of a long-forgotten past rather than the remarks of a liberal judge made less than twenty years previously.

In *Walsh*, the plaintiff, an employee of the defendant security company, collected a large amount of money from a bank in Cork City and drove a van in the direction of Cobh, where he intended to deliver the money to smaller banks and a post office. There was another employee driving with him in the van, which had a Garda escort. They encountered an ambush, in which the van's path was blocked by a tractor and bullets were fired at the windscreen which began to shatter. The plaintiff was eventually forced to open the door of the van and was hit on the head with what he believed to be the butt-end of a rifle. The robbers made off with most of the money.

The plaintiff sued the defendant for negligence. Barrington J held in his favour and the Supreme Court affirmed.

The essence of the plaintiff's case was that the time of delivery had been the same every week for a period of seven years and that, in view of the fact that the journey was by a high-risk route, the time should have been varied periodically. This argument appealed to Egan J, with whose judgment Finlay

CJ and Hederman J concurred. The defendant's contention that it was contractually tied to the delivery time was swept aside with the observation that there had been 'no evidence at all of any discussions at the appropriate levels about the desirability of reviewing or changing the times of delivery from time to time.' Moreover, the evidence supported to Barrington J's finding that the Garda authorities were quite flexible as to even short notice of alteration in time. 'In any event', said Egan J, 'this was a high risk operation and the defendant was bound to avail of every safety precaution, not just the provision of a Garda escort.'

Egan J went on to quote Finlay CJ's statement in *Ryan v Ireland* [1989] IR 177, at 183 that, in his opinion,

> [t]here could . . . be no objective in a master and servant relationship which would justify exposing the servant to a risk of serious injury or death other than the saving of life itself.

Egan J noted that Barrington J had not dealt specifically with the defendants' argument that the attack had been unforeseeable in view of the seven years' experience of safe passage. He rejected this argument because the provision of a Garda escort had minimised, but not eliminated, the risk:

> Every device or precaution must be taken in a high risk operation such as this and there was expert evidence to the effect that it was unwise to retain a clockwork precision in relation to the time factor.

Egan J's analysis of the factors that must be taken into account by a court in deciding whether to stigmatise conduct as negligent is striking. The traditional formula requires consideration of four factors: the likelihood of injury, the gravity of the threatened injury, the social utility (or otherwise) of the defendant's conduct and the cost of prevention: see McMahon & Binchy, *op. cit.*, 110-19. Undoubtedly the recourse to the protection of a Garda escort was a significant element in discharging the defendant's obligation to prevent injury happening, yet it was not sufficient. Egan J's statement that '[e]very device or precaution must be taken in a high risk operation such as this' seems to go further than what courts formerly required. This is not to suggest that a policy of varying times of delivery was too much to ask; but the idea that a relatively small risk of potentially severe injury should inevitably demand the securing of every conceivable precaution to prevent the injury seems novel.

Why should the duty have been expressed in such uncompromising terms? The answer appears to lie in the foreseeability of another's intentional wrongdoing and the Court's reluctance to let an employer wash his or her hands in relation to preventing the potential injury. What *Ryan* and *Walsh* make clear is that employers are obliged to make strong efforts to protect their employees from this kind of injury. They surely are not required to take every precaution that human ingenuity can ordain. Nonetheless, the courts continue to insist on a very high standard of care towards employees of security firms, as is evidenced by Morris J's decision in *McCann v Brinks Allied Ltd*, High Court, 12 May 1995, which we shall analyse in the 1995 Review.

Employee or independent contractor? In *Quinn v Burrell*, High Court, 23 April 1993 the plaintiff was injured when constructing a farm shed on the defendant's land. There was little doubt that there had been wide-ranging breaches of the Safety in Industry Acts 1955-1980: no scaffolding, tobards or safety net had been used. The plaintiff sued the defendant for these breaches and for employer's liability. It was plain, however, that the plaintiff was an independent contractor rather than the defendant's employee. He had sold the shed to the defendant for an agreed price and had also agreed a price for its construction and the labour that this would involve. The plaintiff had directed and controlled what had to be done. The negligence claim therefore failed. The action for breaches of statutory duty also foundered. We examine this aspect of the decision later in the Chapter, below, 562-3.

Causation Every day courts are called on to determine contested issues of fact where expert witnesses give evidence on both sides. Only rarely do they have to take a position on a factual issue of general scientific import. Here courts evince some natural embarrassment. It is one thing to contradict an expert scientific witness in respect of the specific application of agreed scientific principles to a particular case; it is quite another for the court to take a definitive position on an issue of general scientific controversy. Yet it may be necessary to do this in order to do justice in the litigation before the court.

In *Best v Wellcome Foundation Ltd* [1992] ILRM 609; [1993] 3 IR 421, analysed in the 1992 Review, 610-11, Finlay CJ evinced considerable embarrassment about having to determine whether the whooping cough vaccine can cause brain damage. In *O'Leary v Cork Corporation*, High Court, 19 May 1993, the general issue facing the court was whether trauma is capable of causing multiple sclerosis. An influential study published by McAlpine and Conston in 1952 found a relationship between trauma and the onset of multiple sclerosis within three months, in a small percentage of cases. This study was based on anecdotal histories involving retrospective assessments made by patients — not the most reliable method of scientific investigation. A study published in 1987 by Poser of Harvard Medical School cast some doubt on the earlier findings and a study by Sibley *et. al.*, published in 1991, based on eight years' monitoring of patients, came to conclusions directly contrary to those of the 1952 study.

Murphy J was of the view that a sufficient period had not elapsed since the publication of the Sibley paper to obtain a considered response to its findings. He expressed his guarded conclusions as follows:

> In this highly controversial and extremely technical field, I believe that the better view at the present time is that the preponderance of studies, observation and the experience of clinicians suggests that trauma can be precipitating factor of M.S. for some people who have a predisposition whether genetic, viral or otherwise to the disease. However, I would accept the view of [one of the expert witnesses] to the effect that the paper by Doctor Sibley would force any practitioner to look even more closely at a possible connection between trauma and M.S. in any given case than he would have done prior to its publication.

The plaintiff in the instant case sued his employers for negligence. He worked in the cleansing department of the Corporation. In July 1985 a machine which was used for sucking waste materials from roadside gullies disgorged these materials suddenly. They struck the defendant's back with what he described as 'a fair old wallop'. The plaintiff, having done some further work that day, was sent by his superiors to hospital, where his neck was x-rayed.

He returned to work the following day and with the exception of two or three days, probably during September, he continued to work normally until he was made redundant in November 1985. The plaintiff's ability to play darts had deteriorated suddenly in August 1985. Around then his fingers began to clench or lock and he had to jab or flex them out quickly to unlock them. His wife noticed that in the weeks following the accident he could not hold their youngest child because of the weakness in his hand.

Murphy J was greatly impressed with the integrity of the plaintiff and his wife and the honesty and care of their evidence but nonetheless he considered them to be mistaken on certain important details. He did not accept that the plaintiff had suffered from a condition of morbid fatigue in 1985. It seemed clear that the disease had not first manifested itself until April 1986. The plaintiff had not suspected that there could be a relationship between the accident and the development of multiple sclerosis until considerably later.

Murphy J clearly found the obligation to decide the legal issue a daunting one. He admitted that he would 'gladly have left it to a jury' and that, if he had been entitled to do so, he would have been 'glad to alleviate [the plaintiff's] burden by awarding him very substantial damages.' On the balance of probabilities, however, he was not satisfied that the accident had caused the disease. The fact that any accident would cause multiple sclerosis was itself improbable but Murphy J accepted, on balance, that it was possible. He was not satisfied, however, that any symptoms of the disease had manifested themselves before April 1986 and on that basis he did not accept that the plaintiff had discharged the onus of proof falling on him to satisfy the court that the disability was caused by the accident.

NEGLIGENT MISREPRESENTATION

In *Doolan v Murray*, High Court, 21 December 1993, Keane J awarded damages against the owner of a site on which premises had been built and subsequently sold to the plaintiff. The owner of the site had retained a right of way in relation to part of the site. She had successfully applied for outline planning permission for the construction of the premises. The person who built the premises deviated from the plans, so that it was necessary to obtain permission for its retention; in giving the necessary permission, the planning authority required an access capable of admitting cars and also three car spaces. The plaintiff, when she bought the premises, was unaware of this requirement. She and the owner of the site drew up a deed relating to the right of way. The manner in which the owner of the site negotiated and executed the deed implicitly represented that the right of way as originally reserved, had been intended to be for pedestrian use only and was capable of being locked, whereas, in view of the planning permission requirement, vehicular access was necessary. When the plaintiff subsequently sought to erect a barrier on the path, with the provision of keys for those with a right of way, she discovered the existence of the planning authority's requirements for the first time.

Keane J provided a wide-ranging analysis of the principles of negligence law. He considered that Lord Atkin's statement of the 'neighbour' principle in *Donoghue v Stevenson* [1932] AC 562, at 580 was relevant, in conjunction with the speeches of Lords Reid and Devlin in *Hedley Byrne & Co. v Heller & Partners* [1964] AC 465. He noted that, while Lord Atkin's statement had expressly extended to omissions, the authorities in England and other common law jurisdictions had reflected a reluctance to extend liability to 'pure omissions'. He quoted from Slade LJ's judgment in *Banque Financière v Westgate Insurance Co.* [1989] 2 All ER 952, at 1009:

The same reluctance on the part of the courts to give a remedy in tort for pure omission applies, perhaps even more so, when the omission is a failure to prevent economic harm. . . . [A] corresponding distinction is drawn by the law of contract which in general imposes no liability by virtue of a failure to speak as opposed to a misrepresentation.

Keane J commented that, as this citation suggested,

the general principle of *caveat emptor*, based as it is on the recognition by the law that parties should be left free to determine their obligations to each other, is not to be eroded by the inappropriate invocation of tortious liability.

Where, however, a person elected to make a representation on a matter which was capable of being misleading because of its partial nature, there seemed no reason why liability in tort for negligent misstatement should not arise, provided there was a duty to take care in relation to the making of the representation. Whether such a duty of care arose in the circumstances of the instant case had to be determined having regard to the legal principles laid down in *Hedley Byrne* and subsequently adopted by the Irish courts.

The owner of the site had made a misrepresentation as to private rights; such a misrepresentation was capable of being actionable, in contrast to misrepresentation as to the law in general.

Whilst the *Hedley Byrne* doctrine had its most obvious application in cases where persons holding themselves out as having professional or other skills made statements on which others foreseeably relied, it was not necessarily confined to that category:

The authorities demonstrate that what the court must do in each case is to examine the facts and determine whether the circumstances of the case were such that the maker of the statement should have had within his or her contemplation at the time when it was made a person or persons who might reasonably rely on it to their possible detriment. There must be, as the cases make clear, an assumption of responsibility in circumstances where the maker of the statement ought to have foreseen that it would be relied on and it was in fact relied on by the plaintiff.

The owner of the site clearly must have known of the plaintiff's concern in relation to the right of way. In her negotiations prior to the execution of the deed, it must have been obvious to her that her silence as to the true nature of the right of way left the plaintiff under a false impression which could well result in adverse financial consequences to her. She should have been aware that the plaintiff would rely on her silence as indicating that there were no problems of which she knew in regard to the right of way. Accordingly Keane J imposed liability on the owner of the site for negligent misstatement.

An important statement of law by Keane J in respect of two other defendants should be noted. He stated that the fact that they had entered into a contract with the plaintiff did not mean that their duties to the plaintiff were necessarily to be ascertained from the terms of the contract alone. A vendor of property might well be under a duty of care *quoad* the purchaser in accordance with the principles of *Hedley Byrne*.

In *McAnarney v Hanrahan* [1994] 1 ILRM 210, Costello J laid down some important principles in relation to negligent misstatement. The plaintiffs had bought the leasehold interest in a public house for £45,000 on the basis of assurances by the defendant auctioneer that a bid for £54,000 had been received at auction and that previous negotiations with the ground landlords justified the assessment of the purchase price for the freehold at a maximum of £3,000. Neither of these assurances was correct. Some time after buying the property, the plaintiffs sought to acquire the freehold. The ground landlord's price was £40,000 (ultimately reduced to £30,000). They sued the auctioneer and his principal for negligent misstatement.

Costello J held that the case fell within the principles laid down by the House of Lords in *Hedley Byrne v Heller & Partners Ltd* [1964] AC 465. He quoted with approval from Lord Morris's speech (at 502-3):

> If, in a sphere in which a person is so placed that others could reasonably rely upon his judgment or his skill or upon his ability to make careful enquiry, a person takes it upon himself to give information or advice to, or allows his information or advice to be passed on to, another person who, as he knows or should know, would place reliance upon it, then a duty of care will arise.

In the instant case the auctioneer had taken upon himself responsibility for giving his opinion about the purchase of the freehold. He should have known that the plaintiffs would place reliance on what he told them, particularly as he expressly stated that negotiations had already taken place with the ground landlords. A special relationship had thus arisen between the parties, which imposed on the auctioneer the duty of care in giving the information. He had breached that duty in that, before making the statement, he had taken no care to see what price the landlords would require for their interest.

The case was different from *Bank of Ireland v Smith* [1966] IR 646, where Kenny J had held that no duty of care towards prospective purchasers was imposed on an auctioneer placing an advertisement that contained misleading information. In the instant case the responsibility that the auctioneer had taken upon himself and the particular circumstances of the negotiations created a special relationship which was absent in the circumstances which Kenny J was considering.

On the question of damages, Costello J noted that in cases of negligent misstatement, these should be assessed by analogy with claims for damages for deceit, to put the plaintiff in the position he would have been in if the representation had not been made to him. This should be contrasted with claims based on breach of warranty, where damages are assessed on the basis that the warranty is true. This meant that damages should not be assessed on the basis of the loss of a bargain for the purchase of the freehold, which would be £27,000 — the difference between £3,000 mentioned by the auctioneer and the sum of £30,000 that the plaintiffs ultimately paid. Instead, damages should be assessed on the difference between the price actually paid for the premises (£45,000) and the actual market value of the premises at the time of sale. The evidence on this matter led Costello J to assess damages at £5,000. Costello J's approach on this matter is in harmony with that adopted by s. 45(1) of the Sale of Goods and Supply of Services Act 1980 in relation to statutory misrepresentation.

Costello J declined to award any compensation for mental distress. He noted that compensation for injury to feelings may be included in cases of fraud (cf. *Doyle v Olby (Ironmongers) Ltd* [1969] QB 158, at 170) and he thought that 'in principle in suitable cases . . . damages for negligent misrepresentation in respect of mental distress caused to a plaintiff could be assessed.' In the instant case, however, Costello J did not think that the defendants' wrongdoing could 'be measured in any meaningful way' or that 'the justice of the case' required damages to be increased under this heading.

In *O'Brien v Campbell Catering International Ltd*, High Court, 22 March 1993, on appeal from the Circuit Court, Morris J affirmed the dismissal of a claim for negligent misrepresentation where the plaintiff, who held qualifications in food technology, was induced by the defendant to take up a position as meat processing plant technical assistant manager carrying out work in Egypt in a meat processing plant operated by an Egyptian company. The experience turned out unhappily and the plaintiff claimed that the defendant had negligently made a number of representations about the Egyptian company that were not correct.

Among these was the assertion that the company was run by people who were reliable. Morris J was satisfied that this representation had indeed been made but he considered that it 'would have to be related to the ordinary idiosyncrasies and characteristics of Egyptian businessmen and . . . the plaintiff would have taken this assurance on that basis, as he was fully familiar with the situation, having worked in this part of the world for many years.'

In *O'Donoghue v L.V. Nolan (Incorporated)*, High Court, 29 July 1993, Carroll J held that the defendant, engaged in investment and business consultancy, was guilty of negligent misrepresentation in inviting the plaintiff to invest in a publication for pharmacists, where the defendant had failed to make proper enquiries to verify the assertions made by the vendor of the publication concerning its circulation, the frequency of its appearance and the quantum of its advertising revenue. The vendor was held guilty of fraudulent misrepresentation. He had made false statements to the investment consultant, knowing them to be untrue, with the intention of deceiving him and anyone else reading the document prepared by the investment consultant for the purpose of investment. Carroll J did not think that the facts could 'be regarded as merely being "enhanced" for the purpose of attracting an investor'. The plaintiff had been misled by the document; if he had known true facts, he would not have invested his money.

NERVOUS SHOCK

In *Kelly v Hennessy* [1993] ILRM 530, Lavan J adopted the views that Denham J had expressed in *Mullally v Bus Éireann* [1992] ILRM 722 on the subject of liability for 'nervous shock'.

The facts of the case were tragic. The plaintiff was a married woman, the mother of two daughters and a son. One evening in 1987, her husband and her daughters left the family home in County Meath to travel to Dublin Airport to collect the plaintiff's niece, who was arriving on a flight from abroad. Some time after 9.30 p.m. the niece telephoned the plaintiff and informed her that her husband and daughters had been seriously injured in a road accident. The plaintiff 'immediately went into shock, became upset and commenced vomiting'. She was taken to Jervis Street Hospital by her neighbours to see her family. She was ill during the journey. When she arrived at the hospital, she saw her family, 'each of whom w[as] in an appalling condition and one of whom she . . . described as looking like mince meat.'

Thereafter, the plaintiff 'lead a traumatised existence'. Her husband remained in hospital for over three months. He suffered permanent brain damage. Lavan J, describing his position at the time of trial, said: 'He cannot cope with people. He rises at 1 p.m. daily and must be bathed and cared for by the plaintiff'. One of the plaintiff's daughters, who was hospitalised for over a year, was also permanently brain damaged, 'and a serious problem to her mother at home.' The other daughter, who was in hospital for three months, made a full recovery from her injuries.

The plaintiff's husband and daughters had received compensation for their injuries from the defendant, whose negligence had caused the accident. The amount that was awarded included the cost of ongoing care, for the husband and the seriously injured daughter, which was required on a daily and permanent basis. The plaintiff would not take in trained help. She considered that she could not leave her husband and daughter; she expressed the fear that, were she to 'let go', she would never recover.

Lavan J accepted that the plaintiff was 'a genuine, gentle and caring human being'. He added: 'No greater love for one's family have I ever witnessed.' The medical evidence established that the plaintiff had suffered immediate shock resulting in vomiting on receiving the telephone call and that this condition had been 'gravely aggravated by scenes she immediately thereafter witnessed in Jervis Street Hospital'. The post-traumatic stress disorder had continued until 1992, at the earliest; the plaintiff continued to suffer a serious depression and Lavan J doubted whether she would ever fully recover from what he perceived to be a clear psychiatric illness. He rejected the defendant's argument that the plaintiff's failure to acknowledge her pain, grief and depression constituted in law a failure to mitigate her damages. This conclusion would seem eminently sustainable. The doctrine of failure to mitigate damages is not intended to capture complex internal psychological strategies for coping with personal tragedy.

In his legal discussion of the substantive issue of the scope of liability for negligently caused nervous shock, Lavan J noted that *Mullally* was not binding on him but that it was 'of strong persuasive authority, being a judgment of the High Court'. Having considered all of the leading judicial authorities in Ireland and England, he adopted the view of Denham J in *Mullally* and held that the plaintiff entitled to recover as against the defendant for nervous shock. He awarded the plaintiff £75,000.

The Supreme Court affirmed Lavan J: [1996] 1 ILRM 321. We shall examine the Supreme Court judgment in the 1995 Review. We need here merely note that it maintains the traditional policy of the Irish courts, from as far back as the decision of the Court of Appeal in *Byrne v Southern and Western Railway Co.*, unreported, February 1884, of treating 'nervous shock' actions as essentially unproblematic from the standpoint of policy. See N. Mullany & P. Handford, *Tort Liability for Psychiatric Damage: The Law of 'Nervous Shock'* (1993), 149. It is nonetheless true that we have yet to experience litigation in Ireland where the plaintiff's claim is at the outer edges of liability, as, for example, where the plaintiff suffers a post-traumatic stress disorder on being *informed* of the death or injury of a loved one, without actually witnessing the aftermath of the carnage.

PROTECTION OF PRISONERS

The essence of the value judgment underlying the concept of negligence involves, as we have noted, a balance of several factors: the *likelihood* of injury, the *gravity* of the threatened injury, the social utility (or inutility) of the impugned conduct and the social or economic *cost of preventing injury*. *Kavanagh v Governor of Arbour Hill Prison* is a decision in which all of these factors were clearly in focus.

The plaintiff, a prisoner serving a seven-year sentence for burglary, was stabbed with a Stanley knife blade by another prisoner when walking from the recreation hall to his cell in the company of several prisoners. He claimed that the prison authorities had been negligent in two respects: by their failure to supervise the journey adequately and their failure to detect the passing over of the blade from a visitor to a prisoner.

Morris J rejected both grounds. He declined to stigmatise as negligent the brief interruption of direct supervision by prison officers of no more than a few seconds' duration, where the group of prisoners moved from the sight of one officer to that of another. The monitoring regime of visitors was appropriate to the kind of prisoner housed in Arbour Hill. Most of the 140 inmates were sexual offenders. No subversive prisoners were there. Morris J accepted that:

> the requirements and procedures of such a prison must be appropriate to the type of prison that it is and that the requirements appropriate, for instance, for Portlaoise involving as they do strip searching of the visitors and prisoners after visits, would be inappropriate for Arbour Hill.

A rigorous search policy would generate feelings of frustration and ill-will among the group of settled long-term prisoners. Adequate surveillance and searches were carried out at Arbour Hill and no contact, save a handshake, was permitted between prisoners and visitors. The prison authorities accepted that, from time to time, small objects, such as the blade in the instant case, would pass into the prison but there was a need to strike a balance as to what was reasonable and to maintain a humane regime in the prison. In this context, Morris J applied the principles set out in the judgment of Hamilton P in *Muldoon v Ireland* [1988] ILRM 367. See the 1987 Review, 326. *Muldoon* also was concerned with injury resulting from the use of an offensive weapon in Arbour Hill; the President in that case acquitted the prison authorities of negligence.

In *Bond v Ireland*, High Court, 13 May 1993, decided three weeks after *Kavanagh*, Budd J had to deal with the security regime of Portlaoise prison.

The two plaintiffs, prisoners there, had been attacked in the exercise yard by two other prisoners. The instrument of violence was a metal rose of a shower head. Their claim in negligence, based on the known risk that their assailants represented to the prison authorities, failed on the evidence but two other grounds of negligence were also considered, in relation to the failure to search prisoners using the exercise yard and the supervision regime of the yard.

Budd J quoted the relevant passages from *Muldoon* and *Kavanagh*. He referred to the evidence of Mr John Lonergan, Governor of Mountjoy Prison and formerly Governor of Portlaoise to the effect that it was difficult to find contraband items in a prison, since a rub-down search could frequently miss them. There were, he said, many items that could be used as weapons if one prisoner wished to 'get at' another. Budd J considered it clear from Mr Lonergan's evidence and that of other prison officers that one had 'to strike a reasonable balance in respect of supervision and in particular with regard to the number and extent of searches which are carried out.'

The Deputy Governor of Portlaoise Prison testified that it was not the practice to search prisoners from the block where these prisoners were housed as they were going into the exercise yard as by and large they were well behaved. In the past fifteen years, there had been no incidents in the yard.

As to supervision of the yard, Budd J noted that the Deputy Governor had explained that, 'after an incident on 30th December 1974', prison officers and Garda 'had been in the exercise yard but that this had caused constant confrontation between the staff, the prisoners and the Garda'. Eventually the staff had been placed outside a chain-link fence surrounding the yard. There was no need for prison officers to be in the yard and it was also understandable for security reasons. Budd J dismissed the plaintiff's case. In his view, there had been no failure to provide adequate searches of the prisoners or to supervise them adequately.

Bond's case is a good example of how the law of negligence, properly understood and applied, responds sensitively to the realities of life and accepts that the best management regime may be one that has to run an inevitable risk of injury.

PROFESSIONAL NEGLIGENCE

Lawyers In *McMullan v Carthy*, High Court, 13 July 1993, Carroll J exonerated from any negligence a solicitor who had faithfully transmitted her client's instructions and enquiries to the senior counsel engaged in injunction proceedings to restrain an alleged nuisance. The senior counsel had appeared to advise incorrectly that, in spite of a settlement in those proceedings, it would be possible to re- enter them subsequently and proceed again for the injunction at a latter stage. Carroll J was satisfied that, in her communications with the senior counsel and in acting in reliance on his advice, she had fully discharged her duty of care. Carroll J was not required to address the question whether the principles underlying *Rondel v Worsley* [1969] 1 AC 191 and *Saif Ali v Sydney Mitchell & Co. (a firm)* [1980] AC 198 are good law in Ireland. Cf. McMahon & Binchy, *op. cit.*, 272-275. Perhaps some day a litigant disappointed by his or her counsel's performance in court will assert that an immunity from the duty of care frustrates the constitutionally-protected right to litigate: see J. Kelly, *The Irish Constitution* (3rd ed., by G. Hogan & G. Whyte, 1994), 770-773. Of course that right is subject to rational restriction, so it will not prevail against a reasonably-crafted statute of limitations (*O'Brien v Manufacturing Engineering Co.* [1973] IR 334) or the judicial entitlement to dismiss proceedings that are frivolous or vexatious (*D.K. v A.K.* [1993] ILRM 710, analysed in the 1992 Review, 365-7). Nevertheless, the fragile and controversial quality of the rationale for advocacy immunity may encourage a court in the future to invoke the constitutional dimension in departing from the British authorities on this question.

In *Pierse v Allen*, High Court, 9 June 1993, Murphy J had an opportunity to review and explain the rationale of his earlier decision on legal malpractice in *Kelly v Crowley* [1985] IR 212. In *Kelly*, he had imposed liability in negligence on a solicitor who had bought a licensed premises for the plaintiff, knowing that the plaintiff wanted to acquire what is normally called a publican's licence, without enquiring from the vendor's solicitors whether the licence was publican's or a hotel licence. See McMahon & Binchy, *op. cit.*, 281. In *Pierse v Allen*, the solicitor had acted in 1983 for clients who bought premises on the representation of the vendor that it was a hotel. It turned out that it had lost its status as a hotel some time previously. The clients invoked *Kelly v Crowley* but Murphy J distinguished the earlier decision:

> [T]he error of the solicitor in that case was a failure to establish the nature of the property or interest offered for sale. It was not a failure to establish the right or title of the vendor to that property. That is a consideration which in general must be postponed for detailed investigation subsequent to the contract and prior to completion and on the footing that if, for any reason, the vendor is unable to make title to the property which he has contracted to sell, . . . at the very least the purchaser will recover the deposit paid to be discharged of any liability in respect of the balance of the purchase price.

In the instant case there was no doubt whatever about the nature of the property offered for sale. Insofar as it had enjoyed a particular value or status, it had clearly been represented to be a 'hotel'. Murphy J was accordingly of the view that the solicitor had not been guilty of negligence in relation to any specific pre-contract enquiry; expert evidence had been given to the effect that there was not at the time of trial, or more particularly in 1983 had not been, any general practice with regard to making pre-contract enquiries or requisitions. Of course the absence of any such general practice would not inevitably be fatal to the plaintiffs' claim: cf. *Roche v Peilow* [1985] IR 232. Murphy J must have been of the view that there was no question that the practice should be stigmatised as one obviously lacking in due care.

Doctors

(a) Diagnosis There have been many cases in which doctors have made a mistaken diagnosis. Liability does not inevitably follow: only where the diagnosis was one that a reasonable doctor would not have made will the plaintiff have a prospect of success: *Dunne v National Maternity Hospital* [1989] ILRM 735; [1989] IR 91. But what is the position where the doctor is nonplussed and simply *cannot* make a diagnosis? This was the position in *Coughlan v Whelton*, High Court, 22 January 1993.

The plaintiff consulted the defendant consultant, complaining of severe pain in his chest and right arm after consuming small amounts of alcohol. The defendant subjected him to a battery of tests, involving radiography, but these revealed nothing useful. He contacted the plaintiff's general practitioner explaining that he had not been able to make a conclusive diagnosis.

The plaintiff had Hodgkin's disease. Lavan J accepted evidence that 'only two persons in the Irish population of 3.5 million would present with symptoms of Hodgkin's disease including a symptom of alcohol-induced pain' and that there had been no recorded case where a patient presented with only the single system of alcohol-induced pain.

Applying the principles enunciated in *Dunne*, Lavan J acquitted the defendant of negligence. He could:

> not see how a doctor can be guilty of negligence if he carried out all appropriate tests and all of those tests prove normal as a result of which he cannot come to a conclusion and conveys that clear view to the patient's general practitioner.

(b) General practitioners' house calls In *O'Doherty v Whelan*, High Court, 18 January 1993, the important question of the scope of the duty of a general practitioner to make home visits fell for consideration. The plaintiff, a 'very highly-strung and at times hysterical' person, became ill at a time when she was in the eleventh week of pregnancy. She had previously suffered

two miscarriages in the first trimester. She attended the defendant's surgery on Friday afternoon. The defendant, who was aware of her medical history and of her excitable disposition, diagnosed a 'flu like' illness, probably viral, with a probable urinary tract infection. She did not, however, ask the plaintiff to provide her with a urinary sample, on account of time constraints. The surgery time was drawing to a close; laboratory facilities were not readily available at the weekend; it was approaching closing time for the chemists and there was a prescription for antibiotics to be filled.

The plaintiff's condition worsened overnight and the following morning. She vomited up the tablets she had been prescribed. Her husband telephoned the defendant at least twice over the weekend and asked her to come to visit the plaintiff and on each occasion she was unwilling to do so. On the first call, she recommended to the husband that he bring his wife to hospital forthwith. The exchanges between them were acrimonious, the defendant complaining that the husband slammed down the phone on her in mid-sentence on both occasions. On the second occasion, the defendant was very angry and upset that her earlier advice had been disregarded. She repeated that advice to the husband. When eventually, on the following Tuesday, the plaintiff was brought to hospital, her condition continued to deteriorate but, over time, it improved and she was in due course discharged. No definitive diagnosis was ever made. Although the medical staff at the hospital administered antibiotics, they could not determine whether the treatment helped or hindered the plaintiff's recovery.

O'Hanlon J, applying the *Dunne* criteria, imposed liability on the defendant. With regard to the consultation on Friday, he considered that the defendant had been 'remiss' in not seeking a urine specimen to verify her diagnosis. This precautionary measure had been by-passed only because of the lateness of the hour. If postponed, the defendant should have made arrangements to have it carried out later, by way of a check on the treatment she had prescribed. O'Hanlon J did not explicitly characterise this approach as negligent. It is hard to see how, in the circumstances of the case, it should be so considered. The plaintiff's condition had deteriorated so rapidly that the defendant's recommendation that she be brought to hospital surely overtook and discharged any obligation to have the test carried out subsequently as a check on the prescribed treatment.

The crucial question of liability related to the telephone calls and the defendant's failure to visit the plaintiff in her home. O'Hanlon J noted that, although the plaintiff was a very highly-strung person, she was undoubtedly vomiting and unable to retain food or medicine; this was 'calculated to cause in her feelings of alarm and concern for the well-being both of herself and of her baby, at the early stage of her pregnancy.'

O'Hanlon J concluded that the defendant should be regarded as having failed to respond adequately to the situation that arose after the Friday consultation. In an important passage, he observed:

> That is not to say that an obligation can arise in every case where a request is made to a general practitioner to visit the patient at home, to comply with such request. That would be wholly unreasonable. Every case must be judged on its own particular circumstances.

O'Hanlon J had regard to a number of factors. The plaintiff was a young mother, with one child of two years who had to be looked after. She had suffered two miscarriages, both in the first trimester of the pregnancy, and she was now expecting another baby and was in or about the eleventh week of the pregnancy. She was undoubtedly ill when she had attended the defendant's surgery and sufficiently ill in the defendant's opinion to be put on a course of antibiotics. She was known to the defendant to be of a nervous and highly-strung and excitable disposition.

In that situation, when a plea was made for a domiciliary visit within a day or two after the consultation, on the basis that the plaintiff had been unable to keep down the medication prescribed and that her condition had worsened significantly, the request for a house visit should have been treated with greater sympathy than it was accorded even on the evidence given by the defendant herself.

It was a situation where the plaintiff and her husband needed reassurance and where the plaintiff's condition needed to be monitored closely. The defendant felt that she had responded appropriately by telling the husband to have the plaintiff brought to hospital, but on the defendant's own account of the telephone calls there was little to indicate that this direction or suggestion was being well received at the other end or that it was going to be complied with. O'Hanlon J thought it was unfortunate to respond angrily to a young couple who had good reason to be worried about the situation, and a message such as, 'Get her into the hospital and stop telephoning me', was not, in his opinion, an appropriate way to obtain co-operation in having the plaintiff's fears set at rest and in having her illness attended to properly.

On the defendant's account of the two telephone calls O'Hanlon J did not think she was entitled, after either of them, to feel confident that the plaintiff was on her way to hospital and that the defendant need have no further cause for concern.

It appeared to O'Hanlon J that the response given by the defendant to the telephone calls was in all probability affected by the difficulties with which the defendant herself had to contend at the time:

> It was the week-end; she was suffering from a painful and troublesome

back injury; her father was seriously ill; she had a young child of her own to look after, and her husband was dead. She knew from a previous experience that the plaintiff was highly-strung and liable to dramatise her complaints.

These are all ameliorating factors which should not be minimised, but they are not sufficient to provide an answer to the claim that the response of the defendant to the patient's pleas for help was neither adequate nor appropriate.

The damages awarded in the case were the small sum of £1,000 for the pain and distress caused to the plaintiff between the first telephone call and the time she was admitted to the hospital on the following Tuesday. This was because the illness from which she suffered was of unknown origin and it proceeded apparently unaffected by the medical care she received in the hospital. O'Hanlon J considered that it would be entirely speculative to contend that the effects of the plaintiff's illness would have been any less severe if she had been seen at home by the defendant.

(c) Surgery In *Lynskey v Governors and Guardians of the Charitable Infirmary of Jervis Street*, High Court, 23 April 1993, the plaintiff, a married man aged sixty-one, with three children, had an operation conducted by the defendant's medical team, for the removal of bilateral epididymal cysts. During the course of the operation, the testicular artery, with the diameter of a thread, was severed. The person carrying out the operation, who was Registrar in Urology, considering that the best course was orchidectomy, removed the testis on the basis that it had been deprived of its blood supply.

The plaintiff's action for negligence rested on three grounds. First he contended that the operation was of such complexity that it should have been carried out by a person with greater experience. This Costello J rejected on the evidence. The Registrar in Urology had ten years' experience of general surgery and, six months after the operation, had acted as locum for the Consultant Urologist who expressed himself 'quite happy to let him operate on any member of my family.'

The second ground was that the Registrar in Urology had been negligent in severing the artery. Costello J rejected this contention on the basis that, having regard to the nature, size and position of the cysts, there had been a risk of severance even with the exercise of reasonable skill and care.

Finally the plaintiff argued that the testis should not have been removed. An expert witness supported this view. As against this, an expert witness on behalf of the defence contended that the Registrar in Urology had acted correctly in making a balanced decision. Whereas the course suggested by

the plaintiff's expert witness would be applicable to a young boy whose
testicular inability might be perilous, one had to set against this the risk of
the development of an acutely gangrenous condition, or infection or extru-
sion. The expert witness concluded that, '[f]aced in th[ese] circumstances in
a 61-year-old man, one would be tempted not to replace the testis'.

Costello J agreed with this witness. He was satisfied that the Registrar in
Urology, in having to make a balanced decision, had 'exercised reasonable
care in the making of that decision for good reasons. . . .'

PUBLICANS' LIABILITY

In *Walsh v Ryan*, High Court, 12 February 1993, Lavan J imposed liability
on a publican where a female customer was seriously assaulted on the
premises by another customer who had arrived at the premises in a drunken
condition and caused a row. He had been served drink while in the premises.
The publican had evicted the plaintiff and the assailant from the premises
and declined to call an ambulance for the plaintiff. The defendant knew the
assailant and had been aware of his violent or unruly propensity for a
considerable time previously. He had twice had to intervene in the row which
the assailant had caused, which culminated in the assault.

Lavan J's analysis of the legal issues is of very considerable interest. The
plaintiff had argued that, by virtue of ss. 13 and 18 of the Licensing Act 1872,
the defendant was negligent in that he had permitted drunkenness on his
premises and had failed to exclude a drunkard from his premises. Lavan J
rejected this argument, stating:

> These two sections of the Act . . . create two statutory offences [;] they
> do not, in my view, constitute evidence of negligence.

In taking this approach, Lavan J departed from some of the judicial
authorities elsewhere in the common law world, where civil liability has been
imposed on the commercial purveyors of alcohol on the basis of breach of
statute: see Binchy, 'Comment: Drink Now — Sue Later' (1975) 53 *Canadian Bar Rev.* 344, at 348, *Jordan House Ltd. & Menow v Honsberger* (1973)
38 DLR (3d) 105; [1974] SCR 239, A.M. Linden & L.N. Klar, *Canadian
Tort Law: Cases, Notes and Materials* (10th ed., 1994), 285-6. It is arguably
preferable to rest liability on breach of the duty of care in negligence as this
allows the court a greater degree of flexibility than the terms of a statutory
provision that frankly never contemplated the imposition of civil liability
resulting from its enactment.

The plaintiff also contended that the defendant was liable as occupier to the plaintiff, citing *Foley v Musgrave Cash & Carry Ltd*, Supreme Court, 20 December 1985. Lavan J accepted this argument. He took the view, in the circumstances of the plaintiff's being a contractual invitee, the defendant's knowledge of the assailant's drunkenness and propensity towards violence and his two interventions in the row, the defendant occupier owed a duty to take reasonable care to ensure that his premises were 'conducted without risk to his customers'. That duty had been violated in the instant case. (It is interesting to speculate on how the facts of the case would be characterised under the Occupiers' Liability Act 1995, which applies only to dangers 'due to the state of the premises': s.1(1).)

Whilst deciding the case on the basis of occupier's liability, Lavan J made it clear that the general principles of liability set out in *Foley* and in Lord Atkin's test in *Donoghue v Stevenson* [1932] AC 562, at 580, established 'a duty of care owed by the publican to his customers.' Presumably, therefore, in a future case it will be open to a plaintiff injured off the premises, perhaps in a road accident miles away from the public house, to invoke the 'neighbour' principle in seeking to impose a duty of care on the publican. It is unlikely that this duty would be limited to other customers: the risk of injury is in some cases just as foreseeable off the premises: cf. McMahon & Binchy, *op. cit.*, 122.

PONY-TREKKING

In *O'Driscoll v Kavanagh*, High Court, 26 March 1993, Lavan J imposed liability on the owner of a riding school which carried on business providing pony-trekking facilities and tuition in horse-riding. The plaintiff, aged sixteen, fell from a horse which he had hired from the defendant for the purpose of trekking with other students from his school. The accident occurred towards the end of the journey, which was supervised by two employees of the defendant.

The crucial question in the case was one of evidence: whether the horse had spontaneously broken into a gallop or had been encouraged to do so by the plaintiff in a race with his colleagues. Lavan J held in favour of the plaintiff on this issue.

Lavan J accepted that the defendant had the duty to supervise the pony trek properly, to provide a horse which was suitable in all of the circumstances, and to provide a leader of the pony trek so as to ensure that the following ponies would have their speeds controlled.

It was not for every injury occurring in the course of a trek, or other like sporting activity, that a defendant ought to be liable. Once the defendant established the proficiency of the applicant to ride, properly equipped that person, properly selected an appropriate animal and duly supervised the trek from the beginning to the end, then it seemed to Lavan J that he would have acted reasonably in all of the circumstances of the case. Lavan J gave as an example the case of a person who goes on a skiing lesson, properly equipped and taught. The lessons might conclude with the learner falling and breaking his or her wrist, but Lavan J did not consider that this would implicate the proprietor in negligence.

The plaintiff had failed to call expert evidence that supervision was an essential part of the duty of an owner such as the defendant in the instant case. However, that point had never been challenged. Lavan J was satisfied in all of the circumstances that in conducting a party of sixteen year old school boys on a trek, 'supervision, and strict supervision at that,' was an essential part of the duty of care owed to the plaintiff. Accordingly Lavan J found that the defendant failed to properly supervise and control the speed of the trek.

PUBLIC AUTHORITY LIABILITY

In *Gaye v Dublin County Council*, High Court, 30 July 1993, a valiant attempt to circumvent the traditional immunity of highway authorities from liability of nonfeasance failed on the evidence rather than on the law. The plaintiff had tripped on an uneven footpath near her home. She sought to attach liability to the defendant council on several grounds: that it had created the problem when retaining the footpath after sewage work had been carried out on it, at a time when the council had not yet taken the estate into its charge, that it had failed to discover the problem when inspecting the estate prior to taking it over, that the problem constituted a nuisance which the council had adopted when taking charge of the estate and that the council was liable for the negligence of those who had conducted the sewage installation, on the basis of the controversial holding of the majority of the Supreme Court in *Weir v Dun Laoghaire Corporation* [1984] ILRM 113. Cf. McMahon & Binchy, *op. cit.*, at 763, Morgan & Hogan, *Administrative Law in Ireland* (2nd ed., 1991), at 661-2.

Morris J rejected the first and last of these four grounds on the basis that the problem had not been shown to trace its provenance to the sewage installation. There was no need for him to consider whether the majority in *Weir* had gone too far in casting the net of vicarious liability. He rejected the second ground on the basis that there was 'no evidence whatsoever' that the problem existed at the time the council took charge of the estate. He went on to observe that circumstances might arise where a local authority might deem it expedient and proper to take an estate in hand notwithstanding defects, as, for example, where a builder became insolvent:

The local authority, adopting the lesser of two evils, may well be prepared to take the estate in charge fully aware of the defects. In such a circumstance no negligence in failing to inspect would arise.

Might not such a holding concede too great an immunity to local authorities? Even those who act in the public interest can find that they have a duty of care thrust upon them. This may seem to them a curious reward for their contribution to the public weal but tort law has long since accepted that a duty of care may be generated by conduct that was not obligatory. From the standpoint of public policy, it does not impose an undue burden on local authorities: if repair is out of the question, other strategies, however tiresome to users of the path, present themselves. These include warnings and barriers, though it must be admitted that the scope for placing areas of footpaths out of bounds for extended periods is not very great.

The fact that Morris J accepted that the third ground of argument put forward by the plaintiff was sound in law, though unsustainable on the facts, is worthy of reflection. In the law of nuisance, the courts do not concern themselves with the motivation or purpose of the defendant in taking possession of land on which a nuisance already exists. The defendant may not plead that he or she has not adopted the nuisance merely because the purpose was a socially beneficial one. One need not advocate the assimilation of the torts of negligence and nuisance before one can point to the anomaly of resting the plaintiff's prospects of success on strategies of pleading. The Supreme Court displayed a healthy disdain for any resurrection of undue formalism in *Hanrahan v Merck, Sharp & Dohme (Ireland) Ltd* [1988] ILRM 629. This is as it should be.

It is perhaps unfortunate that the evidence was such as to render otiose any judicial consideration of the question whether the *Weir*-based principle of vicarious liability embraces nonfeasance on the part of the person or body for whose negligence the highway authority may be vicariously liable. One could approach the matter formalistically or substantively. A formalist analysis would be that, if a highway authority is not liable for nonfeasance on its part, it should not become so by reason of the fact that it discharges some of its functions through the agency of other actors. We believe that this is an unconvincing analysis and we suggest that a consideration of the substantive issues of policy will yield a better solution.

The highway authorities' traditional immunity from liability for nonfeasance was based on the lack of financial resources of these bodies at a time when local government was a function of essentially private charitable endeavour. With the democratisation of the process and its transformation into an element of the public political process, the idea that a highway authority cannot afford to maintain the roads within its jurisdiction has become completely anachronistic. The truth of the matter is that it is perfectly capable of doing so if there is a political will to do so.

It can be argued that, even if the traditional immunity in respect of nonfeasance still has vitality, and is not unconstitutional on the basis that it amounts to an arbitrary restriction on the right to litigate (or the right to bodily integrity), it should not be extended to cases where the highway authority has a putative vicarious liability, under the *Weir* principle. A liability of this kind, however controversial, is simply grounded on policy considerations that have nothing to do with the reasons invoked for granting immunity to highway authorities for nonfeasance.

BREACH OF STATUTORY DUTY

If I engage you to erect a shed and you do so carelessly and are injured, should I have to compensate you? A simple sense of justice would suggest not. If you invoke the panoply of safety legislation, should you be permitted to enmesh me within its remit so as to require me to compensate you because I cannot escape the language of the legislative provisions ? Again, justice would not seem to be served by forcing me to pay your bill. In *Quinn v Burrell*, High Court, 23 April 1993, the plaintiff, an independent contractor, engaged to build a shed for the defendant, fractured his skull when he fell through the partially constructed roof of the shed. It was clear that there had been substantial breaches of the Construction (Health, Safety and Welfare) Regulations 1972. The status of the plaintiff, though a matter of dispute in the case, seemed incontrovertible. He had advertised in terms that were consistent only with his being an independent contractor. The terms of his contract with the defendant were similar. The contract, which specified the payment of a total sum in respect of all labour engaged on the project, pointed the same way. Moreover, the evidence established that the plaintiff had been in control of the operation at all stages prior to the accident. His claim for negligence therefore failed: see the Employer's Liability section of this Chapter, above 543.

The plaintiff also sought compensation on the basis of s. 43 of the Safety in Industry Act 1980, which provides as follows:

> Where a person undertakes building operations or work of engineering construction to which by virtue of s. 88 or 89 of the [Factories Act 1955] provisions of that Act apply, then any person, other than the first mentioned person or an employee of the first mentioned person, who designs and controls or directs the operation or works or supervises the manner in which or the method by which the operations or works are

carried out, shall be deemed for the purposes of the said provisions, in their application to the operations or works, to be the occupier of a factory.

Hamilton P was satisfied that *the plaintiff* had controlled, directed and supervised the manner in which the work was being carried out. He held that, 'by virtue of the terms of the said s. 43, [the plaintiff] was the occupier of the site. . . .' He held that the defendants had been guilty of neither negligence nor breach of statutory duty.

This conclusion is undoubtedly correct but the President's holding that the plaintiff was occupier of the defendant's premises is not fully convincing. The defendant was undoubtedly the occupier of his own farm. S. 43 characterises the person who controls the building operations as 'the occupier of a factory' only where the person thus in control is one *other than the person who undertakes the building operations*. The plaintiff himself was clearly such a person. Therefore s. 43 was of no assistance to the plaintiff, not because he was occupier of the site but rather because the defendant was not.

In *Barry v Nitrigin Éireann Teo* [1994] 2 ILRM 522, the facts of which we set out in more detail in the section of this Chapter on Employers' Liability, above 538-9, Costello J held that the defendants had been in breach of the Factories (Noise) Regulations 1975 (SI No 235 of 1975) in circumstances giving rise to a successful claim for damages for breach of statutory duty (as well as negligence at common law) by the employee.

Regulation 4(1) protected a person from exposure to a sound pressure level 'of such intensity and duration as is likely to cause him harm'. The medical evidence clearly established such harm: the plaintiff at the time of the proceedings was suffering from bilateral nerve deafness from noise exposure over the years. This condition was not exclusively attributable to his employment but the contribution of other factors was relatively slight, requiring a reduction in the damages from £60,000 to £50,000.

Costello J considered that there had also been a breach of regulation 7(1) of the 1975 Regulations. It provided as follows:

Subject to regulation 4(1) of these regulations, a person employed shall not be exposed to sound pressure levels in excess of 90dBA unless either
—

(a) the duration and level of exposure is controlled so that its cumulative effect is unlikely to cause harm, or
(b) ear protection is provided which effectively reduces to a level which is unlikely to cause harm the sound pressure level at each ear of the person.

The plaintiff had been exposed to pressure levels in excess of 90dBA and the exceptions in the regulation did not excuse what had happened. The defendants had not been able to establish that the duration level of the exposure was controlled so that the cumulative effect was not harmful. Nor did the ear protection that was provided carry out what sub-paragraph (b) required.

The reporter, Paul Coughlan, notes that the 1975 Regulations were revoked and replaced with effect from 1 July 1990 by the European Communities (Protection of Workers) (Exposure to Noise) Regulations 1990 (SI No 157 of 1990). The 1990 Regulations, implementing the Council Directive 86/188/EEC, extend to many places of work not covered by the 1975 Regulations. For further consideration of the 1990 Regulations see Dr. Yvonne Scannell's *Environmental and Planning Law in Ireland* (1995), at 492-3 and John White's *Civil Liability for Industrial Accidents*, volume 1, paras. 19.9.01 *et. seq.* (1993).

CONTRIBUTORY NEGLIGENCE

In *Dyer v Dublin Corporation*, High Court, 10 June 1993, the plaintiff injured his hand when attempting to slam the front door of his home which he rented from the defendant. The door had been damaged by a previous tenant and the defendant Corporation had been dilatory in fixing it. This delay constituted negligence on the part of the defendant in its capacity as landlord. Nonetheless Morris J held that the plaintiff was guilty of contributory negligence to the extent of 50%. The procedure he had adopted of putting his hand around the leading edge of the door and pulling it sharply towards him, attempting to remove his hand before the door slammed was a careless one. The plaintiff was a clerical assistant with An Post, and 'an articulate and intelligent man.' In Morris J's view, he ought to have taken some remedial measures, such as fitting a temporary handle on the door, rather than persist in what his own counsel had stigmatised as the 'Russian Roulette' method of closing the door.

Morris J's reference to the plaintiff's intelligence should not be taken to suggest that the quantum of contributory negligence is to be assessed in the light of the intelligence of the particular plaintiff. Generally courts, when dealing with contributory negligence, as with negligence, apply the objective standard of the reasonable person. Children are different. Intelligence is a factor in assessing their negligence or contributory negligence: see McMahon & Binchy, *op. cit.*, 718-22.

In the section on the Duty of Care, above, 533-4, we have discussed the decision of Flood J in *Gorey v Gorey and P.H. Gorey & Sons Ltd*, High Court,

10 June 1993. The plaintiff was injured when the partially covered body of a hydraulically operated tipper truck fell on him. He was at the time seeking to assist the driver in responding to an earlier breakdown. The driver should have made the truck safer and was thus guilty of negligence. The plaintiff was the director of the company that owned the lorry. The driver, an employee of the company, was his brother.

Flood J acquitted the plaintiff of any contributory negligence. It was reasonable of him to have concluded that his brother was not working in circumstances of imminent peril to his own safety or that of his fellow employees. In approaching the lorry to check the fuel line, the plaintiff was entitled to assume that he was not incurring any greater risk or that, if he was, he would be warned of the nature of the risk by his brother.

In *Galvin v Aer Rianta*, High Court, 13 October 1993 (Circuit Court Appeal) the plaintiff, a disabled person, was injured when she fell on an escalator while embarking on an air pilgrimage with a hundred other invalids to Lourdes. She had not availed herself of a lift which was close to the escalator since a man in a white shirt and dark trousers, who appeared to be an official, told her and her husband that they should use the escalator because the lift was for invalids only.

The carrier was liable under Article 17 of the Warsaw Convention 1929; a crucial question was whether it could successfully plead Article 21 in mitigation or exoneration. Article 21, in essence, is equivalent to s.34 of the Civil Liability Act 1961.

Barr J was satisfied that the plaintiff had not been guilty of contributory negligence. The plaintiff had done what she was told when confronted by a person in apparent authority. She and her husband were 'simple people in late middle-age, who [were] not experienced travellers.'

This holding is useful in showing that the particular experience of the particular plaintiff may be a factor in assessing whether his or her conduct in a particular context amounted to carelessness. In the instant case the plainitff had done her reasonable best in the light of the information available to her. Nevertheless, courts throughout the common law world are very slow to listen to arguments based on lack of experience where the context is an 'everyday' one, even where the plaintiff can establish that it was novel for him or her. One suspects that an accident in a railway station might inspire less judicial sympathy for the argument that the plaintiff was in an environment of which he or she had no previous experience.

Earlier in the chapter, in the section on Traffic Accidents, above 537-8, we discuss O'Hanlon J's decision in *Strick v Treacy*, High Court, 10 June 1993. Briefly, the case involved a collision between the plaintiff, who was driving along a highway and the driver of a fire tender, who drove his vehicle, with flashing lights, into her path against traffic lights showing red. O'Hanlon

J held that the plaintiff, the driver of the fire tender and the driver of a Garda car which was acting as escort to the fire tender and which parked in the fast lane of the highway were all guilty of negligence. He reduced the plaintiff's damages by 50%.

This massive reduction can be explained largely by the plaintiff's failure to wear a seat belt, which O'Hanlon J considered had 'contributed significantly to the seriousness of her injuries.' These injuries were to the chin, neck and knee — just the areas that one might expect would be protected, to a greater or a lesser extent, by the use of a seat belt.

In *Hamilton v The Office of Public Works*, High Court, 22 November 1993, the plaintiff, an electrician employed by the defendant, tripped on a gully that crossed an underground passageway in Leinster House, where he was working. The electric light in the area was defective and the area was in virtual darkness. Liability was admitted but the defendant contended that the plaintiff was guilty of contributory negligence in that, being a regular user of the passage, he ought to have known about and avoided the gully. The defendant also argued that the plaintiff should have repaired the light. Morris J rejected both arguments. He accepted the plaintiff's evidence that he had not used the passageway regularly because some of the rooms in the area were alleged to have had asbestos fittings. He was also satisfied that the plaintiff had 'no function' in repairing the light.

VICARIOUS LIABILITY

Tort law proceeds on the basis of the biblical injunction that no man can serve two masters: if an employee of one employer is 'lent' to another employer, the question of which employer may be vicariously liable for the torts of the employee is answered on an all-or-nothing basis. Only one employer can be attached with vicarious liability. This approach rests uneasily with the 'control' test, which dominates the general question of whether one person should be vicariously liable for another's torts. There is no reason in principle why more than one person should be capable of exercising control over how another person carries out his or her worth.

Nonetheless, in *McGowan v Wicklow County Council*, High Court, 27 May 1993, Morris J applied the traditional test. The plaintiff, an employee of Wicklow County Council, was injured when struck by a JCB driven by the employee of an independent contractor who had rented his machinery, accompanied by the driver, to the Council on an hourly basis to carry out trench-digging operations. The arrangement had been preceded by a 'plant-tender'. The only function which the Council performed, apart from paying for the machine and driver, was to nominate the number of hours as required, to mark out for the driver the line in which the trench was to be dug and to tell him the locations where he was to work. An additional degree of co-operation was obviously necessary between the driver and the County Council workforce so as to synchronise their efforts and to check the depths and slopes of the drains that were being cut. That required the County Council representative to direct when the digging was to be suspended for the purpose of carrying out the checks and, if the depth was found to be unsatisfactory, to repeat the dig.

In Morris J's view, this was not an assumption of control over the driver and was 'no more than the co-operation required between two independent workmen employed on the same job.' He noted the evidence of the engineer in charge of the project, to the effect that the nature of the arrangement had been such that the JCB driver 'would never be given instructions as to how the job was to be done, nor how the driver was to manage his machine.'

DEFAMATION

Publication   In *O'Brien v Ulster Bank Ltd*, High Court, 21 December 1993, Carney J accepted without hesitation that to send a letter to the plaintiff's place of employment in circumstances where it is likely to be opened by the plaintiff's employers' secretarial or office staff will constitute sufficient publication for the tort of libel where in fact such a member of staff opens and reads the letter.

Defamatory connotation   In the Chapter on Practice and Procedure, above, 460, we discuss the decision of the Supreme Court in *Duffy v Newsgroup Newspapers Ltd* [1994] 1 ILRM 364, to the effect that, once the trial judge on an application under O. 25, r. 1 of the Rules of the Superior Courts 1986 rules, as a preliminary point of law, that the words complained of are capable of a defamatory meaning, the rest of the issues, including which of several possible defamatory meanings is or are established and whether the words referred to the plaintiff, are not appropriate for preliminary resolution.

O'Flaherty J (Finlay CJ, Egan, Blayney and Denham JJ concurring) touched on the 'group' cases. His observations give no support to the argument (not apparently canvassed in court) that the denial of a remedy in defamation to a wide class of plaintiffs is unconstitutional.

Discovery procedure   In *Galvin v Graham-Twomey* [1994] 2 ILRM 315 in a Circuit Court appeal, *per* O'Flaherty J, one teacher sued another for libel.

She claimed that two members of the board of management had told her that they had received letters from the defendant regarding her, the contents of which they declined to disclose on the grounds of confidentiality, but that they were 'very strong' and difficult to believe. She sought discovery of these letters.

The Circuit Court judge had declined to order discovery and O'Flaherty J affirmed. He considered it essential for a plaintiff to set forth with some particularity in his pleadings the details of the complaint:

> He cannot be permitted to launch his proceedings and then hope on discovery to be able to amend his pleadings and thereby make his case. In my judgment that is not the purpose of discovery and would be a quite wrong use of the procedural remedy of discovery.

It is of course quite right that a plaintiff with no true foundations of a case should not be entitled to construct them with building bricks exclusively acquired by means of discovery. There is also a difficulty with a case built entirely on hearsay evidence where discovery is sought to cure the inadmissibility of the evidence. (In the instant case the plaintiff could perhaps have surmounted this difficulty on the basis that the demeanour of her informants fell within the *res gestae* doctrine.) Nevertheless, the issue of principle remains: if a plaintiff can establish as a fact that he or she has been defamed but is unable to provide specificity without recourse to discovery, why should discovery be denied? This is not a case of a fishing expedition where the plaintiff has not yet had a catch. There is indeed a fish at the end of the line; the only question relates to its precise description. The plaintiff can truly aver that he or she has been defamed, not merely that this may be the case.

In two decisions in 1993, *McDonagh v Newsgroup Newspapers Ltd*, 23 November 1993 and *Burke v Central Independent Television plc* [1994] 2 IR 61, the Supreme Court made it clear that, to say of any persons within the State that they were active supporters or sympathisers of the Provisional IRA's campaign of violence was 'to defame them in a very serious and important manner' (*per* Finlay CJ, in *Burke*, at 81).

In *Burke*, the Supreme Court, giving priority to protection of the right to life over the right to a good name, held that the defendants were not obliged to deliver up certain documents in proceedings for discovery where doing so might conceivably place informants in jeopardy. The price exacted by the Court was that the defendants should sacrifice their defence of fair comment, since the documents appeared largely to be confined to this issue. The defendants were left free to plead justification if they so desired.

O'Flaherty J's judgment enlarged on the fair comment issue. He gave clear support for Viscount Finlay's characterisation, in *Sutherland v Stopes*

[1925] AC 47, at 62-63, of the 'rolled up' plea as one exclusively of fair comment. The decision of the former Supreme Court in *Campbell v Irish Press Ltd* (1955) 90 ILTR 105 was in accord.

On the question of damages, O'Flaherty J observed that the defeat of a plea of justification, after persistence in it at a trial, 'would call for aggravated damages in the ordinary way'. In his view, the weakness or otherwise of the sources of information on which allegations were based would not affect this head of damages. This may be debated. If, for example, such a seemingly reliable source as the intelligence service were to prove unreliable, it is hard to see why the jury, when assessing aggravated damages, should necessarily be completely insensitive to the rationality of the defendant's reliance. Conversely, a defendant's recklessness in persisting in an allegation that is obviously based on a completely unreliable source should be a reason for enhancing the damages.

It is interesting to discern in O'Flaherty J's attitude little apparent sympathy for the Law Reform Commission' proposal, in its *Report on the Civil Law of Defamation* (LRC 38-1991) that reasonable care should afford a defence (subject to publication of a correction statement) in cases where the plaintiff has suffered no economic loss. (O'Flaherty J has expressed general approval, extra-judicially, for the Commission's proposals:

Burke is an example of how the Commission's proposal regarding reasonable care could yield serious injustice. The allegation that a person is a member of a terrorist organisation no doubt is capable in many cases of causing economic loss, but it also, in some instances, could expose the defamed person's life to danger. The Commission's approach to the contest between property rights and the right to life contrasts strongly with the approach of the Supreme Court in *Burke*.

Fair comment In *Foley v Independent Newspapers (Ireland) Ltd* [1994] 2 ILRM 61, Geoghegan J addressed the important question of the proper scope of the defence of fair comment. The Sunday Independent published an article written by Senator Shane Ross (who was the fourth defendant in the case) in which Senator Ross had commented robustly on the fees charged by the two inspectors into the Greencore saga.

The passage of which the plaintiff, one of the inspectors, complained was as follows:

The inspectors were ripping off the State. They were sent into Greencore to unveil skullduggery. They appear to have done an efficient job, but in the process they have decided to charge fees of an immoral not illegal magnitude.

£250,000 per inspector for six months work is a public scandal in itself. Certainly, a minister could be forgiven for seven or eight impulsive telephone calls when he saw the bill reaching three million mark. Mr. O'Malley has an notoriously short fuse.

The Minister has exposed a piece of institutionalised hypocrisy. The inspectors were appointed to counter the culture of greed; they have turned out to be part of it. Their brief was to protect the tax-payer; they're milking him.

The inspectors' fees are indefensible. They undermine the whole basis of the investigation.; Excesses of capitalism always tread a fine line between legality and illegality. The comparative merits of tax avoidance and tax evasion have no moral difference but simply a legal distinction. These fees come into the tax avoidance category.

The government turns out to be a good mark, an easy target for predators. Public money can be thrown away like confetti, if it is in the name of protecting the tax-payer!

No fees were agreed in advance. The Minister rightly saw the danger. His instincts were correct. It is a pity he offered so many hostages to fortune in his cavalier approach to the solution.

Spain P, in the Circuit Court awarded the maximum sum of £30,000 against the newspaper and Senator Ross, both of whom appealed to the High Court. There was no plea of justification but there was a plea of fair comment in the form of a rolled up plea: cf. McMahon & Binchy, *op. cit.*, 660.

Geoghegan J rejected the defence. The relevant facts had not been truly stated, although they had been described by a series of sentences that were literally accurate. The failure by Senator Ross to state some important facts on which the comment purported to be based, which, had they been mentioned, would falsify or alter the complexion of the facts that were stated was fatal to the defence. The figure of £250,000 was a cumulative one, based on a particular mode and particular rates of remuneration negotiated and agreed with the State within a relatively short period of the inspectors' appointment. Any ordinary reader of the article, unaware of the facts, would have understood the author to be saying that the inspectors had sent in their respective bills without any prior agreement with the State as to the matter of remuneration.

A second reason for rejecting the defence of fair comment was because the offending passage in the article had imputed dishonourable and immoral conduct on the part of the plaintiff as an appointed inspector, especially having regard to his professional position as a senior counsel, where the facts did not warrant this attack. The allegation went further than merely the contention that the plaintiff's fees had been exorbitant: it clearly amounted to the charge that the plaintiff had taken advantage of the State and the taxpayer, 'perceiving the State as a kind of easy target or "soft touch" in order to obtain what he knew was excessive remuneration.' Geoghegan J did not equiparate 'ripping off' with merely 'charging too much'. He observed:

> It is quite true that a patron of a restaurant or a customer of a shop may well complain that the prices are a 'rip-off' without necessarily suggesting immoral conduct on the part of the restaurateur or the shopkeeper but the sentence 'the inspectors were ripping off the State' introduces a direct personal accusation. It implies that the inspectors were stealing in the moral sense though not of course in the sense that a prosecution could be brought under the Larceny Act.

Geoghegan J considered, moreover, that the ordinary reader would interpret the word 'predators' as meaning 'something like moral equivalents of robbers or plunderers,' rather than as an equivalent merely to a protected take-over bidder in the financial world, as Senator Ross had suggested.

It has to be admitted that the conceptual foundations of the defence of fair comment are notoriously unstable. If a comment can be distinguished from an assertion of fact, how can it be that any comment is capable of being defamatory, since it fails to amount to a communication containing any factual proposition about the plaintiff? An expression of outrage or contempt can of course in some contexts suggest an underlying propositional communication, however incoherent, but, if this constitutes actionable defamation, it does so on the basis of its factual propositional content, not on we might call its expostulatory element.

In *Foley*, counsel for the defendants, apart from relying on the common law defence of fair comment, also called in aid Article 40.6.1.i of the Constitution. He referred the court to authorities indicating that the traditional law of contempt of court had been affected by that constitutional provision and he argued that the law of libel might also be affected by it. Geoghegan J was not receptive to this approach:

> Even if that submission as a general proposition is correct any consideration of that particular constitutional provision would have to be balanced by consideration of Article 40.3.2° which requires that the State shall by its laws protect as best it may from unjust attack and in the case of injustice done vindicate the good name of every citizen. As far as this particular case is concerned, I am satisfied that once that balancing is done that plaintiff's entitlement to succeed under the ordinary laws of libel is unaffected.

Geoghegan J thus left to another day the task of entering into a serious

investigation of the constitutional dimensions of speech and reputation and
the balancing of these two entitlements. It could be that Geoghegan J was
suggesting that the Constitution did indeed require a particular calibration to
be attempted and that, although he said nothing about what that calibration
might be, he was willing to conclude that it yielded a result in the plaintiff's
favour. That would seem to be an incorrect interpretation of his remarks,
however. It seems clear that Geoghegan J was of the view that the constitutional provisions left unaffected the application of the common law and
statutory law of libel. He gave no inkling as to why he came to this position
other than to indicate that a balancing process at a constitutional level was
indeed required by the Constitution. The phrase '[a]s far as this particular
case is concerned' might suggest that Geoghegan J envisaged that a partic-
ularised balancing process sensitive to the particular circumstances of every
case, was appropriate. It could also, however, mean that Geoghegan J
regarded the case as raising a generic issue of balancing; we can only guess
at the level of generality that may have been envisaged. It could perhaps be
cast in terms of reputation versus comment or, more specifically, newspaper
commentary versus the reputation of a person in the public spotlight.

Such constitutional implications have been analysed in O'Dell, 'Does
Defamation Value Free Expression?' (1990) 12 *DULJ (ns)* 50, and the whole
issue of the constitutional protection afforded to speech reputation and
privacy interests is insightfully analysed in the same author's 'When Two
Tribes Go To War: Privacy Interests and Media Speech', in Marie McGonagle's *Essays in Law and Media* (forthcoming, 1996). O'Dell criticises
Geoghegan J for having stated, but failed to resolve, the conflict between
speech and good name and for having given no guidance as to how that or
similar conflicts may be resolved in the future. He refers to the Canadian
decision of *Hill v Church of Scientology* (1994) 20 CCLT (2d) 129, affirmed
by the Supreme Court of Canada on 20 July 1995, which reached essentially
the same conclusion as Geoghegan J's but after considerable deliberation and
analysis. On the other hand, in contemporary decisions, the High Court of
Australia reached the opposite conclusion. Irish law has reached the point
that the courts must now squarely face the implications of *Meskell* for the
law of torts and confront the essence of Article 40.6.1.i. One suspects that
we are close to the definitive decision on the subject.

In *Harkin v The Irish Times Ltd*, High Court, 1 April 1993, Carney J, on
appeal from the Circuit Court, dismissed libel proceedings taken by restaurateurs arising from a newspaper article featuring their restaurant. He considered that the article had been hostile and unfair and, in one respect at least,
'seriously and negligently inaccurate', but that did not necessarily make it
actionably defamatory.

Carney J proceeded on the basis that the critic would not be liable for defamation, however severe or 'even, in a sense unjust' the criticism might be, provided the critic did not misrepresent the subject matter of the review, did not go out of her way to attack the character of the proprietor and engaged in criticism that was the honest expression of her real opinion. To lose the defence of fair comment, 'there would have to be misdescription of substance or the introduction of fiction for the purpose of condemnation.'

The plaintiffs had taken great exception to being described, incorrectly, as restaurateurs who served chicken cordon bleu. It did not seem to Carney J that such an assertion could reasonably be said to lower the plaintiffs in the estimation of right-thinking members of society.

The judgment does not give any indication as to whether the tort of injurious falsehood was in issue. In some cases that would offer a more convenient basis of liability than defamation.

Damages Throughout the common law world, courts have in recent years been debating how best to give specificity to criteria for awarding damages in defamation cases. See, for example, *John v MGN Ltd* [1996] 2 All ER 35. In *McEntee v Quinnsworth t/a Crazy Prices*, Supreme Court, 7 December 1993, little light was cast on these principles, the Court preferring to treat the matter very much on its facts.

The plaintiffs, a builder and his fifteen year old son, living near Dundalk, had been forcibly arrested by a store detective employed by the defendant store on suspicion of stealing a miscellany of small items including a packet of rawl plugs, one Pritt Stick, a tape, two tooth brushes and two Cadbury Turkish Delight chocolate bars. They had been taken, resisting, to the manager's office, detained there and interrogated by the Gardaí; their property was searched; eventually they had been released from detention.

Their proceedings against the store had met with startling success in the High Court. The jury had awarded the father £250,000 and the son £100,000 for slander. They had also awarded the father £5,000 for false imprisonment and £5,000 for assault. The son had been awarded £15,000 for false imprisonment and £5,000 for assault.

The defendants' appeal against the quantum of damages was successful. Finlay CJ (Egan and Blayney JJ concurring) considered that there could be no doubt that in a relatively small country town in Ireland, for a man whose credit and general reputation in the neighbourhood were of very considerable importance to his trade, to be seen arrested by the officers of a supermarket and to be heard by even a limited number of people as being accused of theft was a very serious blow to his reputation and a very serious damage to his standing. It was equally clear that the continued attempt to justify an accusation right up to a full and public hearing in the High Court which might easily attract significant publicity was an aggravating factor of considerable significance. Bearing all these matters in mind, however, the Chief Justice was not satisfied that there were any grounds on which the assessment of a figure of £250,000 for damages for slander could be supported, Although the Supreme Court in *Barrett v The Independent Newspapers Ltd* [1986] IR 13 had set out how reluctantly an appellate court should approach an assessment of damages in defamation cases made by a jury, it was clear that the jury's assessment of the damages for slander had gone 'well beyond the top of any range which would be appropriate in principle for the nature of the accusation made, even making full allowance for the defence of justification.'

Finlay CJ was satisfied that the appropriate level of damages for slander would not exceed £75,000. He considered himself obliged to take the assessment of the jury as an indication that they would have viewed the case as one of the more serious of the type of accusation it involved and that therefore, in his assessment of damages he 'should allow for the top of the appropriate range.' The figure of £75,000, in his estimation, represented that figure. When approaching the assessment of whether the amounted awarded to the son was appropriate the Chief Justice considered that he should have regard to the fact that the jury had placed 'a relatively high figure upon the damage to his reputation' and also that the jury assessed it as being significantly less serious than that attached to his father. He did not however, see any logical ground on which he should be in any way bound by the relativity of their two figures. He reduced the quantum of damages from £100,000 to £60,000. The jury's awards to both plaintiffs in respect of false imprisonment and assault were not disturbed on appeal.

In *McDonagh v Newsgroup Newspapers Ltd*, Supreme Court, 23 November 1993, the plaintiff, a member of the Irish Bar, had been briefed by the Irish Government to attend as its representative and observer at the inquest held in Gibraltar upon the deaths of Mairéad Farrell, Sean Savage and Daniel McCann, following an intervention by the Special Air Service regiment of the British Army, very shortly after they had entered Gibraltar. Allegations had been made that their deaths constituted part of a 'shoot-to-kill' policy on the part of the British Army and that unnecessary force had been used. (The European Court of Human Rights subsequently held against Britain on this issue.) The *Sun* newspaper had published a piece criticising the participation of the plaintiff and of the representatives of other organisations (including the National Council for Civil Liberties and Amnesty International) in robust terms.

The plaintiff sued for libel. The jury found that the article had conveyed that the plaintiff was a left-wing spy; that he had attended the inquest for purposes other than the fair and accurate reporting of the proceedings; that he was a sympathiser with terrorist causes, unsuited for and incapable of performing the duties for which he had been appointed by the Irish Government; that his conduct was such as to cause outrage to British Army officers charged with the duty of combating terrorism; and that he was biased, lacking in integrity and incapable of exercising sound judgment. The jury awarded the plaintiff £90,000.

The defendants appealed unsuccessfully to the Supreme Court. Finlay CJ (O'Flaherty, Egan, Blayney and Denham JJ concurring) said, with regard to the claim that the plaintiff was a sympathiser with terrorist causes, that he was satisfied that there were 'not very many general classifications of defamatory accusation which at present in Ireland, in the minds of right-minded people, would be considered significantly more serious'. That seriousness might be somewhat aggravated by the plaintiff's role, as a barrister, in the administration of justice. The other meanings found by the jury to flow from the defendant's assertions constituted in their combined effect an extremely grave accusation of professional misconduct on the part of the plaintiff. The Chief Justice considered that the amount awarded by the jury, 'though undoubtedly high and at the top of the permissible range', should not be disturbed.

DAMAGES

General Damages

(a) Facial disfigurement In *Basmajian v Haire*, High Court, 2 April 1993, Barr J awarded the defendant, suing on a counter-claim, £190,000 general damages for serious injuries she received in a car accident at the age of twenty-four. These injuries included fractures of her skull, jaw palate and femur, a broken nose, loss of hearing, scars to her face, memory loss and a substantial change of personality, involving depression and loss of confidence. Barr J commented that facial disfigurement was 'particularly distressful for a young woman'.

In *Walsh v Ryan*, High Court, 12 February 1993, which we discuss earlier in the Chapter above, 558, in relating to publicans' negligence, Lavan J awarded £30,000 general damages to the victim of a violent assault whose injuries included serious scarring to her face, arm, hand and body, which required one hundred and ten stitches and a skin graft to her arm. Lavan J described the scar on her face as 'noticeable and disfiguring'; it was permanent and would not benefit from plastic surgery.

(b) Loss of hearing In *Barry v Nitrigin Éireann Teo* [1994] 2 ILRM 522, Costello J held that £60,000 would be the appropriate quantum of damages if the defendants had been entirely responsible for causing the plaintiff, their employee, to sustain a moderate hearing loss, which would remain for the

rest of his life. The plaintiff would have to wear a hearing aid. Costello J did not think that the condition would deteriorate, except for the normal inevitable processes of ageing.

(c) Dental injury In *McNamara v Kennedy*, High Court, 13 May 1993, Costello J awarded £45,000 general damages where the plaintiff sustained injury to her teeth in a traffic accident. She had lost six teeth and was obliged to wear a denture and a bridge. Costello J was satisfied that there was no physical basis for her complaint of constant saliva in her mouth. He thought it probable that when the case was over the plaintiff would find that she could use her denture without any discomfort. The plaintiff had 'behaved very unwisely indeed' in going from dentist to dentist over the seven years since the accident but this did not amount, in Costello J's view, to contributory negligence or a failure to mitigate damage. (The negligent failure to mitigate damage is characterised as contributory negligence by s. 34(2)(b) of the Civil Liability Act 1961 as a result of Professor Glanville Williams' advocacy: see McMahon & Binchy, *op. cit.*, 358).

(d) Finger injury In *Dyer v Dublin Corporation*, High Court, 10 June 1993, Morris J awarded £30,000 general damages (reduced by half on account of the plaintiff's contributory negligence) for the amputation of the tip of the plaintiff's right ring finger. The operation had been followed by two days' treatment in the hospital, and by periodic attendance to deal with infection of the finger and the removal of the fragment of nail which grew out of the retained nail bed. There was the possibility that the nail might fail to regrow, which would involve a further procedure for its removal.

(e) Injury to foot In *Dunne v Honeywell Control Systems Ltd*, Supreme Court, 1 July 1993, there was an appeal against quantum of damages only from the High Court decision, [1991] ILRM 595, which we discussed in the 1990 Review, 500-5. Barron J had awarded £125,000 general damages where the plaintiff, aged twenty-eight, had injured his left foot. He had experienced much pain, his toes began to claw and the ball and sole of the foot had become hypersensitive. A successful operation had dealt with the hypersensitivity. Another operation rectified the clawing but the plaintiff had a permanent limp and was destined to develop secondary arthritis in ten to fifteen years, which would require an operation for the fusion of the affected joints.

Invoking McCarthy J's dictum, in *Reddy v Bates* [1984] IR 197, at 203-7, that there should be a difference of at least 25% in so far as general damages were concerned before the Supreme Court should vary an award, Blayney J (Finlay CJ and OFlaherty J concurring) held that the damages, whilst 'at the top end of the scale for an injury of this kind, and perhaps over it', were not so excessive as to warrant interference.

In *Murphy v White Sands Hotel*, High Court, 21 May 1993, Flood J awarded £98,600 for pain and suffering where the plaintiff, a 25-year-old woman, received injuries to her foot, which resulted in severe and lasting pain. He noted that the plaintiff came '[with]in that small group of patients who have a continuance of pain which does not react to treatment[;] the pain undoubtedly is affecting her mood and her lifestyle, her capacity to work and her enjoyment both of her home and her work and social occasions and activities.' The prognosis was discouraging: the pain was likely to continue into the foreseeable future and there was 'no realistic basis upon which she c[ould] hope for even a partial recovery.'

(f) Psychiatric disturbance Elsewhere in the chapter (above, 549-50), we consider the topical issue of liability for causing post-traumatic stress disorder. The controversy about the parameters of liability relates in essence to plaintiffs who have not in fact been otherwise physically injured by the defendant. It has always been plain beyond argument that post-traumatic stress disorder following on physical injury to the plaintiff negligently caused by the defendant should engender compensation.

In *Hamilton v The Office of Public Works*, High Court, 22 December 1993, a question of diagnosis arose in this context. The plaintiff had been physically injured in circumstances where his employers were guilty of negligence to him: see above, 566. He claimed that he had developed a condition of post-traumatic stress disorder and sought compensation for it, over and above the compensation due to him on account of the original physical injury. There was a conflict of expert evidence. Morris J preferred the evidence of the defendants' expert witness. There was no dispute that the plaintiff was suffering from anxiety and stress reaction; the defendants' expert witness attributed this to certain events that had occurred in the plaintiff's career rather than to the trauma of the accident. He was of the opinion that the plaintiff had none of the classic symptoms of post-traumatic stress disorder, such as nightmares, flashbacks to the event, social withdrawal and sweating.

In *McGowan v Wicklow County Council*, High Court, 27 May 1993, Morris J awarded £30,000 general damages where the plaintiff suffered no significant physical injuries in an industrial accident but sustained chronic post-traumatic stress disorder, involving insomnia, nightmares, flashbacks, anxiety and poor concentration. Expert evidence was given to the effect that, in the vast majority of such cases, a recovery is to be expected within five years and that litigation plays a major part in prolonging the condition. Morris J was happy to accept this evidence.

It is relatively rare for a plaintiff to appeal successfully to the Supreme Court seeking an increase in the amount of compensation awarded in personal injury litigation in the High Court. This happened in *Sheriff v Dowling*, Supreme Court, 26 May 1993. The plaintiff had been awarded £90,000 for general damages. At the time of the accident in 1985 she was twenty years old. She received serious back injuries which did not respond well to treatment. Spinal fusion was not successfully completed and pain persisted even after she had had a metal implant in her spine. In spite of a full range of medical treatment, the plaintiff continued to have significant pain and disability; she occasionally wore a brace and used crutches. Her condition resulted in psychiatric disturbance and depression, involving in-patient treatment. She had a difficult pregnancy followed by the birth of her child by Caesarean section which was attributable to her condition.

The Supreme Court increased the sum awarded for general damages to £135,000. Egan J (O'Flaherty and Blayney JJ concurring) observed that the Supreme Court should not interfere unless the amount awarded by the trial judge differed 'substantially' from what the Supreme Court itself would have awarded. Invoking McCarthy J's dictum in *Reddy v Bates* [1984] ILRM 197, at 205 as to the requirement of a difference of at least 25% in so far as general damages were concerned before the Supreme Court should vary an award, Egan J stated that such a difference existed in the present case.

In *Doyle v Fox*, High Court, 10 March 1993, the plaintiff claimed damages, *inter alia*, for depression and for the deterioration of his relationship with his wife, resulting from injuries in an accident caused by the defendant's negligence. He had disclosed to a medical witness that he was drinking forty to fifty pints a week. In awarding him £24,000 general damages, Flood J made it clear that he considered that the plaintiff had exaggerated his depression. He was of the view that 'if [the plaintiff] moved the decimal point a place to the left in the number of pints he drinks per week the depression might be considerably alleviated and indeed that his relationship with his wife would no doubt improve.'

Special damages   In *Sheriff v Dowling*, Supreme Court, 26 May 1993, the Supreme Court held that the trial judge had been mistaken in calculating damages on the assumption that the plaintiff, an executive working at Maynooth University, would have retired at the age of forty six if she had not been injured in the accident which gave rise to the claim. She was a married woman with four children. Egan J (O'Flaherty and Blayney JJ concurring) acknowledged that it was impossible to say with any degree of certainty how long the plaintiff would have worked, but the assumption that a married woman would retire from gainful employment at such an early age seemed to him to be 'somewhat unfair and not justified by the evidence in th[e] case.'

The increase of the quantum for loss of earnings from £27,000 to £40,000 suggests that Egan J pitched the retirement date at around fifty one. Some discussion as to why this age was considered appropriate might have been helpful.

INTERFERENCE WITH ECONOMIC INTERESTS

In *Kent Adhesive Products Co t/a Kapco v Ryan*, High Court, 5 November 1993, the parties had originally been engaged in a joint venture to distribute library products in Ireland. This had not worked out successfully. Some time later, the defendants had incorporated another company. The plaintiff company sought an interlocutory injunction to restrain, *inter alia*, the infringement of its patent rights and the commission of injurious falsehood, passing off and slander of goods.

As to the injurious falsehood, the plaintiff claimed that the defendants had disseminated incorrect information that the plaintiff had ceased to trade in Ireland. The defendants gave an explanation (not enlarged upon in Costello J's judgment) which, if accepted on oral evidence, would constitute the defence of absence of malice: cf McMahon & Binchy, *op. cit.*, 674. Costello J was, however, satisfied that the plaintiff had shown that there was a case of substance to be tried.

Similarly, the plaintiff had raised a substantial issue in relation to passing off. The plaintiff alleged that the defendants had represented the company they had established to be the successor to the original company.

The third matter was in relation to slander of goods. The plaintiff claimed that the defendants' company had suggested that its goods were more 'environmentally friendly than the plaintiff's goods' and that this amounted to slander: *per* Costello J, at p. 7 of his judgment. Costello J did not think that the court could so reasonably hold and he was not satisfied that the plaintiff had made out a case of substance to be tried in relation to slander of goods:

> What was said in the letters, it seems to me, was the ordinary type of puffing remarks that are expected in the commercial world. I do not think that they could amount in any other way to defamation.

In treating slander of goods as a tort separate from injurious falsehood, Costello J was adopting an independent approach: cf. J Fleming, *The Law of Torts* (8th ed., 1992), 710. The conventional stance is to divide litigation in this context into injurious falsehood, on the one hand, and defamation (comprising libel and slander), on the other.

Although the plaintiff had made out a case of substance to be tried, Costello J declined to grant an interlocutory injunction, since the defendants had expressed a willingness, without prejudice, to give undertakings that they would commit no actionable wrong. Costello J required an undertaking from them to print their business letters in accordance with the Business Names Registration Act — and to write to customers to whom they had already written, explaining the true position as to the plaintiff company.

In *An Bord Tráchtála v Waterford Foods plc*, High Court, 25 November 1992, Keane J had to consider how the principles relating to the tort of passing off apply in an international context where the plaintiff is not a conventional business. An Bord Tráchtála, established under the Export Promotion Act 1959, was charged with the task of developing and promoting the export of Irish produce throughout the world. It designed a logo to assist it's marketing of Irish agri-food products abroad, by the creation of a single identity representative of all Irish food-related products. The logo consisted of a symbol representing the sun rising over a valley of green hills leading down to the sea; it was accompanied by the legend 'Food Ireland'. The plaintiffs prominently displayed the logo on all their exhibition stands at international trade fairs, and in supermarket displays abroad, as well as in advertising at home and abroad.

The defendant, a company with a range of milk and cheese products sold extensively abroad, developed a logo consisting of a yellow sun above a blue and green valley, with the accompanying legend 'Waterford Foods.' They consulted with the plaintiffs, seeking to produce a model that would satisfy the plaintiffs' fears of potential confusion with their logo. Ultimately, when negotiations broke down, the plaintiffs sought an interlocutory injunction against the use of the defendants' logo, on the basis that it constituted passing off.

A crucial threshold issue was whether the fact that the plaintiffs' case rested primarily on the dangers affecting the use of their logo for the promotion of their products *abroad* should be a ground for the court's declining to hear the case on the basis of lack of jurisdictional competence. According to the traditional rule of private international law expressed in *Phillips v Eyre* (1870) LR 6 QB 1, the Irish court would have jurisdiction if the wrong would have been actionable if committed here and the act constituting the wrong was not justifiable by the law of the place where it was done. This rule has come under sustained criticism in recent years. Nonetheless Keane J thought it proper to apply it in the instant case. In the Conflicts of Law chapter, above, 139, we examine this aspect of Keane J's judgment.

On the basis of the rule, the question that required resolution at the interlocutory stage was whether the plaintiffs had established that there was a serious issue to be tried as to whether the activities of the defendants in Britain would, if carried on in Ireland, amount to the tort of passing off.

Keane J was satisfied that the plaintiffs had not met this requirement. The first essential in a passing off action was for the plaintiff to prove that the name or other indicia on which he relied had been well known in connection with a business in which he had goodwill, or with goods connected with that business, and had been distinctive of those goods or that business. The authorities cited to the Court made it clear that the word 'business' was to be widely construed and the fact that the plaintiffs were not engaged in any trade or profession in the conventional sense would not of itself be an obstacle. But the plaintiffs had not adduced any evidence that the logo on which they relied was well known, or known at all, in Ireland or any other country in connection with them or any business in which they might be regarded as engaged, principally the promotion of Irish exports abroad. Nor was there the slightest reason why it should be so known:

> [F]rom the point of view of the plaintiffs, provided the logo achieves, or helps to achieve, its object of identifying Irish food products abroad with a pure and pollution-free environment, it is hardly a major consid- eration that the name and reputation of the sponsoring body is not known to the prospective customers in Birmingham or Glasgow. It is 'Food Ireland' that the logo seeks to promote, not 'An Bord Trachtála'.

Even if it could be said that there was a cause of action available to the plaintiffs, provided they could demonstrate some risk of confusion that would lead people in Britain to suppose that the defendants' products enjoyed some unique and official form of endorsement from the plaintiffs (which Keane J described as 'a somewhat innovative claim, to put it no more strongly'), the plaintiffs had failed to adduce any independent evidence as to the risk of such confusion. If was not enough for the plaintiffs to say that specific examples of confusion would not be available until the defendants' logo was launched. If the plaintiffs' apprehensions were justified, it was the defendants' competitors in the British export market who would be primarily affected by the alleged similarity between the two logos; but there was 'simply no evidence' that any of these firms shared the plaintiffs' concern as to the possibility of confusion arising.

Finally, Keane J applied the common-sense test of the first impression produced by the offending logo when placed side by side with the plaintiffs' logo. This test had been favoured by Whitford J in *Laura Ashley Ltd v Coloroll Ltd* (1987) RPC 1. Keane J did not consider the essential feature of the plaintiffs' logo to be the symbol: it was the symbol in conjunction with the words 'Food Ireland'. The possibility of any significant confusion, even supposing it was actionable, was in Keane J's view remote.

Accordingly, Keane J refused to grant an interlocutory injunction. It was thus unnecessary for him to consider the other arguments that had been addressed to him as to the adequacy of damages and the balance of convenience.

TRADE DISPUTES

In the Labour Law Chapter, above, 377-8, we analyse Lardner J's decision in *Draycar Ltd v Whelan* [1993] ELR 119 relating to the entitlement to picket under the Industrial Relations Act 1990.

Transport

AIR TRANSPORT

Aer Lingus restructuring   The Air Companies (Amendment) Act 1993 authorised the investment by the State of a further £175m in Aer Lingus, the State airline, as part of the restructuring plan for the airline, commonly called the Cahill Plan. The Plan, named after the executive chairman of Aer Lingus, had been approved by a decision of the Commission of the European Communities in November 1993. The 1993 Act also provides for the establishment of a holding company, Aer Lingus Group plc. The 1993 Act came into effect on 22 December 1993 on its signature by the President.

Air fares: notification   The European Communities (Fares and Rates for Air Services) Regulations 1993 (SI No. 256) gave full effect to Council Regulation 2409/92 by requiring Community air carriers to notify their air fares on scheduled services to and from Ireland to the Department of Transport, Energy and Communications within a period of 24 hours prior to the air fares coming into effect. The Regulations also provide for a maximum fine of £1,000 on summary conviction for failure to comply with an instruction to withdraw any air fare issued by the Minister or the European Commission under Council Regulation 2409/92. The 1993 Regulations also revoked the European Communities (Scheduled Air Fares) Regulations 1991.

Air operator authorisations, certificates and licences   The Air Navigation (Air Operators' Certificate) Order 1993 (SI No. 325) introduced, in accordance with Council Regulation 3922/91, a requirement for a commercial aircraft operator to be issued with a certificate attesting to the operator's operational and technical competence to conduct an air service. The Air Services Authorisation Order 1993 (SI No. 326), which revoked the 1966 Order of the same title (as amended: see the 1992 Review, 620), grants a general authorisation for certain categories of air operators, including those which possess an operating licence under Council Regulation 2408/92. The Air Navigation and Transport Act 1965 (Section 8) Regulations 1993 (SI No. 324) introduced, in accordance with Council Regulation 2407/92, provisions concerning the licensing of air carriers and fees for operating licences. Finally, the Air Navigation and Transport Act 1965 (Section 8) (No. 2)

Regulations 1993 (SI No. 325) prescribe the basis on which authorisations for various types of flights by air carriers may be granted to air carriers who would not qualify for such authorisations under s. 8 of the 1965 Act.

Civil subsonic jets: noise	The European Communities (Restriction of Civil Subsonic Jet Aeroplane Operations) Regulations 1993 (SI No. 130) implement Directive 92/14/EEC and provide that, subject to certain exceptions, civil subsonic jets must meet certain noise specifications in order to operate in the State. The requirements are effective for some aircraft from 1 April 1995 while others must meet the requirements only by 1 April 2002.

Irish Aviation Authority	The Irish Aviation Authority Act 1993 provides for the establishment of a new entity, the Irish Aviation Authority, to perform functions concerning air traffic control formerly exercised by the Department of Transport, Energy and Communications. Part II of the Act (ss. 11 to 45) contains standard provisions concerning the establishment and composition of the Authority and its staffing. Despite its title, the Authority is not, strictly speaking, a State body, but is a company incorporated under the Act and in accordance with the Companies Acts 1963 to 1990: see ss. 11 and 12 of the Act. However, in many respects the Authority has the attributes normally associated with a State body, including close control by the Minister for of Transport, Energy and Communications: see s. 17 of the Act.

Part III of the Act (ss. 46 to 57) relates to the transfer to the Authority of the functions concerning the Eurocontrol Convention, that is, the 1960 Brussels International Convention relating to Co-Operation for the Safety of Air Navigation, as amended. The Eurocontrol Convention was incorporated into Irish law by the Air Navigation (Eurocontrol) Acts 1963 to 1983, which have now been repealed and replaced by Part III of the 1993 Act.

Part IV of the 1993 Act (ss. 58 to 63) concerns the role of the Authority in connection with other international Conventions on air navigation, notably the Chicago Convention: that is the 1944 Convention on International Civil Aviation, as amended. The Chicago Convention was incorporated into Irish law by the Air Navigation and Transport Act 1946.

Part V (ss. 64 to 74) of the 1993 Act deals with a number of miscellaneous matters, including the investigation of air accidents, the detention of aircraft and the prosecution of offences under the Act. Under s. 65 of the Act, substantial new investigative powers are given to the Authority, though these are without prejudice to existing powers of officers of the Minister for Transport, Energy and Communications. S. 66 of the Act provides that the power of detention of aircraft is transferred to the Authority. Power to initiate summary prosecutions is also given to the Authority in certain cases by s. 73. However, it is also clear that substantial powers concerning air transport remain with the Minister for Transport, Energy and Communications.

The bulk of the 1993 Act came into effect on 8 December 1993, pursuant to the Irish Aviation Authority Act 1993 (Commencement) Order 1993 (SI No. 355), but the Authority itself did not come into being until 1 January 1994, pursuant to the Irish Aviation Authority Act 1993 (Vesting Day) Order 1993 (SI No. 414).

Protected area The Air Navigation (Protected Area) Order 1993 (SI No. 205), made under s. 14 of the Air Navigation and Transport Act 1950, provided for a 300 metres radius protected area around certain navigational equipment in County Clare used by aircraft flying to or from Shannon Airport or within the Shannon Flight Information Region. Proposed developments within this protected area require a permit from the Minister for Transport, Energy and Communications.

Sanctions Although the European Communities (Prohibition of Trade with the Federal Republic of Yugoslavia (Serbia and Montenegro)) Regulations 1993 (SI No. 144) (see the Commercial Law chapter 63, above) revoked the Air Services (Authorisation) (Amendment) (No. 2) Order 1992 (see the 1992 Review, 620), the restrictions on civil aircraft flights to Serbia and Montenegro contained in the 1992 Order continue under the terms of Council Regulation 990/93, which the 1993 Regulations implemented. The Air Services Authorisation Order 1993 (SI No. 326) (discussed in a different context above, 583) gave effect to similar restrictions on civil aircraft flights to Libya under the terms of Council Regulation 945/92 and also revoked the Air Services (Authorisation) (Amendment) Order 1992 (see the 1992 Review, 620). It is of interest that two Council Regulations dealing with similar topics were implemented in Ireland by different statutory means.

INTERNATIONAL CARRIAGE OF GOODS BY ROAD

CMR: Croatia The International Carriage of Goods by Road Act 1990 (CMR Contracting Party) Order 1993 (SI No. 94) adds Croatia to the list of CMR Contracting Parties specified in the International Carriage of Goods by Road Act 1990 (CMR Contracting Parties) Order 1991. See also the 1991 Review, 461 and the 1992 Review, 620.

Perishable foodstuffs The International Carriage of Perishable Foodstuffs (Consolidation) Regulations 1993 (SI No. 188) consolidated all existing Regulations on this topic. The 1993 Regulations were made under the

International Carriage of Perishable Foodstuffs Act 1987 (see the 1987 Review, 348). The 1993 Regulations revoked Regulations of the same title from 1989 (1989 Review, 446) 1991 (1991 Review, 461) and 1993 (SI No. 108).

TIR Carnet The European Communities (TIR Carnet and ATA Carnet-Transit) Regulations 1993 (SI No. 61) give effect to Council Regulation 719/91 and Commission Regulation 1593/91 and provide for fines of up to 1,000 and for the forfeiture of goods where any person fails to produce goods covered by a TIR Carnet or an ATA Carnet at the Customs Office at the point of exit from the European Community/Union or at the office of destination within the Community/Union, as the case may be.

MERCHANT SHIPPING

Collisions The Collision Regulations (Ships and Water Craft on the Water) (Amendment) Order 1993 (SI No. 287) amended the 1984 Order of the same title in order to clarify the use by vessels of inshore traffic zones, which are the areas that lie between the coast and the lanes prescribed in the traffic separation scheme.

Competition rules The European Communities (Application of the Rules on Competition to Maritime Transport) Regulations 1993 (SI No. 386) are discussed in the Commercial Law chapter, 47, above.

Fire drills and life-saving training The Merchant Shipping (Musters and Training) (Amendment) Rules 1993 (SI No. 7) amend the 1990 Rules of the same title (1990 Review, 474) and give effect to 1991 amendments to the 1974 IMO Convention for the Safety of Lives at Sea (SOLAS), whose essential requirements were incorporated into Irish law by the Merchant Shipping Act 1981. More specific requirements than heretofore are laid down on fire drills as well as in training crews in the use of life-saving appliances and fire-fighting equipment.

Life-saving appliances The Merchant Shipping (Life-Saving Appliances) Rules 1993 (SI No. 380) imposed new requirements concerning life-saving appliances in respect of certain classes of ships built after 1 July 1986. The Merchant Shipping (Life-Saving Appliances) Rules 1983 (Amendment) Rules 1993 (SI No. 381) amended the 1983 Rules concerning life-saving appliances in respect of certain classes of ships built before 1 July 1986. Finally, the Merchant Shipping (Life-Saving Appliances) Rules 1983

(Amendment) (No. 2) Rules 1993 (SI No. 382) also amended the 1983 Rules concerning life-saving appliances in respect of certain classes of ships built after 1 July 1986. All three sets of Regulations gave effect to 1983 and 1988 amendments to the 1974 IMO SOLAS Convention referred to above.

Musters: fishing vessels The Merchant Shipping (Musters) (Fishing Vessels) Regulations 1993, made under the Merchant Shipping Act 1992 (see the 1992 Review, 625-6), introduced requirements for musters, preparations for emergencies, inspection and maintenance of life saving and fire fighting equipment and the recording of particulars of these in vessels' logbooks.

Pilot ladders and hoists The Merchant Shipping (Pilot Ladders and Hoists) Rules 1993 (SI No. 55) provided for more detailed requirements in relation to provision of pilot ladders and hoists and revoked the 1967 Rules of the same title in order to give effect to 1991 amendments to the 1974 IMO SOLAS Convention, referred to above. The 1993 Rules also revoked the 1983 Rules of the same title, but only in respect of ships on which equipment and arrangements for pilot transfer are installed on or after 1 January 1994.

Salvage and wrecks The Merchant Shipping (Salvage and Wreck) Act 1993 incorporated into Irish law the 1989 International Convention on Salvage, and also provided for a number of miscelleaneous changes necessary to the Merchant Shipping Acts 1894 to 1992 and the Harbours Act 1946. Brian Hutchinson provides an insightful and comprehensive analysis of the background to the 1993 Act in his Annotation for *Irish Current Law Statutes Annotated*. The 1993 Act came into effect on 1 March 1994: see the Merchant Shipping (Salvage and Wreck) Act 1993 (Commencement) Order 1994 (SI No. 32 of 1994).

Part II of the 1993 Act (ss. 7 to 11) empowers authorised officers to intervene where a vessel is in distress. Such authorised officers, appointed by the Minister for the Marine under s. 3 of the Act, would include officers of the Irish Marine Emergency Service, harbour masters or surveyors from the Marine Survey Office in the Department of the Marine. S. 10 of the 1993 Act also confers wide powers on a member of the Garda Síochána to search, seize and detain any person or property which the garda believes may have been plundered from a vessel in distress.

Part III of the 1993 Act (ss. 12 to 38) contains the main provisions giving effect to the 1989 International Convention on Salvage. Part III also has the effect of repealing and replacing ss. 510 to 517, contained in Part IX, of the Merchant Shipping Act 1894 as well as the Maritime Conventions Act 1911. Part III of the 1993 Act updates substantially the provisions concerning salvage, including the powers and duties of a salvor and the basis for judicial compensation of salvors where disputes arise.

Part IV of the 1993 Act (ss. 39 to 58) deals with wrecked and stranded vessels and had the effect of repealing those provisions of Part IX of the Merchant Shipping Act 1894, ss. 518 to 571, which had not already been repealed by Part III of the 1993 Act. A major element of Part IV of the Act concerns the function of the Receiver of Wrecks, who acts in a type of quasi-arbitral role concerning the disposal of wrecks and reward for salvors. It may be noted that s. 51 of the 1993 Act requires, for the first time, that the owner of a wreck must remove it if it is a navigational hazard. S. 54 of the Act amends s. 57 of the Harbours Act 1946 by expanding the powers of a harbour authority to remove a wreck in the seaward approaches to a harbour.

Part V of the 1993 Act (ss. 59 to 66) contains provisions for offences and penalties under the Act, but also includes some miscellaneous provisions of a general nature. Thus, s. 66 confers for the first time a power in the Minister for the Marine to make Regulations in relation to the burial of human remains at sea.

RAIL TRANSPORT

Competition rules   The European Communities (Application of the Rules on Competition to Rail and Road Transport) Regulations 1993 (SI No. 416) are referred to in the Commercial Law chapter, 48, above.

ROAD TRAFFIC

Roads Act 1993: commencement   The broad elements of the Roads Act 1993 are, *inter alia*, discussed under various sub-headings in this section. The provisions of the 1993 Act were brought into force on various dates between 1 August 1993 and 1 January 1994. The relevant commencement Orders were the Roads Act 1993 (Commencement) Order 1993 (SI No. 197), the Roads Act 1993 (Commencement) (No. 2) Order 1993 (SI No. 406), the Roads Act 1993 (Commencement) Order 1994 (SI No. 118 of 1994) and the Roads Act 1993 (Commencement) (No. 2) Order 1994 (SI No. 399 of 1994).

Classification and maintenance of public roads   Part II of the Roads Act 1993 (ss. 10 to 15) updated the system for the classification of public roads as well as dealing with their maintenance. Previous legislation provided for classification into main roads, county roads, urban roads, trunk roads and link roads. S. 10 of the 1993 Act rationalises these classifications into three categories: national, regional and local roads. S. 13 of the 1993 Act provides that, subject to the functions performed by the National Roads Authority under Part III of the Act (see below, 591), the maintenance and construction of all national and regional roads in an administrative county remains the function of the local authority in that area. S. 13 imposes exclusive maintenance rights on local authorities in respect of local roads. S. 14 of the 1993 Act requires local authorities to enter into agreements and arrangements under s. 59 of the Local Government Act 1955 concerning national roads where requested to do so by the National Roads Authority. Existing agreements and arrangements between local authorities under the 1955 Act concerning regional and local roads may be continued in force under the 1993 Act, but any such agreements concerning national roads require the consent of the National Roads Authority.

Competition rules The European Communities (Application of the Rules on Competition to Rail and Road Transport) Regulations 1993 (SI No. 416) are referred to in the Commercial Law chapter, 48, above.

Construction standards The European Communities (Motor Vehicles Type Approval) Regulations 1993 (SI No. 139) further amended the Regulations of 1978 of the same title to take account of EC Directives 92/62/EEC, 92/97/EEC and 92/114/EEC, which lay down technical specifications for the construction of motor vehicles. The Road Traffic (Control of Supply of Vehicles) (Amendment) Regulations 1993 (SI No. 301) amend the 1991 Regulations of the same title (1991 Review, 463) by updating the list of Regulations which must be complied with to meet the requirements of s. 8 of the Road Traffic Act 1968 as well as the 1991 Regulations themselves.

Cycleways S. 68 of the Roads Act 1993 concerns the regulation of cycleways.

Dangerous structures and trees S. 70 of the Roads Act 1993 provides for the regulation of dangerous structures and trees on or near any public road.

Duty of care of road users S. 67(1) of the Roads Act 1993 imposes a general duty of care on any person using a public road to take reasonable care for his own safety and for that of any other person using the public road. S. 67(2) of the Act states that it shall be the duty of a person using a public road to take all reasonable measures to avoid: (a) injury to himself or to any other person using the public road; and (b) damage to property owned or used by him or by any other person using the public road. While this general duty in large part merely reiterates the common law duty of road users and contains none of the detail to be found in the Road Traffic General Bye-Laws Regulations 1964, as amended (see, for example, immediately below), s. 67

of the 1993 Act provides for an extremely important statement of general principle. This, no doubt, will become a common part of pleadings in future civil claims arising from road traffic accidents.

Emergency services   The Road Traffic General Bye-Laws (Amendment) Regulations 1993 (SI No. 63) amended the Road Traffic General Bye-Laws Regulations 1964 by inserting a new Bye-Law 43 which confers certain exemptions from a number of provisions of the 1964 Bye-laws. The exemptions apply to fire brigade vehicles, ambulances and Garda vehicles being used in emergency situations 'where such use does not thereby endanger the safety of road users.' The exemptions relate to Bye-Laws 6 to 13, 15 to 22, 25(2), 28 and 40(1)(a), the latter inserted by the Road Traffic General Bye-Laws (Amendment) Regulations 1983.

Emission levels   The European Communities (Mechanically Propelled Vehicle Emission Control) Regulations 1993 (SI No. 363) prohibit the issue of first licences for certain new vehicles from 1 January 1994, unless they comply with the air pollutant emission control requirements specified in Directives 91/542/EEC and 92/53/EEC, as amended by Directive 93/81/EEC. Certain limited exemptions up to 30 September 1994 are provided for as well as penalties for non-compliance. For previous Regulations, see the 1992 Review, 627.

Horses on road   The Road Traffic General Bye-Laws (Amendment) Regulations 1993 (SI No. 294) (which should surely be titled the Road Traffic General Bye-Laws (Amendment) (No. 2) Regulations 1993 in view of SI No. 63, above) amend Bye-Law 32 of the 1964 Bye-Laws by providing that any person (whether mounted or on foot) who leads a horse on a road shall do so with their left hand, keeping the horse between themselves and the left hand side of the road. The original Bye-Law 32 had simply provided that any person riding a horse on a road shall do so on the left hand side of the road.

Licences   The Road Traffic (Licensing of Drivers) (Amendment) Regulations 1993 (SI No. 5) amended the 1989 Regulations of the same title by providing for changes in the conditions applying to the granting of provisional licences for motor cyclists. They also extended from five to 10 years the period within which driving licence holders may renew their licences.

Motor cycle helmets   The Road Traffic (Construction, Equipment and Use of Vehicles) (Amendment) (No. 2) Regulations 1993 (SI No. 322) lay down standards in respect of safety helmets for motor cyclists and their pillion passengers. They delete references to obsolete standards and recognise the standards of any member State of the European Community and also certain UN standards.

Motorways, busways and protected roads Part IV of the Roads Act 1993 (ss. 43 to 55) contains additional measures concerning the regulation of motorways, busways and protected roads, the latter referring to roads in respect of which particular restrictions are applied. S. 47 of the Act provides for a road authority making proposed schemes to the Minister for the Environment concerning motorways, busways or protected roads. Such schemes must be in a specified form and will only come into effect on being approved by the Minister under s. 49 of the Act. Ss. 50 and 51 contain provisions concerning the environmental impact statement and environmental impact assessments required in accordance with the EC Directives in this area: see the 1988 Review, 314, and the 1989 Review, 447-8.

National Roads Authority Part III of the Roads Act 1993 (ss. 16 to 42) provides for the establishment of the National Roads Authority (NRA). S. 17 of the 1993 Act provides that the main function of the NRA is in relation to the planning and supervision of works for the construction and maintenance of national roads. S. 18 of the Act requires the NRA to prepare five yearly plans concerning national roads. S. 20 of the Act empowers the NRA to issue directions to local authorities in connection with the construction of national roads, including motorways. S. 21 requires the NRA to prepare such plans and documentation as may be required to obtain financial assistance from the European Communities. Other provisions of Part III concern the normal administrative arrangements concerning the NRA. Finally, while the general commencement of the 1993 Act has been described above, 588, we should note that the National Roads Authority (Establishment) Order 1993 (SI No. 407) provided for the establishment of the NRA itself on 23 December 1993 and the Environmental Research Unit (Establishment) Order 1988 (Revocation) Order 1993 (SI No. 409) revoked the 1988 Order referred to in the title of the Order and provided for the dissolution of the Environmental Research Unit of the Department of the Environment with effect from 1 January 1994 on the establishment of the NRA.

Noise S. 77 of the Roads Act 1993 provides for the control of road traffic noise by means of Regulations made by the Minister for the Environment after consultation with the Environmental Protection Agency, as to which see in general the 1992 Review, 529-34.

Public service vehicles The Road Traffic (Public Service Vehicles) (Amendment) Regulations 1993 (SI No. 29) provided for an extension of time for compliance with SI No. 358 of 1992: see the 1992 Review, 630.

Registration and licensing   The Road Vehicles (Registration and Licensing) (Amendment) Regulations 1993 (SI No. 23) amended the 1992 Regulations of the same title (1992 Review, 630) concerning the format of trade licence plates for the motor trade; amended the provisions concerning surchages for failure to register within the calendar month period; and also prescribed statutory declarations to be completed by certain applicants for licences. The Road Vehicles (Registration and Licensing) (Amendment) (No. 2) Regulations 1993 (SI No. 126) amended the definition of 'registered owner' of a mechanically propelled vehicle contained in Art.1 of the 1992 Regulations of the same title (1992 Review, 630) in order to conform fully with the registration requirememts of the Finance Act 1992 (1992 Review, 502-6). The Vehicle Registration and Taxation Regulations 1993 (SI No. 252) amended the 1992 Regulations of the same title (1992 Review, 630) and provided, *inter alia*, for a new form of certificate of registration. Finally, the Road Vehicles (Registration and Licensing) (Amendment) (No. 3) Regulations 1993 (SI No. 198) and the Road Vehicles (Registration and Licensing) (Amendment) (No. 4) Regulations 1993 (SI No. 263) amended the period for the issue and renewal of vehicle licences (tax discs).

Road races   Ss. 74 and 75 of the Roads Act 1993 provide for the regulation of road races on public roads, including the temporary closing of roads.

Rights of way   S. 73 of the Roads Act 1993 provides for the circumstances in which a local authority may extinguish a public right of way.

Signs: bus lanes   The Road Traffic (Signs) (Bus Lane) (Amendment) Regulations 1993 (SI No. 113) deal with the signification of bus lanes.

Signs: general   S. 72 of the Roads Act 1993 provides for the regulation of unauthorised signs on any public road.

Skips   S. 72 of the Roads Act 1993 provides for the regulation of skips on any public road.

Speed limitation devices   The Road Traffic (Construction, Equipment and Use of Vehicles) (Amendment) Regulations 1993 (SI No. 299) implemented Directive 92/6/EEC, which requires that certain buses and heavy goods vehicles be fitted with speed limitation devices. The European Communities (Speed Limitation Devices) Regulations 1993 (SI No. 300), also involving the implementation of Directive 92/6/EEC, deals with the sealing of such speed limitation devices.

Temporary dwellings Ss. 69 and 71 of the Roads Act 1993 provide for the regulation of temporary dwellings, caravans and vehicles on any public road.

Toll roads Part V of the Roads Act 1993 (ss. 56 to 66) concerns the updating of the regulation of the construction of toll roads.

ROAD TRANSPORT LICENCE

Decision within reasonable time In *Twomey v Minister for Tourism and Transport*, Supreme Court, 12 February 1993, the Court held that a decision on an application for a road freight certificate under the European Communities (Merchandise Road Transport) Regulations 1977 should be made within a reasonable period from the time of application: see the discussion in the Administrative Law chapter, 19, above.

TOUR OPERATORS AND TRAVEL AGENTS

The Tour Operators (Licensing) Regulations 1993 (SI No. 182) and the Travel Agents (Licensing) Regulations 1993 (SI No. 183) consolidated with amendments the respective requirements for the grant of tour operators and travel agents licences as well as the fees for granting these licences and also revoked all previous Regulations in this area (see the 1992 Review, 632). The 1993 Regulations were made under the Transport (Tour Operators and Travel Agents) Act 1982. On the 1982 Act, see the 1987 Review, 242.

Index